Library of Congress Cataloging-in-Publication Data

Gibson, Robert L. (Robert Lewis)
    Introduction to counseling and guidance / Robert L. Gibson.
Marianne H. Mitchell.—5th ed.
      p.   cm.
    Includes bibliographical references (p.   ).
    ISBN 0–13–273533–4
    1. Counseling.   I. Mitchell, Marianne. II. Title.
BF637.C6G48 1999
158′.3—dc21   98–19223
                                   CIP

Cover art: Nicholas Hill
Editor: Kevin M. Davis
Production Editor: Linda Hillis Bayma
Design Coordinator: Diane C. Lorenzo
Production Coordination: Betsy Keefer
Photo Editor: Anthony Magnacca
Cover Designer: TOPEgrafix
Production Manager: Laura Messerly
Director of Marketing: Kevin Flanagan
Marketing Manager: Suzanne Stanton
Advertising/Marketing Coordinator: Krista Groshong

This book was set in Goudy Old Style by BookMasters, Inc., and was printed and bound by Courier/Westford, Inc. The cover was printed by Phoenix Color Corp.

© 1999, 1995 by Prentice-Hall, Inc.
Simon & Schuster/A Viacom Company
Upper Saddle River, New Jersey 07458

Earlier editions © 1990, 1986, 1981 (entitled *Introduction to Guidance*) by Macmillan Publishing Company

Photo credits: pages 2, 178, 194, 228, 310, and 444, Scott Cunningham/Merrill; pages 46, 98, 122, 260, 376, and 394 Anthony Magnacca/Merrill; page 358, Barbara Schwartz/Merrill; and pages 26 and 420, Anne Vega/ Merrill.

Acknowledgments: pages 16 and 19: From *Community Mental Health: A General Introduction*, 2nd edition, by B. L. Bloom. Copyright © 1984 (1977) by Brooks/Cole Publishing Company, a division of International Thomson Publishing, Inc., Grove, CA 93950. Reprinted by permission of the publisher. (*continued on pg 577*)

the United States of America

7 6 5 4 3 2 1

3533–4

rnational (UK) Limited, *London*
stralia Pty. Limited, *Sydney*
Inc., *Toronto*
americana, S.A., *Mexico*
ivate Limited, *New Delhi*
c., *Tokyo*
Ltd., *Singapore*
il, Ltda., *Rio de Janeiro*

Introduction to Counseling and Guidance FIFTH EDITION

Robert L. Gibson
INDIANA UNIVERSITY

Marianne H. Mitchell
INDIANA UNIVERSITY

MERRILL *an impri...*

Upper Saddle River, New
Columbus, Ohio

M
Ack
Copy
Pacific
Printed in
10 9 8
ISBN: 0-13-2
Prentice-Hall Inte
Prentice-Hall of Au
Prentice-Hall Canad
Prentice-Hall Hispano
Prentice-Hall of India P
Prentice-Hall of Japan, In
Simon & Schuster Asia Pre
Editora Prentice-Hall do Bra

About the Authors

Dr. Robert L. Gibson is Professor of Education, Department of Counseling and Educational Psychology at Indiana University, Bloomington, Indiana. In addition to his experiences as a counselor educator, he has been a high school teacher, counselor, and director of guidance, as well as a college counselor. His service activities include Chairperson of the Guidance and Counseling Committee of the North Central Association of Schools and Colleges; member of the state guidance advisory committee in two states; president of two state counseling associations; treasurer of the Association for Counselor Education and Supervision (ACES); plus various state and national committee memberships.

His research activities include directing funded international research projects in the areas of pupil academic achievement, common educational problems of youth, and school dropouts. Recent studies include theoretical preferences of practicing counselors and studies of counselor functions in varied settings.

Dr. Gibson is Co-Director of Indiana University's programs in Bermuda and Scotland.

Dr. Marianne H. Mitchell is Professor of Education, Department of Counseling and Educational Psychology, Indiana University, Bloomington, Indiana. She has served as President of the American Counseling Association and as President of the Association of Counselor Education and Supervision.

Dr. Mitchell's research activities include international investigations of pupil personnel services and pupil achievement and common educational problems in the United States, the United Kingdom, and Europe. She has been the principal investigator in studies of career information delivery systems, career placement programs, and adolescent girls' attitudes towards vocational education. She serves as a consultant to the Ministries of Education and Health and Social Services in Bermuda and to Moray House Institute, Edinburgh, Scotland.

Dr. Mitchell is Co-Director of Indiana University's programs in Bermuda and Scotland.

Preface

This book is primarily designed for use in introductory counseling and guidance courses and in related fields for those who seek a comprehensive overview of counseling services. In this text, readers will find a broad general discussion rather than the in-depth treatment that students majoring in counseling can anticipate later in their specialized preparatory courses.

The objectives of this book are to provide the reader with an overview and general understanding of (1) historical perspectives and current activities of counselors, (2) the role and function of counselors in a variety of settings, (3) techniques utilized by counselors, (4) multicultural considerations in counseling, (5) organization of counseling programs, and (6) legal and ethical guidelines.

Although counselors in both school and nonschool settings adhere to basically the same principles and practices, it is recognized, through special attention in Chapter 3 (schools) and Chapter 4 (community and agency), that counselors are functioning in a variety of settings. We therefore believe that those interested in counseling in both school and nonschool settings will find this book to be an appropriate introduction.

The initial chapters lead the reader from the historical background of the counseling movement through traditional current activities. These activities are then translated into the counselor's role and function in both school and nonschool settings (Chapters 3 and 4). Chapter 5 focuses on the primary and distinguishing activity of counselors—individual counseling. Chapter 6 discusses multicultural counseling. Chapter 7 presents the various group activities in which counselors engage. Chapters 8 through 11 discuss other basic activities of counselors (assessment through standardized and nonstandardized techniques, career counseling, and consultation). Chapter 12 discusses the current trend of increased counselor attention to prevention and wellness. Chapters 13 and 14 address development and management of counseling and guidance programs and their improvement through accountability, evaluation, and research. The final chapter presents ethical and legal considerations. Throughout this text we have sought to raise the reader's multicultural awareness. Special issues and current concerns of the profession have also been addressed.

As an introductory text, we have written and revised this book in a style that we hope is readable and enjoyable as well as informative. Your comments, suggestions, and reactions will be most welcome.

ACKNOWLEDGMENTS

We would like to acknowledge all those who have contributed directly and indirectly to the undertaking and completion of this book. These include, of course, the helpful staff of Merrill/Prentice-Hall, including Linda Hillis Bayma, Production Editor, and particularly our past and present editors, Lloyd C. Chilton, Robert Miller, Linda Sullivan, and Kevin Davis. Special thanks go to Betsy Keefer, whose prompt responses and careful attention to detail kept this writing project on schedule. Ms. Kathy Deselle, copy editor, has been helpful as well. We would also like to acknowledge the valuable comments of our reviewers: Clayton J. Arceneaux, University of Southwestern Louisiana; Willis E. Bartlett, University of Notre Dame; Ronald D. Bingham, Brigham Young University; Brenda Freeman, University of Wyoming; Robert F. McClure, University of Texas at Tyler; Robert C. Nielsen, North Dakota State University; Lee J. Richmond, Loyola College in Maryland; and Jeff Robins, Rutgers University.

We are extremely grateful to the many considerate authors and publishers who granted us permission to quote from their publications. It is appropriate to acknowledge the many useful suggestions from our departmental colleagues at Indiana University and our fellow counselor—educators who volunteered their time and comments for our guidance. In addition, we have been appreciative of the critical comments of our graduate students (who undoubtedly had in mind the well-being of their counterparts of the future). We are particularly thankful for the patient and persistent assistance of our graduate assistants, past and present. For this edition, we especially recognize the contributions of Carrie Hill. In conclusion, we would like to acknowledge our close friends and families, whose support and encouragement have been important to our work on this edition.

R. L. G.
M. H. M.

Brief Contents

Contents

Introduction
to Counseling
and Guidance

Historic Perspectives

COUNSELING: A RESPONSE TO HUMAN NEEDS

Many of you have recently decided to prepare for careers as counselors; some of you may be considering such a decision; still others may be interested in counseling because you are in or are preparing to enter various careers in which some introductory knowledge of this field may be helpful. In this process you probably asked yourself, Why have I selected this field? On occasion, you also may have even thought, Why do I have to work? Both are age-old questions that are vital to society and that have been discussed and researched extensively over the years.

Perhaps an equally important question but one not raised quite as frequently or researched as extensively is, Why do certain careers exist? What were the factors that led to their demand and creation? The answers to these questions are fairly obvious concerning such fields as medicine and law, for the need for physicians and lawyers in society has been clearly and universally recognized since the earliest recordings of civilizations. Less clear to many, however, is the role of less well known occupations, such as ornithology, demography, and cytotechnology. Although a popular understanding and acceptance of the need for all careers are not necessary or expected, those studying the general areas encompassed by counseling will benefit from understanding the nature of the societal needs to which counseling and counselors are responding and, in turn, understanding the nature of those responsibilities and responses.

This first chapter, therefore, briefly reviews the historic antecedents leading to the development of counseling programs and the professional careers they represent. You may determine whether counseling and counselors are a response to human needs or just another fancy that will pass when the need is examined more closely and critically.

OUR HERITAGE FROM THE PAST

It is quite possible that the earliest (although unconfirmed) occasion in which humans sought a counselor was when Adam reaped the consequences of his eating the apple in the Garden of Eden. There is no proof of this early beginning to counseling, but an abundance of evidence suggests that persons throughout the ages have sought the advice and counsel of others believed to possess superior knowledge, insights, or experiences.

Perhaps the first counterparts of the present-day counselor were the chieftains and elders of the ancient tribal societies to whom youths turned or were often sent for advice and guidance. In these primitive societies, tribal members shared fundamental economic enterprises such as hunting, fishing, and farming. No elaborate career guidance programs were developed—or needed—because occupational limitations were usually determined by two criteria: age and sex. Later, as skills became more recognizable and important to societies, the occupational determinant of inheritance became common. Thus, potters passed on the secrets and skills of their trade to their sons, as did the smiths and carpenters. Women passed on their skills to their daughters; however, their occupational opportunities were limited.

A study of early primitive life can lead one to conclude that most of the conflicts existing in present-day society regarding career decision making were absent. This lack of a career decision-making dilemma, however, should not be interpreted to mean that workers did not enjoy or take pride in a job well done. Even the earliest evidence of humankind's existence indicates that pride and pleasure resulted from developing and demonstrating one's skills—in developing one's human potential.

In the early civilizations, philosophers, priests, or other representatives of the gods and religions assumed the function of advising and offering counsel. The historic origins of the concept of developing one's potential may be identified in the early Grecian societies, with their emphasis on developing and strengthening individuals through education so that each could fulfill a role reflecting their greatest potential for themselves and their society. It was believed that within each person were forces that could be stimulated and guided toward goals beneficial to both the individual and the community. Of these early Greek counselors, Plato more than any other person is generally recognized as one of the first to organize psychological insights into a systematic theory. Belkin (1975) notes that Plato's interests

> were varied, and he examined the psychology of the individual in all of its ramifications: in moral issues, in terms of education, in relation to society, in theological perspective, and so on. He dealt with such questions as "What makes a man virtuous—his inheritance, his upbringing, or his formal education?" (Meno), "How can children be most effectively taught" (Republic), and "Why techniques have been successfully used in persuading and influencing people in their decisions and beliefs" (Gorgias). But it is not the specific questions themselves that prove important to counselors, but, rather, the method that Plato used to deal with these questions, a method which, more than any other in the history of human thought, sets the way for the counseling relationship. It is a dramatic method, in which profound questions are dealt with through the dynamics of very real human interactions, a method in which the characters are as important as the things they say. (p. 5)

The second great counselor of the early civilizations was Plato's student, Aristotle, who made many significant contributions to what was to become the field of psychology. One of these was his study of people interacting with their environment and others. Also, Hippocrates and other Greek physicians offered the opinion that mental disorders were diseases originating from natural causes. Physicians' treatments (bleeding, purging, etc.) were hardly humane except by comparison.

Later, in ancient Hebrew society, individuality and the right of self-determination were assumed. The early Christian societies emphasized, at least in theory if not always in practice, many of the humanistic ideals that later became basic to democratic societies and, in the 20th century, the counseling movement.

Philosophers who were also educators, such as Luis Vives (1492–1540), recognized the need to guide persons according to their attitudes and aptitudes. Foreshadowing the more recent women's equity movement and the earlier women's liberation movement, "Vives in his *De subventione pauperum* (Bruges, 1526) even demanded that girls should be prepared for useful occupations" (Mallart, 1955, p. 75).

In the Middle Ages, attempts at counseling increasingly came under the control of the church. By the early Middle Ages, the duty of advising and directing youth had become centered in the parish priest. At that time, education was largely under church jurisdiction. Sporadic efforts at placing youth in appropriate vocations occurred during the rise of European kingdoms and the subsequent expansion of the colonial empires. Books aimed at helping youths choose an occupation began to appear in the 17th century (Zytowski, 1972). A number of picture books also appeared depicting different occupations. One of the more popular publications was Powell's *Tom of all Trades: Or the Plain Path Way to Preferment*, published in 1631 in London. "Powell gives much information on the professions and how to gain access to them, even suggesting sources of financial aid and the preferred schools in which to prepare" (Zytowski, 1972, p. 447).

Also during this time, René Descartes (1596–1650) and others began to study the human body as an organism that reacted or behaved to various stimuli. These studies were to be forerunners for later, more accurate and scientific psychological studies.

In the 18th century, Jean-Jacques Rousseau (1712–1778) suggested that the growing individual can best learn when free to develop according to his or her natural impulses; he advocated permissiveness in learning and learning through doing. At approximately the same time, the famous Swiss educator Johann Pestalozzi (1746–1827) expressed the belief that society could be reformed only to the extent that the individual in that society was assisted to help him- or herself develop.

For centuries, however, many with mental illnesses, as well as those with physical illnesses, went underground and retreated. Although the wealthy could afford the attention of physicians, most mentally ill patients were almost always treated in the home. Those poor who received any treatment at all were cared for in hospitals run by religious orders. For the first 75 years of this new nation, the United States of America, few public facilities existed for the treatment of the mentally ill.

The newly independent United States did have leading citizens with a counseling viewpoint. "One of its most versatile citizens, Thomas Jefferson, called for a plan to recognize and educate its male youth as a source of national leadership" (Gibson & Higgins, 1966, p. 4). The second president, John Adams, called for laws for the liberal education of youths, especially of the lower classes. He felt that no expense for this purpose could be thought extravagant.

The most famous U.S. educator of the 19th century, Horace Mann, included in his *Twelfth Annual Report* a notation of the advantages of the American common school system, advantages that were to be conducive to the development of counseling and guidance programs in U.S. education in the next century. Mann reported that "in teaching the blind and the deaf and dumb, in kindling the latent spark of intelligence that lurks in an idiot's mind, and in the more holy work of reforming abandoned and outcast children, education has proved what it can do by glorious experiments" (Johansen, Collins, & Johnson, 1975, p. 280). Mann also believed that education should have as one of its objectives the reform of society, and he continually stressed this view in his reports to the Massachusetts Board of Education.

In the wake of the political scandals of the Grant administration and other evidence of the decay of Christian morals, methods of moral instruction and moral education became significant in the later 1800s. In 1872, the noted educator A. D. Mayo stated that morality and good citizenship were indistinguishably intermingled and that moral education in the public schools should be based on concepts, principles, and models drawn from the Christian tradition of U.S. Society.

During this period, the biologist Herbert Spencer (1820–1903) set forth his concept of adjustment (Hinshaw, 1942). This biological concept held that forms of life that do not adapt to their environment eventually become extinct. From this, Spencer concluded that perfect life consisted of perfect adjustment. In other words, biological adjustment is a criterion of life. Adaptive behavior is that which maintains life.

Also important to the scientific study of behavior and of special significance to the eventual development of counseling as a psychologically based profession was the emergence of the field of psychology itself during the latter part of the 19th century. Preceded by physicists and physiologists who were conducting experimental investigations that led to reliable information on physical and physiological aspects of behavior, similar investigations launched psychology as a separate science in the late 1800s. Psychology's formal beginnings as a separate science occurred in 1879 when Wilhelm Wundt opened his Psychological Institute at the University of Leipzig. This was the beginning of the movement toward a systematic inquiry into human behavior rather than aimless and often biased observation. With William James (1892–1920) as its early American leader, psychology emerged over the next 100 years as a recognized discipline with its own distinct areas of specialization, inquiry, and training.

The rise of psychiatry as a specialty of medicine was another important and relevant development of this period. This field led to a decline in the support of moral treatment for mental disorders because psychiatry advocated organic treatment for organic causes. During this same time, the state mental hospital movement, led by Dorothea Dix, resulted in the development of these institutions and the removal of much of the care for at least the seriously mentally ill from local communities (Goshen, 1967).

A major contribution to the field of psychiatry and to all the field of mental health were the studies and writings of Sigmund Freud, an Austrian, in the early 1900s. His writings advanced the historical prominence of psychoanalytic theory and influenced later prominent theorists in the field such as Alfred Adler, Albert Ellis, and Fritz Perls. (Freud died in 1939 in London, England, where he resided as a refugee from the Nazi occupation of his country.)

As the United States entered the 20th century, its society was growing more complex, and finding one's appropriate place within it and adjusting to it were becoming increasingly complicated. Many adults were turning to such traditional sources of guidance as their family physician, minister, or employer. However, it would appear that the 20th century was ripe for a considered and genuinely scientific approach to meeting many human needs. The time was now for the development of counseling and other psychologically oriented programs to meet these needs. Let us examine how these emerged in schools and institutional and agency settings in the 20th century.

THE DEVELOPMENT OF COUNSELING AND GUIDANCE IN U.S. EDUCATION

History is often made when a person with an idea coincides with a need and an opportunity. In 1908, Frank Parsons organized the Boston Vocational Bureau to provide vocational assistance to young people and train teachers to serve as vocational counselors. These teachers were to aid in the selection of students for vocational schools and assist students in choosing a vocation wisely and making the transition from school to suitable work. Soon thereafter, Parsons (1909) published *Choosing a Vocation*, a predecessor to this and other basic books in the field. In this publication, he discusses the role of the counselor and techniques that might be employed in vocational counseling. This book is divided into three areas: personal investigation, industrial investigation, and the organization and the work.

Parson's book is interesting reading even today, and few would find fault with what he considered to be three factors necessary for the wise choice of a vocation:

(1) a clear understanding of yourself, your aptitudes, abilities, interests, ambitions, resources, limitations, and other causes; (2) a knowledge of the requirements and conditions of success, advantages and disadvantages, compensation, opportunities, and prospects in different lines of work; and (3) true reasoning on the relations of these two groups of facts. (p. 5)

Parsons goes on to suggest that in initiating the personal investigation, the client should first make an extensive self-study by answering questions on a "schedule of personal data." The counselor then fills in the details by reading between the lines. Parsons states that this approach will give clues to possible flaws such as defective verbal memory and slow auditory reactions. Such a client would, as he puts it, "have difficulty in becoming an expert stenographer" (p. 7). The inventory suggested by Parsons includes such items as "How far can you walk? Habits as to smoking? Drinking? Use of drugs? Other forms of dissipation? How often do you bathe?"

An unusual feature of the intake interview was the observations Parsons suggests regarding the client's physical appearance:

> While I am questioning the applicant about his probable health, education, reading, experience, et cetera, I carefully observe the shape of his head, the relative development above, before, and behind the ears, his features and expression, color, vivacity, voice, manner, pose, general air of vitality, enthusiasm, et cetera.
>
> If the applicant's head is largely developed behind the ears, with big neck, low forehead, and small upper head, he is probably of an animal type, and if the other symptoms coincide, he should be dealt with on that basis. (p. 7)

Parsons advocates getting the client to see him- or herself exactly as others do and giving the client recommendations about methods that can be used for self-improvement—for example, reading suitable books to develop analytical power. Parsons also recommends using biographies of famous people and finding commonalities with the client in biographic details as a form of inspiration.

Parsons insists that counselors be thoroughly familiar with all relevant details concerning job opportunities, the distribution of demand in industries, and courses of study. A detailed analysis should be made of industrial opportunities for men and women, including location and demand, work conditions, and pay. A similar detailed approach was to be given to opportunities in vocational schools.

Parsons also explains the need to train vocational counselors. This training was to be accomplished in one to three terms, and the applicants were to have some relevant occupational background and maturity. In addition to sound judgment, character, and maturity, Parsons (1909) believes the vocational counselor should have the following traits:

1. A practical working knowledge of the fundamental principles and methods of modern psychology.
2. An experience involving sufficient human contact to give him an intimate acquaintance with human nature in a considerable number of its different phases; he must understand the dominant motives, interests, and ambitions that control the lives of men, and be able to recognize the symptoms that indicate the presence or absence of important elements of character.
3. An ability to deal with young people in a sympathetic, earnest, searching, candid, helpful, and attractive way.
4. A knowledge of requirements and conditions of success, compensation, prospects, advantages, and disadvantages, etc., in the different lines of industry.
5. Information relating to courses of study and means of preparing for various callings and developing efficiency therein.
6. Scientific method analysis and principles of investigation by which laws and causes are ascertained, facts are classified, and correct conclusions drawn. The counselor must be able to recognize the essential facts and principles involved in each case, group them according to their true relations, and draw the conclusions they justify. (pp. 94–95)

Parson's pioneer efforts and publications were popular and succeeded in identifying and launching a new helping profession: the guidance counselor. Today, Parsons is generally referred to as the "father of the guidance movement in American education," but he probably did not envision the growth of the movement from the several dozen counselors he trained to the more than 50,000 counselors functioning in schools alone 80 years later.

By 1913, the fledgling guidance movement (as it was initially called) had grown sufficiently in numbers and specialization to warrant the organization of the National Vocational Guidance Association and initiate, two years later, the publication of the first guidance journal, appropriately titled *Vocational Guidance*. The term *guidance* was the popular designation for the counseling movement in schools for well over 50 years. However, in recent generations, *guidance* has been sometimes viewed as an outdated label. Additionally, the early years of the movement had a vocational orientation that was primarily concerned with those aspects of youth guidance dealing with vocational choice, preparation, and placement. (Sixty years later, many of the same characteristics would once again be reasserted in the career education and guidance movements.) Hence, in these early years, the movement was often referred to as one of vocational guidance.

According to Rockwell and Rothney (1961), other early leaders in the U.S. guidance movement were Jessie B. Davis, Anna Y. Reed, Eli W. Weaver, and David S. Hill. Their contributions should also be noted.

Davis's approach was based on self-study and the study of occupations. His descriptions of counseling (Rockwell & Rothney, 1961) seem to suggest that students should be preached to about the moral value of hard work, ambition, honesty, and the development of good character as assets to any person who planned to enter the business world. In their discussion of early pioneers of the guidance movement, Rockwell and Rothney (1961) write:

> Davis's position within the social gospel philosophy was enhanced by his use of the "call" concept of the ministry in relation to the way one should choose a vocation. When an individual was "called," he would approach it with the noblest and highest ideals which would serve society best by uplifting humanity. (p. 351)

In the same era, Anna Reed was an admirer of the then prevailing concepts and ethics of the business world and the free enterprise system. She believed that guidance services could be important to the Seattle school system as a means of developing the best possible educational product. Contrary to today's philosophy, she placed the system's (business world) needs above those of the individual. As a result, the guidance programs she developed were designed to judge a person's worth by the employability of that individual.

Another early leader, Eli Weaver, succeeded in establishing teacher guidance committees in every high school in New York City. These committees worked actively to help youths discover their capabilities and learn how to use those talents to secure the most appropriate employment (Rockwell & Rothney, 1961).

The fourth of these early pioneers, David S. Hill, was a researcher in the New Orleans school system who used scientific methods to study people. Because his research studies pointed out the wide diversity in student populations, he advocated and worked for a diversified curriculum complemented by vocational guidance. He viewed this model as most appropriate if the individual student were to develop fully.

In the first quarter of the 20th century, two other significant developments in psychology profoundly influenced the school guidance movement: (a) the introduction and development of standardized, group-administered psychological tests and (b) the mental health movements.

The French psychologist Alfred Binet and his associate Theodore Simon introduced the first general intelligence test in 1905. In 1916, a translated and revised version was introduced in the United States by Lewis M. Terman and his colleagues at Stanford University, and it enjoyed widespread popularity in the schools. However, when the United States entered World War I and the armed services sought a measure that would enable them to screen and classify inductees, the first so-called group intelligence measure, the Army Alpha Test, was subsequently administered to thousands of draftees. The possibilities of applying these and other psychometric techniques to pupil assessment resulted in the rapid development and expansion of standardized testing in education in the decade immediately following World War I.

The 1920s was a lively decade in many ways. That noble experiment, Prohibition, was launched; in turn, such names as Al Capone and Baby Face Nelson appeared in the nation's newspaper headlines. Socially, jazz, flappers, and bathtub gin were in vogue. For the professional educator, the Progressive movement ensured a lively educational era as well. This movement, the thought of which would influence the further development of a people-oriented philosophy, stressed the uniqueness and dignity of the individual pupil, emphasized the importance of a facilitating classroom environment, and suggested that learning occurred in many ways. Many of today's counselors would have embraced the Progressive education suggestions that pupils and teachers should plan together, that the child's social environment should be improved, that the developmental needs and purposes of the student should be considered, and that the psychological environment of the classroom should be a positive, encouraging one.

Organized guidance programs began to emerge with increasing frequency in secondary schools in the 1920s and more often than not modeled themselves after college student personnel programs, with titles of deans (separately for boys and girls, of course) and similar accompanying functions of discipline, school attendance, and related administrative responsibilities. As a result, many programs of this decade began to have a remedial emphasis, as pupils who experienced academic or personal difficulties were sent to their deans for help modifying their behavior or correcting their deficiencies. Nevertheless, a counselor of the mid-1920s, if projected by a time machine into a school counselor's meeting 80 years later, could converse easily with his present-day counterparts—at least to the point of their concerns and involvement in vocational or career counseling, the use of standardized testing instruments, assistance to students with their educational planning, the need for a more caring school environment, and their role as disciplinarians and quasi-administrators.

It is also probable that the elementary school counseling movement had its beginnings in the mid-1920s and early 1930s, stimulated by the writings and efforts of William Burnham. Faust (1968) indicates that Burnham emphasized the important role of the teacher in the mental health of children in the elementary school. Efforts to develop guidance in elementary schools during this period were scarcely noticeable, but a few notable programs were undertaken. One of these, in Winnetka, Illinois, established a department of elementary counseling with resource personnel for guidance. These personnel included (although not all on a full-time basis) psychiatrists, psychometrists, psychologists, an educational counselor, a psychiatric social worker, and supporting clerical services. Their basic responsibilities were counseling, child study, psychotherapy, pupil analysis, parental assistance, and referrals.

College campuses also began to reflect the influences affecting the guidance movement in the 1920s as student personnel workers began utilizing standardized tests for admission and placement purposes. A few institutions even began to offer vocational guidance. By the end of the 1920s, it was evident that the early guidance pioneers believed that there was a need for guidance services, and the school was the proper institution for the delivery of these services. Some even thought that pupil guidance should encompass all grades.

It is also important to note that the word *counseling* was rarely used during these early years as the label *guidance* was broadly applied to those activities utilized to guide students and other clients into appropriate educational choices and career decisions. The reversal in popularity of these labels is noted by Hoyt (1993) in his article "Guidance is Not a Dirty Word." Perhaps the first delineation of counseling as a psychological process was expressed with the publication of *Workbook in Vocations* by Proctor, Benefield, and Wrenn in 1931 (cited in Lewis, Hayes, & Lewis, 1986).

While the American public debated the policies of FDR and the threat of Hitler to world peace, the guidance movement of the 1930s continued to develop to the point at which it was becoming increasingly popular as a topic for discussion and debate in educational circles. Questions and criticisms concerning guidance activities were increasingly noted in the professional literature of the era. Educational associations appointed committees to study the movement, and many issued reports with descriptions and definitions of guidance and guidance services. The New York State Teachers Association published a report in 1935 in which guidance was defined as "the process of assisting individuals in making life adjustment. It is needed in the home, school, community, and in all other phases of the individual's environment" (p. 10).

As in the 1960s, when concern was often expressed about the interchangeability of the words *guidance* and *counseling*, in the 1930s a similar concern was expressed over the interchangeability of the terms *student personnel* and *guidance*. Adding to the confusion, leading spokespeople for the movement during that period, such as John Brewer (1932), used the terms *education* and *guidance* synonymously.

Sarah M. Sturtevant (1937) sought to deal with some of these growing concerns by addressing a few of the questions regarding the developing secondary school guidance movement: What do we mean by the guidance movement? What are the essentials of a functioning guidance program? What personnel and what qualifications should guidance workers have for a good guidance program? And the inevitable question, What are the costs of individualizing education? These questions would not be outdated more than 60 years later.

During the late 1930s and early 1940s, the trait-factor approach to counseling became increasingly popular. This often-labeled directive theory received stimulus from the writings of E. G. Williamson (*How to Counsel Students: A Manual of Techniques for Clinical Counselors*, 1939) and others. Whereas critics of this measurement-oriented approach claimed it was rigid and dehumanizing, Williamson stresses its worth: "You are trying to improve your understanding by using data with a smaller probable error of estimate, such as test data—instead of judgments, which have a much larger probable error of estimate: variability" (Ewing, 1975, p. 84).

Also during the 1930s, possible directions for guidance in the elementary school were put forth by the child study movement, which took the position that it was the teacher's role to provide guidance for each pupil in the self-contained classroom. Publications by Zirbes (1949) and others described the ways in which the learning experiences of children could be guided. The intensive study of each child was recommended, with the objective of understanding how children achieved or failed to achieve certain developmental tasks. This popular approach found some following at the secondary school level and ultimately led to the suggestion of "every teacher a guidance worker."

As the United States emerged from World War II, the counseling and guidance movement appeared to be taking on new direction. A significant contributor to this revitalization, with an impact on counseling in both school and nonschool settings, was Carl R. Rogers (1902–1987). Rogers set forth a new counseling theory in two significant books, *Counseling and Psychotherapy* (1942) and a refinement of his early position, *Client-Centered Therapy* (1951). In *Counseling and Psychotherapy*, Rogers offers nondirective counseling as an alternative to the older, more traditional methods. He also stresses the client's responsibility in perceiving his or her problem and enhancing the self. This self theory soon was labeled nondirective because it appeared to be the opposite of the traditional counselor-centered approach for dealing with client problems.

Rogers's suggestion that the client assume the major responsibility for solving his or her own problem rather than the therapist solving the client's problem provoked the first serious theoretical controversies in the school guidance and counseling movement. Rogers's follow-up publication, *Client-Centered Therapy*, was the result of this continued research and application effort. The book promotes the semantic change from nondirective to client-centered counseling but, more importantly, places increased emphasis on the growth-producing possibilities of the client.

Perhaps more than any other person, Rogers influenced the way in which American counselors interact with clients. Furthermore, his view of the client as an equal and his positive view of a person's potential seem more consistent with the American way of life and democratic traditions than the European-based theories.

> The extent of [Rogers's] influence was most marked by the overnight replacement of testing by counseling as the key guidance function. In turn, counseling would rise to such eminence in the next few years that it would compete and contend with guidance in regard to the use of the counselor's time and the overall purpose of counseling and guidance. What began as an adjunct tool of guidance would now raise a challenge for ascendancy in its own right. (Aubrey, 1977, p. 292)

Over the years, Rogers continued to research, test, revise, and challenge others to test his theory. In summary, it might be analogous to compare Carl Rogers's impact and contributions to the counseling movement of the 20th century with Henry Ford's contribution to the development of the automotive industry.

Another dimension to the techniques of counselors of the late 1940s and one to which Rogers, again, was a significant contributor was group counseling. Others, utilizing research data gathered by the armed services and their investigations into small group dynamics, developed a theoretical framework within which school counselors could integrate the skills and processes of individual counseling with the dynamic roles and interactions of the individual in a group setting.

Other opportunities also appeared on the horizon for the counseling and guidance movement. Feingold (1947), writing in *School Review*, called for a new approach to guidance. He indicated that guidance counselors cannot stop with mere educational direction—they must go beyond that goal, must provide guidance, "not only for the anointed, but for those pupils who really need it—the pupils who run afoul of rules and regulations" (p. 550). Feingold and others also called for "guidance of the whole child," an outgrowth of the child study movement of the 1930s. Three years later, Traxler (1950), writing in the same publication, identified emerging trends in guidance.

1. More adequate training of guidance personnel.
2. Guidance as an all-faculty function.
3. Closer cooperation with home and community agencies.
4. Orderly accumulation and recording of individual information.
5. Use of objective measures.
6. Differential prediction of success on the basis of test batteries that yield comparable scores in broad areas.
7. Increased interest in improved techniques in the appraisal of personal qualities of pupils and the treatment of maladjustment.
8. Trend toward "eclectic" guidance (rather than directive/nondirective).
9. Recognition of the relationship between remedial work and guidance.
10. Improved case study techniques.
11. Availability and better use of occupational-educational information. (pp. 14–23)

In 1957, the Soviet Union made headlines around the world by successfully launching the first earth satellite, *Sputnik I*. An indirect but nevertheless significant result of this accomplishment was the lift-off of the counseling and guidance movement in the United States. This boost came about through legislation resulting from the public's criticism of education and its failure to supply trained personnel for careers deemed vital for national well-being. This legislation, labeled the National Defense Education Act and passed in September 1958, became an important landmark in American education, as well as the guidance movement, for its acknowledgment of the vital link among our national well-being, personnel needs, and education.

This act provided special benefits for youth guidance in five of its ten titles or sections. Of these, perhaps Title V was the key to the upsurge in counseling and guidance program development. Gibson and Higgins (1966) indicate that this provided for "(1) grants to states for stimulating the establishment and maintenance of local guidance programs, and (2) grants to institutions of higher education for the training of guidance personnel to staff local programs" (p. 7).

Gibson and Higgins go on to point out that six years later (September 1964), the impact of the act could be detected in announcements from the U.S. Department of Health, Education, and Welfare, which pointed out that the act had, in that short period, achieved the following:

- Made grants to states of approximately $30 million, thereby helping bring the number of full-time high school counselors from 12,000 (one for every 960 students) in 1958 to 30,000 (one for every 510 students) in 1964.
- Through the end of the 1964–1965 academic year, supported 480 institutes designed to improve counseling capabilities, which were attended by more than 15,700 secondary school counselors and teachers preparing to become counselors.
- From 1959 to 1964, made it possible for 109 million scholastic aptitude and achievement tests to be given to public secondary school students and over 3 million to private secondary school students.
- Helped 600,000 students obtain or continue their college education with federal loans.
- Trained 42,000 skilled technicians to meet critical manpower needs.
- Granted 8,500 graduate fellowships, a first step toward meeting the need for many more college teachers. (p. 7)

Stimulated by this rapid growth in counseling and guidance, standards for the certification and performance of school counselors were developed and upgraded; the criteria used by accrediting associations for school guidance program evaluation were strengthened; and noticeable progress was made in counselor training. Many writers in the field noted that guidance had come of age, that there was a new era.

For example, Donovan (1959) wrote about a new era for guidance in which he pointed out that "the test expert and professional counselor enter the picture to give scientific aid in getting each child in touch with those teachers and courses best calculated to free his abilities" (p. 241). He and others further discussed the movement from an era of mass education to one in which each child was treated as an individual with "counseling personnel becoming indispensable auxiliaries to administrators and teachers" (p. 241).

The following year, Klopf (1960) called for an expanding role for the high school counselor. He pointed out that "as populations increase, schools will become larger and taxes become greater in most communities. Instructional services will increase in communities, but guidance programs may not increase accordingly" (p. 418). He suggested that new uses and approaches to homeroom group guidance, small discussion groups, and group counseling needed to be explored. He also suggested that guidance workers should view themselves not only as counselors but as individuals concerned with total learning, including the personal and social relations of the student:

> If he has a knowledge of individual behavior, the social structure of the school and the community and awareness of the world of today and the future, this in all the ongoing activities of the school he should share. (p. 418)

In the 1960s, one of the most important developments for the school counseling and guidance movement was the *Statement of Policy for Secondary School Counselors* (1964), which was developed and approved as an official policy statement by the American School Counselor Association (ASCA). This effort to specify the role and function of the school counselor involved more than 6,000 school counselors plus teachers, school administrators, and other educators.

C. Gilbert Wrenn's classic contribution of the 1960s, *The Counselor in a Changing World*, also examined the counselor's role in a society with changing ideas about human behavior and changing schools. Wrenn (1962) noted the growing complexity of the counselor's task:

> It is not enough for the counselor to understand youth in isolation, as it were. More than ever before, the counselor must understand not only the student, but himself and his adult contemporaries as they attempt to adjust to a rapidly changing technology and the world order. (p. 8)

C. Harold McCully (1965) implied that if school counselors were to move toward bona fide professionalization, "they cannot afford to define their function on the basis of a retrospective analysis of what counselors have done in the past as technicians" (p. 405). He forecast needed new directions in which the counselor functioned as a consultant and agent for change, directions that would require substantive study of the dynamics of cultural and social change.

By the 1970s, the school guidance counselor had inherited a series of stereotypes, the value and validity of which had to be determined. What historians recorded about guidance in the 1970s attested to their concern for these generalizations and their behavior in dealing with them. These stereotypes were as follows:

> *The Stereotype of Responsibility.* The belief by parents and others that counselors have certain responsibilities such as ensuring that the student takes the "right" courses, selects the appropriate college, takes necessary standardized examinations, meets application deadlines, and so forth.

The Stereotype of Failure. The belief that the counselor is responsible for keeping individuals from failing—that the counselor is a buffer between success and failure. As a predictor of outcomes that determine decisions, the counselor can assess risks and chances for success or failure.

The Stereotype of Occupational Choice. Perhaps more consistent and widespread than any other is the view of the counselor as the person who can tell a student what occupation to enter—who can make this "once-in-a-lifetime" decision for individuals. After all, the counselor is the one with the various interest and aptitude tests and occupational fields—and one is constantly referred to as the person to see about industrial, armed services and educational recruitment materials. (Munson, 1971, pp. 16–17)

In 1973, the National Commission on the Reform of Secondary Education published its report, with 32 recommendations for the improvement of secondary education. Although the majority of these held implications for the functioning of the secondary school counselor, the following were of particular importance:

- Recommendation 6, dealing with bias in counseling
- Recommendation 9, focusing on career education
- Recommendation 10, emphasizing suitable job placement as a part of career education
- Recommendation 12, recommending alternative routes to high school completion

During the mid-1970s and early 1980s, a number of developments influenced counselors in schools and frequently in other settings as well. As noted in more detail in Chapter 14, the accountability movement of this period influenced many school counseling programs to develop more relevant data-based programs, usually based on objective needs assessments. A major publication of this period, *Guidance and Counseling in the Schools* (Herr, 1979), was the outgrowth of a national survey directed by Dr. Edwin L. Herr and jointly sponsored by the American Personnel and Guidance Association* and the Counseling and Guidance Office of the U.S. Department of Education.

Although state certification laws have in recent generations governed the credentialing of counselors in schools in all states, school counselors have also become increasingly interested in the movement to license counselors for practice outside school settings. By 1997, 44 states plus the District of Columbia had passed legislation to license counselors (Alabama, Arizona, Arkansas, California, Colorado, Connecticut, Delaware, Florida, Georgia, Idaho, Illinois, Indiana, Iowa, Kansas, Kentucky, Louisiana, Maine, Maryland, Massachusetts, Michigan, Mississippi, Missouri, Montana, Nebraska, New Hampshire, New Jersey, New Mexico, North Carolina, North Dakota, Ohio, Oklahoma, Oregon, Rhode Island, South Carolina, South Dakota, Tennessee, Texas, Utah, Vermont, Virginia, Washington, West Virginia, Wisconsin, and Wyoming), and others are preparing to follow suit.

In 1983, the presidentially appointed National Commission on Excellence in Education issued its report, entitled *A Nation at Risk* (Bell, 1983). This report cites as its primary evidence the decline in standardized achievement test results and has brought about recommendations for longer school days, more effective school discipline, a return to basics, and more. Although

---

*The American Personnel and Guidance Association officially changed its name to the American Association for Counseling and Development (AACD) in 1983. Then, in 1992, the AACD changed its name to the American Counseling Association.

there are no specific references to school counseling programs, many inferences for such programs could be drawn. Another significant report, *Keeping the Options Open*, published in 1986 by the College Entrance Examination Board (Commission on Precollege Guidance and Counseling), focuses entirely on school counseling and guidance programs.

During the 1980s and 1990s, a number of social concerns affecting children stimulated an accelerated growth of elementary school counseling. Issues such as substance abuse, child abuse, sexual abuse, and latchkey children, plus increased interest in and attention to prevention led to mandated elementary school counseling in 16 states by 1997.

Another recent influence on school counseling programs is the School-to-Work Opportunities Act of 1994, which provides the framework for creating school-to-work opportunity systems in all states, with career counseling and guidance being a high priority activity.

THE DEVELOPMENT OF INSTITUTIONAL AND AGENCY COUNSELING PROGRAMS

The mental health movement, like the vocational guidance movement, owed much of its impetus in the early 1900s to the efforts of one person. This was Clifford Beers, who was neither a physician nor a psychologist, but for several years a patient in a mental institution suffering from schizophrenia. During his confinement, Beers (1908) wrote:

> I soon observed that the only patients who were not likely to be subjected to abuse were the ones least in need of care and treatment. The violent, noisy, and troublesome patient was abused because he was violent, noisy, and troublesome. The patient too weak, physically or mentally, to attend to his own wants was frequently abused because of that very helplessness which made it necessary for the attendants to wait upon him. Usually a restless or troublesome patient placed in the violent ward was assaulted the very first day. This procedure seemed to be a part of the established code of dishonor. The attendants imagined that the best way to gain control of a patient was to cow him from the first. In fact, these fellows—nearly all of them ignorant and untrained—seemed to believe that violent cases could not be handled in any other way. (pp. 164–165)

In another statement, Beers (1908) wrote:

> Most sane people think that no insane person can reason logically. But that is not so. Upon unreasonable premises I made most reasonable deductions, and at that time when my mind was in its most disturbed condition. Had the newspapers which I read on that day which I supposed to be February 1st borne a January date, I might not then, for so long a time, have believed in special editions. Probably I should have inferred that the regular editions had been held back. But the newspapers I had were dated about two weeks ahead. Now if a sane person on February 1st receives a newspaper dated February 14, he will be fully justified in thinking something wrong, either with the publication or with himself. But the shifted calendar which had planted itself in my mind meant as much to me as the true calendar does to any sane businessman. During the seven hundred and ninety-eight days of depression I drew countless incorrect deductions, and essentially the mental process was not other than that which takes place in a well-ordered mind. (pp. 57–58)

These and similar descriptions aroused the public to initiate humanitarian reforms and scientific inquiry into the problems of mental illnesses and their treatment. With the help of a few psychologists of the time, such as William James and Adolph Meyer, the mental hygiene movement was launched to educate the general public on a better appreciation of the plight and treatment of disturbed persons.

At the same time, the viewpoint that persons are products of both their environment and their heredity was reemerging. As a result, a new type of institution for dealing locally with mental illness was gaining support. This institution was to become the forerunner of our present-day community mental health center. It was called a psychopathic hospital. According to Bloom (1984):

> It was to be located in the community, and it was to provide treatment rather than custodial care. The rationale for the psychopathic hospital was based on a set of what were then quite radical ideas. First, it was believed that patients should be identified and treated soon after the onset of their disorder. Second, it was believed that patients should not be isolated from their families, friends, and other sources of support. Third, it was believed that patients' families could provide very useful information to those persons responsible for the patients' treatment and that such information would be far easier to obtain if the treatment facility were in the community. Finally, the psychopathic hospital was designed to stimulate in local physicians an increased interest in the problem of mental illness. (p. 15)

Along with psychopathic hospitals, community aftercare services for former psychiatric patients emerged, and local hospitals began to develop psychiatric diagnostic and outpatient clinics. Community efforts also increased to raise the standards of treatment and prevention of mental disorders and to establish local clinics for disturbed children. As the public became increasingly aware of the extent and impact of mental illness, the possibility of preventive or early treatment began to be discussed.

World War I not only stimulated the development and postwar usage of standardized group psychological tests, it also resulted in two acts significant to the development of one of the early specializations in counseling, rehabilitation counseling. The first of these, the Civilian Vocational Rehabilitation Act (Public Law 236, 1920), was followed in 1921 by Public Law 47. The latter created the Veteran's Bureau and provided, among other benefits, a continuation of vocational rehabilitation services for veterans, including counseling and guidance:

> The counseling provided for veterans was one of the most important features of the Veterans Administration's vocational rehabilitation and education program. It had been observed early in the vocational rehabilitation program for the disabled veterans of World War I that good vocational counseling and guidance was of crucial importance. The lesson was not overlooked in the legislation for World War II veterans and in the implementation of that legislation. All Public Law 16 trainees were required to select their vocational objectives only after formal vocational evaluation and counseling. Those training under Public Law 346 could receive counseling services if they requested them. (Obermann, 1965, p. 190)

The term *rehabilitation counselor*, however, did not appear in professional literature until the late 1930s. Since then, rehabilitation counseling has generally come to be recognized as basically psychological counseling that specializes in the rehabilitation of persons with physical as well as social and emotional problems. In the history of its development, the practice of rehabilitation counseling seems to have gone through several models, described by Jacques (1969) as

1. Vocational agent, trainer, or worker model.
2. Vocational counselor or coordinator of services model.
3. Psychotherapeutic model.
4. Community-centered team counselor model. (p. 17)

The quarter century from 1904 to 1929 was a period of rapid growth in solid scientific research in many different areas. As Mueller (1979) reports:

> While there may have been an overly optimistic view of the fruits of mathematization and postulated procedures, it was a period in which the foundations for such techniques as factor analysis, test theory, scaling, etc., were broadly expanded. In areas such as physiological and sensory psychology, human and animal learning, and social and abnormal psychology, the empirical bases of psychology as science were made as firm in that period as they have ever been. This period established psychology as a provable science, not just an "in-principle" science. (p. 20)

One of the prominent theorists of this period was another Austrian, Alfred Adler, a one-time disciple of Freud, who migrated to the United States in 1932 to avoid the Nazi rise to power in his country. His lectures and writings formed the basis for Adlerian counseling. Adler was one of the pioneers of family counseling and his theories have, in recent years, also influenced the counseling of children.

During the first half of the 20th century, the community mental health movement reflected a good deal of diversity and encompassed both ideological and practical features. Jeger and Slotnick (1982) note:

> As a philosophy, it has its roots in the fields of social psychiatry and public health, which recognized the iatrogenic effects of institutionalization, redefined "mental illness" as a social problem, advocated alternatives to hospitalization and called for community change for purposes of preventing mental health problems. As a methodology, community mental health refers to specific programs that sought to translate this ideology into practice. (p. 15)

After World War II, a series of federal legislative acts defined the mandates of agencies and in so doing provided operational definitions of community mental health practices. The federal government's first major entrance into the public mental health arena began with the passage of the National Mental Health Act of 1946, which established the National Institute of Mental Health. The National Mental Health Act also encouraged each state to designate a single agency as the state mental health authority and initiated a state grant-in-aid program to assist these authorities in the improvement of community mental health services.

In 1944, the Veterans Administration (VA) established centers to provide counseling for those receiving benefits under the GI Bill, which provided training and education for veterans. Many counselors were trained in VA-supported counseling services on college campuses. The VA did much to broaden and professionalize the role of the vocational counselor. In 1951, the VA established the position of counseling psychologist, in line with new concepts from psychology and related disciplines (Borow, 1964, cited in Humes, 1987, p. 16).

During and immediately after World War II, counselors also found increasing opportunities in the VA vocational rehabilitation and educational services as these were rapidly expanded to accommodate the needs of U.S. Armed Services personnel and ex-service personnel.

Counseling, as a recognized speciality in the field of psychology, also emerged during this time. In 1946, Division 17 (Counseling Psychology) of the American Psychological Association was recognized with Dr. E. G. Williamson as the first president. The speciality gained further recognition and acceptance in 1951 following a conference at Northwestern University called by Dr. C. Gilbert Wrenn. Another prominent contributor to the movement was Dr. Carl R. Rogers, whose writings (noted earlier in this chapter) promoted psychological and public interest in psychotherapy.

Another counseling specialty began to emerge in the 1950s in the form of marriage and family counseling. Although historically this movement appeared to have been initiated in the early 1930s, the dramatic post–World War II increase in the separation and divorce rate of young couples led to rapid developments in marital therapy. In the 1960s, dramatic increases in new styles of coupling, marriage, and living together further stimulated interest in providing professional counseling assistance to couples and families. During this period, marital therapy moved increasingly from individual analysis to conjoint marital therapy (Brown & Christensen, 1986).

This period after World War II also saw a rapid expansion of community mental health services. In 1955, Congress passed a Mental Health Study Act, which established a joint commission on mental illness and health. This study resulted in a report entitled *Action for Mental Health* (1961), which led in 1963 to the Community Mental Health Centers Act (Public Law 88-164) (Jeger & Slotnick, 1982).

The initial 2,000 centers were expected to provide five essential services:

1. Inpatient (for short-term stays);
2. Outpatient;
3. Partial hospitalization (i.e., day and/or night hospitals);
4. Emergency care (i.e., 24-hour crisis services); and
5. Consultation (i.e., indirect service) and community education (i.e., prevention).

For a center to be considered comprehensive, five additional services were required: (a) diagnostic, (b) rehabilitation, (c) precare and aftercare, (d) training, and (e) research and evaluation (Jeger & Slotnick, 1982).

The first decline in the number of patients in state mental institutions was recorded in 1955. This decline was to continue steadily over the next 20 years despite increases in the number of admissions. This trend had obvious implications for the growth of local mental health services.

The trauma of the Vietnam War and the postwar era for many veterans and their families created another population needing mental health counseling. Also during the 1960s and 1970s, increased substance abuse and public awareness of the extent and seriousness of the problem at all age levels led to research, the development of training programs, and the growth of another area of specialization for counselors. Special attention to preparing specialists for correctional counseling and counseling the elderly reflected a concern for the needs of these populations as well.

The Community Mental Health Centers Amendments of 1975 (Public Law 94-63) redefined the notion of a comprehensive community mental health center from the 5 minimum and 5 optional services to a mandated set of 12 services. They include the 5 originally established services plus 7 additional services as follows:

1. Special services for children
2. Special services for the elderly
3. Preinstitutional screening and alternative treatment (as pertains to the courts and other public agencies)
4. Follow-up for persons discharged from state mental hospitals
5. Transitional living for persons discharged from state mental hospitals
6. Alcoholism services (prevention, treatment, and rehabilitation)
7. Drug abuse services

In addition, the 1975 amendments also obligated centers to allocate 2% of their operating budgets for program evaluation.

The mandated delivery of these 12 services was further modified in the Community Mental Health Extension Act of 1978 (Public Law 95-622). Specifically, new centers were required to provide 6 services (inpatient, outpatient, emergency, screening, follow-up of discharged inpatients, and consultation/education) and were allowed to phase in gradually the remaining 6 of the 12 services over their initial three years of operation (i.e., partial hospitalization, children's services, elderly services, transitional halfway houses, alcohol abuse, and drug abuse services).

In considering all the various provisions for services mandated by legislation since the 1970s, we can convey the spirit of the community mental health movement. The ten characteristics delineated by Bloom (1984) as differentiating community mental health from traditional clinical practice can serve to identify both the ideological and operational aspects of the movement:

- First, as opposed to institutional (i.e., mental hospital) practice, the *community* provides the practice setting.
- Second, rather than an individual patient, a *total population* or community is the target; hence the term *catchment area* to define a given center's area of responsibility.
- A third feature concerns the type of service delivered, that is, offering *preventive services* rather than just treatment.
- *Continuity of care* among the components of a comprehensive system of services constitutes the fourth dimension.
- The emphasis on *indirect services*, that is, consultation, is the fifth characteristic.
- A sixth characteristic lies in the area of *clinical innovations*—brief psychotherapy and crisis intervention.
- The emphasis on *systematic planning* for services by considering the demographics of a population, specifying unmet needs, and identifying "high-risk" groups represents a seventh characteristic.
- Utilizing new *person-power resources*, especially nonprofessional mental health workers, constitutes the eighth dimension.
- The ninth dimension is defined in terms of the *community control* concept, which holds that consumers should play central roles in establishing service priorities and evaluating programs.
- Finally, the tenth characteristic identifies community mental health as seeking *environmental causes* of human distress, in contrast to the traditional intrapsychic emphasis. (Jeger & Slotnick, 1982, p. 17)

Although a majority of community mental health workers might agree that these characteristics reflect the orientation of community mental health, there is much less agreement on the emphasis of these concepts in practice. (Bloom, 1984, p. 38)

In the 1970s, significant federal legislation in the form of the Mental Health Systems Act passed Congress and was signed into law by President Carter. In addition to continuing many of the provisions of the original act, other provisions broadened the scope of care for disturbed children and adolescents. President Reagan's election in 1980, however, led to new economic policies at the federal level, which included repealing the budgetary authorizations of this act. As a result, in the 1980s, states and local communities were increasingly called on to assume the financing of mental health care facilities and programs.

The United States entered the 1990s with great fanfare—trumpeting the many accomplishments of the first 90 years of the century and anticipating triumphs in the remaining

10 years. Not to be overlooked, however, was the fact that the nation faced significant societal problems that affected millions of its citizens.

These problems included the ever-increasing AIDS epidemic; the continuing addiction of millions to drugs and alcohol; the alarming numbers of abused children and spouses; increases in teen pregnancies, teen suicides, and teens engaged in criminal activities; the persistent school dropout problem; the disgraceful numbers of homeless; the resurfacing of various forms of prejudice; a bankruptcy of values ranging from the political to the private sector; and a myriad of career needs affecting all age groups and socioeconomic levels. The United States could be labeled a nation on the verge of being psychologically and sociologically at risk.

Further, in examining these problems, we would note that many of these issues require not only remedial treatment but, even more importantly, preventive efforts of our profession if they are to be ameliorated to any degree. Treatment or punitive actions cannot alone solve societal problems. Only prevention has the prospect for diminishing the numbers of potential victims of nearly all these social ills. In this context, then, we can conclude that most of these problems are in our realm. Of all the helping professions, counselors, more than any other, have access to and work with populations and emphasize prevention as well as early intervention and treatment.

Thus, as we begin a new century, we see the opportunity for counseling to become *the* helping profession and respond to society's needs in the coming years. The chapters that follow will acquaint you with the skills and knowledge counselors must acquire to serve society's mental health needs and the settings in which counselors will function to provide their services in meeting these great challenges in the years ahead.

SUMMARY

We have examined the need of humankind, from the time of Adam down through the ages, for advice and counsel, to understand themselves and their relationships to their fellow human beings, and to recognize and develop their own potential. In responding to these needs, chieftains and elders of ancient tribal societies were perhaps the first forerunners, the ancient counterparts, of the present-day counselor. Later, in the early civilizations, philosophers, priests, or other representatives of the gods filled roles offering advice and counseling. Often so-called treatment for the mentally ill was cruel, even when administered by physicians. The role of religion in the counsel and advice of the young in particular, but not exclusively, continued through the Middle Ages, supplemented by sporadic efforts of talent identification and development and even planned career placement. From the Middle Ages onward, teachers also were increasingly expected to provide guidance for their pupils, often of the most directive kind. To supplement these efforts, books began to appear with increasing frequency from the 18th century onward that focused on providing advice and counsel to youth in meeting many of the problems of the times, especially those concerning occupational choice. Meanwhile, many leading statesmen, philosophers, scientists, and educators were laying a philosophical groundwork that would eventually support and nurture an embryonic movement to establish psychology as a science and academic discipline in its own right, with an impact on school and community settings.

The school counseling and guidance movement, which for many years was unique to U.S. Education, in its beginnings had a vocational guidance emphasis but was shortly to be influenced by a multitude of other movements, especially psychological testing, mental health, and progressive education. Later in the 20th century, the interdisciplinary character of the movement was further emphasized through influences from such movements as group dynamics, counseling psychology, education of the gifted, career education, and placement.

The public or community aspects of the mental health movement initially focused on home confinement and treatment, if at all. An early significant development was state support for the establishment of state mental hospitals in the United States in the 19th century. However, at the turn of the century (1908), the mental health movement was stirred by the writings of Clifford Beers, and local mental health treatment centers began to emerge. These community aftercare services were the forerunners of the present-day community mental health centers.

Three significant legislative acts that further stimulated the counseling movement were the Civilian Vocational Rehabilitation Act (1920), the Mental Health Study Act (1955), and the Community Mental Health Center Act (1963). Later in this century, public need led to the development of specializations in marriage and family, substance abuse, corrections, and gerontological counseling.

Over the years, the movement has not been without its pioneers and heroes. Of course, the great humanistic teachers of history—Christ, Mohammed, Buddha—and farsighted leaders such as Plato, Aristotle, Rousseau and Pestalozzi, would have been charter members and undoubtedly elected officers of any counseling association of their time in history. In the United States, one can easily envision Franklin, Jefferson, Lincoln, and the Roosevelts receiving honorary life memberships in the American Counseling Association for their contributions to the eventual growth of the movement. But the real heroes have been persons such as Parsons, Beers, Davis, Reed, Weaver, and Hill—those early, persistent, and farsighted pioneers of the movement whose efforts were later recognized and advanced and then further enriched by the giants of the last half of the 20th century: Carl R. Rogers, E. G. Williamson, C. Gilbert Wrenn, Albert Ellis, and Donald Super.

It is said that a movement must have a cause and leadership to survive. This brief review of some historic highlights of the development of counseling and guidance in the United States should indicate that neither has been lacking. As the past illuminates the future, it is possible to predict that, regardless of the wonderful scientific and technological advances that await humankind, many persons will search out the counsel and advice of the trained, while others will still seek self- and other understandings for the development of their potential or the solution of their problems. Also, as we look at current major social concerns, we see unprecedented opportunities for the counseling profession to serve society. Let us therefore proceed to the next chapter to examine some of the activities of the trained professional counselor.

DISCUSSION QUESTIONS

1.   Discuss factors and events that influenced your decision to enter or consider entering the counseling profession.

2.   Have you had your fortune told? If so, who and when, how accurate, and what results? Which do you believe is most likely to be accurate in predicting futures: palmists, astrologists, graphologists, or others? Defend your selection.

3.   National and state legislative acts have had significant impact on the counseling profession. In view of current national social problems, what new legislation might you suggest that would affect the field of counseling?

4.   Discuss differences and similarities in the historic development of counseling in schools versus counseling in agency and institutional settings.

CLASS ACTIVITIES

1.   Go to the library and find the earliest article you can on the subject of counseling and guidance. Report your article, its date, author, publication, and content to the class.

2.   Identify significant characteristics of today's society and examine these to see whether they have implications for the development of any new careers or occupations. What are the implications of these developments for the counseling profession? Discuss in small groups.

3.   Review current newspapers and popular publications for reports or articles that would imply a

useful role that the counseling profession can play in responding to human needs in today's society.

4.   Go to the library and examine the major journals in the field of guidance and counseling today. Select three journals and examine issues that are focused on today and compare them with the issues discussed 20 and 30 years ago. What changes do you see in the contents?

SELECTED HISTORICAL READINGS

Adler, A. (1959). *Understanding human nature*. New York: Premier Books.

Anastasi, A. (1954). The measurements of abilities. *Journal of Counseling Psychology, 1*, 164–168.

Conant, J. (1959). *The American high school today*. New York: McGraw-Hill.

Cross, H. I. (1964). The outcome of psychotherapy: A selected analysis of research findings. *Journal of Consulting Psychology, 28*, 413–417.

Dugan, W. (1962). An inward look: Assumptions and expectations. *Counselor Education and Supervision, 1*, 174–180.

Dymond, R. F. (1953). Can clinicians predict individual behavior? *Journal of Personality, 22*, 151–161.

Ellis, A. (1957). Outcome of employing three techniques of psychotherapy. *Journal of Clinical Psychology, 13*, 334–350.

Gummere, R. (1988). The counselor as prophet: Frank Parsons. *Journal of Counseling and Development, 66*, 402–405.

History of psychology [Special section] (1997, July). *American Psychologist, 52* (7).

Hooper, D. (1996). Counselling psychology: Into the new millenium. In R. Woolfe & W. Dryden (Eds.), *Handbook of counselling psychology* (pp. 630–648). London: Sage.

Howard, G. S. (1992). Behold our creation! What counseling psychology has become and might yet become. *Journal of Counseling Psychology, 39*, 419–442.

Murphy, G. (1955). The cultural context of guidance. *Personnel and Guidance Journal, 34*, 4–9.

Odegaard, C. (1987). A historical perspective on the dilemmas confronting psychologists. *American Psychologist, 42*, 1048–1051.

Professional counseling: Spotlight on specialties [Special issue]. (1995, November/December). *Journal of Counseling and Development, 74* (2).

Strawbridge, S., & Woolfe, R. (1996). Counselling psychology: A sociological perspective. In R. Woolfe & W. Dryden (Eds.), *Handbook of counselling psychology* (pp. 605–629). London: Sage.

Tiedeman, D. V., & Field, F. L. (1962). Guidance: The science of purposeful action applied through education. *Harvard Educational Review, 32*, 483–501.

Watkins, C. E. (1994). On hope, promise, and possibility in counseling psychology or some simple, but meaningful observations about our specialty. *Counseling Psychologist, 22*, 315–334.

Whitely, J. (Ed.). (1984). Counseling psychology: A historical perspective. *The Counseling Psychologist, 12*, 1–126.

Williamson, E. G. (1964). An historical perspective of the vocational guidance movement. *Personnel and Guidance Journal, 42*, 854–859.

Woolfe, R. (1996). The nature of counselling psychology. In R. Woolfe & W. Dryden (Eds.), *Handbook of counselling psychology* (pp. 3–20). London: Sage.

Wynkoop, T. F., & Dixon, D. N. (1994). Organizational and political issues in counseling psychology: An accounting of the Georgia Conference recommendations. *Counseling Psychologist, 22*, 342–356.

RESEARCH OF INTEREST

Beale, A. V. (1986). Trivial pursuit: The history of guidance. *School Counselor, 34* (1), 14–17.

Abstract

This article quizzes the reader with 15 trivia questions and provides the answers regarding the history of guidance. Additional resources, as well as references to the article, are provided for readers who are interested in learning more about the history of the school guidance movement.

Campbell, D. P. (1965). Achievements of counseled and non-counseled students twenty-five years after counseling. *Journal of Counseling Psychology, 12*, 287–293.

Abstract

During the mid-1930s, 400 students who had obtained counseling at a university counseling center were matched individually with noncounseled students of similar academic and socioeconomic background. One year later comparisons revealed that counseled students had significantly better grades and had made a better adjustment to college. Few comparisons can be made between the pairs 25 years later because of historic factors and experimental mortality. Remaining comparisons revealed a mild difference in achievement in favor of counseled over noncounseled students 25 years later.

Helwig, A. A. (1993). Employment counselor training and professional issues in the United States. *Journal of Employment Counseling, 30* (4), 153–167.

Abstract

This article discusses employment counseling as practiced by the U.S. Employment Service (currently called Job Service) during the past 30 years. A brief outline emphasizes the rapid expansion of employment counseling services in the 1960s, decentralization of employment and training services in the 1970s, and elimination of counseling consultants to each region by 1973. The development of the competency-based counseling model in the early 1970s provided a performance-based program in which skills (e.g., relationship, assessment, guidance and counseling, professional development skills) necessary for the job of employment counselor were identified. More recent training initiatives include the Veterans Assessment Program, advanced group counseling training, and the National Veterans Training Institute. Because few new counselors have been hired for Job Service during the past 15 years, it is asserted that the existing corps is well trained, experienced, and skilled.

Ray, C. G., & Finley, J. K. (1994). Did CMHCs fail or succeed? Analysis of the expectations and outcomes of the community mental health movement. *Administration and Policy in Mental Health, 21* (4), 283–293.

Abstract

This article establishes a historical context for assessing the impact of the Community Mental Health Center (CMHC) program. The program was based on the social-engineering themes of comprehensiveness, centralized service delivery to meet all needs within a catchment area, and self-sustainment that would be integrated over time with mainstream health care. However, competition for valuable economic resources and the rise of social ills (including family disintegration, drug abuse, and urban violence) required that CMHCs target their services to specialized areas. Deinstitutionalization caused CMHCs to face large numbers of nonpaying patients who, in the past, would have been hospitalized. Although CMHCs today contribute substantially to meeting mental health service needs, their services are severely limited.

Resnick, R. J. (1997). A brief history of practice—expanded. *American Psychologist, 52* (4), 463–468.

Abstract

Psychology can trace its origins from philosophy, through experiential introspection and behaviorism, to a major branch in the evolution of the discipline called practice. This article presents a history of practice, with emphasis on major events that altered the direction and focus of practice. The history begins with the first patient of Lightner Witmer and traces the movement into assessment, psychotherapy, and primary health care. It examines the impact of the federal government, the Veterans Administration system, and World Wars I and II on the evolution of practice. The expansion of the availability of services along with the movement to credential-qualified professionals are delineated within the context of licensure laws, freedom of choice acts, and third-party reimbursement. Finally, the impact of health reform on psychological practice is described. These events are viewed as an integral part of the history of psychology as well as the evolution of practice.

Truax, C. B. (1966). Reinforcement and nonreinforcement in Rogerian psychotherapy. *Journal of Abnormal Psychology, 71*, 1–9.

Abstract

This article explores the possibility of important reinforcement effects from therapy encounters with a client-centered therapist. Four eclectic and one analytic clinical psychologist rate three therapist behaviors identified as potential reinforcers and nine patient behaviors identified as theoretically significant, from an unbiased sample of 40 typewritten (TPT, Therapist, Patient, Therapist) interaction units. Findings support the Skinnerian view that reinforcement occurs and influences behaviors in Rogerian therapeutic encounters.

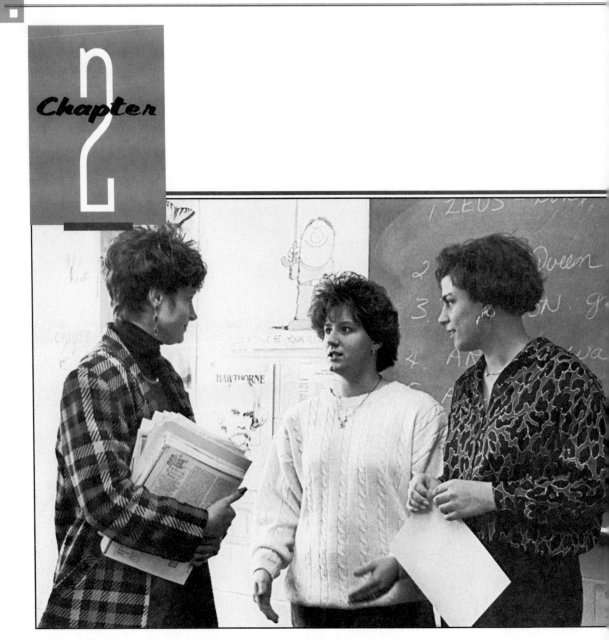

Chapter 2

Traditional and Current Activities of Counselors

In studying any profession one may ask, What is the profession of . . . (i.e., counseling)? What do they (i.e., counselors) do? This chapter's objective is to respond to those questions. We begin by examining counseling as a helping profession and then identify activities through which the professional counselor carries out his or her responsibilities.

COUNSELING AS A HELPING PROFESSION

Counseling as a helping profession is a concept that forms the basis for the role and function of the counselor in today's society. A helping profession may be described as one in which the members are specially trained and licensed or certified to perform a unique and needed service for fellow human beings. Helping professionals serve; they are recognized by society as the sole professional providers of the unique and needed services.

The helping professions include medicine, law, dentistry, education, psychology, and social work. The roots of each lie in the nature of humankind and society, past and present. It is on these bases that services are determined and programs for providing these services are developed. We will briefly review some of the basic concepts of humankind and society as a basis for the helping professions in general and the counseling profession in particular.

In the instance of the helping professions, including counseling, it is appropriate to begin with the very foundation of their existence—namely, the human client. This client has certain distinguishing characteristics that provide a basis for the counseling profession and the institutions and agencies through which this profession contributes its special knowledge and skills. Although any attempt to characterize such a versatile and ever-changing species as human beings is perilous, we have certain stable yet unique traits that set us apart from other living species. In the main, these are what we might term the privileges of the human race. They provide not only the basis or focus of our being, but the basis for our doing as well. They also suggest roles that human beings can play in helping their fellow human beings. These distinguishing characteristics include the following:

- *Humans are among the weakest species at birth.*
  We are born without the genetically imprinted behaviors possessed by many forms of life. Young animal life in the forests and jungles of the world can survive without adult help; young human life cannot. Our early survival is dependent solely upon the attention, care, and affection of others. The human need for love and care and the degree to which it is provided becomes a critical basis for the lifelong adjustment or lack of it for the individual.
- *Humankind has the greatest potential for growth and development of all the species.*
  The brain itself triples in physical size and multiplies even more in capacity as a child grows. This brainpower, coupled with a surplus of energy (over all other species) gives us almost limitless possibilities. The realization of human potential does not, however, rest with the individual alone but also depends on many environmental variables and assistance in recognizing and developing one's potential.
- *Humankind has the highest level of communication skills, skills that enable us to express our thoughts in detail to many others; to teach our language to others (even other animal species at certain levels); to record, send, and receive.*
  These dual capacities, sending and receiving, in both word and gesture, form the bases for human relationship skills and for love and affection, which in turn form the

27

primary stimulus for the human race. This ability to relate to others thus becomes the core of a happy, well-adjusted life.

- *The human species exhibits a wider range of differences than any other.*
  These differences not only clearly distinguish each human from every other human but also multiply the potential of the society and stimulate the advancement of civilizations. The concept of individual differences provides the rationale for client analysis in the helping professions.

- *Human beings manipulate and are manipulated by their environment.*
  The behavior of a human being cannot be adequately understood apart from the environmental context within which it occurs. Thus, environmental analysis is becoming increasingly important to the professional counselor.

- *Humankind is the only living organism that captures the time stream.*
  We can recall the past, act in the present, and plan for the future. This gives us the capability for building on our past experiences, avoiding past mistakes, anticipating the future, and planning for the development of our potential.

- *Humankind has the ability to reason and to gain insight.*
  These twin factors enable us to make reasoned choices among alternatives and to change. This aptitude for planned individual change is significant in the important arenas of individual development and social adjustment (relationships with one's peers). Our ability to understand ourselves and act rationally also contributes to the maturing process.

From images of the human species, McCully (1969) draws inferences for counseling and other helping relationships as follows:

1. All [people] at birth possess the potential for the distinguishing characteristics of the human species; and
2. The environmental conditions the individual experiences from birth on may either nourish or suppress their realization. (pp. 134, 135)

In light of these premises, we can suggest at even this early point in our discussion that a fundamental basis for counseling program development must be rooted in our understanding of the characteristics and needs of all our clientele, plus an understanding of the environment that shapes them. For counselors, this implies learning about human growth and development and our sociocultural foundations.

Societal needs and expectancies also play an important role in a profession's development and functioning. The brief historic review in Chapter 1 indicated some of the social influences on the development of the counseling profession.

THE PROFESSIONAL COUNSELOR

As a beginning student in a counselor preparation program, you have made a commitment to prepare yourself for entry into the counseling profession. Membership in a profession mandates that the member assumes the expectancies and characteristics of a professional. The term *professional counselor* distinguishes the professional from those who may use the title counselor in conjunction with another primary occupation (i.e., loan counselor, sales counselor, investment counselor, etc.). Professionals are full-time active representatives of their profession. They accept the responsibilities of professionalism. For the professional counselor, these responsibilities include the following:

1. The professional counselor must become fully trained and qualified to meet the needs of the client population he/she elects or is designated to serve. Training requires an appropriate graduate level (master's degree at least) program, which includes an understanding and awareness of the systematic theories that guide professional practice.

2. The professional counselor needs to be professionally and personally committed to constantly updating and upgrading the skills and knowledge to reflect the latest and ongoing progress in one's professional field.

3. The professional counselor is aware of and contributes to the advancement of the profession through the conducting of and participation in research studies designed to advance knowledge for the profession. In addition, he or she assures the dissemination of such studies to the profession through professional writings and program presentations at professional meetings.

4. The professional counselor is an active participating member of the appropriate professional organizations at all levels (national, regional, state, local).

5. The professional counselor is aware of and adheres to all legal and ethical guidelines pertaining to the profession and the practice of counseling. It should be noted that in the majority of states the use of the title counselor is protected by law.

COUNSELING AS A DISCIPLINE

While examining our roots and the emergence of counseling as a helping profession, it is also appropriate to note the foundations for counseling as a discipline. Much of this foundation has been derived from the field of psychology. The contributions from psychology have included counseling theory and process, standardized assessment, individual and group counseling techniques, and career development and decision-making theories.

Specialty areas within the field of psychology have further contributed to a knowledge base for counselors to draw on. These include *educational psychology* and its studies of learning theories and human growth and development and their implications for educational settings. *Social psychology* helps us understand the impact of social situations on individuals, including the environment's influence on behavior. *Ecological psychology* is also concerned with the study of environments and how individuals perceive and are shaped by, as well as influence in turn, their environments. *Developmental psychology* helps us understand why and how individuals grow and change over their life span.

While acknowledging that our strongest disciplinary ties are to the field of psychology, we must also recognize the important contributions of other sciences to the counseling profession. For example, sociology has contributed to our understanding of human groups and their influence on human behavior. Anthropology has provided counselors with insights into the cultures of peoples, cultures that in turn provide guidelines for the behaviors and viewpoints of their members. (Chapter 9 will discuss the contributions of sociology and anthropology to human assessment.) Biology has helped us understand the human organism and its uniqueness. The health professions have made us aware of the importance of wellness and prevention.

TRADITIONAL ACTIVITIES

The historic review of the counseling movement in Chapter 1 noted the contributions of the many disciplines and influences that have consistently been adding and expanding their areas of emphasis. Noted were eras of vocational or career guidance, mental health, standardized testing for client analysis, education as guidance, group activities, and the identification and college placement of the gifted. Other movements included the community mental health agency movement; the counseling psychology movement; the development of specialized counseling programs for rehabilitation, substance abuse, correctional, marriage and family, and elderly counseling; the reemphasis of the impact of environment on the individual's growth and development; and a currently renewed stress on preventive intervention. However, despite the relatively short time that counseling has existed as a profession, certain traditional activities, basic principles, and identifiable patterns of program organization have emerged. An understanding of these can provide some insights into the not infrequently asked question, How come counselors do what they do the way they do it?

Because many of the early training programs emphasized school counselor preparation, many of the influential texts had this orientation as well. These authors tended to discuss counselor functions in terms of services. For example, approximately 40 years ago, Froehlich (1958), in discussing counseling and guidance services to pupils in schools, identified basic services to pupils in groups and individually, services to the instructional staff, services to the administration, and research services. Due to the National Defense Education Act (NDEA) of 1958, the 1960s were a period of rapid growth for counseling programs, especially in schools. Publications of that period, such as that by Hatch and Costar (1961) also noted that

> it seems more desirable to think of the guidance program as a program of services—services which can be defined, recognized, administered, and evaluated. It is then possible to define a guidance program as a program of services specially designed to improve the adjustment of the individual for whom it was organized. (p. 14)

These authors go on to make the following suggestions:

- Guidance services are for all concerned.
- Guidance services are for all school levels.
- Guidance services are primarily preventive in nature.
- The teacher plays a major role in the guidance program.
- The program of guidance services needs trained personnel.
- The program of guidance services requires coordination.
- The guidance program uses and improves on present practices.
- Guidance services are not an added activity.
- Guidance services are a group of facilitating services.
- The training background of guidance workers presupposes certain elements.

Hatch and Costar conclude their first chapter by identifying the following services as desirable for a school counseling program:

- Pupil inventory service
- Information service

- Counseling service
- Placement service
- Follow-up and evaluation service

Other references of this period include Zeran and Riccio (1962), who identify basic services as analysis of the individual, counseling, placement, and follow-up and informational services. Gibson and Higgins (1966) note that although semantics and labels varied, the basic services were usually identified as pupil analysis, individual counseling, informational activities, group guidance, placement and follow-up, and evaluation and research.

Later, in the 1980s, Shertzer and Stone (1981) enumerated components of guidance programs in schools as follows: (1) an appraisal component; (2) an information component; (3) a counseling component; (4) a consulting component; (5) a planning, placement, and follow-up component; and (6) an evaluation component. Blocher and Biggs (1983) note in their discussion of counseling in community settings that counseling psychologists engage in individual and small group counseling centered around concerns involving educational and vocational planning, personal problem-solving and decision making, family problems, and other activities related to personal growth, prevention, consultation, and, at times, as a psychological educator. They state that assessment strategies must be developed and mastered that permit an understanding of individuals as they interact in natural environments. Counselors must understand processes of human development as they apply to both individuals and social organizations.

Additional insight into the basic services expected from counselors and counseling programs may be discerned by noting that the Council for Accreditation of Counseling and Related Educational Programs (CACREP) specifies that all counselors should study eight core areas: human growth and development, social-cultural foundations, helping relations, group work, career and lifestyle development, appraisal, research and program evaluation, and professional orientation.

In summary, these and numerous other authors over the years have pointed toward certain traditional or basic activities for counselors across all settings, although emphasis may vary, of course. Those prominently identified include individual assessment, environmental assessment, individual counseling, group counseling and guidance, career assistance, and placement and follow-up. Currently, these traditional activities have expanded to include referral, consultation, research, evaluation and accountability, and prevention. Preventive intervention has also received renewed attention. These are discussed briefly in the sections that follow and will be considered in greater detail in later chapters.

Individual Assessment

Individual assessment is that activity that seeks, systematically, to identify the characteristics and potential of every client. This activity is often considered a primary skill of the professional counselor because it provides a database for more readily understanding the person in the counseling setting, the effective planning of group counseling activities that reflect client interests and needs, the development of responsive career and human potential development programs, and the organization of systematic placement and follow-up programs. Often referred to as *individual inventory, assessment,* or *appraisal,* this activity promotes the client's self-understanding as well as better understandings by counselors and other helping professionals.

This activity received initial stimulus as a result of the standardized testing movement. Even today, standardized test results are the most frequently used objective data in individual analysis. Other popular and traditional techniques are observation and observation reports, self-reporting techniques such as the autobiography, and, in recent years, an increasing use of values clarification techniques. It should be noted that other helping professional specialists also have diagnostic skills and responsibilities. For example, a school counselor will often consult with school psychologists and psychometrists as specialists in psychological assessment, including individual testing, and with school social workers as specialists in environmental and case study analysis. Chapters 8 and 9 will discuss these and other techniques for human resource assessment in greater detail.

Individual Counseling

Individual counseling, since the early days of the counseling movement, has been identified as the core activity through which all the other activities become meaningful. Counseling is a one-to-one helping relationship that focuses on a person's growth and adjustment and problem-solving and decision-making needs. It is a client-centered process that demands confidentiality. This process is initiated by establishing a state of psychological contact or relationship between the counselor and the client and progresses as certain conditions essential to the success of the counseling process prevail. Many practitioners believe that these include counselor genuineness or congruence, respect for the client, and an empathic understanding of the client's internal frame of reference.

Although each counselor will, in time, develop his or her own personal theory to guide personal practice, established theories provide a basis for examination and learning. Effective counseling not only requires counselors with the highest levels of training and professional skills, but a certain type of person as well. Counseling programs will suffer in effectiveness and credibility unless counselors exhibit understanding, warmth, humaneness, and positive attitudes toward humankind. Chapter 5 will discuss individual counseling in greater detail.

Group Counseling and Guidance

Groups have become increasingly popular as a means of providing organized and planned assistance to individuals for a wide range of needs. Counselors provide such assistance through *group counseling* or *group guidance*. In schools, students have been organized into groups for what might be called guidance purposes since long before any counseling or guidance label was bestowed on the activity. The organization of courses and group meetings to dispense primarily occupational information can be traced back to before the evolution of the counseling movement. Homeroom grouping served a guidance as well as an administrative function long before being labeled as such. However, in 1934, a textbook by H. C. McKown bore the title *Home Room Guidance*. With the increasing importance and attention given to extracurricular activities in schools in the 1920s and 1930s, some suggested these activities also were a type of group guidance experience.

Although various activities from time to time have been given the label group guidance, the most consistent definition of this service is one that views it as an activity designed to provide individuals with information or experiences that promote their career or educational understandings and personal social growth and adjustment. Some traditional group guidance activities that have become familiar to most high school students are career days, college days, and orientation days.

In recent generations, group counseling has also been viewed as a basic but different activity than group guidance. Whereas group guidance focuses on providing information and developmental experiences, group counseling tends to focus more on the problem-solving and adjustment needs of persons through a process very similar to individual counseling. Gazda (1984) makes distinctions between group guidance and group counseling in the school setting as follows:

Group Guidance

Group guidance was organized to prevent the development of problems. The content included educational–vocational–personal–social information not otherwise systematically taught in academic courses. The typical setting was the classroom. Typical class size ranged from approximately 20 to 35. Providing accurate information for use in improved understanding of self and others was the direct emphasis in group guidance; attitude change frequently was an indirect outcome or goal. The leadership was provided by a classroom teacher or counselor who utilized a variety of instructional media and group dynamics concepts in motivating students and in obtaining group interaction. Instructional media included unfinished stories, puppet plays, movies, films, filmstrips, guest speakers, audio and videotaped interviews, student reports, and the like. Group dynamics concepts referred to the process employed in group guidance, such as sociodramas, buzz groups, panels, and other related techniques. (p. 6)

Group Counseling

Whereas the goal of group guidance is to provide students with accurate information that will help them make more appropriate plans and life decisions and in this sense is prevention oriented, group counseling is growth engendering and prevention and remediation oriented. Group counseling is prevention oriented in the sense that the counselees or clients are capable of functioning in society but may be experiencing some "rough spots" in their lives. If counseling is successful, the rough spots may be successfully smoothed with no serious personality defects incurred.

Group counseling is growth engendering insofar as it provides the participants incentive and motivation to make changes that are in their best interest (that is, the participants are motivated to take actions that maximize their potential through self-actualizing behaviors).

Group counseling is remedial for those individuals who have entered into a spiral of self-defeating behavior but who are nevertheless capable of reversing the spiral without counseling intervention. However, with counseling intervention, the counselee is likely to recover, and recover more quickly and with fewer emotional scars.

Although the content of group counseling is very similar to group guidance—including educational, vocational, personal, and social concerns—a number of other factors are quite different. First *group guidance* is recommended for all students on a regularly scheduled basis; *group counseling* is generally recommended only for those who are experiencing continuing or temporary problems that information alone will not resolve.

Group guidance makes an *indirect* attempt to change attitudes and behaviors through accurate information or an emphasis on cognitive or intellective functioning; group counseling makes a *direct* attempt to modify attitudes and behaviors by emphasizing total involvement. Group guidance is applicable to classroom-size groups, whereas group counseling is dependent upon the development of strong group cohesiveness and the sharing of personal concerns, which are most applicable to small, intimate groups. (pp. 7–8)

We might conclude that group guidance activities are most likely to be found in schools. Group counseling will be popular in agency and institutional settings and utilized somewhat, though not as frequently as group guidance, in school settings, whereas group psychotherapy will most frequently occur in clinics and agency or institutional settings. Group counseling and other group responsibilities of the counselor will be discussed in greater detail in Chapter 7.

Career Assistance

Since their earliest inception, both the school guidance movement and the counseling psychology movement have had a strong vocational influence. Traditionally, this activity has been viewed as one in which standardized tests were used for career assessment and planning. Descriptive materials and media were accumulated, organized, and then disseminated through planned group activities, as well as used in individual advising and counseling.

For many years in school settings this activity was referred to as the *information service* (providing occupational and educational information). In the 1970s, the concept of this basic service was broadened and a new (now more appropriate) label assigned: *career guidance*. This term seemed more compatible with the rapidly developing career education movement and also represented in the minds of many (but not all) a broadening of the school counseling program's responsibility in the career development of school-aged youths. This approach, a developmental one, suggests certain experiences and understandings at each stage of one's growth that will provide for the building of appropriate foundations for later career planning and decision making.

The attention to and preparation for providing career assistance to client populations is one of the distinguishing and unique characteristics of the counseling profession. Dramatic changes taking place in the world of work have greatly altered the workplace and affected the traditional planning and careers of millions of workers. As a result, the counseling profession is being called upon once again to renew and update its efforts in one of its most traditional areas of service and to provide career guidance and counseling, not at selected stages in life's development, but across the entire life span.

Too, technology is keeping pace with the rapid change affecting work, workers, and preparation for work. Computer-based programs, the Internet, distance learning, and interactive learning systems are but a few of the technological developments impacting how counselors provide career assistance and information to their clients.

Counselors in both school and nonschool settings are called upon to provide career planning and adjustment assistance to clients. In some agencies, such as community career centers and career centers for special populations, the focus is almost exclusively on the career needs of individuals. Counselors in government employment offices and rehabilitation services have an obvious responsibility to provide career counseling and guidance. Even those counselors in more broadly based programs such as community agencies, secondary schools, and institutions of higher education are expected to provide for the career-oriented needs of the populations they are designed to serve.

Placement and Follow-Up

Placement and *follow-up* have more traditionally been a service of school counseling programs with an emphasis on educational placement in courses and programs. In actual practice, this has meant that many school counselors have had responsibility for student scheduling, a very time-consuming task that has been viewed with considerable controversy as an administrative rather than a counseling function. Another aspect of educational placement is those activities associated with college admissions.

The other obvious component of the placement service—employment placement—has had much less emphasis and planning in schools. However, concerns for youth unemployment in the 1990s has resulted in increasing attention to this aspect of placement in schools. Job placement in school counseling programs strives to match students seeking part-time or regular employment with available jobs. It also frequently involves a form of referral as well, in which the individual is referred to a particular job setting.

Follow-up activities are a means of assessing the effectiveness of a program's placement activities. Placement and follow-up activities have taken on increasing significance in schools in which career education and planning are emphasized. Of course, employment counselors and rehabilitation counselors are very active in the referral, placement, and follow-up of their clients. Also, as counselors are increasingly employed in business and industrial settings, these procedures will be an important aspect of their services. Counselors in all settings should use follow-up procedures for assessing counseling outcomes. Placement and follow-up activities are discussed further in Chapter 10.

Referral

Referral is the practice of aiding clients in finding needed expert assistance that the referring counselor cannot provide. This assistance provides the client with a higher level of training or special expertise related to the client's needs. Counselors in all settings will find it an advantage to their clients to establish a network of qualified helping professionals for referral purposes. Of course, counselors themselves will be the recipients of referrals from their various work settings and the populations they are expected to serve.

Consultation

Consultation is a process for helping a client through a third party or helping a system improve its services to its clientele. The former, usually labeled *triadic consultation,* is popular in working with parents of troubled children or teachers with problem pupils. The latter, appropriately labeled *process consultation,* focuses primarily on the processes that an agency or institution may be using to carry out its mission. Thus, consultation is a form of outreach in which counselors function as team members to assist individual clients or systems that serve clients.

In community and other agency settings, consultation is receiving increased attention as a way of preventing severe mental illnesses. In fact, the Community Mental Health Centers Act requires centers to provide consultation as one of five essential services. In school settings, especially elementary schools, the counselor is being increasingly used as a consultant to teachers and parents. Consultation is discussed in greater detail in Chapter 11.

Research

Research is necessary to the advancement of the profession of counseling. It provides a major source of empirically based hypotheses relevant to the ultimate goal of implementing effective counseling. It is a means for producing additional knowledge in our field, providing factual data to reinforce or guide the counselors' professional judgments, and seeking answers to questions and issues of professional concern. Research results and the research process are important to program managers and other counselors who find it advantageous to have factual data to reinforce or guide their professional judgment.

Whether one is an active researcher or not, a counseling professional cannot afford to ignore or gloss over important research in the field. Different client populations, more diverse and usually more intense client problems, plus greater variation in staff backgrounds and, hence, treatment approaches, offer counselor-researchers the opportunity for unique and significant research investigations. The Community Mental Health Center Amendment of 1975 emphasizes research with local application.

Interest has grown recently in *outcome research*—research that measures the outcomes of various counseling practices and activities. The American Counseling Association Foundation has sponsored studies of counseling outcome research. The professional publications of the American Counseling Association and the American Psychological Association regularly report the findings of counseling research studies. A brief sampling of counseling research studies is provided at the end of each chapter, and research is discussed in general in Chapter 14.

Evaluation and Accountability

Although *evaluation* and *accountability* are not synonymous terms, they are interrelated and counselors and counseling programs are expected to engage in both. *Evaluation* is a means or process for assessing the effectiveness of the counselor's activities. It is fundamental to the verification and improvement of professional and program performance.

The use of the term *accountability* is an outgrowth of demands that schools and other tax-supported institutions and agencies be held accountable for their actions. In other words, some evidence of accomplishments must be provided in return for tax investments. Accountability also implies that these accomplishments must be provided in return for tax investments, and that these accomplishments be relevant to the purpose for which the agencies or organizations were established.

Accountability establishes a basis for relevance, effectiveness, and efficiency. In this context, evaluation can be viewed as a component of the accountability model. More attention is given to accountability and evaluation in Chapter 14.

Prevention

The past 20 years have seen a substantial number of reports of important studies that examined the promotion of mental health through primary prevention using a social-psychological perspective. These include the Hahnemann Group (Spivack & Shure, 1974), the Connecticut Group (Allen, Chinsky, Larsen, Lochman, & Selinger, 1976), Project Aware (Thomson-Rountree & Woodruff, 1982), and the Rochester Pilot Program (1976–1977) (Weissberg & Gesten, 1982). The protective factors that operate in children's responses to stress and disadvantage have also been used to profile invulnerable, that is, stress-resistant, children (Garmezy, 1978; Rutter, 1980).

These and other studies suggest that a most attractive alternative to traditional remedial mental health practices is primary prevention, which seeks to prevent the occurrence of the disorder in the first place. Such an alternative suggests a shift in focus to the settings and life conditions that shape early adaptation. In this regard, the school and the family are those social institutions that most profoundly affect early human development. Increasingly, this focus is on the school as a vital, ongoing shaping force with organizational advantages for the initiation and development of mental health programs for primary prevention.

Thus, potential benefits for society may be derived from devising programs in schools that facilitate positive mental health interacting with a mastery of cognitive development. Because basic human needs, both sociological and psychological, are to a large measure met either successfully or unsuccessfully in major social institutions, for youth the schools become not only a resource for intellectual achievement but institutions that, in a larger and more important sense, shape the entire social group, subject to its experiences. As such, the schools have a major role in the promotion of positive mental health. In this effort, a significant contribution can be made through effective primary intervention strategies.

Community and other mental health–oriented agencies are becoming active in working with families to head off anticipated stresses, as well as in working with other stress-prone groups, such as divorced individuals, widows and widowers, and so forth. We can anticipate that counselors in a wide range of settings will be increasingly called on to develop and implement prevention strategies for serving their clientele. Chapter 12 gives further attention to prevention and wellness.

Closely allied with prevention is the concept of *wellness*, which recognizes both the mental and physical well-being of the individual. Although the professional counselor may assist clients more directly in becoming mentally healthy, the possible interrelationships between mental and physical health cannot be overlooked. Counselors will, therefore, work to establish links with health care professionals. Too, as we are concerned with the total well-being of the individual, we may consider the *holistic approach* to counseling, which embodies the dimensions of body, mind, spirit, and emotions.

BASIC PRINCIPLES

Principles tend to form a philosophical framework within which programs are organized and activities developed. They are guidelines that are derived from the experiences and values of the profession, and they represent the views of the majority of the profession's membership. As such, they become fundamental assumptions or a system of beliefs regarding a profession and its role, function, and activities.

For Schools

Indicated here are some principles suggesting how school counseling programs can make their contributions more effectively:

1. School counseling and guidance programs are designed to serve the developmental and adjustment needs of all youth.
2. The school counseling program should be concerned with the total development of the students it serves. This program also recognizes that individual development is a continuous, ongoing process; therefore, school counseling programs must themselves be developmental.
3. Pupil guidance is viewed as a process that is continuous throughout the child's formal education.
4. Trained professional counseling personnel are essential for ensuring professional competencies, leadership, and direction. (This does not imply that paraprofessionals cannot make worthwhile contributions.)
5. Certain basic activities are essential to program effectiveness, and these must be specifically planned and developed if they are to be effective.
6. The school counseling program must reflect the uniqueness of the population it serves and the environment in which it seeks to render this service; thus, like individuals, each school guidance program will be different from other programs.

7. Relevant to the preceding point, the school counseling program should base its uniqueness on a regular, systematic assessment of the student clientele's needs and the characteristics of the program's environmental setting.

8. An effective instructional program in the school requires an effective program of pupil counseling and guidance. Good education and good guidance are interrelated. They support and complement each other to the student's advantage.

9. Relevant to statement 7, teacher understanding and support of the school counseling program is significant to the success of such programs.

10. The school counseling program is accountable. It recognizes the need to provide objective evidence of accomplishments and the value of those accomplishments.

11. The school counselor is a team member. The counselor shares a concern and programs for youths with psychologists, social workers, teachers, administrators, and other educational professionals and staff.

12. The school counseling program must recognize the right and capability of the individual to make decisions and plans.

13. The school counseling program must respect the worth and dignity of the individual— every individual.

14. The school counseling program must recognize the uniqueness of the individual and the individual's right to that uniqueness.

15. The school counselor should be a role model of positive human relations—of unbiased, equal treatment.

Although counseling is a relatively young profession, counselors are developing traditions, establishing their role and worth, and will cope resourcefully and imaginatively with the demands of the future. The following discussion considers some traditions, activities, and effective counseling program organization and functioning.

For Community Agencies

Counseling programs in community and other institutional or agency settings represent a wide range of approaches for delivering services. The development and implementation of these services is based on certain underlying assumptions and basic principles. The basic assumption that community involvement is essential for relevant and accountable community mental health agencies has implications for the basic principles of those agencies that are community-based. Bloom (1984) has suggested seven such principles for the guidance of professional personnel employed in community mental health agencies as follows (these might be paraphrased slightly for noncommunity-based mental health agencies):

Principle 1:

Regardless of where your paycheck comes from, think of yourself as working for the community.

Principle 2:

If you want to know about a community's mental health needs, ask the community.

Principle 3:

As you learn about community-mental-health-related needs, you have the responsibility to tell the community what you are learning.

Principle 4:

Help the community establish its own priorities.

Principle 5:

You can help the community decide among various courses of action in its efforts to solve its own problems.

Principle 6:

In the event that the community being served is so disorganized that representatives of various facets of the community cannot be found, you have the responsibility to find such representatives.

Principle 7:

You should work toward the equitable distribution of power in the community. (pp. 429–431)

FUTURE DIRECTIONS FOR THE PROFESSION

As we enter a new century, we are mindful that the future and change are inseparable. Progress for the counseling profession itself depends on the generation of new knowledge and the changes new knowledge stimulates. Certainly a number of these changes affecting our profession are already under way so we can not lay claim to any crystal ball magic in noting the following future directions for the counseling profession.

1. Increasing standards for counselor preparation: It may be of some small solace to those of you currently anticipating the work ahead in your master's program in counseling to realize that counselor preparation programs, which have moved from 32–36 credit-hour programs to 45–48 master's credit-hour programs in the last decades of the 20th century, are anticipated to move to 65 hours and beyond in the early generations of the 21st century. Increases in new knowledge and the broadening of counselor responsibilities will be the major contributors reflected in new and additional course work requirements. Additionally, as in other professions, counselors must increasingly in the years ahead anticipate a lifetime of learning—of constantly updating their skills and knowledge if they are optimally to serve their clients and the public in general.

2. Increasing attention to speciality fields: As professions develop and increasingly gain public confidence, there is a tendency for specialty fields to emerge. For example, specialties have proliferated in the traditional helping professions of medicine and law. Specialties are also emerging in the counseling profession. We note such specialties as marriage and family counseling, multicultural counseling, crisis counseling, substance abuse counseling, career counseling, elementary school counseling, secondary school counseling, community/agency counseling, gerontological counseling, rehabilitation counseling, mental health counseling, and so forth. As we look to the future, we anticipate that increased attention will be given to these specialty fields, which have already evolved in our profession, and it is appropriate to project that new and, perhaps at this point, unidentified specialty fields will emerge.

3. Increasing use of technology: The technology explosion projected for the 21st century will undoubtedly impact and influence all of the helping professions, including counseling. We are already aware of the influence that computers, automated testing programs, fax machines, electronic mail, and distance learning have made on the workplace and within counseling

organizations. Those involved in the worlds of developing technology indicate that "we ain't seen nuthin' yet!," that we are really just experiencing the tip of the iceberg. Among the projections are that clients will be able to receive face-to-face counseling without leaving home through the use of what we today might call closed-circuit television. Some are also suggesting that clients will be able to use computers again within the comfort of their own home to access career opportunities, to assess their career capabilities, and so forth.

Many in the counseling profession question the use of technology to the exclusion of the personal interaction that occurs between client and counselor. Many also question the ability to retain the confidentiality of various electronic means of communication. In any event, we can anticipate an exciting era in which counselors and the counseling profession will be called upon to adjust to, utilize, and cope with rapid technological advancements.

4. Increasing focus upon empirical results: Although not necessarily justified, counseling has long been considered suspect by many of its critics due to a presumed lack of empirical evidence supporting counselor activities and results. In recent years, the profession has devoted more attention to informing the public of factual evidence documented by empirical research supporting counselor activities and ensuing results. This trend must continue and, in fact, be accelerated with particular attention to counselor effectiveness in prevention programs, human relationships, and other areas of critical national need. Not only prospective clients but the general public must be made aware of what our profession can do to improve our national well-being.

5. Updating the profession's traditional theories: The counseling profession's traditional theories of counseling and career development have been under scrutiny in recent years as many have challenged their relevancy in view of the changing characteristics and dynamics of society and the world of work. It has been suggested that the original data and bases on which the theories were founded are no longer appropriate. Without involving ourselves in this debate, we would simply note that most of the leading theorists today are engaged actively in researching and updating the traditional theories of our profession. We can assume that others are researching and testing new theories that may well emerge in the 21st century. (Attention to these traditional theories and possible new and emerging ones as well will be provided in Chapters 5 and 10.)

6. Renewing attention as well as expanding career counseling parameters: The world of work has undergone dramatic and, in many instances, unanticipated changes in the last generation of the 20th century. Among the prominent influencers of these changes are the closing out of certain traditional careers and the emerging of completely new careers. The U.S. economy's expansion into the world marketplace and the necessity of competing in a global economy resulting in many industries and careers being shifted out of the country; downsizing which has affected the stability of heretofore lifetime career paths; the concept of career counseling across the life span as retirement barriers fall; and legislative activities stimulating school-to-work transition planning are but a few of the well-known examples of the sweeping changes that have occurred in recent years in the world of work. These shifts have produced an upheaval in the career planning of countless adults as well as confusing young people planning their entries into a career and the world of work. This has focused new attention on the counseling profession as *the* profession with specialized training in the area of career counseling. It is also resulting in increased opportunities for counselors to function in specialized career settings. This renewed attention to a traditional area of concern and expertise in the counseling

profession offers many exciting possibilities for our profession to provide special expertise and service to the general public in the years ahead.

7. Increasing attention to public communication and political activity: Many leaders in the counseling profession have called upon counselors to become more politically active (not in a partisan sense but in a public information sense) to publicly communicate what counselors do, what they are accomplishing, and so forth. All too frequently, the general public appears to be misinformed, partially informed, or uninformed regarding the significant contributions that the counseling profession can make to individuals and to society's wellness. Although there is no challenge to our recognized expertise to communicating in a "counseling booth," we very frequently appear to have let our communication skills stop at that point. It is now apparent that if we are to compete and be recognized for what we do in the public service area, we must make the public aware of our skills and contributions. This has been a major deficit standing in the way of our profession's advancement which is only now beginning to be recognized and remedied. This action must continue.

8. Increasing attention to program relevancy: The accountability movement over the last 20 years of the 20th century has brought about a recognition that to adequately serve our client populations we must be relevant. Programs must attend to the real needs of their client populations, not to theoretical or assumed needs. The basis for developing relevant programs are objective needs assessments which then lead to the development of relevant and accountable counseling programs.

9. Increasing multicultural sensitivity and activity: Although as a profession we justifiably claim to be experts in human relationships, we have failed to transform our skills in individual counseling and small group relationships to the broader community and even national relationship issues. Certainly progress has been made in recent decades in the area of racial relationships; however, the overall picture of relationships among our population indicates many elements of our citizenry are at odds with each other. These differences are expressed in everything from subtle prejudices to extreme violence which constantly threaten our national stability and well-being. There appears to be little concerted effort to mitigate or improve these situations. As a profession espousing positive human relationships, it is time we step forward and assume a national leadership role in dealing with this human crisis.

SUMMARY

Most of the basic principles and traditional activities enumerated here have, as Chapter 1 suggested, a historic relationship with the development of the counseling movement. Although the organization of these activities into program formats differs across the various settings, the mention of the importance of individual assessment, one-to-one counseling, group activities, career information, and placement and follow-up would evoke a ringing round of applause from our professional forebears. Additionally, in recent generations we have come to view consul-

tation as an expected professional service, and the current emphasis on prevention indicates it will be a major role for counselors in the future.

Traditions are the hallmarks of a profession. They are often seen as indices of the professional maturity of a discipline and synonymous with the guiding principles for a profession. They represent guidelines for newcomers (and reminiscences for the old-timers) to the profession. They become powerful determinants of the profession's goals and actions and, in time, extremely resistant to elimination or alteration. Thus, although we sometimes hear a call for drastic change (even elimination of counseling programs in some settings), it is not the fundamental beliefs or traditional activities of the counselor that must change, but rather how the activity is interpreted or viewed and carried out that will determine the merits of a counseling program in any setting.

Relevancy is a key to the success or failure of a program's activities and services. For example, it is doubtful that the counseling skills and understandings that we possessed when we first entered the profession would be relevant to the demands of today's youths, and it is certain that both the concept of careers and the career information at our disposal then would not be in any way relevant today. As C. Gilbert Wrenn stressed in his classic book *The World of the Contemporary Counselor* (1973), "the need of the counselor is to attempt to understand contemporary youth and the world in which they live" (p. 3). That is relevancy—seeing and understanding the environment that surrounds our clients, as well as our clients themselves.

We move from this broad overview of counselor activities to more specifically examining how counselors may function in school settings (Chapter 3) and community and agency settings (Chapter 4).

DISCUSSION QUESTIONS

1.   When you hear the term *professional*, what does this imply to you? What does the label profession mean to you?

2.   Discuss characteristics attributable to those in the helping professions (medicine, law, dentistry, education, psychology, and social work) and how these characteristics help and/or hinder professional performance.

3.   Do some current societal needs have implications for new directions in educational or societal services? Identify and discuss.

4.   List five environmental variables that positively influenced the development of your human potential as well as five environmental variables that detracted from your human potential growth. Next, examine present environmental variables.

5.   Are there traditions you associate with other professions such as medicine and law? Discuss these and how you believe they may have evolved.

6.   Are there any special responsibilities that a profession has to the public? Identify and discuss.

7.   In view of current societal needs, what changes in the traditional counselor role and function might be envisioned, if any?

CLASS ACTIVITIES

1.   Organize the class into small groups to interview professionals in medicine, dentistry, law, nursing, and teaching. Interviewers should seek information regarding (1) training, (2) regulation of the profession by the profession, and (3) traditions of the profession. Report findings orally to the class.

2.   Have class members interview counselors in various settings to ascertain the major activities they typically engage in as professional counselors. Report these findings to the class.

3.   Organize the class into small groups and have each group member discuss his or her contact with counseling programs and the perceptions of those programs for each of the educational levels: elementary, secondary, and higher education. Have each group come up with a list of recommendations based on its experiences for improving school counseling programs.

SELECTED READINGS

Etringer, B. D., Hillerbrand, E., & Claiborn, C. D. (1995). The transition from novice to expert counselor. *Counselor Education & Supervision, 35* (1), 4–17.

Herr, E. L. (1982). *Why counseling?* [Monograph]. Washington, DC: American Personnel and Guidance Association.

Hollis, J. W. (1997). *Counselor preparation, 1996–1998: Programs, faculty, trends* (9th ed.). Washington, DC: Accelerated Development/NBCC (National Board for Certified Counselors).

Hutson, P. W. (1962). On professionalism. *Personnel and Guidance Journal, 41* (1), 63–64.

McCully, C. H. (1962). The school counselor: Strategy for professionalization. *Personnel and Guidance Journal, 40* (8), 681–689.

Meier, S. T., & Davis, S. R. (1997). *The elements of counseling* (3rd ed.). Pacific Grove, CA: Brooks/Cole.

Miller, G. M. (1988). Counselor functions in excellent schools: Elementary through secondary. *The School Counselor, 36* (2), 88–93.

Pedersen, P., & Leong, F. (1997). Counseling in an international context. *Counseling Psychologist, 25,* 117–121.

Tiedeman, D. V. (1980). Status and prospect in counseling psychology: 1962. In J. M. Whiteley (Ed.), *The history of counseling psychology* (pp. 125–132). Monterey, CA: Brooks/Cole.

Whiteley, J. M. (1980). Counseling psychology in the year 2000 A.D. *Counseling Psychologist, 8* (4), 2–62.

RESEARCH OF INTEREST

Brehms, C., & Johnson, M. C. (1997). Comparison of recent graduates of clinical versus counseling psychology programs. *Journal of Psychology, 131* (1), 91–99.

Abstract

This study assessed similarities and differences of aspects of programs and job-related activity in 129 recent graduates (aged 28 to 56 years) from clinical or counseling graduate psychology programs. Subjects were given a graduate activities questionnaire, which was developed specifically for this study, and the short version of a theoretical orientation survey. Results revealed only minor differences. Counseling psychologists were more likely to (a) provide group therapy, career counseling and assessment, public lectures and workshops; (b) have more knowledge of the Strong-Campbell Interest Inventory; (c) be more likely to work in university counseling centers; and (d) endorse humanistic theoretical orientations. Clinical psychologists were more likely to (a) work in medical school settings; (b) ascribe human behavior to internal states rather than to social causes; and (c) have greater knowledge of the Rorschach. However, the similarities between the two specialties relative to work setting, theoretical orientation, service, research, and teaching activities far outweigh these minor differences. Implications of these findings are placed in the context of previous research that has suggested the possible merger of the two specialties.

Brehms, C., Johnson, M. E., & Gallucci, P. (1996). Publication productivity of clinical and counseling psychologists. *Journal of Clinical Psychology, 52* (6), 723–725.

Abstract

This study compared the research productivity of 500 clinical versus 500 counseling psychologists and found surprisingly few differences. A serendipitous finding was low productivity across the board, and a question was raised about the success of the scientist-practitioner model in both clinical and counseling psychology doctoral programs in instilling a research-publication ethic among professional (as opposed to experimental, social, etc.) psychologists.

Dees, M. S., III, Buck, P., Walker, C. E., & Nicewarder, A. (1985, August). *Survey of the public perception of psychology, psychologists, and psychiatrists.* Paper presented at the Annual Convention of the American Psychological Association, Los Angeles, CA.

Abstract

The public perception of psychology, psychologists, and psychiatrists has not been examined for 20 years. Participants for this study were randomly selected from an urban area (Oklahoma City) and a rural area (Okarche, Oklahoma). Questionnaires about the usefulness and competency of these professionals were admin-istered by telephone; half of the questionnaires used the term *psychologist* (N = 225) and the other half substituted the word *psychiatrist* (N = 225). Additionally, urban *psychologists* (N = 47) and *psychiatrists* (N = 25) responded to the questionnaire as if they were members of the public. Psychiatrists were favored for intel-ligence testing, career counseling, sexual dys-function, and alcohol and drug abuse whereas psychologists were favored for stress manage-ment. The findings indicated that the percep-tion of psychologists' competence had improved since a 1965 study, but confusion about professional domain continued. Rural residents also recognized the need for psychia-trists and psychologists, but they desired less in-formation than urban residents about a potential therapist. The psychologists and psy-chiatrists who responded to the questionnaire reported that the public had a higher percent-age of confidence in their abilities to solve problems than the public reported.

Forsyth, D. R., & Leary, M. R. (1997). Achieving the goals of the scientist-practitioner model: The seven interfaces of social and counseling psychology. *Counseling Psychologist*, 25 (2), 180–200.

Abstract

   Counseling and social psychology have commingled theoretically and empirically for many years, but both fields have much to gain from a more complete integration across seven domains: educational (learning, teaching, and training), professional (relationships between researchers and practitioners), practical (inte-grated attempts to solve individual and societal problems), methodological (shared empirical procedures and standards), theoretical (attempts to construct conceptual models that span disci-plines), metatheoretical (shared assumptions about the phenomena under study), and episte-mological (fundamental assumptions held in common about how knowledge is expanded). After estimating the strength of the union be-tween social and counseling psychology on each of these seven planes, suggestions for fortifying the weaker links and enhancing the vitality of the stronger links are offered.

Livneh, C. (1988). Characteristics of lifelong learn-ers in the human service professions. *Adult Edu-cation Quarterly*, 8 (2), 149–159.

Abstract

   The characteristics of Lifelong Learners in the Professions instrument was administered to 195 human service professionals, and responses were subjected to principal components analy-sis, Varimax rotation, and multiple regression analysis. Two factors emerged as potential pre-dictors of lifelong learning: educability and fu-ture orientation.

Sawatzky, D. D., Jevne, R. F., & Clark, G. T. (1994). Becoming empowered: A study of counsellor development. *Canadian Journal of Counselling*, 28 (3), 177–192.

Abstract

   This study examined the experiences of nine doctoral students in counseling that contributed to the development of their effectiveness as coun-selors. Data were collected from interviews with subjects in the final stages of their internship at a variety of professional settings. Based on a the-matic analysis of the interviews, a cyclical model of counselor development, Becoming Empow-ered, was proposed. This model included four recurring themes: experiencing dissonance, re-sponding to dissonance, relating to supervision, and feeling empowered. The model developed from recognizing gaps in skills, knowledge, and experience and experiencing emotional turmoil to acquiring new skills and experiences and changing attitudes. Feelings of empowerment were enhanced by changing perspectives and ex-periencing increased competence.

The School Counselor's Role and Function

Counselors in any work setting need to be aware of what services school counselors and school counseling provide. Therefore, a purpose of this chapter is to orient potential counselors, including those interested in school settings, to the

- Training of counselors
- Credentialing of counselors
- Role and function of counselors and their supporting professionals in differing educational settings.

TRAINING PROGRAMS FOR COUNSELORS

As previously noted, counseling and guidance programs in schools are an educational development of the 20th century, and they have, until recent years, been unique to the United States and Canadian educational systems. The same is true of training programs for counselors. Similarly, since the initial years of the National Defense Education Act (1958–1960), both the number and size of counselor training programs has grown rapidly. The supporting facts indicate that in 1964 there were 327 institutions of higher education supporting counselor preparation programs with 706 faculty. Hollis and Wantz (1994) report that by 1992 this number of programs had increased to 798. Also, if you had entered a counselor training program in 1964, you could have anticipated a training staff of slightly more than two full-time faculty members; however, if you delayed your entry until 1990, you could have expected, on the average, a staff of eight full-time faculty members.

Because many of you may already be enrolled in programs of counselor education, this chapter's initial discussion may serve only to remind you to see your adviser about the course work that lies ahead or how your own program may differ from others. We are certain, however, that you recognize the significant relationship between what you are trained to do and your role and function once you are on the job. Also, as Thomas (1973) noted in *The Schools Next Time:*

> Control of the lower schools (elementary and secondary) by the colleges is again obvious when one remembers that all certified school personnel are college trained—they cannot be licensed without such training. Teachers, counselors, and administrators are all enculturated with the biases of academia. (p. 216)

As a means of putting into perspective who functions at what level and with what training or expertise, Table 3-1 indicates that persons with appropriate experience or training and the skills to communicate can function at the advice-giving level. In the school setting, for example, all teachers and most staff would qualify as advisers for many occasions and should serve in this important role in the school's program of pupil guidance. At the second level, special training to at least the master's degree is required, which provides the school counselor with special expertise as a counselor. Such expertise sets the counselor apart from other professionals in the school setting and establishes the unique qualifications to interact with or on behalf of students in meeting their routine development, adjustment, planning, and decision-making needs. The third level represents the highest degree of professional training available, usually an earned doctorate. As practicing counselors, these professionals are most frequently used as resource personnel for referrals and consultation. Their clients usually have serious personality disorders requiring intensive and long-term counseling. In addition to counseling,

TABLE 3-1   Levels of Training and Responsibility

Level	Training	Responsibility
First	Appropriate educational and/or experience background	Advising; information-giving
Second	Master's degree in counseling and guidance	Developmental and normal adjustment counseling
Third	Doctorate in counseling and guidance, clinical mental health, or counseling psychology, or M.D. with specialty in psychiatry	Serious personality disorders

these higher trained counselors may also seek careers in research or university teaching or in supervisory positions.

Additional insights into the relationship between levels of training and the counselor's role and function in educational settings as represented by initial employment may be noted in Table 3-2, which depicts the initial placement of graduates of master's degree programs in school counseling. Table 4-1 in Chapter 4 will depict the initial employment of community and other mental health majors.

In examining the content of training programs available, one cannot help but note course content consistent among master's programs across the United States and Canada. In

TABLE 3-2   Placement of Graduates from School Counseling Entry Level Master's Degree Program the First Year After Graduation

Placement Settings	1993		1996	
	Number of Programs Reporting Placement	Percent of all Graduates	Number of Programs Reporting Placement	Percent of all Graduates
Advanced graduate programs	152	7	116	5
Managed care	0	0	1	0
Private practice/agency	0	0	17	0
Public agency	0	0	17	1
School: Elementary	225	29	229	30
Middle	211	23	220	21
Secondary	207	34	238	37
Higher education student affairs	0	0	29	2
Other settings	74	7	50	5
Total		100		101
Number of programs supplying data	235		248	

the United States, much of this conformity is undoubtedly the result of state certification patterns for school counselors, which reflect, with little deviation, an expectancy of training to perform the traditional basic services noted in Chapter 2.

A number of counselor training institutions also offer a specialist or sixth-year degree. In many states, this degree qualifies one with appropriate experience for director or supervisor of guidance or director of pupil personnel services certificates. The current trend toward a two-year master's degree will probably result in the elimination of the specialist degree in many institutions.

Approximately 175 counselor training institutions in the United States and Canada offer programs leading to an earned doctorate. These programs tend, according to the nature of the program, to prepare their candidates for positions in mental health clinics, hospitals, crisis and therapy agencies, for positions on university counselor education or counseling psychology faculties, in college and university counseling centers, and for rehabilitation counseling, student personnel work in higher education, and other agency or institutional settings. Some may also elect to enter private practice. Variations in program emphasis and preparation patterns are more commonplace than at the master's level. Also, in many institutions, several counselor education or related programs may exist because of specialized training (i.e., departments of counselor education, rehabilitation counseling, counseling psychology, marriage and family, etc.).

THE CREDENTIALING OF SCHOOL COUNSELORS

Today, the title counselor seems to be used with ever-increasing frequency in a variety of settings. There are home-buyer counselors, financial counselors, landscape counselors, used car counselors, and diet counselors. There are also counselors who may be distinguished from the first group on the basis of certification or legal licensure. These include legal counselors, investment counselors, psychological counselors, and school guidance counselors. Differences between licensure and certification will be discussed in Chapter 4. The licensure or certification indicates that the holder has successfully completed and has been examined on learning and experience criteria recommended by the representative professional organizations and the appropriate licensing boards or agencies. The late C. Harold McCully, in his classic discussion "The School Counselor: Strategy for Professionalization" (1962), suggested

> A profession is an occupation in which the members of a corporate group assure minimum competence for entry into the occupation by setting and enforcing standards for selection, training, and licensure or certification. (p. 682)

Certification is a process that certifies the qualifications of individuals to engage in professional practice, usually in specific settings such as schools, utilizing a title authorized by the certification agency. Education and its subspecialties is an example of a profession that certifies qualifications usually through state departments of education guided, in many instances, by state legislative enactments. In addition to state laws, certification may be awarded by agencies and volunteer organizations. School counselors are required to be certified under such guidelines in all states.

The process requires that the candidate for certification produce evidence of meeting the criteria for such certification. Minimally, for those seeking certification as counselors, this process requires evidence of appropriate academic course work at a recognized and, in some states, regionally accredited institution of higher education. In addition, at this writing, 21 states require teaching experience although 10 of them will substitute an internship in a school setting for this requirement. Five states require undergraduate degrees in education. A few states also require specific course work in areas such as state history, special education, computers, and so on. Thirty-five states also require candidates to satisfactorily pass some type of written examination.

Because credentialing for school counselors is usually through certification, the other major process of credentialing, licensure, will be covered in the following chapter's discussion of counselors in noneducational settings.

Another activity that has significance for the credentialing process, whether it be certification or licensure, is *accreditation*. We will note briefly at this point that most programs preparing school counselors are accredited by their regional accrediting associations. Counselor training programs in schools or colleges of education may also have accreditation by the National Council for Accreditation of Teacher Education (NCATE), and programs both within and outside education may qualify for approval by the Council for Accreditation of Counseling and Related Educational Programs (CACREP). Doctoral programs preparing counseling psychologists may seek accreditation by the American Psychological Association. In addition, many state departments of public instruction accredit higher education training programs within their jurisdictions.

As previously mentioned, all states require certification for those who will be school counselors. Generally very similar across states, these requirements account for the considerable degree of reciprocity by which candidates certified in one state may be eligible for certification in other states. For example, the vast majority of certification programs require a counselor's minimal completion of a master's degree. Also, most certification patterns require course work appropriate to the basic guidance services. That includes courses in appraisal or, sometimes, standardized testing, career and educational information, career guidance or career development, individual counseling, group guidance and counseling, and principles of counseling and guidance. Courses in consultation and organization of school counseling programs are also frequent requirements. In addition, some sort of supervised practicum experience is typically required. Again, 12 states also demand one to three years of prior teaching experience for certification to counsel in schools. An increasing number of states have, however, recently amended their certification requirements to provide for an alternative experience to teaching, such as an internship.

It is probably a chicken-or-egg situation to attempt to determine whether training influences practice or vice versa, and it is not the intent of this chapter to bias that argument. We have, by choice, discussed training and resulting certification first. In the paragraphs that follow, counseling practices in various educational settings will be described. One may note the relationship between these practices and training patterns previously presented. Remember, though, that this discussion is a brief overview only, and greater detail and specificity will be provided later.

Advantages

The following advantages accrue from some sort of a credentialing process:

1. *Credentialing protects the public against those who would masquerade as possessing certain skills and training.* A number of years ago, an article in the old *Look* magazine entitled "Beware of

the Psycho-Quacks" gave examples of the various guises for preying on the public under counseling and psychological titles. Many have read the book or seen the movie *The Great Imposter,* in which one individual successfully assumed a variety of professional careers. Although such reports sometimes amuse and often attract admirers for those who have beat the system, very few people would knowingly like to be seen by a physician who is not a physician, a lawyer who is not a lawyer, or a counselor who is not a counselor. These examples remind us of the need for some sort of a procedure that protects the public against professional misrepresentation and fraud.

2. *It provides, at the very least, minimally accepted training and experience requirements.* Credentialing and training requirements (and experiences) are closely interrelated. This interrelationship provides for a common core of learning experiences and achievement expectancies. These are related to the profession's concept of preparatory standards for entry into the profession. These standards are not only helpful to candidates considering entry into training programs and protect them from misleading training schemes, but they also reassure employers as well as the general public who use the services.

3. *Credentialing can provide a legal base for the protection of the membership of the profession.* Because credentialing suggests standards that benefit the public, law-making bodies are prone to provide the profession and its membership with certain legal forms of protection. For example, individuals cannot legally practice medicine without a license, and lawyers legally have the right of privileged communication with their clients. In many states, the right to enter private practice in such fields as psychology and professional counseling is limited by law.

4. *It may provide a basis for special benefits.* In addition to legal benefits, credentialed professionals may also qualify for certain financial benefits. Physicians' and lawyers' fees may qualify for insurance payments. Physicians, including psychiatrists, also qualify for national health insurance payments such as Medicaid. Psychologists may also qualify as mental health providers for insurance payments in some states. Credentialed school counselors have, on occasion, been qualified to receive special training grants to increase their qualifications. Because credentialing qualifies individuals for membership in professional organizations, they become eligible for the benefits such memberships provide (e.g., special training, publications, and group insurance).

THE ROLE AND FUNCTION OF COUNSELORS IN SCHOOL SETTINGS

An Overview

The counselor's role and function, as described in an official American School Counselor Association statement is presented in Appendix A.

One view of the role and function of school counselors may be based on how they spend their time. A study by Partin (1993) identified school counselors' perceived distribution of time categorized by elementary, middle/junior high, and senior high school (see Table 3-3). Later in this chapter, we will present results of a recent role and function study (1996–1997) that we conducted.

Individual counseling, guidance activities, consultation, and group counseling are major activities as measured by time commitments. Administrative and clerical responsibilities increase from elementary to senior high school. In fact, Partin (1993) notes in his study that

TABLE 3-3   Counselors' Perceived Distribution of Time

Activity	Elementary		Middle/Junior High		Senior High	
	M%	SD	M%	SD	M%	SD
Testing, appraisal	6.29	6.70	7.27	5.39	6.68	4.02
Guidance activities	24.19*	21.16	13.18[a]	11.75	11.47[a]	8.23
Individual counseling	27.31	18.99	28.60	13.91	30.96	16.56
Group counseling	11.21	8.19	12.44	11.94	8.77	6.26
Professional development	3.64	2.92	3.78	2.70	4.55	2.98
Consultation	12.10	6.45	13.50	8.11	11.32	6.24
Resource coordination	5.43	4.58	6.38	5.38	6.11	3.30
Administrative & clerical	7.02[a]	7.42	11.83[a]	10.16	17.27*	13.06
Other, nonguidance activities	4.43	12.99	5.08	5.31	3.98	7.18

[a] Means are significantly lower than means marked with an asterisk (*).
$p < .05$

Source: From "School Counselors' Time: Where Does It Go?," by R. L. Partin, 1993, *The School Counselor, 40* (4), 1993, p. 278. Copyright © American Counseling Association. Reprinted by permission. No further reproduction authorized without written permission of the American Counseling Association.

"for senior high counselors, paperwork, scheduling, and administrative tasks are seen as significant time robbers that deter counselors from allotting more time for individual and group counseling" (p. 279).

The variety in school settings, of course, will account for some differences in the ways counselors may carry out their roles. However, some common influences determine the role and function of counselors, regardless of the setting. The first of these is what might be called *professional constants* or determinants that indicate what is appropriate and not appropriate to the counselor's role. These include guidelines and policy statements of professional organizations, licensing or certification limitations, accreditation guidelines and requirements, and the expectancies of professional training programs. In addition to these professional constants, personal factors inevitably influence role and function. These include the interest of the counselor, such as what he or she likes to do; what the counselor gets encouraged to do and is rewarded for doing by the school, community, or his or her peers; what the counselor has resources to do; what the counselor perceives as the appropriate role and function for a given setting; and finally, how life in general is going for the counselor. The counselor's attitudes, values, and experiences both on and off the job can influence how he or she views the job.

Counselors and other professional helpers are recognizing more and more that traditional roles and delivery systems in human services may have imposed real limitations on their ability to deal directly and effectively with clients' critical needs. We would also note the current call for counselors and counseling programs to become increasingly active in preventive interventions and developmental guidance. Thus, as we further view the role and function of counselors, we are seeking to integrate for you, our reader, not only those concepts that have proven themselves over the years but also current and promising directions that seem necessary for the counselor to remain a viable entity in the school setting.

How Counselors in Educational Settings Spend Their Time

During the 1996–1997 school year, we conducted a role and function study of practicing counselors in school and nonschool settings. Participants in the study were randomly selected from the membership directory of the American Counseling Association and asked to complete a survey form indicating the comparative amount of time (good amount, fair or average amount, little, or none) spent on 14 possible activities. Space was also provided to indicate additional activities. School respondents were summarized according to educational levels (i.e., elementary, middle/junior high, and secondary education). A numerical value was given to each of the time-spent categories (i.e., good amount = 3; fair or average amount = 2; little = 1; and none = 0). Total scores were then tabulated for each activity, resulting in an unscientific but reasonably accurate indication of the rank order of time spent on various common activities that practicing counselors engage in for each of the specified settings. Table 3-4 presents results from counselors in elementary, middle/junior high school, and senior high school settings.

Hardesty and Dillard (1994) in an earlier study examined the tasks and functions counselors at different grade levels view as important. Three hundred and sixty-nine elementary, middle, and high school counselors were surveyed regarding activities in schools. They found three major differences in the ranking of counselor activities by elementary

TABLE 3-4   How Practicing Counselors Spend Their Time

Activity	Elementary	Middle/ Junior High	Senior High
Individual counseling	2.5	2	2
Organizing & conducting counseling groups	10	10.5	10.5
Classroom & other group guidance activities	4	6	10.5
Standardized test administration and/or interpretation	7	6	
Nonstandardized assessment (i.e., case studies, observation, information gathering interviews, questionnaires, etc.)	5	4	
Needs assessment (to determine priority needs of the target population)	9		
Consultation activities	1		8
Providing career guidance and information		3	5
Providing educational guidance & information (including scholarships, college placement, student scheduling, etc.)		9	1
Prevention planning & implementation activities	2.5	8	4
Developmental activities	7	10.5	9
Administrative activities	6	1	3
Information dissemination, public communications, and public relations	8	5	7
Other			

Source: Based on a survey by Robert L. Gibson and Marianne H. Mitchell, 1997.

counselors compared with their middle and secondary school counterparts: (1) elementary subjects perform more consultative and coordination activities; (2) elementary subjects may perform less administrative-like activities (scheduling and paperwork); and (3) whereas secondary school subjects and middle school subjects seem to work with student concerns on an individual basis, elementary subjects tend to work systematically with families, teachers, and community agencies.

The Elementary School Counselor

Elementary schools are a powerful socializing force in human development. For better or worse, virtually all members of modern society carry important imprints of their elementary school experiences throughout their lives. In this setting, the young pupil is expected to acquire basic mastery of increasingly difficult bodies of knowledge as well as learn to meet the school's behavior and social expectancies. Failure to learn generates behavioral problems just as inappropriate behaviors and social skills handicap learning.

In the 1970s, it had become increasingly evident that the developmental requirements of elementary-age youth were often neglected and even unrecognized (Stevens & Phil, 1982; White, 1985). As a result, a number of states (15 by 1997) have mandated elementary school counseling. We believe this trend will continue as the public becomes increasingly aware of the vital role of the elementary school in primary prevention.

The characteristics of the elementary pupil and the elementary school dictate certain features in program organization that distinguish elementary school counseling programs from those in secondary schools and at other educational levels. Thus, the elementary school counselor's role and function will also reflect these differences. The differences, however, are not so much in what elementary school counselors do, but in *how* they do it.

For example, counselors and other elementary school specialists must work closely and effectively with classroom teachers. Guidance activities, usually classroom oriented, are a major time consumer. (See Table 3-5 for a rank ordering of elementary school counselor activities as indicated by counselors.) This context naturally leads to an emphasis on consultation and coordination. In addition to counseling, consulting, and coordination functions, the elementary school counselor has responsibilities for pupils' orientation, assessment, and career

TABLE 3-5   Major Functions of Elementary School Counselors

Order	Function	Percentage Engaged In
1	Individual counseling	98.8
2	Group guidance and counseling	81.0
3	Working with parents	79.2
4	Consultation with teachers and administrators	78.9
5	Classroom guidance instruction	65.5
6	Assessment activity	39.3
7	Coordination with community agencies	39.1

Source: Reprinted from "Prevention and the Elementary School Counselor," by R. L. Gibson, 1989, *Elementary School Guidance and Counseling, 24* (1), p. 34. © 1989 American Counseling Association. Reprinted by permission. No further reproduction authorized without written permission of the American Counseling Association.

and other development needs as well as significant attention to the prevention of undesirable habits and behaviors.

Counselor

Although one-to-one counseling in the elementary school may take correspondingly less of the counselor's time than counseling at other levels, the counselor should be available to meet individually or in groups with children referred by teachers or parents or identified by the counselor or other helping professionals in need of counseling. Too, counselors in elementary schools can anticipate individual pupils coming to the counseling offices for assistance, advice, or support. Such current social issues as substance abuse, child abuse, divorce, and discrimination are a frequent basis for individual counseling in the elementary school.

Consultant

As a consultant, the counselor may confer directly with teachers, parents, administrators, and other helping professionals to help an identified third party such as a student, in the school setting. In this role, the counselor helps others to assist the student-client in dealing more effectively with developmental or adjustment needs.

Coordinator

Elementary school counselors have a responsibility for the coordination of the various guidance activities in the schools. Coordinating these with ongoing classroom and school activities is also desirable. As the only building-based helping professional, the elementary school counselor may be called on to coordinate the contributions of school psychologists, social workers, and others. Other coordination activities could include intraschool and interagency referrals.

Agent for Orientation

As a human development facilitator, the elementary school counselor recognizes the importance of the child's orientation to the goals and environment of the elementary school. It is important that the child's initial education experiences be positive ones. In this regard, the counselor may plan group activities and consult with teachers to help children learn and practice the relationship skills necessary in the school setting.

Agent of Assessment

The counselor in the elementary school can anticipate being called on to interpret and often gather both test and nontest data. To the counselor will also fall the task of putting these data into focus, not only to see but to be able to interpret the child as a total being. Beyond the traditional data used for pupil understanding, the counselor should also understand the impact of culture, the sociology of the school, and other environmental influences on pupil behavior.

Career Developer

The importance of the elementary school years as a foundation for later significant decisions underscores the desirability of planned attention being given to the elementary pupil's career development. Although the responsibility for career education planning rests with the classroom teachers, the elementary school counselor can make a major contribution as a co-ordinator and consultant in developing a continuous, sequential, and integrated program.

Agent of Prevention

In the elementary school, there are early warning signs of future problems for young children: learning difficulties, general moodiness (unhappiness or depression), and acting-out behaviors (fights, quarrels, disruptions, restlessness, impulsiveness, and obstinacy). There is an accumulation of evidence to demonstrate that children who cannot adjust during their elementary school years are at high risk for a variety of later problems. Further, substance abuse, violence among peers, vandalism, problems associated with latchkey children, and so forth have increased among elementary school pupils, raising additional concerns and public calls for preventive efforts.

A study (Gibson, 1989) of 96 elementary school programs recommended as outstanding by their state departments of public instruction indicated that prevention was a major program emphasis in 85% of these programs. Elementary school counselors will be increasingly called on and challenged to develop programs that seek to anticipate, intervene in, and prevent the development of these problems. Table 3-6 ranks the emphasis of the programs in this 1989 study.

In our 1996–1997 role and function study, a survey of 224 elementary school counselors indicated that they spend their professional time engaged in the following activities, in order from highest to lowest:

1. Consultation with teachers, parents, and other educational personnel
2. Prevention planning and implementation; individual counseling
3. Classroom and other group guidance activities
4. Nonstandardized assessment of pupils such as case studies, observation, individual interview, and so forth
5. Administrative duties, such as record keeping, reporting, and preparation of materials
6. Developmental activities

TABLE 3-6   Prevention Objectives of Elementary School Counseling and Guidance Programs

Rank	Objective	Percentage
1	To prevent child and/or sexual abuse	69.7
2	To prevent substance abuse	64.9
3	To promote self-concept development	35.8
4	To promote personal safety	17.6
5	To promote social-skills development	15.0
6	To prevent teenage pregnancy	6.3
7	To prevent premature school leaving	4.4
8	To prevent school vandalism	2.1

Source: From "Prevention and the Elementary School Counselor," by Gibson, R. L., 1989, *Elementary School Guidance and Counseling, 24* (1), p. 34. © 1989 American Counseling Association. Reprinted by permission. No further reproduction authorized without written permission of the American Counseling Association.

7. Information sharing, dissemination, and public communications and relations
8. Needs assessment
9. Organizing and conducting counseling groups

Other activities frequently noted were administration and/or interpretation of standardized tests; providing for educational guidance, such as study skills, assistance, and peer tutoring; and participation in orientation programs and various parental assistance groups. A few elementary school counselors reported their involvement in such nonprofessional activities as lunchroom monitoring, recess and playground duties, and crossing guard and school bus duties.

The benefits of counseling programs in elementary schools are outlined in Table 3-7.

An Overview of the Elementary School Counselor's Role

The following description of a day in the life of an elementary school counselor was written by Sherry K. Basile, Ph.D., at that time an elementary school counselor at Berkeley Elementary School, Monck's Corner, South Carolina. Dr. Basile is currently an assistant professor of education at Indiana University.

> Children are scattered on the sidewalks, laughing, playing, crying, some hugging poles. It's early morning and as I walk through the safety of the gate, I am welcomed with a deluge of hugs from what seems like a thousand arms. In the distance there are faces with eyes eagerly waiting their turn for mine to acknowledge theirs.

TABLE 3-7   Benefits of Counseling Programs in Elementary Schools

The elementary school exists to provide:	The counseling program in the elementary school can contribute by:	This implies the following:
1. Foundations for learning and living	1. Providing classroom guidance to enhance learning and relate learning to preparation	1.1 Classroom guidance 1.2 Consultation with teachers and administrators
2. Transmission of our culture and historical heritage	2. Developing multicultural awareness; pride in our cultural diversity and respect for the uniqueness of all cultural/ethnic groups	2.1 Classroom guidance activities 2.2 Consultation with teachers and administrators 2.3 Group guidance and counseling
3. Development as a social-psychological being	3. Providing for the socialization (social development) of all children, including respect for self and others	3.1 Group guidance and counseling focusing on prevention, development, and remediation 3.2 Individual counseling 3.3 Consultation with parent
4. Preparation for citizenship	4. Providing for the development of each individual's human potential	4.1 Career development 4.2 Individual assessment 4.3 Talent and skill enhancement

The elementary school is a gloriously fulfilling environment for a school counselor. In my opinion the elementary school counselor is the ultimate human resource for hundreds of children. We are perceived by them as an adult who never judges or belittles them. We are their friend. Children depend on us to be loving, understanding, happy, always willing to help, incredibly flexible and genuine. In essence we are our positions.

Truly, our jobs are energizing and rewarding. In the lives of many children, we are possibly the only positive force. Our presence in schools allows all children to experience feeling warm and fuzzy and accepted.

The multifarious position of an elementary school counselor begins as I enter the gate of the school yard. Following my regal entrance into the building, most often I am greeted by teachers who need consultation on discipline problems or to refer a child. They follow me inside. Once in my office, I can find paper and pencil to take necessary notes.

With all their needs met, I get ready for the parent conference that is scheduled next. Many parents work and are unable to come in after school, so they prefer early morning appointments. Teachers may or may not be included depending on the issue.

This type of conference is intervention. When a problem or concern exists, the counselor intervenes, for example, by suggesting ways of modifying behavior or some other form of problem solving.

In addition to intervention, another major thrust is toward prevention. The purpose and underlying hope is to help children, early in their lives, to become problem solvers, to develop self-confidence, to become more responsible and thoroughly practice being the best they can be.

We incorporate prevention strategies primarily through classroom guidance activities. In my school, teachers are allowed to choose either the first period of the day or their period before lunch for classroom guidance.

It is now time to gather audiovisual equipment and scurry off to a classroom. Sometimes I pack a cassette player, puppets, posters, handout sheets, books, stickers, but always high energy and a smile. Also, the rule at my school is that, as the counselor walks by, it is not acceptable to get out of line to give hugs. They all raise their hand for a high-five as I walk by their line. This saves the teacher frustration from lining up again, and I am not late for my scheduled activity.

As I open the door and enter the classroom, there's clapping and happy glowing faces. The children are thrilled that I have come to be with them. The teachers sit in the back of the room or at their desks. I invite the children to enter the world of affective education—feelings, thoughts, decision making, understanding who they are and how to be the best they can be. Through clever and outwardly unacademic techniques of teaching, whether it is musical or magical, the children gain understanding of themselves and life skills that will forever be useful to them. In addition, they are uplifted, excited, and eager to learn.

On my way back to the office, I am inevitably stopped by a teacher or two for a quick suggestion or a follow-up comment on a child they referred. Since I am often stopped on my way to or from a classroom, it is necessary to invite them to come to my office at their activity period or after school.

With a few minutes before my next scheduled activity, I stop in the attendance office to welcome any new students who have registered.

Next is a small-group counseling session consisting of children who have been referred for similar reasons. My group size is limited to six children. Guidelines for conducting group counseling are followed.

After group, there are phone calls to return to parents, district office personnel, the school psychologist, doctors, or other counselors.

Now it's time to administer a series of screening tests and counsel with individuals before leaving for the next classroom guidance presentation. If time permits I will join a class for lunch. It's always a treat for children when the counselor shares extra time.

After lunch, again there are phone calls to return and messages that need attention. It may be necessary to visit a classroom to do an observation or go to the rescue in an emergency situation. This time is also used for paperwork. On days when I make an abuse or neglect report to the Department of Social Services, three copies of the report must be made and sent to appropriate agencies. Afternoons are scheduled for individual and small-group counseling also.

After children leave for the day, typically there is a constant flow of teachers in the guidance office. This time is also used for parent-teacher conferences and staffings of children into programs for students with disabilities.

On days when the school psychologist is working in my school, I work closely with her as a liaison for teachers who have referred children for psychological testing. Teachers depend on the counselor to make accurate reports to the school psychologist related to the special needs of their children. It is often advisable to set up times for her to observe in these classrooms.

After testing and proper discussion of test results, we set up staffing dates and parent conferences to explain test scores and recommendations. I send letters of invitation to parents and teachers a week in advance of the meetings. Administrators are also included in these staffings.

By now, the school day has come to an end. I pack my school bag, exchange hugs, and say my good-byes. It could be an evening when I'm conducting a parenting class at school. If so, things at home are put into fast-forward so I can leave again for school. There are parents who are a little nervous yet eager to learn how to better care for their children and relieved that other parents share their woes. Parenting groups are very supportive and encouraging ways to reach the children. Our jobs are made easier because of them.

Elementary school counselors are special, caring people who are dedicated to educating children in the affective domain. We help them become more self-confident, productive, and successful adults. Our day is ended with a feeling of accomplishment because of the constant feedback we get from children, parents, and teachers about the difference we make in the lives of people they care about. Elementary school counselors: every child deserves one!

The Middle/Junior High School Counselor

In the 1970s, there was a trend away from a junior high school concept toward a middle school concept. These changes have not been without their attending controversies, but the middle school in concept and function may not really be all that different from the more traditional junior high school. For example, many contend that the junior high school was originally conceived as an institution to meet the developmental and transitional needs of youth from puberty to adolescence, from elementary to secondary school. Early in the middle school movement, it was suggested that a rationale for the middle school concept was based on data indicating that modern youth reach physical, social, and intellectual maturity at a younger age than did previous generations and that the junior high school may no longer meet the developmental needs of these students.

Regardless of whether a school system adopts a middle school type of intermediate school or stays with the more traditional junior high school, it would appear that either institution will reflect such characteristics as providing for (a) the orientation and transitional needs and (b) the educational and social-developmental needs of their populations. In such a setting, middle or junior high school counselors will be actively involved in the following roles.

Student Orientation

This would include the initial orientation of students and their parents to the programs, policies, facilities, and counseling activities of their new school and, later, their pre-entry orientation to the high school they will attend.

Appraisal or Assessment Activities

In addition to typical school record and standardized test data, counselors may increasingly encourage the use of observation and other techniques to identify emerging traits of individual students during this critical development period.

Counseling

Both individual and group counseling should be used by school counselors at this level. In practice, it appears that middle and junior high school counselors tend to use group counseling more frequently than individual counseling.

Consultation

Counselors will provide consultation to faculty, parents, and, on occasion, school administrators regarding the developmental and adjustment needs of individual students. Counselors will also consult with other members of the school system's pupil personnel services team.

Placement

Counselors are usually involved in course and curricular placement of pupils, not only within their own schools but also cooperatively with their counterparts in the feeder secondary schools.

Student Development

As one notes the role of the middle school, it is obviously important that student development be given specific attention by school counselors, faculty, and other helping professionals (i.e., social workers, psychologists, etc.). This means understanding the developmental characteristics of this age group and their attending developmental tasks and planning programs that are appropriately responsive.

Seventy-one middle and junior high school counselors reported (in our 1996–1997 survey) that they spent their professional time involved in the following activities, in order from highest to lowest:

1. Administrative activities
2. Individual counseling
3. Providing career guidance assistance and materials
4. Student assessment using nonstandardized procedures
5. Dissemination of information regarding program; public relations activities
6. Group guidance activities
7. Standardized test administration and/or interpretation
8. Planning and implementation of prevention activities
9. Providing educational guidance and information
10. Group counseling; developmental activities

A number of the responding counselors mentioned significant amounts of time spent in meetings, serving on committees, meetings with parents, and sponsoring student organizations.

An Overview of the Middle School Counselor's Role

The following description of a middle school counselor's responsibilities was written by Rochelle House, a middle school counselor at Central Middle School in Columbus, Indiana.

Part of my joy as a middle school counselor is the endless variety that exists; part of my challenge is being not only prepared but flexible for that variety. There is rarely a "typical" day, but if there were, it would begin early with smiles for staff arriving early to prepare for a day with young adolescents. Leftover business from yesterday receives attention; a discussion with a teacher about the student who needs encouragement to keep working hard even though that test score was discouragingly low; a discussion about the student who needs extra support during difficult family changes; support for a teacher who seeks suggestions for motivating and connecting with a hard-to-reach young student; acknowledging the information from an administrator about a parent concern; and thank you's to the secretaries for yesterday's assistance and wishing them an outstanding day.

At 7:45 A.M. the early bell announces the opening of the day. Students stream into the Guidance Office for appointment passes, to set a time to discuss a concern, to look for or turn in lost items, to make a phone call home to ask a parent to retrieve and deliver forgotten items. At this time of day, there are multiple reminders that these young adolescents can be quite forgetful and quite needy. A bit of extra attention brings open smiles and can set the student off to a positive day.

Shortly after the day begins, a new student and parent arrive to enroll. Following a meeting with the Dean to register and go over all required documents, it is my turn to welcome the student and parent, find out about their likes, dislikes, and preferences; introduce them to the academic program they will experience; discuss elective options; devise a schedule; provide a tour (using a student assistant as ambassador, if available); and introduce them to one or more of their teachers. A typical orientation for a new student takes up about one hour. A very important role for me is to make the student feel welcome and important and to present an open and warm atmosphere for them.

Upon returning to the office, a quick check of phone calls and the daily schedule occurs. On tap for today are: a meeting with one of the academic teams to discuss student needs and teacher concerns; a parent/team conference to consider the special needs for a particular student; a classroom presentation on career skills; and appointments with students to follow up on academic progress reports. An important part of my focus is to assist in ensuring the success of all students. This occurs through individual sessions with students that touch on accountability, motivation and skill building, small group counseling, classroom guidance, consultation with parents, teachers, teaching teams, outside counselors, and administrators.

As the day moves forward, students frequently present themselves with a desire for assistance with a peer conflict to talk about a family or personal concern, to question how to achieve in a given teacher's class, especially when the student believes the teacher does not like him or her. Phone calls and personal consultation with the Dean of Students, the School Nurse, and caseworkers from Child Protection fill the time between scheduled meetings, classroom visits, and student conferences. Informal visits with students occur during "lunch duty" supervision and chance meetings in the hallways during passing periods. Students respond well to "hellos" and being called by name when seen in the hallway. A school of 700+ can seem overwhelming for a young adolescent. Being known by adults helps make it seem less scary!

As students leave for the day, time is spent returning phone calls to parents and making phone calls to community members for assistance with career activities. Upcoming activities include our program, "Catch Your Dream," giving students and parents feedback from the Career Interest Inventory. Another is "Reality Store," a collaborative effort with the local Business and Professional Women's Association in which students experience a day in adult life. Career Day is when students hear a variety of career speakers. Organization of each of these activities requires many phone calls and follow-up calls as well as meetings to finalize these important events.

Some days require other meetings: a community-wide committee "Care Teams," a district-wide K-12 Guidance Steering Committee, a district Pupil Services Network, middle school Parent Advisory Committee, Team Representative Committee, Remediation Committee, as well as faculty meetings. These meetings are all important to the functions of a middle school as well as the effectiveness of the developmental counseling program.

In addition, my own professional development provides support for the energy required to be effective in my work. Attending professional conferences and meetings enhances my effectiveness as a middle school counselor. All that I do is underscored by an effort to positively support success by all students. It is a privilege to be involved in this work.

The Secondary School Counselor

Although the role and function of the secondary school counselor has expanded over the years, it is clearly the most traditional and most readily identified, even though it has been more frequently and seriously challenged than that of elementary or collegiate counselors. However, despite these challenges, any drastic changes are unlikely. Although the emphasis and techniques will undoubtedly change, the role and function of the secondary school counselor will continue to be built around the traditional expectancies discussed in Chapter 2. These expectations are, for the most part, confirmed in a study of the goals of secondary school guidance programs reported by Moles (1991) (see Table 3-8) and our more recent 1996–1997 study as illustrated in Table 3-4.

TABLE 3-8   Goals for Guidance Programs: Means of Rankings

Goal	Currently Emphasized	Desired by Guidance Staff	Desired by School Administrators	Desired by Teachers	Desired by Parents
Help students with their academic achievement in high school[a]	2.7	2.6	3.2	3.6	2.9
Help students plan and prepare for postsecondary schooling	2.7	2.3	2.4	2.1	2.2
Help students with personal growth and development	2.5	3.1	2.4	2.6	2.6
Help students plan and prepare for their work roles after high school	2.0	2.0	2.0	1.7	2.3

Note: 1 is lowest, and 4 is highest emphasis.

[a]Phrased as "Help students improve their achievement in high school courses" in the question for columns 2–5.

Source: From "Guidance Programs in American High Schools: A Descriptive Portrait," by O. C. Moles, 1991, *School Counselor, 38* (3), p. 167. Copyright © American Counseling Association. Reprinted by permission. No further reproduction authorized without written permission of the American Counseling Association.

The 109 secondary school counselors who responded to our function and role survey (1996–1997) reported their involvement in the following activities in order from highest to lowest:

1. Providing educational guidance and information, including student scheduling, college placement, and scholarship information
2. Individual counseling
3. Administrative activities and record keeping
4. Prevention activities
5. Providing career guidance and assistance
6. Standardized test administration and/or interpretation
7. Information dissemination: public communication and human relations
8. Consultation activities
9. Student development activities
10. Group guidance; group counseling

As with their elementary and middle/junior high school counterparts, secondary school counselors were engaged in noncounseling activities. Prominent among these were hall duty and monitoring student lunchrooms. Some also indicated duties as substitute teachers.

In a study of teacher opinions of secondary school counseling programs, Gibson (1989) reports that teachers view the most important functions of counselors as (a) providing individual counseling, (b) offering career planning assistance and information, (c) administering and interpreting standardized test results, and (d) assisting in college guidance and placement.

The roles and functions of the secondary school counselor are not dissimilar to those of counselors in the elementary and middle/junior high schools. The differences occur in how counselors in the secondary school discharge their role and function and in the various emphases appropriate to the secondary school setting. For example, the emphasis at the secondary school level shifts slightly from the preventive to the remedial in dealing with many common counseling concerns. Many of these issues are potentially serious life problems, such as addiction to drugs and alcohol, sexual concerns, and interpersonal relationship adjustments. Furthermore, there is less client emphasis on preparing for decisions and more emphasis on making decisions. These include immediate or impending career decisions or further education decisions, decisions relevant to relationships with the opposite sex and perhaps marriage, and decisions involved in developing personal values systems.

In addition to these different emphases in contrast to counseling needs at other educational levels, counselors anticipate more emphasis on consultation and on a broader understanding of the impact of environment on students' behavior; a shifting emphasis toward a closer relationship with the classroom teacher in the school environment, as opposed to the traditional "medical" model (in which the client in need comes to the office for a "prescription"); and, finally, a shift in emphasis from a reactive to proactive change agent in both the school and the community.

An Overview of the Secondary School Counselor's Role

Ms. De Klocke, a counselor at North Side High School in Fort Wayne, Indiana, lists her activities in a typical day as a high school counselor.

Typical Day's Activities of a High School Counselor

- Typically arrive at 7:00 A.M. and leave at 5:00 P.M.
- Host parent calls to explain her foreign student's broken elbow and premature return to Brazil
- Coordinator of Career Academy calls to see whether student who was recommended for the special program and put on a waiting list last semester is still interested in participating
- Student from Czech Republic discusses schedule change
- Student from Germany adds two classes to his schedule for second semester; checked with teachers for approval
- Senior brings in college application and wants school recommendation completed by tomorrow
- Local employer calls for recommendation for a 1993 graduate who is seeking employment
- Interpretation of PSAT/NMSQT test results to 200+ juniors and sophomores
- Conference with former student's parent (her daughter graduated in 1979; currently her granddaughter is a freshman at NSHS) who is concerned with her granddaughter's well-being
- Conference with a sophomore who is interested in participating in an international exchange program for his junior year
- Conference with senior who needs help with college application
- Phone call from senior parent re FAFSA form and Financial Aids Workshop
- Conference with senior (returning from a semester of study in Japan at our sister city school) who will be returning for his eighth semester at North Side; also needed help with college applications
- Conference with senior and Student Assistance Counselor re possible abuse by parent
- Conference with parent (whose daughter graduated in 1993) and daughter's fiancé who wants to get GED certificate
- Phone conversation with soccer coach who had borrowed a videotape of soccer game from one of our Spanish exchange students and had not returned it
- Conference with female junior who is interested in hosting a Japanese girl
- Phone conversation with former student (who was a peer facilitator and now a teacher at South Side High School) who is interested in starting such a program at his school and wanted some help in writing his proposal
- Conference with Japanese businessman who brought me a present from parents of one of our exchange students
- Conference with a journalism student who was writing an article on the FAFSA and financial aid
- Chat with senior football player whom I had moved, at his request, from an Essentials of English class to an Academic English class, checking on his grades; currently earning a B+
- Conference with sophomore soccer player to see whether his family would consider taking the Rotary Exchange student from Turkey for the second semester

- Phone conversation with counselor from Educational Opportunity Center regarding one of our students
- Phone conversation with probation officer downtown to discuss the student's being transported to North Side to take the SAT test
- Appointment downtown with Media Services person in Fort Wayne Community School Channel 20 regarding production of a videotape about PURSUITS career development program (which I coordinate)
- Phone conversation with Educational Testing Service regarding providing test center for the PLUS Academic Abilities Assessment Program (for sixth graders)
- Conference with parent of junior dropout regarding plans to reenter school next semester
- Area coordinator for Center for Cultural Interchange needs signature for student from Argentina who will enter North Side High School second semester
- Phone conversation with Indiana University Admissions Office regarding appeal process for senior who was not admitted; followed up with letter confirming the telephone conversation
- Phone conversation with mother of senior transfer student who is experiencing adjustment problems
- Parent request for progress reports for student; advised secretary to prepare reports
- Conference with teacher regarding need to find shadowing sites for Advanced Biology students
- Phone conversation with tutor at Benet Learning Center regarding a student he is tutoring
- Conversation with North Side graduate who is currently a professor at Earlham College
- Conference with parent of sophomore regarding college opportunities for minority students
- Discussion with athletic director regarding NCAA Clearinghouse for student-athletes
- Prepared memo for science and math teachers regarding National Engineers Week and the need to recommend seniors who are serious about pursuing a career in engineering
- Senior Interview (all counselors assist in interviewing each senior individually)
- Phone conversation with Purdue nutritionist who will teach the "Have a Healthy Baby" class
- Case conference with student-athlete, his mother, and a teacher to discuss inappropriate behavior and attitude
- Conference with student regarding possibility of sexually transmitted disease; referral to Board of Health; appointment scheduled
- Letter to mayor regarding nomination of student for Mayor's Youth Achievement Award
- Letter and applications completed for Hoosier Girls state delegates and alternates
- Meeting with two community consultants and Student Assistance Counselor regarding plans for conflict management training sessions
- Conference with *Journal-Gazette* reporter regarding teens and "Sexuality in the 1990s"
- Phone conversation with two counselors in our feeder middle schools arranging for home stays for eleven Japanese middle school students and one teacher

- Financial Aid workshop, 7–9 P.M. with 96 parents participating
- This is a typical day!

Additional Responsibilities on a Regular Basis

Monthly Meetings

- Faculty Advisory Committee (first Tuesday 2:45–4:00)
- Faculty meetings (first Thursday, during teachers' plan periods)
- Family and Children's Service board meeting (third Thursday, 11:30–1:00); PR Committee meets second Tuesday for lunch
- Sister Cities Committee (first Wednesday, 5:00–6:15)
- Integrated Guidance Program staff (first Thursday, 8–10 A.M.)
- Curriculum and Instruction division (second Tuesday, 8–10 A.M.)

Other Meetings

- North Side High School administrative staff and guidance staff meet weekly for about 2 hours each
- Performance Based Accreditation Steering Committee meets weekly at 7 A.M.; School Climate Committee (which I chair) meets weekly at either 7 A.M. or 2:45 P.M.
- Peer facilitator training, 7 A.M. on Tuesday, Thursday, Friday
- PURSUITS (career development program) board meets quarterly; I serve as coordinator of this program, which is funded by a private foundation, currently serves all high schools in Allen County and 11 Fort Wayne Community Schools middle schools, and pilots a career development program for elementary schools
- Dave Hefner International Exchange Fund Board meets twice a year; I serve as president
- Indiana Counseling Association Foundation meets yearly; I serve as treasurer
- North Side Area Guidance Leadership Project (3-year project funded by the Lilly Endowment) core team meets quarterly; North Side High School CAIT (Child Advocacy/Inquiry Team) meets regularly
- Regularly attend professional conferences and workshops as well as serve on various ad hoc committees (e.g., the State of Indiana GED study group)
- Supervise test center for the American College Testing, Scholastic Aptitude Testing, ASE Technician Test, PLUS, and U.S. Postal Service exams
- Prepare college applications/scholarship recommendations on an ongoing basis (usually after school and on weekends)
- Attend/supervise various fine arts programs, athletic events, dances, and other programs

Counselors in Vocational Schools

The image and the significance of vocational education changed markedly in the 1970s. Once regarded as a dumping ground for the unwilling or unable student (with facilities usually appropriate to this image), vocational education programs have made a dramatic turnaround. Today they are some of the finest educational facilities in the country, attracting students at all ability levels and preparing them for jobs in demand. School counselors need to become aware of both the nature of vocational education programs and the opportunities available to those who complete them. Additionally, counselors in preparation need to recognize some differences in the role and function of the counselor in the vocational school.

Counselors in Higher Education

A wide variety of counseling services are available to students in programs of higher education across the United States and Canada. Some of these counselors function in specialized facilities such as career centers and college admissions and placement offices. The majority of counselors, however, are employed in university counseling, mental health, or psychological service centers. These centers typically offer personal, academic, and vocational counseling, although group counseling has increased in popularity in recent years. Many of these centers are interdisciplinary in terms of staffing.

Some insight into anticipated responsibilities of counselors on college campuses may be provided by noting the CACREP standards for the training of college counselors. These standards suggest that college counselors will need preparation in (a) career counseling, (b) group work, (c) prevention and intervention methods and procedures, and (d) additional studies (i.e., academic assistance, promoting interpersonal relationships, leadership training, consultation, etc.).

A noticeable trend in the activities of college counseling center programs is their move to assist larger numbers of students on their campuses through such activities as outreach programs, special workshops, residence hall groups, and peer counseling. On some campuses, counselors are also becoming more active in consultation with their faculty peers, campus administrators, and leaders of student organizations.

Counseling Services in Community and Junior Colleges

Counselors in community colleges play a significant role in the educational, social, and emotional development of the student. They provide a variety of services for students with distinct socioeconomic and cultural backgrounds and varying levels of academic abilities and motivation toward education (Paradise & Long, 1981).

Community and junior colleges are often challenged with the task of educating students who have not developed the necessary skill to engage in adequate college work (Higbee, Dwinell, McAdams, GoldbergBelle, & Tardola, 1991). Higbee et al. explain that these students generally had not planned to attend college and therefore failed to choose an academic curriculum in high school, may have dropped out of high school and later decided further education was necessary, have been absent from the academic setting for an extended period of time, experienced poor instruction or a weak curriculum in high school, or have little motivation. They insist that counseling services for these students must address intellectual as well as emotional development by focusing on the following issues:

- Academic policies and procedures
- Study skills
- Time management strategies
- Communication skill development
- Cultural pluralism
- Relationship enhancement

- Stress reduction
- Health and wellness
- Career exploration
- Decision-making skills
- Goal-setting strategies
- Motivational strategies
- Personal empowerment strategies

Counseling services are noted by Burnham and Satcher (1990) as among the services provided for enhancing the educational opportunities of individuals with learning disabilities in more than 40 community colleges in Mississippi, Alabama, Georgia, Tennessee, and Alabama. Activities offered include advising, remedial skills courses, training programs, support groups, orientation programs, career development, and study skills courses. Through involvement in such activities, students have a stronger chance of gaining the most from their education and becoming involved in a career that contributes not only to societal needs but also to their own image of themselves as an important contributing factor in our society. Delco (1988) claims that enhancement of this self-image is just as important as enhancement of educational skills and that counselors play a vital role in promoting this positive self-image.

As the U.S. economy has become more and more dependent on technology, community colleges are playing a significant role in the training and retraining of the workforce for business and industries (Hirshberg, 1991). Hirshberg identifies the activities of management and technical assistance for new and small businesses, tech prep programs with high schools, cooperative education programs, partnerships with state agencies, and customized and contract job training for industries as roles of community colleges in promoting the economic development of our society. She emphasizes further the important role that counseling services play in promoting the appropriate education and training of students in these programs.

Quimbita (1991) maintains that community colleges are in a position to take a significant role in increasing the number of individuals in scientific careers as well as promoting diversification in terms of ethnic and gender composition. Vocational counseling and career guidance services are among the strategies she identifies as being utilized by community colleges in successfully recruiting and educating more women and minorities into two-year college science, math, and engineering programs.

TEACHER AND ADMINISTRATOR ROLES IN THE SCHOOL COUNSELING PROGRAM

The Classroom Teacher

Although it seems heresy to the counseling profession, it has been and could continue to be possible for schools to exist without the benefit of counselors. Many students possibly would not achieve their potential, solve their problems, or make appropriate decisions and plans, but nonetheless most of them would learn, progress, and be viewed as educated. It is also possible for schools to exist without the presence of an even more prominent member—the school principal. Although teachers would be even more overburdened with administrative responsibilities, and their teaching effectiveness would undoubtedly suffer, students would still be taught, learn (perhaps at a slower rate), graduate (even without the principal's handshake), and be viewed as educated.

Schools without teachers, however, cease to be schools. They become, instead, detention centers, social clubs, or temporary shelters, and any learning that takes place would be both incidental and accidental. It therefore becomes obvious, and has been since the beginning of schooling, that the teacher is the most important professional in the school setting. Teacher support and participation are crucial to any program that involves students. The school counseling program is no exception. Further, today's teachers, as indicated in a study (Gibson, 1990), feel that they should have responsibilities in the school counseling program beyond those performed in the classroom. Gibson (1990) also notes:

> Notwithstanding changing roles and calls for new directions, it can be concluded that secondary school teachers continue to believe that counseling and guidance programs make a positive contribution to the total program of their schools. Interviews further confirmed that teachers have high respect for the skills and dedication of the counselors in their schools. This was especially noted in those schools in which counselors interacted with every teacher on a one-to-one basis at least once per semester. (p. 254)

It is therefore important to examine the role and function of the classroom teacher in the counseling program, recognizing, of course, that differences may be anticipated at differing educational levels and in different educational settings.

Listener-Adviser

Most classroom teachers see their pupils every day, five days a week, for at least 45 minutes per day on the average of 180 school days per year, often for several years, all of which represents a staggering amount of contact time exceeded by no other adults except parents, and that exception does not always hold true. Inevitably, the teacher more than any other professional in the school setting is in the position to know the students best, to communicate with them on an almost daily basis, and to establish a relationship based on mutual trust and respect. The teacher thus becomes the first line of contact between the student and the school counseling program; a contact in which the teacher will frequently be called upon to serve in a listening/advising capacity.

Referral and Receiving Agent

The classroom teacher is the major source of student referrals to the school counselor. Because the counselor's daily personal contacts with students are necessarily limited, the counselor's personal awareness of students needing counseling is similarly limited. The counseling program must, therefore, depend on an alert faculty to ensure that students with counseling needs will not go unnoticed and uncounseled. School counselors need to encourage their teacher colleagues to actively search for these students, because much evidence exists to suggest that only the tip of the proverbial iceberg has been touched in efforts to identify all students with serious counseling needs.

Of course, simply identifying these students to a counselor may not be enough. In many instances, the teacher must orient and encourage the student to seek counselor assistance. Nor does the teacher's responsibility necessarily end when the student has entered a counseling relationship. The teacher may still be involved, if only in the role of supporting the student's continuation with the counseling process. Teachers may also anticipate a role as a receiving agent, not only for those students they have referred but for others in their classes as well. In such situations, the teacher in a sense receives the counseled student back into the classroom environment and, it is hoped, supports and reinforces the outcome of the counseling. The importance of this reinforcer role cannot be overemphasized. Teachers can also play a valuable role as a member of study teams for pupils they refer.

Discoverer of Human Potential

Each year teachers witness a talent parade through their respective classes. Most teachers have the expertise to identify those who may have some special talents for their own particular career specialty. That expertise, multiplied across the many career specialties, represents a near army of talent scouts that should ensure that each student will have his or her talents and potentials identified and his or her development encouraged and assisted. This teacher role as a discoverer of human potential is significant in fulfilling not only a mission of the school counseling program but also in meeting the responsibility of education to the individual and to society.

Career Educator

Closely related to the foregoing is the teacher's central role in the school's career education program. Because career education is recognized as a part of students' total education, it is important also to recognize the classroom teacher's responsibility to integrate career education into teaching subject matter. Career education cannot succeed without career guidance and vice versa. The success of the career guidance program is tied to the success of the career education program, a success that rests largely with the classroom teacher.

The career education responsibilities of the teacher include developing positive attitudes and respect for all honest work, a challenging responsibility in view of the many adult-imposed biases with which the student is constantly confronted. Additionally, the teacher must promote the parallel development of positive student attitudes toward education and its relationship to career preparation and decision making. Students must also have the opportunity to examine and test concepts, skills, and roles and develop values appropriate to their future career planning. The security of the classroom group provides an ideal setting for these experiences.

Human Relations Facilitator

The potential for success of any school counseling program depends to a considerable degree upon the climate of the school, an environment that is conducive to the development and practice of positive human relations. The influence of the classroom teacher on that environment is dominant, as ably expressed by Haim Ginott:

> I have come to the frightening conclusion
> I am the decisive element in the classroom
> It is my personal approach that creates the climate
> It is my daily mood that makes the weather
> As a teacher I possess tremendous power to make a child's life miserable or joyous
> I can humiliate or humor, hurt or heal
> In all situations it is my response that decides whether a crisis will be escalated or de-escalated, and a child humanized or dehumanized. (cited in Gross & Gross, 1974, p. 39)

Among the research emphasizing the importance of a favorable classroom and school environment for learning is that reported in Benjamin Bloom's book *Human Characteristics and School Learning* (1976). Bloom suggests that it is possible for 95% of the students to learn all that the school has to teach at or near the same achievement level. His research indicates that most students will be very similar in both learning and their motivation to learn when they are provided the favorable conditions or environment for learning. His research also demonstrates that when the environment in the classroom is unfavorable, differences occur that widen the gap between high and low achievers. In this role as a human relations facilitator, the classroom teacher has the opportunity to be a model to demonstrate positive human relations. The teaching and practicing of these skills should occur as a regular procedure in the classroom as the teacher plans and directs group interactions that promise positive human relationship experiences for each individual participant.

Counseling Program Supporter

Someone once said, "Counselors are the most human of all humans." Be that as it may, counselors, like all humans, need and respond to the encouragement and support of their fellow beings. Therefore, a significant contribution that the classroom teacher can make to the school counseling program is one of counselor encouragement and support and the creation of a motivating environment. Support can be especially influential in determining how pupils view and use the services of the school's counseling program. Teachers' reactions also do not go unnoticed by school administrators and supervisors. Of course, evidence of teacher support for counseling ideally should extend to parents and others in the community as well.

Despite the importance of the classroom teacher in any school counseling program at any educational level, evidence indicates that, in far too many settings, the classroom teacher is still only incidentally involved in the program. Many classroom teachers may feel uncertain about the goals of their school programs and may lack communication and involvement in the counseling programs. In such situations, the student is the real loser, and both the counselor and the teacher must share the blame.

Because the school counseling program is the responsibility of counselors, they must initiate communications and interaction with their teaching faculties; they must actively pursue teachers' involvement and assistance, and they must exemplify their claim to human relations expertise. Blum (1986) suggests the importance of the counselor having visibility—being seen—and sociability—being known by the teachers in their school. They must also recognize that although most teachers are willing to accept their role in the school counseling program, as many studies have indicated, they may lack some understanding of what that role and function are.

Of course, not all teachers will or can be "all things," as suggested in this section. Hopefully, most can and will accept many of the roles, however. These role opportunities also can be enhanced by preparing teachers to recognize, accept, and enjoy their roles in the school counseling program. Unfortunately, most teachers do not seek and are not required to take course work in counseling and guidance and, therefore, are limited in realizing their full potential as team members.

The Chief School Administrator

Whether a building principal or a university president, the chief on-site administrator is potentially (and usually) the most important person in the development of any educational program in his or her respective setting. Most school staff members (including principals and college presidents) think of chief administrators in terms of power—what the chief administrators permit them to do and not to do. Previous studies (Gibson, Mitchell, & Higgins, 1983) have noted that administrative support was ranked in the highest priority category in the establishment and development of school counseling programs. These studies emphasize the significant role the school principal and other educational leadership can and should play in any program of counseling within their jurisdiction. This role may be appropriately expressed through leadership, consultation, advice, and resource support. Some of the characteristics of these activities are described next.

Program Leader and Supporter

The leadership behavior of the school principal on behalf of the school counseling program is a major determinant of the program's prospects for success. Because school administrators represent the educational leadership in both the school and the community, they have the responsibility of giving clear, open, and recognized support for the school program. This will include responsibilities for communicating program characteristics, achievements, and needs to school boards and others within the educational system and to the tax-supporting public.

Program Consultant and Adviser

The chief school administrator has the best overview of all activities and planning within the institution. This position enables the chief administrator to make a valuable contribution to the school counseling program as adviser and consultant on school needs that can be served by the school program, school policies that affect counseling program functioning, resolution of problems encountered by the program, and procedures or directions for program development and improvement.

Resource Provider

Chief school administrators are usually responsible for the institution's budget—its makeup and utilization. In this role, they provide advice and direction to all school programs regarding budget expectations, staffing possibilities, facilities, and equipment. They may also be aware of possible external resources such as state or federal funding, which the school counseling program may wish to explore.

THE COUNSELOR AND RELATIONSHIPS WITH OTHER HELPING PROFESSIONS

As already noted, one of the school counselor's important roles is as a team member. Unlike the gifted athlete who may have to limit membership to one team, the counselor may play on several teams. One of the most important and logical of these is the *pupil personnel services* or helping professions team. This team typically includes the school psychologist, social worker, speech and hearing specialists, and health personnel. To work effectively with each other, members must understand the expertise and responsibilities of their fellow team members and how they support each other. This is not always easy because their roles often seem to overlap, especially at the elementary school level. The All Handicapped Children's Act of 1975 has had the most consistent influence over the past 20 years in role determination for elementary school personnel. Unfortunately, most training programs do little in the way of interdisciplinary planning or training. Therefore, it becomes the responsibility of the school counselor and other helping professionals to initiate and develop positive, cooperative working relationships consistent with the team concept.

The School Psychologist*

Recent estimates indicate that more than 22,000 school psychologists practice in the United States today (Fagan & Wise, 1994). These psychologists received their professional preparation in one of the approximately 235 training programs that emphasize the application of knowledge in psychological and educational foundations to the academic, behavioral, and social problems that students experience in a school setting.

During the 1970s and 1980s, the number of school psychologists increased dramatically in public schools as a result of state and federal laws mandating free and appropriate educational services for students with disabilities. As a result of the expansive growth in special education, the role and services provided by most school psychologists have been heavily tied to federal and state requirements for comprehensive evaluation of students to determine eligibility for special education services. Federal laws such as the Individuals with Disabilities Education Act (IDEA) indicate that the services of school psychologists include assessment, consultation, and the provision of psychological services to students with disabilities and their families (Humes & Hohenshil, 1987). Consistent with these mandates, recent studies have reported that school psychologists spend approximately 50% of their time involved in assessment-related activities, with the remaining 50% evenly distributed across consultation and intervention activities (Smith, 1984; Reschly & Wilson, 1993).

As the focus in special education and other remedial education programs switched during the 1980s from eligibility and identification to intervention and prevention for students with mild disabilities and others at risk for school failure, school psychologists became increasingly involved in intervention and remediation programs for all students. The school psychologists' skill with individual assessment tools—including measures of cognitive ability; academic achievement; and behavioral, personality, or adaptive behavior—are often used to meet specific student needs and deliver possible intervention alternatives. Increasingly, these assessment skills are expanding beyond individual test administration to include interviewing, observation, and alternative techniques such as curriculum-based assessment.

Because the school psychologist is heavily trained in the use of clinical tools such as those that measure the mental and personality characteristics of the individual, counselors may often find it desirable to refer students to the school psychologist for clinical diagnosis. And the school psychologist will often identify, through his or her diagnostic evaluations, pupils in need of counseling.

School counselors will often work directly with school psychologists in providing psychological and support services to students with disabilities, families, and classroom teachers working with these students. Thus, school counselors and school psychologists will frequently collaborate on building-based and student support teams that consult with

*Information regarding school psychology was provided by Nancy Waldron, Ph.D., Assistant Professor, Indiana University.

teachers and parents and provide direct services to students with academic and/or behavioral problems in school.

The School Social Worker

Crouch (1979) defines social work as "the attempt to assist those who do not command the means to human subsistence in acquiring them and in attaining the highest possible degree of independence" (p. 46). The school social worker provides helping services for those children who are unable to make proper use of their educational opportunities and who find it difficult to function effectively in the school environment. In this role, the social worker is a referral source for those children who appear to have emotional or social problems that are handicapping their learning and social adjustment to school. The school social worker has special interviewing and casework skills that are used within a school-child-parent context. The school social worker works closely with community agencies and nonschool professional helpers, such as physicians, lawyers, and ministers.

Meares (1977) reports a study that ranked the importance of the tasks performed by school social workers. Four major interrelated priority activities were identified: (a) clarifying the nature of the child's problem and the parameters of social work services; (b) assessing the child's specific problem; (c) facilitating better relationships among school, community, and pupils; and (d) educational counseling with the child and his or her parents. Most activities emphasize the importance of the liaison role. Thus, there has been a transition from the primarily clinical casework approach to serving children in schools to that of home-school-community liaison and educational counseling with the child and his or her parents (p. 198).

The school social worker is an important member of the school services team. Counselors and other helping professionals may depend on the social worker to provide better understanding of the child, especially in regard to the home environment and the nature of the pupil's behavioral problems.

Special Educator

In 1975, The Education for All Handicapped Children Act (Public Law 94-142) was signed into law. This law's intent was to provide normal and integrated educational opportunities for children with disabilities. A major impact of the act, stemming from the desire to educate the student in the least restrictive environment, was the mainstreaming of most students with disabilities into regular classrooms. The regular classroom teacher was also made responsible for the progress of such students in his or her classroom, and the law forbade any categorical labels (i.e., *emotionally disturbed, retarded,* etc.). Other aspects of the law provided for due process or the equal protection of the rights of people with disabilities and individualized programs designed to maximize the potential of each student.

One outcome of these provisions has been the addition of the special educator to the school's helping services team. Obviously, the school counselor has special skills in terms of assessment and placement, individual counseling, group guidance, and career assistance that can help this population. Consulting with parents can also be helpful. In all of these aspects, the school counselor will work closely with the special educator and others concerned with maximizing the educational opportunities for these students.

School Health Personnel

Most school systems employ professional health services personnel, at least on a part-time basis. Most common are the school nurse and the dental hygienist; a number of school systems also employ school physicians. Your personal recall of these helping professionals may consist of memories of immunization shots, opening your mouth to say "Ahh," the taste of the tongue depressor, and the admonition of the dental hygienist when she discovered you weren't brushing regularly. Such recalls are fairly characteristic of the role of these providers of basic, preventive health services for all school children. These professionals also identify children who need special medical treatment or referrals for the correction or alleviation of defects. Counselors will find these medical specialists a resource for making referrals and determining whether or to what extent physical ailments or defects are an obstacle to a student's anticipated development or adjustment.

Psychiatrists

Psychiatrists are physicians with specialized training in the treatment of behavioral abnormalities. As physicians, psychiatrists are permitted by law to use drugs and other physical means of treatment for mental problems. Counselors often suggest to parents that they refer their son or daughter to a psychiatrist if it is suspected that the child may have an emotional disturbance requiring the use of medication. Many psychiatrists perform an important consultative role to pupil personnel workers, as well.

> It is clear that there are many overlapping functions—especially among school counselors, school psychologists, and school social workers, particularly in the elementary school. There remains a uniqueness to each specialty, however. The question to be answered, then, is: Who does what? It can be argued that there is enough work to spread around if the dollars and jobs exist. Student non-adjustment and incidence of social ills suggest that there are not enough mental health professionals. Then what is the issue? The problem seems to be territoriality. The three specialties (elementary school counselors, school psychologists, school social workers) remain eager to protect professional boundaries even though similarities are acknowledged when actual situations require broad services to pupils. Perhaps the main solution to the teamwork dilemma is a multidisciplinary examination of organizational patterns and line-staff relationships. (Kameen, Robinson, & Rotter, 1985, cited in Humes & Hohenshil, 1987, p. 43)

Working together as a team is clearly desirable, enabling each helping professional to enhance the contributions of the other.

Computers and Counseling in the Schools

Cooperation among the various helping professions has been enhanced significantly by the advent of computer technology in recent generations. This development has promoted abundant use of computers in schools today, and counselors are currently offering a variety of computer-assisted services to students.

Initially (in the 1980s), counselors were beginning to utilize computers primarily for career counseling and guidance. However, in the 1990s, computers and computer programs were being increasingly used to assist students in a wide range of developmental needs, decision making and problem-solving, and prevention programs.

Gerler (1995) noted:

> A most promising new approach to the Internet and the World Wide Web is by way of software programs such as NETSCAPE or MOSAIC, which are often free to nonprofit organizations. These programs, in conjunction with public domain software, allow for easy manipulation of QuickTime movies, audio, and impressive graphics. The public domain software for Macintosh users, for example, includes GraphicConverter, JPEGView, Simple Player, Sound Machine, and Sparkle.
>
> GraphicConverter is a public domain program developed by Thorsten Lemke to convert pictures of different formats into images that can be viewed on specific computer systems.
>
> JPEGView is a fast, easy-to-use image viewer for JPEG, GIF, and PICT images. Information about the program can be obtained by writing Aaron Giles, 182 E. 95th Street 11E, New York, NY 10128 or at the following E-mail address: giles@med.cornell.edu.
>
> Simple Player, developed by Rich Williams and Chris Thorman, is used to play and edit movies. Information about the program can be obtained by calling Apple Computer at 1-800-767-2775.
>
> Sound Machine is a program that allows for playing audio, including voice. The program was developed by Rod Kennedy. Information can be obtained at the following E-mail address: rod@faceng.anu.edu.au.
>
> Sparkle was developed by Naynard Handley. Information can be obtained at the following E-mail address: maynard@elwing.otago.ac.nz.
>
> All of these programs can be downloaded easily onto personal computers that have access to the Internet. Taken together, these programs make the Internet a tool for educators from kindergarten through the doctoral level. School counselors and counselor educators will need hardware capable of accessing and using what is available on the Internet to participate fully in counselor networks that will surely be available in the future. School counselors will need computer hardware with adequate RAM (random-access memory) and sufficient hard drive storage capability to create, capture, and communicate audiovisual presentations. (p. 11)

Many counselors, realizing the influence of home entertainment software such as Nintendo, have utilized video games in attempts to enhance the relationship-building process with students. For example, the Print Shop game is used to encourage the expression of feelings among resistant clients; Wheel of Fortune and MacConcentration are used with students with learning disabilities to encourage their engagement with the counselor and to provide the opportunity for success in the counselor's presence. Nonverbal games such as the Hot Air Balloon are used by counselors who do not speak the same language as the student in order for the two to find a commonality between themselves without having to speak.

Clearly, video games have become a dominant aspect in many students' lives. Gifford (1991) identifies six attributes of such games that contribute to their success as counseling and learning tools: They (a) encourage free play by allowing children to exercise fantasies without the limitations of the real world; (b) encourage easy movement between electronic "microworlds" from one graphic environment to another; (c) provide instant replays of performances that allow students to study, edit, or make another attempt at a task in a safe environment that supports risk taking; (d) let children be in control even to the point where they can turn the game off when frustrated; (e) serve as partners with the students in the learning process; and (f) provide an opportunity to work toward a clear goal that enhances motivation.

Another application of computer-assisted counseling involves a MacMentoring Project. In attempting to reconnect disenfranchised youth back to school through this program, counselors have successfully facilitated the students' development of greater self-esteem while also teaching them transferable computer skills (Casey & Ramsammy, 1992). Students involved have shown improvement in task behaviors, gained knowledge and skills in word processing and computer graphic procedures, and benefited from a nondirective relationship with the counselor as the computer facilitates the counseling relationship.

The computer is a vital resource in the educational system, and all students must become knowledgeable and comfortable with the use of this tool. Campbell and Dobson (1987) explain that often students may experience computer anxiety, avoid interacting with computers, and consequently eliminate present educational opportunities as well as future employment choices. They insist that counselors must take the initiative in identifying these students and implementing appropriate interventions that would assist students in dealing with these problems. Crosbie-Burnett and Pulvino (1990) support Campbell and Dobson's contention that children who are not computer competent will be at a significant disadvantage in school as well as the job market. They recommend a multimodal group counseling approach through which counselors are able to help those who are uncomfortable with computers become more confident and familiar with computers. The program is called PRO-TECH (Crosbie-Burnett & Pulvino, 1990) and is based on

P—practice on the computer

R—risk-taking imagery and behaviors through the computer

O—organization and planning of computer projects

T—tactile exploration with the computer

E—emotions associated with trying new things

C—cognitions or developing positive self-talk

H—helping others learn

Through involvement in such group activities, students have the opportunity to realize that others have similar fears and doubts as they do about using computers, have access to supportive individuals during their process of learning about computers, and, as a result, experience increased feelings of self-efficacy in regard to computer use. Counselors play a significant part in providing an environment through which students can become less threatened and more motivated in terms of working with computers.

School counselors also have a major role in serving as the communications link in schools, as they are responsible for communicating such information as school policies, graduation requirements, and special programs and activities being offered (Lucking & Mitchum, 1990). Lucking and Mitchum identify the computer as a necessary resource that facilitates this communication to students, parents, administrators, and other interested parties. They refer to *desktop publishing,* a term "given to the production of documents with a recent generation of software and newly developed printer technology" (p. 270), as a computer tool providing high-quality printed material. Desktop publishing allows the counselor to produce high-quality documents, avoid the expense of commercial documents, and have more time for providing counseling services to students.

Assessment of students is a common task for school counselors. Computerized programs are available to assist in analyzing all available assessment data, generating hypotheses, making interpretations, and suggesting recommendations about the examinee. Sattler (1992, p. 790) warns that anyone utilizing such computerized assessment strategies must be aware of their limitations. Among these limitations are that "computerized reports are usually based on one, two, or three tests; they usually do not take into account either the examinee's unique clinical history or the complete assessment results (Matarazzo, 1986)." Counselors are still the ones responsible for communicating results in a nontechnical and understandable manner. If a computer report is used by a counselor who is untrained regarding the limitations and use of such reports, results might be misinterpreted and interventions would be based on inaccurate conclusions. This situation would clearly pose the potential for more harm than good for the student. In addition, counselors are responsible for ensuring that their computer-based assessment programs function properly so accurate results are obtained (American Counseling Association, 1995).

Of further concern in regard to using computer-assisted counseling strategies is the aspect of confidentiality. Abuse of confidentiality is more likely when student information is maintained on electronic data storage systems, although counselors can avoid problems in this area by using identification codes and passwords and placing restrictions on individuals who may have access to student information (Zunker, 1990). School counselors must take serious precautions in order to ensure the maintenance of confidentiality regarding student information.

The American Counseling Association (1995) addresses these concerns regarding computer use in their ethical guidelines. (See Appendix B for the *American Counseling Association Code of Ethics and Standards of Practice*.) Counselors have additional responsibilities when using computer-based assessment procedures (American Counseling Association, 1995). Although counselors need to provide equal access to computer-based counseling applications, it must be determined whether the client being evaluated is intellectually, emotionally, and physically capable of completing the computer-based administration. The program should be appropriate to the client's needs, and the client should have a solid understanding of the purpose and procedures for the activity. Limitations of computer-based applications need to be explained to the client. Finally, counselors are responsible for following up with clients after use of computer-based applications to determine if any misconceptions or inappropriate uses may misconstrue the results.

Of course, it should be noted that computers and technology are intended to complement and upgrade the activities that counselors engage in, not replace them. The human element in the whole range of counseling services is too significant to be downsized by any technology.

PATTERNS OF COUNSELING PROGRAM ORGANIZATION IN EDUCATIONAL SETTINGS

Because it was noted earlier in this chapter that school counseling programs must reflect the differences in their populations and settings, it is appropriate to assume that these differences will also result in differing organizational structures for programs. Consequently, it must be recognized that there are many successful yet differing patterns of program organization for all educational levels. Furthermore, these structures differ according to the educational levels (elementary, middle, secondary, or higher education) they serve. This section attempts to briefly illustrate only a few of the most traditional and popular program formats.

In Elementary Schools

As has been already noted in the discussions of the historical development of guidance in American education, counseling programs are just beginning to emerge in the elementary schools of this country, despite the fact that there have been supporters of this concept for more than 50 years. Because there are no established, traditional organizational formats with which the subject of elementary counseling programs might be comfortably introduced, let us examine some possible considerations.

In determining appropriate approaches to program organization and development in the elementary school, elementary educators have considered those characteristics and goals of the elementary school, especially those that highlight the special role of the elementary school as an educational institution. These include the missions of orienting the elementary school child to the educational environment and providing the elementary school pupil with the basic educational-developmental experiences that are essential for future development. Other special characteristics of the elementary school are also important as considerations in the organization and development of their counseling programs, including the following:

- Most elementary schools are homeroom-teacher–centered. The elementary pupil is in a self-contained classroom with one teacher for most of the day, and the pupil is with this teacher for at least one academic year. As a result, pupil and teacher get to know each other better in the elementary school than in schools at higher levels.
- There is an emphasis on learning through activity. Physical activity and exercises related to learning are characteristic of the elementary school.
- The elementary school pupil is a member of a reasonably stable group. Although some school populations are relatively transient, it is common for a child to be with the same group of fellow pupils for most of each school year and, in many elementary school situations, with many of the same children throughout one's elementary school years.
- Elementary schools are usually smaller and less complex than secondary schools.
- Parental interest and involvement are generally greater at the elementary school level.

Further reflected in the educational approach and structure of the elementary school are the characteristics of the elementary school children. It must be noted by anyone who has ever set foot in an elementary school that there is no such thing as the typical elementary school pupil. And parents and teachers who interact with these children on a daily basis can further testify to the difficulties of characterizing this age group. It is therefore appropriate to suggest that the common characteristic all elementary youths share is that no two are alike. Despite this, it is not inappropriate to briefly note some broadly recognized needs and characteristics of this youthful population, even though there have been and will continue to be innumerable studies made and volumes written about the needs of children.

As a basis for guidance in the elementary school, we will view these needs from two standpoints: (1) those basic needs which continuously demand satisfaction, and (2) those developmental needs which must be met during different life stages.

People's basic needs have been presented by Maslow in a hierarchy or priority ordering of needs in which the higher-order needs will emerge only when the lower-order needs have been fairly well satisfied. Maslow points out that the best way to repress the higher motivation of humankind is to keep individuals chronically hungry, insecure, or unloved. According to Maslow's theory, as the teacher and counselor view the elementary pupil and the ability to become self-actualized and develop potential, the teacher or counselor must be concerned with the degree to which the pupil's lower-order needs are being met.

The developmental needs of humankind, according to his life stage theory, have been well presented by Havighurst (1953) in his popular "developmental tasks." Counselors and teachers in the elementary school should take note of the following developmental tasks for middle childhood:

1. Learning physical skills necessary for ordinary games
2. Building wholesome attitudes toward oneself as a growing organism
3. Learning to get along with age mates
4. Learning an appropriate masculine or feminine social role
5. Developing fundamental skills in reading, writing, and calculating
6. Developing concepts necessary for everyday living
7. Developing conscience, morality, and a scale of values
8. Achieving personal independence
9. Developing attitudes toward social groups and institutions

The presentations of Maslow and Havighurst stress both the personal and the cultural nature of the needs of children as they grow and develop. There is also an implied developmental task for educational programs: the task of providing learning experiences appropriate to the needs, both basic and developmental, of the elementary school child.

In addition to the needs of children, plans for counseling in the elementary school should take into consideration the following characteristics of the student:

- The elementary school student is experiencing continuous growth, development, and change.
- The elementary school student is constantly integrating experiences.
- The elementary school student is relatively limited in the ability to verbalize.
- The reasoning powers of the elementary school pupil are not fully developed.
- The ability of the elementary school pupil to concentrate over long periods of time is limited.
- The enthusiasm and interest of the elementary school pupil can be easily aroused.
- The decisions and goals of the elementary school pupil serve immediate purposes—he or she does not yet make long-range plans.
- The elementary school pupil displays feelings more or less openly.

The implications of these characteristics and needs for programs of counseling in the elementary school must be reflected in both counseling program structure and counselor role and function.

On the basis of these identifiable features of the elementary school and the characteristics and needs of elementary school students, any successful program in the elementary school that focuses on the student must have not only the approval but also significant involvement of the faculty. It must be teacher-centered. Furthermore, close and frequent contact with parents must be anticipated, especially in the primary years. Any program that relies too heavily on "talking at" the elementary school student, even when supplemented with films and other media or material aids, is doomed to failure. The elementary school is activity oriented, and the counseling program in this setting must "do as the Romans do." Finally, the elementary school years are noted as developmental years. The elementary school guidance program must, therefore, respond accordingly with a developmental rather than a remedial emphasis—an emphasis that suggests, for example, less individual adjustment counseling and more developmental group guidance activities.

In Secondary Schools

Since their early, sometimes timorous, and sometimes tenuous beginnings in the 20 years after Parsons through their experimental growth years of the 1930s and 1940s into the boom years of the 1950s and 1960s, school counseling and guidance programs have been almost the exclusive property of high schools in the United States. Although different influences and emphases in both the secondary school and the counseling and guidance movement have often altered concepts of program structure and function, the movement maintained a steady growth in both numbers and professionalization through the last half of the 20th century and developed recognizable images of program structure, role, and function. These, however, may also be more readily understood if one renews acquaintance with the characteristics of the secondary school (so well eulogized in *Is There Life After High School*, Keyes, 1976) and with the high school student as well.

Although adolescence is identified as that period between puberty and adulthood, nothing defies standard definition or description more than the adolescent. They are as varied, unpredictable, and uncontrollable as their peer group permits. They give meaning to the expression "generation gap," of which many adolescents are proud and, before it's over, for which many adults are thankful. Most persons view their adolescent years as different from those of today. They probably were, for adolescents today not only exhibit a wide variation in individual characteristics, but the group characteristics also seem to change rapidly from generation to generation. As an extreme example, many may recall that some of their grandparents seemed to go directly from childhood to work and adulthood. They completed their eight to ten years of schooling and went to work. Today, some youths stretch their adolescence into their 20s, resisting growing up, or accepting responsibility, and rejecting independence. For all who are concerned with youth during these magical years, for those who may hope to ease their passage, it is important to recognize some of the characteristics of adolescents:

- It is a period of continuous physical growth, not the least of which is the awakening of sexual impulses. Girls discover boys, and boys discover girls who discover boys. Puppy love becomes a serious crush that becomes undying love (at least for the moment).
- It is a period of movement toward maturity with all its implications for independence, responsibility, and self-discipline; a period often very trying to parents who want to keep little Sasha tied to her mother's apron strings or Johnnie still passing the football to old "butter fingers" Dad.
- Reveling in their newly acquired independence and the discovery of their rapidly developing abilities to reason and hypothesize, many adolescents exaggerate their ability to solve the problems of the world and those that are personal for them. At the same time, many become critical of adult solutions to social problems, lifestyles, and values but deny that adults are in a position to evaluate life among the adolescents.

- Furthermore, with the acquisition of the privileges of adulthood—independence, responsibility, and self-direction—there is a movement from childish to adult forms of expression, reaction, and behavior. For better or worse, adult behavior is mimicked and often exaggerated.
- Self-selected (not adult-imposed) peer group memberships are important to the adolescent. The peer group becomes the center of most of their significant social-recreational activities and, in the eyes of many parents (and many authorities as well), their initial sex education "program." Also, while demanding their independence from parents and other adult controls, adolescents in turn may surrender much of their independence and individuality to peer group conformity.
- It is a period when they seek direction, a set of values, and their own personal identity. The latter demands treatment as an individual—a demand that the home and the school often appear to overlook. In the quest for this new identity, the adolescent encounters, with peers, many of the common problems of this journey. Although a multitude of studies have investigated the priority concerns of youths, most of these tend to be outdated immediately after their publication. Recognizing this limitation, we would use three categories to classify a consensus of common adolescent problems from current studies.
  a. *Developing as a social being.* This includes problems of one-to-one personal relationships, particularly dating, love, sex, and marriage. It also involves group living and acceptance and, in general, the development of human relationship skills.
  b. *Developing as a unique being.* The adolescent is concerned with the development and recognition of the uniqueness of individuals. It is a time when they are seeking to develop their own value system and often find they face value conflicts. Anxieties are often created as a result of constant demands to measure up made by evaluative testing and other appraisal techniques that appear to standardize them. They are also concerned when they fail to gain parental or other support for their new self.
  c. *Developing as a productive being.* In this regard, youths are concerned with their educational adjustments and achievements, their career decisions, future educational directions, impending financial needs, and employment prospects. Many become concerned because school is not providing them with a marketable skill. Others feel that staying in school is delaying earning a living.

Let us now briefly note some of the significant characteristics of the secondary school. Although there are, of course, many exceptions to any attempt to characterize schools at any level, the following are generally appropriate for many secondary schools in the United States and Canada.

- Secondary schools are generally large, complex institutions populated by a heterogeneous student body. The size and complexity of the secondary school have implications for both counseling program development and program activities. Because the larger student bodies tend to be more heterogeneous, often representing many cultural minority groups, the identification of these groups and the response to their needs can represent a major challenge to the program.
- Secondary school faculties represent a variety of academic specialties. The secondary school faculty member tends to concentrate on a particular subject area. As a result, the secondary school faculty represents a variety of specializations, which provides a reser-

voir of resources that the school counseling program may use in the career, educational, and personal-social development of students.

- Secondary school years are important decision-making years for the individual student. During a student's secondary schooling, one is usually confronted with at least two lifetime-influencing decisions. The first of these decisions is whether to complete secondary schooling. Various dropout studies indicate that approximately one fourth of high school youth make the decision to leave school before finishing their secondary school program. Secondly, many students make important decisions regarding careers or choice of college. The wide variety of course offerings and activities available in most secondary schools prompts a nearly continuous series of minor decisions for the students as well. They may also be confronted with significant personal decisions regarding sex and marriage, use of tobacco, alcohol and drugs, and friends and friendship.

- Secondary schools are subject-matter oriented. Schedules and classes tend to be formal and rigidly organized in many secondary schools, with considerable emphasis on academic standards, homework, and grades (rather than personal growth). Emphasis on standardized test achievements and school discipline can be expected. The homeroom that many students have experienced in the elementary school years ceases to exist in most high schools, except as an administrative checkpoint. As a result, at a time when students are accelerating their development as social beings, the secondary school structure often tends to inhibit this growth and development by placing them in a series of formal, academically-oriented subject-matter class experiences. At the same time, many schools fail to provide students with an organized scheduled group (such as homeroom) where they might develop social skills and attitudes. This suggests a challenge to the subject-matter teacher and the counselor to work cooperatively to incorporate social development experiences into the academic program.

- School spirit, or esprit de corps, is usually more evident in secondary schools than in any other educational institution. This school spirit is usually reflected in the quest for winning athletic events, championship bands, and other public indications of excellence. Often the competition among students for participation in significant school events is keen. Social divisions may often arise between those who have made it and those who have not in terms of these activities. On the positive side, however, school spirit in competitive activities can often be a potential factor in motivating students to remain in school, making them seek higher academic achievements, and promoting pride in the school. Recently, frequent suggestions and efforts have been made to increase the visibility of academic competition as well.

- The school principal is the single most influential person in the secondary school setting. Decisions, policy development, and practices all emanate or are subject to the approval of the school principal. Unlike the elementary school principal, the secondary principal is frequently assisted by several assistant principals, supervisors, department heads, and specialty chairs. In addition, probably no other person is so significant in establishing the tone or atmosphere of the school and its inhabitants.

Although the adolescent and the adolescent's school share many characteristics in common, wide variations also prevail between them. Counseling programs in secondary schools seem to reflect these ambivalences as counselors engage in many of the same basic activities but within a variety of organizational structures. Figures 3-1 through 3-3 present three of the

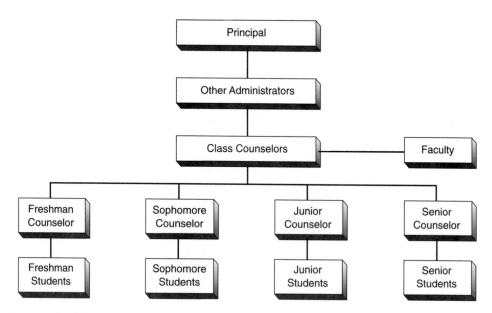

Figure 3-1 Class Counselor Model.

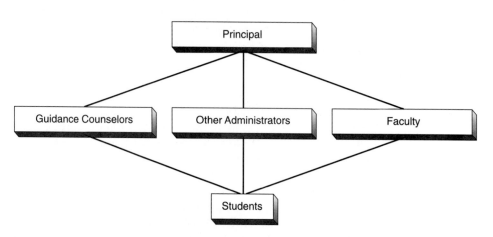

Figure 3-2 Guidance Counselor (Generalist) Model.

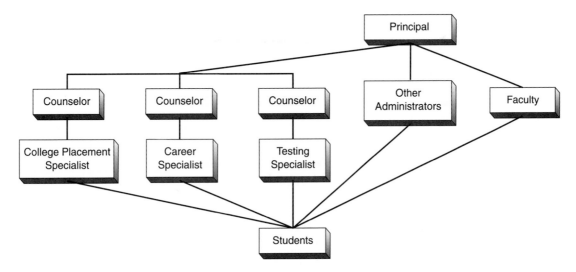

Figure 3-3 Guidance Counselor (Specialist) Model.

more traditional organizational models of school counseling programs. Bigger schools in larger school systems may have resource specialists and specialized services (computer and data processing, test scoring) available in the administrative offices of the school system. These resources are available to supplement the efforts of the local building counselors. Small schools may often have to share counseling and other specialized personnel. These personnel may operate out of the central administrative offices of the school system and be available on certain days to each school that shares their assignment.

In Institutions of Higher Education

Although the popular view from the ivory tower seems to most frequently focus on the football stadium, the attractive students, and sometimes (but rarely) the distinguished professor, a serious look at most college and university campuses confirms the existence of counselors and attending programs of counseling and other student services or student development, as it is now called. As might be anticipated, these programs are as unusual or as traditional as the institutions they represent. The burgeoning junior and community college movement appears to be developing programs that often suggest an open marriage between elements of secondary school counseling programs and traditional university student personnel services programs. Four-year colleges and universities maintain, although often with interesting innovations, programs based on traditional student personnel services models—programs in which counseling services are frequently provided through campus counseling centers or clinics, residential counselors, and career counseling offices. Today, the field continues to grow.

Figure 3-4 illustrates an organizational chart for a four-year college with counseling services provided as a part of the student services of the college or university. Figure 3-5 displays counseling services as a unit of a large university program.

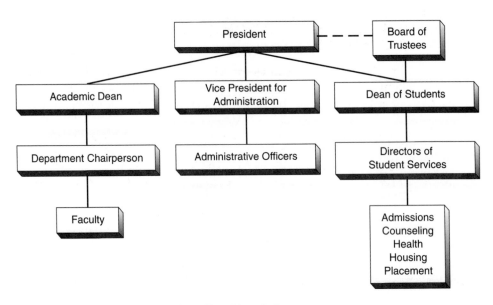

Figure 3-4 Organization Chart for a Four-Year College.

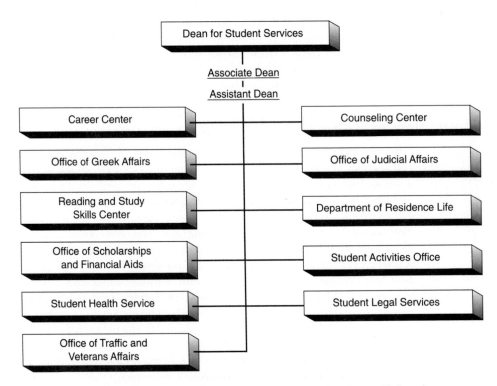

Figure 3-5 Organization Chart for Student Service Division in a Large University.

FUTURE DIRECTIONS FOR SCHOOL COUNSELING PROGRAMS

All of us engage in predicting the future. Much of our speculation on what lies ahead is, of course, short-range—we predict that the weather will be better tomorrow, the price of coffee will go up again next month, or the football team will be a winner next fall.

Predicting the future is fun, but it is also risky, especially if one is bold enough to put these speculations in print. However, despite the many uncertainties attending even the most scientific efforts (and highly reputable scientific institutes are engaged in such studies today), we still read our horoscopes and annual New Year's predictions, have our palms read or hand-writing analyzed, and note that books such as Naisbitt and Aburdene's *Megatrends 2000* (1990) have become international best-sellers.

Although the high level of interest in knowing what the future holds for us and our societies does not appear to have diminished over the centuries, both the nature and need for future insights have undergone significant change. We have noted the emergence since World War II of a futuristic science, with an emphasis on scientific, data-based, and computer-assisted forecasting, and the development of organizations such as the Institute for the Future (Middletown, Connecticut), the World Future Society (formed in Washington, DC), and the Hudson Institute (Indianapolis, Indiana). The need for some form of reasonably accurate future forecasting has become increasingly evident.

One indicator that change will probably take place in product, activity, or organization is strong and significant criticism of their present state. For example, even those who "see no evil, hear no evil, speak no evil" are well aware of the volume and intensity of critical charges leveled at education over the years, criticisms that have and will continue to promote change in the future.

For example, increased emphasis on basics was called for since President Reagan's 1984 Task Force on Education. The publication of this task force, *A Nation at Risk* (Bell, 1983), led to a nationwide educational reform movement characterized by a return to no-nonsense basics, greater attention to student discipline and management, and measurement of student growth through standardized achievement testing. Of special interest to school counselors was the report of the College Entrance Examination Board's Commission on Precollege Guidance and Counseling, *Keeping the Options Open* (1986), which found:

- Adequate counseling and guidance services are essential for all students, particularly for those who suffer disadvantages from poverty, discrimination, and family stress or disruption.
- Counseling is a profession in trouble. (Too often counselors are assigned tasks—administrative routines, maintaining records, and supervising students—that make inadequate use of their special skills and talents. In many states the student/counselor ratios are rising beyond the level at which counselors can perform effectively.)
- Provision for guidance and counseling follows an all too well-established pattern in the distribution of public services: Those with the least at home often get the least help from public institutions and programs. (College Entrance Examination Board, 1986, pp. 2–3)

The College Board Commission made four priority recommendations for future action in our schools.

1. Establish a broad-based process in each local school district for determining the particular guidance and counseling needs of the students within each school and for planning how best to meet these needs.

2. Develop a program under the leadership of each school principal that emphasizes the importance of the guidance counselor as a monitor and promoter of student potential, as well as
coordinator of the school's guidance plans.

3. Mount programs to inform and involve parents and other members of the family influential in
the choices, plans, decisions, and learning activities of the student.

4. Provide a program of guidance and counseling during the early and middle years of schooling,
especially for students who traditionally have not been well-served by the schools. (College
Entrance Examination Board, 1986, pp. 5–6)

They also made four other major recommendations that involve a variety of actors and institutions outside the schools and provide essential support for school-based change.

- Strengthen collaboration among schools, community agencies, colleges, businesses, and other
community resources to enhance services available to students.
- Establish a process in each state to determine the guidance and counseling needs of specific student populations and give support to local initiatives that address these needs.
- Increase support of federal programs that help disadvantaged students to enter and remain in
college.
- Revise the training of school counselors to include the specific skills and knowledge necessary
to enable them to take a more central role in schools. (College Entrance Examination Board,
1986, p. 6)

We must also recognize that a new wave of counselors are now entering our schools as
many of the NDEA (National Defense Education Act) trained counselors of the 1960s move
into retirement. This, coupled with the increased nationwide demand for elementary school
counselors, could result in an acceleration in employment opportunities for counselors in
schools. Many states are also revising training and certification requirements.

This new generation of counselors must be computer competent and alert to the technological advancements of the information age that have implications for their practice.
Electronic learning and multimedia approaches, among others, will dramatically influence
new approaches to learning. Too, counselors will increasingly network via the Internet with
counselors locally and nationally, as well as internationally, to exchange ideas, solutions, and
information.

New curricular emphases will include increased attention to technological and vocational curricula, plus renewed attention to the arts. The schools may also stress the importance of environmental conservation. Increased international orientation may also be
anticipated. A longer school day and school year may be part of future school systems in the
United States. Finally, the schools are being envisioned as centers for lifelong learning.

As in the past, counselors will continue to counsel and consult and give attention to
the career development needs of student populations. These needs, however, will be dramatically different from the past one person, one career approach as we view a century when individuals entering the workforce (with the exception of the professions) can anticipate three
to seven distinctly different careers over their working lifetime. Many of these will require a
return to educational settings, adapting to new technologies, and movement to new geographic locations. School career programs must prepare youthful workers for both adaptability and flexibility. Counselors must ensure that youth are prepared for tomorrow's career world
rather than yesterday's.

There will be a greatly increased program emphasis on prevention and early intervention, with special attention to such societal concerns as child abuse, substance abuse, teen pregnancies, AIDS and other human sexuality concerns, and the seemingly perennial problems of school dropouts and youth unemployment. The increasing recognition that prevention programs are needed—and more promising—than the after-the-incident treatment of these social issues will present school counselors with unprecedented opportunities to establish their uniqueness and, at the same time, their unprecedented value to society. Too, counselors will be expected, as the school's human relations experts, to take a much more active role in preventing prejudice by promoting multicultural understandings and relationships. As noted previously, we are a profession dedicated to caring and respecting the worth of every individual. Further, as a discipline, we are experts in communication and human relations. Thus, our values and skills would suggest an increasingly important role for the profession of counseling in promoting positive and productive relationships among all racial/cultural/ethnic and religious populations.

The urgent need for counselor involvement is further suggested by the recognition that although considerable progress has been made in legislative enactments and judicial decisions, much more remains to be accomplished at the levels of personal awareness, understanding, respect, and acceptance. The urgency for this progress is further highlighted when we note that an estimated 25% of our population represents minorities. This is projected to increase to 32% by 2010 and 47% by 2050 (U.S. Department of Commerce, Economics and Statistics Administration, Bureau of the Census, 1993). Here again we note that the elimination of prejudice and the substitution of respect and understanding in human relations must begin in the school setting. To achieve this goal, counselors must themselves be models of awareness, understanding, and acceptance. Counselors of the 2000s will also be expected to be more professionally competent in assessing differing environments (i.e., community, school, and so forth) and their impact on their clients.

Accountability mandates will demand increased counselor knowledge in the areas of measurement and standardized testing. The rapidly developing field of family therapy will influence school counseling in the immediate decades ahead. In this regard, Peeks (1993) writes:

> The changes occurring in the fields of counseling and education are traversed within the walls of U.S. public schools. As counseling has made a shift toward the systems paradigm, the student is viewed as a part of a larger unit, his family. As education makes a shift toward expanded effectiveness, parents are viewed as an important and integral part of the educational process. Both of the changes acknowledge the importance of a student's extended social unit to the success of his or her education. Students are first members of a family. (p. 248)

Counselors in schools will be called upon in the near future to direct more attention to family lifestyles and their impact on school youth. Peeks (1993, p. 249) predicts:

> The increasing changes in education and the expanded counseling function will bring counseling and education closer together within the context of the schools. It is predicted that the schools of the future will become family centers (Cetron, 1985), where family health and employment services are offered for stress-laden families. A typical school district may provide training for students ages 3 to 21 years and for adults 21 to 80-plus years. These expanded services will be offered either through satellites or widely expanded professional staffs. Schools will need programs to protect children against the ravages of social disorganization and family collapse (London, 1987).

The establishment of such programs will necessitate family involvement in the context of the school by school counselors who understand the powerful systemic connection between the student and family. Parent involvement in the school in almost any form seems to produce measurable gains in student achievement (Henderson, 1988).

Additionally, the vast majority of homes in the United States with children will be either dual-career or single-parent homes. The implications of these new models of family life are many, not the least of which will be, What happens to the children? So far, there has been little planning to provide for these latchkey youth. Obviously, the failure to make adequate provisions guarantees disastrous consequences to both the individual and society. School counseling programs must take the lead in developing comprehensive and effective programs for all school youth, including latchkey children.

According to Peeks (1993, p. 248), it is also important in the decades ahead for counselors to work for parental involvement in their child's academic efforts.

> Decades of research document that families are critically important to the academic success of students. Studies have shown that, for most students, the schools they attend make less difference to academic success than the families from which they come (Gandara, 1989). Further research has shown that parent-school conferences not only enhance family-school relationships, but that they also have an impact on student performance (Turnbull & Turnbull, 1990).

We believe that school counselors of the future increasingly will be called on to engage in research in their settings to hasten the solutions to many constant youth problems such as those previously noted. Only through an all-out professional effort involving those on the scene can we hope to make real headway in dealing with these problems.

In addition, another responsibility of schools in the future will be to prepare students to enter a rapidly changing job market. If the United States is to continue to compete in the worldwide marketplace, American workers will need to be more highly trained than at present. Schools will be responsible for preparing students who are adaptable, able to respond quickly to the changing requirements of new technologies. Many workers' jobs will change dramatically, often in the span of just a few years. This means schools will train and retrain both youth and adults. As noted earlier, future workers will be displaced frequently, and they will be moving constantly from one occupation to another. They will need periodic retraining because each new job will be different from the previous one.

THE ECOLOGY OF THE SCHOOL

In discussing the ecology of the school, we are, in fact, examining the climate of the school, its environment. Ecological psychology has, since the early pronouncements of Kurt Lewin (1936), stressed the importance of the environment on individual behavior. The growing field of specialists in ecological psychology are concerned with how individuals perceive, are shaped by, value, influence, and are influenced by their environments.

Certainly, the school is a significant environment and one that will influence the behavior, values, and plans of its student inhabitants. However, Conyne (1987) notes that only recently has increased interest in the application of this viewpoint to the practice of counseling been noted. Within this context, school counselors can improve their understanding of their student-client population by recognizing the following concepts:

1. Environment is a significant influence on behavior. Therefore, school counselors must understand this influence if they are to predict, modify, or prevent undesirable behaviors in their student clientele.

2. Because stable, long-term settings such as the school pass on expectations and norms for behaviors, values, and attitudes, school counselors, with their teaching colleagues, must plan accordingly.

3. Environmental understandings provide a basis for the development of meaningful prevention programs.

4. Students, like all others, strive for optimal environments in which to develop adequate self-concepts, fulfill their needs, and maximize their potential. Such settings provide supportive relationships and a climate that is motivational and enjoyable.

Schools and students cannot be understood on the basis of records and data (i.e., test scores, grades, attendance, etc.) alone. They are performers on the stage of life. To understand the roles they are playing, we must understand the setting. Ecological psychology thus helps us better understand students by understanding their psychological interplay with their environment.

SUMMARY

An article in *Better Homes and Gardens* noted that "if you graduated from high school before 1960, chances are the only school counselors you have known are your child's (Daly, 1979, p. 15). This chapter assumes that most of those who graduated from high school before 1960 also knew little about how their counselors were trained or licensed and had little familiarity with their role and function. Perhaps this very lack of understanding has led the counseling professionals in the past decade to move more energetically into the public communications arena to "tell what they're about," upgrade their training, and seek protection of their profession from unqualified intruders through certification and licensure. Much has been accomplished in a short period if one considers that at the turn of the 20th century there were no counselors in schools. Almost 100 years and approximately 200,000 school counselors later, we can identify tremendous progress in training, certification, and practice.

Counselor training today is available at the master's, specialist, and doctoral levels, with the possibility of undergraduate and postdoctoral courses as well. All states specify some type of counselor preparation or certification for employment in school settings, with the exception of postsecondary institutions. These requirements in general reflect role and function expectancies. Differing characteristics of various school levels, settings, and clientele, by necessity, result in variations in that role and function. However, school counselors cannot go it alone. They must view themselves as member players on the school team and work for the cooperation and contributions of teachers, administrators, and other helping professionals who are vital to the success of any school counseling program.

Finally, we noted that school counselors and school counseling programs must be able to adapt to the demands of the future if they are to become or remain relevant and valuable to the populations they are intended to serve. This is, of course, no less true for counselors functioning in various community and agency settings. Chapter 4 will describe counselors in these various settings.

DISCUSSION QUESTIONS

1. Discuss contacts that you can recall during your schooling with differing helping professionals (i.e., school psychologist, school social worker,

school counselor, school nurse, and other health personnel). Compare the role of each of these in the school program.

2.   As a potential counselor, are there some special preparations or subject matters that you would like to see as a part of your training program? Identify and present a rationale.

3.   Should school counselors be required to have teaching experience? Why or why not?

4.   Discuss your own elementary, junior/middle, and/or high school counseling programs as you experienced them.

5.   What do you envision the professional activities of a school counselor will be in 2025?

6.   How should school counseling and guidance programs respond to major societal programs such as substance abuse, child abuse, AIDS, school dropouts, underemployment, the homeless? Are there other major societal problems that school counseling programs should address? If so, what are these problems and how should school counseling programs respond to them?

CLASS ACTIVITIES

1.   Shadow a school counselor for a day or two and report your observations to the class.

2.   Interview a teacher, school principal, or other helping professional regarding their relationship and contribution to the school counseling program. Report your findings.

3.   Assume you (the class) are a group of experts called together to formulate a model school counselor preparation program for the first years of the 21st century. Outline such a model.

SELECTED READINGS

Bell, T. (1983). *A nation at risk: The imperative for educational reform.* Washington, DC: The National Commission on Excellence in Education.

Casey, J. A. (1995). Developmental issues for school counselors using technology. *Elementary School Guidance and Counseling, 30* (1), 26–34.

College Entrance Examination Board. (1986). *Keeping the options open.* New York: Author, Commission on Precollege Guidance and Counseling.

Dean, L., & Meadows, M. (1995). College counseling: Union and intersection. *Journal of Counseling and Development, 74* (2), 139–142.

Dennis, D. L., Buckner, J. C., Lipton, F. R., & Levine, I. S. (1991). A decade of research and services for homeless mentally ill persons. *American Psychologist, 46,* 1129–1138.

Gibson, R. L. (1990). Teacher opinions of high school guidance programs: Then and now. *The School Counselor, 37,* 248–255.

Kelly, J. A., Murphy, D. A., Sikkema, K. J., & Kalichman, S. C. (1993). Psychological interventions to prevent HIV infection are urgently needed: New priorities for behavioral research in the second decade of AIDS. *American Psychologist, 48,* 1023–1034.

McAuliffe, G. J. (1992). A case presentation approach to group supervision for community college counselors. *Counselor Education and Supervision, 31,* 163–174.

Milburn, N., & D'Ercole, A. (1991). Homeless women. *American Psychologist, 46,* 1161–1169.

Neukrug, E. S. (1991). Computer-assisted live supervision in counselor skills training. *Counselor Education and Supervision, 31,* 132–138.

Paisley, P., & Borders, D. (1995). School counseling: An evolving specialty. *Journal of Counseling and Development, 74* (2), 150–153.

Rafferty, Y., & Shinn, M. (1991). The impact of homelessness on children. *American Psychologist, 46,* 1170–1179.

Robbins, S. B., Lese, K. P., & Herrick, S. M. (1993). Interactions between goal instability and social support on college freshman adjustment. *Journal of Counseling and Development, 71,* 343–348.

Short, R. J., & Talley, R. C. (1997). Rethinking psychology and the schools: Implications of recent national policy. *American Psychologist, 52,* 234–240.

Srebalus, D. J., Schwartz, J. L., Vaughan, R. V., & Tunick, R. H. (1996). Youth violence in rural schools: Counselor perceptions and treatment resources. *School Counselor, 44* (1), 48–54.

Worthington, R. L., & Juntunen, C. L. (1997). The vocational development of non–college-bound youth: Counseling psychology and the school-to-work transition movement. *Counseling Psychologist, 25*, 323–363.

RESEARCH OF INTEREST

Brooks, D. K., & Gerstein, L. H. (1990). Counselor credentialing and interprofessional collaboration. *Journal of Counseling and Development, 68*, 477–484.

Abstract

This article presents the history and development of the counselor credentialing process. It includes aspects of standards, accreditation, certification, and licensure, as well as future trends in the licensure movement pertaining to preparation and training, examinations, accountability, and consumer protection. Collaboration and reimbursement are also discussed.

Casey, J., & Ramsammy, R. (1992, February). *MacMentoring: Using technology and counseling with at-risk youth.* Paper presented at the Annual Conference of the California Association for Counseling and Development, San Francisco.

Abstract

The MacMentoring Project was designed to reconnect disenfranchised youth back into school through activities focused on enhancing self-esteem while also teaching them transferable computer skills. Among the subjects ($N = 45$), improvements of on-task behaviors, expression of creativity, benefits from a nondirective counseling strategy, and success at meeting expectations were demonstrated.

Corders, L. D., & Drury, S. M. (1992). Comprehensive school counseling programs: A review for policymakers and practitioners. *Journal of Counseling and Development, 70*, 487–498.

Abstract

An overview of the components of effective school counseling programs that have surfaced over the period from 1960–1990 are presented. Results and discussion are categorized in seven sections, including core principles of school counseling programs, program resources, interventions utilized by programs, evaluation procedures, written policies, program climate, and renewal process.

Fagan, T. K., & Jenkins, W. M. (1989). People with disabilities: An update. *Journal of Counseling and Development, 68*, 140–143.

Abstract

This article provides information regarding disabling conditions in school-age and adult populations. It presents changes in federal legislation and interpretations of this legislation. The focus is on adult disabling conditions and rehabilitation services.

Fairchild, T. N., & Seeley, T. J. (1996). Evaluation of school psychological services: A case illustration. *Psychology in the Schools, 33* (1), 46–55.

Abstract

This article describes how school psychological services were evaluated in two elementary schools serviced by the same school psychologist. Twenty-one students who had received individual counseling services and 183 students who had participated in classroom guidance activities were asked to complete questionnaires evaluating their experience. Forty-four teachers completed the one-page School Psychological Services Evaluation Scale, and 37 partners of students who had participated in psychoeducational assessment were asked to complete the Assessment Service Evaluation: Parent Rating Scale. The school psychologist also provided an accountability report. Results from the available sample show that school psychological services were positively viewed by students, teachers, and parents. Based on suggestions obtained during the evaluation, the school psychologist was also able to make improvements to the service.

Fisher, P. J., & Breakey, W. R. (1991). The epidemiology of alcohol, drug, and mental disorders among homeless persons. *American Psychologist, 46*, 1115–1128.

Abstract

This article discusses recent research regarding the prevalence of alcohol, drugs, and mental (ADM) disorders and the personal characteristics of homeless substance abusers and individuals with mental disorders. It emphasizes that these individuals are impacted by extreme poverty; underutilization of public entitlements; isolation from family, friends, and other networks of support; frequent contacts with correctional agencies; and poor overall health. The conclusion is that awareness of those issues must take place in advocating more suitable services for persons experiencing homelessness.

Hardesty, P. H., & Dillard, J. M. (1994). The role of elementary school counselors compared with their middle and secondary school counterparts. *Elementary School Guidance & Counseling, 29* (2), 83–91.

Abstract

This study examined the tasks and functions counselors at different grade levels view as important. Three hundred and sixty-nine elementary, middle, and high school counselors were surveyed regarding activities in schools. Three major differences in the ranking of counselor activities by elementary counselors were found compared with their middle and secondary school counterparts: (a) elementary subjects perform more consultative and coordination activities; (b) elementary subjects may perform less administrative-like activities (scheduling and paperwork); and (c) whereas secondary subjects and middle school subjects seem to work with student concerns on an individual basis, elementary subjects tend to work systematically with families, teachers, and community agencies. Elementary school counselors need to actively demonstrate how their work contributes to the overall school environment and the development of students.

Leigh, B. C., & Stall, R. (1993). Substance use and risky sexual behavior for exposure to HIV. *American Psychologist, 48*, 1035–1045.

Abstract

This article reviews research literature on the relationship between substance use and high-risk sexual behavior through global association studies, situational association studies, and event analysis procedures. It concludes that both sex and substance abuse are complicated behaviors and wonders whether related comprehension of the dynamics of the relationship is necessary.

Lombana, J. H. (1989). Counseling persons with disabilities: Summary and projections. *Journal of Counseling and Development, 68*, 177–179.

Abstract

The findings of various articles pertaining to counseling individuals with disabilities and the progress recently made regarding provision of services to these individuals is presented here. Issues of concern in counseling persons with disabilities are discussed and guidelines for counselors in their future work with persons with disabilities are provided.

Mooney, S. P., Sherman, M. F., & Lo Presto, C. T. (1991). Academic locus of control, self-esteem, and perceived distance from home as predictors of college adjustment. *Journal of Counseling and Development, 69*, 445–448.

Abstract

This article examines the academic locus of control, self-esteem, and geographic distance from home (actual and perceived) as predictors of college adjustment for female college freshmen ($N = 88$). Results indicate that internal academic locus of control, high levels of self-esteem, and a belief that the distance from home was "just right" for the individual related to personal, academic, social, and attachment adjustment.

Olson, M. J., & Dilley, J. S. (1988). A new look at stress and the school counselor. *The School Counselor, 35*, 194–198.

Abstract

This review of research on school counselors' stress concludes that stress is not so much a function of conflict between roles that are differentially endorsed by different publics as it is of the sheer number of roles that are strongly endorsed. It claims mental health and quality of work of counselors is adversely affected by the stress of inability to meet demands.

Paulson, B. L., & Edwards, M. H. (1997). Parent expectations of an elementary school counselor: A concept-mapping approach. *Canadian Journal of Counselling, 31* (1) 67–81.

Abstract

A concept-mapping process was used to understand parental expectations of an Edmonton elementary school counselor's role. The 25 parents who participated generated 91 statements that were subsequently sorted by each parent and analyzed to develop a seven-theme conceptualization of parental expectations. Parents requested that the counselor become highly involved in providing services that involve support, referral, education, and information. In addition to perceiving the counselor as a provider of direct counseling services, parents expected that the school counselor would collaborate extensively with them. Additional expectations include developmental programming for all children in the school and services involving teacher consultation, special needs programming, and community liaison.

Roberts, A. H., & Rust, J. O. (1994). Role and function of school psychologists, 1992–1993: A comparative study. *Psychology in the Schools, 31* (2), 113–199.

Abstract

This study examined the roles and functions of 52 school psychologists from Iowa and Tennessee. Three multivariate analyses of variance (MANOVAs) were used to test differences between (a) reported time spent on prereferral, assessment, intervention, consultation, and curriculum-based assessment; (b) reported actual time spent and desired time spent; and (c) desired time spent on the five variables. Significant differences were found for the time spent in all areas, in actual time spent versus desired time spent in consultation, and in desired time spent in curriculum-based assessment. Results suggest that school psychologists in Tennessee and Iowa occupy different roles. School psychologists in Tennessee reported spending the majority of their time on assessment activities, whereas the Iowa sample balances their time among the five functions.

Schmidt, J. J. (1995). Assessing school counseling programs through external reviews. *School Counselor, 43* (2), 114–123.

Abstract

External reviews were performed in two southeastern school systems to respond to questions each school system had about the services being provided by counselors; the perceptions of students, parents, and teachers about those services; and the extent to which the current staff was meeting the needs of these audiences. Results indicated that accountability continues to be an important issue for the school counseling profession. Neither school system had a clearly defined school counseling program. The lack of evidence to support a comprehensive program with stated goals and objectives, a job description for school counselors, and guidelines for professional practice prevented either review team from recommending an increase in counseling positions. Findings reveal perceptions of school counselors as being overwhelmed with case loads, administrative duties, clerical tasks, and crises that occur in schools.

Vacc, N. A., & Loesch, L. C. (1993). A content analysis of opinions about the National Counselor Exam. *Journal of Counseling and Development, 71*, 418–421.

Abstract

This analysis explores the degree of professional satisfaction among candidates ($N = 363$) taking the National Counselor Examination (NCE) between 1986 and 1990. Responses refer to specific test items, overall content of the examination, professional value of the examination, and the examination process. Both negative and positive comments are reported.

Wiggins, J. D., & Moody, A. H. (1987). Student evaluations of counseling programs: An added dimension. *The School Counselor, 34*, 535–561.

Abstract

School counseling programs in seven junior high and four senior high schools are evaluated by focusing on student perceptions of various parts of the counseling program and then relating these evaluations to reported time-task emphasis of counselors. Counselors who spent the most time in direct delivery of services through individual and group counseling were rated as most effective.

Wilson, N. S. (1986). Counselor interventions with low-achieving and underachieving elementary, middle, and high school students: A review of the literature. *Journal of Counseling and Development, 64*, 628–634.

Abstract

This article reviews experimental studies and evaluates the effects of counselor interventions on the grade point average of underachieving or low-achieving students in elementary, middle, and high schools. Includes characteristics of programs associated with improved achievement.

Chapter 4

Counselors in Community and Agency Settings

Many of you may eventually consider employment as counselors in community, agency, or other nonschool professional situations. This chapter's objective is to acquaint you with the counselor's role and function in a variety of these settings. They include community mental health agencies, employment and rehabilitation agencies, correctional settings, and marriage and family practice. Pastoral counseling, gerontology counseling, and private practice are also discussed.

Table 4-1 through Table 4-4 identifies first-year job placements of community, marriage and family, mental health, and rehabilitation counselors. You may gain insights into possible employment opportunities if you are interested in nonschool settings.

TRAINING PROGRAMS FOR COUNSELORS IN COMMUNITY AND AGENCY SETTINGS

The training of counselors for the various community and agency settings is very similar to the training of school counselors, and in the past there was little distinction in many master's degree programs with the possible exceptions of practicum and internship settings and perhaps a few specialized courses. However, professional organizations have pushed for new standards in training counselors in specialty areas. The result is an increase in specialized courses. In some schools, counselors may be trained in separate departments or in programs with distinctly different emphases. Even greater distinctions will be noted at the doctoral degree level, where preparation tends to focus on the anticipated professional work setting.

The Council for Accreditation of Counseling and Related Educational Programs (CACREP; 1994) specifies that community agency counselor preparation programs will require a minimum of 48 semester-hours or 72 quarter-hours of graduate course work. This course work will include studies in each of eight common core areas: human growth and development, social-cultural foundations, helping relations, group work, career and lifestyle development, appraisal, research, and program evaluation and professional orientation. Programs in mental health counseling and/or marriage and family counseling/therapy are comprised of graduate-level study, with a minimum of 60 semester-hour or 90 quarter-hour credits. Additional course work is required in three specialty areas: foundations of community counseling, contextual dimensions for community counseling, and knowledge and skills for the practice of community counseling. A 600-hour internship in a community setting is also required.

Further insights into both training and on-the-job functioning may also be noted by examining the provisions of the Community Mental Health Centers Act of 1963, which provided for the establishment of a network of mental health centers throughout the nation. Each center was to provide at least the five basic services of (a) inpatient care; (b) outpatient care; (c) partial hospitalization; (d) emergency care; and (e) consultation, education, and information.

Many counselors and managers in community mental health centers are Ph.D. graduates of counseling psychology programs. In addition to their preparation in individual and group counseling, their training programs typically include course work in psychological measurement, research design, biological and cognitive and other bases of human behavior, and intervention strategies and service delivery systems, plus course work leading to competency in an area of specialization.

TABLE 4-1 Placement of Graduates from Community Counseling Entry Level Master's Programs the First Year After Graduation

	1993		1996	
Placement Settings	Number of Programs Reporting Placement	Percent of all Graduates	Number of Programs Reporting Placement	Percent of all Graduates
Advanced graduate programs	125	10	122	11
Managed care	81	8	89	8
Private practice/agency	119	24	125	22
Public agency	130	49	141	48
School: Elementary	0	0	53	7
Middle	0	0	8	0
Secondary	0	0	6	0
Higher education student affairs	0	0	9	0
Other settings	44	8	30	2
Total		99		100
Number of programs supplying data	143		149	

Source: From Counselor Preparation, 1996–98: Programs, Faculty, Trends, p. 80, by J. W. Hollis, 1997, Muncie, IN: Accelerated Development, Inc., and National Board for Certified Counselors. Reprinted with permission of Taylor & Francis, Inc.

TABLE 4-2 Placement of Graduates from Marriage and Family Counseling/Therapy Entry Level Master's Programs the First Year After Graduation

	1993		1996	
Placement Settings	Number of Programs Reporting Placement	Percent of all Graduates	Number of Programs Reporting Placement	Percent of all Graduates
Advanced graduate programs	43	12	59	13
Managed care	34	9	40	9
Private practice/agency	52	37	60	26
Public agency	46	37	67	41
School: Elementary	0	0	4	0
Middle	0	0	3	0
Secondary	0	0	4	0
Higher education student affairs	0	0	4	0
Other settings	14	4	25	9
Total		99		98
Number of programs supplying data	53		74	

Source: From Counselor Preparation, 1996–98: Programs, Faculty, Trends, p. 89, by J. W. Hollis, 1997, Muncie, IN: Accelerated Development, Inc., and National Board for Certified Counselors. Reprinted with permission of Taylor & Francis, Inc.

TABLE 4-3 Placement of Graduates from Mental Health Counseling Entry Level Master's Programs the First Year After Graduation

Placement Settings	1993		1996	
	Number of Programs Reporting Placement	Percent of all Graduates	Number of Programs Reporting Placement	Percent of all Graduates
Advanced graduate programs	47	14	61	14
Managed care	32	7	46	11
Private practice/agency	46	25	60	21
Public agency	53	48	68	46
School: Elementary	0	0	3	0
Middle	0	0	1	0
Secondary	0	0	0	0
Higher education student affairs	0	0	6	2
Other settings	20	6	24	6
Total		100		100
Number of programs supplying data	56		74	

Source: From *Counselor Preparation, 1996–98: Programs, Faculty, Trends,* p. 98, by J. W. Hollis, 1997, Muncie, IN: Accelerated Development, Inc., and National Board for Certified Counselors. Reprinted with permission of Taylor & Francis, Inc.

TABLE 4-4 Placement of Graduates from Rehabilitation Counseling Entry Level Master's Programs the First Year After Graduation

Placement Settings	1993		1996	
	Number of Programs Reporting Placement	Percent of all Graduates	Number of Programs Reporting Placement	Percent of all Graduates
Advanced graduate programs	46	5	47	7
Managed care	36	7	30	5
Private practice/agency	59	28	56	28
Public agency	62	50	64	51
School: Elementary	0	0	1	0
Middle	0	0	0	0
Secondary	0	0	3	0
Higher education student affairs	0	0	4	0
Other settings	23	8	25	8
Total		98		99
Number of programs supplying data	75		67	

Source: From *Counselor Preparation, 1996–98: Programs, Faculty, Trends,* p. 113, by J. W. Hollis, 1997, Muncie, IN: Accelerated Development, Inc., and National Board for Certified Counselors. Reprinted with permission of Taylor & Francis, Inc.

Thus, as we proceed to examine the role of the counselor in a variety of community, agency, and institutional settings, we emphasize that these counselors deal with the developmental and growth needs of clients as well as the more traditional remedial and adjustment concerns.

THE IMPORTANCE OF LICENSURE

As noted in Chapter 3, the movement toward licensure is one that, in the long run, will protect both the public and the profession. Licensure is particularly important to many professional counselors practicing in community agencies or private practices, in which client reimbursement is significant to the agency's or individual's fiscal wellness. This reimbursement, usually referred to as third-party payment, is based on insurance companies' and Medicare provisions to pay for services rendered to clients by eligible (licensed) providers. The process of licensure in each state is established by legislative action. State licensure boards administer the legislated licensing program.

Currently, counseling psychologists may be credentialed in any of the 50 states. To be eligible for such licensure, candidates must hold an earned doctorate in psychology, have completed a predoctoral internship, and have passed the national licensure examination and whatever special examination an individual state may require.

Professional counselors trained in programs of counselor education may currently secure licensure in 44 states and the District of Columbia. Although this process differs from state to state, it typically requires candidates to have an earned master's degree and often to have passed the National Board for Certified Counselors examination. Graduates of programs accredited by CACREP may, in some instances, be eligible to take this examination upon completing their graduate training program, rather than having to wait to gain experience before being eligible to take the examination.

COMMUNITY MENTAL HEALTH AGENCIES

Community mental health agencies provide counseling services for the general population within a specified geographic locale. Many community mental health agencies have been initiated under the provisions of the Community Mental Health Act of 1963, which provides initial funding for such centers that must be developed following the guidelines of the National Institute of Mental Health. These agencies were designed to provide preventive community mental health services. Typically, such centers offer inpatient and outpatient services, emergency services, and educational and consultation services. Many centers also provide partial hospitalization services, diagnostic services, and precare and aftercare in the community through programs of home visitations, foster home placement, and halfway houses.

Senator Edward M. Kennedy (1990) notes:

Experience has demonstrated that a number of key features must be included in any effective community-based program of care for the seriously mentally ill. They include the following:

• Quantitative analysis of the population to be served, so that the number of people to be helped and their specific needs can be determined.

- Case management, so that someone is responsible for coordinating and monitoring necessary services.
- A program of support and rehabilitation to provide services appropriate for each client's age, functional level, and individual needs. Psychotherapy, regular social contact to assist reintegration into the community, vocational training, supervised work, and assistance in obtaining and keeping competitive employment should be available to adults, and an appropriate range of services should also be available to children. The goal is to enable individuals to function at the maximum feasible level.
- Medical treatment and mental health care, available on a continuum from day hospitalization to periodic appointments, to regulate medication and monitor mental status.
- Assistance to families who often provide the frontline care for the mentally ill in the community and who are often left to cope with the severe strains of mental illness without assistance from the society at large.
- Housing services, ranging from half-way houses with staff in residence who provide continuous supervision to largely independent living. Outreach to the homeless mentally ill should be seen as an essential part of these services. (pp. 1238–1239)

Table 4-5 indicates how agency counselors spend their professional time, in order of time consumption from highest to lowest. These data come from our counselor's role and function study (1996–1997).

TABLE 4-5 How Practicing Counselors Spend Their Time[a]

Activity	Agency
Individual counseling	1
Group counseling	8
Couples/family counseling	4.5
Crisis intervention	
Standardized test administration and/or interpretation	
Nonstandardized assessment (i.e., case studies, information gathering interviews, questionnaires, etc.)	6.5
Needs assessment (to determine priority needs of your target population)	6.5
Consultation activities	3
Case management	4.5
Dealing with Managed Care Organizations (MCOs) as a provider (i.e., making application, precertification, concurrent review of cases, appealing decisions, etc.)	
Prevention activities	10
Clinical supervision activities	9
Administrative activities	2
Information dissemination: public communication and public relations	
Other	

[a]Based on a survey by Robert L. Gibson and Marianne H. Mitchell, 1997.

The Agency Team

In most community mental health agencies, counselors are employed as team members with other helping professionals. These typically include psychiatrists, clinical and counseling psychologists, and psychiatric social workers. Psychiatrists are usually considered to be the team leaders, inasmuch as they have a medical background and may perform physical examinations, prescribe drugs, and admit people to hospitals in the treatment of behavior abnormalities. In addition to basic medical training, certification as a psychiatrist typically requires three years of residency in a psychiatric institution plus two years of further practice.

Counseling or clinical psychologists are prepared in programs that require a minimum of three academic years of full-time resident graduate study, plus a full year's internship in an appropriate setting. Although emphases in programs will vary somewhat from institution to institution and depend on whether one is trained in a clinical or counseling psychology program, the psychologist receives general training in basic psychology, counseling and psychotherapy, psychological assessment, and psychological research.

Some contend that the difference between clinical and counseling psychology has never been entirely clear, but distinctions do exist. One distinction might be that clinical psychologists appear to work more frequently with behavioral abnormalities and personality reorganization, whereas counseling psychologists emphasize increased understanding of the adjustment problems of normal persons.

Psychiatric social workers are trained minimally to the master's degree level in two-year programs. One year of this program is devoted to supervised internship in a clinical or hospital setting. Social workers are trained to help people experiencing economic or other problems. This assistance is facilitated through welfare and other programs. The psychiatric social worker, however, is more frequently found in hospital or community mental health settings. In such settings, they may gather data regarding patients and their families and often will work with the patient's family in assisting the client's adjustment. In many community mental health centers, psychiatric social workers may also conduct treatment of a nonmedical nature.

Counseling in the Agency Setting*

What is it like to counsel in an agency setting? The following represents a day in the life of a counselor at the South Central Community Mental Health Agency, Bloomington, Indiana.

Typical Day of a Counselor at a Community Mental Health Center

8:00 A.M.	Pick up any messages with secretary regarding schedule changes, important meetings scheduled.
8:05 A.M.	Drop by medical records and get three charts for clients scheduled to be seen today.
8:10 A.M.	Review case notes for client #1 scheduled at 8:30.
8:30 A.M.	Meet with client #1 for 50 minutes—27-year-old married woman with two children dealing with the recent death of her father—grief issues.
9:20 A.M.	Write summary report on client #1.
9:45 A.M.	Make phone calls: (1) social worker assigned to case seen yesterday regarding special services needed for client's child; (2) psychiatrist regarding referral of client needing psychiatric evaluation for current functioning.

---

*Written by Louise Dunn Miracle, Ph.D.

10:00 A.M.	Meet with new client for scheduled intake.
11:15 A.M.	Rewrite intake notes for new client just seen for presentation of client in team meeting later today.
11:45 A.M.	Call client seen two days ago to give information about a new support group formed for AMA (adults molested as children) victims.
12:00 P.M.	Eat lunch and pick up new messages.
12:30 P.M.	Go over notes in preparation for presentation of morning's intake to team—and previous case notes for client to be seen at 2:00 P.M.
1:00 P.M.	Team meeting: Meet with adult outpatient team; listen to the presentation of five new cases; pick up two of the new cases to fill two slots left by client terminations; present new case to team (client seen at intake earlier).
2:00 P.M.	Meet with client #2—36-year-old recently divorced male with two small children, having problems coping with new situation.
3:00 P.M.	Write case summary note for client #2.
3:20 P.M.	Make phone calls: (1) confirm appointment regarding phone message from client; (2) call new clients picked up in team to reschedule appointment—able to reach one and set up appointment—other unavailable: dictate letter to other client to be typed by secretary.
3:45 P.M.	Go to Center library to seek a reference for assertiveness training as refresher to use with client scheduled the next day.
4:00 P.M.	Meet with client #3—72-year-old woman complaining of morning dizziness and anxiety attacks.
4:50 P.M.	Write case summary notes for client #3.
5:10 P.M.	Return charts to medical records.
5:15 P.M.	Leave for the day.

Counselors in community settings deal with widely diverse populations and a great variety in both the type and nature of human concerns. These range from continuous developmental needs of people to crises requiring immediate emergency attention.

In addition to community mental health agencies, a variety of what might be labeled alternative and nontraditional yet related community counseling services have developed over the past several generations. These nontraditional service centers have had different titles, but most of them can be categorized under the labels of hot lines or crisis centers, drop-in or open-door centers, and specialized counseling centers such as those catering to drug and alcohol abusers or centers dealing with special populations such as women, minorities, or the aged.

Hot lines or crisis phones have been one of the most popular and older alternative services offered. They are frequently staffed by nonprofessionals or paraprofessionals with, in some settings, professional volunteers available or a professional supervisor on call. Usually hot lines or crisis phones are designed to provide sympathetic and helpful listeners and reliable information for dealing with common concerns such as drug overdoses, suicide, spouse abuse, alcoholism, and mental breakdown.

Open-door or drop-in centers provide havens for persons who need a place to come to and, in larger cities, to get off the streets—a place where they can feel secure and receive sympathetic attention and counseling assistance. Some of these centers actually provide minimal accommodations where a person can "sleep it off." For the most part, however, they simply provide an opportunity for the person to face emergency counseling assistance. In many of these centers, record keeping is at a minimum and clients may not even be required to give their name or other personal data unless they wish.

In a number of more populous communities, various specialized counseling service centers are on the increase. These centers tend to serve special populations, defined either by the nature of the problem, such as alcohol or drug addiction, spouse abuse, marital relations, or sexual problems; or by age classifications or racial or religious groups. These specialty centers tend to be staffed by a mixture of professionals, paraprofessionals, and volunteers. Facilities are equally diverse. For example, the Norfolk, Virginia, Redevelopment and Housing Authority has established a system of community-based counselors who function with aides to assist individuals and families living in 11 public housing parks in that city. These counselors and their aides give support to residents in crisis situations and provide the information they need to cope with their problems, including the rules and regulations of the housing authority. Counseling activities tend to focus particularly on strengthening families.

Figure 4-1 depicts how an agency may be organized.

EMPLOYMENT COUNSELING

In 1933, the Department of Labor established the Employment Security offices, which were to provide job placement and attending advising or counseling functions for the unemployed. Counseling was more specifically provided for in the GI Bill of 1944, which provided job counseling for veterans returning from World War II. By the 1960s, the Department of Labor was encouraging states to upgrade their counselors to the professional or master's degree level of training.

Within the Department of Labor, an employment counselor is defined as one who performs counseling duties and who meets the minimum standards for employment counselor classification. The employment service system is designed to bring together workers seeking employment with employers seeking workers in order to improve the functioning of the nation's labor markets. Each state is expected to administer a labor exchange system to facilitate this service and to participate in a system for sharing information between the states, including the use of standardized classification systems issued by the Secretary of Labor. Employment counselors may also administer the work test requirements of the state unemployment compensation system.

Although the focus of employment counselors, as with other employees of the U.S. Employment Service (now called Job Service), is appropriate job placement of its clientele, the counselors are expected in the process to counsel clients on personal problems and assist them in developing attitudes, skills, and abilities that will facilitate their employment. Counselors are also involved in gathering data from their clients and in the administration and interpretation of standardized tests. Employment counselors tend to consider the National Employment Counseling Association (an organizational affiliate of the American Counseling Association) as their professional organization.

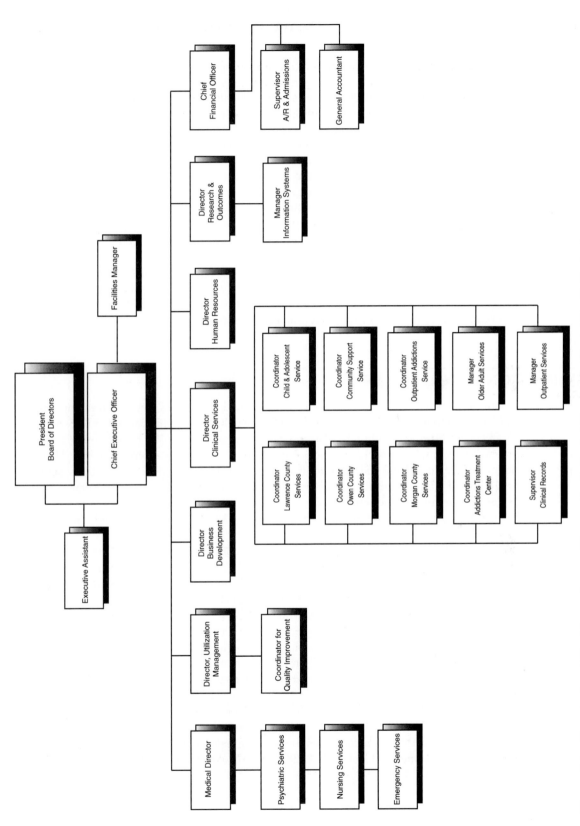

Figure 4-1 Organizational Chart for an Agency. (*Source:* South Central Community Mental Health Center.)

Employee Assistance Counselors

More and more counselors are practicing in business and industrial work settings. The impact of substance abuse on the workforce, plus a heightened recognition of the importance of employees' general mental health to productivity, stimulated the initial development of many programs. Economic opportunity and labor legislation also created opportunities. However, as counselors proved their worth in the industrial sectors, many programs expanded their activities to include career assistance, retirement planning, educational guidance, and family counseling. Additionally, the rapidly changing nature of the employment picture in the decades ahead continues to create challenges for employers and employees alike and their programs for assisting employees. Recent trends toward downsizing, merging, the hiring of temps (temporaries), and the movement of whole industrial complexes to new geographic locales are examples of just a few of these new and emerging challenges.

Counselors in business and industrial settings are frequently organized into Employee Assistance Programs (EAPs). Most counseling in EAPs would be labeled brief or short-term therapy. Too, the diversity of worker needs in most settings require that EAP counselors have an extensive knowledge of referral sources and client options.

CORRECTIONAL COUNSELING

Practitioners of correctional counseling are employed in various law enforcement settings, ranging from those involved with first-time juvenile probationary offenders to persons incarcerated in penal institutions. Counselors in these settings usually have training backgrounds in counseling, psychology, sociology, criminal justice, or forensic studies. Their duties include counseling and interviewing; the use of various analytical techniques, such as the use of standardized testing; referrals; parole recommendations; and placement. In some juvenile institutional settings, counselors may be employed as live-in advisers. Counselors working with youthful juvenile offenders work closely with police officers and other authorities.

Examples of counselors functioning in juvenile correctional institutions may be found in the differential treatment approach of the Kennedy Youth Center of Morgantown, West Virginia, and the Indiana Boys' School, Plainfield, Indiana. These and other similar institutions utilize the differential treatment approach, which seeks to take into account individual differences in matching inmates with counseling staff on the basis of personality or behavioral categories. In other correctional settings, counselors function as key agents in converting closed, traditional punitive systems into those that are more positive, helping, and rehabilitative. In these settings, the emphasis is on the formation of positive interpersonal climates and open lines of communication among the various members of the prison community, including inmates and correctional officers, or guards. An example of such an activity in recent decades has been the training by correctional counselors of prison guards and other security personnel in racial relations and/or multicultural awareness.

Counselors in the field of correctional counseling may join the International Association of Addictions and Offender Counselors, a division of the American Counseling Association.

REHABILITATION COUNSELING

History reflects the admiration that society has always held for those who have overcome physical handicaps to achieve notable success: the man (Franklin D. Roosevelt) who was paralyzed by polio in both legs at age 39 but later became President of the United States of America and a wartime world leader; the woman (Helen Keller) who was deaf and blind from the age of 2 but became a successful author and lecturer; the deaf musician (Ludwig van Beethoven); or the amputee actress (Sarah Bernhardt), to name but a few. Clifford Beers, who was mentioned in Chapter 1, is an example of individual triumph over mental illness.

The achievements of these and others, despite their handicaps, were notable; but history has failed to record the tragic losses in human potential that were allowed to occur because of lack of attention, other than medical, for people with disabilities. Since World War II, however, rehabilitation counseling has expanded into public agencies so that these individuals may receive special counseling assistance in overcoming their disabilities.

Although the central role of the rehabilitation counselor has remained quite consistent over the years, the functions and required knowledge and skill competencies of the rehabilitation counselor have expanded. Regardless of their employment setting and client population, most rehabilitation counselors (a) assess client needs, (b) develop goals and individualized plans to meet identified needs, and (c) provide or arrange for the therapeutic services and interventions (e.g., psychological, medical, social, or behavioral) needed by clients that may include job placement and follow-up services. Counseling skills are considered an essential component of all of these activities (Jenkins, Patterson, & Szymanski, 1992) as seen in Leahy and Szymanski, (1995):

> x Research by Leahy, Szymanski, and Linkowski (1993) indicated that the following ten knowledge domains represent the core competency requirements of rehabilitation counselors: (a) vocational counseling and consultation services; (b) medical and psychological aspects; (c) individual and group counseling; (d) program evaluation and research; (e) case management and service coordination; (f) family, gender, and multicultural issues; (g) foundations of rehabilitation; (h) workers' compensation; (i) environmental and attitudinal barriers; and (j) assessment. The specialized knowledge of disabilities and of environmental factors that interact with disabilities, as well as the range of knowledge and skills required in addition to counseling, differentiates the rehabilitation counselor from other types of counselors in today's service delivery environments. (Jenkins, Patterson, & Szymanski, 1992, p. 163)

Rehabilitation counselors help clients overcome deficits in their skills. They may work with a special type of client such as the deaf, the blind, the mentally ill, or the physically disabled, or, in some settings, all of these plus people with other kinds of disabilities as well.

For example, vocational rehabilitation counseling seeks to help clients with disabilities prepare for gainful employment, frequently assisting in appropriate job placement. In recent decades, much effort has been expended on the rehabilitation of substance abusers, with counselors prominent in both inpatient and outpatient facilities. We have also noted increased efforts to rehabilitate those with mental disabilities. Rehabilitation counselors also work with ex-offenders in preparing for adjustment to life in society's mainstream.

The role of rehabilitation counselors is a complex one; they provide a broad range of psychological and career-oriented services and work with and often coordinate the efforts of community agencies in their client's behalf. They also function as resource persons who seek to encourage the optimum adjustment and development of their clients.

Capuzzi and Gross (1997) note:

> Academic training of counselors whose interest lies in working with clients with disabilities is accomplished almost invariably through Rehabilitation Counselor Education (RCE) programs. These training programs are typically graduate (master's level) programs and are offered by Counselor Education or Counseling Psychology departments. Completing the programs normally requires two years of academic and clinical training when pursued full time.
>
> The curriculum content pursued in most of these training programs has been developed and verified by the Council on Rehabilitation Education (CORE). CORE was established in 1971 as an accreditation body to oversee the academic and clinical training of rehabilitation counselors and to promote effective delivery of rehabilitation services to people with disabilities. Of the approximately 100 RCE programs in the United States, 84 are currently CORE-accredited. These programs must show evidence of a graduate-level curriculum that provides its trainee with a course of study that includes, but is not limited to, the following knowledge and/or skill areas: (1) history and philosophy of rehabilitation; (2) rehabilitation legislation; (3) organizational structure of the rehabilitation system (public and private, nonprofit and for-profit service delivery); (4) counseling theories, approaches, and techniques; (5) case management; (6) career development and vocational counseling theories and practices; (7) vocational evaluation, occupational information, job analysis, and work adjustment techniques; (8) job development and placement; (9) medical aspects of disability; (10) psychosocial aspects of disability; (11) knowledge of community resources and services; (12) rehabilitation research; (13) measurement and testing; (14) legal and ethical issues in rehabilitation counseling; (15) independent living; and (16) special topics in rehabilitation (such as transition from school to work, supported employment, rehabilitation engineering).
>
> In addition, rehabilitation counseling trainees are required to participate in supervised practicum and internship experiences totaling a minimum of 600 clock hours in approved rehabilitation sites and under the supervision of a certified rehabilitation counselor. (pp. 487–488)

MARRIAGE AND FAMILY COUNSELING

Although the marriage vows read "until death do us part," the high divorce rate in this country in recent decades indicates that thousands of couples have decided they cannot wait until their entry into eternity to part. In addition, thousands of other couples suffer through phases of their marriages or seek adjustment to marriage difficulties by means other than separation or divorce.

Certainly, an abundance of statistical empirical evidence indicates that family discord and divorce is continuing to increase. The stresses of the actual divorce process for spouses and children and the later adjustment requirements for all involved are well documented and include such problems as the feelings of failure that often accompany divorce, and other emotions such as anger, regret, and depression. Adjustment problems may also arise in terms of separation, child rearing, and single-parent roles. In addition to these emotional and psychological stresses, there are those practical concerns that center on the legal issues and financial responsibilities for persons in divorce or separation. Also, the adjustment problems of children in the divorcing of parents cannot be overlooked. Concerns about loyalty, parental dating, and custody can have severe psychological consequences, especially when coupled with the feelings of guilt and devalued self-concept commonplace in children of divorce.

We can conclude that the traditional image of the home and family as a cozy nest of love, security, togetherness, and never-ending happiness has been severely battered (as have many of the nest's inhabitants) in recent generations. The need for counselors who can effectively counsel outside the one-to-one relationship, who can work in this new dimension—the family or family system—has evolved. Yet, providing effective counseling assistance to families and couples in today's complex and stressful society is a challenging and often difficult task, frequently complicated by advice from nonprofessionals, cultural traditions, and environmental pressures.

Although the first marriage and family help centers were established in the 1930s, it is only within the past several decades that marriage and family therapy has emerged as a counseling speciality. With more than 40,000 counselors engaged in the practice, the American Association of Marriage and Family Counselors represents this specialty area as does Division 43 of the American Psychological Association, the International Association for Marriage and Family Counselors, and the division of the American Counseling Association entitled the International Association of Marriage and Family Counseling.

Whereas individual counseling focuses on the individual person and his or her concerns, family therapy tends to focus on the family system. Even if only one member of the family is being counseled, if the counseling is concerned primarily with the family system, it can be viewed as family counseling.

> Family and couples counseling/therapy is a treatment approach which views and treats the family as a system. The system has properties all its own: a set of rules, assigned and ascribed roles for its members, an organized power structure, intricate overt and covert forms of communication, and elaborate ways of negotiating and problem solving that permit various tasks to be performed effectively (Goldenberg & Goldenberg, 1991). Family counselors/therapists engage in the clinical practice of treating individuals, couples, or families. Regardless of the number of clients being treated, the family counselor conceptualizes problems in terms of the systems perspective. The family counselor therefore focuses on the context in which individuals exist and intervene on the relational level. (Carlson, 1993, p. 63)

An objective of family therapy may be to bring about change in the family structure and the behavior of family members. Communication among the family will probably be examined as well as how the family resolves its conflicts.

We must continue to recognize the rising numbers of dual-career couples, single-parent families, and latchkey children as issues in family living that are more characteristic of recent generations. These stresses, plus those accompanying the necessitated major career changes predicted for most adult workers in the immediate decades ahead, would indicate complex factors challenging marriage and family counselors.

An outgrowth of the increased recognition of the extent and popularity of marital problems has been the development of a specialty area within the field of marriage counseling. This group, represented by the American Association of Marriage and Family Therapy, includes memberships from diverse professional preparation backgrounds, including psychiatrists, psychologists, law, and the ministry. Another representative organization of this group is the National Council on Family Relations.

Many counselor education programs offer courses in the marriage and family area. Popular courses include marriage counseling, family counseling, human sexuality, and marriage/family counseling. For those who wish to specialize in the field of family therapy, credentials can be earned in one of two ways. An individual can complete an advanced degree in one of the traditional disciplines, such as clinical psychology, counseling, pastoral counseling, expressive therapies, social work, or psychiatry. Either within the course of study for that degree or after completing the degree, the student must complete specific course work that meets the educational requirements for a degree in marriage and family counseling.

PASTORAL COUNSELING

From the standpoint of sheer numbers and geographic coverage, pastoral counseling provides a significant mental health resource. Not only are clergy members generally available to listen to the concerns and personal problems of their parishioners, but they also are frequently the first source to which people in trouble turn. In fact, many churches offer counseling on family issues including marriage problems, bereavement counseling, and youth counseling and guidance. The American Association of Pastoral Counselors certifies individuals and also accredits training programs.

Churches are also increasingly utilizing professional counselors in their youth programs. In recognition of the mental health function of the clergy, many theological training programs include courses in pastoral counseling, related psychology, and general counseling subjects. Special programs have also been developed in clinical pastoral education for theology students and clergy wanting further training. Although many of these specialized programs are comparatively short-term, others provide intensive training in clinical settings.

GERONTOLOGY COUNSELING

The "graying of America" is the phrase frequently used to note the dramatic increase in the older population. The *U.S. Bureau of the Census Current Population Reports* (1995) noted that the group 65 years of age and older constitutes approximately 11% of our total population, contrasted to 4.1% in 1900, with predictions of continued increases well beyond the turn of the century. "People now live from two thirds to three fourths of their lives as older persons. In the next 20 years, one in five persons in the United States will be over the age of 60 (American Association of Retired Persons, 1988)" (Myers, 1992, p. 35).

With increased representation has also come an increased sensitivity to the needs, including counseling, of this special population. Also, as this group becomes more politically potent and active, the aged themselves are demanding the same range of social services and attention to their needs that are provided for other age groups.

Development in later life can be viewed from at least two perspectives: developmental sequences and life transitions. The developmental perspective assumes a unidirectional, stepwise progression of events. Certain tasks must be mastered for successful development. The positive theme here is that development occurs and can be fostered throughout the life span. Older persons are not viewed as static, rigid, or poor prospects for therapeutic change. . . .

Gerontologists, those who study older persons, have devoted much attention to the study of successful aging. Those who age successfully tend to have a strong sense of life satisfaction, high self-esteem, and positive morale. Persons who do not age successfully experience depression and low self-esteem. (Myers, 1990, p. 248)

Retirement is a dramatic change occuring in the lives of most of the working elderly. For many workers, including the elderly, their job is an important source of their identity; that is, I'm a teacher, I'm a salesperson, I'm a secretary, and so on. The loss of this identity, through retirement, can be difficult for the elderly, who, in addition, may have most of their contacts with others on their job. Loneliness is not uncommon problem among aging retirees. Further, retirees as well as many older individuals have not developed avocational interests or leisure time pursuits, resulting in boredom and frustration for many. The loss of spouses and other loved ones is particularly noticeable among the elderly. Bereavement counseling should be available during these difficult periods. Depression, stress, and alcoholism are also common among the elderly.

The increased recognition of the needs of this population are further reflected in the growth of course offerings in counselor preparation programs and substantive increases in professional publications addressing the counseling of older individuals. It is also now possible for gerontological counselors to be certified.

> Any National Certified Counselor (NCC) may apply for specialty certification as a National Certified Gerontological Counselor (NCGC). The certification does not require an examination, but a review of training, experience, and supervisory evaluations. A 2-year "alternate entry period" was established at the time the credential became available to encourage practicing counselors to seek certification.
>
> As of January 1, 1993, applicants will meet these criteria (NBCC, 1990): (a) 2 years of professional gerontological counseling experience; (b) three graduate courses in gerontology (or the equivalent in 120 hours of related gerontological counseling continuing education), and a 600-hour internship or supervised experience (25% of which is with or on behalf of persons age 55 or older) or a 600-hour internship or supervised experience in a gerontological setting; (c) completion of a self-assessment of competence; and (d) two professional assessments of competence. The NCC certification is awarded after a successful review of credentials and competencies. (Myers, 1992, pp. 37–38)

PRIVATE PRACTICE

The possibility of establishing a full-time private practice has appealed to an increasing number of counselors and many, employed by other institutions or agencies, have done so on a part-time basis. Those interested in private practice may consider whether they wish to practice alone or in a partnership or group practice. They must also determine whether to enter general practice or specialize (i.e., addictions, career, children, etc.).

A basic consideration in entering private practice is whether one's professional interest and expertise are relevant to a sufficient client population in the geographic area of practice to adequately support the private practitioner. Legal and ethical guidelines are critical. And the importance of licensure and eligibility for third-party payment must be examined. A 1992 study of professional developmental needs of 288 mental health counselors (Wilcoxon & Puleo, 1992) reported that two top professional concerns were (a) third-party reimbursement (54.5%) and (b) licensure (46.5%). Other concerns that the individual private practitioner must address are fiscal (fees, billing policies, insurance, office overhead), logistical (office location, hours, furnishings, record keeping, secretarial help), and public relations or communications, including advertising of services.

FUTURE DIRECTIONS

In 1980, *The Counseling Psychologist* had a special theme issue (volume 8, number 4) entitled "Counseling Psychology in the Year 2000." In this issue, Whiteley concludes:

> In order to have an increased impact in the changed world of 2000 A.D., counseling psychology will have to enlarge its substantive bases to include environmental psychology and environmental planning; life-span developmental psychology including aging, developmental tasks, and transitions between phases of life; the psychology of men and women, the growth of men and women within relationships, sex roles, parenting, sexuality, and child rearing; more refined approaches to building a psychological sense of community; assertion training and social organization; self-renewal, psychobiology; information and computer science; and, finally, systematic study of the expected future and its alternatives. (p. 7)

In 1987, Division 17, the Counseling Psychology division of the American Psychological Association, held its third national conference focusing on the theme "Planning the Future." Rude, Weissberg, and Gazda (1988) note:

> Across the five work groups that comprised the Third National Conference for Counseling Psychology a number of common themes emerged. Discussions of identity affirmed the value of the scientist-practitioner model and of traditional strengths such as prevention, life-span development, and skill-building as well as innovative and nontraditional functions. Among the ideas that were endorsed multiple work groups were strategies to enhance counseling psychology's visibility and political strength and to build mechanisms for proactive planning into governance. Ways to improve the training of counseling psychologists by enhancing rigor, scientific thinking, professional identity, and ability to work in diverse and emerging settings also received substantial attention. Overall, deliberations of the groups resulted in substantial convergence and a set of specific goals and plans for the future. (p. 423)

Details of the conference were reported when another special issue of *The Counseling Psychologist* (Fretz, 1988) featured the theme and reports from this conference on "Planning the Future."

> Leona Tyler (1980) discussed the implications for the year 2000: "It means that counseling psychology (and counseling psychologists) will be dealing with the significant reality problems of that day, just as they have been oriented toward the reality problems of the '40s, '50s, '60s, and '70s.
>
> What are these reality problems of 2000 likely to be? (Fortunately, I can treat this as an academic exercise). No one really knows, of course, but it is useful to speculate. Here are my speculations concerning those trends that are likely to involve counseling psychologists:
>
> 1. The single-cycle sequence of family life, education, work and labor-force retirement will break down. Education will be a life-long process, interspersed and interacting with work and family.
> 2. There will be more explicit attention to a broader scope of life skills. Just as we now have organized training in educational skills and job skills, so there will be organized training in family skills, community skills, recreational skills, and so on.
>
> Mental health will be a recognized aspect of our total health system. Just as we go to the dentist twice a year and have an annual medical exam, so we will periodically go to the psychologist for a 'psychological check-up.'

In all of the above, counseling psychologists, with their history of dealing with the normal, everyday reality problems of the entire spectrum of age and level of adjustment will have an increasingly important role to play. They will be located in a variety of settings—educational institutions, government, community and social agencies, and private business and industry. And if psychology ever develops a 'general practitioner' (as I think it will) professional training in counseling psychology will be the best preparation for this role." (p. 22)

Many of these predicted futures of a decade ago are already emerging as reality. We would note also that advancements in "futuristic science," as in other fields, are making it possible to be increasingly accurate in seeing the future.

For community, agency, and other counselor settings, it is appropriate to note that the increased attention to prevention, multicultural, family, and career issues will apply to nonschool counselor settings as well. For example, the growing European and Asian economic competition as well as U.S. companies threatening to take their production to where workforces are more efficient and/or cheaper will mandate the United States' development of a world-class workforce. This will necessitate training and retraining, plus worker transitions to new careers and locations. For orderly and meaningful career planning and development, career counseling should be increasingly in demand in the public sector.

Because of the potential for at least temporary unemployment or underemployment and the accompanying frustrations, people abuse, substance abuse, and crime will continue to be national social concerns unless the major nonschool institutions of society (government, business, and industry) demonstrate more caring through counselor-directed human assistance programs.

Counselors in nonschool settings must be prepared for the fall-out from an older workforce; a drastic scaling down of traditional promotional opportunities in many fields; more women in management positions; the downsizing of government, military, and related industries leaving the former workers of these organizations seeking new options; and the creation of a large pool of workers in temporary or transitional jobs. Thus, although the future will present many opportunities for counselors, whether we as a profession serve the population will depend to a large degree on how vigorous and successful we are in communicating to the political and general publics our capabilities and readiness for rendering our much-needed services in the decades ahead.

SUMMARY

You have a problem and you need to see a counselor, but you are no longer in school, and, besides, your old school counselor is too busy with the current student body. So what are your options? This chapter has suggested a number of opportunities both for employment as counselors and assistance for clients in nonschool settings.

Community mental health agencies are perhaps the most versatile in terms of their readiness to deal with a wide range of developmental as well as remedial needs. Also, the staffing of these agencies is usually more diverse, often including professionals trained in medicine and social work as well as psychology. If one is seeking less conventional settings, many communities have crisis centers, hot line counseling, open-door agencies, centers for human growth, and other nontraditional approaches to providing mental health services.

If your problem is one of career decision making or job placement, you might want to seek the assistance of a government employment office counselor. (Unlike private employment agencies, government employment offices charge no fees and are more likely to employ trained counselors.) Additionally, career counseling centers, both government and nongovernment sponsored, are available in a number of communities. These specialized centers are also popular on college campuses.

Of course, if you are confined to a correctional institution, your only option may be your institutional counselor. Unfortunately, in many such institutions counseling personnel may not be employed.

For assistance in overcoming a physical or mental disability, rehabilitation counselors can be a valuable resource because they have received special training to work with the developmental needs of the handicapped. Rehab counselors may be found in community and other government agencies and hospitals. A small number are in private practice.

If your problem is marriage- or family-related, there can be help for you, too, because marriage and family counseling is a growing area of specialization. Like many of your friends and neighbors, you may turn to your family clergy. The likelihood is increasing that your minister, priest, or rabbi will have received some counseling preparation in his or her ministerial studies, or will have some assistant specially trained to provide counseling services. Another source of counseling assistance, if you are by chance a member of the armed services, would be your service counselor. If you are among our older readers, specialized counseling assistance may also be available to you to help you plan for your retirement or other needs.

A final option, one that would probably cost you more dollars, is to seek out a counselor in private practice. Large population centers, university-oriented communities, and upper socioeconomic suburbs are the more likely habitats of the private practitioners. Obviously, evidence of appropriate training, such as licensure, is important for private practitioners.

Having examined the historical development of our profession, the activities of counselors and their role and function in various school and nonschool settings, we now move to a more detailed examination of specific counselor services and activities. We shall begin in the next chapter with our most important skill and service: individual counseling.

DISCUSSION QUESTIONS

1. Discuss your familiarity with the role and function of counselors in nonschool settings.

2. Discuss differences in lifestyle one might anticipate among the following:

- School counselors
- Correctional counselors
- Counselors in private practice

3. Should all counselors for school and nonschool settings come under one broad general counseling license? Discuss.

4. Should counselors in community agencies be involved in such community problems as substance abuse, crime and delinquency, the homeless, unemployment, and so on? If so, in what way?

5. Discuss the growth of specialty areas in the counseling profession (i.e., marriage and family, sports, gerontology, etc.). Are there other areas of counseling specialization that you see emerging in the next 25 years?

6. Suggest prevention or enrichment program ideas for nonschool counseling agencies.

CLASS ACTIVITIES

1. Shadow a marriage and family counselor, an employment counselor, a counselor in private practice, or a counselor in an agency or institutional setting and report your experiences to the class.

2. Interview a minister, rabbi, or priest regarding the counseling aspects of his or her assignment.

3. Visit your local community mental health center and prepare a written report covering the following topics:

- Scope of jurisdiction
- Services offered

- Population served
- Internal administrative hierarchy
- Fees charged
- Sources of funding

4. Survey a small sample of your community population to ascertain their perceptions of the counseling profession and their awareness of local counseling agencies and services. Discuss the implications of your findings.

SELECTED READINGS

Egbert, A. (1985). Employment counseling for the handicapped can be easier through linkages. *Journal of Employment Counseling, 22* (1), 31–38.

Herr, E. L., & Fabian, E. S. (Eds.). (1995). Professional counseling: Spotlight on specialties [Special issue]. *Journal of Counseling and Development, 74,* 113–224.

Kunkel, M. A., & Newsom, S. (1996). Presenting problems for mental health services: A concept map. *Journal of Mental Health Counseling, 18* (1), 53–63.

Leahy, M. J., & Holt, E. (1993). Certification in rehabilitation counseling: History and process. *Rehabilitation Counseling Bulletin, 37* (2), 71–80.

Parker, W. M., & McDavis, R. J. (1983). Attitudes of Blacks toward mental health agencies and counselors. *Journal of Non-White Concerns in Personnel and Guidance, 11* (3), 89–98.

Quackenbos, S., Privette, G., & Klentz, B. (1985). Psychotherapy: Sacred or secular? *Journal of Counseling and Development, 63* (5), 290–293.

Schlossberg, N. (1984). *Counseling adults in transition.* New York: Spring Publishing (212 pages).

Schmolling, P., Yaukeles, M., & Burger, W. (1985). *Human services in contemporary America.* Monterey, CA: Brooks/Cole.

Seligman, L., & Dougherty, E. (1987). Establishing and maintaining a private practice. *Counseling and Human Development, 19* (5), 1–11.

Watkins, C. E., Jr., Lopez, F. G., Campbell, V. L., & Himmell, C. D. (1986). Contemporary counseling psychology: Results of a national survey. *Journal of Counseling Psychology, 33* (3), 301–309.

Worthington, E. L. (1986). Religious counseling: A review of published empirical research. *Journal of Counseling and Development, 84* (7), 421–431.

RESEARCH OF INTEREST

Benjamin, B. A. (1992). Career counseling with couples. *Journal of Counseling and Development, 70,* 544–549.

Abstract

This article examines a career counseling model that takes into account the couple dynamics active in the career choice process of the adult individual. It describes facilitative elements of career counseling with couples, the role of couple assessment, precautions in counseling couples, and future directions.

Bernal, G. (1987). Families with depression, school, marital, family and situational problems: A research note. *American Journal of Family Therapy, 15* (1), 44–51.

Abstract

Improvement rates for families in family therapy for depression, school, family, marital, and situational problems are reported here. Marital problems showed the lowest rate of improvement, whereas depression improved in fewer sessions. Family and situational problems improved most with the help of many sessions.

Cooper, S. E. (1986). The effects of group and individual vocational counseling on career indecision and personal indecisiveness. *Journal of College Student Personnel, 27* (1), 39–42.

Abstract

Decreases in career indecision and personal indecision were found in both group and individual vocational counseling for a sample of 34 students.

Crane, D. R., Griffin, W., & Hill, R. D. (1986). Influence of therapist skills on client perceptions of marriage and family therapy outcome: Implications for supervision. *Journal of Marital and Family Therapy, 12* (1), 91–96.

Abstract

Marriage and family therapy training clinic clients rated their therapist's skill level on several therapist variables including experience, confidence, concern, and how well the treatment seemed to fit their view of the problem. Suggestions for using these results in supervision of beginning therapists are given.

Dion, G. L., & Anthony, W. A. (1987). Research in psychiatric rehabilitation: A review of experimental and quasi-experimental studies. *Rehabilitation Counseling Bulletin, 30* (3), 177–203.

Abstract

Studies on the outcomes of psychiatric rehabilitation are described in terms of setting predominant focus of the intervention outcome measures and interventions used. The article shows the effectiveness of rehabilitation interventions for decreased recidivism, increased time spent in the community, increased rates of employment and productivity, increased skill development, increased satisfaction, and decreased costs.

Giblin, P. (1986). Research and assessment in marriage and family enrichment: A meta-analysis study. *Journal of Psychotherapy and the Family, 2* (1), 79–96.

Abstract

This study attempts to integrate and evaluate existing enrichment research literature using meta-analysis. Eighty-five studies from 1971 to 1982 of premarital, marital, and family enrichment, representing 3,886 couples or families, were gathered and their results statistically aggregated. Results show that enrichment programs affected the lives of participants, particularly in the areas of communications skills and constructive problem-solving techniques. Participants underwent negative changes initially. Findings are discussed in terms of overall enrichment effectiveness as well as salient programs, design, and measurement characteristics.

Giblin, P., Sprenkle, D. H., & Sheehan, R. (1985). Enrichment outcome research: A meta-analysis of premarital, marital, and family interventions. *Journal of Marital and Family Therapy, 11* (3), 257–271.

Abstract

This article presents findings from meta-analysis of 85 studies of premarital, marital, and family enrichment, representing 3,886 couples or families. The findings are discussed in terms of overall enrichment effectiveness and salient program, subject, design, measurement, and analysis characteristics. The most powerful factors related to outcome were measurement variables.

Hosie, T. W., West, J. D., & Mackey, J. A. (1993). Employment and roles of counselors in employee assistance programs. *Journal of Counseling and Development, 71*, 355–359.

Abstract

Employment and roles of master's-level counselors in employee assistance programs (EAPs) as well as the services offered by the diverse EAP organizations are examined. It was found that master's-level counselors were similar to individuals with master's degrees in social work in employment rate and percentages among EAP staff. Differences in the roles of counselors among the EAP types are presented.

Prout, H. T., & Demartino, R. A. (1986). A meta-analysis of school-based studies of psychotherapy. *Journal of School Psychology, 24* (3), 285–292.

Abstract

The meta-analysis technique is applied to school-based studies of psychotherapy. Thirty-three controlled studies were identified that met the criteria for meta-analysis. Although research efforts in this area offer a relatively small number of appropriate studies, the results of the meta-analysis indicate that psychotherapy in the schools can be viewed as at least moderately effective. Evidence was also found of the greater efficacy of group and behavioral theory interventions and interventions that target observed behaviors and problem-solving abilities.

Shelby, J. S., & Tredinick, M. G. (1995). Crisis intervention with survivors of natural disaster: Lessons from Hurricane Andrew. *Journal of Counseling and Development*, 73 (5), 491–497.

Abstract

This article presents anecdotal evidence from mental health work with Hurricane Andrew survivors in south Florida and discusses implications for general disaster counseling. The mental health workers served a predominantly lower SES group with diverse ethnic identities, all of whom had been left homeless by the 1992 hurricane. Interventions were based on the belief that enhancing clients' perceived power would restore or improve predisaster functioning. Issues presented by adults included helplessness and a sense of loss, both of which were dealt with through individual counseling, stress reduction techniques, and helping the adults increase their sense of mastery. Children experienced regression and anxiety and were treated through play therapy, drawing, and positive reframing. The effects of multicultural issues are noted.

Silverman, W. H., & Beech, R. P. (1984). Length of intervention and client assessed outcome. *Journal of Clinical Psychology*, 40 (2), 475–480.

Abstract

The relationship between length of intervention and client-assessed outcome in clients ($N = 47$) seen in an outpatient program of a community mental health center is explored. The results indicated no differences between single-session and multiple-session clients in terms of demographic background, presenting problems, assessments of agency helpfulness, or problem improvement.

Stinnett, T. A., Havey, J. M., & Oehler-Stinnett, J. (1994). Current test usage by practicing school psychologists: A national survey. *Journal of Psychoeducational Assessment*, 12 (4), 331–350.

Abstract

This study surveyed 123 members of the National Association of School Psychologists to examine the assessment activity of practicing school psychologists. Results indicate that assessment activities still account for about 50% of the practice hours of school psychologists, followed by consultation (20%) and treatment (19%). Subjects reported frequent use of intellectual, behavioral-social-emotional, achievement, and perceptual assessment methods but were less likely to be involved in vocational or preschool assessment. Familiar instruments, such as the Wechsler scales, the Woodcock-Johnson Psychoeducational Battery—Revised, the Wide Range Achievement Test—Revised, and the Vineland Adaptive Behavior Scales were the most used tests. In the social-emotional domain, direct assessment methods (e.g., interview and observation) were more frequently used and were rated as more important than standardized measures.

Syzmanski, E. M., Leahy, M. J., & Linkowski, D. C. (1993). Reported preparedness of certified counselors in rehabilitation counseling knowledge areas. *Rehabilitation Counseling Bulletin*, 37 (2), 146–162.

Abstract

This study investigated the perceived preparedness of certified rehabilitation counselors and assessed differences in perceived preparedness across respondent characteristics. A sample of 1,535 rehabilitation counselors who renewed their certification between March 1991 and October 1992 reported that they were at least moderately prepared in the following areas that constituted the majority of rehabilitation counseling knowledge: vocational services; foundations of rehabilitation; case management and services; group and family counseling; medical and psychosocial aspects; workers' compensation, employer services, and technology; individual counseling and development; social, cultural, and environmental issues; research; and assessment. Significant differences in perceived preparedness on at least one subscale were found for preservice education level, gender, job setting, job title, and years of experience.

Watts, R. E., Trusty, J., Erdman, P., & Canada, R. (1996). Texas LPCs' perceptions of their counselor training: A brief report. *TCA Journal, 24* (1), 9–14.

Abstract

This study examined counseling professionals' perceptions of how well their counselor training program prepared them for their work as professional counselors. Two hundred and twelve master's-level counselors licensed by the Texas State Board of Examiners of Professional Counselors were surveyed. Results show the subjects to be somewhat neutral regarding the effectiveness of their preparation. Subjects perceived their training in normal human development and theories of counseling to be adequate, whereas their training in substance abuse counseling, treatment planning, private practice, and the DSM system was perceived as inadequate.

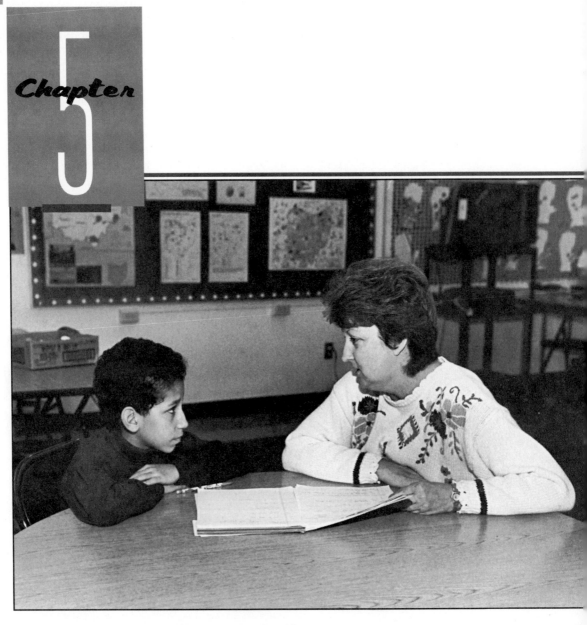

Chapter 5

Individual Counseling

Counseling is, of course, the single most important activity in which counselors engage. They are called counselors not because they give tests, offer career planning information, or provide consultation, but because they counsel. Counseling is a skill and process distinguished from advising, directing, perhaps listening sympathetically, and appearing to be interested in many of the same concerns as professional counselors. To introduce this topic, the objectives of this chapter are to (a) orient the reader to traditional and popular theories of counseling, (b) introduce and briefly discuss the counseling process, and (c) examine some basic counseling skills.

Individual counseling has, since the early days of the movement into both school and nonschool settings, been identified as the heart of any program of counseling services. All other professional activities of the counselor lead to this most important function. Test results, career information, and autobiographies are all relatively meaningless if they do not provide information that enhances the effectiveness of the counseling process.

Many definitions of counseling are available to students of counseling. There are semantic differences, of course, but most definitions begin by suggesting that individual counseling is a one-to-one relationship involving a trained counselor and focuses on some aspects of a client's adjustment, developmental, or decision-making needs. This process provides a relationship and communications base from which the client can develop understanding, explore possibilities, and initiate change. In this setting, it is the counselor's competence that makes positive outcomes possible. The counselor's skills and knowledge provide the appropriate framework and direction that maximize the client's potential for positive results. Untrained and unskilled helpers, regardless of their best intentions, cannot duplicate the functions of the professional counselor.

Though counseling is viewed as a helping relationship, with the counselor as the helper, it is also a relationship in which the client must assume some responsibility to participate fully, cooperatively, and willingly. Only then can the potential benefits of the counseling relationship and process be possible.

THEORIES OF COUNSELING

Because the various definitions of counseling differ little in actual meaning, one might assume that all counselors function similarly in like situations; that, like so many robots, we would all respond similarly, interpret client information in the same manner, and agree on desired outcomes in specific counseling situations. Thus, a chapter on counseling techniques might read like a cookbook in which recipes were specified for the kinds of situations and the kinds of outcomes desired for these situations. Of course, nothing could be further from the truth. As definitions vary in counseling, the approaches that professional counselors use vary even more. Although the variety of these approaches may, at times, confuse the beginning student and the general public as well, it is fair to say that unlike recipes, they have proven useful in the provision of counseling services to various populations. These approaches are usually distinguished and described under their theoretical labels.

Theoretical models for counseling have their origins in the values and beliefs of persons who, in turn, have converted these into a philosophy and a theoretical model for counseling. These values and beliefs form a rationale for what one does, how one does it, and under what

circumstance. It predicts probable outcomes for different sets of conditions. Theory summarizes the information base of the philosophy and enables one to draw conclusions.

For the beginner as well as the experienced counselor, theories provide guidelines that
have been tested by experienced counselors. They explain behaviors. They may predict desirable or undesirable outcomes in given circumstances. Theories can also assist counselors in
organizing client data into a coherent and meaningful framework and developing counseling
strategies appropriate to the situation.

Of course, for the established theories, research has played an important part in bridging the gap between theory and practice through verifying or proving theoretical premises.
This progress from theory to practice is depicted in Figure 5-1.

In the next section, we will present brief descriptions of some of the popular counseling
theories. Counselors in training, and certainly the proactive professional counselor, should be
knowledgeable about the popularly recognized theories of counseling—their premises, characteristics, differences or similarities, and implications for practice. It should be stated, however, that these and other recognized theories in the field of counseling provide only a base
that the practicing counselor will modify in order to suit the unique situation in which he or
she functions and his or her unique personality.

As these traditional theories of counseling are examined, it is important to recognize
their roots in European and North American cultures. The pioneering theorists did not consider multicultural perspectives in their origins. Thus, all these theories can be enhanced by
multicultural awareness and considerations. In fact, the counselor's failure to recognize the
unique cultural background of clients from diverse backgrounds will handicap her or his client
interaction. All this suggests that counselors consider the extended background—family, support networks, coping styles, and so forth—plus the cultural context of the client for integration into their theoretical orientation.

Finally, we believe that eventually every counselor will adopt that theory or combination of theories, plus a multicultural perspective, that is most appropriate for him or her; with
which he or she is most comfortable and effective; and that reflects what he or she is as a person *and* a professional.

Psychoanalytic Theory

For beginning counselors, the study of psychoanalytic theory is more important from a historic perspective rather than as a model for adoption. Sigmund Freud and Freudian therapy
have been prominently associated with the practice of psychoanalysis and psychotherapy
throughout the 20th century and influenced the development of numerous other theories as
well. Freud developed and popularized worldwide the first accepted comprehensive theory of
personality development, which included not only a theory of personality but a method of
therapy as well. Freud broadened the field of psychology and gave it a new and exciting look,
though not without controversy, and assured himself of a prominent place in the history of
the fields of counseling, psychology, and psychotherapy.

Psychoanalytic theory views the personality as divided into three major systems; the id, the
ego, and the superego. The id is inherited and thus is present from birth. The id is believed by
many to work on the pleasure principle and provides the drive for the pursuit of personal wants.

The ego is viewed as the only rational element of the personality. The ego also has contact with the world of reality. Because of this contact with reality, it controls consciousness and
provides realistic and logical thinking and planning and will moderate the desires of the id.

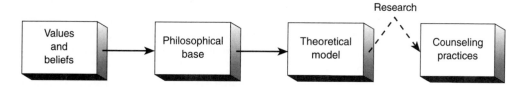

Figure 5-1   Bridging the Gap from Theory to Practice.

The superego represents the mind's conscience and operates on a principle of moral realism. It represents a person'a moral code, usually based on one's perceptions of the moralities and values of society. As a result of its role, the superego in a sense is responsible for providing rewards, such as pride and self-love, and punishments, such as feelings of guilt or inferiority to its owner.

In this triangle, the superego, because it resides largely in the subconscious, is most aware of the impulses of the id and seeks to direct the ego to control the id. As a result, psychoanalytic theory views tension, conflict, and anxiety as inevitable and that human behavior is therefore directed toward reducing this tension. In this context (reduction of tension), Freud's daughter Anna further advanced psychoanalytic theory when she expanded on the concept of defense mechanisms. These may be characterized as mechanisms that help individuals reduce tensions, adapting or adjusting to situations through distortion or denial which would otherwise create high levels of stress or anxiety. It is fair to say that all of us use these techniques on occasion—perhaps to assuage our guilt feelings regarding something we failed to do or to tell ourselves (and maybe others) that we were not supposed to do it in the first place. For the most part, these are normal and operate at an unconscious level. Of course, excuses can be of concern, for example, the individual who rationalizes his or her consistently inappropriate and destructive behavior.

Here are several commonly employed defense mechanisms.

- *Repression* represents those memories, feelings, and thoughts that are stored in the unconscious because their recall may be painful or fearful. Much of what is repressed occurs in childhood and, therefore, may not be readily verbalized. Because repression is usually limited to specific areas or topics, only behavior related to the area will be affected. Repression is viewed as the basic defense mechanism, and psychoanalysis seeks to bring the repressed into the conscious.

- *Rationalization* is a commonly practiced defense mechanism that seeks to justify or provide a seemingly reasonable explanation in order to make undesirable or questionable behaviors appear logical, reasonable, or acceptable. It is frequently used to modify guilt feelings because the valid or true explanation for the behavior would produce feelings of guilt or anxiety.

- The return to an earlier form of behavior or stage of development is called *regression*. This usually occurs when the more mature or appropriate behavior is blocked by feelings of uncertainty, anxiety, fear, conflict, or lack of reward. In some instances, it will also represent a retreat to earlier more automatic responses.

- *Identification* gives one satisfaction or compensation by identifying with others and their achievements. In identification with others, an individual may actually acquire new and useful behaviors.

- *Displacement* represents movement away from one object to another that is less threatening or anxiety producing. A common form of displacement is sublimation, wherein unacceptable urges may be channeled into more acceptable behaviors as, for example, the conversion of sexual interests and energy into nonsexual activities such as sports, religion, work, and so on.
- *Overcompensation* (reaction formation) is the display of behaviors as attitudes that represent the opposite of one's repressed feelings. Anxiety and guilt feelings are repressed and their opposites expressed instead.

In summary, these and other defense mechanisms represent behavioral responses designed to protect the individual's current self-concept against threat.

In the psychoanalytical context, then, reducing tension becomes a major goal of counseling. Because personality conflict is present in all people, nearly everyone can benefit from professional counseling. Inasmuch as the psychoanalytic approach requires insights that in turn rely on openness and self-disclosure, multiculturally oriented counselors would be aware that some Asian, African, and Native Americans would see these traits as signs of immaturity.

Psychoanalytic theory usually views the client as weak and uncertain and in need of assistance in reconstructing a normal personality. The counselor plays the role of the expert who will facilitate or direct this restructuring. The client will be encouraged to talk freely, to disclose unpleasant, difficult, or embarrassing thoughts. The counselor will provide interpretation as appropriate, attempting to increase client insights. This, in turn, may lead to working through the unconscious and eventually to achieve the ability to cope realistically with the demands of the client's world and society as a whole. In this process, among the techniques the psychoanalytic counselor may employ are projective tests, play therapy, dream analysis, and free association, all of which require special training, usually available only at the doctoral level.

Individual Psychology

Individual Psychology is often called Adlerian therapy after its initial developer, Alfred Adler. Adler was a colleague of Freud who disagreed with him on some basic issues. This disagreement led Adler to break away entirely from Freud's circle. Adler's works have had, in turn, a profound impact on many therapists who followed, such as Albert Ellis, Victor Frankl, Rudolf Dreikurs, Rollo May, and William Glasser.

Individual Psychology sees the person holistically and focuses on the uniqueness of individuals. Adler's view of humans offered a positive and refreshing alternative focus to Freudian psychoanalytic theory. At the core of his theory was the belief that there exists within the human being an innate drive to overcome perceived inferiorities and to develop one's own potential for self-actualization, and, that given a positive environment, this growth will take place.

What is it that keeps a person from moving in a fast and easy manner toward this full realization of self? For Adler it was feelings of inferiority. A person permits himself or herself to experience these feelings through three sources: (1) our biological dependency and dependency in general as infants, (2) our image of ourselves in relationship to the grandeur of the universe, and (3) organ inferiority. The drive within ourselves, however, enables us to compensate for these feelings and strive for superiority and perfection.

Adlerian theory has been, on occasion, referred to as *socioteleological* for its viewpoint of individuals constantly striving to achieve their goals. He also stressed the importance of developing the client's social interests and reeducating clients so that they can live in society as one who gives to the society as well as receives from it.

When a person comes for therapy, it is assumed that she or he is experiencing incongruence and discomfort in either work, friendship, or love. The counseling process, then, is seen as a means by which the therapist and counselee work together to help the counselee develop awareness as well as healthier attitudes and behaviors so as to function more fully in society. Developing social interest is seen as the salient variable of one's mental health.

The Adlerian counseling process involves four stages: (1) establishing relationship, (2) diagnosis, (3) insight/interpretation, and (4) reorientation. In the first session, the counselor establishes a relationship with the client through a subjective/objective interview in which the client is helped to feel comfortable, accepted, respected, and cared about. Through an objective component of the interview, the client is encouraged to explain what specifically has helped him or her determine the need for counseling. The client is asked to discuss how things are going in each of the life task areas. Also during this first session, the counseling process is explained and discussed with the client. The diagnostic stage involves the lifestyle interview, a formal assessment procedure that looks at things such as family constellation, perceptions of self in relationship to siblings, perceptions of parents, early recollections, and recurrent dreams.

The interpretation phase is the time during which the counselor and the client develop insight from the lifestyle interview into the client's basic mistakes by analyzing and discussing the convictions, goals, and movement that the client developed early in life and the ensuing thought, emotional, and behavioral patterns and attitudes.

The reorientation stage is perhaps the most critical, for it is in this stage that the therapist helps the counselee to move from intellectual insight to actual development and expression of healthier attitudes and behaviors. Here the client—with the counselor's support, encouragement, and direction—actively pursues changing unhealthy ways of thinking, feeling, and behaving to ways that are more satisfying and healthy for herself or himself and society.

Adler was one of the pioneers in family therapy, which made spin off contributions to the field of elementary counseling. Today, concepts of Adlerian counseling are also being used in working with children of divorce and/or remarriage.

Client-Centered Theory

Client-centered (now frequently referred to as person-centered) counseling is another historically significant and influential theory. This theory was originally developed and described by Carl R. Rogers as a reaction against what he considered the basic limitations of psychoanalysis. As a result of his influence, this particular approach is often referred to as Rogerian counseling.

The Rogerian approach stresses the client's capability and responsibility to create ways to more accurately identify and cope with reality. The better clients know themselves, the more likely they are to identify the most appropriate behaviors for themselves. Rogers emphasized the importance of the counselor being a warm, genuine, empathic, and caring individual.

In understanding the client-, or person-centered, approach to counseling, it is helpful to be aware of the personality basis for this theory, as presented by Rogers (1959a) in the form of 19 propositions. The lead statements for each of these propositions follows.

1. Every individual exists in a continually changing world of experience of which he is the center.
2. The organism reacts to the field as it is experienced and perceived. This perceptual field is, for the individual, "reality."

3. The organism reacts as an organized whole to this phenomenal field.

4. The organism has one basic tendency and striving—to actualize, maintain, and enhance the experiencing organism.

5. Behavior is basically the goal-directed attempt of the organism to satisfy its needs as experienced, in the field as perceived.

6. Emotion accompanies and in general facilitates goal-directed behavior, the kind of emotion being related to the seeking versus the consummatory aspects of the behavior, and the intensity of the emotion being related to the perceived significance of the behavior for the maintenance and enhancement of the organism.

7. The best vantage point for understanding behavior is from the internal frame of reference of the individual himself.

8. A portion of the total perceptual field gradually becomes differentiated as the self.

9. As a result of interaction with the environment, and particularly as a result of evaluational interaction with others, the structure of self is formed—an organized, fluid, but consistent conceptual pattern of perceptions of characteristics and relationships of the "I" or the "me," together with values attached to these concepts.

10. The values attached to experiences and the values which are a part of the self-structure, in some instances, are values experienced directly by the organism, and in some instances are values introjected or taken over from others, but perceived in distorted fashion, as if they had been experienced directly.

11. As experiences occur in the life of the individual, they are either (a) symbolized, perceived, and organized into some relationship to the self; (b) ignored because there is no perceived relationship to the self-structure; (c) denied symbolization or given a distorted symbolization because the experience is inconsistent with the structure of the self.

12. Most of the ways of behaving which are adopted by the organism are those which are consistent with the concept of self.

13. Behavior may, in some instances, be brought about by organic experiences and needs which have not been symbolized. Such behavior may be inconsistent with the structure of the self, but in such instances the behavior is not "owned" by the individual.

14. Psychological maladjustment exists when the organism denies to awareness significant sensory and visceral experiences, which consequently are not symbolized and organized into the gestalt of the self-structure. When this situation exists, there is a basic or potential psychological tension.

15. Psychological adjustment exists when the concept of the self is such that all the sensory and visceral experiences of the organism are, or may be assimilated on a symbolic level into a consistent relationship with the concept of self.

16. Any experience which is inconsistent with the organization or structure of self may be perceived as a threat, and the more of these perceptions there are, the more rigidly the self-structure is organized to maintain itself.

17. Under certain conditions, involving primarily complete absence of any threat to the self-structure, experiences which are inconsistent with it may be perceived, and examined, and the structure of self revised to assimilate and include such experiences.

18. When the individual perceives and accepts into one consistent and integrated system all his sensory and visceral experiences, then he is necessarily more understanding of others and is more accepting of others as separate individuals.

19. As the individual perceives and accepts into his self-structure more of his organic experiences, he finds that he is replacing his present value system—based so largely upon introjections

which have been distortedly symbolized—with a continuing organismic valuing process.*
(pp. 483–524)

In the counseling relationship, six conditions account for personality change in the client. These were presented by Rogers (1959a, 1967a).

1. Two people (a therapist and a client) are in psychological contact. (1967a, p. 73)
2. The client is experiencing a state of anxiety, distress, or incongruence.
3. The therapist is genuine (truly himself or herself) in relating to the client.
4. The therapist feels or exhibits unconditional positive regard for the client.
5. The therapist exhibits empathetic understanding of the client's frame of reference and conveys this understanding to the client.
6. The therapist succeeds to a minimum degree in communicating empathetic understanding and unconditional positive regard to the client. (1959a, p. 213)

Some of the changes expected from a successful utilization of this approach are

- The person comes to see himself differently.
- He accepts himself and his feelings more fully.
- He becomes more self-confident and self-directing.
- He becomes more the person he would like to be.
- He becomes more flexible, less rigid, in his perceptions.
- He adopts more realistic goals for himself.
- He behaves in a more mature fashion.
- He changes his maladjustive behaviors, even such a long-established one as chronic alcoholism.
- He becomes more acceptant of others.
- He becomes more open to the evidence, both to what is going on outside of himself, and to what is going on inside of himself.
- He changes in his basic personality characteristics in constructive ways. (Rogers, 1959b, p. 232)

Thus, the client-centered model is optimistic in its view of humankind. Clients are seen as being basically good and possessing the capabilities for self-understanding, insight, problem solving, decision making, change, and growth.

The counselor's role is that of a facilitator and reflector. The counselor facilitates a counselee's self-understanding and clarifies and reflects back to the client the expressed feelings and attitudes of the client. Giving information for problem solving in a client-centered context is not usually considered a counselor responsibility. The client-centered counselor also would not seek to direct the mediation of the counselee's inner world, but, rather, to provide a climate in which the counselee could bring about change in himself or herself.

In recent years, another label, *self-theory*, has been increasingly used instead of the traditional client-centered, nondirective, or Rogerian labels. This has probably resulted from the emphasis on enhancement of the self, the capacity of one's self, self-actualization, and self-

---

*From C. R. Rogers (1959), "A Theory of Therapy, Personality and Interpersonal Relationships as Developed in the Client-Centered Framework" in S. Koch, *Psychology: A Study of Science*, Vol. 3. Copyright © 1959. Reprinted with permission of McGraw-Hill, Inc.

perceptions. Regardless of one's choice of label, this theory, originated by Rogers, continues to exert its influence on the field of counseling.

From a multicultural frame of reference, Ivey, Ivey, and Simek-Morgan (1993) indicate

> the emphasis in Rogerian theory on ideal self and real self tends to obscure relational and broader environmental issues. As such, you may find it helpful to add a broader focus when working with many clients. For example, it would be within the Rogerian tradition to help clients focus on *real relationships and ideal relationships*. Such a focus would help individuals think of themselves as persons in relation to significant others. This focus would entail a change in the style of counseling and therapy usually associated with Rogers. But when one considers Rogers's life development, one would suspect that these concepts are not too distant from where he was heading at the end of his life. Clearly, Rogers was focusing on a more *ideal world* as contrasted with the *real world* (*Umwelt*). (p. 304)

During the National Defense Education Act (NDEA) era, Rogers's popular writings further advanced the public image of the counselor and counseling. His tremendous contributions to the profession itself in the areas of both individual and group counseling created a whole new wave of nondirective counselors and left a positive lasting impact on the whole field of mental health and the helping professions.

Behavioral Theory

Each of us have our own unique patterns of behavior, and most of us believe we understand at least why we behave the way we do and, perhaps, even the behavior of identifiable others as well. Although we may have only anecdotal rather than scientific evidence, we may, nonetheless, as countless others do, develop our own personal theory of behavior. The scientific development of behavioral theory and conditioning can be traced directly from Pavlov's 19th-century discoveries in classical conditioning. Important foundations for the behavioral approach later were discovered from the system of psychology called behaviorism, founded by American psychologist John B. Watson (1913) and expressed initially in his article "Psychology as the Behaviorist Views It."

Significant research and publication on the subject were conducted by Watson, Thorndike, and others, but it was not until B. F. Skinner systematically refined and developed his principles of behaviorism that the behavioral theory moved toward its current popularity. The behaviorist views behavior as a set of learned responses to events, experiences, or stimuli in a person's life history. The behaviorist believes that behavior can be modified by providing appropriate learning conditions and experiences. The experimental origins of the behaviorist's approach explain their indifference to concepts that cannot be empirically observed or measured. Thus, rather than being concerned with the emotional dynamics of behavior characteristic of the insight approaches of either Freudians or Rogerians, the behaviorist focuses on specific behavioral goals, emphasizing precise and repeatable methods. The behavioral theoretical approach to counseling has grown steadily since the 1950s and today is utilized by therapists in a wide variety of settings. This approach has been successful in the treatment of smoking, weight control and other eating disorders, substance abuse, speech difficulties, behavior problems, and so forth.

For the behaviorist, counseling involves the systematic use of a variety of procedures that are intended specifically to change behavior in terms of mutually established goals between a client and a counselor. The procedures employed encompass a wide variety of techniques drawn from knowledge of learning processes. A current leader in behavioral psychology, John D. Krumboltz (1966), historically placed these procedures into four categories.

1. *Operant Learning.* This approach is based on the usefulness of reinforcers and the timing of their presentation in producing change. Reinforcers may be concrete rewards or expressed as approval or attention.
2. *Imitative Learning.* This approach facilitates acquisition of new responses by exposure to models performing the desired behaviors.
3. *Cognitive Learning.* This technique fosters learning of appropriate responses by simply instructing the client how he may better adapt.
4. *Emotional Learning.* Involves substitution of acceptable emotional responses for unpleasant emotional reactions, using techniques derived from classical conditioning. (pp. 13–20)

John Krumboltz popularized behavioral approaches to counseling, as he identified counseling as a way to help people learn to solve their problems. Learning and relearning are viewed as ways to help people make changes. Krumboltz also applied behavioral theory in terms of quantifying and measuring baselines and successes in counseling.

Arnold Lazarus developed a systematic multimodal approach to counseling and psychotherapy based on a behavioral model. In his model, he uses the acronym BASIC-ID to account for all of the facets of a client's life. Multimodal therapy is not considered behavioral purely because it is based on reconditioning, but rather, it is behavioral because it is action oriented and focuses on what is observable.

The cognitive-behaviorists helped popularize behavioral methods of skill practice and homework assignments. Meichenbaum, for example, has created a cognitive-behavioral approach to skill improvement, using self-monitoring and self-verbalization.

Behaviorists believe that stating the goals of counseling in terms of observable behavior is more useful than stating goals that are more broadly defined, such as self-understanding or acceptance of self. This means that counseling outcomes should be identifiable in terms of overt behavior changes. Three examples of behavioral change appropriate to counseling are the altering of behavior that is not satisfactory, the learning of the decision-making process, and problem prevention.

In many ways, practicing behavioral counselors follow a similar approach as other counselors in clarifying and understanding the needs of their clients. They use reflection, summarization, and open-ended inquiries. But, rather than probing for deeper feelings, they are seeking to better understand dimensions of the client's situation and environment. Feelings are secondary to behaviors. Behavioral counselors attempt to uncover the specific antecedents, circumstances, and consequences of client situations so that they will be able to develop specific goals, objectives, and treatment plans.

Behavioral counselors, however, take a more directive role than many counselors in initiating and directing therapeutic activities. Sessions tend to be structured and action oriented. Behavioral counselors often take on roles of teacher or coach.

Counselors utilizing behavioral theory assume that the client's behavior is the result of conditioning. The counselor further assumes that each individual reacts in a predictable way to any given situation or stimulus, depending on what has been learned.

Ivey, Ivey, and Simek-Morgan (1993) warn that:

the behavioral approach can run into problems in multicultural situations over the issue of *control*. Early ventures in behavioral psychology often gave the therapist, counselor, or teacher almost complete power, and decisions sometimes focused on controlling the client rather than helping the client control him- or herself. Behavioral psychology has been forced to overcome some of these early problems and the resultant fears among minority clients and their advocates. (p. 219)

Gilliland, James, and Bowman (1998) point out that:

most modern behavioral counselors approach the helping process from a much broader perspective than was the case a few years ago. Rather than viewing the counselor as the expert who scientifically develops and imposes behavior-modifying processes on the client, the modern approach strives to involve the client in the analysis, planning, process, and evaluation of his or her behavior-management program. Modern behavioral counselors seek to help the client extinguish a wide range of maladaptive behaviors and learn adaptive behaviors needed to establish and maintain targeted goals and consequences. The counselor collaborates with the client. The counselor is expected to have training and experience in human behavior modification and also to serve as consultant, teacher, adviser, reinforcer, and facilitator. (p. 206)

Hackney and Cormier (1996) point out that:

characteristics of clients who seem to have the most success with behavioral interventions include:

- People with a strong goal orientation—motivated by achieving goals or getting results.
- People who are action-oriented—need to be active, goal-focused, participating in the helping process (this includes several cultural groups, including Asians and African Americans).
- People who are interested in changing a discrete and limited (two to three) number of behaviors. (p. 213)

Rational Emotive Therapy

As is often the case, a person is associated with the formulation and development of a theory, such as Carl R. Rogers and client-centered therapy. A comparatively recent movement, rational emotive therapy (RET), has been formulated by Albert Ellis. This theory is based on the assumption that people have the capacity to act in either a rational or irrational manner. Rational behavior is viewed as effective and potentially productive, whereas irrational behavior results in unhappiness and nonproductivity. Ellis assumes that many types of emotional problems result from irrational patterns of thinking. This irrational pattern may begin early and be reinforced by significant others in the individual's life as well as by the general culture and environment. According to Ellis, people with emotional problems develop belief systems that lead to implicit verbalizations or self-talk resting on faulty logic and assumptions. And what a person tells her- or himself is intimately related to the way that person feels and acts.

The basic foundation of Ellis's theorizing is contained in this ABCDEF paradigm. Ivey et al. (1993) note that:

perhaps Ellis's most important contribution is his A-B-C theory of personality, which can be summarized as follows:

A—the "objective" facts, events, behavior that an individual encounters.

B—the person's beliefs about A.

C—the emotional consequences, or how a person feels and acts about A. (p. 259)

The D-E-Fs of the paradigm are aimed at the promotion and maintaining of change. D indicates the counselor's disputing of the client's irrational thoughts, E refers to the presumed consequences of the therapist's interventions, and F stands for the new feelings the client has regarding the situation.

Ellis identified a series of 11 values or ideas that are universal in Western societies and inevitably lead to neurotic behaviors.

1. I believe I must be loved or approved of by virtually everyone with whom I come in contact.
2. I believe I should be perfectly competent, adequate, and achieving to be considered worthwhile.
3. Some people are bad, wicked, or villainous, and therefore should be blamed and punished.
4. It is a terrible catastrophe when things are not as I would want them to be.
5. Unhappiness is caused by circumstances that are out of my control.
6. Dangerous or fearsome things are sources of great concern and their possibility for harm should be a constant concern for me.
7. It is easier to avoid certain difficulties and responsibilities than it is to face them.
8. I should be dependent to some extent on other persons and should have some person on whom I can rely to take care of me.
9. Past experiences and events are what determine my present behavior; the influence of the past cannot ever be erased.
10. I should be quite upset over other peoples' problems and disturbances.
11. There is always a right or perfect solution to every problem, and it must be found or the results will be catastrophic. (Hackney & Cormier, 1996, p. 182)

The goal of RET is to reduce or eliminate irrational behavior. In order to change this undesired behavior, clients have to learn how their thinking, emotions, and behavior are interrelated. Negative and self-defeating thoughts and emotions must be reorganized so that the client's thinking becomes logical and rational.

The RET therapist does not believe that a personal relationship between the client and counselor is a prerequisite to successful counseling. In fact, the therapist may frequently challenge, provoke, and probe the irrational beliefs of the client. In the relationship, the counselor is viewed more as a teacher and the client as a student. As a result, procedures may include not only teaching and related activities such as reading or other assignments but also questioning and challenging, even confrontation tactics, contracts, suggestions, and persuasion. RET can be applied not only to individual therapy but also to group therapy, marathon encounter groups, marriage counseling, and family therapy.

RET is frequently relatively short-term and is not helpful with the seriously disturbed. Clients usually have little difficulty in learning the underlying principles and terminology of RET. Although RET therapists may challenge clients, such confrontations with minority clients should not bring into question the client's cultural values and background.

Reality Therapy

Another theory of counseling that has gained popularity in recent decades is that of reality therapy, largely developed by William Glasser. Glasser's fairly straightforward approach places confidence in the counselee's ability to deal with his or her needs through a realistic or rational process. From a reality therapy standpoint, counseling is simply a special kind of training that attempts to teach an individual what he should have learned during normal growth in a rather short time.

Glasser (1984) suggested that reality therapy is

applicable to individuals with any sort of psychological problem, from mild emotional upset to complete psychotic withdrawal. It works well with behavior disorders of the aged and the young, and with drug- and alcohol-related problems. It has been applied widely in schools, corrections institutions, mental hospitals, general hospitals, and business management. It focuses on the present and upon getting people to understand that they choose essentially all their actions in an attempt to fulfill basic needs. When they are unable to do this they suffer, or cause others to suffer. The therapist's task is to lead them toward better or more responsible choices that are almost always available. (p. 320)

Glasser (1981) conceptualized reality therapy in eight steps.

1. Make friends or get involved, or get along; create a relationship or gain rapport.
2. Deemphasize the patient's history and find out what you are doing *now*.
3. Help the patient learn to make an evaluation of his or her behavior. Help the patient find out if what he or she is saying is really *helpful*.
4. Once you have evaluated the behavior, then you can begin to explore alternative behaviors—behaviors that may prove more helpful.
5. Get a commitment to a plan of change.
6. Maintain an attitude of "No excuses if you don't do it." By now the patient is committed to the change and must learn to be responsible in carrying it out.
7. Be tough without punishment. Teach people to do things without being punished if they do not; it creates a more positive motivation.
8. Refuse to give up. Once clients realize the counselor will not give up, they feel more support and work proceeds with more efficiency and promise.

In 1989, Glasser's *Control Theory* was published, elaborating upon his reality theory. In his control theory, Glasser identified his concept of the components of total behavior as: (1) active behavior, (2) thinking, (3) feeling, and (4) physiology as the capacity to produce voluntary and involuntary body mechanisms. Glasser believes that control theory could help individuals take more effective control of their lives; that human beings are control systems, and this is how they function to fulfill their needs. Reality therapy (and control theory) suggest that humans have four needs, as follows, which are encoded in their genes.

- The need to belong, to love, cooperate, and share
- The need for power
- The need for freedom
- The need for fun and recreation

Reality therapy focuses on present behavior and, consequently, does not emphasize the client's past history. When using this approach, the counselor functions as a teacher and a model. Reality therapy is based on the premise that there is a single psychological need that is present throughout life: the need for identity, which includes a need to feel a sense of uniqueness, separateness, and distinctiveness. The need for identity, which accounts for the dynamics of behavior, is seen as universal among all cultures.

Reality therapy is based on the anticipation that the client will assume personal responsibility for her or his well-being. The acceptance of this responsibility, in a sense, helps a person to achieve autonomy or a state of maturity whereby she or he relies on her or his own internal support. Whereas many of the counseling theories suggest that the counselor should function in a noncommital way, reality therapists praise clients when they act responsibly and indicate disapproval when they do not.

Glasser had an intense interest in education. In his book *Reality Therapy* (1965), he described his concepts for helping children in problem solving. Glasser believed that the public schools were failure-prone and promoted a success model for schools, rather than what he saw as the traditional model of failure. As a result, reality therapy has been successfully implemented in not only agencies and mental health institutions but also in many schools and school systems. He went on to publish his ideas regarding education in his best-seller book, *Schools Without Failure* (1969), in which he suggested a program to eliminate failure and to replace the traditional model of memory work, irrelevant instruction, and discipline with a model stressing relevance, prevention, and success. He sought to create an environment that would motivate and involve students in the development of responsible behavior. He also sought to establish ways of involving parents and the community in the schools and in their children's education.

Both in and out of school, reality therapy stresses the importance of making a plan through which the client can improve his or her behavior. This plan should lead to behavior that enables the client to gain satisfaction and, even at times, favorable recognition as well.

Transactional Analysis

Transactional analysis (TA) is a cognitive-behavioral approach that assumes a person has the potential for choosing and redirecting or reshaping one's own destiny. Eric Berne did much to develop and popularize this theory in the 1960s. It is designed to help a client review and evaluate early decisions and to make new, more appropriate choices.

TA views normal personality as a product of healthy parenting (I'm OK, You're OK). Abnormal personality results when the child must play games to gain approval. Transactional analysis then seeks to understand the transactions between individuals in order to understand the different personalities that are a part of each of us. Each of these personalities behave in their own distinct patterns and are, at different times, in control of the individual. When one of the three ego states is unwilling to relinquish its control and asserts it rigidly, especially at inappropriate times, the client is in difficulty and in need of psychological assistance. Transactional analysis will seek to restore a damaged ego and develop the client's capacity to use all ego states appropriately, especially the adult, which is needed to govern one's life.

Thus, transactional analysis places a great deal of emphasis on the ego, which, from this viewpoint, consists of three states: child, parent, and adult.

Child: A set of behaviors, feelings and/or attitudes that are the relics of the individual's childhood and are important in building a person's adult self-concept.

Parent: A product of "recordings" from an individual's parents that are passed on and/or acted on. This is sometimes referred to as parental conditioning.

Adult: This ego state develops from the assimilation of the individual's unique experiences from childhood on. These are translated into facts which then become regulatory in the individual's life and thus, the "adult" is the most changeable of the three ego states.

Each of these states can take charge of the individual to the point that his or her observable behavior indicates "who's in charge" (adult, parent, or child). The client is assisted in gaining social control of his or her life by learning to use all ego states where appropriate. The ultimate goal is to help the client change from inappropriate life positions and behaviors (life scripts) to new more productive behaviors while coming from an "I'm OK" position.* (Gibson, Mitchell, & Basile, 1993, p. 74)

An essential technique in TA counseling is the contract that precedes each counseling step. This contract between counselor and counselee is a way of training or preparing people to make their own important decisions. In addition to the contract technique, transactional analysis also utilizes questionnaires, life scripts, structural analysis, role-playing, analysis of games and rituals, and "stroking" (reinforcement). Although not a counseling technique, transactional analysis sessions are tape-recorded in their entirety.

At each stage of counseling, the decision to go ahead is squarely up to the counselee. (This is the way the counselor protects himself or herself from implications that the counseling is being forced on the counselee.) The counselor may specify conditions to client participation in contracts, such as requiring the counselee to define, in advance, what advantage might ensue from their joint effort.

Transactional analysis, of course, focuses on the individual, but it is a procedure for counseling persons within a group setting. TA counselors feel that the group setting facilitates the process of providing feedback to persons about the kind of transactions in which they engage. The counseling group, then, represents a microcosm of the real world. In this setting, the individual group members are there to work on their own objectives and the counselor acts as the group leader.

Gestalt Counseling

"Gestalt therapy, developed by Frederick Perls, is a therapeutic approach in which the therapist assists the client toward self-integration and toward learning to utilize his energy in appropriate ways to grow, develop, and actualize" (George & Cristiani, 1995, p. 66). The primary focus of this approach is the present—the here and now. This approach implies that the past is gone and the future has yet to arrive; therefore, only the present is important.

Gestalt counseling also has as its major objective the integration of the person. In popular terminology, this might be called getting it all together. Perls (1948) writes

> The treatment is finished when the patient has achieved the basic requirements: a change in outlook, a technique of adequate self-expression and assimilation, and the ability to extend awareness to the verbal level. He has then reached that state of integration which facilitates its own development, and he can now be safely left to himself. (p. 58)

In order to achieve this togetherness, the counselor seeks to increase the client's awareness. As a result, the counselor functions in a way that provides the client with an atmosphere conducive to the discovery of client needs, or what the client has lost because of environmental demands, and in which the client can experience the necessary discovery and growth.

In this process, the counselor will engage the client in what Perls labels a here and now discussion. The counselor attempts to provide the client assistance in identifying what she needs to become independent—to not be dependent on others. In order to accomplish this, the client must work on getting her act together in order to function as a systematic whole

---

*From Gibson, Robert L., Mitchell, Marianne H., and Basile, Sherry K., *Counseling in the Elementary School: A Comprehensive Approach.* Copyright © 1993 by Allyn and Bacon. Reprinted by permission.

encompassing behaviors, feelings, thoughts, and attitudes. In this process, the client must also learn to take responsibility for herself.

Gestalt counselors believe that people always act to organize stimuli into total pictures or wholes. Several of the principles that have been developed to explain this process were stated by Hansen, Stevic, and Warner (1986).

> *Principle of Closure:* When we perceive a figure that is incomplete, our mind acts to finish the figure and perceives it as complete.
>
> *Principle of Proximity:* The relative distance of stimuli from each other within the perceptual field determines how they are seen.
>
> *Principle of Similarity:* The similarity of stimuli in the perceptual field causes us to group them together.
>
> Each of these three principles illustrates how the human mind seeks to make sense from the vast array of stimuli in the phenomenal field by pulling things together. The important point is that the stimuli have meaning only as they are organized in the mind by the individual. (p. 130)

Cited by George and Cristiani (1995), Passons lists eight assumptions about the nature of humans that act as the framework for Gestalt counseling.

> 1. Individuals are composite wholes made up of interrelated parts. None of these parts—body, emotions, thoughts, sensations, and perceptions—can be understood outside the context of the whole person.
> 2. Individuals are also part of their own environment and cannot be understood apart from it.
> 3. People choose how they respond to external and internal stimuli; they are actors, not reactors.
> 4. People have the potential to be fully aware of all their sensations, thoughts, emotions, and perceptions.
> 5. Individuals are capable of making choices because they are aware.
> 6. Individuals have the capacity to govern their own lives effectively.
> 7. People cannot experience the past and the future; they can experience only themselves in the present.
> 8. People are neither basically good nor bad. (p. 66)

From these assumptions we can conclude that the Gestalt therapist has a positive view of the individual's capacity for self-direction. Furthermore, the client must be encouraged to utilize this capacity and take responsibility for his own life—and do that *now*, in the present; he must experience the here and now. Counseling techniques may include "how" and "what" questions, confrontations, "I" statements, and sharing awareness with clients emphasizing this moment.

Other Theories

In addition to the traditional theories of counseling previously described, there are several other popular theoretical approaches of which the beginning counselor should be aware and which can be explored further if of special interest. Then, there is the traditional eclectic approach which enables the counselor to employ the strengths of the various approaches without being wedded to any one specific theory.

Existential Approach

Individuals define who they are by their choices, even though there may be factors beyond one's control that restrict one's choices. It is important for the individual to find meaning in one's life through awareness. However, with freedom comes responsibility. Rollo May and Victor Frankl are well-known existential theorists and writers.

Counseling helps clients recognize outmoded ways of life and become willing to take the responsibility to change, to expand, and to find meaning in their life that is unique to them.

Family Systems Therapy

Family systems theory is based on the assumption that the client cannot be completely understood apart from his or her family. For example, when dramatic changes take place in the family unit, all members of the unit will be affected. Interactions between the individual and her or his family members are usually significant. Mentally healthy persons have both good family relations and also satisfactory relationships outside the family. Counselors help individuals who need better relationships with important people in their lives in or out of the family unit.

Integrated Theories

In recent years, we have seen continued efforts not only to reinforce and expand on the many traditional counseling theories, but, additionally, to develop new multidimensional and integrated models. One of these, Actualizing Counseling and Psychotherapy, presented by Brammer, Shostrom, and Abrego (1989), represents a creative synthesis approach to counseling theory and human growth. Actualizing counseling is based, in part, upon assumptions drawn from major theoretical approaches.

Actualization counseling represents a developmental therapy derived from *historical and psychodynamic approaches* to counseling. The person is viewed from a perspective of development over time: past, present, and future.

1. Development is cumulative in the sense that early experiences influence the kinds of later experiences a person will have. The meaning and impact of events is influenced by past history, which shapes our expectations and desires.
2. Unresolved conflicts and grief from previous generations can become transmitted in an intergenerational process, which may constrict current personal growth and contribute toward symptom development.
3. Personal development becomes actualized as individuals develop clear internal boundaries. Clear boundaries within oneself involves an awareness of one's own moment-to-moment thoughts and feelings, inner polarities and conflicts, and defensive style.
4. Personality development is dynamic, changing its focus and pattern over time.
5. Development is enhanced by a consistent core identity, which can orchestrate changing life structures or "season," and a broad repertoire of skills to anticipate and manage situational and developmental stress.
6. Insight into one's development over time can be an invaluable assistance in self-actualization. However, insight is of limited usefulness unless it is accompanied by the experience of changed behavior patterns.

Actualization therapy derives important assumptions from *phenomenological approaches* to counseling.

7. We affirm the uniqueness of each individual. We believe that personal development involves learning to become aware of one's own unique strengths, limitations, and purpose.

8. One's representation of events determines behavior more than events themselves. These internal beliefs guide one's behavior with others. Concurrently, circular recursive interactional patterns with others shape one's expectations and interpretations of events. This ongoing feedback from others intentionally or unintentionally confirms or disconfirms existing internal psychological beliefs and structures.

9. One has freedom to choose much of one's future. While much of human behavior is shaped by personal history and systemic forces, the actualizing process assumes that one's future is largely undetermined and a person has wide ranges of freedom to choose.

10. The assumption of freedom places corresponding responsibility on the person for his or her own actualizing. Even though growth takes place in a social context, each person is responsible for initiating and maintaining changes for his or her own life, based on an examined and considered choice of values and principles. The therapist maintains an active neutrality, emphasizing accurate empathic understanding while valuing the person's responsibility to choose his or her own goals.

Behavior therapy contributes an action focus to actualizing therapy as well as an understanding of how change occurs.

11. While some primitive behaviors are reflexive, hence largely genetically determined, and some are the result of chemical or neurological changes, a fundamental assumption of actualization counseling is that social behavior is learned and changes in behavior follow an active learning process. Important life skill deficits, such as competencies in social and work roles, may be mastered through new learning.

12. Most human learning is not automatic but is mediated by cognitive processes. A reciprocal interaction takes place between thoughts, emotions, actions, and feedback from others. Change can begin at any of these processes.

Systems approaches remind us that each individual is embedded within a larger relational context.

13. Actualization is achieved primarily in social interaction with a counselor, teacher, minister, group, friend, or family, but it can also be achieved through self-help methods, such as meditation and imagery. Social interaction becomes the main vehicle for conditions of actualization such as honesty with feelings, awareness of self, freedom of expression, and trust in oneself and others. Therapist support is an important component in helping others to achieve their potential.

14. Transactional patterns play an important role in shaping behavior. Therapeutic change is facilitated by disrupting dysfunctional interactional patterns and providing new feedback. This usually involves altering either the client's interpretation of other people's behavior or the behavior itself.

15. Actualization involves learning to set clear external boundaries with others. These boundaries are evidenced by the ability to maintain a clear sense of self in the midst of an anxious emotional field. Additionally, an actualized person has a capacity for intimacy and a readiness for closeness based on a firm sense of identity to risk the self with others.

16. Actualization is reflected in an attitude of interdependency. An actualizing person has a systemic ethic of responsibility. Personal decisions are made in terms of their impact on the total

web of relationships that the person is involved in, both in the present and in the future. An interdependent person attempts to balance his or her own rights against the claims of others and learns to deal with the inevitable tensions that this will involve.

17. Actualization is in part a by-product of an interdependent attitude in which one transcends self-interest to cooperate with others working for the common good of justice and love. Actualization involves widening the inclusiveness of the circle of those we consider as our "neighbor" from the narrowness of our familiar beginnings toward real solidarity with a commonwealth of people. Pursuit of self-actualization apart from an attitude of interdependency produces alienation from others. (Brammer, Shostrom, & Abrego, pp. 54–55)

Ivey, Ivey, and Simek-Downing (1987) note that an integrated knowledge of skills, theory, and practice is essential for culturally intentional counseling and therapy. Further,

skills form the foundation of effective theory and practice: The culturally intentional therapist knows how to construct a creative decision-making interview and can use microskills to attend to and influence clients in a predicted direction. Important in this process are individual and cultural empathy, client observation skills, assessment of person and environment, and the application of positive techniques of growth and change.

Theory provides organizing principles for counseling and therapy: The culturally intentional counselor has knowledge of alternative theoretical approaches and treatment modalities.

Practice is the integration of skills and theory: The culturally intentional counselor or therapist is competent in skills and theory, and is able to apply them to research and practice for client benefit.

Undergirding integrated competence in skills, theory, and practice is an intentional awareness of one's own personal world-view and how that world-view may be similar to and/or different from the world-view and personal constructions of the client and other professionals.* (p. 413)

Ivey, Ivey, and Simek-Morgan (1997) indicate that

integrative theories are currently becoming more numerous and influential. Meichenbaum's construction of cognitive-behavioral theory brings diverse theories together in a coherent fashion and thus offers a broader scope than traditional behavioral frames of reference. Developmental counseling and therapy integrates theory and practice in a different format and provides an overall rationale for moving from sensory to behavioral to cognitive to systemic approaches. Developmental counseling and therapy, perhaps more than other theories, emphasizes sensorimotor and systemic/cultural foundations of experience, arguing that a network approach is essential if change is to be maintained over time. (p. 407)

Eclectic Counseling

The eclectic approach to counseling is one of long-standing tradition and equally long-standing controversy. It originally provided a safe, middle-of-the-road theory for those counselors in the early years of the profession who neither desired nor felt capable of functioning as purely directive or nondirective. The directive approach, championed by E. G. Williamson and others at the University of Minnesota, took control and, in effect, influenced directly the client's decision making and exerted major influence on the outcomes of the counseling process. The nondirective approach, with Carl R. Rogers as its chief spokesperson, believes that the counselor's role was more that of facilitator than decision maker and that the client must achieve the necessary insights and self-confidence to make one's own decisions.

Defenders of the theory suggested eclecticism as an approach that allowed each individual to construct one's own theory by drawing on established theories. It has often been suggested that the eclectic counselor can choose the best of all counseling worlds. Others contend that eclecticism encourages counselors to become theoretical "jacks of all trades." Certainly, the many theoretical models currently available can be confusing in the absence of a model or definitive guidelines for theory and technique selection.

Eclecticism is not intended to compound the confusion. Rather, it enables the counselor to build a personalized, yet professional system that embodies components of various established theories to blur into an integrated whole. Eclecticism assumes the diversity among individuals and the diversity in human needs and concerns and the environments in which they occur can be best responded to when the counselor has theoretical options and the flexibility to use these within a conceptual and organized framework.

Lazarus and Beutler (1993) explain the differences between unsystematic eclecticism, theoretical integrationism, and technical eclecticism. Unsystematic eclecticism is a "ragtag, shotgun collection of miscellaneous methods" (p. 381) that precludes sound decision making and coherent treatment planning. Theoretical integrationism and technical eclecticism have been offered as alternative approaches to unsystematic eclecticism.

Theoretical integrationism consists of integrating theoretical concepts from two or more counseling theories. It operates under the assumption that the convergence of theories produces enhanced therapeutic procedures. Lazarus and Beutler (1993) suggest that this approach may slow therapeutic progress and lead the counseling process in unproductive directions. The argument is based on their experience that theoretical integration "results in a gallimaufry of methods and ideas that have no consistent rationale and cannot be evaluated" (p. 383).

In response to their concerns, Lazarus and Beutler (1993) offer another approach to counseling and psychotherapy: technical eclecticism. This strategy asserts that

> effective combinations of therapeutic procedures do not necessarily arise from integrating disparate views of psychopathology and even counseling or psychotherapy. Indeed, an effective program of counseling can be based on a systematic process for selecting therapeutic procedures if this decision-making system is, itself, built on empirical demonstrations of the conditions, problems, and clients with whom different procedures are effective. (p. 383)

Technical eclecticism is explained as a systematic method of treatment planning and intervention based on a thorough multimodal assessment of the client (Lazarus, 1989). Such an assessment identifies problems in the following seven areas: behavior, affect, sensation, imagery, cognition, interpersonal, and drugs/biology (BASIC-ID). After the multimodal appraisal, techniques are chosen that (a) fit the needs of the particular client and (b) are supported by data in regard to their efficacy under identified circumstances. Lazarus and Beutler (1993) have found that technical eclecticism is effective and avoids any "recourse to unsystematic eclecticism or needless integration" (p. 383). Furthermore, they explain that technical eclecticism is not atheoretical; theories are necessary in that they yield new interventions that fit the unique qualities of various client problems and situations. However, the theories utilized are grounded "in empirical roots and direct applications to treatment decisions and assessment of efficacy" (p. 384).

We conclude our discussion of eclecticism by noting Wallace's (1986) warning.

Student-counselors cannot shelve their responsibility for constructing a personal theory of counseling by turning it into an intellectual game or academic exercise. Their obligation to their clients is far too real for that. Developing an eclectic approach to therapy requires an enterprising juxtaposition and a genuine confrontation of their work with the values, thoughts, and research of others. And, while independence of observation and thought is essential to an eclectic stance, so are understanding, respect, and tolerance for other theorists. Before students in search of a personal theory of counseling and psychotherapy can choose the best, they must become fully aware of all that are available—no small achievement in a discipline overburdened with diverse and contradictory theories. The eclectic approach, then, is no shortcut to theory formulation. Indeed, when properly traveled, it is a most difficult path to follow. (p. 310)

Theoretical Preferences of Practicing Counselors in Educational Settings

Which theories are the most popular in practice? This question may very appropriately be asked by students in counselor preparation programs, beginning counselors, and even experienced practicing counselors. In an effort to provide some current indications, we conducted a brief, simplistic survey in 1996–1997 of 420 practicing counselors (randomly selected from the American Counseling Association membership directory). (An initial pilot study involved Indiana counselors only.) The results of this survey are displayed in Table 5-1. It should

TABLE 5-1   Survey of Theoretical Preferences of Practicing Counselors

Theory	Schools		Agencies and Nonschool Settings	
	Percentage Preferring	Rank	Percentage Preferring	Rank
Psychoanalytic (Freudian)	0	13.5	5	10.5
Individual psychology (Adlerian)	14	2	10	5.5
Person-centered (Rogerian)	22	1	14	2.5
Rational emotive	12	4	12	4
Reality	10	5	5	10.5
Existential	2	10	2	12
Directive	13	3	10	5.5
Behavior	3	9	6	8
Family systems	1	11.5	14	2.5
Solution-based	4	7.5	2	12
Gestalt	1	11.5	2	12
Transactional analysis	0	13.5	6	8
Eclectic	7	6	16	1
Other	4	7.5	6	8
	N = 170	N = 116		

*Source: From a survey conducted by Robert L. Gibson and Marianne H. Mitchell, 1996–1997.

be noted that while a total of 286 responses were received (representing a return rate of 68%), the number of theoretical orientations that practicing counselors reported frequently drawing upon in their practice ranged from two to seven with a mean of 4.1, indicating a desire for flexibility in meeting the needs of different clients and situations. Table 5-1 represents responses from 170 counselors in educational settings and 116 counselors in nonschool settings. Somewhat surprisingly, only insignificant differences were noted for the differing educational levels, thus the responses are summarized.

BUILDING A PERSONAL THEORY

As Table 5-1 demonstrates, most counselors can identify a traditional theory that has greatly influenced their own personal theory and practice of the art of counseling. It is therefore appropriate to note at this point that, although beginning counseling students should become familiar with the traditional and proven theories, eventually in practice they will develop their own variation or eclectic approach. Your own personal theory will be modified to fit you as a unique individual and perhaps adjusted to more effectively serve special client populations.

As George and Cristiani (1995) point out,

> all counselors interact with clients on the basis of a set of beliefs they have about people and how people change; therefore, the importance of counselors clarifying those beliefs and developing them into a theoretical foundation is emphasized. (p. 119)

In the last analysis, counselors must develop a theoretical framework that fits them personally; a framework in which they can work comfortably, be themselves, and be maximally effective.

We conclude this discussion of counseling theories by noting that theories are like a road map—they indicate to you, the counselor, differing but established routes for reaching a final destination—in this instance, the goal of providing maximum assistance to the client in an efficient and enhancing way. As a beginning counselor, when your experience and professionalism grows, you may develop your own personal eclectic theory. In so doing, you are seeking to identify a framework or system of harmonious parts which will be in harmony with who you are as a person and as a professional—what you believe in, value, and stand for as a person and as a professional. In all endeavors we are most comfortable when we are engaged in something we are sure about and competent in doing. If you know yourself—your strengths and limitations—and have a valid theoretical framework that is understood and comfortable to you, you may proceed with ever-increasing confidence to providing counseling assistance to your clients.

THE CASE OF GEORGE

Applying the differing counseling theories in practice can, of course, lead to differing approaches and interactions with clients experiencing similar needs, and, though approached from different perspectives, each has high probabilities of success in the hands of the skilled theoretician-counselor.

In this section, we present the case of George to illustrate how George might be counseled from seven different theoretical orientations. (We recognize also that not all therapists of a given theoretical orientation will approach the same client concern in the same manner.)

Client: George, 28-year-old male
              Two-year technical college degree in air conditioning and refrigeration
              Twice divorced; no children; three different jobs in eight years

Problem: Interpersonal relationships
              (Can't interact positively with people)
              (Easily irritated by others, especially supervisors)

Psychoanalytic

Counselor in charge. Initial focus on recall of earliest childhood experiences. Were his parents aggressive personalities? What angered him then? Are there particular events in the past that especially angered him? Discuss his history of personal relationships. Be alert to resistance or transference. Free association, dream analysis, hypnosis may be used. Resistance is confronted. Role of sexuality may be explored. Analysis and interpretation precedes treatment, which will be long term.

Adlerian (Individual Psychology)

Process is a joint responsibility of client and counselor. Client's inappropriate social beliefs will be challenged in a humanistic way. Client is encouraged and assisted in developing social skills. Basic assumptions about self (weaknesses) are restructured.

Person-Centered (Rogerian)

Counselor as helper; major responsibility is the client's. Relationship building with George is the first task; trust must be developed. At the same time, George is encouraged to believe in himself; that he has the capacity to get along with others—to make friends. Case histories, analysis in a traditional sense, probing and questioning is out—focus is on building a relationship that is facilitative.

Behaviorism

A relatively short-term approach in which the counselor becomes a teacher to the client. First step would probably be developing a case study of George. George's inappropriate behaviors will be examined and he will be taught new, more appropriate behaviors (hence, the term *behavior modification*).

Rational Emotive Therapy (RET)

Counselor-client almost a business or teacher-student relationship. Client will be shown that anger, hostility, and suspicion are nonproductive emotions. George may be asked to examine how one would normally or rationally react in his circumstances. George may be taught more appropriate behaviors.

Reality

Time will initially be spent building a relationship with George, but, here again, the counselor assumes a teaching role. George will be helped to realistically view his problem and to become more responsible in solving it. Contracts would probably be used.

Gestalt

A warm, caring relationship is established with George. George will be encouraged to become more aware of his inappropriate behaviors and to take responsibility for changing them *now*.

(Action *now*—not talk.) Confrontation, role playing, questioning (how?, why?) may be used, but always in a caring sense.

GOALS OF COUNSELING

Another approach to viewing the various theoretical models is to examine goals in relationship to theories. Table 5-2 outlines a framework in the form of counseling goals that are presented through a developmental continuum. It incorporates various counseling models and integrates Maslow's (1970) hierarchy of needs.

In Table 5-2, the continuum moves from the top (primary goals/needs) to the bottom (secondary goals/needs).

> It is proposed that client goals/needs that are most basic (at the top of the continuum) need to be addressed in counseling before a client can work effectively on higher level goals/needs (at the bottom of the continuum). The continuum is seen as fluid, however, and a counselor might well be working up and down the continuum at different times with a client. (Bruce, 1984, p. 259)

Obviously, counseling goals may also be more simply classified in terms of counselor goals and client goals or the immediate, intermediate, or long-range goals of therapy. Regardless of how one chooses to classify counseling goals, counseling, like all other meaningful activities, must be goal driven, have a purpose, or seek to attain an objective. Broadly speaking, counseling goals may also be separated into the following categories.

Developmental Goals: Developmental goals are those wherein the client is assisted in meeting or advancing her or his anticipated human growth and development (that is, socially, personally, emotionally, cognitively, physical wellness, and so on).

Preventive Goals: Prevention is a goal in which the counselor helps the client avoid some undesired outcome.

Enhancement Goals: If the client possesses special skills and abilities, enhancement means they can be identified and/or further developed through the assistance of a counselor.

Remedial Goals: Remediation involves assisting a client to overcome and/or treat an undesirable development.

Exploratory Goals: Exploration represents goals appropriate to the examining of options, testing of skills, and trying new and different activities, environments, relationships, and so on.

Reinforcement Goals: Reinforcement is used in those instances where clients need help in recognizing that what they are doing, thinking, and/or feeling is okay.

Cognitive Goals: Cognition involves acquiring the basic foundations of learning and cognitive skills.

Physiological Goals: Physiology involves acquiring the basic understandings and habits for good health.

Psychological Goals: Psychology aids in developing good social interaction skills, learning emotional control, developing a positive self-concept, and so on.* (Gibson, Mitchell, Basile, 1993, pp. 87–89)

---

*From Gibson, Robert L., Mitchell, Marianne H., and Basile, Sherry K., *Counseling in the Elementary School: A Comprehensive Approach.* Copyright © 1993 by Allyn and Bacon. Reprinted by permission.

TABLE 5-2   Continuum of Counseling Goals

Counseling Process Goals	Corresponding Counseling Process Models	Maslow's Hierarchy of Needs, Expanded (Physiological Needs)
Ego development (Inception) Anxiety reduction Personal adjustment	Clinical/analytical model Ego psychotherapy	Security/safety needs Dependency Ego defenses
Socialization Role/self-identity Social adjustment Behavior change	Behavioral counseling Behavior modification Reality therapy	Belongingness needs Affiliation Identification Character development
Developmental competence Resolving developmental conflicts and challenges Coping/mastery Problem solving Decision making Self-sufficiency	Developmental counseling Adlerian counseling Transactional analysis Rational-emotive therapy Problem solving Decision making	(Developmental/cognitive needs) to know and understand, curiosity
Self-esteem Self-awareness Self-acceptance Self-confidence Congruence of self	Client-centered/relationship counseling	Esteem needs, value development
Self-realization Actualizing potential: Intellectual, emotional, social, spiritual	Gestalt counseling Existential counseling	Actualization needs

Source: Reprinted by Bruce, P., "Continuum of Counseling Goals: A Framework for Differentiating Counseling Strategies," *Personnel and Guidance Journal, 62,* 1984, p. 260. © American Counseling Association. Reprinted with permission. No further reproduction authorized without further permission of the American Counseling Association.

Hackney and Cormier (1996) note that

goals serve three important functions in the counseling process. First, goals can have a motivational function in counseling. Secondly, goals can also have an educational function in counseling in that they can help clients acquire new responses and three, goals can also meet an evaluative function in counseling whereby the client's goals help the counselor to select and evaluate various counseling strategies appropriate to the client's goals. (pp. 104–105)

THE COUNSELING PROCESS

Having briefly introduced some of the popular counseling theories, let us now move on to examine the translation of these theories into action. This action is frequently referred to as the counseling process. This process is usually specified by a sequence of interactions or steps. Although various authors will conceptualize these stages or phases differently because of different theoretical models, there is considerable agreement that initially the process is concerned with relationship establishment, followed by some method of problem identification and patterns of exploration, leading to planning for problem solution and remediation and concluding with action and termination. The stages might be identified as follows:

1. relationship building
2. problem identification and exploration
3. planning for problem solving
4. solution application and termination.

A brief description of each of these stages will be helpful.

Relationship Building

As often stated in definitions, counseling is a relationship. Furthermore, it is defined as a helping relationship. It therefore follows that if it is to be a relationship that is helpful, the counselor must take the initiative in the initial interview to establish a climate conducive to mutual respect, trust, free and open communication, and understanding in general of what the counseling process involves.

Within a formal context, Brammer (1988) asserted that this relationship takes the form of an interview—a structured helping relationship to which many variables contribute. Figure 5-2 illustrates these variables.

Although responsibility will later shift increasingly to the client, at this stage the responsibility for the counseling process rests primarily with the counselor. Among the techniques the counselor may use are those designed to relieve tensions and open communication. Both the counselor's attitude and verbal communications are significant to the development of a satisfactory relationship. In the latter instance, all of the counselor's communication skills are brought into play. These include attentive listening, understanding, and feeling with the client. Certainly, the quality of counselor-client relationship will influence counseling outcomes.

Among the factors that are important in the establishment of this counselor-client relationship are positive regard and respect, accurate empathy, and genuineness. These conditions imply counselor openness, an ability to understand and feel with the client, as well as

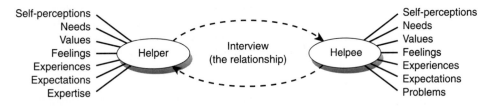

Figure 5-2   The Helping Relationship in the Interview.
Source: From Brammer, L. M., *The Helping Relationship: Process and Skills.* Copyright © 1988 by Allyn and Bacon. Reprinted by permission.

valuing the client. This counselor-client relationship serves not only to increase the opportunity for clients to attain their goals but also to be a potential model of a good interpersonal relationship, one that clients can use to improve the quality of their other relationships outside the therapy setting.

Counselors must keep in mind that the purpose of a counseling relationship is to meet, insofar as possible, client needs (not counselor needs). The counseling process within this relationship seeks to assist the client in assuming the responsibilities for his or her problem and its solution. This will be facilitated by the counselor's communications skills, the ability to identify and reflect clients' feelings and the ability to identify and gain insights into the clients' concerns and needs.

Establishing a helpful relationship with the client must be achieved early in the counseling process, inasmuch as this will often determine whether or not the client will continue. Suggested goals for the initial counseling interviews might include the following.

λ *Counselor's Goals*

- Establish a comfortable and positive relationship.
- Explain the counseling process and mutual responsibilities to the client.
- Facilitate communications.
- Identify and verify the client's concerns which brought her or him to seek counseling assistance.
- Plan, with the client, to obtain assessment data needed to proceed with the counseling process.

Client's Goals

- Understand the counseling process and his or her responsibilities in this process.
- Share and amplify reasons for seeking counseling.
- Cooperate in the assessment of both the problem and self.

Problem Identification and Exploration

Once an adequate relationship has been established, clients will be more receptive to the indepth discussion and exploration of their concerns. At this stage, clients assume more responsibility, because it is their problem and it is their willingness to communicate as much of the nature of the problem to the counselor that will determine to a large extent the assistance the counselor can give.

During this phase, the counselor continues to exhibit attending behavior and may place particular emphasis on such communication skills as paraphrasing, clarification, perception checking, or feedback. The counselor may question the client, but the questions are stated in such a way as to facilitate the continued exploration of the client's concern. Questions that would embarrass, challenge, or threaten the client are avoided. Throughout this phase, the counselor will recognize cultural differences and their implications in terms of how techniques should be modified to be culturally appropriate.

Now the counselor is seeking to distinguish between what might be called surface problems and those that are more complex. The counselor also strives to determine whether the stated problem is, in fact, the concern that has brought the client to the counselor's attention. This may be a time for information gathering. The more usable information the counselor has, the greater the prospects of accurate assessment of the client's needs. It is therefore helpful for counselors to recognize the various areas of information that must be tapped.

We have, rather arbitrarily, grouped the information desired under three headings: the time dimension, the feeling dimension, and the cognitive dimension. Subsets of information under each of these headings are indicated as follows.

1. The *time dimension* includes the client's past experiences, especially those which he or she may view as influencing experiences. The present dimension would cover how well the person is functioning presently, especially those current experiences which may have influenced the client to seek counseling. The future time dimension would include future hopes, plans and goals, and also how the client plans to achieve these.
2. The *feeling dimension* includes the emotions and feelings of the client towards him- or herself, as well as significant others, including groups, attitudes, values, and self-concept. All are a part of the feeling dimension.
3. The *cognitive dimension* includes how the client solves problems, the coping styles which she or he employs, rationality in making daily decisions, and the client's capacity and readiness for learning.

At this point, some counselors may use appraisal techniques such as standardized tests for problem diagnosis. Subproblems of the problem may also be identified. During this stage, the client not only explores experiences and behaviors but also may reveal feelings and the relationship of concern to the way she or he is living life in general. The counselor is seeking to secure as much relevant data as possible and to integrate it into an overall picture of the client and her or his concern. The counselor also shares these perceptions with the client. A goal of this stage is for both the counselor and the client to perceive the problem and its ramifications similarly. One of the counselor's goals during this stage is to help the client develop a self-understanding that recognizes the need for dealing with a concern—the need for change and action.

Obviously, this is a busy stage of the counseling process. Much of the real work occurs now, especially where extensive exploration is needed. Facilitative conditions must continue in order to promote client understandings of action plans for resolving problems. Although problem-solving activities are likely to be initiated during this stage, the major steps in implementing the activities take place in the third stage.

We identify the steps or stages in problem identification and exploration as follows.

1. *Define the problem.* The counselor, with the cooperation of the client, is seeking to describe or identify the problem as specifically and objectively as possible. It is important that the counselor's and client's understanding of the problem are in harmony. In addition to the accuracy desired in defining the problem, it is important to identify the components or contributing factors and the severity of the problem to the client, its recency, and longevity.
2. *Explore the problem.* The kinds of information needed in order to fully understand the problem and its background are gathered at this point. Once the kinds of needed information have been identified, then counselor and client must determine how this information can be obtained, whose responsibility it will be, and establish timelines for gathering them. Within this context, decisions may be made regarding the administering,

for example, of standardized psychological measures. To test or not to test is a decision in which the client must have a major voice, regardless of how desirable it may be to obtain data through the use of standardized psychological measures, the effect on the client and his or her willingness to participate fully in the counseling process may be threatened by this data-gathering technique. In some situations, the counselor may wish to complete a detailed case study. Obviously, this is a decision that will depend on the seriousness of the situation, the amount of data needed, and the amount of time available to both counselor and client for this purpose. In many agency settings, intake interviews will gather basic information that is deemed useful in most counseling situations. In this process, it is obviously important that the counselor continue to employ facilitative behavior.

3. *Integrate the information.* In this step, it is important that all of the information collected be systematically organized and integrated into a meaningful profile of the client and the client's problem. Too, at this point it would be appropriate to begin the exploration of changes that may be needed and barriers that may exist to these changes. The actual identification of possible solutions will be discussed in the next section. We note that in brief therapy, also discussed later in this chapter, this stage, as well as all stages in the counseling process, is condensed or collapsed in such a way as to expedite the process.

Planning for Problem Solving

Once the counselor has determined that all relevant information regarding the client's concern is available and understood, and once the client has accepted the need for doing something about a specific problem, the time is ripe for developing a plan to solve or remediate the concern of the client.

At this point, effective goal setting becomes the vital part of the counseling activity. Mistakes in goal setting can lead to nonproductive procedures and the client's loss of confidence in the counseling process. In this stage, we again suggest certain steps in sequence whereby we might view the processes involved.

1. *Define the problem.* It is important that both the counselor and the client view the problem from a similar perspective and have the same understandings of its ramifications.
2. *Identify and list all possible solutions.* At this point, it is appropriate to brainstorm all possibilities. Both the client and counselor participate, but the client should be given the opportunity to list as many possibilities as may come to her or his mind. If there are some obvious solutions that are overlooked, the counselor may suggest to the client "have you also thought of———?" When listing solutions none should be eliminated simply because at first glance they appear to be impossible to implement. Those that will be eliminated for various reasons will be taken care of in the next step.
3. *Explore the consequences of the suggested solutions.* Here the client, with encouragement from the counselor and even occasional suggestion, will identify the procedures needed to implement each of the suggested solutions. In so doing, it will be noted that some procedures may be too complex or, for other reasons, impossible to apply. Other solutions may produce more problems or more serious consequences than the problem which is the focus for solution in this counseling sequence. In any event, the projected outcomes for each solution must also be explored thoroughly.

4. *Prioritize the solutions.* Following exploratory stage 3, the client again with the counselor's encouragement will prioritize the solutions from best possibility down to least likely to produce the desired results. Once the decision has been made and the best solution selected, the client is now ready to move on to application and implementation.

In the further development of this plan, the counselor recognizes that the client will frequently not arrive at basic insights, implications, or probabilities as fast as the counselor will. However, most counselors will agree that it is better to guide the client toward realizing these understandings him- or herself, rather than just telling the client outright. To facilitate the client's understanding, the counselor may use techniques of repetition, mild confrontation, interpretation, information, and, obviously, encouragement.

Solution Application and Termination

In this final stage, the responsibilities are clear-cut. The client has the responsibility for applying the determined solution, and the counselor, for determining the point of termination. In the first instance, the counselor has a responsibility to encourage the client's acting on his or her determined problem solution. During the time that the client is actively engaged in applying the problem solution, the counselor will often maintain contact as a source of follow-up, support, and encouragement. The client may also need the counselor's assistance in the event things do not go according to plan. Once it has been determined, however, that the counselor and the client have dealt with the client's concern to the extent possible and practical, the process should be terminated. As noted before, this responsibility is primarily the counselor's, although the client has the right to terminate at any time. The counselor usually gives some indication that the next interview should just about wrap it up and may conclude by summarizing the main points of the counseling process. Usually, the counselor will leave the door open for the client's possible return in the event additional assistance is needed. Because counseling is a learning process, the counselor hopes that the client has not only learned to deal with this particular problem but has also learned problem-solving skills that will decrease the probability of the client's need for further counseling in the future.

In concluding this section on the counseling process, we are aware of our frequent reference to the client's "problem," and we would like to remind our readers that problems are not always based on perceived inadequacies or failures requiring remediation and restorative therapy. Clients can have equally pressing needs resulting from concerns for developing their human potential—for capitalizing on their strengths. In these instances, the emphasis is on development, growth, or enhancement, rather than remediation.

Finally, we note the five-stage decisional counseling model presented by Ivey et al. (1993).

> The central theoretical point of the five-stage model is that *counseling and therapy are not only about decisions, but the interview itself also may be structured using a decision-making framework.* Mastering the five-stage interview, gaining an understanding of key empathic dimensions, and developing competence in interviewing microskills will give you a framework for understanding many different approaches to helping theory.
>
> You can structure a very effective interview using the following five stages as a model or checklist:

1. Establishing rapport and structure ("Hello" and "This is what we'll be doing today.")
2. Gathering data and identifying assets ("What's the problem or concern?" and "What are your strengths?")
3. Determining outcomes ("What do you want to have happen?")
4. Generating alternative solutions ("What are we going to do to generate new ideas?")
5. Generalizing and transferring learning ("Will you do it?") (pp. 76–77)

Table 5-3 presents a description of some influencing skills and their motivation function in the interview.

COUNSELING SKILLS

Thus far in this chapter we have discussed the importance of the counselor having a theoretical framework within which to function and a knowledge of the process or stages through which client counseling moves. Equally important are the skills that the counselor must possess to apply a given theory and implement the process.

The skills of counseling have their roots in both theory and process and have been reinforced through practice and research. The counselor acquires these skills through learning and practice. The primary counseling skill is communication, both nonverbal and verbal.

Communications Skills

Nonverbal Communications Skills

All of us communicate nonverbally. Through the use of facial expressions, body posture, and physical movements we send messages, usually intentional but sometimes not intentional. We also usually "read" messages that others communicate to us in a similar manner. In our society, nonverbal language is a popular means of communication, and, in counseling, it is a social interaction process important to both the counselor and the counselee. For example, from the onset and throughout the counseling process, visual clues will influence the client's perception of the counselor. As noted earlier in this chapter, one of the nonverbal ways in which the counselor deals with this factor is by exhibiting attending behavior, by communicating nonverbally, "I am interested in you and your concerns, I respect you, and I'm going to give you my undivided attention," and so forth. Attending behavior accomplishes several purposes.

First, it indicates to the client that she or he is the object of your undivided attention. It further indicates the respect that you have for him or her as an individual. It also indicates your acceptance of the client and your readiness to assist with his or her concerns to the full limit of your professional abilities. Further, it facilitates the flow of communication by demonstrating your undivided attention. This conveys to the client your interest and will encourage further verbalization on the client's part. It also tells the client that not everything that she or he needs to communicate has to be put into words. Attending behavior keeps you, the counselor, aware and alert at all times. It enables you to follow the client's communication. Finally, attending behavior enables you to identify clues that the client may subconsciously or even consciously reveal during the course of the counseling interview.

More than 20 years ago Gazda, Asbury, Balzer, Childers, and Walters (1977) categorized nonverbal behaviors into four modalities still popular today. It should be emphasized that non-

TABLE 5-3 Influencing Skills

Skill	Description	Function in Interview
Interpretation/ reframing	Provides an alternative frame of reference from which the client may view a situation. May be drawn from a theory or from one's own personal observations. *Interpretation may be viewed as the core influencing skill.*	Attempts to provide the client with a new way to view the situation. The interpretation provides the client with a clear-cut alternative perception of "reality." This perception may enable a change of view that in turn may result in changes in thoughts, constructs, or behaviors.
Directive	Tells the client what action to take. May be a simple suggestion stated in command form or may be a sophisticated technique from a specific theory.	Clearly indicates to clients what action counselors or therapists with them to take. The prediction with a directive is that the client will do what is suggested. . . .
Advice/information	Provides suggestions, instructional ideas, homework, advice on how to act, think, or behave.	Used sparingly, may provide client with new and useful information. Specific vocational information is an example of necessary use of this skill.
Self-disclosure	The interviewer shares personal experience from the past or may share present reactions to the client.	Emphasizes counselor "I" statements. This skill is closely allied to feedback and may build trust and openness, leading to a more mutual relationship with the client.
Feedback	Provides clients with specific data on how they are seen by the counselor or by others.	Provides concrete data that may help clients realize how others perceive behavior and thinking patterns, thus enabling an alternative self-perception.
Logical consequences	Interviewer explains to the client the logical outcome of thinking and behavior— if/then.	Provides an alternative frame of reference for the client. This skills helps clients anticipate the consequences or results of their actions.
Influencing summary	Often used at or near the end of a session to summarize counselor comments; most often used in combination with the attending summarization.	Clarifies what has happened in the interview and summarizes what the therapist has said. This skill is designed to help generalization from the interview to daily life.

Source: From *Counseling and Psychotherapy: A Multicultural Perspective,* 4th ed., p. 66, by A. E. Ivey, M. B. Ivey, and L. Simek-Morgan, 1997, Boston: Allyn and Bacon.

verbal behaviors are highly idiosyncratic; interpretation of these clues must be tentative and based on the context in which they are sent.

1. Nonverbal Communication Behaviors Using Time

Recognition

Promptness or delay in recognizing the presence of another or in responding to his or her communication

Priorities

Amount of time another is willing to spend communicating with a person

Relative amounts of time spent on various topics

2. Nonverbal Communication Behaviors Using the Body

Eye contact (important in regulating the relationship)

Looking at a specific object

Looking down

Steady to helper

Defiantly at helper ("hard" eyes), glaring

Shifting eyes from object to object

Looking at helper but looking away when looked at

Covering eyes with hand(s)

Frequency of looking at another

Eyes

"Sparkling"

Tears

"Wild-eyed"

Position of eyelids

Skin

Pallor

Perspiration

Blushing

"Goose bumps"

Posture (often indicative of physical alertness or tiredness)

"Eager," as if ready for activity

Slouching, slovenly, tired looking, slumping

Arms crossed in front as if to protect self

Crossing legs

Sits facing the other person rather than sideways or away from

Hanging head, looking at floor, head down

Body positioned to exclude others from joining a group or dyad

Facial expression (primary site for display of affects; thought by researchers to be subject to involuntary responses)

No change

Wrinkled forehead (lines of worry), frown

Wrinkled nose

Smiling, laughing

"Sad" mouth

Biting lip

Hand and arm gestures

Symbolic hand and arm gestures

Literal hand and arm gestures to indicate size or shape

Demonstration of how something happened or how to do something

Self-inflicting behaviors

Nail biting

Scratching

Cracking knuckles

Tugging at hair

Rubbing or stroking

Repetitive behaviors (often interpreted as signs of nervousness or restlessness but may be organic in origin)

Tapping foot, drumming or thumping with fingers

Fidgeting, squirming

Trembling

Playing with button, hair, or clothing

Signals or commands

Snapping fingers

Holding finger to lips for silence

Pointing

Staring directly to indicate disapproval

Shrugging shoulders

Waving

Nodding in recognition

Winking

Nodding in agreement, shaking head in disagreement

Touching

To get attention, such as tapping on shoulder

Affectionate, tender

Sexual

Challenging, such as poking finger into chest

Symbols of camaraderie, such as slapping on back

Belittling, such as a pat on top of head

3. Nonverbal Communication Behaviors Using Vocal Media

Tone of voice

Flat, monotone, absence of feelings

Bright, vivid changes of inflection

Strong, confident, firm

Weak, hesitant, shaky

Broken, faltering

Rate of speech

Fast

Medium

Slow

Loudness of voice

Loud

Medium

Soft

Diction

Precise versus careless

Regional (colloquial) differences

Consistency of diction

4. Nonverbal Communication Behavior Using the Environment
Distance

Moves away when the other moves toward

Moves toward when the other moves away

Takes initiative in moving toward or away from

Distance widens gradually

Distance narrows gradually

Arrangement of the physical setting

Neat, well-ordered, organized

Untidy, haphazard, careless

Casual versus formal

Warm versus cold colors

Soft versus hard materials

Slick versus varied textures

Cheerful and lively versus dull and drab

"Discriminating" taste versus tawdry

Expensive or luxurious versus shabby or spartan

Clothing (often used to tell others what a person wants them to believe about him/her)

Bold versus unobtrusive

Stylish versus nondescript

Position in the room

Protects or fortifies self in position by having objects such as desk or table between self and other person.

Takes an open or vulnerable position, such as in the center of the room, side by side on a sofa, or in a simple chair. Nothing between self and other person.

Takes an attacking or dominating position. May block exit from area or may maneuver other person into boxed-in position.

Moves about the room.

Moves in and out of other person's territory.

Stands when other person sits, or gets in higher position than other person.* (pp. 89–92)

Verbal Communications Skills

Strange as it may seem, we will initiate our discussion of verbal communications skills by discussing listening. Listening is a prerequisite to effective verbal communicating. Listening also is implied in attending behavior, but because of its importance, we emphasize the point again because listening is the basis of counselor competence.

Effective listening enables counselors to adroitly manipulate their verbal counseling skills. These skills include using attending responses that indicate to the client that you are listening (i.e., "I understand," "I see") and what we might label as stimulus responses, those that encourage the client to continue to comment (i.e., "Can you tell me more about that?" "Could you clarify that for me?" "Please continue if you wish.").

Effective listening is mandatory for feedback, another important verbal (as well as nonverbal) communication skill. Feedback is the verbalization of the counselor's perceptions and reactions to the client's behaviors, feelings, concerns, actions, expressions, and so forth. It offers the client the opportunity in turn to feedback-react, perhaps validate or expand on the counselor's feedback. It offers the counselor the opportunity to periodically summarize and validate what has transpired and ensure that both counselor and counselee are accurately receiving each other's messages before moving further in the counseling process.

The art of questioning is also important in verbal communications. Skill in questioning involves timing, wording, and type of questions. The competent counselor does not inject questions that will stop, alter, or slow down a client's open discussion of a concern. Questions are injected to keep the discussion moving (i.e., "Why do you think they reacted that way to your behavior?"); to clarify (i.e., "What do you mean? Am I right in understanding you?"); and to validate (i.e., "How do you know? Give me an example.").

The type of question used should be appropriate to the desired outcome. Open questions (i.e., "How did you feel about that?") provide opportunities for the client to express feelings, provide greater detail, and gain new insights, whereas closed questions (i.e., "Will you go back next week?") get an answer rather than an evasive or rambling reply. The counselor may also decide when to use direct questions (i.e., "Tell me, are you an alcoholic?") or nondirect questions (i.e., "What do you think about alcoholism today?"), which do not directly identify the client with a problem or issue.

Effective communication is also facilitated by knowing what not to do. George and Cristiani (1995) list several barriers to communications.

1. Giving advice
2. Offering solutions
3. Moralizing and preaching
4. Analyzing and diagnosing

---

*From Gazda, George M., Asbury, Frank R., Balzer, Fred J., Childers, William C., and Walters, Richard P., *Human Relations Development*. Copyright © 1977 by Allyn and Bacon. Reprinted by permission.

5. Judging or criticizing
6. Praising and agreeing; giving positive evaluations
7. Reassuring (p. 126–128)

Short-Term Counseling or Brief Therapy

Recent years have witnessed increased interest in and practice of short-term, or brief, therapy. Although in practice brief therapy is probably as old as therapy itself, it has only been written about in recent generations as a recognized and viable approach for the delivery of counseling assistance. This new popularity can be attributed to a number of factors, including the escalating costs of treatment; the managed care movement; limitations on payments imposed by insurance companies; a busy public that wants as much time as possible to devote to career and family; and the results of studies, some highly publicized in the popular media, indicating that for most situations short-term therapy is at least, if not more, effective than long-term; evidence of lasting or durable results; and because it more frequently responds to the client's anticipation of treatment time.

Although descriptions of what constitutes short term seem to vary somewhat, it would appear to be in the range of one to five sessions with an average length of one hour each. The process itself is characterized by (1) promptness of treatment (no lengthy intake interviews); (2) openness and cooperation; (3) rapid assessment and focus on the problem; (4) an emphasis on the client's positive traits in solution identification; and, of course, (5) some attention to time limitations. In addition to the goals of responding to the client's needs which brought the client to counseling, short-term therapy also seeks the development and enhancement of the individual's potential for fruitful behaviors, including learning to solve one's own problems.

Good (although not the only) candidates for brief therapy are (1) motivated to change; (2) can establish positive personal relationships readily and easily; (3) expect and want only a brief treatment; and (4) are not psychologically impaired.

Basile (1996) summarized strategies that contribute to the effective application of a solution-based brief therapy model as follows.

1. Foster the development of a therapeutic or working alliance
2. Assess the client's motivation for change (as a visitor, a complainant, or a customer)
3. Establish a goal for treatment
4. Use presuppositional and solution-focused language
5. Search for strengths, solutions, and exceptions
6. Connect and stay connected with your client's sense of humor
7. Be pragmatic
8. Brief therapy moves slowly; stay on track (pp. 8–9)

SPECIAL COUNSELING POPULATIONS

Counselors in nearly all settings deal with a variety of individual problems and concerns. Because increasing attention is being given to certain populations, it seems appropriate to note several of these special clients.

Substance Abusers

Increases in the use of alcohol and drugs and the ill effects of their abuse are well publicized. These social ills are spelled out in such dramatic numbers as minimally 9 million estimated alcoholics, 550,000 heroin addicts, and 4 million regular users of marijuana. Nor is the outlook for future generations bright as data indicate there are 3 million teen alcoholics, 5 out of 10 adolescents use marijuana, and 1 out of 10 youth have tried cocaine. Persons are considered abusers of any substance when it is used to the extent that it causes or threatens damage to the individual or society or both.

Individuals who abuse alcohol are labeled *alcoholics*. An alcoholic is an individual who has habitually consumed alcohol to the point where he or she can no longer control his or her intake of alcohol or stop drinking for any appreciable period. Although a variety of classification systems may be used, the American Psychiatric Association recognizes the following types of alcoholism.

> *Episodic excessive drinking.* If alcoholism is present and the individual becomes intoxicated as frequently as four times a year, the condition should be classified here. Intoxication is defined as a state in which the individual's coordination or speech is definitely impaired or his behavior is clearly altered.
>
> *Habitual excessive drinking.* This diagnosis is given to persons who are alcoholic and who either become intoxicated more than 12 times a year or are recognizably under the influence of alcohol more than once a week, even though not intoxicated.
>
> *Alcoholic addiction.* This condition should be diagnosed when there is direct or strong presumptive evidence that the patient is dependent on alcohol. If available, the best directive evidence of such dependence is the appearance of withdrawal symptoms. The inability of the patient to go one day without drinking is presumptive evidence. When heavy drinking continues for three months or more it is reasonable to presume addiction to alcohol has been established. (Kinney & Leaton, 1978, p. 42)

Belkin (1988) points out that

> some drugs are inherently dangerous and may always be considered instances of drug abuse unless taken under the supervision of a physician. Heroin, a synthetic derivative of morphine, is a highly addictive substance with no legitimate medical uses. Crack, a derivative of cocaine, gained a deadly prominence during the mid-1980s. The hallucinogenic (psychedelic) drugs produce gross distortions of reality, hallucinations, and erratic behavior and thinking. Barbiturates and other depressant drugs produce a feeling of relaxation and blissfulness that enables the user to forget all the problems that must be faced in life. Such drugs are highly addictive and may result in fatality upon withdrawal. Cases of suicide under the influence of barbiturates are not uncommon. Amphetamines are stimulant drugs that result in great feelings of optimism as well as mania. They are used by adolescents as sleep inhibitors, appetite suppressants, and for relief of depression. Prolonged use of amphetamines may result in hallucinations, psychosis, and violent behavior. (p. 322)

Beginning in the mid-1970s, alcohol has been the single most abused drug in adolescent culture. It is estimated that more than three million teenagers today are alcoholics, most of them enrolled in schools. No one knows exactly why this is, but it may represent a characteristic of adolescent rebellion against the adult—what they view as a restricting and nonunderstanding adult society.

The symptoms of alcoholism among teenagers are much more readily observed and therefore easier to detect than the use of many other substances. Characteristics of the alcoholic adolescent are excessive absenteeism; poor academic achievement; poor relationships with adults; and lack of participation or interest in school activities. As with alcoholic adults, adolescents may also have an alcoholic aroma.

The counselor may be involved in prevention, intervention, and crisis treatment or remediation. However, counseling programs stress the importance of specialized training for counselors who are working with substance abusers. Because such clients are very resistant to change and the facilitating conditions are often beyond the therapist's control, counselors working with these clients must be especially trained in those dramatically different techniques proven to have some chance of success with substance abuse clients. Too, counselors must be aware of client conditions which merit referral to more highly trained specialists for long-term treatment and monitoring.

In addition to having a thorough and well-grounded understanding of the drug problem, the counselor should also be engaged in a continual interaction with teachers, ministers, juvenile authorities, industrial personnel managers, and others who can assist in the implementation of prevention, early intervention and/or addictive treatment programs.

In many programs, both individual and group counseling methods are used. In some settings, counseling teams have been found to be effective for group counseling. It is also obviously important that counselors who work with drug and alcohol abuse have more than a superficial knowledge of the causes, symptoms, and potential outcomes of the problem. Furthermore, in many individual situations, medical treatment may be needed, and referral to or teaming with a psychiatrist may be necessary.

Counselors in all settings, therefore, need to be aware of the resources available for the treatment of substance abuse clients. These may include emergency clinics, specialized centers, hospital care (both inpatient and outpatient), halfway houses, crisis centers, and special assistance groups such as Alcoholics Anonymous and Narcotics Anonymous. Counselors working with such populations generally have a specialized knowledge of the pharmacological, physiological, psychological, and sociocultural aspects of the use of alcohol and drugs.

Women

Even though federal and state legislation has sought to promote opportunities for women to achieve their potential by stimulating legal equality of the sexes, abundant evidence indicates a lack of consistency at both the national and state levels in the application and enforcement of such legislation. In many ways, discrimination has become much more subtle since the Civil Rights Act of 1964.

Further, the changing role of women in the world of work has produced resultant changes in both the lives of women and family life. For example, working women have greater financial freedom; and they experience later marriages, more living together, and higher divorce rates than did their mothers' mothers. Although the majority of women work because of economic necessity, they continue to have a history of working for less money. In most organizations, men still control the fiscal management and decision making, thus reinforcing the glass ceiling. Further, of the single-parent families living in poverty, approximately 58% are headed by women. Teenage girls and poverty environments are especially at risk. A dramatic increase in the number of dual-career couples has created issues regarding whose career takes priority; the division of household responsibilities; and the bothersome issue of latchkey children, often left without supervision for long periods.

The counselor's role in counseling women is often further complicated by not only the woman's perception of what is appropriate for her but also by society's viewpoints. Another complicating factor in counseling women is the multiple role expectations held for women as wife, mother, and employee. With increasingly greater numbers of women seeking counseling, especially for career planning and decision making, there is a need to be alert that sexist counseling does not limit their career opportunities. The counselor has the responsibility to help women understand their own values, abilities, aptitudes, and interests and to utilize these to develop their fullest potential. In so doing, the counselor must, as always, function as a nonbiased, nonstereotyping helper.

Older Adults

In the 1980s, we became increasingly aware that our population was growing older, living longer and more actively, and becoming another special population for counseling services. Although in the past the elderly were in a sense often "out of sight, out of mind," it is clear that in the 1990s they increasingly came into the mainstream of public thought and activity. Popular books like *Old Friends* by Tracy Kielder (1993) and *The Fountain of Age* by Betty Friedan (1993) told us of the increasing age of our population and awareness of this aging. (In the latter publication, it is noted that life expectancy in the United States has increased 30 years in the 20th century and that from 1970 to 1985, the number of people over age 65 increased by 30%!) As we enter the next century, we can anticipate an elderly population (age 65 and older) of more than 31 million. Further, this population will live and may work longer if they choose, because the Employment Act of 1967, as amended in 1986, makes it possible for workers to work beyond age 65.

It is interesting to note that even though older individuals are now living longer and healthier with the option of continuing to work, they are, as a group, declining to do so, as the age at which people retire continues to gradually move downward. Of course, some of these will return to work when they experience boredom in retirement; but for many, the option of early retirement may offer an escape from boring and unsatisfying jobs. Too, retirees seeking reentry into the workforce rarely find opportunities equal to the positions they left or commensurate with their abilities and experiences.

Regardless of when an elderly worker chooses to retire, the experience can be both significant and traumatic. For many retirees, adjusting to life without work is difficult because they feel a loss of status as workers are more valued in our society than nonworkers; for many it means a loss of planned involvement with other people; and some have developed so few supplemental leisure time or recreational activities that life suddenly becomes boring or meaningless because they have excess time on their hands. But there is promise of a better transition for these older adults, and this promise appears to rely heavily on counseling.

As employee assistance programs (EAPs) are increasingly helping older workers plan for their retirements and make psychological adjustments, such assistance is becoming an increasingly significant employee benefit and opportunity for counseling.

Counseling assistance would tend to stress orientation to retirement with attending personal adjustment counseling, financial planning, career assessment and assistance for those desirous of some form (part-time or full-time) of continued employment, and leisure planning. Additionally, most older adults will face other major changes in their twilight years, including the loss of one's spouse; the decline of physical and often mental capacity and well-being; a decline in financial security; a decline in mobility—not just their own physical ability but also a time when they can no longer drive, which in itself may increase one's isolation; a decline in social contacts and increased loneliness; and an increase in mental health problems.

Counselors will thus have the opportunities to meet, primarily through community services and outreach programs, the needs of another distinct and worthy segment of our population. Counselors working with older clients must again exhibit acceptance, openness, and respect of clients and their values. Even the oldest client must be permitted to look ahead and plan for a different future if this is the client's desire. If a lack of awareness and attitudes is not inhibiting, counselors can help older clients find new meanings and roles in life.

Business and Industry

Recent generations have witnessed a steady broadening of the opportunities for counselors to function in a variety of settings. This is due in part to organizations, agencies, and special populations recognizing that they share needs and concerns in common with other populations and settings where these needs and concerns are recognized and dealt with. Increasingly, business and industrial organizations and their workforces have realized that they may benefit, from both a corporate and individual viewpoint, from programs of counseling assistance. Certainly, the development of EAPs has provided increased opportunities for counselors and other helping professionals to assist individuals in their work settings.

Counselors can provide worthwhile programs to facilitate the career development and placement or replacement of workers and management personnel. Personnel training, especially in human relationship and communications skills, is another area of promise and as noted previously in this chapter, retirement counseling is also an area of potential counseling service. Increased emphasis is also noted on prevention and wellness programs for employees.

Toomer (1982) suggested possible roles and functions in business and industry as outlined in Figure 5-3. Additional discussion of EAPs will be presented in Chapter 10.

AIDS Patients

Acquired Immunodeficiency Syndrome (AIDS) was recognized and labeled a little more than a decade ago. Since that time it has become one of the most feared of diseases and health epidemics. The swift spread of AIDS and its incurability and rapid fatality rate have caused widespread public concern. In 1995, the Centers for Disease Control and Prevention reported 501,310 cases of AIDS in the United States (p. 98). (See Table 5-4 and for additional information, see Tables 5-5 and 5-6.)

The February 28, 1997, *Morbidity and Mortality Weekly Report*, published by the Centers for Disease Control and Prevention, indicates that

From 1981 through 1996, a total of 573,800 persons aged ≥13 years with AIDS were reported to the Centers for Disease Control by state and local health departments [see Table 5-7]. The expansion of the AIDS surveillance case definition in 1993 resulted in a large increase in reported cases during 1993 followed by declines in numbers of AIDS cases reported each year from 1994 through

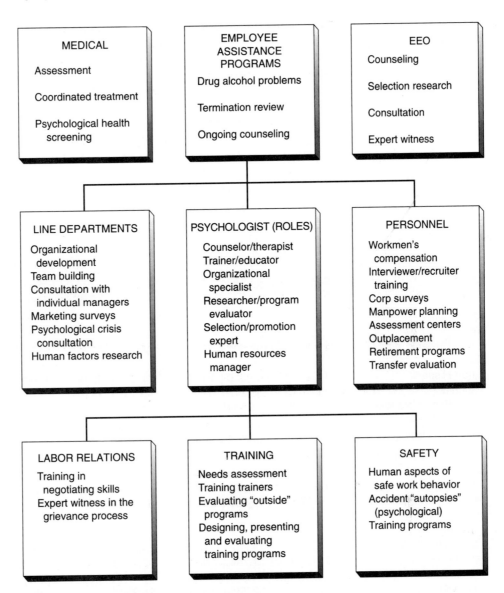

Figure 5-3   Counseling Psychologists in Business and Industry: Roles and Relationships.
Source: From J. E. Toomer, *Counseling Psychologists in Business and Industry*, p. 13, 1982. Copyright ©
1984 Sage Publications. Reprinted by permission from Sage Publications and author.

1996. The 68,473 AIDS cases reported during 1996 was substantially higher (47%) than the number reported during 1992.

From 1992 through 1996, non-Hispanic blacks, Hispanics, and women accounted for increasing proportions of persons reported with AIDS. In 1996, non-Hispanic blacks accounted for 41% of adults reported with AIDS, exceeding for the first time the proportion who were non-Hispanic white, and women accounted for an all-time high of 20% of adults reported with AIDS. (pp. 166–167)

TABLE 5-4   Number and Percentage of Persons with AIDS, by Selected Characteristics and Period of Report—United States, 1981–October 1995

Characteristic	1981–1987 Number (%)	1988–1992 Number (%)	1993–October 1995 Number (%)	Cumulative Number (%)
Sex				
Male	46,317 (92.0)	177,807 (87.5)	204,356 (82.5)	428,480 (85.5)
Female	4,035 (8.0)	25,410 (12.5)	43,383 (17.5)	72,828 (14.5)
Age groups (yrs)				
0–4	653 (1.3)	2,766 (1.4)	2,013 (0.8)	5,432 (1.1)
5–12	100 (0.2)	669 (0.3)	616 (0.2)	1,385 (0.3)
13–19	199 (0.4)	758 (0.4)	1,343 (0.5)	2,300 (0.5)
20–29	10,531 (20.9)	38,662 (19.0)	41,861 (16.9)	91,054 (18.2)
30–39	23,269 (46.2)	92,493 (45.5)	111,992 (45.3)	227,754 (45.4)
40–49	10,491 (20.8)	47,088 (23.1)	64,990 (26.2)	122,569 (24.4)
50–59	3,690 (7.3)	14,537 (7.2)	18,413 (7.5)	36,640 (7.3)
≥60	1,419 (2.8)	6,244 (3.1)	6,513 (2.6)	14,176 (2.8)
Race/ethnicity				
White, non-Hispanic	30,104 (59.8)	102,551 (50.5)	105,516 (42.6)	238,171 (47.5)
Black, non-Hispanic	12,794 (25.4)	63,319 (31.2)	94,158 (38.0)	170,271 (34.0)
Hispanic*	7,039 (14.0)	35,213 (17.3)	45,135 (18.2)	87,387 (17.4)
Asian/ Pacific Islander	309 (0.6)	1,339 (0.7)	1,809 (0.7)	3,457 (0.7)
American Indian/ Alaskan Native	67 (0.1)	433 (0.2)	783 (0.3)	1,283 (0.3)
HIV-exposure category				
Men who have sex with men	32,246 (64.0)	110,934 (54.6)	111,257 (44.9)	254,437 (50.8)
Injecting-drug use	8,639 (17.2)	49,093 (24.2)	67,708 (27.3)	125,440 (25.0)
Men who have sex with men and inject drugs	4,193 (8.3)	14,252 (7.0)	13,984 (5.6)	32,429 (6.5)
Hemophilia	505 (1.0)	1,744 (0.9)	2,009 (0.8)	4,258 (0.8)
Heterosexual contact	1,248 (2.5)	12,335 (6.1)	24,958 (10.1)	38,541 (7.7)
Transfusion recipients	1,285 (2.6)	3,894 (1.9)	2,521 (1.0)	7,700 (1.6)
Perinatal transmission	608 (1.2)	3,084 (1.5)	2,432 (1.0)	6,124 (1.2)
No risk reported	1,628 (3.2)	7,881 (3.9)	22,872 (9.2)	32,381 (6.4)
Region†				
Northeast	19,544 (38.8)	62,282 (30.6)	74,769 (30.2)	156,595 (31.2)
Midwest	3,770 (7.5)	20,352 (10.0)	24,914 (10.1)	49,036 (9.8)
South	12,960 (25.7)	65,926 (32.4)	86,462 (34.9)	165,348 (33.0)
West	13,550 (26.9)	46,675 (23.0)	53,729 (21.7)	113,954 (22.7)
U.S. territories	516 (1.0)	7,889 (3.9)	7,566 (3.1)	15,971 (3.2)

TABLE 5-4 (*Continued*)

Characteristic	1981–1987 Number (%)	1988–1992 Number (%)	1993–October 1995 Number (%)	Cumulative Number (%)
Vital status				
Living	2,779 (5.5)	32,144 (15.8)	155,006 (62.6)	189,929 (37.9)
Deceased	47,573 (94.5)	171,073 (84.2)	92,735 (37.4)	311,381 (62.1)
Total‡	**50,352 (100.0)**	**203,217 (100.0)**	**247,741 (100.0)**	**501,310 (100.0)**

*Persons of Hispanic origin may be of any race.
†*Northeast* = Connecticut, Maine, Massachusetts, New Hampshire, New Jersey, New York, Pennsylvania, Rhode Island, and Vermont; *Midwest* = Illinois, Iowa, Kansas, Michigan, Minnesota, Missouri, Nebraska, North Dakota, Ohio, South Dakota, and Wisconsin; *South* = Alabama, Arkansas, Delaware, District of Columbia, Florida, Georgia, Kentucky, Louisiana, Maryland, Mississippi, North Carolina, Oklahoma, South Carolina, Tennessee, Texas, Virginia, and West Virginia; *West* = Alaska, Arizona, California, Colorado, Hawaii, Idaho, Montana, Nevada, New Mexico, Oregon, Utah, Washington, and Wyoming.
‡Includes persons for whom sex, race/ethnicity, or region are missing.
Source: Reports on HIV/AIDS 1995 Morbidity and Mortality Weekly Report: A Compilation of 1995 MMWR Articles on HIV Infection and AIDS, Centers for Disease Control and Prevention, Nov. 24 1995, Vol. 44(46), pp. 849–853.

Reports on HIV/AIDS 1995: Morbidity and Mortality Weekly Report reports that

> During 1994 state, local and territorial health departments reported to the Centers for Disease Control and Prevention 80,691 cases of acquired immunodeficiency syndrome (AIDS) among persons in the United States, which followed the 106,618 cases reported in 1993.
>
> Of the total 80,691 reported cases, 79,674 (99%) occurred among adolescents and adults (i.e., persons aged ≥ 13 years) and 1017 among children < 13 years. The number of cases reported in children during 1994 (1017) increased 8% over those reported during 1993 (942). Of the 1017 children, 50% were female, most were black (62%) or Hispanic (23%) and 92% were infected through perinatal transmission (p. 1).

AIDS is also a disease of the young, with 16.4% of the victims in their twenties, 45.3% in their thirties, and 26.3% in their forties. Treatments to extend the life of victims are continuing to be developed. AIDS patients are also looking to improve their quality of life including their psychological well-being.

As patients and their close friends and relatives increasingly seek counseling to help them cope with the emotional stresses resulting from AIDS, counselors must become more knowledgeable about the disease and the psychological reactions most likely to occur. Initial shock and panic are typical reactions of those learning they have contracted AIDS. Additionally, they frequently feel isolated and punished (Why me?!). Low self-esteem is often reinforced by discrimination, including difficulty in securing and holding a job and developing and maintaining social relationships.

Counselors providing assistance to AIDS-infected clients must recognize that they (the clients) have frequently lost social support from both friends and family, which results in their loss of ability to cope. Serious depression is not uncommon among this group. Many will also react with anger and frustration. Counselors can help assist and educate the support systems of patients—families, friends, employers—and help the AIDS patient focus on life and living.

TABLE 5-5   Estimated Persons Living with AIDS, by Age Group, Sex, Exposure Category, and Year, 1991 through 1996, United States*

Male adult/adolescent exposure category	Year					
	1991	1992	1993	1994	1995	1996
Men who have sex with men	55,400	72,800	86,900	95,500	102,000	111,900
Injecting drug use	17,900	25,800	34,100	39,700	43,800	48,000
Men who have sex with men and inject drugs	8,100	10,900	12,800	13,600	14,200	14,700
Hemophilia/ coagulation disorder	970	1,400	1,575	1,650	1,650	1,650
Heterosexual contact	2,375	4,000	6,000	7,700	9,600	12,300
Receipt of blood transfusion, blood components, or tissue	700	860	970	1,050	1,150	1,275
Risk not reported or identified	910	1,125	1,225	1,175	1,200	1,275
Male subtotal	86,400	116,800	143,500	160,400	173,600	191,000
Female adult/adolescent exposure category						
Injecting drug use	6,900	10,100	13,500	15,800	17,800	19,700
Hemophilia/ coagulation disorder	40	60	80	90	110	130
Heterosexual contact	4,750	7,900	11,800	15,100	18,600	22,900
Receipt of blood transfusion, blood components, or tissue	550	690	830	950	1,050	1,225
Risk not reported or identified	340	420	460	460	470	510
Female subtotal	12,500	19,200	26,700	32,500	38,100	44,400
Pediatric (<13 years old) exposure category	2,125	2,650	3,000	3,250	3,400	3,450
Total†	**101,000**	**138,600**	**173,100**	**196,200**	**215,000**	**239,000**

*Estimates of persons living with AIDS are derived by subtracting the estimated cumulative number of deaths in persons with AIDS from the estimated cumulative number of persons with AIDS. Estimated AIDS cases and estimated deaths are adjusted for reporting delays, but not for incomplete reporting. Total estimates of less than 1,000, 1,000 to 2,499, 2,500 to 4,999, and 5,000 or more are rounded to the nearest 10, 25, 50, and 100, respectively. Annual estimates are through the most recent year for which reliable estimates are available. Because there is uncertainty in the estimates of persons living with AIDS; changes over time in the estimates of persons living with AIDS should not be computed from these rounded estimates. See Technical Notes.
†The sum of exposure category estimates may not equal the total annual estimates because of rounding.
Source: HIV/AIDS Surveillance Report, June 1997, Vol. 9 (1), p. 25.

TABLE 5-6 Adult/Adolescent AIDS Cases by Single and Multiple Exposure Categories, Reported through June 1997, United States

	AIDS cases	
Exposure category	Number	(%)
Single mode of exposure		
Men who have sex with men	286,611	(47)
Injecting drug use	124,684	(21)
Hemophilia/coagulation disorder	3,673	(1)
Heterosexual contact	53,119	(9)
Receipt of transfusion*	8,063	(1)
Receipt of transplant of tissues, organs, or artificial insemination†	12	(0)
Other‡	95	(0)
Single mode of exposure subtotal	**476,257**	**(79)**
Multiple modes of exposure		
Men who have sex with men; injecting drug use	33,600	(6)
Men who have sex with men; hemophilia/coagulation disorder	151	(0)
Men who have sex with men; heterosexual contact	8,366	(1)
Men who have sex with men; receipt of transfusion/transplant	3,260	(1)
Injecting drug use; hemophilia/coagulation disorder	182	(0)
Injecting drug use; heterosexual contact	27,251	(5)
Injecting drug use; receipt of transfusion/transplant	1,541	(0)
Hemophilia/coagulation disorder; heterosexual contact	83	(0)
Hemophilia/coagulation disorder;receipt of transfusion/transplant	779	(0)
Heterosexual contact; receipt of transfusion/transplant	1,452	(0)
Men who have sex with men; injecting drug use; hemophilia/coagulation disorder	43	(0)
Men who have sex with men; injecting drug use; heterosexual contact	4,528	(1)
Men who have sex with men; injecting drug use; receipt of transfusion/transplant	573	(0)
Men who have sex with men; hemophilia/coagulation disorder; heterosexual contact	20	(0)
Men who have sex with men; hemophilia/coagulation disorder; receipt of transfusion/transplant	34	(0)
Men who have sex with men; heterosexual contact; receipt of transfusion/transplant	252	(0)
Injecting drug use; hemophilia/coagulation disorder; heterosexual contact	60	(0)
Injecting drug use; hemophilia/coagulation disorder; receipt of transfusion/transplant	36	(0)
Injecting drug use; heterosexual contact; receipt of transfusion/transplant	892	(0)
Hemophilia/coagulation disorder; heterosexual contact; receipt of transfusion/transplant	32	(0)
Men who have sex with men; injecting drug use; hemophilia/coagulation, heterosexual contact	8	(0)
Men who have sex with men; injecting drug use; hemophilia/coagulation disorder; receipt of transfusion/transplant	13	

(continued)

TABLE 5-6   (*Continued*)

Exposure category	AIDS cases	
	Number	**(%)**
Men who have sex with men; injecting drug use; heterosexual contact; receipt of transfusion/transplant	153	(0)
Men who have sex with men; hemophilia/coagulation disorder; heterosexual contact; receipt of transfusion/transplant	5	
Injecting drug use; hemophilia/coagulation disorder; heterosexual contact; receipt of transfusion/transplant	18	(0)
Men who have sex with men; injecting drug use; hemophilia/coagulation disorder; heterosexual contact; receipt of transfusion/transplant	5	(0)
Multiple modes of exposure subtotal	**83,337**	**(14)**
Risk not reported or identified	**44,582**	**(7)**
Total	**604,176**	**(100)**

*Includes 37 adult/adolescents who developed AIDS after receiving blood screened negative for HIV antibody.
†Twelve adults developed AIDS after receiving tissue, organs, or artificial insemination from HIV-infected donors. Four of the 12 received tissue or organs from a single donor who was negative for HIV antibody at the time of donation. See *New England Journal of Medicine,* 1992; 326: 726–32.
‡"Other" also includes 63 persons who acquired HIV infection perinatally, but were diagnosed with AIDS after age 13.
Source: HIV/AIDS Surveillance Report, 1997, Vol. 9(1), p. 16.

This may include the development of adequate coping styles, identifying and entering careers they can achieve in, and joining AIDS support groups. Counseling AIDS clients requires great sensitivity and understanding of the complexities of the disease. Counselors must also guard against their own possible prejudices and fears.

Abuse Victims

With legal responsibilities for reporting suspected cases, the number of children abused annually is estimated to be more than one million. Domestic violence characterized by spouse abuse and/or child abuse is rampant in the United States, and the personal, social, and economic costs are inestimable. Reports indicate that one third of all married people engage in spouse abuse. As public awareness of the extent of the problem has increased, so have efforts to provide assistance and refuge for the adult victims and, frequently, relocation for the children.

Spouse abuse is often associated with poverty, substance abuse, and career disappointments. For abused spouses, the most popular response has been providing shelters and crisis lines. Most of the personnel for these settings are drawn from the ranks of paraprofessional

TABLE 5-7 Number and Percentage of Persons Aged ≥13 Years Reported with AIDS, by Sex and Race/Ethnicity—United States 1981–1996

	Year of Report											
	1992		1993*		1994		1995		1996		1981–1996	
Characteristic	Number	(%)	Number	(%)	Number	(%)	Number	(%)	Number	(%)	Number	(%)
Sex												
Male	40,330	(86)	87,945	(84)	64,730	(82)	59,285	(81)	54,653	(80)	488,300	(85)
Female	6,307	(14)	16,671	(16)	13,830	(18)	13,682	(19)	13,820	(20)	85,500	(15)
Race/Ethnicity												
White, non-Hispanic	22,320	(48)	47,468	(45)	32,677	(42)	29,402	(40)	26,229	(38)	267,487	(47)
Black, non-Hispanic	15,576	(33)	37,523	(36)	30,373	(39)	28,729	(39)	28,346	(41)	198,780	(35)
Hispanic	8,223	(18)	18,410	(18)	14,612	(19)	13,961	(19)	12,966	(19)	101,253	(18)
Asian/Pacific Islander	334	(<1)	761	(<1)	573	(<1)	558	(<1)	561	(<1)	4,090	(<1)
American Indian/ Alaskan Native	121	(<1)	369	(<1)	246	(<1)	237	(<1)	207	(<1)	1,544	(<1)
Total†	46,637	(100)	104,616	(100)	78,560	(100)	72,967	(100)	68,473	(100)	573,800	(100)

*Year the expanded AIDS surveillance case definition was implemented.
†Totals include persons with unknown or missing race/ethnicity.
Source: Morbidity and Mortality Weekly Report, Feb. 28, 1997, Centers for Disease Control and Prevention Vol. 46 (8), p. 166.

and volunteer workers, although helping professionals such as counselors, social workers, and/or psychologists are increasingly being utilized.

In recent years, the public has become more aware of the nature and extent of child abuse in the United States. Even so, we suspect the real extent of this national tragedy is largely unreported. Not only does child abuse destroy the joys and memories of youth, but its damaging aftereffects can cause psychological problems throughout the victims' adult life. The federal government and all states have passed legislation to stop child abuse. School counselors are mandated reporters of suspected child abuse in most states and, as a result, can be penalized for failing to report such cases.

Baker (1996) suggests steps as follows in reporting child abuse as a school system employee.

1. Report suspected cases of child abuse to the building principal immediately; that is, children under age eighteen who exhibit evidence of serious physical or mental injury not explained by the available medical history as being accidental; sexual abuse or serious physical neglect, if injury, abuse, or neglect has been caused by the acts or omissions of the child's parents or by a person responsible for the child's welfare.

2. Each building principal will designate a person to act in his or her stead when unavailable.

3. The principal may wish to form a team of consultants with whom to confer (e.g., school nurse, home and school visitor, counselor) before making an oral report to public welfare service representatives. This should be done within twenty-four hours of the first report.

4. It is not the responsibility of the reporter to prove abuse or neglect. Reports must be made in good faith, however.

5. Any person willfully failing to report suspected abuse may be subject to school board disciplinary action. (p. 287)

Additionally,

school counselors are the central helpers in any school system's child abuse prevention efforts. They must recognize the symptoms of possible abuse and their legal reporting responsibilities. They must also recognize their responsibility to take a leadership role in developing and implementing an effective program of child abuse prevention. Allsopp and Prosen (1988) emphasize the increasing need for counselors to provide appropriate training and information for school personnel who might be involved in cases of suspected child abuse. They discuss a model program which has been successfully implemented in the training of over 2,000 teachers and administrators to deal with sexual abuse cases. The program consisted of: (a) information related to offenders, victims, and non-offending family members; (b) present laws and proposed legislation; (c) requirements and procedures for school systems in reporting suspected child sexual abuse; and (d) available community resources for victim's use. Ninety-eight percent of teachers reported that the program increased their awareness of victims and offenders; 92 percent stated that the program provided them with a clearer understanding of the school system's procedures for reporting child sexual abuse; 93 percent expressed they had increased their knowledge of county services currently available to victims; and 98 percent reported that as a result of participation in the program, they felt more adequately prepared to deal with a situation in which a child was sexually abused.* (Gibson et al., 1993, p. 109)

*From Gibson, Robert L., Mitchell, Marianne H., and Basile, Sherry K., *Counseling in the Elementary School: A Comprehensive Approach*. Copyright © 1993 by Allyn and Bacon. Reprinted by permission.

The American School Counselor Association (1993) indicates that

> It is the responsibility of the school counselor to report suspected cases of child abuse/neglect to the proper authorities. Recognizing that the abuse of children is not limited to the home and that corporal punishment by school authorities might well be considered child abuse, the ASCA supports any legislation which specifically bans the use of corporal punishment as a disciplinary tool within the schools.

Please refer to Appendix M for the full text of the American School Counselor Association (ASCA) Child Abuse Statement (1993).

In recent years, we have also been made much more aware of the incidence of sexual abuse as the victims come forward and discuss the harmful effects of their experiences.

- Incidence research shows that between 8% to 38% of women and 5% to 9% of men in the United States have been victimized.
- Sexual abuse is an international concern, although specific statistics are not available.
- Sexual abuse essentially, by definition, is harmful.
- The most common ages of victims are 8 through 12, with many cases outside of that span.
- Stepfathers may be five times as likely to victimize a daughter sexually than fathers are, although other family members (brothers, uncles, grandfathers) could be offenders.
- Most female victimization occurs within the family.
- Boys are more likely to be abused outside the family than are girls. (Rencken, 1989, p. 3)

We can only assume that the extent of reported sexual abuse is minimal and that because of guilt, stigma, and fear, many, many incidents continue to go unreported. Regardless, the effect can be traumatic. Cooney (1991) indicates that the emotional effects of childhood sexual abuse include the *loss of childhood* because those who have been abused experience the adult world of sexuality; *guilt* and a sense of being responsible for the abuse; *low self-esteem* and the feeling that they are not as good as their peers; many kinds of *fear; confusion; depression; anger; inability to trust others; helplessness;* and *altered attitudes toward sexuality.*

Again, it is important to note the role of prevention programs. Such programs require careful planning and a coordinated effort involving school and community agency counselors, social workers, school teachers, administrators, nurses, and significant community groups. Parents obviously should be involved and educated regarding their responsibilities. Children themselves need to be educated and informed regarding sources of help if needed. The local media should also be requested to fully publicize the efforts to prevent child sexual abuse.

Sexual abuse is, of course, not limited to children. Adolescents are also frequently victimized, and rape, including date rape, is being increasingly reported. Although prevention is the desired antidote, we must still be prepared to assist the victims through crisis lines, crisis centers, and specialized rape assistance programs.

The victims of child abuse may be placed in temporary shelters or, in extreme cases, foster homes. The current trend, however, is to hold the family together if at all possible. An effort is made to give the parents the training and support they need to become adequate parents. Groups are commonly used for this purpose. The goal is to help them break the cycle of abuse. It should be emphasized that effective parenting does not come naturally but must be learned in a step-by-step fashion.

Counselors functioning in those settings serving abused spouses or children need special skills in individual and group counseling and crisis and short-time interventions, plus a knowledge of marriage and family dynamics.

Gays and Lesbians

In recent generations, the counseling profession has become more aware of issues relating to the counseling of lesbian women and gay men. Too, as many of this population are now readily acknowledging their sexual orientations and moving more openly into the public mainstream, more members of this group can be expected to seek assistance from counseling professionals.

Given that the research on the lesbian and gay populations to date is complex, often contradictory, and, in some cases, biased as well, counselors may find it confusing to find agreed-upon guidelines for providing effective counseling. However, in practice, many of the profession's proven approaches would appear to provide a basis for assistance inasmuch as many of the common problems faced by gays and lesbians are not unique to this population. These include the problems of (a) societal prejudice, (b) family conflict, (c) peer ridicule and rejection, and (d) health fears (especially AIDS).

In counseling, then, we would assume that awareness, acceptance, and understanding would provide a basic foundation. Going beyond these basics, in assisting adolescent gays and lesbians, Teague (1992) points out that

> homosexuality as a life-style can be many things to many people. For the gay or lesbian adolescent, it can lead to confusion, isolation, or a number of other serious problems such as attempted suicide. As a means of finding support and accurate information, these teens may seek out a mental health professional. (p. 422)

He concludes that

> effective intervention with gay and lesbian adolescents requires that mental health counselors take a positive approach that entails more than a simple acceptance of homoerotic people and life-styles. It requires a willingness to work with clients in accordance with the realities of a gay life-style rather than non-gay interpretations of those realities. It is a time to move beyond merely helping gays cope and adjust. As mental health counselors, we need to help them develop innovative and satisfying ways to grow as gay people. (Moses & Hawkins, 1982, as seen in Teague, 1992, p. 422)

In assisting gay and lesbian clients across a range of ages, Fassinger (1991) suggests

> a variety of theoretical approaches and techniques may be effective with gay and lesbian clients. Cognitive approaches, for example, may be useful in overcoming negative thinking and self-talk about gayness, whereas client-centered approaches may have great utility in encouraging expression of repressed affect. Gestalt "empty chair" techniques may be particularly effective in bringing into awareness all sides of the ambivalence and confusion about gay and non-gay affiliation, as well as helping individuals vicariously confront family, friends, co-workers and others about their identity. Feminist approaches are empowering in their examination of oppression and sex-role socialization, as well as their emphasis on equality in relationships (including the therapeutic alliance). Bibliotherapy is particularly important for this population, because so little is known about healthy gay people and life-styles due to societal invisibility and the lack of diverse role models. Family/ systems approaches and couples counseling are important for working with relationship issues, and group therapy is an effective means for reducing shame and alienation and developing social sup-

port. Cross-cultural approaches provide an important foundation for work with culturally diverse gay and lesbian clients. Overall, any theoretical approach or intervention should be carefully examined and re-examined throughout implementation for inherent bias and should be applied with sensitivity and professional self-awareness. (pp. 171–172)

Counselors should anticipate gays and lesbians among their clientele at all ages and be comfortable as well as knowledgeable in working with this population. The latter includes understanding the lifestyle and gender-specific issues common at different stages across the life span of gays and lesbians. In some settings and situations, counselors may find it useful to identify therapists who are themselves gays or lesbians for referral or consultative purposes.

SUMMARY

Counseling is the heart of the counselor's activity. Although there is general agreement in broadly defining counseling, a variety of theoretical concepts have emerged over the years. Traditional approaches such as psychoanalytic and client-centered theories are still popular, but in recent generations, behavioral theory, rational emotive therapy, reality therapy, and integrative theory have attracted followers. However, as noted in concluding our discussion of theory, counselors may still opt for the eclectic approach, one that gives the option of selecting from any and all of the existing theories.

The counseling process initially focuses on relationship establishment, then seeks to identify and explore the client's problem with the objective of establishing client goals. The process then proceeds to the planning and problem-solving stage and, finally, to the applying of the solution and termination of the counseling relationship. Although these stages tend to blend into each other, they serve as a guide to a logical sequence of events for the counseling process. The effective application of the process is dependent upon the basic counseling skills required of the counselor.

More and more attention has been given to the counselor's responsibility and need for special preparation in dealing with our population's diversity and a range of special problems. Recent generations have also noted increased usage of group counseling and other group techniques by counselors. These will be discussed in Chapter 7.

DISCUSSION QUESTIONS

1.   What theoretical orientation would you prefer for your own counselor?

2.   How can counseling help improve the quality of life for (a) children of elementary school age? (b) the elderly of postretirement age?

3.   When, or under what circumstances, would you encourage a friend to see a counselor?

4.   How do you interact in establishing a relationship when you meet someone for the first time? What impresses you most about an individual when you meet him or her for the first time?

5.   What are the differences and similarities between advising, providing guidance, and/or counseling an individual?

6.   Discuss counseling as a growth enhancement and/or development activity.

CLASS ACTIVITIES

1.   Interview a practicing counselor regarding his or her theoretical orientation and how he or she determined that this theory was the most appropriate.

2.   Identify the counseling theory that, at this early point in your training, you feel would be most appropriate for you. Share your rationale (in a group) with others in the class who have selected the same theory.

3.   Conscientiously practice the basic counseling skills of attending behavior in your interactions

with others for a week. Report your reactions and/or results.

4. Keep a log noting the effectiveness of your communications skills with others over a three-day period. What are the implications of your findings?

5. Organize the class into groups of three. Each individual in the triad is to alternate playing the role of counselor, client, and observer. The student-client has a problem; each of the three role-playing counselors is to practice, in the first round, the skill of attending behavior; in the second round, attending behavior plus reflection of feelings; in the third round, attending behavior, reflection of feelings, and facilitative communications. The observer, in addition to observing the process, is to evaluate the effectiveness of the counselor in practicing the basic skill or skills and be the time keeper for each session (approximately 5–7 minutes for the first round, 10 minutes for the second and third rounds). After the conclusion of each counseling session, counselor and client should also assess the process (allow about 15–20 minutes after each session for this activity).

SELECTED READINGS

Brammer, L. (1988). *The helping relationship* (4th ed.). Englewood Cliffs, NJ: Prentice-Hall (181 pages).

Claibourne, C., & Ibrahim, F. (Eds.). (1987). Counseling and violence [Special issue]. *Journal of Counseling and Development, 65* (7), 338–390.

Cooney, J. (1988). Child abuse: A developmental perspective. *Counseling and Human Development, 20* (5), 1–10.

Davenport, D. S., & Woolley, K. K. (1997). Innovative brief pithy psychotherapy: A contribution from corporate managed mental health care. *Professional Psychology: Research and Practice, 28,* 197–200.

Gold, J. R. (1996). *Key concepts in psychotherapy integration.* New York: Plenum Press.

Hill, C., Helmer, J., Tichenor, V., Spiegel, S., O'Grady, K., & Perry, E. (1988). Effects of

therapist response made in brief psychotherapy. *Journal of Counseling Psychology, 35* (3), 222–233.

Ivey, A., & Goncalves, O. (1986). Developmental therapy: Integrating developmental processes into the clinical practice. *Journal of Counseling and Development, 66* (9), 406–413.

Maki, R. H., & Syman, E. M. (1997). Teaching of controversial and empirically validated treatments in APA-accredited clinical and counseling psychology programs. *Psychotherapy, 34* (1), 44–57.

Okum, B. (1987). *Effective helping: Interviewing and counseling techniques* (3rd ed.). Monterey, CA: Brooks/Cole (293 pages).

Shaikur, B. (1988). The measurement and treatment of client anger in counseling. *Journal of Counseling and Development, 66* (8), 361–365.

Smith, D. (1982). Trends in counseling and psychotherapy. *American Psychologist, 37* (7), 802–809.

Stalikas, A., & Fitzpatrick, M. (1996). Relationships between counsellor interventions, client experiencing, and emotional expressiveness: An exploratory study. *Canadian Journal of Counselling, 30,* 262–271.

Switzky, H. N. (1997). Individual differences in personality and motivational systems in persons with mental retardation. In W. E. MacLean, Jr. (Ed.), *Ellis' handbook of mental deficiency, psychological theory and research* (3rd ed.) (pp. 343–377). Mahwah, NJ: Lawrence Erlbaum Associates.

Tracey, T., & Dundon, M. (1988). Role anticipation and preparations over the course of counseling. *Journal of Counseling Psychology, 35* (1), 3–14.

Weinrach, S. (1987). Microcounseling and beyond: A dialogue with Allen Ivey. *Journal of Counseling and Development, 65* (10), 532–537.

RESEARCH OF INTEREST

Bieschke, D. J., Bowman, G. D., Hopkins, M., & Levine, H. (1995). Improvement and satisfaction with short-term therapy at a university counseling center. *Journal of College Student Development, 35* (6), 553–559.

Abstract

This study examined satisfaction and variables that contributed to improvement among university counseling center clients. Ninety-eight 17–47-year-old students (74 female) who received short-term (3–10 sessions) individual counseling completed pre- and post-treatment evaluations. Therapists consisted of advanced psychology graduate students, psychology interns, part-time counselors, and senior staff. Ninety-four percent of the clients expressed satisfaction with services and demonstrated a reduction in distress. Clients' perceptions of the therapeutic working alliance significantly contributed to their satisfaction.

Bloch, S., Szmukler, G. I., Herrman, H., & Benson, A. (1995). Counseling caregivers of relatives with schizophrenia: Themes, interventions, and caveats. *Family Process, 34* (4), 413–425.

Abstract

This study evaluated an intervention designed to reduce burden and increase physical and emotional well-being in sixty caregivers of patients with schizophrenia. Subjects were randomly assigned to experimental or control groups. Experimental subjects underwent six one-hour weekly individual counseling sessions. Coping, family, and social themes arose among subjects. Cases associated with those themes are described. Principle interventions applied by the counselors included active listening, recognition of the caregiver's experience, clarification of problems arising in counseling, and use of educational approaches. Counselors were given caveats to treatment as the program evolved. Caveats addressed issues including therapists' blurring of professional boundaries and subjects addressing concerns other than those unique to caregiving. Thirteen themes emerged.

Holloway, E. L., & Wampold, B. E. (1986). Relation between conceptual level and counseling-related tasks: A meta-analysis. *Journal of Counseling Psychology, 33* (3), 310–319.

Abstract

Meta-analysis was used to review 24 studies that applied conceptual systems theory (CST) (a) to investigate the effect of counselor's conceptual level (CL) on the counselor's performance and (b) to investigate the matching of CL and environmental structure. Results corroborate the predictive power of CST in the context of the counseling situation. The prediction that counselors who were matched with a compatible environment (i.e., low-CLs with high structure and high-CLs with low structure) would perform better than those who were mismatched was corroborated. It was also found that low CLs generally performed significantly better in more highly structured environments, whereas high CLs showed only a slight improvement in their matched low CL environment. Due to the lack of standardization in the task stimulus, it was unclear whether higher CLs generally performed better than low CLs. Methodological, conceptual, and training issues are discussed.

Howard, K. I., Orlinsky, D. E., & Lueger, R. J. (1994). Clinically relevant outcome research in individual psychotherapy: New models guide the researcher and clinician. *British Journal of Psychiatry, 165* (1), 4–8.

Abstract

This article recommends a more systematic exploratory methodology for clinical research, emphasizing the generalizability and constructive replication of findings. This quasi-experimental, case-study approach entails the use of objective data, continuous assessment, a model of problem stability, diverse and heterogeneous samples, and clear evidence of an effect that can be ensured for magnitude and treatment applicability.

Lambert, M. J., & Okiishi, J. C. (1997). The effects of the individual psychotherapist and implications for future research. *Clinical Psychology Science and Practice, 4* (1), 66–75.

Abstract

A body of research concerning psychotherapy outcome is reviewed with the intent of establishing the importance of the individual psychotherapist to treatment process and outcome. Although particular therapy techniques have not been shown to be especially important in therapy process and outcome, they have been the focus of most research and training for the past two decades. In the past, extensive study of the individual therapist was difficult, but the rising trend of managed health care organizations has created opportunities to conduct research on this topic. Hypothetical outcome data for individual clinicians are presented in graphical form. An attempt is made to show how patient typing can be used to adjust outcome by case-mix methods. Suggestions for future research are made.

Waller, G. (1997). Drop-out and failure to engage in individual outpatient cognitive behavior therapy for bulimic disorders. *International Journal of Eating Disorders, 22* (1), 35–41.

Abstract

This study explored the characteristics of bulimics who fail to complete therapy. Noncompleters were divided into those who failed to engage and those who dropped out, so that these groups could be directly compared. Subjects were 50 women (bulimia nervosa or anorexia nervosa of the bulimic subtype) recruited from a case series of referrals to an eating disorders clinic, who were offered individual cognitive-behavior therapy. The women (28 completers; mean age 22.3 years) were compared on standardized measures of eating, psychological, and family characteristics. The noncompleting groups both had high levels of borderline psychopathology and more severe perceived bulimic characteristics than the completers. However, the dropouts and failures-to-engage subjects had very different patterns of perceived family emotional involvement, with the failures-to-engage subjects reporting relatively healthy functioning.

Weisz, J. R., Weiss, B., Alicke, M. D., & Klotz, M. L. (1987). Effectiveness of psychotherapy with children and adolescents: A meta-analysis for clinicians. *Journal of Consulting and Clinical Psychology, 55* (4), 542–549.

Abstract

This team conducted a meta-analysis of 108 well-designed outcome studies using 4- through 18-year-old subjects to examine effectiveness of psychotherapy with children and adolescents. Overall, findings revealed significant, durable effects of treatment that differed somewhat with client age and treatment method but which were reliably greater than zero for most groups, most problems, and most methods.

Chapter

6

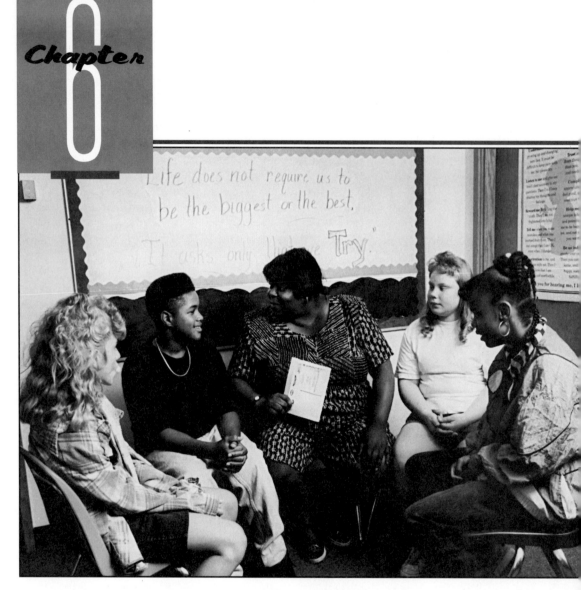

Life does not require us to be the biggest or the best.

"It asks only that we Try."

Multicultural Counseling

The United States has always been known as a country of considerable population diversity where many cultures have contributed to its greatness. Over the past 40 years, increasing attention has been given to the uniqueness and rights of these minority cultures. The Civil and Equal Rights movements and attending legislation focused attention on racial as well as gender inequalities in the last quarter of the 20th century. Additionally, projected growth in numbers and percentages of America's minority populations in the decades immediately ahead increases the urgency of developing positive helping relationships among all our cultures. This heightened national attention has also been reflected in the counseling profession, in which a noticeable increase in attention to the needs and issues of cross-cultural counseling has occurred over the past 25 years. In this context, counseling as a human relationship and helping profession must become a significant and positive national influence—and of course, in our specialty area of individual counseling, we must demonstrate consistently and conclusively that we are truly multiculturally oriented in both theory and practice; that we are effective as multicultural counselors.

Attending to these needs is further mandated by all the major associations that accredit the preparation of counselors (Council for the Accreditation of Counseling and Related Programs, Council on Rehabilitation Education, American Psychological Association, National Association for the Accreditation of Teacher Education, and all the regional accreditation associations).

ETHNIC GROUPS AND CROSS-CULTURAL COUNSELING

xMulticultural counseling is a process in which desired outcomes are not impeded by cultural differences between counselor and client. How the counselor arrives at this higher level of functioning and factors that must be considered are discussed in this chapter.

Certainly, our often stated philosophical assumptions of the inherent worth and dignity of the individual, respect for the individual's uniqueness, the right of the individual to self-actualization, and so forth, would indicate our commitment to effective cross-cultural counseling.

In addition, counselors must move beyond commitment, as important as it may be, to an active pursuit of appropriate theoretical foundation and effective practices. In our pursuit of positive and meaningful multicultural counseling and guidance, we must be constantly aware that the term *multi* means "many" and that we are sensitizing ourselves to the uniqueness of the many different cultures that comprise our population. In so doing, we recognize that many of the traditional characteristics of the mainstream counseling process (i.e., openness, emotional expression, sharing of intimate feelings, etc.) may actually inhibit effectiveness with clients of minority cultures.

Ridley (1995) notes that multicultural clients are more likely than White clients to have unfavorable experiences in some of the major aspects of counseling including the following.

- **Diagnosis.** Minority clients tend to receive a misdiagnosis, usually involving more severe psychopathology but occasionally involving less severe psychopathology, more often than is warranted.
- **Staff assignment.** Minority clients tend to be assigned to junior professionals, paraprofessionals, or nonprofessionals for counseling rather than senior and more highly trained professionals.

- **Treatment modality.** Minority clients tend to receive low-cost, less preferred treatment consisting of minimal contact, medication only, or custodial care rather than intensive psychotherapy.
- **Utilization.** Minority clients tend to be represented disproportionately in mental health facilities. Specifically, minority clients are underrepresented in private treatment facilities and overrepresented in public treatment facilities.
- **Treatment duration.** Minority clients show a much higher rate of premature termination and dropout from therapy, or they are confined to much longer inpatient care.
- **Attitudes.** Minority clients report more dissatisfaction and unfavorable impressions regarding treatment. (p. 9)

Lee (1991) emphasizes that counseling professionals must consider language differences that may exist between themselves and their culturally different clients.

> Multiculturism is a pervasive force in modern society that acknowledges the complexity of culture. During the last 20 years, multiculturalism has become recognized as a powerful force, not just for understanding "exotic" groups but also for understanding ourselves and those with whom we work in a complicated social context. Multiculturalism has gained the status of a general theory, complementing other scientific theories to explain human behavior (Pedersen, 1991, p. 6)
>
> Whether or not multiculturalism emerges as a truly generic approach to counseling and whether or not it emerges as a fourth force with an articulated impact on counseling equivalent to behaviorism, psychodynamics, and humanism, culture does provide a valuable metaphor for understanding ourselves and others. It is no longer possible for counselors to ignore their own culture or the culture of their clients. Until the multicultural perspective is understood as making the counselor's job easier instead of harder and increasing rather than decreasing the quality of a counselor's life, however, little real change is likely to happen. (Pedersen, 1991, p. 11)

It is especially important that counselors in schools be sensitive to the differing cultures represented there. This not only increases their effectiveness as professional counselors and makes them more acceptable and approachable to all students, but it also enables them to serve as adults modeling appropriate behaviors and attitudes toward all ethnic and cultural groups.

Further, "school counselors in particular must be aware that minority children and adolescents are the most rapidly growing segment of the youth population but that there is little information available about their problems or needs" (Gibbs, Huang, & Associates, 1989). Counselors who work with children have an added responsibility because children cannot control their environment. The understanding or lack of understanding demonstrated by others about cultural differences can influence the core of the child's developing personality. Children are in the early stages of cultural awareness and may not recognize that their experiences differ from others (Anderson & Cranston-Gingras, 1991, p. 91) and that forms of discrimination may exist.

"A major developmental task is to discover and integrate one's ethnicity, culture, and race as these affect oneself and others (Christensen, 1989). Children may internalize the beliefs of the majority about their own cultural group. One of the goals of culturally sensitive counselors is to foster the child's environment so that the emphasis is on the child's uniqueness and not on conformity with the norm" (Anderson & Cranston-Gingras, 1991, p. 91).

Pedersen (1988) recommends that students in counselor preparation programs need to develop awareness that would require an individual to have

- ability to recognize direct and indirect communication styles;
- sensitivity to nonverbal cues;

- awareness of cultural and linguistic differences;
- interest in the culture;
- sensitivity to the myths and stereotypes of the culture;
- concern for the welfare of persons from another culture;
- ability to articulate elements of his or her own culture;
- appreciation of the importance of multicultural teaching;
- awareness of the relationships between cultural groups; and
- accurate criteria for objectively judging "goodness" and "badness" in the other culture. (p. 9)

In further heightening awareness of multicultural issues and practices in counseling, we call your attention to the Association for Multicultural Counseling and Development (AMCD), a division of the American Counseling Association (ACA), which publishes a journal of the same name as well as a newsletter.

> We also note the importance of increasing the number and ratio of counselors from culturally different or minority backgrounds in our elementary schools. Not only should minority children have access to counselors of similar ethnicity, but all children should have exposure to role models representing the great cultural diversity of our country.
>
> Our country is no longer considered a "melting pot" of many cultures, one in which emphasis is placed on all cultures becoming the same as the majority culture. Rather, the concept of cultural pluralism has been adopted which focuses on the retention and value of the diverse aspects of every culture that constitutes our nation. In this regard, counselors can advocate the preservation of cultural diversity and model the respect and acceptance that all minorities deserve.
>
> In schools, counselors can ensure that minorities are included in group activities and that classroom guidance activities are utilized to educate the school population about cultural diversity. Too, counselors must always be mindful that diversity exists within every cultural/racial population. There are no exact profiles for any minority group. The only "stereotype" is that individual differences exist in all populations. (Gibson, Mitchell, Basile, 1993, p. 121)

Sue (1981) presents sources of conflict and misinterpretation in cross-cultural counseling, as noted in Tables 6-1 and 6-2. Sue (1978) also proposes characteristics that distinguish culturally effective counselors. First, culturally effective counselors understand their own values and assumptions of human behavior and recognize that those held by others may differ. Second, culturally effective counselors realize that "no theory of counseling is politically or morally neutral." Third, culturally effective counselors also understand that external sociopolitical forces may have influenced and shaped culturally different groups. Fourth, culturally effective counselors are able to share the world-view of their clients rather than being culturally encapsulated. Finally, culturally effective counselors are truly eclectic in their counseling, using counseling skills because of their appropriateness to the experiences and lifestyles of the culturally different.

Minorities, as a label, implies less than full-time or majority membership in a society. It is important that counselors convey through their attitudes and actions that these populations are full, equal members of society. Because understanding alone will not accomplish the task, it is vitally important that counselors educate themselves about different ethnic peoples. The counselor must learn to communicate both verbally and nonverbally in a manner and style that is recognizable and comfortable for the client. The counselor must convey his or her own attitude of acceptance and respect for the ethnic client, and the counselor must genuinely feel this respect if he or she is to convey it successfully.

TABLE 6-1   Generic Characteristics of Counseling

Language	Middle Class	Culture
Standard English	Standard English	Standard English
Verbal communication	Verbal communication	Verbal communication
	Adherence to time schedules (50-minute session)	Individual centered
	Long-range goals	Verbal/emotional/behavioral expressiveness
	Ambiguity	Client-counselor communication
		Openness and intimacy
		Cause-effect orientation
		Clear distinction between physical and mental well-being

Source: From D. W. Sue, *Counseling the Culturally Different: Theory and Practice,* p. 31. Copyright ©
1981 John Wiley & Sons, Inc. Reprinted by permission of John Wiley & Sons, Inc.

African Americans

In 1996, African Americans were the largest minority in the United States, with an estimated
population of more than 33 million. This population has historically been a victim of racism,
prejudice, and discrimination. Although legislative, educational, and humanitarian efforts are
being made to overcome these abusive elements, programs have been slow to develop, and
not without resistance. Disturbing data even today indicates the high percentage of Black
youths in the criminal justice system; high numbers of unemployed and underemployed; and
lack of adequate population representation in higher education (both as students and faculty),
the professions, and supervisory and management positions. The counseling profession has a
responsibility to be proactive, contributing to the righting of these social wrongs, and to be
effective in working with African American clients.

The previous chapter discussed the importance of getting off to a good start in the counseling relationship. It is also important to integrate an appropriate multicultural dimension
when assisting African American clients. Some suggestions about the elements necessary in
the vital first few sessions follow.

1. Identify the expectations of the Black clients, find out what they believe counseling is, and explore their feelings about counseling.
2. Indicate what you feel counseling is and what you do during counseling. Find out if they feel
   that will be useful to them.
3. Indicate the limits of confidentiality. If the client was referred, explain your relationship with
   that agency and the information, if any, that you will share with the agency.
4. If you are not Black, find out how the client feels about working with an individual from a different ethnic group.
5. If there is difficulty with self-disclosure, attempt to identify the reasons for this.

TABLE 6-2   Third World Group Variables

Language	Lower Class	Culture
	Asian Americans	

Bilingual background	Nonstandard English
	Action oriented
	Different time perspective
	Immediate, short-range goals
	Concrete, tangible,
	    structured approach
		Asian language
		Family centered
		Restraint of feelings
		One-way communication
		    from authority figure to person
		Silence is respect
		Advice seeking
		Well-defined patterns of
		    interaction (concrete
		    structured)
		Private versus public display
		    (shame/disgrace/pride)
		Physical and mental
		    well-being defined differently

	Blacks	

Black language	Nonstandard English
	Action oriented
	Different time perspective
	Immediate, short-range goals
	Concrete, tangible,
	    structured approach
		Black language
		Sense of "peoplehood"
		Action oriented
		Paranorm due to oppression
		Importance placed on
		    nonverbal behavior

	Hispanics	

Bilingual background	Nonstandard English
	Action oriented
	Different time perspective
	Immediate, short-range goals
	Concrete, tangible,
	    structured approach
		Spanish speaking
		Group-centered cooperation
		Temporal difference
		Family orientation
		Different pattern of
		    communication
		A religious distinction
		    between mind/body

	American Indians	

Bilingual background	Nonstandard English
	Action oriented
	Different time perspective
	Immediate, short-range goals
	Concrete, tangible,
	    structured approach
		Tribal dialects
		Cooperative not competitive
		    individualism
		Present-time orientation
		Creative/experiential/
		    intuitive/nonverbal
		Satisfy present needs
		Use of folk or super natural
		    explanations

Source: From D. W. Sue, *Counseling the Culturally Different: Theory and Practice,* pp. 31-32. Copyright © 1981 John Wiley & Sons, Inc. Reprinted by permission of John Wiley & Sons, Inc.

6. Find out information on the history of the problem and the client's perception of the causes. Also, what would the client see as a valuable outcome of counseling?

7. Gather information on the family (nuclear or extended). It is important to determine who helps out and who is living with the family.

8. Identify the strengths of the clients and their families. What resources are available to them? How have they handled problems successfully before?

9. Examine external factors that might be related to the presenting problem, including the impact of racism and concerns for health, education, employment. Identify agencies they come in contact with. Identify any additional stressors.

10. If appropriate, examine issues revolving around racial identity and associated personal conflicts.

11. After information about the problem has been gathered, establish mutually agreed-upon goals.

12. Talk about and consider the means to achieve the goals.

13. Discuss the number of sessions necessary to achieve the goals and the responsibilities of the counselor and the client.

14. Determine whether the client feels the two of you can work together. Also, consider other options that are available. (Sue & Sue, 1990, p. 225)

Of course, these elements can be shifted about and some even omitted on occasion.

It is also important for counselors to recognize that within the African American population there is great diversity. This means that the counselor must be alert and sensitive to individual differences and avoid the trap of cultural stereotyping. Exum and Moore (1993) suggest four basic strategies for an out-of-culture counselor working with African American clients.

1. Rely on the core conditions.
2. Use directive rather than passive or nondirective methods.
3. Attend to nonverbal behavior.
4. Be available. (pp. 204–207, cited in McFadden, 1993)

Client characteristics common to African Americans which counselors should be sensitive to are such psychological strengths as flexibility, forgiveness, resilience, and persistence. In general, they value God and family, getting along with others, and believing the best about everyone. Their most common coping mechanisms are denial, isolation, repression, and introjection.

Latin Americans

Latin Americans represent the fastest growing minority in the United States, with an estimated 27 million plus population in 1996. The overwhelming majority (60%) of this population is Mexican, followed by Puerto Rican (15%) and Cuban (6%). The remaining are almost exclusively from other Central and South American countries. The continued rapid growth of this group, aided by legal immigration influx, further accentuates the need for the preparedness of counselors who can function effectively with Latin American clients.

Perhaps the most informative perspective for counseling professionals is one that is limited to values orientation in the context of family values and sex roles (Arredondo, 1991). This perspective notes the significant role of the family as the predominant and most valued of social institutions in Latin cultures. Parental authority is unquestioned and family loyalty is a given. Sex roles are also clearly defined, with males being dominant in the more traditional settings. Males are expected wage earners outside the home, although Latin women in the United States are increasingly entering the workforce. These changing roles and values are often a source of conflict within the Latin American family and society.

In working with Latin American clients, counselors must be aware, as with other cultures, of stereotyping. There are many Latin American subcultures, each with its own uniqueness. As with other cultures, it is important that the client be treated with dignity by correctly pronouncing his or her name. Respect for the Latin American client is of utmost importance if the counseling process is to succeed. Too, in common with other minority clients, counselors must anticipate that most Latin Americans will have little understanding of counseling and counselors. As a result, counselors will usually be more successful if they use a directive approach with Latin American clients and avoid the use of psychodynamic terminology and assessment measures that are apt to turn the client away.

Asian Americans

Another rapidly growing minority population in the United States are Asian Americans. This population was estimated at 9.5 million in 1995. Within this population are numerous distinct national groups, including Japanese Americans, Chinese Americans, Phillipino Americans, Korean Americans, and so on. This diversity within the global group again highlights the importance of avoiding broad include-all categorizations. Even so, there are several areas of commonality which culturally conscientious counselors should be aware of including family roles and values, control and restraint of emotions, and deference to and respect for authority. The cultural values of the various national groups are also important to recognize. Counseling and related mental health therapies are not well known or accepted by the vast majority of Asian Americans. It may, therefore, be appropriate to consider treatment strategies for immigrants and refugees as suggested by Ishisaka, Nguyen, and Okimoto (1985); Lorenzo and Adler (1984); Nidorf (1985); and Tung (1985).

1. Use restraint when gathering information. Because of the stigma against mental illness, the norm against sharing private matters with outsiders, the lack of client knowledge of the mental health field, the therapist should refrain from asking too many questions.
2. Prepare the clients for counseling by engaging in role preparation. Lambert and Lambert (1984) found that Asian immigrants who were told about (a) what happens in therapy, (b) the need for verbal disclosure, (c) problems typically encountered by clients in therapy, (d) the role of the therapist and client, (e) misconceptions of therapy, and (f) the need for attendance adjusted better to counseling than a control group who did not receive role preparation. The clients who were prepared developed more accurate perceptions of therapy, saw their therapist as more interested and respectful, perceived more positive changes on their part, and were more satisfied with their adjustment.
3. Focus on the specific problem brought in by the client, and help the client develop his or her goals for therapy. This allows the concerns of the client to be presented and reduces the chance that the world-view of the therapist will be imposed on the client.
4. Take an active and directive role. Because of cultural expectations and a lack of experience with mental health therapy, the clients will rely on the counselor to furnish direction.
5. Do a thorough analysis of current environmental concerns, such as the need for food and shelter. The clients may need help filling out forms, need information on services that are available to them, and help in interacting with agencies. Assess financial and social needs.

6. In working with families, consider intergenerational conflicts especially due to changes in role, culture conflict, and differences in acculturation levels.

7. The therapy should be time limited, focus on concrete resolution of problems, and deal with the present or immediate future. (Sue & Sue, 1990, pp. 199–200)

Arabian Americans

An emerging minority of recent decades has been the Arabian Americans. In 1996 there were an estimated three million plus Arabs residing in the United States plus 40,000 people with student visas. Due to their relatively recent emergence as a recognizable minority, the counseling profession has focused little attention on their uniqueness and needs. We are aware of discriminations and stereotypes generated in the public opinion sector by media attention to terrorist activities attributed to individuals of Arabian descent. The hostility and suspicion between many in the two cultures (Arabian American and Caucasian American) has handicapped both opportunities and positive outcomes for counseling with this population.

In seeking to assist Arabian American clients, counselors must display extra sensitivity to their clients' cultural background. Again, keeping in mind the diversity within this minority population, some generalizations can be made that most Arabian Americans share the following beliefs and practices.

1. Marriage and children are essential for a complete and happy adult life.
2. Men are the heads of their families and the designated decision makers. In other words, authority and family identification are patrilineal.
3. The extended family is valued across generations. Young people owe profound respect to their elders, and often even to older siblings.
4. Children are expected to care for their parents and older relatives, usually inviting them to live in their homes, particularly after an older person is widowed.
5. Family honor is most easily damaged by the behavior of women, so they have a great responsibility toward the entire extended family to comport themselves in an honorable way.
6. Family ties and duties have precedence over work or career aspirations.
7. Religious identity and belief in God are essential. (McFadden, 1993, p. 264)

Counselors can test their cultural sensitivity and levels of awareness for counseling Arabian American clients by responding to the following questions.

• Am I able to recognize direct and indirect communication styles?
• Am I sensitive to nonverbal cues?
• Am I aware of cultural and linguistic differences among Arab groups?
• What are some common myths and stereotypes about Arabs?
• What stereotypes do Arabs have about Americans?
• Am I aware of my own feelings about Arabs and Arab society and culture? (Pedersen, 1988)

Counselors must constantly strive to improve their therapeutic relationships and effectiveness with this minority. Of even more importance is our profession's responsibility as human relationship specialists that we become an active force in building positive and productive relationships between Arab minorities and mainstream populations. The greatness and idealism of this nation was not built on prejudice and hostilities among our diverse populations. We must join the effort to reverse this undesirable trend.

Native Americans

Native Americans numbered over two million in 1996. Though not large in numbers compared with other minorities, American Indians have suffered long and disgraceful discrimination. Discrimination has been stimulated over the generations by federal government policies and politics, in which tribal welfare was rarely a consideration. Living on desecrated reservations, they have been isolated from the mainstream American culture and all too frequently have lived in deprivation and poverty.

As with other minority cultures, counselors must first of all understand the diversity that exists within the Native American population. Today, the U.S. government recognizes more than 500 tribes, each with its own traditions, values, spiritual beliefs, and family and tribal structure. Complicating this already complex mosaic are various federal legislation enactments and their interpretations.

All of this is to say to the would-be counselor of Native Americans that there is no stereotype or cultural profile that can be drawn on as absolute. It may be suggested that many Native Americans manifest a respect and desire for harmony with nature and their family and tribal systems. Giving, sharing, and cooperation are also common values of long standing. Counselors must approach their Native American clients with sensitivity and understanding and the realization that they may be viewed in the same sense as a tribal elder—meaning more talk and advice giving on the part of the counselor. Of course, by explaining the counseling process to the client, this may be somewhat mitigated.

> Arredondo (1986) has proposed a systematic model for working with refugees that is also applicable to working with Indian/Native clients. This model is holistic, in that it encompasses six dimensions of the client's life: the historical era, sociopolitical factors, sociocultural factors, individual variables, developmental tasks, and esteem and identity themes.
>
> By using these six dimensions and combining them with social cognitive interventions, the counselor will be using a framework that is considered less culturally biased than other theoretical approaches (LaFromboise & Rowe, 1983). This approach is considered less biased because it recognizes the impact of culture on personal and environmental variables and allows each culture to define its own appropriate behaviors or targets for intervention. It is culturally sensitive in that it provides for the differences across tribes. (Peregoy, 1993, p. 184)

THE CULTURALLY SKILLED COUNSELOR

The concept of our country as a melting pot where all of our many cultures become one is no longer appropriate. Rather, we view the strength of our nation as one in which our various cultures, in preserving their own uniqueness, contribute to our national well-being. Counselors have the opportunity to make significant contributions to the preservation of cultural diversity and the well-being of all culture and as advocates and role models, of course, in their professional practice as effective counselors to culturally diverse populations.

Counselors need a set of principles to guide them in their practice and at the same time respect the individuality of every client. These principles will assist counselors in more effectively counseling clients from culturally diverse backgrounds.

1. Every client should be understood from his or her unique frame of reference.
2. Nomothetic, normative information does not always fit a particular client.
3. People are a dynamic blend of multiple roles and identities.
4. The idiographic perspective is compatible with the biopsychosocial model of mental health.
5. The idiographic perspective is transtheoretical. (Ridley, 1995, pp. 82–83)

The following therapeutic actions will assist counselors in becoming more effective with minority clients.

1. Develop cultural self-awareness.
2. Avoid value imposition.
3. Accept your naiveté as a multicultural counselor.
4. Show cultural empathy.
5. Incorporate cultural considerations into counseling.
6. Do not stereotype.
7. Weigh and determine the relative importance of the client's primary cultural roles.
8. Do not blame the victim.
9. Remain flexible in your selection of interventions.
10. Examine your counseling theories for bias.
11. Build on the client's strengths.
12. Do not protect clients from emotional pain. (Ridley, 1995, pp. 88–100)

Understanding the impact of cultural values, beliefs, behaviors, and other influences is obviously important when individuals (i.e., counselor and client) from different cultural backgrounds seek to relate and understand each other.

Ivey, Ivey, and Simek-Morgan (1993, p. 105) developed a cube illustrating the various types of multicultural concerns clients can present in therapy. All clients are combinations of many multicultural issues, and differing ones may be prepotent at different times. A range of multicultural issues affecting the counseling relationship make up one side of the multicultural cube (see Figure 6-1).

Along the left side of the cube is the locus of the issue. Although therapists traditionally tend to locate the concern in the individual, an individual issue may actually derive from the family, and the family issue may derive from problems in the group, community, state, or even country. This points to the need to engage in family therapy, group work, or even community and political action to promote change.

Clients also have differing levels of awareness of multicultural issues. Four stages of cultural identity are listed in Figure 6-1 (Ivey et al., 1993, pp. 105–106).

To conclude, we note that to serve all cultures counseling programs should have at least one minority counselor; ensure that all professional and staff are multiculturally attuned (use consultants if necessary); address issues that may be the concerns of minorities only; consider—are public announcements of services appealing and appropriate to *all* populations; involve minority community members in planning; and be advocates for all cultures.

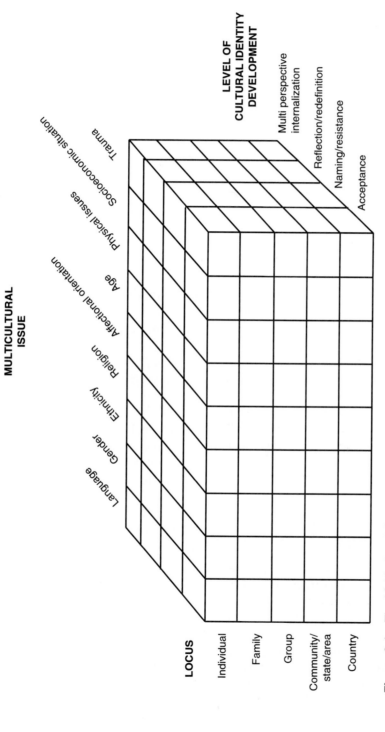

Figure 6-1 The Multicultural Cube.

Source: From A. E. Ivey, M. B. Ivey, and L. Simek-Morgan, *Counseling and Psychotherapy: A Multicultural Perspective*, 3rd ed., p. 106, 1993. Copyright © 1993 Allyn and Bacon.

SUMMARY

Multicultural counseling is a process in which desired outcomes are not impeded by cultural differences between the counselor and the client. This chapter discussed how the counselor can arrive at this higher level of functioning and factors that must be considered. These factors were discussed in relationship to African Americans, Latin Americans, Asian Americans, Arabian Americans, and Native Americans. The importance of the counselor understanding his or her own culture and how this affects his or her interaction with clients of differing cultures was also noted.

DISCUSSION QUESTIONS

1.   How would multicultural issues affect the way you assess a client and arrive at a clinical diagnosis? Do multicultural issues only affect assessment when the client is culturally different from the counselor? Why or why not?

2.   As a culturally effective counselor, how will you integrate multicultural skills and recommendations into your own personal theory of counseling?

3.   When conducting assessments from a multicultural perspective, how will you apply culturally relevant data to your clients without engaging in stereotyping or bias? How will you attend to individual, or idiographic, client data without ignoring cultural norms?

CLASS ACTIVITIES

1.   Divide into small groups. In each group, discuss what cultural biases and assumptions are held and have group members challenge unfounded biases and stereotypes.

2.   Consider the following scenario:

A Korean child is transferred to a predominantly White school. Discuss among the class how the school counselor would help the child adjust to the new environment. What cultural issues should the counselor consider?

3.   Divide into small groups. In each group, have each person answer the following questions: (a) How would I describe my own ethnicity? (b) What would I identify as my race? (c) What do I identify as my culture? Then discuss what one would look for in a client in order to determine the client's ethnicity, race, and cultural background.

4.   Divide into pairs. Describe a time when you exhibited intentional or unintentional racism, and what could have been done differently to avoid exhibiting the racist behavior. Then discuss your own experiences with being victims of racism. Finally, discuss times you exhibited cultural sensitivity.

SELECTED READINGS

American Psychological Association, Office of Ethnic Minority Affairs (1993). Guidelines for providers of psychological services to ethnic, linguistic, and culturally diverse populations. *American Psychologist, 48,* 45–48.

Canino, I. A., & Spurlock, J. (1994). *Culturally diverse children and adolescents: Assessment, diagnosis, and treatment.* New York: The Guilford Press.

Coleman, H. L. K. (1995). Cultural factors and the counseling process: Implications for school counselors. *The School Counselor, 42,* 180–185.

Dana, R. H. (1993). *Multicultural assessment perspectives for professional psychology.* Boston: Allyn & Bacon.

LaFromboise, T. (1988). American Indian mental health policy. *American Psychologist, 33* (5), 388–397.

Locke, D. C. (1992). *Increasing multicultural understanding: A comprehensive model.* Newbury Park, CA: Sage Publications.

Paniagua, F. A. (1994). *Assessing and treating culturally diverse clients: A practical guide.* Thousand Oaks, CA: Sage Publications.

Pedersen, P. (1987). Ten frequent assumptions of cultural bias in counseling. *Journal of Multicultural Counseling and Development, 15* (1), 16–24.

Pedersen, P. B., Draguns, J. G., Lonner, W. J., & Trimble, J. E. (Eds.). (1996). *Counseling across cultures*. Thousand Oaks, CA: Sage Publications.

Ponterotto, J. G., & Pedersen, P. B. (1993). *Preventing prejudice: A guide for counselors and educators*. Newbury Park, CA: Sage Publications.

Ridley, C. R. (1995). *Overcoming unintentional racism in counseling and therapy*. Thousand Oaks, CA: Sage Publications.

Ridley, C. R., Mendoza, D. W., Kanitz, B. E., Angermeier, L., & Zenk, R. (1994). Cultural sensitivity in multicultural counseling: A perceptual schema model. *Journal of Counseling Psychology, 41*, 125–126.

Sinacore-Guinn, A. L. (1995). The diagnostic window: Culture and gender sensitive diagnosis and training. *Counselor Education and Supervision, 35*, 18–31.

Smith, E., & Vasquez, M. (Eds.). Cross-cultural counseling [Special issue]. *The Counseling Psychologist, 13* (4), 531–720.

Sue, D. W., Ivey, A. E., & Pedersen, P. B. (Eds.). (1996). *A theory of multicultural counseling and therapy*. Pacific Grove, CA: Brooks/Cole.

Sue, D. W., & Sue, D. (1990). *Counseling the culturally different: Theory and practice* (2nd ed.). New York: John Wiley.

Zayes, L. H., Torres, L. R., Malcolm, J., & DesRosiers, F. S. (1996). Clinicians' definitions of ethnically sensitive therapy. *Professional Psychology: Research and Practice, 27*, 78–82.

RESEARCH OF INTEREST

Atkinson, D. R. (1985). A meta-review of research on cross-cultural counseling and psychotherapy. *Journal of Multicultural Counseling and Development, 13* (4), 138–153.

Abstract

This article analyzes four major reviews of the research on the effects of race on counseling and psychotherapy (S. I. Abramowitz & J. Murray, 1983; D. R. Atkinson, 1983; D. K. Harrison, 1975; and J. M. Sattler, 1977) in terms of client use of mental health services, client preferences for counselor race or ethnicity, counselor prejudice and sterotyping, differential diagnosis of client problems, differential counseling process, differential treatment strategies, and differential outcomes. An attempt was made to examine research outcomes across ethnic groups, research designs, and research settings. Several observations regarding methodology are discussed, and several conclusions derived from analog, survey, and archival studies are reached. Recommendations for future research on cross-cultural counseling and psychotherapy are presented.

Atkinson, D. R. (1990). Minority students' reasons for not seeking counseling and suggestions for improving services. *Journal of College Student Development, 31*, 342–350.

Abstract

In this study, ethnic minority students were surveyed to determine the relationships between cultural commitment and counseling utilization, reasons for not seeking counseling, and suggestions for improving counseling services. Results indicate that past utilization of counseling or psychological services by ethnic minority students is not related to their cultural commitment. Rather, the availability of culturally similar or culturally sensitive counselors is an important determinant of counseling service utilization. Culturally sensitive counselors are most important to ethnic-identified minorities and least important to mainstream-identified minorities.

Bishop, J. B., & Richards, T. F. (1987). Counselor intake judgments about White and Black clients in a university counseling center. *Journal of Counseling Psychology, 34*, 96–98.

Abstract

Counselor intake judgments about White and Black clients at a university counseling center were compared. There were no significant differences found between the two groups on 10 of the 11 variables studied. Counselors reported significantly higher ratings only on the judged potential for change in Black clients when compared with that in White clients. Ratings on the type and severity of presenting problem, client anxiety level, ease of expression, motivation, realism of goals, and physical appearance were not significantly different. Counselors' feelings about clients and the predicted number of counseling sessions were also similar for Black and White subjects. The findings are discussed in light of previous research studies about racial diagnostic bias. Recommendations are made for future research efforts.

Folensbee, R. W., Draguns, J. G., & Danish, S. J. (1986). Impact of two types of counselor intervention on Black American, Puerto Rican, and Anglo-American analogue clients. *Journal of Counseling Psychology, 33,* 446–453.

Abstract

This study tested the hypothesis that types of counseling intervention may be differentially effective depending on the client's cultural background. A total of 84 female community college students of Black American, Puerto Rican, or Anglo-American backgrounds received either affective responses or closed questions from a counselor in an analogue counseling situation that permitted subject-generated responses. Content analyses and ratings of counselors revealed that affective responses were superior to closed questions on all dependent measures for Anglo-American subjects. For Black American subjects, all content variables and two of three ratings of counselors suggested superiority of affective responses. For Puerto Rican subjects, all ratings of counselors and three of four content variables suggested superiority of affective responses. The researchers concluded, in consideration of present and previous research, that affective responses are superior to closed questions in initial counseling interviews with Anglo-American college students. The same may be true for Black American and Puerto Rican community college students, but inconsistencies in results indicate that further research is necessary.

Ford, D. Y., Harris, J. J., III, & Schuerger, J. M. (1993). Racial identity development among gifted Black students: Counseling issues and concerns. *Journal of Counseling and Development, 71,* 409–417.

Abstract

This article discusses a review of the literature regarding the paucity of information pertaining to culture-specific issues of being African American and gifted. Psychological issues of being African American and gifted and perspectives on racial identity development are presented. Components of counseling interventions are indicated.

Neimeyer, G. J., & Gonzales, M. (1982, August). *Duration, satisfaction, and perceived effectiveness of cross-cultural counseling.* Paper presented at the Annual Convention of the American Psychological Association, Washington, DC.

Abstract

It is generally acknowledged that racial groups differ in their values, beliefs, and behaviors as well as counseling needs, but evidence is mixed as to the effects of racial differences in the counseling process. A sample of 70 clients participated in a study to examine the differences in the duration, satisfaction, and effectiveness resulting from combinations of White and non-White counselors and clients. Results indicated that White counselors provided fewer sessions and that non-White clients expressed lower levels of overall satisfaction with counseling regardless of counselor race. No differences in counseling effectiveness were observed. White clients seeing White counselors attributed their change more to counseling than to other outside factors.

The results suggest that racial factors may be associated with the duration, satisfaction, and attribution of perceived change in counseling, but not with perceived effectivenss.

Ponterotto, J. G., Rieger, B. P., Barrett, A., & Sparks, R. (1994). Assessing multicultural counseling competence: A review of instrumentation. *Journal of Counseling and Development, 72* (3), 316–322.

Abstract

This article reviews four instruments designed to assess multicultural counseling competence in trainees and practicing professionals. The Cross-Cultural Counseling Inventory—Revised (CCCI–R), the Multicultural Counseling Awareness Scale–Form B (MCAS–B), the Multicultural Counseling Inventory (MCI), and the Multicultural Awareness-Knowledge-and-Skills Survey (MAKSS) were each critically reviewed in terms of item development, psychometric properties, and pragmatic utility. Specific research suggestions for continued empirical validation on the instruments are posited, and strong cautions regarding their use in training are leveled.

Wade, P., & Bernstein, B. L. (1991). Culture sensitivity training and counselor's race: Effects on Black female clients' perceptions and attrition. *Journal of Counseling Psychology, 38,* 9–15.

Abstract

Effects of brief culture sensitivity training for counselors, effects of counselors' race on Black female clients' perceptions of counselor characteristics, and the counseling relationship and clients' satisfaction with counseling were examined in an actual counseling situation. Client attrition across three sessions was also assessed. Clients assigned to experienced counselors who had received culture sensitivity training rated their counselor higher on credibility and relationship measures, returned for more follow-up sessions, and expressed greater satisfaction with counseling than did clients assigned to experienced counselors who had not received the additional training (control condition). Although same-race counseling dyads resulted in less client attrition, this factor did not influence client perceptions of counselors and the counseling process.

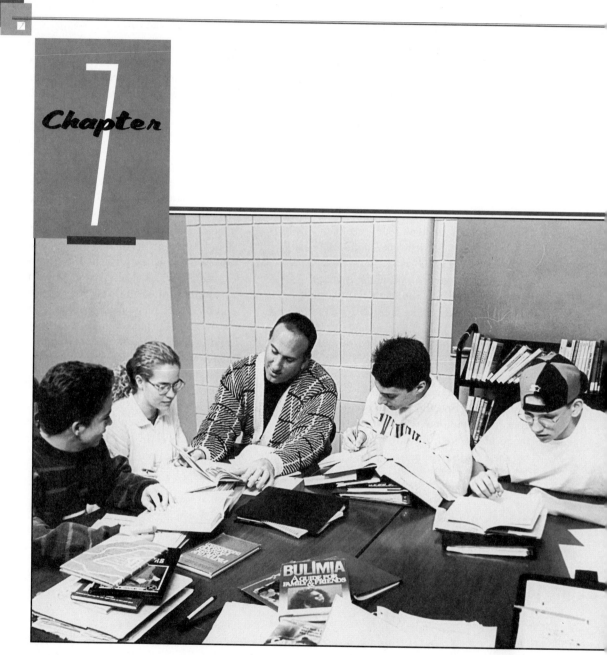

Group Techniques for Counselors

The rugged individualist has been extolled over the years in United States history. The sagas and accomplishments of Daniel Boone, Davy Crockett, Wild Bill Hickok, Wyatt Earp, Buffalo Bill, Susan B. Anthony, Charles Lindbergh, and others have been told and retold. We still pay certain homage today to the lone wolf who can make it alone, ignore the system, or shun the spotlight. Perhaps one of the reasons we so admire this rugged individualist is that we recognize it is almost impossible to go it alone in today's group-oriented, group-dominated, and group-processed society. In fact, today, to be well adjusted in a given society usually means that the individual has mastered the society's norms of social interaction—of functioning appropriately in groups.

This chapter's objectives are therefore to (a) identify the various types of group settings used by counselors to assist their clients and (b) introduce the process and values of group counseling, group guidance, and values clarification techniques.

Suggestions of the influence and dependence on groups result from an examination of the individual's functioning in today's society. Such an examination leads to several conclusions.

1. Humans are group oriented. People are meant to complement, assist, and enjoy each other. Groups are natural for these processes to occur.
2. Humans seek to meet most of their basic and personal-social needs through groups, including the need to know and grow mentally; thus, groups are a most natural and expeditious way to learn.
3. Consequently, groups are most influential in how a person grows, learns, and develops behavioral patterns, coping styles, values, career potentials, and adjustment techniques.

For counselors, teachers, and others who work with groups in leadership, facilitative, and teaching capacities, the following additional assumptions can be made.

1. An understanding of the influences and dynamics of groups can help further assessments and understandings of the individuals.
2. An understanding of the organization and utilization of groups can help in the teaching and guidance of others.
3. Group counseling may be more effective for some people and some situations than individual counseling.
4. Special populations can benefit from groups specially designed to recognize their uniqueness and/or their needs.

DEFINITIONS AND EXPLANATIONS

In any study of groups, particularly of an introductory nature, it is important at the onset to clarify the various labels in group counseling and guidance, including a definition of *group*. Webster's *Third New World International Dictionary* (unabridged) defines a group as "a number of individuals bound together by a community of interest, purpose, or function." However, within and across the professional disciplines engaged in the study and practice of groups, there are wide variations in defining a group. To narrow the definition of *group* for discussion here, it should be noted that counseling groups are characterized by interaction. They are functional or goal-oriented groups. Aggregate groups without interaction of the members are not functioning groups.

Counselors may view various group activities as occurring at three levels. These are the guidance level, the counseling level, and the therapy level. In brief, the levels may be defined as follows.

Group Guidance

Group guidance refers to group activities that focus on providing information or experiences through a planned and organized group activity. Examples of group guidance activities are orientation groups, career exploration groups, college visitation days, and classroom guidance (discussed later in this chapter). Group guidance is also organized to prevent the development of problems. The content could include educational, vocational, personal, or social information, with a goal of providing students with accurate information that will help them make more appropriate plans and life decisions.

Group Counseling

Group counseling is the routine adjustment or developmental experiences provided in a group setting. Group counseling focuses on assisting counselees to cope with their day-to-day adjustment and development concerns. Examples might focus on behavior modification, developing personal relationship skills, concerns of human sexuality, values or attitudes, or career decision making.

Gazda (1989) suggests that group counseling can be growth engendering insofar as it provides participation incentives and motivation to make changes that are in the clients' best interests. However, it is remedial for those persons who have entered into a spiral of self-defeating behavior but who are, nevertheless, capable of reversing the spiral with counseling intervention.

Group Therapy

Group therapy provides intense experiences for people with serious adjustment, emotional, or developmental needs. Therapy groups are usually distinguished from counseling groups by both the length of time and the depth of the experience for those involved. Therapy group participants often are individuals with chronic mental or emotional disorders requiring major personality reconstruction. Group therapists obviously require a higher level of training.

Gazda's (1989) continuum, describing relationships among the group processes, is presented in Figure 7-1.

T-Groups

T-groups are derivatives of training groups. They represent the application of laboratory training methods to group work. T-groups are an effort to create a society in miniature in which an environment is created for learning.

T-groups are relatively unstructured groups in which the participants become responsible for what they learn and how they learn it. This learning experience also usually includes learning about how people function in groups and about one's own behavior in groups. A basic assumption appropriate to T-groups is that learning is more effective when the individual establishes authentic relationships with others.

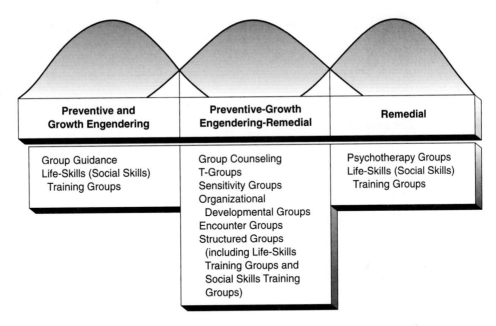

Figure 7-1   Relationships Among Group Processes.
Source: From Gazda, George M., *Group Counseling,* p. 9. Copyright © 1989 by Allyn and Bacon.
Reprinted by permission.

Sensitivity Groups

In actual practice, the label *sensitivity groups* appears to be applied so frequently and broadly as to be almost meaningless. In a more technical sense, however, a sensitivity group is a form of T-group that focuses on personal and interpersonal issues and on the personal growth of the individual. There is an emphasis in sensitivity groups on self-insight, which means that the central focus is not the group and its progress, but, rather, the individual member.

Encounter Groups

Encounter groups are also in the T-group family, although they are more therapy oriented. Rogers (1967b) defines an encounter group as a group that stresses personal growth through the development and improvement of interpersonal relationships via an experiential group process. Such groups seek to release the potential of the participant.

> In an intensive group, with much freedom and little structure, the individual will gradually feel safe enough to drop some of his defenses and facades; he will relate more directly on the feeling basis (come into a basic encounter) with other members of the group; he will come to understand himself and his relationship to others more accurately; he will change in his personal attitudes and behavior; and he will subsequently relate more effectively to others in his everyday life situation. (Rogers, 1967b, p. 262)

Extended encounter groups are often referred to as *marathon groups*. The marathon encounter group uses an extended block of time in which massed experience and accompanying fatigue are used to break through the participants' defenses.

Although encounter groups offer great potential for the group members' increased self-awareness and sensitivity to others, such groups can also create high levels of anxiety and frustration. It is, therefore, obvious that if encounter groups are to have maximum potential and minimal risk, they must be conducted by highly skilled and experienced counselor leaders.

Task Groups

Task groups are organized to meet organizational needs through task forces or other organizational groups or to serve individual needs of clients through such activities as social action groups. These groups are frequently useful to organizations seeking ways to improve their functioning. In agency counseling centers, task groups may be organized to assist clients in dealing with a wide range of needs from spiritual to educational.

Psychoeducation Groups

Psychoeducation groups emphasize cognitive and behavioral skill development in groups structured to teach these skills and knowledge. Psychoeducational groups are more guidance in nature than counseling or therapy oriented.

Minigroups

Although technically two or more people can constitute a group, the use of the term *minigroup* has become increasingly popular in recent years to denote a counseling group that is smaller than usual. A minigroup usually consists of one counselor and a maximum of four clients. Because of the smaller number of participants, the potential exists for certain advantages resulting from the more frequent and direct interaction of its members. Withdrawal by individuals and the development of factions or cliques are less likely in minigroups.

Group Process and Group Dynamics

Two terms commonly used in describing group activities are *process* and *dynamics*. Although often used interchangeably, they do have different meanings when used to describe group counseling activities. The beginning counseling student should note that *group process* is the continuous, ongoing movement of the group toward achievement of its goals. It represents the flow of the group from its starting point to its termination. It is a means of identifying or describing the stages through which the group passes.

Group dynamics, however, refers to the social forces and interplay operative within the group at any given time. It describes the interaction of a group, which may include a focus on the impact of leadership, group roles, and membership participation in groups. It is a means of analyzing the interaction between and among the individuals within a group. Group dynamics is also used on occasion to refer to certain group techniques such as role playing, decision making, rap sessions, and observation.

In-Groups and Out-Groups

Although these are not groups organized or overseen by counselors, they are often important in understanding influences on client behaviors. These groups can be based on almost any criteria, such as socioeconomic status, athletic or artistic accomplishments (in schools especially), a particular ability, racial-cultural origins, and so forth. *In-groups* are characterized by associations largely limited with peers of like characteristics, whereas *out-groups* consist of those excluded from in-groups. For example, there are nonparticipants in athletics or drama who have not been invited to participate in such things as social clubs. In many counseling situations, it is important for counselors to understand how clients see themselves and others in terms of in or out.

Social Networks

Although not a group in a formal sense, *social networks* result from the choices that individuals make in becoming members of various groups. As counselors, we may be concerned with how these choices are made and their impacts on individuals. Sociologists engage in social network analyses to determine how the interconnectedness of certain individuals in a society can produce interaction patterns influencing others both within and without the network.

PROFESSIONAL STANDARDS FOR THE TRAINING OF GROUP WORKERS

The Association for Specialists in Group Work (ASGW) advocates the incorporation of core group competencies as part of the master's-level training required in all counselor education programs. It also supports preparation of group work specialists at the master's degree level and the continued preparation of group work specialists at the post-master's level (Education Specialist, Ed.S., or certification, doctoral, continuing education, etc.), recognizing that recommended levels of group work specialty training in many programs will need to be accomplished following completion of the master's degree.

The 1990 revision of the *Professional Standards for Training of Group Workers* contains two levels of competencies and related training that have been identified by the ASGW Standards Committee.

1. *Core Group Competencies:* The minimum core of group worker competencies and related training necessary for all counselors, including knowledge, skills, and practice (minimum: 10 clock hours; recommended: 20 clock hours)

2. *Group Work Specialists:* Advanced competencies that build on the generalist core in the four identified group work specialties of
   - Task/work groups, including knowledge, skills, and supervised practice beyond core group training (additional minimum: 30 clock hours; recommended: 45 clock hours);
   - Guidance/psychoeducation groups, including knowledge, skills, and supervised practice beyond core group training (additional minimum: 30 clock hours; recommended: 45 clock hours);
   - Counseling/interpersonal problem-solving groups, including knowledge, skills, and supervised practice beyond core group training (additional minimum: 45 clock hours; recommended: 60 clock hours); and
   - Psychotherapy/personality reconstruction groups, including knowledge, skills, and supervised practice beyond core group training (additional minimum: 45 clock hours; recommended: 60 clock hours). (Association for Specialists in Group Work, 1990, p. 13)

For the training of those who engage in group psychotherapy, the distinguished scholar in the field, Irvin D. Yalom (1995), suggests four major components essential to a comprehensive training program beyond the didactic and theoretical as (1) observing experienced group therapists at work, (2) close clinical supervision of their maiden groups, (3) a personal group experience, and (4) personal psychotherapeutic work (p. 512).

GROUP COUNSELING

More than 100 years ago, the psychologist William James (1890) wrote

> We are not only gregarious animals liking to be in sight of our fellows, but we have an innate propensity to get ourselves noticed and noticed favorably, by our kind. No more fiendish punishment could be devised, were such a thing physically possible, than that one should be turned loose in society and remain absolutely unnoticed by all the members thereof. (p. 293)

James, as well as others, have noted over the years the importance of human relationships in meeting basic needs and influencing the personal development and adjustment of persons. For most people, the vast majority of these relationships are established and maintained in a group setting, and for many, daily routine adjustment problems and developmental needs also have their origins in groups. Interest has increased in group social skills development in the elementary grades and in the development of group relationships and communications skills across all ages of the adult population.

Counseling, as a facilitative science, has a helping relationship base, which must also be a human relationship. Because the most frequent and common human relationship experiences occur in groups, groups also hold the potential to provide positive developmental and adjustment experiences for many people. The following sections examine some of the potential values of group counseling and how these values are realized. The careful selection of participants and formations of groups and the skillful utilization by the counselor of appropriate group techniques are also discussed.

Theoretical Considerations

In Chapter 5, the important rationale base that theory provides for good counseling practice was discussed, as were popular theoretical orientations. As in individual counseling, effective group counseling emanates from a sound theoretical base. Therefore, let us briefly reexamine the popular counseling theories in the context of their application to group rather than individual counseling settings.

In groups led by counselors with a *psychoanalytic* theoretical orientation, the counselor interprets transference and resistances in order to free the unconscious. The analysis may focus on the behavior of individual members of the group and/or the behavior of the group as a whole.

Individual or *Adlerian* group leaders are somewhat direct and active in the group process while recognizing that the group members can decide what to do for themselves. The group setting is viewed as a safe opportunity for members to examine themselves, develop self-respect, and improve their social interactions as they strive to develop their potential.

Client-centered counselors have always had an active interest in group counseling. Carl Rogers coupled his beliefs of human behavior with his observations of therapeutic groups to formulate his ideas of group counseling and therapy, labeled a *basic encounter group*. The client-centered approach assumes that people have a natural tendency to grow and improve themselves. Group counseling can provide an atmosphere within which members feel safe to reveal their needs and ultimately to improve their lives. The group leader also models behavior that facilitates a positive group environment and the overall group process.

The *behavioral* counselor in the group setting proceeds to systematically identify the members' problems in behavioral terms. Behavioral objectives are established for members and the counselor reinforces those behaviors clients wish to acquire.

In group counseling, the *rational emotive* therapist, not the environment, is prominent in promoting client change. He or she does this through reason, persuasion, role playing, and so forth. The counselor seeks to bring about cognitive and rational behavior change. Within the group, members help each other in identifying illogical, emotionally driven behaviors.

Reality-oriented groups provide a caring environment in which clients can feel worthwhile and secure enough to explore more satisfying behavior. The counselor may function as teacher in order to lead the group members to adapt more appropriate behaviors and make more realistic choices.

As noted in Chapter 5, *transactional analysis* (TA) is essentially a process for counseling individuals within the group setting. TA counselors usually feel that the first step in establishing a TA group is the teaching of the recognition of ego stages.

Gestalt therapists focus on the integration of the person—getting it all together—with counselor-client interaction a key. This focus does not change in the group setting, as may be noticed in the goals of such groups as identified in Table 7-1.

Eclectic counselors, will, in group counseling situations, as in individual counseling, utilize a variety of theoretical perspectives to respond to the variety of clients, interactions, and problems. Table 7-1 offers a comparison of the group goals of the different theoretical viewpoints.

Values of Group Counseling

Group counseling is not a team sport. The goal is not to have a winning group. Group counseling, rather, attempts to achieve the goals, meet the needs, and provide a valuable experience to the individual members who constitute the group. The following opportunities may be provided by group counseling.

1. *Exploration, with the reinforcement of a support group, of one's developmental and adjustment needs, concerns and problems, may be possible.* Groups can provide a realistic social setting in which the client can interact with peers who not only are likely to have some understanding of the problem or concern that the client brings to the group, but who will, in many instances, also be sharing the same or a similar concern. The counseling group can provide the sense of security needed by the group members to interact spontaneously and freely and take risks, thus promoting the likelihood that the needs of each of the members will be touched on and that the resources of peers will be utilized. The old saying that misery loves company may in fact provide a rationale for group counseling. One is more comfortable in sharing a problem with others who have similar experiences and may also be more motivated to change under these conditions.

2. *Group counseling may give the client an opportunity to gain insights into his or her own feelings and behavior.* A freely interactive group, with few structural restrictions, will, in time, develop into a social microcosm of the participant members. Given enough time in the

TABLE 7-1 Comparative Overview of Group Goals

Model	Goals
Psychoanalytic	To provide a climate that helps clients reexperience early family relationships. To uncover buried feelings associated with past events that carry over into current behavior. To facilitate insight into the origins of faulty psychological development and stimulate a corrective emotional experience.
Adlerian	To create a therapeutic relationship that encourages participants to explore their basic life assumptions and to achieve a broader understanding of lifestyles. To help clients recognize their strengths and their power to change. To encourage them to accept full responsibility for their chosen lifestyle and for any changes they want to make.
Psychodrama	To facilitate the release of pent-up feelings, provide insight, and help clients develop new and more effective behaviors. To open up unexplored possibilities for solving conflicts and experiencing dominant sides of oneself.
Existential	To provide conditions that maximize self-awareness and reduce blocks to growth. To help clients discover and use freedom of choice and assume responsibility for their own choices.
Person-centered	To provide a safe climate in which members can explore the full range of their feelings. To help members become increasingly open to new experiences and develop confidence in themselves and their own judgments. To encourage clients to live in the present. To develop openness, honesty, and spontaneity. To make it possible for clients to encounter others in the here and now and to use the group as a place to overcoming feelings of alienation.
Gestalt	To enable members to pay close attention to their moment-to-moment experiencing, so they can recognize and integrate disowned aspects of themselves.
Transactional analysis	To assist clients in becoming free of scripts and games in their interactions. To challenge members to reexamine early decisions and make new ones based on awareness.
Behavior therapy	To help group members eliminate maladaptive behaviors and learn new and more effective behavioral patterns. (Broad goals are broken down into precise subgoals.)
Rational-emotive therapy	To teach group members that they are responsible for their own disturbances and to help them identify and abandon the process of self-indoctrination by which they keep their disturbances alive. To eliminate the clients' irrational and self-defeating outlook on life and replace it with a more tolerant and rational one.
Reality therapy	To guide members toward learning realistic and responsible behavior and developing a "success identity." To assist group members in making value judgments about their behaviors and in deciding on a plan of action for change.

Source: From *Theory and Practice of Group Counseling,* Third Edition, p. 53, by Gerald Corey. Copyright © 1990, 1985, 1981 by Wadsworth, Inc. Reprinted by permission of Brooks/Cole Publishing Company, Pacific Grove, CA 93950.

group setting, clients will begin to be themselves, interact with others, and create the same interpersonal universe they have experienced, including the display of maladaptive, interpersonal behavior to the group. Yalom (1995) states that

the corrective emotional experience in group therapy has several components:

1. A strong expression of emotion, which is interpersonally directed and is a risk taken by the patient.
2. A group supportive enough to permit this risk taking.
3. Reality testing, which allows the patient to examine the incident with the aid of consensual validation from the other members.
   - Reality testing which allows the patient to examine the incident with the aid of consensual validation from the other members
   - A recognition of the inappropriateness of certain interpersonal feelings and behavior or of the inappropriateness of certain avoided interpersonal behaviors
   - The ultimate facilitation of the individual's ability to interact with others more deeply and honestly. (pp. 25–26)

As the client gains new insights into behaviors and feelings as a result of interactions with members of the counseling group, influences on self-concept formation may also occur. Because of the significant influence of self-concept on one's personal-social adjustment, perception of school, and career decision making, the opportunity to bring about positive change in self-concept through new insights provided by the group counseling experience is a value not to be overlooked.

3. *Group counseling provides clients with an opportunity to develop positive, natural relationships with others.* The personal interactions that take place within the group counseling structure provide an excellent and continuous opportunity for the group member to experiment with and learn to manage interpersonal relations. This includes developing sensitivities to others, their needs, and feelings. It also provides opportunities to learn of the impact one's behavior has on others. Thus, through the group process and its interactions and sharing of experiences, the client may learn to modify earlier behavior patterns and seek new, more appropriate behaviors in situations that require interpersonal skills.

4. *Group counseling offers opportunities for the client to learn responsibility to self and others.* Becoming a member of a counseling group implies the assumption of responsibilities. Even when there are initial tendencies to avoid assuming responsibility for one's behavior, contributing to the group's interactions, or accepting one's assignment within the group, these avoidance techniques will usually fade away as group relationships develop and group goals are established.

Selection of Group Members

All of us have had experience in organizing groups. When deciding on group members for a social occasion, we select good old Charlie because he is a laugh a minute; Diane, because she gets along with everybody; Tomás, in case we need some serious conversation; and Ming, because she is a good listener. But if the group's purpose is a more serious one, such as planning a neighborhood park, we might choose Rosalita, because of her know-how with flowers and shrubbery; Jim, because he is a landscaping expert; Luca, because of her architectural skills;

and Manuel, because of his proven fund-raising abilities. In each instance, people are usually selected because they can contribute something to the group and its interaction.

The formation of counseling groups is obviously not as casually attended to as social groups. Professionally, we need some criteria beyond guesstimates as to what is needed. An approach to gathering objective data to support the formation of counseling groups dealing with specific and identifiable needs is the needs assessment.

> A needs assessment is important to stay fully informed about the current needs of your constituents. Without tapping into them on a regular basis, you may be providing services that are not relevant or that do not accurately meet their requirements. Not only does a needs assessment tell you what topics are important, it provides you with data useful in persuading reluctant administrators and teachers to permit children to leave the classroom for the group experience.
>
> There are formal and informal ways to conduct a needs assessment. In a school setting, you could informally poll parents, teachers, children, and administrators by directly asking them for their opinions on what group topics/issues need to be addressed. A more formal way to gather these important data is to develop a simple survey instrument that can more accurately assess the current state of needs, thus providing more in-depth information for both planning and evaluating future groups. (Smead, 1995, p. 23)

Although group counseling focuses on the needs of the individual members, the importance of group membership to the achievement and adjustments of individuals in the group cannot be overestimated. Group member selection is one key to a successful counseling group.

The following are possible criteria for the selection of group members: (a) common interest, (b) volunteer or self-referred, (c) willingness to participate in the group process, and (d) ability to participate in the group process. A popular criterion for group selection also may be a common interest of the potential members in a similar problem, concern, or issue.

Many group specialists believe that the best group member is a self-referred group member. Group counseling should be an option chosen by the group participants. Choice guarantees the protection of the client's rights. It also further enhances the motivation for counseling should the client decide to be in a counseling group.

Corey (1995) notes that

> screening should be a two-way process. Therefore, the potential members should have an opportunity at the private screening interview to ask questions to determine whether the group is right for them. Group leaders should encourage prospective members to be involved in the decision concerning the appropriateness of their participation in the group. (p. 87)

In the selection of potential group participants, Corey (1990) states that

> careful screening will lessen the psychological risks of inappropriate participation in a group. During the screening session the leader can spend some time exploring with potential members any fears or concerns they have about participating in a group. The leader can help them make an assessment of their readiness for a group and discuss the potential life changes that might come about. (p. 88)

In some instances, potential group members may lack the ability or desire to communicate with others or to relate to and assist others. From a temperament viewpoint, not everyone will be a suitable group member. In short, a person must possess certain abilities or aptitudes if he or she is to profit from and contribute to the group experience. Thus, although there are any number of procedures that may be used by counselors to form a group, inviting clients to participate once the counselor has become familiar with the individual and his or her concerns is a procedure that is the most realistic and professionally sound. We cannot emphasize enough the importance of the client being comfortable and satisfied with her or his decision to participate.

During the process of screening interviews for possible group membership, the counselor may want to specify the ground rules group members are expected to follow. Gazda (1989) presents the following example.

1. Set a goal or goals for yourself before you enter the group, or at the very latest, as early as you can isolate and define your direction of change. Revise these goals as clarification and/or experience dictates.

2. Discuss as honestly and concretely as you can the nature of your trouble, including the successful and unsuccessful coping behaviors you have employed.

3. When you are not discussing your own difficulties, listen intently to the other group members and try to help them say what they are trying to say and to communicate your understanding, caring, and empathy for them.

4. Maintain the confidentiality of all that is discussed in the group. (There are no exceptions to this rule other than those things that pertain to you only.)

5. Be on time and attend regularly until termination of the group (if a closed group) and until you have met your goals (if the group is open ended).

6. Give the counselor the privilege of removing you from the group if the counselor deems it necessary for your health and for the overall benefit of the group.

7. Concur that all decisions affecting the group as a whole will be made by consensus only.

8. Inform the group counselor in private, before the group is constituted, of individuals who would for various reasons constitute a serious impediment to your group participation. (I feel that the "cards should be stacked in the counselee's favor" as much as possible; therefore those individuals who could inhibit the counselee should be excluded from the group if at all possible.)

9. You may request individual counseling interviews, but what is discussed in these interviews should be shared with the group at the appropriate time and at the discretion of the counselor and yourself.

10. When fees are involved, concurrence on amounts and payment schedules is made with the counselor before counseling begins.* (pp. 37–38)

Another consideration in the formation of the counseling group is "What should the size of the group be to get the best results?" Yalom (1995) notes that his own experience and a consensus of the clinical literature implies that the

> ideal size of an interactional therapy group is approximately seven or eight with an acceptable range of five to ten members. The lower limit of the group is determined by the fact that a critical mass is required for an aggregation of individuals to become an interacting group. When a group is reduced to a size of four or three, it often ceases to operate as a group; member interaction diminishes, and therapists often find themselves engaged in individual therapy within the group. Many of the advantages of a group—the opportunity for broad consensual validation, the opportunity to interact and to analyze one's interaction with a large variety of individuals—are compromised as the group size diminishes. (p. 276)

---

*From Gazda, George M., *Group Counseling*. Copyright © 1989 by Allyn and Bacon. Reprinted by permission.

The upper limit is determined by sheer economic principles; as the group increases in size, less and less time is available for the working through of any individual's problems. (p. 277)

It is certainly appropriate to note that as group sizes increase, that intimacy and comfort which exists in small or modest-size groups may begin to diminish. The number of group members can also influence the difficulty of scheduling meetings and, hence, the number of and time between meetings. Larger groups often have a tendency to become less personal and more mechanical in their process. Larger groups also increase the risks that some members may be inadvertently overlooked to the extent that their needs are not satisfied.

At the other end of the size continuum, the two- or three-person group, despite the advantages of closeness and feelings of security, often suffers from a deficit in the human experiences, viewpoints, and value resources found in groups of five to eight, for example.

Meeting time for groups in nonschool settings should be based on predetermined or mutually convenient times. In schools, however, Stockton and Toth (1993) note that

it is important to involve teachers in the group planning process (i.e., how many times, and when, will students be called out of class?). Some counselors have found it effective, at the middle or high school level, to schedule the group during different class periods each meeting time so as not to have a student miss the same class time over and over again. (p. 74)

GROUP LEADERSHIP

In his book *Leadership*, James M. Burns (1978, p. 2) refers to the activity of leadership as "that most observed and least understood phenomenon," a viewpoint that few would dispute. The nature and quest for leadership at all levels and across all settings has been a continuing challenge to humankind. However, Burns's suggestion that "true leaders emerge from, and always return to, the wants and needs of their followers" (cited in Goodwin, 1978, p. 48) appears to have some relevance for leaders of counseling groups.

In discussing the personal characteristics of the effective group leader, George and Dustin (1988) note that

there is general agreement as to the characteristics of an effective leader. Honesty and openness are important in that they imply a willingness to accept feedback and a willingness for the leader to self-examine needs and values to determine their impact on the group. These qualities suggest the leader's interest in personal and professional growth as well as the personal growth of the group members. Such a leader can be nonjudgmental and accepting, can value personal relationships, and can have positive relationships. Without narrow or rigid behavior patterns the effective group counselor takes risks, is flexible and spontaneous, and has a healthy degree of self-confidence and enthusiasm. (p. 37)

Within this framework of the group counselor as a leader-member nourisher, what are the leadership responsibilities or functions? Helen Driver (1958), an early leader in the group counseling movement, identifies leadership techniques for the group counselor.

1. Support: giving commendation; showing appreciation.
2. Reflection: mirroring feelings.
3. Clarification: making meanings clear, showing implications of an idea.
4. Questioning: bringing out deeper feelings, inviting further response.
5. Information: providing data for examination, serving as a resource person, teaching.

6. Interpretation: explaining the significance of data, using analogy.
7. Summary: asking for client summary first, pointing out progress, alternatives. (pp. 100–102)

In preparation for group leadership responsibility, Stockton (1980) reviewed the importance of training in four areas.

(1) didactic knowledge (e.g., potential group leaders should understand theories of group counseling, ethical principles, research); (2) individual clinical skills such as those involving assessment, interpreting nonverbal behaviors, ability to use self-disclosure, confrontation and other standard therapeutic tools; (3) knowledge of group dynamics, most particularly developing a keen sense of the importance of timing and knowing how to pace a variety of specific group leader techniques and interventions; and (4) achieving a healthy personality oneself. (p. 57)

Stockton and Morran (1982) surveyed the group leadership research and report that the results are inconclusive: "There is very little research that provides clear evidence for a particular style of leadership as being most effective" (p. 48). Some of the more significant results from their survey is that leadership is multidimensional, which thus makes it difficult to control for unidimensional examination. Stockton and Morran also conclude that the Lieberman, Yalom, and Miles (1973) study of encounter groups comes closest to supporting a specific style of leadership. This study's results are summarized as follows.

The most effective encounter group leaders (a) were moderate in amount of emotional stimulation (emphasizing disclosure of feelings, challenging, confronting, etc.), (b) were high in caring (offering support, encouragement, protection, etc), (c) had meaning-attribution utilization (providing concepts for how to understand, clarifying, interpreting, etc), and (d) were moderate in expression of executive functions (setting rules, limits, norms, time management, etc.). (Stockton & Morran, 1982, pp. 70–71)

Corey and Corey (1997) point out personal characteristics of effective group leaders, which include the following.

- Courage
- Willingness to model
- Presence
- Goodwill and caring
- Belief in group process
- Openness
- Becoming aware of your own culture
- Nondefensiveness in coping with attacks
- Personal power
- Stamina
- Willingness to seek new experiences
- Self-awareness
- Sense of humor
- Inventiveness
- Personal dedication and commitment

An examination of these suggestions for group leadership indicates the group counselor's responsibility for the structure, conduct, and general overseeing of the group sessions. It should also be mentioned that conscientious group leaders do not become involved in group activities beyond their depth of professional preparation. Group counseling emphasizes factors of association rather than deep emotional disturbances. The counselor's depth of psychological understanding and skill in group dynamics are individual considerations in the level of group counseling that she or he undertakes. For those counseling groups that focus on specific and narrow concerns, such as family relations, human sexuality, or substance abuse, it is obviously desirable that the counselor-leader have some special understanding of the topic.

GROUP PROCESS

The elements of the group counseling process share much in common with those identified with individual counseling. These may be separated into their logical sequence of occurrence.

The Establishment of the Group

The initial group time is used to acquaint the new group members with the format and processes of the group, to orient them to such practical considerations as frequency of meetings, duration of group, and length of group meeting time. Additionally, the beginning session is used to initiate relationships and open communications among the participants. The counselor also may use beginning sessions to answer questions that clarify the purpose and processes of the group. The establishment of the group is a time to further prepare members for meaningful group participation and set a positive and promising group climate.

The group counselor must remember that in the initial group sessions the general climate of the group may be a mixture of uncertainty, anxiety, and awkwardness. It is not uncommon for group members to be unfamiliar with one another and uncertain regarding the process and expectancies of the group regardless of previous explanations or the establishing of ground rules.

It is important in this initial stage of group establishment that sufficient time be taken to ensure that all of the group's members have their questions and concerns addressed; that they understand the process and are beginning to feel comfortable in the group. Of course, the impression that the group counselor makes in this initial stage is of utmost importance to the smooth and successful process of the group.

Identification: Group Role and Goal

Once an appropriate climate has been established that at least facilitates a level of discussion, the group may then move toward a second, distinct stage—that of identification. In this stage, a group identity should unfold, the identification of individual roles should emerge, and group and individual goals be established. These may all develop simultaneously or at different paces. They are, however, significant at this stage of the group counseling process. It is also important to make operational the group counseling goals.

Most of us have few undirected, non–goal-oriented activities in our typical everyday plan of action. Those who work with groups frequently, whether in teaching or other capacities, can well predict the outcome if one were to appear before such a group with the question, "How would you like to spend your time today?" At worst, chaos would result, and at best, considerable time would be lost before determining how the group could best utilize the time available.

Goal setting is no less important in group counseling than in any other activity that seeks to be meaningful. The early identification of goals in group counseling will facilitate the group's movement toward a meaningful process and outcomes. The process of establishing these goals is the joint responsibility of the counselor and group members. These goals are most readily identified and implemented when they are specified in behavioral terms. Certainly, it is important to make the group counseling goals operational from the outset. These goals should be stated in objectives that are not only measurable but also attainable and observable and likely to be realized in view of the group strategies planned. It is also important in this process that the subgoals of each individual group member be recognized and responded to.

It is important for counselors to be aware of the probable, or, at least possible, conflict and confrontation during this stage of the group's development. Yalom (1995) labels this second phase as "the conflict, dominance/rebellion stage." He adds that it is a time when

> the group shifts from preoccupation with acceptance, approval, commitment to the group, definitions of accepted behavior, and the search for orientation, structure, and meaning, to a preoccupation with dominance, control, and power. The conflict characteristic of this phase is between members or between members and the leader. Each member attempts to establish for himself his preferred amount of initiative and power, and gradually a control hierarchy, a social pecking order, emerges. (p. 297)

This second stage, often referred to as the confrontation stage, is one in which conflict and even open hostility will often occur. As members attempt new patterns of behavior and new approaches to group goals, differing perceptions as well as differences in solutions generated by the individual members can lead to a range of behaviors from normal discussions to active and open confrontations. In this stage, the counselor must function to keep the discussions in-bounds and prevent them from becoming personal attacks on individuals' values and integrity.

The counselor should not misjudge silence as a sign of group compliance in this stage, but rather, the counselor must be alert to the possibility that silence may signal resistance on the part of the group members. Not all groups will experience this stage in the same degree of intensity or conflict. In groups with younger clients, such as high school students, the perception of the counselor as an authority figure may inhibit expressions of conflict, doubt, anger, and so on.

Hansen, Warner, and Smith (1980) describe this second stage as one in which the group members manifest their dissatisfaction with the operation of the group. It is a time following the initial acquaintance period when

> members are frequently frustrated in their attempts to evolve new patterns of behavior through which to work toward group goals. The discrepancy between individuals' real selves and their stereotyped images of the group may lead to conflict. Group members may challenge others' reactions to them and insist on their own rights. Some conflict may erupt when certain issues are discovered to be more complex than the group members originally perceived. The process of conflict and confrontation also occurs as group members begin to perceive and experience difficulty implementing changes in behavior. (p. 502)

When conflicts and confrontations, as previously described, do occur, a more cohesive group usually emerges, with increased openness in communication, consensual group action and cooperation, and mutual support among the members. A concern at this point may also be the tendency of some group members to withdraw. Stockton, Barr, and Klein (1981) warned that not only does the group member lose, but premature termination can result in negative effects on the group from which the member has dropped. Initial work stages of the group require membership stability in order to develop therapeutic potential from group treatment, and loss of members makes this task more difficult.

Productivity

In the third stage of the group's development, a clear progression toward productivity is noted. As the group has achieved some degree of stability in its pattern of behaving, the productivity process can begin. Also, because the members are now more deeply committed to the group, they may be ready to reveal more of themselves and their problems. This is the period of problem clarification and exploration, usually followed by an examination of possible alternate solutions.

The emphasis of this stage is on recognizable progress toward the group's and individual members' goals. In this process, however, each group member is exploring and seeking an understanding of self, situation, and problem or concern; and each member develops a personal plan integrating these understandings. The three subphases of this stage may be (1) assessment, (2) understanding, and (3) planning. The group structure tends to be functional.

In group counseling, productivity can be frequently translated as successful problem solving. Group counseling thus often becomes a process seeking to promote change. In this regard, the group counselor must (1) determine where the group is; (2) identify where the group wants to go, what it desires to accomplish; (3) identify the most promising process to facilitate the movement of the group from where it is to where it desires to go; and then (4) proceed to employ the selected processes in order, to achieve the desired outcomes. Here again, it is important to have agreement and, hence, participation of all involved in assessing where the group is, where it wants to go, how it can best get there, and then doing it!

Although group strategies may be selected by the group for any or all of these phases, it is important that they make sense to each member in terms of their individual needs. The counselor may note that progress is being made when progress can be seen. Of course, progress is not always constant during this time, and occasionally regression, stagnation, or even confusion may occur. Certainly whenever the group does not understand what it is doing, it is important to stop until understanding is achieved. Sometimes uncertainty occurs when a member (or members) don't understand how they are to participate. Sometimes they may feel they have nothing to contribute.

On these occasions, the counselor is alert to prevent process problems from handicapping progress and group achievement. Often, a simple reminder by the counselor of the stated goals or objectives of the group can prevent activities or discussions that tend to sidetrack members or the group as a whole from maintaining progress. However, because of the relationships and the group climate previously established, groups should overcome these difficulties and regain their productivity.

During this phase, the problem or concern should be clarified to everyone's satisfaction, and ownership should be verified. This clarification includes a thorough understanding of the nature of the problem and its causes. It is only when this has been achieved that resources for problem solutions can be realistically examined. This phase may be successfully concluded when all possible solutions have been considered and examined in terms of their consequences. These solutions should be practical or capable of being realized (obtainable), and the final choice of a solution should be made only after appropriate consideration and discussion. It should be emphasized that this is not the time for snap judgments and hurried commitments. At this point, then, the group members have examined themselves and the problem as it applies to them and have explored these considerations in depth; have looked at possible solutions and their consequences; have determined the course of action that appears most appropriate; and are ready to move into the next stage, one in which they will try out or experiment with their chosen solution. In this process, they have, by making their own decisions, also established their ownership of the problem and the chosen solution.

Realization

When members of the group recognize the inappropriateness of past behaviors and begin to try out their selected solutions or new behaviors, progress is being made toward realization of their individual goals. At this time, responsibility has been established with the individual members to act upon their own decisions. The counselor encourages the sharing of individual experiences and goal achievement both within and outside the group. Although general success with the new behaviors may provide sufficient reinforcement for many members to continue, for others a support base of significant others outside the group should now be developed to facilitate a maintenance of the change once the counseling group is terminated. In school settings, counselors might, for example, consult with parents and teachers to implement this strategy.

Termination

Most of us have experienced occasions of regret and even sorrow when temporary groups to which we have belonged reach the break-up point. Regardless of the purpose for which the group is organized, we may try to prolong its eventual dissolution by promising get-togethers, planning social activities, and in general agreeing that "this has been too much fun to let it end." On many such occasions, casual strangers have become the best of friends in relatively short periods of time, and the threatened termination of the relationships is at least psychologically resisted.

For these same reasons, members may resist the termination of a counseling group. The very nature of counseling groups, with their emphasis on interpersonal relationships, open communication, trust, and support, promises the development of a group that the membership may want to continue indefinitely. It is therefore important from the very beginning that the group counselor emphasize the temporary nature of the group and establish, if appropriate, specific time limitations. The counselor also reminds the group, as the time approaches, of the impending termination. This does not mean that the counselor alone is responsible for determining the termination point of a group. Although the counselor may, of course, assume this responsibility, termination may also be determined by the group members or by the group members and the counselor together.

Termination, like all other phases or stages of the group counseling experience, also requires skill and planning on the part of the counselor. Termination is obviously most appropriate when the group goals and the goals of the individual members have been achieved and new behaviors or learnings have been put into practice in everyday life outside the group. The group will also be ready to terminate when, in a positive sense, it has ceased to serve a meaningful purpose for the members. Under less favorable circumstances, groups may be terminated when their continuation promises to be nonproductive, harmful, or when group progress is slow, and long-term continuation might create overdependency on the group by its members.

Members may be terminated from a group at any time during the group's existence. Members who are disruptive, seriously handicap the other members, may be more effectively assisted through individual counseling, or personally desire to terminate are not uncommon subjects for individual terminations. Group counselors should be aware that this is common, especially in the beginning stages of a group, when several members may voluntarily terminate. It is important that the counselor accept this as a matter of course and refrain from exerting pressure on such persons to remain in the group. At the same time, however, the counselor may indicate a willingness to see the person(s) on an individual basis.

The point of termination is a time for review and summary by both counselor and clients. With some groups, time will be needed to work through the feelings of the members regarding termination. Even though strong ties may have developed and there are pressures from the group to extend the termination time, those pressures must be resisted, and the group must be firmly, though gently, moved toward the inevitable termination.

An excellent summary of essential counseling skills related to stages of the group process is presented by Gill and Barry (1982) in Table 7-2.

GROUP GUIDANCE ACTIVITIES

In a broad, general context, group guidance is probably as old as formal schooling. Good teachers through the years have used groups for what today would be called pupil guidance purposes. In schools, group guidance activities have been designed to provide information to students in groups or experiences beyond those associated with the day-to-day learning activities in the classroom. In nonschool settings, group activities have been planned to provide information, skill building, opportunities for personal growth and development, orientation, and assistance in decision making.

Values

Over the years, certain values have been attributed to group activities of a guidance nature. Some of these will be discussed in the following sections.

Facilitating Personal Development

Certain experiences that lead to personal development can take place only in the group setting. These include the opportunity to learn and play certain roles, such as group leader, group

TABLE 7-2 Classification System for Group-Focused Counseling Skills

Stage I	Stage II	Stage III
Group Formation: Facilitating cooperation toward common goals through development of group identity	*Group Awareness:* Facilitating a shared understanding of the group's behavior	*Group Action:* Facilitating cooperative decision making and problem solving

Stage I — *Group Formation:* Facilitating cooperation toward common goals through development of group identity

1. *Norming*
   Stating explicitly the expected group behavior
2. *Eliciting Group Responses*
   Inquiries or invitation to members that encourage comments, questions, or observations
3. *Eliciting Sympathetic Reactions*
   Inquiries or invitations to members that encourage disclosure of experiences or feeling similar to those being expressed
4. *Identifying Commonalities and Differences*
   Describing comparative characteristics of participants
5. *Eliciting Empathic Reactions*
   Inquiries or invitations to members that encourage reflection of one member's expressed content or feeling
6. *Task Focusing*
   Redirecting conversation to immediate objectives; restating themes being expressed by more than one member

Stage II — *Group Awareness:* Facilitating a shared understanding of the group's behavior

1. *Labeling Group Behavior*
   Identifying and describing group feelings and performance
2. *Implicit Norming*
   Describing behavior that has become typical of the group through common practice
3. *Eliciting Group Observations*
   Inquiries or invitation to members that encourage observations about group process
4. *Eliciting Mutual Feedback*
   Inquiries or invitations to members that encourage sharing of perceptions about each other's behavior
5. *Identifying Conflict*
   Labeling discordant elements of communication between members
6. *Identifying Nonverbal Behavior*
   Labeling unspoken communications between members (facial expression, posture, hand gestures, voice tone and intensity)
7. *Validating*
   Requesting group confirmation of the accuracy of leader or members' perceptions
8. *Transitioning*
   Changing the group's focus on content or feelings being expressed
9. *Connecting*
   Relating material from group events at a particular time or session to current situation
10. *Extinguishing*
    Ignoring, cutting off, diverting members' inappropriate talk/actions

Stage III — *Group Action:* Facilitating cooperative decision making and problem solving

1. *Identifying Group Needs*
   Asking questions and making statements that clarify the wants and needs of the group
2. *Identifying Group Goals*
   Asking questions and making statements that clarify group objectives
3. *Attributing Meaning*
   Providing concepts for understanding group thought, feelings, and behavior
4. *Eliciting Alternatives*
   Providing descriptions of possible courses of action and inviting members to contribute alternatives
5. *Exploring Consequences*
   Inquiries or invitations to the group that evaluate actions and potential outcomes
6. *Consensus Testing*
   Requesting group agreement on a decision or course of action

follower, or member; the development of patterns of cooperation with others; and the learning of group communication skills.

Stimulation of Learning and Understanding

Group settings can provide people with opportunities to learn more about and understand
themselves and their relations with others better. Group members can also acquire information about the external world. In this context, group guidance activities are important in providing learning and understanding—relevant to career and educational decision making, and
making personal-social adjustments. Care must be taken in how the information is presented
and perceived. Clients must feel that the information is important to them if they are to assimilate it.

Advantages of Group Interaction

By actively participating in groups organized for guidance purposes, members have the opportunity to broaden their scope of understanding regarding the subject or purpose for which
the group is organized. Additionally, participants should grow in their understanding of group
interactions and dynamics as well as understanding their own behavior in groups.

Economy

Groups should not be organized for guidance purposes solely on the basis of economy. However, when effectiveness in terms of outcome is not lessened, the saving of both counselor's
and clients' time through the use of groups can be of considerable value.

Organizing Group Guidance Activities

All of us have experienced being participants in some type of group activity, social or otherwise, that has been organized on the spur of the moment. Occasionally, these unanticipated
activities have been enjoyable or worthwhile, but probably more often they have resulted in
confusion, uncertainty, perhaps even frustration, and have been considered a waste of time.
The popularity of group activities has, in some instances, led to their scheduling without appropriate preparation, but that is not and should not be the pattern. If group guidance activities are to achieve their potential, a great deal of consideration and organization must go into
their planning, conducting, and evaluation. Although the organization process is very similar to group counseling, discussed earlier in this chapter, the differences, though often subtle,
should be noted and the similarities should be reemphasized. The following guidelines therefore may be helpful.

Determining That There Is a Need for Group Guidance

All too often group guidance activities are simply scheduled. On occasion, the scheduled activities may be responding to an actual need. If we are to ensure their success, it must be determined beforehand that there is a need that a group shares in common and for which a group
guidance response is appropriate. Questionnaires, problem surveys, or checklists administered

to specific populations often will provide a factual basis for determining possible group guidance activities.

Determining That Group Guidance Is the Most Appropriate or Effective Response

Once needs have been determined, the counseling staff must identify those for which a group guidance activity would be appropriate, in contrast to group counseling or individual counseling, or perhaps even some form of instruction. Group guidance activities are those that may be useful to nearly every one in a specific population or setting, hence the total group would experience the activity. Examples might be a stress management program for employees in an industrial setting; a behavior workshop for public relations workers; or a career day for high school students.

Small group guidance activities, in broad general terms, are those designed for specific outcomes, which cater to the needs of smaller subgroups within the total population served by the school or agency counseling and guidance program. These activities may focus on providing information for decision-making and planning purposes, activities for personal development purposes, and assistance for educational adjustments. Small group guidance activities can emphasize smaller components or follow-up activities for the larger college, career, or orientation programs. Other specific examples are guidance groups organized to develop job-seeking and interviewing skills, study techniques, assertiveness training, career education, values clarification activities, discussion groups, and experiences in nonverbal communications.

Determining the Characteristics of the Group

Once the nature of the group guidance activity has been established, certain group characteristics must be determined. Obviously, size of the group must be one consideration. Here, the counselor must determine what size group will be most appropriate for the activities planned and outcomes anticipated. Size will also have an influence on the operational format of the group. Format planning includes determining the types of activities of the group, the length of time allotted for each group session, the number of sessions, and the setting.

A final consideration affecting the group characteristics will be the role of the counselor. Will the counselor be an active participant or an inactive observer who remains in the background once the group's activities are under way? Will the counselor direct the group? Will the counselor be a group arbitrator? What information will the leader provide the group? Will roles be assigned or will roles evolve as the group progresses?

Establishing the Group

Once the characteristics of the group have been determined, members may be selected. They may volunteer or they may be invited to participate. Invitation includes the right of the persons to refuse participation. In establishing the membership of the group, it must be verified that the planned activity will respond to the needs of the individual member and that the structure or operational format will be comfortable for the group member. In large groups, such as those organized for orientation purposes, career needs, or other special information purposes, this is not necessarily essential, but for smaller, intimate groups, it is an important consideration.

Monitoring the Ongoing Activities

Once the group has been established and the members oriented to its purpose and processes, the counselor or facilitator assumes the responsibility for keeping the group on track. It is relatively easy, especially considering the participants' lack of experience and understanding of the group process, to deviate from the purposes of the group, become bogged down in irrelevant discussions and activities, or encounter personal factors that inhibit or impede the functioning of the group. The counselor must, therefore, be constantly on the alert to detect such symptoms and to use her or his skills to minimize these effects. The ongoing activities of the group are meaningful only as long as they promote the progress of the group and its members toward their goals.

Evaluating Outcomes

The importance of evaluation in assessing the outcomes of groups cannot be overemphasized, and evaluation and the accountability process will be discussed in greater detail in Chapter 14. The goals or projected outcomes of the group must be stated in clear, objective, and measurable terms. The criteria for measuring goal achievement must be identified and stated, and data then collected that, when analyzed, will present an objective evaluation of outcomes. Such evaluations can assist counselors and others involved to determine which group guidance activities are most effective and which techniques within groups are most and least effective. Implications for group membership, roles, and leadership may also result.

Classroom Guidance Activities

Classroom guidance is a planned process for assisting school populations in acquiring useful and needed information, skills, and/or experiences. It is also determined that the classroom is the most effective setting for carrying out the designated program and that the program will not detract from but, in fact, may even enhance the regular ongoing curricular offerings.

Classroom guidance activities are characterized by being (a) developmental, (b) ongoing, and (c) having counselors as instructors (but they may be planned with faculty assistance). The substance of the instruction is based on specific needs of the population for which the program is designed to serve. This provides a rationale for the program, which in turn is translated into program goals. Program procedures (including timetables), feedback, and evaluation planning follow. In this context, school counselors will have responsibility for developing a communications plan for orienting all interested parties to their role and function. They will also be responsible for identifying the topics needing attention, gathering resource materials, and preparing handouts.

School counselors will note that programs of classroom guidance help ally them with the teaching faculty. Classroom guidance provides additional opportunities for student interactions and natural settings for identifying and reacting to student needs.

VALUES CLARIFICATION TECHNIQUES FOR GROUPS: AN OVERVIEW

When we state that we believe in free speech, freedom of the press, equal rights for women, and access to education for all, we are, in effect, expressing values. Those values might appropriately reflect the consensual values of our society. Each society is characterized by well-defined, articulated values that are passed on to and practiced by the members of the society. When we extol the pleasures of travel abroad, the virtues of exercise and careful diets, and the inspiration of a specific religious faith, we may, in effect, be expressing our personal values. Thus, values also represent what a person considers important in life, and these ideas of what is good or worthwhile are acquired through the modeling of the society and the personal experiences of the individual.

A discussion of values is basically a discussion of what people believe in, what they stand for, and what is important in life. In recent years, we have seen a dramatic increase in public and political attention to values in relationship to violence and other crimes, political and corporate scandals, the decline in morality, and disrespect for laws and rights. There has also been much discussion regarding who is responsible for imparting desirable values.

We do know that values are the reasons people behave and even think the way they do. They motivate one to plan and act and serve as a standard for judging the worth of activities, achievements, things, and places. In short, it has been claimed that values give direction to one's life and, hence, one's behavior. People who do not know what they value often engage in meaningless, nonproductive, and usually frustrating behavior. In both individual and group counseling, an understanding of the client's values can facilitate the counselor's understanding of the client's behavior, goals, or lack of goals, and what is or has been of significance in the client's life.

Values Defined

Values have become increasingly a topic of frequent discussion and concern in recent years. Government leaders, magazine and newspaper editors, and leading educators as well as countless concerned citizens have suggested that as a nation we are on the verge of moral bankruptcy. They cite financial scandals, political abuses, Medicare fraud, misleading advertising, child molestation, pushing the sale of drugs, and the list goes on and on, evidencing a loss of values. One result has been a renewed call for efforts to re-instill our traditional national values, with school populations being especially targeted. This resulting proliferation of values clarification techniques and the increasing examination of values education in the school curriculum, as with any popular movement, have clouded traditional definitions and brought forth complex explanations of what is meant by values. We do not propose to add to this confusion but rather to present several of the more popular definitions appropriate to those engaged in counseling.

First, the dictionary defines *values* as ideals, customs, and institutions that arouse an emotional response, for or against them in a given society or a given person—a simple straightforward, and, we think, acceptable definition. Another equally clear definition is that values represent the comparative worth we attach to anything (behaviors, people, material goods, experiences, environments, etc.). Values may be generated and reflected in individuals, organizations, institutions, and societies.

In the development of the individual's value system, children are constantly examining, testing and acquiring values based on their experiences and learning. In these early—and formative—years, the developing child and adolescent is also influenced by the impact of significant others; the impact of socializing institutions, such as schools; the perceived values of the cultures in which one is immersed; and the influence of groups one may associate with or hold membership in.

It is in this last instance, groups, that counselors, as group experts, have a role to play in both school and nonschool settings. Too, values and counseling have always been intertwined, have always complemented each other.

VALUES AND COUNSELING

Historic Concerns

Rockwell and Rothney (1961) indicate that from the very beginning of the counseling and guidance movement in the United States, leaders in this movement have expressed concern with values. The father of this movement, Frank Parsons, has been described as a utopian social reformer, believing in the perfectibility of humanity. He viewed guidance as a means to a mutualistic society and the counselor's role as one leading to social goals by offering prescriptive advice. Jessie Davis preached the moral values of hard work, ambition, honesty, and the development of good character as assets in the business world.

Later, Carl Rogers stated his beliefs in the goodness and worthwhileness of people and their abilities to chart their own destiny. C. Gilbert Wrenn, in *The Counselor in a Changing World* (1962) and *The World of the Contemporary Counselor* (1973), discussed the values of the counselor and his or her clients. In the former book, he writes that

> it has become increasingly clear that the counselor cannot and does not remain neutral in the face of the student's value conflicts. Even the counselors who believe most strongly in letting the student work out his own solutions have firm values of their own and cannot help communicating them. They communicate their values in what they do and don't do even if they never mention their beliefs verbally. Furthermore, we expect more and more of the counselor with reference to the needs of society. Just to accept the need for the full development of abilities in the interest of a stronger nation as well as the interest of the individual is a manifest expression of a social value. Because the counselor cannot escape dealing with values and expressing values in his own behavior, he must be clear about the nature of his own values and how they influence his relationships with other people.
>
> A second developing conviction about values is that they are now seen by some psychologists as the central difficulty for many troubled people. Fifty years ago values were clearly defined, and acute maladjustment seemed to result from a willful violation of them. Psychological treatment consisted primarily of freeing the individual from an overwhelming sense of guilt over his transgression against his parents and other representatives of society. But today the picture seems almost the reverse of what it was. The maladjusted person feels himself more lost than guilty. Social expectations have become more diverse, less well defined, less insistent. The social processes of inculcating strong values are less effective today, in part because family and community are less cohesive.
>
> As a consequence the individual feels a lack of purpose and direction. He feels estranged from others and even from himself; he feels worthless and unsure of his identity. He must discover character in himself for himself. Values strongly felt are the foundation upon which he can build an increasingly satisfying personal existence. Thus, clarifying values and perhaps acquiring new values becomes a major task for the individual in counseling, as in education generally. (pp. 62–63)

In the later publication, *The World of the Contemporary Counselor*, Wrenn discusses the counselor's and client's values.

The Counselor's Values

A first concern is that the counselor examine his own hierarchy of values and check it against the contemporary scene. I do not suggest that the counselor must change his values to meet changing assumptions, but rather that he attempt to increase his openness to the intrusions of change. A feeling of great certainty that what he now thinks is right and is right for all time can become a simple rigidity. It is too easy to retreat into a secure castle of one's own construction and close the gates to all that might disturb. It is healthy to be disturbed, for this means that one is required to think, to test assumptions, to question thoughtfully the bases for conduct. It is more realistic to confess confusion than to parade conviction.

On the other hand, admitting confusion could be interpreted as justifying having no convictions, no assurances of vital values. I must anticipate at this point what I want to discuss more carefully later, that one can be committed to values and goals even though they are tentative. In fact, one must be committed to be real, but the commitment may be to values which are seen as subject to modification, as changing with experience. "Tentativeness and commitment" paralleling each other are powerful principles.

The Client's Values

The second area of concern is the acceptance of the client's right to be different in his values. This difference between the values of the client and those of the counselor is often a difference between generations or between cultures. Always, of course, the values of the client are the product of his life experience, unique to him and often markedly different from the experience of the counselor. The 30-year-old, middle-class, socially accepted, college-educated counselor cannot be expected to understand in all cases the values of a 16-year-old, ghetto-reared, socially rejected boy or girl or those of an affluent, socially amoral, parentally rejected youth. In fact, experiential understanding of another is rare. What is most important, however, is that the counselor accept the client's values as being as real and as "right" for him as the counselor's values are for the counselor. There is too frequently a tendency to protest inwardly, "He can't really mean that," when the value expressed by the client is in sharp contrast to a related value held by the counselor. The point is that the client does mean that; his value assumption is as justifiable to him as yours is to you.

So far I have said nothing about the counselor's responsibility for helping the client to examine a given value assumption, particularly if the value is likely to result in behavior harmful to another or to society. He has such a responsibility, I am sure, differing widely from client to client and varying often with the client's psychological readiness to examine values. Basic to the success of any such confrontation, however, is the counselor's acceptance of the "right" of the client to have different values. If a counselor enters into a discussion of another's point of view with the implicit assumption that he is "right" and the other is "wrong," failure is assured. (pp. 34–35)

Relationship to Counseling Theory

As we proceed to examine values or moral education and values clarification and its relationship and potential usefulness for counselors and other helping professionals, let us examine its relationship to some of the traditional, theoretical approaches to counseling. For example, Simon and deSherbinin (1975) note that values clarification skills were natural companions of other skills that help people to develop their potential and live life more fully. Values clarification skills, it was suggested, go hand in hand with the work of Carl R. Rogers, emphasizing warmth and genuineness among people. Simon and deSherbinin go on to state that

values clarification can borrow something from Harvey Jackin's re-evaluation counseling model, in which people make commitments to help each other grow. Generally, people divide the time they have for each other into two equal segments during which each works as both client and counselor. This reciprocity generates power that penetrates deeply into people's lives; values clarification techniques can be used in exactly the same way.

More and more, people working in T-groups are also coming to see that values clarification exercises rapidly advance their aims of getting people close to others' thoughts and feelings.

It has also found its way into the training of Gestalt therapists. Gestalt teachers have sensed that its various strategies are useful in clarifying the way people respond to each other's problems.

Other counselors simply fit a values clarification exercise into a transactional analysis technique. One way that transactional analysis workers have used values clarification is to ask a client to respond to a values question as if the child inside of him or her is speaking, then the parent inside, and then the adult. (p. 683)

Another concern for counselors using values clarification techniques was the criticism of these techniques in the early 1980s. These criticisms, frequently expressed on behalf of religious groups, often portray values clarification techniques as encouraging permissiveness, associated with secular humanism, and detracting from the role of the home and church in teaching values.

Values Theory and Process

In the development of values theory, no individual has made a greater contribution than that of Lawrence Kohlberg. His research was significant in formulating a theoretical viewpoint on moral (or values) development. Kohlberg's early conclusions were that children go through six stages of moral development as follows.

1. Heteronomous morality—obeying the rules to avoid punishment.
2. Individualism, instrumental—purpose and change—Following rules when it is in one's best interest. Serving one's own interests.
3. Mutual interpersonal expectations, relationships and interpersonal conformity—Living up to what is expected of you by others. Being a good person in your own eyes.
4. Social system and conscience—Fulfilling duties, contributing to the group and society. Satisfying your conscience.
5. Social contract or utility and individual rights—Obligation to the law—commitment to family, friends, work.
6. Universal ethical principles—Follows universal principles of morality. (McCandless and Coop, 1979, pp. 163–164)

Kohlberg believed that the individual's development could become fixed at any one of the six stages. He

proposed a moral education program centered around discussions of real and hypothetical dilemmas. The ultimate goal of the program was the moral maturity of the student with moral maturity being defined as "the principled sense of justice." Realizing there might be a disparity between the values the schools said they wished to foster and those they exemplified in their hidden curriculum, he insisted that the hidden curriculum be made "explicit in intellectual and verbal discussions of justice and morality." (Pyszkowski, 1986, p. 22)

A major hypothesis of values clarification that has significant implications for counselors utilizing these techniques suggests that the skillful and consistent use of the valuing process by an individual increases the likelihood that the individual will make appropriate decisions that will be satisfying both to the individual and to society. Raths, Harmin, and Simon (1978) translated this theory into a process consisting of seven subprocesses grouped under three categories. They then suggest that a value in one's life must meet the following criteria.

Choosing

1. freely
2. from alternatives
3. after thoughtful consideration of each alternative

Prizing

4. cherishing, being happy with the choice
5. willing to affirm the choice publicly

Acting

6. doing something with the choice
7. repeatedly, in some pattern of life. (p. 28)

Howe and Howe (1975) suggested a process that seems particularly adaptable to counseling strategies.

1. Developing a climate of acceptance, trust, and open communication
2. Building self-concepts
3. Creating awareness of prizing and publicly affirming values
4. Helping individuals choose freely from alternatives after weighing the consequences
5. Helping individuals learn to set goals and take actions on their values

This process is applicable in both individual and group counseling settings.

Having broadly viewed values and their impact on behavior, noted a basis for values theory, and described similarities between the valuing and counseling processes, let us examine further some of the relationships between values and counseling.

VALUES CLARIFICATION TECHNIQUES AND COUNSELING PRACTICE

The process of counseling and that of values clarification share much in common. As depicted in Table 7-3, both depend heavily on relationship establishment and maintenance; both seek to identify and explore the consequences of appropriate options; both emphasize that choices or decisions are made by the client; and both processes recognize the importance of carrying out decisions through action.

Most values clarification techniques appear to emphasize group participation—and although this is true, it does not necessarily limit their utilization or inclusion in the process of individual counseling. Many of the techniques can be completed by an individual client and then shared and examined within the framework of the counseling process. Such exercises (some of which will be described in more detail later in exercises at the end of this chapter) as drawing a hobby plaque, listing 20 things you like to do, selecting from alternatives, and discussing situational anecdotes are examples of those that can be satisfactorily completed by the client, then discussed and examined with the counselor. They may in turn help the client confirm and practice more appropriate and satisfying behavior.

TABLE 7-3 Similarities Between Values Clarification and Counseling Processes

Stage	Values Clarification	Counseling
1	Getting acquainted Develops a climate of • Trust • Acceptance • Open communication	1. Relationship establishment Developing a helping relationship that facilitates the client's communication of his or her reasons for seeking counseling assistance
2	Builds an individual's self-concept	2. Identification and exploration of client's concern
3	Helps an individual become aware of his or her values	3. Awareness and examination of options available to client
4	Helps individuals choose and affirm their values freely from alternatives after weighing the consequences	4. Client makes decisions after weighing consequences of each option
5	Helps individuals set goals and take action on their values	5. Implementation of decision Goals are set and client takes action

THE COUNSELOR AND VALUES CLARIFICATION TECHNIQUES

Values clarification theory and practice has much in common with counseling theory and practice. In theory, both are seeking to assist individuals in realizing their fullest potential. In practice, both values clarification and counseling seek to assist the individual in developing better self-understanding and a positive self-concept, making appropriate decisions and meaningful choices, and satisfactorily adjusting to the demands of everyday living.

Because values clarification techniques are popularly practiced in groups, their potential for group counseling and guidance is considerable. For example, numerous values clarification techniques designed to promote getting acquainted and developing interpersonal relationship and communication skills would have their appropriate moments in group counseling and guidance. Group values exercises designed to facilitate self-assessment, self-concept clarification, and reinforcement for change would have their usefulness for the group counselor. Exercises that give a person the opportunity to compare, examine, and defend his or her behavior, values, and interests against the norms of others can also be useful in group counseling.

MULTICULTURAL ISSUES AND GROUPS

Counseling and/or guidance groups can provide counselors with both challenges and opportunities for promoting multicultural awareness and sensitivity to their group clients. This assumption is based on recognizing (1) the opportunities groups provide for promoting positive multicultural relationships and (2) the opportunities for counselors themselves to model and be perceived as individuals who are aware, sensitive, and attend to a diversity of populations in an appropriate manner. Coleaders of groups in which one leader is from a cultural minority can be helpful. Here again, as in individual counseling with multicultural clients, counselors must be aware of their own cultural background and how it influences their perceptions and behaviors. Counselors, whatever their background, must conscientiously prepare themselves to work with the wide range of culturally diverse groups that populate our country. Whatever their professional position, counselors must be prepared and ready, even assertive, to step forward to assist their communities in overcoming the misunderstandings, biases, insensitivity, and so on, that threaten the fabric of their community life and our national well-being.

SUMMARY

Today's society is group oriented, and each person belongs to many groups. These groups serve a variety of purposes, and in them one plays a variety of roles. Because of this group orientation, group counseling and guidance have become increasingly recognized as a means of assisting individuals in meeting their adjustment and developmental needs in both school and nonschool settings. These group activities are distinguished by the nature of their concern and the type of group experience provided. Group guidance activities are primarily confined to school settings with an emphasis on providing information or experiences helpful in decision making. Group counseling tends to focus on routine adjustments and developmental needs or problems of individuals, whereas group therapy provides an intense experience that may last for a considerable length of time for individuals with serious adjustment, emotional, or developmental needs. The counselor's role and leadership are important to the success of both guidance and counseling groups. The group counselor must also be skillful and aware of the steps through which the group process moves. This process begins with the selection of members and the initial establishment of the group, the identification of group goals, the clarification and exploration of the group's and its individual members' problems and/or concerns, the exploration of solutions and consequences, decision making regarding solutions, implementation of the decision, and, finally, termination and evaluation.

In recent years, much media attention has been given to the values of youths, the shifting values of the adult world, and the significance of personal values for satisfaction in the world of work. Values have also become increasingly important to professional counselors. Values clarification techniques can provide a helpful and nonthreatening approach for assisting clients in groups and appraising individuals. In a planned program of values clarification and development, the individual initially engages in exercises designed to identify his or her values, then shares them; next, examines them; confirms them, and finally, practices values. Varied group exercises are available for utilization by counselors.

Of course, for counseling—whether group or individual—to be maximally effective, it is important to know the client as well as possible. Assessment techniques which counselors may utilize for this purpose are discussed in the next two chapters.

DISCUSSION QUESTIONS

1. In how many different groups do you actively participate during a typical day? How does your role and function differ across groups?

2. What are the differences among group counseling, group guidance, and group therapy?

3. What are some typical guidance needs of school-aged youth that can be dealt with effectively in groups?

4.   Identify counseling situations in which you believe group counseling might be more effective than individual counseling.

5.   How do you account for the great popularity of sensitivity groups, T-groups, and encounter groups in recent years? Do you see any potential dangers in the popularity of these groups?

6.   Can individuals with differing personality traits be equally effective as group leaders?

7.   Discuss differences in the values generally held by three different client populations: adolescents; working, middle-aged adults; and older Americans approaching retirement.

8.   Are there any general societal values that ought to be taught to all youth through a deliberate program of values education?

CLASS ACTIVITIES

1.   Divide into small groups. Each group member's goal is to identify a new behavior that she or he would like to develop. Then work together to write a contract to be used by all group members. In one week reconvene to discuss progress or setbacks as well as possible changes in the contract.

2.   In small groups, discuss in which situations you would like to improve your communications skills with others. Include both school and career settings.

3.   Organize the class into small groups. Each group identifies a growth or learning activity agreed on by the group members and proceeds to accomplish the goal of their group (insofar as time will permit). Each group then analyzes the dynamics and varying roles of members in the group.

4.   Organize the class into small groups. Groups are to assume they are being exiled to an island for one week. Transportation to the island will be furnished by a rowboat. In addition to normal clothing for mild, but rainy, fall weather, each member of the group may bring six items (not to exceed 20 pounds) for the group's survival. These items should include the necessary foodstuffs and liquids for the group's nourishment during their period of internment. Following the conclusion of the exer-

cise and the reporting of it to the class, each group should reconvene to analyze the dynamics of the group experience, noting the various roles played by members of the group.

5.   Organize the class into small groups. Each group will design a meaningful group activity and demonstrate this activity. (You may use another classroom group for the demonstration if this would be more meaningful.)

6.   Observe the dynamics of a group outside this class and report your observations.

SELECTED READINGS

The following special issues of *The Journal for Specialists in Group Work:* "Critical issues in group work: Now and 2001," *10* (1), 115 pages; and "Support groups," *11* (2), 122 pages.

Brantley, L. S., Brantley, P. S., & Baer-Barkley, K. (1996). Transforming acting-out behavior: A group counseling program for inner-city elementary school pupils. *Elementary School Guidance and Counseling, 31* (2), 96–105.

Bretzing, B. H., & Caterino, L. C. (1984). Group counseling with elementary students. *School Psychology Review, 3* (4), 515–518.

Gilbert, M., & Shmukler, D. (1996). Counselling psychology in groups. In R. Woolfe & W. Dryden (Eds.), *Handbook of counselling psychology* (pp. 442–459). London: Sage.

Karniauski, C. (1988). Using group development theory in business and industry. *The Journal for Specialists in Group Work, 13* (1), 30–43.

Kivlighan, D. M., Multon, K. D., & Brossart, D. F. (1996). Helpful impacts in group counseling: Development of a multidimensional rating system. *Journal of Counseling Psychology, 43,* 347–355.

Mallinckrodt, B. (1997). Interpersonal relationship processes in individual and group psychotherapy. In S. Duck (Ed.), *Handbook of personal relationships: Theory, research and interventions* (2nd ed.) (pp. 671–693). Chichester, England: John Wiley & Sons.

Riordan, R. J., Beggs, M. S., & Karniauski, C. (1988). Some critical differences between self-help and therapy groups. *The Journal for Specialists in Group Work, 13* (1), 24–29.

Stockton, R., & Morran, K. (1985). Perceptions on group research programs. *The Journal for Specialists in Group Work, 10* (4), 186–191.

RESEARCH OF INTEREST

Hines, P. L., Stockton, R., & Morran, D. K. (1995). Self-talk of group therapists. *Journal of Counseling Psychology, 42* (2), 242–248.

Abstract

To identify group leader cognitions and the role experience may play in leader cognitive schemas, 60 participants were placed in one of three groups on the basis of group-leading experience and were exposed to a 20-minute videotape of the group session, during which they completed a thought-listing instrument. Two judges free-sorted the 1,299 collected thoughts and identified and defined 17 distinct thought categories. Three trained judges then placed 1,271 (97.8%) of the thoughts into these categories. Differences among experience levels were also explored through correlation and stepwise multiple regression analysis. Two thoughts, interpretation of group process and internal question regarding member, were found to account for 56% of the variance in experience level. Findings are discussed in terms of group leader cognitive processing, and suggestions for future research are provided.

MacKenzie, D. R. (1994). Where is here and when is now? The adaptational challenge of mental health reform for group psychotherapy. *International Journal of Group Psychotherapy, 44* (4), 407–428.

Abstract

This article outlines the present state of group psychotherapy from the perspectives of the health care and psychotherapy service delivery systems and emphasizes the importance of designing a comprehensive group program, adapting group psychotherapy to a managed care environment, and adapting to professional changes. An examination of psychotherapy service-use patterns shows the importance of time categories and the relevance of group techniques and clinical investigations. The author suggests that traditional interpersonal and psychodynamic group techniques may be modified for time-limited use without sacrificing basic values and with demonstrated effectiveness. Clinicians must also undertake a process of transition in adapting to a more fiscally stringent practice environment. Psychotherapists must let the health care system know that proper practice guidelines are necessary to achieve effective treatment for patients.

MacNair, R. R., & Corazzini, J. G. (1994). Client factors influencing group therapy dropout. *Psychotherapy, 31* (2), 352–362.

Abstract

This study investigated client factors influencing group therapy dropout and continuation in 155 groups. Clients (aged 17–48 years) were assigned to open-ended interpersonal therapy groups and classified as either dropouts or continuers as defined by the therapist, pattern of attendance, and method of leaving the group. Predictor and criterion variables were coded, and interpersonal variables were condensed using principal component analysis. A discriminant analysis found six significant variables predicting dropout: alcohol/drug problem, somatic complaints, roommate difficulties, general fighting, fighting with partner, and introversion. The strongest variable in the discriminant function was alcohol/drug problem. Previous individual counseling was found to predict continuation in group. The discriminant analysis correctly classified more than 76% of cases as dropouts or continuers.

Marcus, D. K., & Holahan, W. (1994). Interpersonal perception in group therapy: A social relations analysis. *Journal of Consulting and Clinical Psychology, 62* (4), 776–782.

Abstract

Although group therapists have emphasized the importance of interpersonal perception and feedback during therapy, there has been little systematic research on how group members form impressions of one another. D. J. Kiesler's interpersonal circle provided a framework for studying interpersonal perception and relations. Twenty-seven women and 18 men from nine time-limited therapy groups reported their impressions of their fellow group members using the Impact Message Inventory, and they also completed two self-report scales. A social relations analysis of these data indicated that subjects' perceptions included both assimilation and consensus. There was also a relationship between how subjects saw themselves before therapy and how they were seen by other group members. The results demonstrated the utility of the social relations model for group therapy research and provided modest support for Kiesler's interpersonal circle.

Merta, R. J., Johnson, P., & McNeil, K. (1995). Updated research on group work: Educators, course work theory, and teaching methods. *The Journal for Specialists in Group Work, 20* (3), 132–142.

Abstract

This article updates research on various aspects of training group counselors, using the results of a national survey of counselor educators. Two hundred and thirty-six responses were analyzed. Group counselor educators are described, required course work in group work and theoretical or philosophical bases for group work are examined, and training components and teaching methods used to educate group counselors are presented. Training practices of counselor educators possessing combined membership in the American Counseling Association and the Association for Specialists in Group Work are compared with those who do not. Implications for training specialists in group work are discussed.

Merta, R. J., Wolfgang, L., & McNeil, K. (1993). Five models for using the experiential group in the preparation of group counselors. *The Journal for Specialists in Group Work, 18* (4), 200–207.

Abstract

Two hundred and seventy-two academic units responding to a national survey indicated which of five experiential group models they are using to train group counselors, and which of four safeguards are employed against such unethical practices as invasion of privacy and abuse of power by an instructor. The traditional instructor-led group is the most widely used (39%) of the models. Although this model is one of two in which students are at greatest risk for experiencing adverse dual relationships, 29% of counselor educators using the model did not indicate using any safeguards. The diversity that exists in the way counselor educators are employing alternative models and safeguards translates into considerable variation in the extent to which students are at risk for experiencing dual relationships or receiving poor training. Results indicate that efforts to avoid adverse dual relationships in experiential groups have not significantly reduced the use of this traditional training component.

Newman, J. A., & Lovell, M. (1993). A description of a supervisory group for group counselors. *Counselor Education and Supervision, 33* (1), 22–31.

Abstract

This article describes a case example and evaluation of group supervision of 43 counselors-in-training (two coleadership pairs) responsible for implementing a 16-week interpersonal skills program. Experiential client-centered and didactic techniques were used to achieve four supervision goals: nurturing effective theory, highlighting counselor self-investigation, and promoting counselor cultural sensitivity. Following completion of the program, counselors filled out open-ended evaluations. Findings indicate that choosing a metaphor to symbolize counselors' leadership role helped to clarify their role, boosted confidence and creativity, and promoted coleader differentiation. The supervisors' ability to be flexible, listen attentively, and validate counselors was cited as both professionally and personally significant.

Omizo, M. M., & Omizo, S. A. (1987). Group counseling with children of divorce: New findings. *Elementary School Guidance and Counseling, 22* (1), 46–52.

Abstract

Sixty children of divorce were assigned to experimental or control conditions, with experimental subjects participating in group counseling intervention. Comparison of the two groups revealed that participation in group counseling appeared beneficial for enhancing self-concept and internal locus of control among elementary school children experiencing parental divorce.

Oppenheimer, B. T. (1984). Short-term small group intervention for college freshmen. *Journal of Counseling Psychology, 31* (1), 45–53.

Abstract

This study examined the effectiveness of a short-term small group intervention in facilitating the social adjustment of 99 college freshmen. The social adjustment of vulnerable subjects was significantly enhanced by group participation, whereas nonvulnerable subjects were unaffected, demonstrating the value of a small group experience in facilitating the transition to college.

Zimpfer, D., & Waltman, D. (1982). Correlates of effectiveness in group counseling. *Small Group Behavior, 13* (3), 275–290.

Abstract

The researchers used multiple groups ($N = 9$) and multiple counselors ($N = 9$) to study correlates of effectiveness in group counseling. Results indicated that both counselor and group composition variables related significantly to member interaction, to how much they valued the group, and to changes in member self-images.

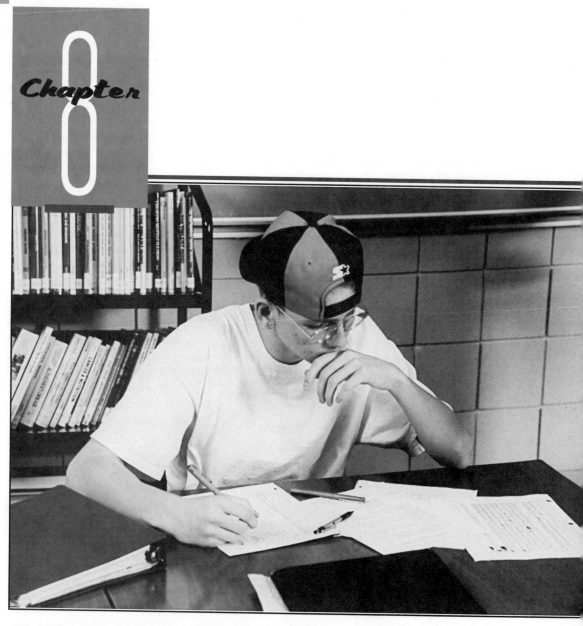

Chapter 8

Standardized Testing and Human Assessment

This chapter will acquaint you with the role of standardized testing in assessment for counseling purposes. We will begin by acknowledging some of the controversies attending standardized testing then move to a brief overview of test interpretation. Criteria for test selection and the different kinds of standardized tests will also be presented.

Few activities in education and psychology have remained as consistent an issue over the past 60 years or have been subject to the controversy and debate that has accompanied the standardized testing movement, not only in schools, but in government agencies and business and industry as well. From statements in Cubberly's (1934) *Public Education in the United States* and Gross's (1963) *The Brain Watchers*, to "Use and Misuse of Tests in Education: Legal Implications" (Nolte, 1975), "IQ Tests and the Culture Issue" (Ornstein, 1976), and "Standardized Tests: Are They Worth the Cost?" (Herndon, 1976) through Robinson's (1983) "Nader versus ETS [Educational Testing Services]," "America's Test Mania" (Fiske, 1988), and the special issue of *Educational Horizons*, "Assessment: The Winter of Our Discontent" (1993, fall), the pros and cons of standardized test usage have been publicly dissected.

Social issues have been raised and legal implications have been tested. Prominent psychologists and educators have also expressed concern over the continued uses and abuses of standardized testing. Many authorities have cautioned counselors and other users of the risks of clients drawing unwarranted conclusions from test results, whereas others have lamented the overemphasis on test scores by individuals, school systems, government agencies, and many businesses and industries. In addition, tests are also misused because of

> the too human desire for shortcuts, quick solutions, and clear-cut answers to our questions. This common human weakness has been capitalized on by soothsayers over the centuries, from phrenologists to astrologers and other self-styled expert advisers. People seeking guidance are often attracted by the facile promises of charlatans, in contrast to the slower, deliberate considerations and the carefully qualified suggestions of the scientifically trained professional. Similarly, if one or two short tests—whatever their technical limitations and defects—seem to offer a simple answer to questions about career choice, interpersonal difficulties, emotional problems, or learning deficiencies, many test takers will be temporarily satisfied. At another level, some misuse of tests by a counselor or other test user may arise from time pressure or work overload, which renders shortcuts attractive. (Anastasi, 1992, p. 610)

Albert Shanker, the former president of the American Federation of Teachers, writes that "exams fail the test" (1988) for the following reasons.

- Since the reputation of a school, its principal, its teachers and the school board and superintendent depends largely on these test scores, schools are devoting less time to reading real books, writing essays, and discussing current events and more and more time teaching kids strategies for filling in blanks and choosing the answers to multiple-choice questions. This destroys much of the value of these tests, which only tell you something if they are an independent measure of what the student knows. School districts are now engaged in a process called "curriculum alignment." That means that course content, textbooks, lesson plans, etc. are all being geared to items that will be on the test. These tests only tap a sample of skills, so it's possible for kids to do well and still not be able to understand real books. But since there's only so much time, schools now minimize or totally leave out those things that are not on these tests. This is the tail wagging the dog. Schools and teachers should not be pressured to drop content they believe to be valuable just because it won't be on the test.
- The tests are very costly in terms of both time and money. Coaching and testing time has increased so much that it is significantly taking away blocks of time from teaching and learning.

- The test scores published by schools and districts are misleading if not downright fraudulent.
- Students who take these tests are not being measured against their peers, but against norm groups who took the test as much as 3 to 10 years earlier. (p. E-7)

In 1983, the popular report of the National Commission on Excellence in Education entitled *A Nation at Risk* based much of its negative findings on standardized test results, fueling once again the controversies over the role of testing in educational evaluation. In 1990, the National Commission on Testing and Public Policy called for a broad overhaul of educational and employment testing. In the 1990s, the continued impact of the accountability movement plus demands that schools measure up have resulted in the continued and, yes, increased use of standardized tests despite the controversies.

Although critics of standardized testing abound, and standardized measurement continues to draw fire, much of the criticism may be as appropriately directed at the misuse and misinterpretation of the instruments as at the tests themselves. The misuse of tests in schools, especially, appears to stem from test users who are inadequately prepared in administering and interpreting standardized tests. At the same time, however, in many schools and school systems, as well as a wide variety of agency settings, tests are used with prudence and caution by adequately trained counselors and psychologists. In most institutional or agency settings where counseling takes place, including schools, standardized tests have been the counselor's basic instrument for objective assessment of the personality traits, aptitudes, interests, and other characteristics of individuals. Clearly, individual counseling demands a knowledge and recognition of the individuality of clients. Measurement of individual differences is a part of the mainstream of personnel psychology.

It therefore is most appropriate to introduce potential counselors to this important area of counselor understanding and skill, recognizing the continuing debates and issues. Such knowledge plus a basic understanding of these areas of testing will enable you to more effectively discriminate between uses and abuses and to retain in your counseling repertoire a useful analytical tool.

STANDARDIZED TEST SCORES—WHAT DO THEY MEAN?

Whenever we evaluate someone, we do it in terms of some kind of comparison or point of reference. (See Oakwood High School hypothetical example discussed later in this chapter.) For instance, we may refer to Juan as the most handsome one in the group, Kathy as the best student in the class, and Mariah as the hardest worker in the bookstore. Here, we are comparing Juan to all others in the group, Kathy to the other students in the class, and Mariah to the other workers in the bookstore. Although we might attempt to make some predictions or deduce some other traits for Juan, Kathy, and Mariah from our observation, these would amount to nothing more than speculations, and we could justifiably be accused of unreliable procedures and data. If Kathy, Juan, and Mariah were to seek counseling, their counselor would want more objective and valid data before attempting to describe their traits and performances against the average traits and performances of others with comparable characteristics and experiences. An elementary understanding of statistics and statistically based tests, however, would enable the counselor to do this.

These basic understandings of educational and psychological statistics enable the counselor to (a) describe the characteristics of an individual or group in comparison with a specific group or population, (b) predict the probability of future success or failure in a given area on the basis of present or past behavior, and (c) infer the characteristics of a population from a sample of that population. It therefore follows that a good working knowledge of elementary statistical concepts is important for anyone who uses the various techniques of individual analysis and mandatory for all who use tests and other tools of measurement. This section offers a brief overview of descriptive statistics, the basic statistical terms, and essential computational procedures, beginning with perhaps the most common—and most commonly misunderstood—of all statistical terms, average.

Averages

When Latonya reports to her parents that she scored 70 on her history test, should they be pleased, satisfied, disappointed, or what? Until they have more information, they cannot be sure how to react, because 70 could represent 70% of the questions answered correctly, 70 answered correctly out of 75 asked, a formula score of 70 (i.e., rights minus wrongs), or 70th in a class of 120 taking the examination. In this example, you may note that a score in and of itself is of little value. A score only becomes meaningful when it provides an index of how well or how poorly one performed in comparison with others taking the same test and, knowing that, what other significance can be interpreted from the results. Latonya's parents are asking what an average performance is on this test and how she differs from the average. Also, one might ask to what does her score relate—what does it mean? Let us begin then by reviewing what is meant by averages.

Most educational and psychological evaluation is based on a person's position in a group compared with others who constitute the group. The average position in a group becomes an important point of mathematical reference in standardized testing for human assessment. There are three distinct statistical types of averages, known as *measures of central tendency*: the mean, the median, and the mode. For most nonstatisticians, the definition of the mean is commonly associated with the term *average*, for the *mean* is defined as the mathematical average of a group of scores. The *median* is the midpoint of a set of scores with 50% of the scores being distributed above and 50% below that point. The *mode* represents the most frequent score in a set of scores. Of these three averages, the mean is the most useful and popular, and the mode, having little statistical value, is the least popular.

Variations from the Average

Once we have determined what is average, we must utilize a statistical methodology to measure the degree to which each person varies from this established average, or *point of central tendency*. Such statistical measures are called *measures of variability*. Two common measures of variability are the range and the standard deviation. The *range* is the spread from the lowest score to the highest score in a distribution. The actual statistical formula is the highest score in a group, minus the lowest score plus one. (The plus one in this formula extends the range to its real limits, which are one-half of a score unit below the lowest.) The range is a relatively simple measurement device with limited descriptive value. The *standard deviation*, however, is a statistical process that allows for an exact determination of distances of scores from the mean.

The mean and the standard deviation, when computed for a specific set of test scores, enable a counselor to determine how well an individual performed in relation to the group. This interpretation is made by specifying standard deviation distance from the mean and determining the proportion of the population that will be beyond or deviate from it, assuming that the scores are normally distributed. This normally distributed population is most popularly viewed as a normal curve, as shown in Figure 8-1. (Note: Rarely are the mean, median, and mode the same.)

In Figure 8-2, the normal curve is, in effect, sliced into bands one standard deviation wide, with a fixed percentage of cases always falling in each band. Figure 8-2 then illustrates a significant fact: The mean plus and minus one standard deviation encompasses approximately 68% of a normally distributed population; the mean plus and minus two standard deviations encompasses approximately 95% of that population; and the mean plus and minus three standard deviations encompasses 99.7% of that population. This information, which re-

Figure 8-1   The Normal Curve.

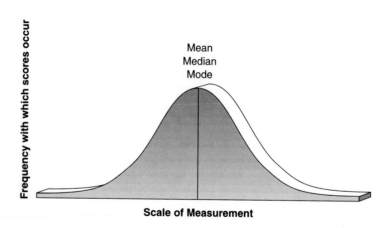

Figure 8-2   Scores in a Normal Distribution.

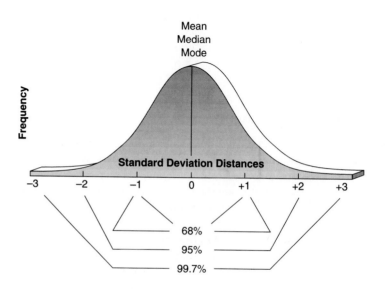

mains constant for any normally distributed set of scores or values, makes possible a meaningful interpretation of any score in a group. As you view the normal curve and its segmentation into standard deviations, note that these facts are handy for interpreting standard scores. Furthermore, whenever you can assume a normal distribution, you can convert standard scores to percentile scores and vice versa. Thus, three basic facts for deriving a statistical evaluation of a person's performance on a psychological test are the person's raw score, mean, and standard deviation for the group with which the individual is being compared.

Relationships

Once you have determined the meaning of an individual's score in relation to others who have been administered the same measure, you must ask what are the other relationships of this score. The score and its comparative standing will take on meaning when it can be related to some meaningful purpose. For example, if students who score high on a college entrance examination actually perform at a high academic level in college, then one can assume that there is a relationship between scores on the examination and performance in college. The test score then becomes meaningful in terms of its prediction of college success, a meaningful purpose.

When you look for a statistical method to express relationships between two variables such as test scores and academic performance, you can compute a *correlation coefficient*. Correlation coefficients range from plus one through zero to minus one. A plus one indicates a perfect positive correlation; that is, the rank order of those taking the college entrance examination and their academic rank order in the college program are identical. A correlation of minus one means that the scores go in exactly the reverse direction. Thus, a correlation of minus one would indicate that persons who score highest on the entrance examination achieve the lowest in college. A zero correlation would represent a complete lack of relationship between two sets of data. A frequently computed coefficient of correlation is the Pearson product-moment coefficient.

Statistical Symbols

The counselor, teacher, or others who read test manuals, interpret test data, or in other ways seek to interpret simple statistical data should be familiar with basic statistical symbols. Although there is no universal statistical language, the following are some of the more commonly recognized symbols and their meanings.

M	Mean
Σ	Sum of
Σfb	The sum of frequencies below the class in which the median will fall
SD (or S)	Standard deviation for a particular set of scores
X	Actual or raw scores obtained
MD	Median
x	Distance (or score difference) of a score from the mean
N	Number of cases
i	Size of a class interval in scale units
M'	Assumed mean
r	Coefficient of correlation
z	Scale value of the standard normal distribution; the standard deviation of distance of a given score from the mean

l The lower limit of the class in which the median will fall
fw The total of the frequencies within the class in which the median will fall
f Frequency; the number of times a particular score occurs
p Percentage of persons getting a test item correct
q Percentage of persons getting a test item wrong ($p + q = 100$)

Presenting Test Scores

Inasmuch as raw test scores are in themselves meaningless, they have little value for the reporting of individual test results. As previously indicated, a raw score becomes meaningful only when it can be converted into some type of comparative score—one that enables an individual to be compared against others of a group. Most standardized tests, therefore, utilize one or more of the following methods of converting raw scores into a more meaningful method of presenting an individual's test results.

Percentiles

A percentile score represents the percentage of persons in the standardized sample for a given test who fall below a given raw score. A person's percentile ranking indicates his or her relative position in a normative sample. For example, if 60% of the students answer fewer than 30 problems correctly on an English usage test, then a raw score of 30 corresponds to the 60th percentile.

Percentiles are probably the most common method of presenting scores and are fairly easy to interpret. Due to their relative ease of interpretation, however, several cautions should be noted. In working with non–test-sophisticated groups, such as parents, students, and most general populations, it is important to emphasize that percentiles do not represent percentages. Because percentiles represent comparison scores, it is also important to note the population with which an individual is being compared and the valid purposes for which comparisons can be made. It should also be noted that there are inequalities in percentile units.

The reason such distortion occurs is quite simple. When a raw-score distribution approximates the normal curve, there are many more moderate scores, which fall in the middle of the distribution, than either high or low scores, which occur at the ends. Because percentiles are based on the raw-score distance encompassed by a specified percentage of the total group, percentile distances near the median, with its high concentration of cases, will encompass a much smaller raw-score difference than the same percentile distance farther from the median. Hence, the 15 points of raw-score difference between the 5th and 10th percentiles may shrink to 5 points of difference between the 40th and 45th.

These distortions make it difficult to use percentiles for profiling and other comparisons of a student's performance on two or more tests. To overcome the limitations in test interpretation resulting from the inequality of percentiles, more and more test publishers are turning to some type of standard score for norming.

Computing Percentiles. To expedite test interpretation, one may want to compute percentiles for a given group. The formula for computing percentiles from a grouped frequency distribution is

$$P_x = l + \left(\frac{P_r N - \Sigma fb}{fw} \right) i$$

Thus, if the 75th percentile is desired, $P_x = 0.75$; if the 40th percentile is desired, $P_x = 0.40$.

A grouped frequency table—once it is properly prepared—can be used for computing most of the elementary statistics a counselor might need for that set of scores. However, the computation of percentiles is made easier by adding to the table a column showing progressive accumulation of frequencies. This is called a cf (cumulative frequency) column; it is shown at the left in Table 8-1, which uses hypothetical data for Oakwood High School.

The following steps show how one would go about finding the 25th percentile for the Oakwood High School data given in Table 8-1.

1. Multiply N by the desired percentile (converted to a decimal) to determine the class in which this percentile falls. For the Oakwood group, N is 250 and the desired percentile is 25. The product of 0.25×250 is 62.5; the cf column indicates that the score value of the individual ranking 62.5 from the bottom is found within the class 50–54, so it is established that P_{25} lies between 49.5 and 54.5.

2. Determine the necessary values for the formula.

$$P_{25}N = 62.5$$
$$\Sigma fb = 40$$
$$fw = 28$$
$$i = 5$$

3. Insert the values in the formula and perform the indicated computations.

$$P_{25} = 49.5 + \left(\frac{62.5 - 40}{28}\right) 5$$

$$= 49.5 + \frac{22.5 \times 5}{28}$$

$$= 49.5 + 4.02$$

$$= 52.53 \text{ or, rounded, } 54$$

TABLE 8-1 Computation of Percentiles

cf	X	f	d	fd
250	95–99	2	7	14
248	90–94	3	6	18
245	85–89	5	5	25
240	80–84	10	4	40
230	75–79	15	3	45
215	70–74	22	2	44
193	65–69	38	1	38
155	60–64	55	0	0
100	55–59	32	−1	−32
68	50–54	28	−2	−56
40	45–49	17	−3	−51
23	40–44	14	−4	−56
9	35–39	5	−5	−25
4	30–34	4	−6	−24
	N = 250			Σfd = −20

Deciles and Quartiles

Chase (1984) described deciles and quartiles as follows.

> Two kinds of figures besides percentiles are also frequently used to show relative standing in a group. These are *deciles* and *quartiles*, both of which are similar to, and indeed can be read from, percentile tables. Deciles are points that divide the distribution of raw scores into segments of 10 percent each. Thus, the first decile D1 would be that point on the distribution below which 10 percent of the cases fall, D2 the point below which 20 percent of the cases fall, etc. Deciles can be computed in the same manner as percentiles, since D1 is P10, D2 is P20, etc.
>
> Deciles, like percentiles, are points on a scale. Therefore, a score can be between the third and the fourth deciles, i.e., in the fourth lowest 10 percent of the group, but it cannot be in the third decile, since that decile is only a point on the scale. Quartiles divide the distribution of raw scores into segments of 25 percent each. Thus, the first quartile, Q1 is the point that cuts off the lowest 25 percent, Q2 the lowest 50 percent of the group (what is another name for this point? [median]), and Q3 the lowest 75 percent of the distribution.
>
> It should be emphasized, however, that deciles and quartiles, like percentiles, are points along the scale. They are not segments of that scale. It is wrong to say that case X *is in the third quartile* or something similar. This is an error because the third quartile is only a point on the scale. (p. 77)

Standard Scores

Standard scores have become increasingly popular with standardized test developers. A standard score expresses a person's distance from the mean in terms of the standardized deviation of the distribution. For example, let us return to Kathy, Juan, and Mariah and their scores on a test.

Mean of the test takers	75
Standard deviation	15
Kathy's score	90
Juan's score	65
Mariah's score	45

Using the formula $\dfrac{X(\text{raw score}) - M(\text{mean})}{SD(\text{standard deviation})}$, the following standard scores are obtained.

$$\text{Kathy:} \frac{90 - 75}{15} = +1.0$$

$$\text{Juan:} \frac{65 - 75}{15} = -0.7$$

$$\text{Mariah:} \frac{45 - 75}{15} = -2.0$$

Because both decimal points and plus and minus signs may be confusing or easily misplaced, they can be transformed into a more convenient form by multiplying each standard score with some constant. For example, if we multiply these scores by 10, we have +10, −7, and −20. We can then eliminate the plus and minuses by adding a constant of 100. Thus, Kathy's score becomes 110, Juan's 93, and Mariah's 80.

Stanines

Another variation for normalizing standard scores was developed by the United States Air Force in World War II. The name *stanine* is a contraction of standard nine, a nine-point scale having a mean of five and a standard deviation of two. The percentages of a normal distribution that fall within each of the nine stanines are as follows.

Stanine	1	2	3	4	5	6	7	8	9
Percentage	4	7	12	17	20	17	12	7	4

Relationships among various types of test scores and the normal curve may be noted in Figure 8-3.

Norms

A favorite expression of soldiers in the ranks is *snafu* (situation normal—all fouled up). We label persons as normal or abnormal if they deviate from our concept of normalcy, and we use such expressions as "He would normally do this" or "Under normal conditions you can expect that." The term *norm* or *normal* is a popular one that most persons use frequently to denote the expected or that which can be reasonably anticipated. The concept of normal or norm as used in standardized testing terminology also implies normal or average performance on a given test. Norms are derived during the process of standardizing a test. As a basis for determining the norms, a test is administered to a sample (usually large) that is representative of the population for whom the test is designed. This group then comprises the standardization sample to establish the norms for the test. These norms reflect not only the average performances but also the relative frequency of the varying degrees of deviation below and above the average.

Age Norms. The use of age norms or standards is a fairly popular one in the nonscientific sense. We often suggest that José is as big as a 10-year-old or Janie has the vocabulary of a 6-year-old. The use of this concept in reporting standardized testing results became popular when the term *mental age* was used during the translations and adaptations of the original Binet scales. From this initial usage, age norms were frequently used to measure any trait that showed progressive change with age. For example, in physical development, it would be relatively simple to prepare norms for the height or weight of growing children by years. In testing, age norms represent the test performance of persons grouped and normed according to their chronological age. This type of score is more likely to be noted in the reporting of achievement tests, especially in the elementary school grades.

There are two shortcomings to this concept of scoring and reporting results. First, there is a lack of agreement regarding when children should be introduced to certain basic academic subjects, at what rates, and what comprehension level should normally be expected in these subjects. Also, age norms assume uniform growth from year to year, an assumption of questionable validity.

Figure 8-3   Relationships Among Different Types of Test Scores in a Normal Distribution.
Source: Reprinted from *Measurement and Evaluation in Psychology and Education,* 4th ed., by Robert M. Thorndike and Elizabeth P. Hagen (New York: Macmillan College Publishing Company, 1977), p.133. From the *Test Service Bulletin No. 48,* January 1955, by the Psychological Corporation.

Grade Norms.   Grade norms are similar to age norms inasmuch as they are based on the average score earned by students at a specific grade level. Again, grade norms are popular for reporting achievement test results in terms of grade equivalents. This method of report-ing standardized test results, however, suffers from the same shortcomings as do age norms but is more readily viewed as suggesting standards to which teachers should aspire. Table 8-2 contrasts the main type of norms for educational and psychological tests.

TABLE 8-2 Main Types of Norms for Educational and Psychological Tests

Type of Norm	Type of Comparison	Type of Group
Age norms	Individual matched to groups whose performance he equals	Successive age groups
Grade norms	Same as above	Successive grade groups
Percentile norms	Percent of group surpassed by individual	Single age or grade group to which individual belongs
Standard score norms	Number of standard deviations individual falls above or below average of group	Same as above

Source: Reprinted from *Measurement and Evaluation in Psychology and Education,* 4th ed., by Robert M. Thorndike and Elizabeth P. Hagen (New York: Macmillan College Publishing Company, 1977), p. 117. From the *Test Service Bulletin No. 48,* January 1955, by the Psychological Association.

SELECTING A TEST—WHAT CRITERIA?

The numbers and variety of standardized tests available to counselors and other users today require a recognition and application of appropriate criteria in test selection. Furthermore, much of the criticism of standardized testing over the years has focused on poorly designed instruments and poorly prepared users, which implies the need of criteria for both. Certainly, there are clinical as well as research-based reasons for concern with the trustworthiness of the data produced by assessment devices.

For obvious reasons, counselors should not use standardized tests that do not give accurate measures or that they (the counselors) are not competent to interpret. An error in measurement and/or interpretation can lead to an error in client decision making.

Validity

Validity is traditionally defined as the degree to which an instrument measures what it claims to measure or is used to measure. For example, does the Whiffenpoof Mechanical Aptitude Test really measure one's aptitude for mechanical activities as claimed, or does it simply reflect one's previous experiences in the areas being tested? Or to raise a question of traditional controversy, do IQ tests really measure basic or native intelligence, or do they more appropriately reflect one's cultural and educational experiences? In establishing validity, one must note the appropriateness of test or interview questions and of situational samples to the evaluation objectives. Because it is impossible to include all possible questions or situations in an evaluation tool, those selected for inclusion must be representative of the content areas or behavioral patterns being assessed and appropriate for the individual under study and the given circumstances. When an instrument meets these conditions, it is said to have *content validity.*

When the foregoing types of validity do not or cannot provide sufficient evidence of a test's validity, its construct validity may be cited. *Construct validity* pertains to the adequacy of the theory or concept underlying a specific instrument. In other words, it involves logically ascertaining the psychological attributes that account for variations in test scores or other derived data. Construct validity is reported in terms of the kinds of responses the test should elicit, and the ways in which those responses should be interpreted on the basis of logical inferences about the behavior the test is designed to assess.

Reliability

The second major criterion to be applied in standardized test selection is reliability. *Reliability* represents the consistency with which a test will obtain the same results from the same population but on different occasions. An instrument's reliability enables a counselor or other user to determine the degree to which predictions based on the established consistency of the test can be made.

Two techniques are popularly used to establish reliability. One is the *test-retest method*. When this method is used, timing between the tests is crucial because growth or decline in performance could occur if the interval is too long, whereas recall of original test items might occur if the interval is too short. A second approach for determining reliability is by establishing an instrument's *internal consistency*. This consistency is set by comparing persons' responses to the odd-numbered questions with the consistency of their responses to the even-numbered questions.

Practicality

A third important, but often overlooked, criterion in the selection of a standardized instrument is that of *practicality*. First and foremost of the practical considerations is whether trained personnel are available to administer, score (if necessary), and interpret the particular standardized test under consideration. The importance of users' understanding the fine points of interpretation cannot be overemphasized.

A second and not unimportant practical consideration is the cost of the instrument and accompanying materials. The expense of scoring is included in this consideration. Additionally, many standardized tests can be used only for one testing, so replacement costs may become another factor. Time required for administration is also a practical consideration, especially, but not exclusively, in school settings.

TYPES OF STANDARDIZED TESTS

Having briefly examined statistical concepts, methods of scoring, and criteria for the selection of standardized tests, let us now consider the specific areas for which standardized tests are available. These include aptitude, achievement, interest, and personality testing. There is admittedly some overlap in these categories, especially in interest and personality, but we will examine them as discrete, though not exclusive, areas for the classification of standardized tests. This discussion will focus on group standardized tests. Although recognizing the value of individual tests and that counselors and psychologists in a variety of nonschool settings frequently use individual tests, beginning counselors, especially in educational settings, work almost exclusively with group tests.

Intelligence or Aptitude?

The terms *aptitude* and *intelligence* are often used synonymously. However, in the discussion of standardized tests, one should examine the subtle differences that distinguish measures of intelligence from measures of aptitude. One distinction is that intelligence tests tend to provide a broad measure of overall or general ability, primarily related to one's potential for learning, whereas aptitude measures tend to focus more narrowly on specific factors. Stating it another way, intelligence tests tend to measure one human characteristic, the intellectual or mental capabilities of the individual, whereas aptitude tests can be used to measure a wide range of primarily career learning and/or performance potentials. Both intelligence and aptitude measures have been the subject of the nature/nurture debates. Additionally, the overlap between intelligence and scholastic aptitude tests has, at times, blurred the differences between these two areas of standardized psychological measurement.

Intelligence Testing

The most popular area of aptitude or ability testing is the category that includes tests purporting to evaluate general academic ability, mental ability, and intelligence. Of these subsets, intelligence, or IQ, testing is the oldest and most controversial. Much of this controversy has centered around the various views of what constitutes intelligence, what influences it—heredity versus environment—and whether intelligence changes. These controversies have led to some more popularly accepted labels such as *academic ability, mental maturity, scholastic ability,* or *academic aptitude tests*. Some of these latter labels are probably more appropriate inasmuch as many of the earlier IQ tests were largely normed on school populations and developed to predict performance in school.

Other shortcomings of general intelligence assessment are that different people arrive at the same end by different intellectual means. The reading level of the test taker can bias the results. Judgments about intelligence can be linked with judgments about the worth of the individual. Finally, there has been a strong tendency to overlook the cultural and value relativity of intelligence judgments.

The first intelligence tests were designed for individual administering by a Frenchman, Alfred Binet, and, in the early 1900s, several American versions were developed. The most popular of these, the Stanford-Binet, based on the work of Lewis Terman at Stanford University, was published in 1916. This test has remained popular in the decades following, with the most recent revisions reflected in the fourth edition (1986, Riverdale Publishing Company). The other popular and perhaps most individually administered intelligence tests are the various Wechsler Scales.

The Wechsler Scales were developed by David Wechsler, a clinical psychologist, and were based on the assumption that intelligence was the sum total of the individual's abilities to think in a rational manner, to act purposely, and to deal in an effective manner with one's environment. Wechsler Scales were developed for both preschool and primary children and adult populations. For school children, tests such as the Wechsler are required under PL 94-142 in order to identify pupils in need of special services. The scales produce three scores: verbal ability, performance ability, and general ability. The Wechsler Test III (WISC-III, 1991) for ages 6 to 16, also allows for the computing of four index scores of verbal comprehension, perceptual organization, freedom from distractability, and processing speed.

One of the most popular group intelligence tests over the years has been the Otis, or, as currently labeled, the Otis-Lennon School Ability Test (OLSAT), and it is in its sixth edition. The first Otis test appeared in 1918 as the Otis Group Intelligence Scale and later achieved great popularity in both industry and education as the Otis-Quick Scoring Mental Abilities Tests. The current edition has five levels ranging from grades 1 to 12, with working times of 60 or 75 minutes, depending on the level.

Two other popular group intelligence tests are the Lorge-Thorndike and the Henmon-Nelson Tests of Mental Ability. The Lorge-Thorndike intelligence test is available in two forms for grades 3 to 13. It provides both verbal and nonverbal batteries for those grades in a single reusable booklet. The verbal battery is made up of five subtests, using only verbal items: vocabulary, verbal classification, sentence completion, arithmetic reasoning, and verbal analogy. The nonverbal battery uses items that are either pictorial or numerical. The three subtests involved are pictorial classification, pictorial analogy, and numerical relationships. The tests in this battery yield an estimate of scholastic aptitude that is not dependent on an ability to read. The working times are verbal battery, 35 minutes; nonverbal battery, 27 minutes.

The Henmon-Nelson Tests of Mental Ability are available in two editions: Form 1 for grades 3 through 12, and a primary battery for kindergarten through grade 2. The primary battery is normatively integrated with Form 1, permitting school systems to use the Henmon-Nelson tests throughout the entire kindergarten through grade 12 range.

Form 1 for grades 3 through 12 has three levels (3 to 6, 6 to 9, and 9 to 12), consisting of 90 items presented in order of increasing difficulty. Form 1 of the Henmon-Nelson Tests of Mental Ability was standardized in the fall of 1972 on a national sample of 35,000 subjects in grades 3 through 12.

The primary battery for kindergarten through grade 2 consists of three separate subtests: a listening test (general information, 30 items); a picture vocabulary test (33 items); and a size and number test (23 items). These short subtests measure simple verbal and quantitative skills considered important in assessing readiness for schoolwork.

Standardization in grade 2 was carried out concurrently with the norming of the Henmon-Nelson in grades 3 through 12 during the fall of 1972. For kindergarten and grade 1, standardization was done in early 1973 on a sample of approximately 5,000 pupils drawn from the same schools that participated in the grade 2 through 12 norming program.

Counselors who elect to use intelligence or mental abilities tests must be ever alert to the very sensitive nature of what they are measuring. Intelligence is at the core of the individual's view of their self-worth and their potential. How does the counselor tell the client that they have scored below average on an IQ test—or a parent that their child has a measured IQ below normal? Obviously serious psychological damage can occur and has in many unfortunate instances over the years.

Counselors should also be aware that many IQ tests have for years been suspected of cultural bias—a bias that would discriminate against minorities and populations in special environments. The use of intelligence tests should, therefore, be approached with extreme caution, if in fact, they are to be used at all.

Aptitude Tests

Aptitude may be defined as a trait that characterizes an individual's ability to perform in a given area or to acquire the learning necessary for performance in a given area. It presumes an inherent or native ability that can be developed to its maximum through learning or other experiences. However, it cannot be expanded beyond this certain point, even by learning. Although that may be a debatable concept, it is stated here as a basis on which aptitude tests are developed. In theory, then, an aptitude test measures the potential of one to achieve in a given activity or to learn to achieve in that activity.

Aptitude tests would most likely be used by counselors and others because they may (a) identify potential abilities of which the person is not aware; (b) encourage the development of special or potential abilities of a given person; (c) provide information to assist a person in making educational and career decisions or other choices between competing alternatives; (d) help predict the level of academic or vocational success a person might anticipate; and (e) be useful in grouping persons with similar aptitudes for developmental and other educational purposes. It should be emphasized that these are *potential* advantages and will accrue only under optimal conditions, which include initially the use of appropriate and proper measurement instruments relevant to the client's needs.

Although we usually anticipate that a person is likely to demonstrate considerable differences across a range of aptitudes, we should also be alert to the possibility that a person will not demonstrate or measure at the same level for a given aptitude every time. In other words, a track star may run the 100-yard dash in 10 seconds one day and the same distance under the same conditions in 10.4 seconds the next day. Aptitude measures are thus actuarial rather than absolute.

Special Aptitude Tests

Special aptitude tests usually refer to those tests that seek to measure a person's potential ability to perform or to acquire proficiency in a specific occupation or other type of activity. Tests that measure special aptitudes are sometimes referred to as *single aptitude tests* or *component ability tests* because they only secure a measure for one specific aptitude or a single special ability. Tests of special aptitude have generally declined in popularity as aptitude batteries have increased in popularity. Counselors must frequently use standardized tests to measure a single aptitude in areas of mechanical, clerical, or artistic abilities. Single-aptitude tests have also been developed for use in various graduate and professional schools. Aptitude tests are also available for particular school subjects, especially in the areas of mathematics and foreign languages.

Vocational Aptitude Batteries

Aptitude batteries are developed on the assumption that different career fields have their own set of criteria. Further, being able to profile and contrast results for differing careers is an advantage.

Multiple-aptitude tests are an outgrowth of factorial studies of intelligence. Anastasi (1996) discusses the objective of factor analysis.

> The principle objective of factor analysis is to simplify the description of data by reducing the number of necessary variables, or dimensions. Thus, if we find that five factors are sufficient to account for all the common variance in a battery of 20 tests, we can for most purposes substitute five scores for the original 20 without sacrificing any essential information. The usual practice is to retain from among the original tests those providing the best measures of each of the factors. (p. 303)

These batteries typically consist of a series of subtests related in varying combinations to a series of occupations or occupationally related activities. The major advantages of batteries over single-aptitude tests are (a) convenience in administration as a result of having in one package a test that can be used to measure potential in a variety of activities; (b) the norming of all the battery's subtests on the same population, which thus yields comparable subtest norms; and (c) the opportunity to compare potential in a wide variety of areas with one test.

The oldest and most widely used of these multiple-aptitude batteries are the General Aptitude Test Battery (GATB), used by the United States Employment Service, and the Differential Aptitude Battery (DAT). The Flanigan Aptitude Classification Test (FACT), and the Armed Services Vocational Aptitude Battery (ASVAB) are also extensively used. A brief examination of the characteristics of these tests may help you further understand the nature of aptitude batteries.

General Aptitude Test Battery.   The General Aptitude Test Battery is administered through the United States Employment Service. However, it is available to nonprofit institutions such as schools for counseling purposes. This battery has 12 subtests, which yield nine scores (see Figure 8-4). It should also be noted that these aptitudes are not all independent as some of the subtests are used in determining more than one aptitude score. As might be anticipated, this battery is primarily used in career counseling for job placement for individuals age 16 or older.

Differential Aptitude Test.   The Differential Aptitude Test consists of a battery of eight subtests. The current (1990) edition features two levels. Level 1 is primarily for students in grades 7 to 9 and level 2, for those in grades 10 to 12. Both versions may be appropriate for

Figure 8-4   Nine Aptitudes Measured by 12 Tests in the General Aptitude Test Battery B1002.

older populations as well. The subtests are verbal reasoning, numerical ability, abstract reasoning, clerical speed and accuracy, mechanical reasoning, space relations, language usage—spelling, and language usage—grammar. This battery has for many years been one of the most popular in common use in schools as a means of assisting counseling for vocational and educational decision making.

Flanigan Aptitude Classification Test.   The Flanigan Aptitude Classification Test is one of the more time-consuming multiple-aptitude tests, requiring approximately eight hours to administer. This comprehensive aptitude test battery was based on the job elements approach basic to performance in a wide range of job classifications. The battery consists of 19 subtests.

1. Inspection
2. Mechanics
3. Tables
4. Reasoning
5. Vocabulary
6. Assembly
7. Judgment and comprehension
8. Components
9. Planning
10. Memory
11. Arithmetic
12. Ingenuity
13. Scales
14. Expression
15. Precision
16. Alertness
17. Coordination
18. Patterns
19. Coding

The results of these tests are profiled for various occupational areas. Counselors may use these findings as an aid in job placement or career and educational planning.

The Armed Services Vocational Aptitude Battery.   Since 1972, approximately one million high school students per year have taken the ASVAB, a service that is available to local high schools at no cost or obligation to either the school or student. This battery, also used throughout the military services and the Department of Defense, consists of ten tests, namely arithmetic reasoning, numerical operations, paragraph comprehension, work knowledge, coding speed, general science, mathematics knowledge, electronics information, mechanical comprehension, and automotive and shop information. Approximately three hours' administration time is needed for the current edition of the battery.

Scholastic Aptitude Tests

Scholastic, or academic, aptitude tests propose to measure a person's potential for performing in academic situations. Such tests as those that constitute the School and College Ability Test (SCAT) and Scholastic Aptitude Test (SAT) batteries have merit insofar as predicting academic performance at higher educational levels. However, more appropriate labels would be academic achievement or academic predictions, because they tend to predict future academic achievement on the basis of past learning rather than of native ability.

A popular academic aptitude test for the high school level is the advanced level of the School and College Ability Test (SCAT III), designed for grades 9 to 12. This test yields a verbal, quantitative, and total score. In line with current trends in testing theory, SCAT seeks to measure developed abilities. Thus, the SCAT draws freely on word knowledge and math processes presumed learned in the earlier school grades.

Two popular tests used for the admission, placement, and counseling of college students are the Scholastic Aptitude Test (SAT) of the College Entrance Examinations Board and the American College Testing Program (ACT), introduced in 1959, which is also used by many institutions of higher education. The ACT consists of four tests: English usage, mathematical usage, social studies reading, and natural sciences reading.

Many high school counselors and college admissions officials have frequently noted that the best single predictor of college student academic performance in college is one's high school academic grade point average. However, this prediction is enhanced when combined with standardized admission test scores such as the Scholastic Aptitude Test (SAT).

The proponents of such tests for admissions purposes suggest that they measure, in a uniform way, the basic knowledge expected in a field, they compensate for differences in grading practices and differing content emphases among schools. Some critics, however, complain that they discriminate against minorities and students attending schools serving lower socio-economic populations.

Achievement Tests

Achievement measurement is an area of standardized testing to which most students have been subject, not on just a single occasion or two, but probably numerous times during their educational programs. Of all the areas of standardized testing, achievement tests are the most popular in terms of numbers administered. Literally hundreds of thousands of achievement tests are administered on an annual basis in the overwhelming majority of schools throughout the country. The accountability movement of recent generations has sparked additional growth in the use of achievement tests to measure and, all too frequently, evaluate teachers, schools, and school systems.

This emphasis on achievement testing as indices of educational excellence in school reform movements of the late 1980s and 1990s has stimulated both the use of achievement tests and attention to their results. Despite the widespread popularity of achievement tests, they are frequently confused with other measures, especially aptitude tests.

Drummond (1996) identifies the various types of achievement tests as follows.

1. *Survey achievement batteries.* Partially norm-referenced and partially criterion-referenced tests that measure knowledge and skill in reading, mathematics, language arts, social studies, and science

2. *Subject area tests.* Achievement tests in a single subject area, such as math or spelling

3. *Criterion-referenced tests.* Tests that measure knowledge and comprehension of a specific skill or competency, for example, the ability to draw specified inferences from pictorial or written content or the ability to read a metric scale and give the weight of an object in metric and English units of weight

4. *Minimum level skills tests.* Tests that measure objectives or skills identified as the minimum skills to be achieved in order to pass from one level or grade to another

5. *Individual achievement tests.* Tests that are administered individually across a wide age or grade range to measure achievement

6. *Diagnostic tests.* Tests that are used to assess the strengths and weaknesses of individuals in a given subject area by measuring a limited number of skills thoroughly (p. 155)

Achievement tests are used to provide measures of (a) the amount of learning, (b) the rate of learning, (c) comparisons with others or with achievement of self in other areas, (d) level of learning in subareas, (e) strengths and weaknesses in a subject matter area, and, in some instances, (f) predictions of future learning. Because of their extensive use and the relatively easy task of identifying appropriate content measures, achievement tests are among the best designed standardized measures available to counselors. There are, however, certain considerations that users must keep in mind if such instruments are to be used appropriately.

First, it is important that the content of the test is relevant to the subject-matter content the student has experienced. In other words, the test should measure what the student has had the opportunity to learn. Further, it is important that the emphasis within the test, in terms of topical areas covered, is appropriate for the emphasis the student has experienced in the subject-matter class. Additionally, the level of difficulty of the test items must be appropriate for the age/grade level being tested. A final consideration, one that bears repeating, is the norming sample on which the test has been standardized.

If this sample is representative of the general population appropriate to the age/grade level being tested, comparison with this general population may be appropriate. If the population of the sample is similar to the population being tested, that would usually be desirable. However, if the norming population is considerably dissimilar, it may not be an appropriate group against which to compare the group being tested.

Although achievement tests that measure only a single subject matter are available, batteries that measure and compare across a series of subject-matter areas are far more popular. This popularity is no doubt due in part to the fact that an achievement battery is less expensive than a collection of subject-matter tests and will probably require considerably less time to administer. This latter advantage occurs because the subject-matter tests within a battery follow uniform procedures for administration of all tests. Too, each subject-matter test has been normed on the same population, making test selection and comparison of students' scores easier.

One of the popular achievement test batteries is the Iowa Test of Basic Skills. This series is available in two forms for kindergarten through grade 8. Depending on which level and form are used, testing time is 60 to 80 minutes. The five major areas tested by this battery are vocabulary, reading comprehension, language skills, work-study skills, and mathematical skills. The test developers point out that this battery measures pupils' abilities to use and acquire skills, for no test or subtest is concerned with only the repetition or identification of facts.

The Iowa Tests of Educational Development are normed for grades 9 through 12 and consist of seven subtests measuring subject-matter areas appropriate for secondary school curricula. Standard scores, grade equivalent scores, national percentile ranks, normal curve equivalent scores, stanines, and large-city norms are available for all tests and for the composites. Local norms are available from the Riverside Scoring Service and the Riverside Publishing Company in Chicago.

The Metropolitan Achievement Test consists of eight battery levels for measuring performance from the beginning of kindergarten through grade 12. This battery consists of single tests for reading comprehension, mathematics, language, social studies, and science. The basic battery consists of the first three tests. The complete battery utilizes all five tests. This battery is available from the Psychological Corporation, a subsidiary of Harcourt Brace Jovanovich, Inc., New York.

Interest Inventories

In a discussion on career planning, one might hear such statements as "I've always been interested in nursing," "The thought of teaching really turns me off," "I know I'd enjoy selling cars," or "Being a flight attendant would be the most exciting career I could imagine!"

Such pronouncements of career interests are common among adolescents and young adults. Equally common are statements of uncertainty and frustration regarding career choices, such as "I wish somebody would just tell me what career I should enter," "I can't make up my mind between engineering or coaching," or "I'm really upset because I can't think of any job I'm interested in."

Although interest testing has, for many years, been a popular psychometric aid to adolescents and young adults in career planning, recently it has been increasingly used for older populations considering mid-life or other career changes.

Discussions and other explorations of interest are valuable aids for career planning and related career counseling and guidance; even a simple listing in hierarchical order of possible careers may be as valid in some instances as standardized, inventoried interests.

However, certain values may result from the use of standardized interest inventories of which counselors, teachers, and others who assist youth and adults in career and related decision making should be aware. Such potential values are

- A comparative and contrasting inventory of a person's interests
- Verification of a person's claimed interest or tentative choice
- Identification of previously unrecognized interests
- Identification of the possible level of interests for various (usually career) activities
- Contrast of interest with abilities and achievements
- Identification of problems associated with career decision making (no areas of adequate interest; high stated interest versus low inventoried interest in a career field)
- A stimulus for career exploration or career counseling

If, however, these values are to be realized, certain guidelines should be followed in deciding when to use interest tests. Hood and Johnson (1991) suggest the following guidelines.

First, counselors should keep in mind that interest inventories measure likes and dislikes, *not* abilities. . . .

Second, clients should be positively motivated to participate in the assessment process. . . .

Third, general interest inventories are of limited value for people who must make rather fine distinctions, such as choosing between civil and electrical engineering. . . .

Fourth, interest inventories may be inappropriate for people with emotional problems (Brandt & Hood, 1968). Disturbed people make more negative responses and endorse more passive interests than do people who are not disturbed (Drasgow & Carkhuff, 1964). Personal issues can interfere with decision making. Counselors usually must address the emotional difficulties before career planning can take place.

Fifth, scores on interest inventories can show significant changes for clients who are young or after long time periods (Johansson & Campbell, 1971). . . .

Sixth, interest scores should be particularly helpful for clients who are undecided about their career plans. . . .

Finally, counselors may wish to use an interest card sort instead of an interest inventory if they are interested in the underlying reasons for the client's choices (Dolliver, 1982). (pp. 108–109)

The popular development of interest tests evolved from studies indicating that people in a given occupation seemed to be characterized by a cluster of common interests that distinguish them from people in other occupations. It was also noted that these differences in interests extended beyond those associated with job performance and that persons in a given occupation also had different nonvocational interests—hobbies and recreational activities that could distinguish them from those in other occupations. Thus, interest inventories could be designed to assess one's interests and relate them to those of various occupational areas. Two of the more popular of these are based on inventories developed by Frederic Kuder and E. K. Strong, Jr.

The Kuder Preference Record is the original and most popular of the various Kuder interest inventories. It provides a series of interest items arranged in triads, from which the respondents choose the one they would like most and the one they would like least. The results are scored and profiled for the occupational areas of outdoor, mechanical, computational, scientific, persuasive, artistic, literary, music, social service, and clerical. Revision of the original preference record, the Kuder General Interest Survey, extends the use downward to the sixth grade by employing a simpler vocabulary that requires only a sixth-grade reading ability (the original version was usually considered appropriate for use in grades 9 through 12). The Kuder Occupational Interest Survey is still another version that provides scores showing similarities with occupational and college-level areas. This form differs from previous Kuder tests in expressing a person's score on each occupational scale as a correlation between her or his interest pattern and the pattern of a particular occupational group.

The Strong Interest Inventory is a revision of the earlier forms of the Strong Vocational Interest Blank, which was first published in 1933. Its latest edition was published in 1994. The various Strong inventories have been based on the assumption that individuals who are attracted to and enjoy a specific occupation have similar interest profiles and, therefore, by assessing and matching the interests of individuals exploring careers against those of workers in the field, better career decisions can be made.

The various interest inventories have been suggested as usable with older adolescents and adults who may be considering higher-level professional or skilled occupations. The Strong Interest Inventory can be scored only by computer. The six general occupational theme scales based on Holland's six personality types provide scores for realistic, investigative, artistic, social, enterprising, and conventional categories. The major and most popular scales for the Strong Vocational Interest series are the 211 occupational scales, plus 4 personal style scales. Fourteen new growth occupations and contemporary careers have also been added. The Strong Interest Inventory is related to the Pathfinder career decision-making system using interactive video. A microcomputer version is also available. The Strong Interest Inventory is published by the Stanford University Press, Stanford, California, and distributed by Consulting Psychologists Press.

The Ohio Vocational Interest Survey (OVIS) is one of a number of somewhat newer interest inventories developed for use with high school students and adults. It was developed after the model on which the Dictionary of Occupational Titles is based (a cubistic model of data, people, and things). The OVIS is separated into three parts: (a) a questionnaire, (b) a local information survey, and (c) the interest inventory. The OVIS reports its results on 25 scales and is available through Harcourt Brace Jovanovich, Inc., New York.

Another approach to the assessment of career interests is the Self-Directed Search (SDS). This instrument was developed by John Holland, whose hexagonal model of six occupational themes is represented in the six summary scores of realistic, investigative, artistic, social, enterprising, and conventional. The SDS is designed to be self-administered, self-scored, and self-interpreted.

When an individual completes the SDS, she uses a summary code comprising the types that rank first and second across all the subtests. Utilizing this code, she refers to a Job Finder, which presents information about 456 jobs listed in terms of two-letter SDS codes. Once a person gets her lists of careers that match a summary code, suggested next steps are listed for her organized career planning. The Self-Directed Search is marketed by Consulting Psychologists Press, Palo Alto, California.

The Career Maturity Inventory, although not precisely an interest inventory, has been designed to measure the maturity of attitudes and competencies that are involved in career decision making. The attitude scale surveys five attitudinal clusters: (a) involvement in the career choice process, (b) orientation toward work, (c) independence in decision making, (d) preference for career choice factors, and (e) conceptions of the career choice process. In contrast, the competency test measures the more cognitive variables involved in choosing an occupation. The five parts of the competency test are (a) self-appraisal, (b) occupational information, (c) goal selection, (d) planning, and (e) problem solving. The Career Maturity Inventory is available from McGraw-Hill Book Company, New York.

Personality Tests

Of all the areas of standardized testing, none is more intriguing to the general public, and perhaps to the counseling profession as well, as personality assessment. From the do-it-yourself personality test in the daily newspaper to sophisticated, projective techniques requiring highly specialized psychological training, personality testing represents a universal quest of the individual to understand what makes him or her and fellow human beings tick. But personality testing is as complex as what it seeks to measure. Let us examine some of the questions or concerns that must be taken into consideration.

What Is Personality?

Aiken (1988) notes that

> the term *personality* has many different meanings. To some, it refers to a mysterious charisma possessed by Hollywood stars and other popular, influential people but not by everyone. To others, personality is the same as temperament, a natural, genetically based predisposition to think, feel, and act in a particular way. To still others, personality consists of a person's unique mixture of emotional, intellectual, and character (honesty, courage, and so forth) traits. And to more behaviorally oriented psychologists, personality is not something internal but rather the externally observable pattern of organized behavior typical of an individual. (p. 321)

You can readily discern the wide variations in viewpoints regarding this topic by asking a group, "What is personality?" and noting the wide range of responses. The concept of personality is a difficult one to treat with the precision usually associated with standardized tests. Thus, constructors of personality tests face the challenge of determining what workable definition of personality they will use and what aspect or aspects of that definition they will measure. Generally speaking, however, in conventional psychometric terminology, "personality tests are instruments for the measurement of emotional, motivational, interpersonal, and attitudinal characteristics, as distinguished from abilities" (Anastasi, 1996, p. 348).

What Is Normal Personality?

This question would probably elicit a variety of answers from the public. Most persons tend to view normal in terms of their own behavioral personality traits and values. Thus, an extremely extroverted person viewed as normal by one group may be viewed as abnormal by another group. Even if one is able to objectively identify norms for specific behavioral responses, one still must determine at what point the deviations from those norms become abnormal.

Can Personality Be Measured?

This question has objectively been answered affirmatively by many authors of standardized personality measures and has further been affirmed by many practicing counselors, psychologists, and psychiatrists utilizing observation and other nonstandardized techniques. Some of the difficulties involved in obtaining accurate assessments are client-based and must be the concern of the test interpreter.

1. The capability of a person to accurately analyze many aspects of his or her own personality is questionable. In some instances, the client may not possess the insight to respond accurately. Although the client's view of self is important, it may not be appropriate to the intent of the measuring instrument. In other instances, one must recognize that the individual's view of self can be distorted, differ from the perceptions of others, and be misleading to the test interpreter.

2. Some persons may deliberately falsify their responses. Most often, deception occurs when a person responds in a manner that he or she views as more socially acceptable than perhaps his or her true response might be. For example, little children almost inevitably respond that they love their parents, even when they do not know them or when they actively dislike them. Also, one can anticipate that some respondents will project an ideal self rather than the real self in their answers. Some persons may respond as the friendly and popular person they wish they were, rather than the withdrawn individual with few friends they recognize themselves to be. The intimate nature of a question may dissuade the respondent from answering accurately. Most notable examples in this category are questions dealing with a person's sexual activities, beliefs, and values.

Several of the more popular personality inventories or standardized personality assessment instruments are the Myers-Briggs Type Indicator, the Mooney Problem Checklist, the Edwards Personal Preference Schedule, and the Minnesota Multiphasic Personality Inventory. The latter two instruments require special training and supervised experience before their use in school or clinical settings.

The Myers-Briggs Type Indicator is a widely used personality test. The standard Form G contains 126 items that determine preferences on the four scales of (1) extroversion/introversion, (2) sensing/intuition, (3) thinking/feeling, and (4) judging/perceiving. The various combinations of these preferences result in 16 personality types helpful in making career and other decisions.

The Mooney Problem Checklist consists of a series of problems to which the client reacts by underlining the problems that are of some concern, circling the problems that are of the most concern, and then writing a summary in his or her own words. It is obviously not standardized in a psychometric sense because it is designed to identify problems for group or individual counseling.

In this sense, the Mooney Problem Checklist is useful for conducting group surveys and identifying persons who want or need counseling assistance with personal problems. Cohen, Montague, Nathanson, Swerdlik (1988) state

> Some personality tests are closely tied to a particular theory of personality, and all of the items on such a test are designed to measure traits or states presumed to exist on the basis of that theory. For example, a personality test constructed within a psychoanalytic framework might have items on it designed to assess id, ego, and super-ego functioning. (p. 307)

The Edwards Personal Preference Schedule (EPPS) is a personality inventory based on the theory of personality presented by Henry Murray (Murray, Barrett, Honburger, 1938). The EPPS is designed to show the relative importance to the individual of 15 key needs or motives

Achievement	Affiliation	Nurturance
Deference	Intraception	Change
Order	Succorance	Endurance
Exhibition	Dominance	Heterosexuality
Autonomy	Abasement	Aggression

Another clinically oriented instrument is the Minnesota Multiphasic Personality Inventory (MMPI). This is a very widely used personality assessment test, especially in clinical settings. Revised in 1992, it is constructed entirely on the basis of clinical criteria. MMPI-II contains 567 statements covering a wide range of subject matters related to the instrument's 10 scales, as follows.

Hypochondriasis	Paranoia
Depression	Psychasthenia
Hysteria	Schizophrenia
Psychopathic deviate	Hypomania
Masculinity-femininity	Social introversion

In addition to the ten clinical scales, the MMPI and MMPI-II contain three validity scales. These are an L, or Lie, score; an F score, which may indicate the seriousness with which the individual responded to the test items; and the K score, a suppressor variable refining the discrimination of five of the clinical variables. As mentioned earlier, all of the MMPI editions require special training and supervised experience before their utilization.

CRITERION-REFERENCED TESTING

One of the most frequently raised issues in the 1970s and 1980s was that of criterion-referenced testing versus norm-referenced testing. Many educators will suggest that it is not a case of either/or—that, in fact, criterion-referenced testing complements norm-referenced testing and vice versa. The inference cannot be ignored, however, when in many school systems criterion-referenced testing has increased as norm-referenced testing has decreased. One cannot deny the rapid gains in popularity that criterion-referenced testing, aided by the accountability movement, has made in recent years.

A criterion-referenced test measures whether a person has attained the desired or maximum goal in a learning experience. If we were to contrast criterion-referenced testing with norm-referenced testing by using a practical example, we might note that a sixth-grade class could achieve an average score ahead of 52% of other sixth-grade classes in a representative nationwide sample. This information, on the one hand, might not tell those interested, such as teachers, parents, and students, more specifically how well this sixth-grade class reads or what they have learned to read. On the other hand, a typical criterion-referenced test result would indicate how many pupils in this sixth-grade class can read at a certain rate of reading, comprehend at a certain level of comprehension, and recall with reasonable accuracy what they have read after passage of a specific period of time. In the first instance, a class is competing against other classes to demonstrate to what degree pupils have learned or not learned to read. In the latter case, however, pupils are competing against a locally established standard, a learning objective, a criterion.

The big debate (Rowntree, 1987, p. 178) in the professional literature appears to be split between the following questions.

1. How well has the individual done compared with norms established by his peer groups (norm referenced)?

versus

2. How well has the individual done by comparison with some predetermined criteria (criteria referenced)?

These questions seem to omit one very important possibility.

3. How well has the individual done by comparison with him- or herself?

Rather than noting the range of individual differences in test scores, criterion-referenced tests place persons in one of two groups: those who have attained the criterion and those who have not.

Perhaps Hawes (1973) best expressed the popularity of criterion-referenced testing by entitling his article "Criterion-Referenced Testing—No More Losers, No More Norms, No More Parents Raising Storms."

COMPUTERIZED ADAPTIVE TESTING

Another popular as well as innovative movement in testing is computerized adaptive testing. In this approach, a computer selects different questions from an item pool to administer to different students. Worthen, White, and Borg (1993) describe the process.

The computer selects each question from a pool of items of known difficulty. The question is displayed on a TV screen, and the student either types the letter of the correct multiple-choice response or touches the screen at the location of the correct response. The computer records whether the response is correct or incorrect and selects the next question, based on the student's response to the previous question. If the student's response is correct, the next item selected will be more difficult; if the student's response is incorrect, the next item selected will be easier. As more items are administered, the computer considers the student's performance on all previous items in estimating his mastery level and selecting the next item to be administered. As a result, the items are adapted to the level of the student. That is, on the whole they will be neither too easy nor too difficult for the individual. The main advantage of this method over conventional testing is that in *computer adaptive testing*, because each student is administered a different combination of items, the teacher cannot teach to the test, and the student cannot help his peers by passing on the test items he remembers, because most of the items administered to other students will be different. (p. 212)

Because each student responds to different sets of questions, their resulting scores are not comparable.

DEVELOPING A TESTING PROGRAM

In many school settings, testing programs may be mandated by state legislative bodies or agencies or set by local school boards with limited input from the schools and their counselors. In nonschool settings, counselors may find that organizational policies dictate, at least in part, the nature of the organization's utilization of standardized tests. However, in those more ideal circumstances where counselors and their fellow helping professionals can determine the nature of the organization's standardized assessment program, it is obviously desirable to develop a logical, sequential approach that provides for accountability. The following steps present one such procedure that, although appropriate perhaps to school settings, may also be suitable for some community and business and industrial settings as well.

1. *Determine the needs.* This is obviously the initial and critical step that defines the degree to which the testing program will be relevant. Here the key question is "What new information do we need to provide good (not just adequate) service to the organization's target population? The word *new* implies that a specific type of test data should not be a priority if it duplicates information already available through other sources. In other words, priority goes to that needed data not already available. Second priority would be for that information that tests can provide for supplementing already existing data.

2. *Determine the program's objectives.* Once the testing needs have been identified, these needs should be translated into the testing program's objectives. For accountability purposes, these objectives should be stated in concise, measurable terms.

3. *Select the appropriate instruments.* In determining which tests are best to serve the program's objectives, obviously the basic criteria of validity, reliability, norming appropriateness, and administrative practicality are applied. In addition, the skills needed to administer and interpret the tests must be available. Costs are always an important consideration.

4. *Determine the testing schedule.* Tests should be scheduled for specific dates to provide data at the time it is most needed or most appropriate. Spacing is also important to avoid testing overload for both those administering and those taking the tests.

5. *Evaluate the outcomes.* Data indicating the degree to which the objectives have been achieved should be collected and utilized. Appropriateness of the instruments should be examined. Results should lead to continuous program improvement.

In testing program planning, one must always bear in mind that testing is not an end in itself, but rather, an opportunity to develop a more complete picture of the client—a picture mutually shared by both the client and the counselor.

Multicultural Issues

The controversies associated with standardized testing noted at the beginning of this chapter have almost from the outset of the psychological measurement movement included charges of bias and discrimination based on gender, race, socioeconomic background, and so forth. Legal recognition of these possibilities were spelled out in Title VII of the Civil Rights Act of 1964, which included prohibiting the use of tests for employment discrimination. Subsequent court decisions have further refined concepts of bias in tests, with the majority of cases being decided in favor of plaintiffs over test companies.

However, beyond the legal guidelines, counselors and other test administrators and interpreters have the professional responsibility to be sensitive and alert to the multicultural clients they serve. For example, test-taking anxiety may be higher with some populations. Verbal inflections, implied implications of results, and the attitude of the counselor can also appear discriminatory. Economic environments can limit some populations, and the verbal directions for some tests may unintentionally bias the test. Also, the client's reading level and rate of reading may be a factor in some instances.

Technology and Testing

The technology boom of the last quarter of the 20th century has not been without its impact on the field of psychological testing. Computerized administering, scoring, and interpretation can be found for a wide selection of specific instruments in all of the major assessment areas.

Although expense was a concern in the beginning, many users now point out that initial outlays are continuing to drop in cost and that following this investment, the computerized systems, including testing on terminals, are becoming cost effective. Advocates also point out that clients tend to like computer testing, especially when adaptive testing is programmed.

Another feature of the computerized program is the near instant feedback of results. Further, the increasing development of narrative interpretations, presented through computer printouts, will obviously speed up the total assessment process. These interpretations are based on the consensus of experts and/or research and does provide for uniformity in interpretations and lessen the likelihood of counselor error or bias. However, many counselors are concerned for the limits imposed on counselor-client interactions and the mechanization of the whole process as opposed to the traditional humanistic approach.

Other questions have also arisen regarding the application of norms generated on paper-and-pencil tests to computerized versions of the same tests, differing administration procedures, and, for some clients, a deviation from the familiar format of classroom and previously taken standardized tests. Confidentiality and other ethical issues have also been examined. Although these and other questions are being debated and studied, it should be abundantly clear that we must adapt to the new technologies and learn to use these new advances to enhance our own performances as professional counselors.

A CONCLUDING THOUGHT

As we conclude this overview on standardized assessment, we note for our readers that the intent of this chapter is to provide only a brief orientation to this very important area of counselor preparation. Subsequent courses in psychological measurement will be required—and should be looked forward to—before a helping professional can ethically and appropriately administer, score, and/or interpret such test results.

SUMMARY

Standardized testing and computerized testing programs have become popular benchmarks for measuring educational attainment of individuals and schools. Most of us have experienced at least the receiving end of this phenomenon. Standardized testing is also a traditional and important tool in the counselor's array of techniques for understanding the client. Despite the historic and extensive use of standardized tests, counselors and other users must be aware of the many criticisms and concerns that have been voiced regarding their use for diagnostic purposes. An understanding of these criticisms and concerns and the degree to which they are valid will enable users to administer standardized tests effectively but safely in their practices.

The importance of comprehending basic statistical processes should not be underestimated. An understanding of averages and variations from the average, as expressed in statistical terminology, and relationships as computed mathematically, is basic to the interpretation of standardized tests. The user of standardized tests also must be aware of and be able to apply the criteria for test selection. These basic criteria are the validity, reliability, and practical characteristics of the test under consideration. Strengths and weaknesses of the common areas of standardized testing should be understood. It is also important that the user recognize the limitations as well as the strengths of a given instrument if it is to be intelligently used in practice. Counselors and others may also want to consider criterion-referenced tests as a substitute or supplement to their programs of standardized testing. Counselors

should be aware of the contributions other disciplines make to the understanding of human behavior. In addition, a wide variety of nonstandardized techniques for human assessment, utilized across many disciplines, is available to the counselor who is knowledgeable in their construction and usage. The next chapter will provide an overview of these possibilities.

DISCUSSION QUESTIONS

1.   What standardized tests have you taken? (Poll the class.) Did the results ever influence your planning or decision making?

2.   How do you feel about being measured by standardized tests? How do you feel about the use of standardized tests to measure traits of your clients?

3.   Under what circumstances would you recommend standardized (norm-referenced) testing over criterion-referenced testing and vice versa?

4.   Are you aware of or have you been involved in public controversies regarding standardized testing? If so, describe and analyze the situation.

5.   What standardized tests would you recommend, if any, to screen potential candidates seeking admission to a counselor training program. Defend your answer.

6.   Are there any measurement voids—areas of performances, behaviors, circumstances, and so on, where it would be helpful to have standardized tests developed?

7.   What would you do in the following situations? (Briefly explain.)

a. An honor student makes a score of 90 on a group intelligence test.

b. A problem student who is failing makes scores at the 95th percentile on an achievement battery.

c. Several parents call you and want to know their child's college placement test scores—also those of their neighbor's children.

d. A student breaks his or her pencil in the middle of a standardized test.

CLASS ACTIVITIES

1. Develop a profile of the so-called normal personality.

2. Develop an interest checklist that might distinguish potential counselors from those who would not enjoy careers as counselors.

3. Develop test items for a standardized test designed to measure an individual's potential for entering a counselor preparation program.

4. Administer the test to students, score in class, and discuss the process.

SELECTED READINGS

Achenback, T. M., & McConaughy, S. H. (1997). *Empirically based assessment of child and adolescent psychopathology: Practical applications* (2nd ed.). Thousand Oaks, CA: Sage.

Anderson, K. E. (1984). Testing and the counselor. *School Guidance Worker, 39* (4), 6–30.

Campbell, V. (1987). Strong-Campbell Interest Inventory: fourth edition. *Journal of Counseling and Development, 66* (1), 53–56.

Duckworth, J. C., & Anderson, W. P. (1995). *MMPI & MMPI-2: Interpretation manual for counselors and clinicians* (4th ed.). Bristol, PA: Accelerated Development.

Eaves, R. C. (1985). Educational assessment in the United States. *Diagnostique, 10* (4), 5–39. [Theme issue: Assessment in Special Education.]

Gottfredson, L. S., & Crouse, J. (1986). Validity versus utility of mental tests: Example of the SAT. *Journal of Vocational Behavior, 29* (3), 363–378.

Healey, C. C., & Mourton, D. L. (1984). The Self-Directed Search personality scales and career maturity. *Measurement and Evaluation in Guidance, 17* (1), 3–13.

Lynch, A. Q. (1985). The Myers-Briggs Type Indicator: A tool for appreciating employee and client diversity. *Journal of Employment Counseling, 22* (3), 104–109.

Miller, G. (1982). Deriving meaning from standardized tests: Interpreting test results to clients. *Measurement and Evaluation in Guidance, 15* (1), 87–94.

Sampson, J. (Ed.). (1986). Computer applications in testing and assessment [Special issue]. *Measurement and Evaluation in Counseling and Development, 19* (1), 5–61.

RESEARCH OF INTEREST

Crouse, J. (1985). Does the SAT help colleges make better selection decisions? *Harvard Educational Review, 55* (2), 195–219.

Abstract

Using data from the National Longitudinal Survey of high school students to calculate the actual improvement in freshmen grade point average, college completion, and total years of schooling from colleges' use of the Scholastic Aptitude Test (SAT), Crouse compares predictions based on high school rank to argue that the SAT's costs do not justify its limited predictive ability.

Grougeon, D. (1985). CEEB SAT mathematics scores and their correlation with college performance in math. *Educational Research Quarterly, 9* (2), 8–11.

Abstract

This study investigated whether the constant decline in Scholastic Aptitude Test (SAT) mathematics scores since 1963 reflected a decrease in student mathematical ability or the SAT's inadequacy in measuring mathematical ability. Findings indicated a very low correlation between SAT math scores and overall college math grades of six graduating classes at one university.

Milner, M., McNeil, J. S., & King, S. W. (1984). The GRE: A question of validity in predicting performance in professional schools of social work. *Educational and Psychological Measurement*, 44 (4), 945–950.

Abstract

Based on a sample of 145 graduate students in social work, results indicated that the Graduate Record Examination, as a primary basis for admission, is not a valid predictor of future performance in schools of social work. Moreover, its elimination does not produce a lower quality of students.

Ornduff, S. R. (1997). TAT assessment of object relations: Implications for child abuse. *Bulletin of the Menninger Clinic*, 61 (1), 1–15.

Abstract

Several recent empirical studies have documented impaired object relations in victims of childhood maltreatment. The consistency of these findings, despite sampling and other methodological differences, highlights the applicability of object relations theory to the study of abuse sequelae. This article illustrates the use of the Social Cognition and Object Relations Scales in the clinical assessment of maltreated children by applying it to selected TAT stories of a sexually abused girl, a physically abused girl, and a distressed but nonabused peer. The stories were randomly selected from a data archive that includes a social history and psychological testing data on some 300 children, all of whom were outpatients at a child guidance clinic. Results revealed impairments in object relations among maltreated children and demonstrated the applicability of the TAT

and the Social Cognition and Object Relations Scales in child assessment.

Powell, B., & Steelman, L. C. (1984). Variations in state SAT performance: Meaningful or misleading? *Harvard Educational Review*, 54 (4), 389–412.

Abstract

The authors attempt to show how the dissemination of uncorrected state Scholastic Aptitude Test (SAT) scores may have created an inaccurate public and governmental perception of the variation in educational quality. Their research demonstrates that comparing state SAT averages is ill-advised unless these ratings are corrected for compositional and demographic factors.

Prediger, D. J. (1994). Multicultural assessment standards: A compilation for counselors. *Measurement and Evaluation in Counseling and Development*, 27, 68–73.

Abstract

This article presents a compilation of standards relevant to multicultural populations drawn from source documents of the American Counseling Association (ACA). Thirty-nine standards were identified in the five source documents. These standards are divided into four groups by assessment tasks: (a) content considerations in the selection of assessment instruments (AIs); (b) norming, reliability, and validity considerations in the selection of AIs; (c) administration and scoring of AIs; and (d) use/interpretation of assessment results. The source documents are the Code of Fair Testing Practices in Education, the Ethical Standards of the ACA, "Multicultural Counseling Competencies and Standards", Responsibility of Users of Standardized Tests, and Standards for Educational and Psychological Testing.

Sandhu, D. S., Poetes, P. R., & McPhee, S. A. (1996). Assessing cultural adaptation: Psychometric properties of the Cultural Adaptation Pain Scale. *Journal of Multicultural Counseling and Development, 24* (1), 15–25.

Abstract

This article explores the psychometric properties of a newly developed Cultural Adaptation Pain Scale, using a sample of 1,932 college students. This scale is designed to assess the degree of subjective pain, social distance, and discouragement that may be related to cultural adaptation. Factor analyses revealed four factors in the scale that had an overall Cronbach's alpha of .85: pain, learned helplessness, positive adaptation, and bigoted. The scale was generally reliable and had face validity. Implications for multicultural counseling are discussed.

Scott, R. R., & Shaw, M. E. (1985). Black and White performance in graduate school and policy implications of the use of Graduate Record Examination scores in admissions. *Journal of Negro Education, 54* (1), 14–23.

Abstract

A significant number of Black graduate students enrolled at the University of Florida in 1982 had higher grades than White students who had performed better than they on the Graduate Record Examination (GRE). This suggests that the GRE is insensitive to the factors that affect Blacks' academic performance.

Tinsley, D. J., Tinsley, H. E., Boone, S., & Shim-Li, C. (1993). Prediction of scientist-practitioner behavior using personality scores obtained during graduate school. *Journal of Counseling Psychology, 40* (4), 511–517.

Abstract

This study investigated the usefulness of personality measures obtained during graduate training in predicting the scientist-practitioner behavior of counseling psychologists. Personality scale scores on the Self-Directed Search, Strong-Campbell Interest Inventory (General Occupational Theme scores), Minnesota Importance Questionnaire, Omnibus Personality Inventory, Tennessee Self-Concept Scale, and MMPI obtained during students' first semester of graduate study were used as predictors. Scientist-practitioner orientation scores calculated for participants reflected their scientist-practitioner interests, preferred job, and publication record. Only scores on the Independence Scale of the Minnesota Importance Questionnaire and on the Social Extraversion Scale of the Omnibus Personality Inventory were statistically significant predictors of actual scientist-practitioner orientation.

Trusheim, D. W., & Crouse, J. H. (1984). The SAT and traditional predictive validity: A critical assessment. *Journal of College Admissions,* (104), 9–12.

Abstract

The benefits to an admissions office using the Scholastic Aptitude Test (SAT) in predicting freshmen grades ($N = 169$ and $N = 172$) were examined. Results suggested the SAT does not increase predictive validity substantially beyond the high school record. It presents an alternative admissions strategy based on multiple regression.

Watkins, E. O., & Wiebe, M. J. (1984). Factorial validity of the Stanford Achievement Test for first-grade children. *Educational and Psychological Measurement, 44* (4), 951–954.

Abstract

The factorial validity of the Stanford Achievement Test (SAT) was investigated with a sample of first graders ($N = 393$). Although eight areas are proposed from the SAT, this analysis produced only one general factor. Results suggest limiting SAT interpretation for first graders to a total score approach.

Nonstandardized Techniques for Human Assessment

Sometimes we are called on to explain, even justify, why one of our close friends acts the way he or she does. The reply may, at least subconsciously, draw on our knowledge of our friend's home and family background; the environment in which he or she grew up or now lives; the cultural background; the physical and psychological characteristics, as we perceive them; or the experiences of the friend. In these instances, a wealth of background information provides insights into the behavior of those we know well. Nor is this knowledge limited by our own particular occupation or discipline. Some of what we know might be classified as cultural or anthropological, some as environmental or sociological, and some as psychological.

In a similar vein, most of us feel more confident with a family physician who has looked after our ailments for years, who knows us from a broader standpoint than what we are as a physical specimen, who understands us totally. It is a situation that an equally competent but newcomer physician cannot duplicate.

In the world of sporting competition, there are frequent references to psyching out the opposition. This psyching out attempts to go beyond understanding the athletic skills of the opponent, implying that the better we know our competition, the better we can play them.

These examples suggest this chapter's objective, namely, to describe nonstandardized assessment techniques for increasing and broadening our understanding of our client population. Thorough assessment increases the potential for maximum treatment efficacy. Interdisciplinary concepts of human assessment are presented, followed by some suggested guidelines or principles of human assessment. We then focus on the nonstandardized techniques commonly employed for individual analysis by counselors in various settings. It should be noted that standardized techniques, such as psychological testing, are those with a precise and fixed format, set of procedures, and method of scoring that enable the instrument to be used for the same purpose in a variety of settings and times. Standardization suggests uniformity and objectivity. Nonstandardization suggests a broader, variable, and more subjective approach to gathering and interpreting data for human assessment.

CONCEPTS OF HUMAN ASSESSMENT

The most intelligent yet most complicated and difficult to understand living organism known to civilization today is the human being. When we place human beings in their environment, a rapidly changing and complex society, we cannot help but recognize the enormity of the task of those who seek to understand, predict, and assist the development of human behavior. In undertaking this responsibility, we are quick to recognize that no one discipline or area of expertise alone possesses the theoretical or technical basis for a comprehensive understanding of modern people in modern society. To this end, then, those who study human behavior—whether from an individual or societal viewpoint; whether from the viewpoint of an anthropologist, sociologist, or psychologist; whether from the viewpoint of an American, Japanese, or German—must be willing to both learn and share with those who have this common interest. It is in this context that we suggest that counselors, regardless of the setting in which they function, can better understand their clients' behavior through the insights gained by studying behavior in the context of other disciplines and cultures. The following is not intended to substitute for such study but only to examine briefly these other perspectives and their implications for counselors.

Sociology

Sociology is a social and behavioral science that focuses on the study of individuals and groups in society and how they behave and interact with one another. The science of sociology contributes to an understanding of the social networks and their impact on individuals, individual roles, and relationships within those networks. Furthermore, sociology is concerned with the study of socialization agents or institutions. These institutions, such as the family, church, school, and government, assume the responsibility of teaching people within that environment what constitutes normal and abnormal behavior for the society. These patterns of normal and abnormal behavior are further shaped by customs, folkways, mores, and laws. Sociology also helps in understanding behavior that deviates from the norms of a group or society. The study of social deviance helps in understanding behaviors, including alcoholism and crime, that are defined as social problems. Such study also helps us to recognize that what is considered normal behavior in one group may be defined as deviant behavior in another group. Furthermore, study in this area can help the counselor recognize the influence of social controls or pressures on the behavior of clients, students, and others. For counselors, it is also important to keep in mind that human beings are social beings, affected by the society of which they are members and, at the same time, expected to contribute to that society.

Counselors will find knowledge of sociology contributes to their understanding of the groups and structures within the society of which they are a part. It is particularly important to understand the significance of the groupings and roles of clients, the influences on clients' behavior of the various groups of which they are members, the roles and relationships that are most significant to clients, and the restriction on clients' behavior and behavior change of the social system of which they are a part. The counselor must understand the various roles of people and the behavior that occurs or is anticipated as a result of these roles. That also includes an understanding of the significance of status, as already noted in many psychological studies. Some suggest that perhaps there has never been a more status-conscious society than our own. Sociologists help us understand status and its implications through the study of social stratification, which involves social classes, social mobilities, social structures, and, in general, the ranking of social positions within society.

The sociologist, like the psychologist, is also concerned with the study of the development of a person's self-concept. Sociological study focuses on self-concept development through the socialization process and its influence by others. It is especially important for counselors to recognize the impact of significant others and reference groups (both within the domain of sociological study) on the development of a person's self-concept. Who are the people whose judgments, imagined or otherwise, are significant to one's self-concept, and what are the groups that one uses to develop and test attitudes, beliefs, and so forth?

Psychology

As we examine the various scientific disciplines, we should note that psychology has been the one most closely associated with the counseling profession. Over the years, psychology has made numerous significant contributions to the development and practice of counseling, including counseling theory and processes, individual and group counseling, standardized assessment, and career development and decision-making theories.

Traditionally, the discipline of psychology has been closely related to the study of school-aged groups and their education. Such fields as educational psychology and human development have been offsprings of these interests. Learning theory has also been extended through work by psychologists. Developmental theorists have assisted counselors and others in understanding why and how humans grow and develop over the life span. Social psychology has provided counselors with insight into the socialization process and social influences, attitudes, attribution, group dynamics, and interpersonal interactions. Ecological theorists have alerted us to the importance of the environment and how it influences individuals and their behavior.

Anthropology

Anthropology is the study of the culture of a society and the characteristics of its social behavior. It involves recording, describing, and analyzing cultures throughout the world and throughout history. In these studies, anthropology identifies the traditions, norms, patterns of learning, coping styles, and other behaviors from both current and historic perspectives. Among the understandings that counselors can glean from the study of anthropology are recognizing (a) that different cultures have different and similar concepts; (b) the importance of the ethnic and cultural background of the client; (c) the importance of the ethnic and cultural background of the counselor; and (d) the significance of subcultures within the larger societal or cultural context. Anthropology, when applied to counseling, suggests the importance of understanding a culture in order to effectively counsel clients from that culture.

In this context, culture is viewed as the beliefs and practices of people within a society, including guidelines for their behavior in given situations (such as religious ceremonies, funerals, weddings, reaching puberty, maturity, and so forth). Human development depends on environmental characteristics. The characteristics of the environment that have been developed by the past inhabitants of the environment constitute the culture with which a person interacts. That culture provides people with their initial values, behavioral guidelines, and expectancies for the future. As just noted, the self-concept is central to the study of personality and behavior by psychologists and sociologists, and the study of anthropology contributes through an understanding of the nature of self as culturally defined. We also view ourselves as influenced by the perspective we have of self in relation to culture. The study of anthropology alerts us to the fact that personality, as it develops, seeks to prepare the individual for living in her or his culture and, by the same token, that a culture functions only through the personalities of those who constitute it, which thus enables predictions regarding overt behavior on the basis of a knowledge of a culture and its traditions.

Today, we are aware that different subcultures often have different values and lifestyles. For example, counselors should be able to understand the lifestyles and values of such populations as African Americans, Native Americans, Asians, Hispanics, Jews, Poles, and others. It is beneficial not only to be able to function free of ignorance in helping relationships with clients from various backgrounds but also to interact without prejudice and bias.

Finally, and related to the study of both anthropology and sociology, we note an increased interest in the field of counseling on cultural and environmental influences on events. In this regard, Blocher and Biggs (1983) described the movement beyond the traditional community mental health approaches to one that examines relationships between human beings and their environment. They suggest that (a) human beings are characterized by a basic and inherent drive toward competence or mastery of an environment and (b) the development of competence needs to be studied as it occurs in natural settings.

Economics

Economics is a science that studies human production, consumption, and distribution. Its significance in the creation of status and influences on our wants shapes many of our behaviors.

Economics is another social science concerned with individual behavior and human relationships. Economists' concern is with people living in various types of economic systems. Economists, like sociologists, are interested in one's economic position, the socioeconomic status of people in a society. Economic attainment interacts with other factors in a culture to determine status. This socioeconomic status can be significant as a determinant of client feelings, attitudes, behavior, and so forth.

Three major socioeconomic strata have been identified: upper, middle, and lower class. Within each of these levels are three sublevels of upper, middle, and lower (e.g., lower middle class). The most reliable indicators of status are income, education, occupation, and geographic location. Because the economic environment in which people live is so closely interwoven with nearly every activity in which counselors engage, we cannot be uninvolved in this area.

C. Gilbert Wrenn (1962) notes the importance of economic learning to counselors when he comments that "the school counselor cannot afford to be a graduate student in psychology and a second-grader in economics" (p. 42). For the counselor, understanding the influences economic systems and theories have on career choices can be meaningful. In addition, the impact of economic systems on human behavior should not go unnoticed by counselors who propose to assess human behavior. The influence of the socioeconomic level of the home on the self-concept of the developing child is also of concern to the counselor.

Interdisciplinary Implications for Counseling

The preceding sections presented a brief overview of perspectives from other disciplines. From these perspectives, implications can be drawn that have relevance to counselors and their functioning in a variety of settings.

1. Counselors must reflect a greater awareness of the various cultures that may be represented within the client population they are hoping to serve.
2. To be effective and relevant, counselors must increase their understanding of the language that is vital to communicating with different cultures, which results from living in one culture and learning in another, the role expectancies of cultures, and cultural biases in schools and other basic institutions that create tensions, hostilities, and distrust among subcultures.
3. Counselors must have an understanding of the social structures of the communities and institutions within which they function. They must also recognize the impact of these and other social structures on how a person views him- or herself, his or her work, education, and other experiences.
4. Counselors must recognize that behavior is a function of an individual's interaction with his or her environment.
5. Counselors must recognize the potential relationships between clients' socioeconomic characteristics and their behaviors and concerns.
6. Counselors should acquire a deeper understanding of the various societal influences on behavior, growth, and development of the individual based on an interdisciplinary approach.
7. Counselors must function more effectively as consultants. In this capacity, the counselor has the opportunity to interpret the social and cultural characteristics of clients and their implications for specific programs and settings.

Guidelines for Human Assessment

Before we examine specific tools and techniques available to counselors for assessing human characteristics, we must first recognize some basic principles or guidelines. These guidelines provide a framework for effectively and professionally functioning in the sometimes delicate task of individual assessment.

1. *Each individual human being is unique, and this uniqueness is to be valued.* Although the principle of individual differences has been eulogized throughout educational and societal circles the better part of the 20th century, in practice, constant pressures encourage conformity and standardization. Counselors must not enlarge this gap between principle and practice but should stress the principle that assessment is a means of increasing understanding of the uniqueness of the individual, a uniqueness that sets one apart from all other people, that provides each person with the basis for his or her own personal worth. That uniqueness is to be valued, not standardized.

2. *Variations exist within individuals.* Each person is unique as well as distinct from others. This principle notes that individual assessment seeks to identify, for example, the special talents, skills, and interests of a person and, at the same time, forestall tendencies to generalize from a single or several characteristics of a person, such as "Anyone who excels in math can excel in anything," or "You give me an all-American in one sport and I'll make them all-American in another." Nor do we overlook the shortcomings. Although the emphasis of assessment is on the strengths and positive attributes of a person, all of us have our weaknesses—shortcomings that we must recognize if we are to overcome, bypass, or compensate for them.

3. *Human assessment presumes the direct participation of the person in her or his own assessment.* For human assessment to be as meaningful and accurate as possible, the person must be willingly and directly involved. This involvement includes input by the client; feedback, clarification, and interpretation, as appropriate, by both the client and counselor; and evaluation by the client. This principle presumes more than the client's one-way feeding in of data, such as taking a standardized test or completing a questionnaire. It assumes her or his right to interpretation and response to that interpretation. It presumes the client's right to clarify and expand her or his response and, as others come to know the client better, to gain better understandings of her- or himself as well.

4. *Accurate human assessment is limited by instruments and personnel.* The effective use of assessment techniques depends on a recognition of the limitations of instruments and personnel as well as acceptance of their potential. These limitations begin with the human element—ourselves, our knowledge and skill in the techniques we would use. Counselors should not under any circumstances use assessment techniques, including standardized tests, in which they have not been thoroughly trained. Additionally, the limitations of clients in responding to individual items as well as instruments must be taken into account. These limitations may include an unwillingness as well as an inability to respond. In addition to these human elements, there are the limitations of the instruments themselves to consider. These include an awareness of the particular shortcomings unique to a given instrument or technique and the general recognition that any of these provide at best only a sample, only clues, not absolutes, and that results may vary among similar instruments and techniques.

5. *Human assessment accepts the positive.* A goal of human resource assessment is the identification of the potential of each person. It is a positive process that, as noted earlier, seeks to identify the unique worth of each person. Assessment can lead to identifying worthwhile goals and positive planning. It should be a process clothed in optimism rather than, as so often is

the case, fear of outcomes and predictions of doom. The counselor's own attitude becomes important in establishing a positive environment for assessment and in using results for client's best interests.

6. *Human assessment follows established professional guidelines.* It is important for counselors, and all other helping professionals who use human assessment techniques, to be aware of the relevant ethical guidelines established by their professional organizations. These guidelines are aimed at protecting both the client and the professional practitioner. Ethical standards for counselors, which address assessment as well as other aspects of practice, are presented in Appendices B, C, G, and H.

DOING WHAT COMES NATURALLY—OBSERVATION

On any given day most of us are the subjects of informal analysis by others and vice versa. These analysts are not among the handful of psychiatrists, psychologists, or counselors with whom we may be acquainted, but they are amateurs doing what comes naturally—observing their fellow human beings, both friend and stranger, and drawing some conclusions about the kinds of persons they are based on what is observed. Depending on what we see and how we interpret it, we may variously categorize people as executive types, models, drifters, untrustworthy, fun-loving, and so on. Furthermore, we are often prone to defend or validate our observations by noting, "I knew there was something that just didn't look right about her," or "You could tell he was a real athlete by the way he walked," and, on other occasions, calling on old clichés (many of which are sexist) as back-up evidence, such as "Just another dumb blonde" or "Watch out for those fiery redheads."

When we make observations au naturel, we are, in effect, studying behavior as it is occurring in real life. Although we must recognize—and we will help you to do this—the weakness of the uncontrolled observation method, we must at the same time recognize that many important questions about a person's natural social behavior cannot be determined through a controlled or clinical approach, much less be measured by standardized instruments. Counselors are also being encouraged to adopt an ecological perspective that suggests the study of behavior intact within the natural setting of the person being observed. As we begin an examination of the various techniques counselors use for gaining a better understanding of their clients, let us start with the most natural and popular of all these techniques: observation. As previously noted, we all employ this technique to varying degrees in drawing conclusions about others, but this is not to suggest that all observations are equally useful for human assessment. As a basis for classifying the differing approaches to observation, we make the following points.

Forms of Observation

Blocher (1987) suggests that systematic observation takes one of three basic forms: (a) naturalistic observation, where we might observe clients or subjects in a natural setting; (b) the survey method, where we survey (observe) particular samples of individuals' behavior we wish to assess; and (c) experimentation, whereby we not only observe but impose specific conditions on those being observed.

⅄ Observations may also be classified by the level of sophistication and training required as noted here.

First Level: Casual Information Observation. The daily, unstructured, and usually unplanned observations that provide casual impressions; engaged in daily by nearly everyone. No training or instrumentation expected or required.

Second Level: Guided Observation. Planned, directed observations for a purpose. Observation at this level is usually facilitated by simple instruments such as checklists and rating scales. Some training desired.

Third Level: Clinical Level. Observations, often prolonged, and frequently with controlled conditions. Sophisticated techniques and instruments used with training, usually at a doctoral level.

At this level and in many clinical settings, the counselor may need to make a diagnosis of mental disorders or may receive a client case history with psychiatric diagnostic nomenclature. The American Psychiatric Association's most recent effort to categorize mental disorders, *The Diagnostic and Statistical Manual of Mental Disorders [DSM-IV]* is frequently used for this purpose [(APA, 1994)].

The Diagnostic and Statistical Manual of Mental Disorders [DSM-IV] (American Psychiatric Association, 1994) contains authoritative information and "official opinions" about the range of mental problems. Counselors rely on the *[DSM-IV]* (1) as a source of standardized terminology in which to communicate with other mental health specialists, (2) to satisfy the record-keeping requirements of insurance companies or credentialing agencies like the Joint Commission on Accreditation of Hospitals, (3) for classifying clientele in statistical categories, as is necessary for research and accountability, (4) to predict the course of a disorder and the progress of treatment based on available evidence, and (5) to construct a treatment plan that will guide interventions (Seligman, 1983). The actual process of differential diagnosis with the *[DSM-IV]* is complex, and mastery of the system requires considerable study. (Kottler & Brown, 1985, p. 161)

Common Weaknesses of Observation

It has been said, "Anticipation is a wonderful thing. It often ensures that we will see what we want to see whether it is there or not." Because observation is a technique we all use frequently, it is only natural that we assume we are reasonably accurate in our observations. However, this is a misleading assumption. Observation can be one of the most abused techniques in human assessment. Let us therefore proceed to examine some of these abuses or common weaknesses, followed by suggestions for increasing the effectiveness of this valuable assessment technique.

One of the popular questions on written examinations for drivers' licenses in many states is to ask the applicant to identify, by shape only, the meaning of various traffic signs. Perhaps you would like to pause and test your recall of these signs, which all of us see every day:

Now compare your responses to the following answers: stop, yield, warning, information, railroad. How did you do? For many at least, this points up one of the glaring weaknesses in undirected observation.

Casual observations do not lend themselves to consistent accurate recall.

Envision yourself on the witness stand in the classical courtroom scene in which you are matching wits with the prosecuting attorney. In a fine you-are-guilty voice, the prosecutor asks, "Who were the first three people you observed on the morning of October 13th a year ago?" Some witnesses might have their recall saved by habit (the wife and kids) or a special event (the minister, a best friend, or my future in-law), but most would have difficulty recalling with accuracy and certainty the first three people they observed on that fateful day and even more difficulty in accurately describing what they were wearing. Although most of us have confidence in our ability to accurately recall what we have observed in the past, courtroom witnesses, witnesses to accidents, observers of historic or sensational events, and even news reporters are so frequently wrong as definitely to suggest that we are not so accurate in our recall of the past, especially the details, as we often assume. Another weakness of undirected observations, then, would be

Complete and accurate recall of undirected or casual observations tends to decrease with the passage of time.

Now assume that you are a devout sports fan. Your favorite team is involved in a close game in the final minutes when an official calls a penalty that could conceivably cost your team the game. Regardless of how flagrant that offense or the call, it would be highly predictable that you, and those supporting your team, would have observed the call differently from the officials and the supporters of the other team. An impartial witness would note that different observers were viewing the same situation differently. Similar illustrations may occur when two different observers describe the same western desert scene as "blending by nature of sand, greenery, and beautiful hills" and "a wasteland of sand and drab plants running into bleak mountains." All of us have experienced the discrepancies that often occur as someone describes a boyfriend or girlfriend and as the same person appears to us. The point is that people differ in how they view the same event, person, or place, and also in the details they observe. We would note this as another weakness in casual and informal observations for assessment purposes.

Similar observations will be viewed differently because each person has his or her own unique frame of reference for interpreting what he or she sees.

These and other shortcomings suggest that undirected and casual observations of our clients may result in incomplete, misleading, or erroneous assessments. The values and opportunities of observation in client analysis are recognized, but some guidelines and instruments must be developed for increasing the accuracy and effectiveness of this technique. Here are some guiding principles for client analysis through observation, followed by a discussion of some useful instruments for reporting and recording our observations of others.

Guidelines for Client Analysis Through Observation

1. *Observe one client at a time.* Observation for individual analysis is just that; it focuses on the person. We are intent on noticing every observable detail of client behavior that may be meaningful in the counseling context. This is just as desirable an objective for observations of people in external group settings as in the more restricted setting of the counseling office.

2. *Have specific criteria for making observations.* We observe our clients for a purpose. We are watching for characteristics of the person appropriate to this purpose. These provide a basis for the identification of specific criteria, which in effect tell us what to look for. For example, if we are observing young persons for the purpose of determining their relationships with adults, we might decide to specifically observe two criteria or characteristics of this relationship: interactions with teachers and interactions with parents. Of course, it is important that the criteria we use be appropriate to our observational objectives.

3. *Observations should be made over time.* Although there is no specific time span formula for conducting observations, they should take place over a period that is long and frequent enough to establish the reliability of our observation. A single sample of behavior is seldom enough for us to say with certainty that this is characteristic of the person. An illustration of this principle is to recall how your later impressions of people often differ from your first impressions, once you have had the opportunity to observe them over time. Also, although concentrated periods of observation may be appropriate, the amount of observational time should not be confused with the span of time over which observations take place.

4. *The client should be observed in differing and natural situations.* Natural behavior is most likely to occur in natural situations. Although these situations vary somewhat among persons, for most youth, the school, home, neighborhood, and favorite recreational locales will be natural; with adults, the place one works will replace the school. Even within these natural settings, people will behave differently but naturally in different locales. For example, a student in school may behave differently in the classroom, the cafeteria, the gym, the hallways, and on the playground. If possible, therefore, clients should be observed in those settings and situations that are typical for them. Furthermore, this means a reasonable variety of those settings. For example, a school-aged youth may exhibit different behavior in one class at school than in others, and completely different behavior in social-recreational settings. An adult may behave differently on the job than at home and differently again in other social settings. Observing in these different settings may help us determine whether some behaviors are limited to or conditioned by specific environments or situations.

5. *Observe the client in the context of the total situation.* In observation for human analysis, it is important to avoid a tunnel vision approach, or one in which we are so visually intent on observing just the client that we may miss noting those interactions and other factors in the setting that cause the person to behave the way he or she does. An example might be a classroom situation in which we observe that at the conclusion of nearly every math class, Nancy always leaves in tears, but we fail to observe that her classroom neighbors Joseph and Jamal appear to tease her throughout the class every day. We have observed the results but not the cause.

6. *Data from observations should be integrated with other data.* In individual analysis, it is important to bring together all that we know about our client. Because we are seeking to see the client as a whole person, we would combine the impressions we gained from our observations with all other pertinent information available to us. The case-study technique used by most helping professionals illustrates this point of integrating and relating data before interpretation.

7. *Observations should be made under favorable conditions.* Anyone who has tried to witness a parade three rows back or watch a key play at a game when the crowd jumps up in front can bear witness to the importance of favorable conditions for making observations. In planned observation, we want to be in a position to clearly view what we are planning to report. Ideally, we should be able to conduct our observation for a sufficient time period without either obstructions or distractions. There are also attitudinal considerations in creating favorable conditions for observation. These include an approach that is free from bias toward the client, any pro-

jections of expected behavior, or permitting one trait to predict another. It is just as important to have a clear psychological viewpoint as a physical viewpoint for observation for individual analysis. We should also be alert to another form of bias that may occur when the person being observed modifies her or his behavior because she or he is aware of being observed.

OBSERVATION INSTRUMENTS

A variety of instruments are available to counselors for use in recording their observations. Most are designed to eliminate one or more of the common weaknesses of undirected or casual observation. They provide a means of recording and preserving an impression of what was observed—an impression that is as accurate a year later as when it was initially recorded. Additionally, many instruments for reporting observations (checklists, rating scales, observation guides) provide specific directions or traits to guide the observer. Some instruments such as rating scales also provide for some degree of discrimination among the traits observed. Because many of these instruments include definitions or descriptions of their items that users are to accept and follow, they can also form a mutual frame of reference that may promote some consistency among observers viewing the same subject. The most popular of these instruments are rating scales, checklists, inventories, and anecdotal and observation reports.

Rating Scales

Rating scales, as the name implies, are scales for rating each of the characteristics or activities one is seeking to observe or assess. They enable an observer to systematically and objectively observe a person and record those observations. Although such scales are not limited to the recording and evaluating of observations, those are the common and popular uses of the instrument.

Rating scales have long been valued as an observation instrument by counselors. They are useful as a means of focusing on specific characteristics, increasing the objectivity of the rater, and providing for comparability of observations among observers; and they are easy to use.

Designing a Rating Scale*

Although there are commercially designed rating scales available, counselors may find it more desirable under most circumstances to design their own. A good self-designed scale will be more appropriate for both the situation and the rater or raters, can be revised if needed, and, of course, is economical. The potential of any rating scale, however, is first determined by its design. There are five steps in designing a rating scale.

Determine the Purpose(s).   An obvious initial step is to determine the potential population and the purpose of the observations or ratings. Usually, the purposes or objectives of such an instrument should be limited in both number and scope. This tends to prohibit the development of scales that are too lengthy and overlapping and that discourage user completion. Scales that are clear, concise, and directed toward limited and precise objectives also increase the likelihood of accurate responses.

Identify the Items.   Once the purposes or objectives of the scale have been established, the developer next identifies appropriate criteria or items to be rated. These items should be

---

*See Example 9-1, "Developing the Rating Scale."

clearly and directly related to the objectives of the observation. Also, they should be easy to understand, observe, and assess.

Identify the Descriptors.   Although there is often a subtle difference between items and descriptors, it is important to honor this difference. Items may not be ratable, so descriptors are used to effect a transition between an identifying item or statement and an objective description. An example of an item could be "appearance," and an example of a descriptor could be "neat and well-groomed at all times."

Identify Evaluators.   As the label implies, evaluations or ratings in some kind of a scale are an anticipated characteristic of this particular technique for making and reporting observations. There are a variety of options for this purpose, such as the number of intervals or points on the scale, the defining of the evaluators, and deciding whether to provide space for comments.

Determine the Format.   A part of the format will be determined by the identification of evaluators, as described in the previous step. Additionally, the organization usually relates items together; the length—not too long—and the directions for completion will all be items to attend to in determining the final format for the instrument.

Limitations of the Rating Scale

Limitations in using rating scales are basically those to which all instruments administered and developed by humans are subject—the limitations of the instrument and the limitations imposed by the user. The most common instrument limitations are (a) the result of poor and unclear directions for the scales' use; (b) a failure to adequately define terms; (c) limited scales for rating; (d) items that tend to prejudice how one responds; (e) overlapping items; and (f) excessive length.

The limitations that raters impose are equally prevalent and can be even more serious, because they can distort or misrepresent the characteristics of a person. The following are common examples.

1. *Ratings made without sufficient observations.* Many raters have an apparent need to complete all the items on a scale and, as a result, will take a stab at items with which they are unfamiliar. Others, in their haste to complete the scale, will make a rating on the basis of limited observation.

2. *Overrating.* There is a growing conviction among those who frequently use rating scales that overrating is a common practice among raters. For example, a recent review of rating scales used in conjunction with admissions to graduate work in a Big Ten university revealed that all 324 candidates were rated "considerably above average" or higher in three categories: appearance, social skills, and leadership.

3. *Middle rating.* Another group of raters appear to play it safe by using only the average or middle categories on a scale, thus avoiding either extremes of high or low assessments. Such ratings tend to misrepresent everyone as being just about average in everything.

4. *Biased ratings.* In addition to personal bias, bias may occur in ratings when raters permit one item that they particularly value or emphasize to set a pattern for the rating of other items.

Although the focus of this discussion has centered on the use of rating scales in reporting observations, this instrument is not limited to only the reporting of observations. Rating scales are also used extensively by counselors and others for performance ratings; evaluations (both personal and institutional); and measurement of attitudes, aspirations, and experiences.

Example 9-1 is a rating scale for identifying potential school dropouts.

Checklists

Another instrument that may be used for recording observations is the observer checklist. This instrument is typically designed to direct the observer's attention to specific, observable personality traits and characteristics. It is relatively easy to use inasmuch as it not only directs the observer's attention to certain specific traits but provides a simple means of indicating whether those traits are characteristic to the person being observed. Unlike the rating scale, the observer checklist does not require the observer to indicate the degree or extent to which a characteristic is present. Figure 9-1 is an example of a simple form of a checklist.

Inventories

Self-report inventories typically consist of structured questions or statements to which the respondent answers "yes" or " no," or "yes," "?," or "no" (Hopkins and Stanley, 1981). Like rat-

---

EXAMPLE 9–1   DEVELOPING THE RATING SCALE

The Beatty-Tingley High School has a history of high incidence of pupil dropout before graduation. The problem has become particularly severe in the past 3 years, and various remedial efforts have had little effect. The school board has therefore determined that a concerted effort will be made to identify potential early leavers and then to design possible preventive measures. The counseling staff has been requested to design an instrument that will lead to the identification of these potential early leavers through the observation of certain behavioral traits. They proceeded to develop a rating scale by first stating the purpose as follows:

Purpose

1. To identify potential dropouts

Following a review of relevant research, the counselors agreed on four possible criteria of potential school leavers:

1. Interest in school
2. Relations with peers
3. Relations with teachers
4. Coping styles

Having identified criteria, they next had to agree on descriptors appropriate for the designing of items on the rating scale. These were determined to be as follows:

1. *Interest in school:* attention in class, participation in class activities, preparation for class
2. *Relations with peers:* frequency of interaction with peers, nature of interaction with peers, attitude of peers, friendships with peers
3. *Relations with teachers:* frequency and nature of interaction with teachers, attitudes toward teachers, attitudes of teachers
4. *Coping styles:* problem-solving skills, dealing with frustration and failure, work habits

---

EXAMPLE 9–1

(continued)

They then began designing the rating scale. The first items were designed to assess the interest of students in their classes.

Interest in School (check most appropriate category)

Class attention:
Consistent and general
alertness to ongoing
activities in the sub-
ject matter class

Never   Rarely   Sometimes   Usually   Always

Comments:

Class participation:
Quality of participation:
knowedgeable and
appropriate contribu-
tions and interactions

Poor   Below   Average   Superior   Excellent
              Average

Comments:

Frequency of participation:

Never   Seldom   Occasionally   Often   Always

Comments:

Preparation for class:
Readiness in terms of
reading and other as-
signments for mean-
ingful participation in
class

Never   Seldom   Occasionally   Usually   Always

Comments:

---

ing scales, they use objective statements and responses in eliciting a person's view of self in regard to the listed items. Self-report inventories are often used to assess self-concept, study habits, and attitudes.

Anecdotal Reports

Anecdotal reports, as the label implies, are descriptions of a client's behavior in a given situation or event. Such reports are subjective and descriptive in nature and are recorded in a narrative form. Often a counselor will collect several of these reports, which then become an anecdotal record of a client's behavior over a period of time or situations.

Design of Anecdotal Records

The format for anecdotal records usually consists of three parts. They are (a) recording identifying data; (b) reporting of the observations; and (c) comments of the observer. This format

<u>Observation Checklist</u>

Personal characteristics of _____
                                                         (name of student)
Observed by (name or code) _____

Periods (dates of observation): from _____ to _____

Conditions under which student was observed: _____

_____

Instructions: Place a check mark in the blanks to the left of any of the following traits you believe to be characteristic of the student.

	Positive Traits		Negative Traits
_____	1. Neat in appearance	_____	16. Unreliable
_____	2. Enjoys good health	_____	17. Uncooperative
_____	3. Regular in attendance	_____	18. Domineering
_____	4. Courteous	_____	19. Self-centered
_____	5. Concerned for others	_____	20. Rude
_____	6. Popular with other students	_____	21. Sarcastic
_____	7. Displays leadership ability	_____	22. Boastful
_____	8. Has a good sense of humor	_____	23. Dishonest
_____	9. Shows initiative	_____	24. Resists authority
_____	10. Industrious	_____	25. A bully
_____	11. Has a pleasant disposition	_____	26. Overly aggressive
_____	12. Mature	_____	27. Shy and withdrawn
_____	13. Respects property of others	_____	28. Cries easily
_____	14. Nearly always does his/her best	_____	29. Deceitful
_____	15. Adjusts easily to different situations	_____	30. Oversolicitous

Comments: _____

_____

_____

_____

_____

Figure 9-1   Observation Checklist.

has several variations, as may be noted by examining three different designs for anecdotal records. Figure 9-2 presents a format that follows in sequence the three parts previously identified. Figure 9-3 alters this format to provide space for comments alongside that are appropriate to particular statements of the anecdotal description. Figure 9-4 provides space for comments of additional observers, if desired.

Anecdotal Report Form
Henry H. Higgins High School

Name _____   Observed by _____

Where observed _____   When: Date _____

                                                   Time _____ to_____

_____

Description:

Comments:

Figure 9-2   Anecdotal Record: Form A.

Anecdote
                                                                              Return to:
                                                                              Counseling Offices
                                                                              Basile Elementary
                                                                              School
Student's name

Description of incident observed	Comments:

Observed by _____

Time _____   Place _____

Figure 9-3   Anecdotal Record: Form B.

Using the Anecdotal Reporting Method

The first consideration in anecdotal reporting is the selection of incidents that may be significant to report. There may be incidents that are typical of a client's behavior and are relevant for the counselor's or client's better understanding of the client. There may also be incidents so atypical of the client's behavior that their reporting and understanding are advisable. In some situations, a series of anecdotes reporting similar behaviors over time would increasingly suggest that the observed characteristics are typical of the client's behavior. Different observers making similar observations of a client's behavior on a specific occasion, or over time, would have similar implications. Also, anecdotal reporting covering a period of time may identify trends or changes in client behaviors.

```
┌─────────────────────────────────────────────────────────────────────────┐
│                                                                           │
│   Anecdotal report for                                                    │
│     Name                                          Date                     │
│                                                                           │
│     Situation                                                             │
│ ─────────────────────────────────────────────────────────────────────── │
│   Description                                                             │
│                                                                           │
│                                                                           │
│ - - - - - - - - - - - - - - - - - - - - - - - - - - - - - - - - - - - - - │
│   Comments:                                                               │
│                                                                           │
│   Observer:                                                               │
│ - - - - - - - - - - - - - - - - - - - - - - - - - - - - - - - - - - - - - │
│   Comments:                                                               │
│                                                                           │
│   Observer:                                                               │
│                                                                           │
│                                                                           │
└─────────────────────────────────────────────────────────────────────────┘
```

Figure 9-4   Anecdotal Record: Form C.

In school settings, teachers may be encouraged to use anecdotal reports in calling counselor attention to students who may need their assistance or in contributing to case studies or just a better understanding of individual students. Example 9-2 illustrates uses of anecdotal reporting in school settings, as well as the counselor's interpretations of these reports.

Example 9-2 illustrates how a series of anecdotes can lead to the identification of a student in need of counseling assistance. In some situations, however, even a single anecdote is enough to alert the counselor to a person in need of assistance.

Advantages Versus Disadvantages

Because anecdotal reports are designed to subjectively describe what has been observed, they become more lifelike than more objective measures. They present a broader, more complete viewpoint of a situation, which at the same time avoids the bleakness of the more quantitative or objective methods of reporting.

The major limitations of anecdotal reporting are those imposed by the observer-reporter. Most common of these are the reporting of feelings about rather than actual behavior of the person observed. The tendency to read in biases or expectancies can result in misleading reports. Overinterpretation or misinterpretation by inexperienced observers are not uncommon. Reporting insignificant, rather than meaningful, behavior can also limit the usefulness of anecdotal reporting.

Time-Based Observations

Observations of behavior based on periods of time may be useful. One strategy of measuring behavior is based upon units of time rather than discrete response units. Kazdin (1981) describes this as follows.

Behavior is recorded during short time intervals for the total time that it is observed. With interval recording, behavior is observed for a single block of time (e.g., 30 minutes) once per day. A block of time is divided into a series of short intervals (10 or 15 seconds), and the behavior of the

EXAMPLE 9-2   USES OF ANECDOTAL REPORTING IN SCHOOL

Student's Name:	Therese
Incident 1:	Mr. Michael
Reported by:	History teacher
Date:	January 16 (Monday)

Therese was not herself in class today. She usually is very active in the class discussions and always responds to questions when no one else seems to have the answer. However, today she sat quietly in her seat. At one point, when the discussion was bogging down, I called on Therese as always, asking her, "What were some of the factors that kept the United States from joining the League of Nations after World War I?" I could barely hear her response, but I thought she said, "Who cares?" and then in a louder voice that bordered on breaking into tears, "I'm sorry, I don't know the answer."

Teacher's Comments: Therese is one of my more mature and capable students. Something is upsetting her, and it would be helpful if a counselor could talk with her.

Student's Name:	Therese
Incident 2:	Ms. Chevez
Reported by:	Chemistry teacher
Date:	January 18 (Wednesday)

For the first time in the 2 years I have known Therese as a student, she has fallen behind in her work in my class. Furthermore, her behavior has been almost disruptive. For example, today, when one of her best friends, Ann, asked her if she could borrow a test tube from her, Therese snapped back at her, saying, "Don't you ever have enough stuff to do your own assignments? No, I'm not lending you anything anymore!" The exchange obviously was unexpected to Ann, who didn't exchange another word with Therese for the rest of the period, while Therese seemed to spend most of the period simply staring at her lab book.

Teacher's Comments: Something is clearly wrong with this girl. This behavior is not typical at all. She needs to see a counselor.

Student's Name:	Therese
Incident 3:	Mrs. Kemp
Reported by:	Physical education teacher
Date:	January 19 (Thursday)

Today, Therese approached me before my fifth period in which she is enrolled and said, "Mrs. Kemp, I am quitting the gymnastics team and I don't want to talk about it." When I put my arm around her and said, "That's OK, Therese, I hope you're all right," she broke into tears and said, "I'll never be all right again!" and then ran into the locker room. I decided to leave her alone and didn't follow up on our conversation at this time.

EXAMPLE 9–2

(continued)

Teacher's Comments: I have noted for the past couple of weeks that Therese hasn't seemed to be herself, but today things seemed to explode. I don't know what the difficulty is, but I do intend to follow up on her problem, whatever it may be, when I see her next week. Do you have any suggestions?

In this situation it is obvious that the school counselor, by the end of the week, is able to put together a picture of a young lady who is clearly upset. Although there are no indications of cause in the incidents described, the counselor has sufficient reason to either call in Therese or, through consultation with Mrs. Kemp, attempt to provide her with appropriate help.

The previous discussion illustrates how a series of anecdotes can lead to the identification of a student in need of counseling assistance. In some situations, however, even a single anecdote is enough to alert the counselor to a person in need of assistance.

---

client is observed during each of them. The target behavior is scored as having occurred or not occurred during each interval. If a discrete behavior, such as hitting someone, occurs one or more times in a single interval, the response is scored as having occurred. Several response occurrences within an interval are not counted separately. If the behavior is ongoing with an unclear beginning or end, such as talking, playing, or sitting, or occurs for a long period of time, it is scored during each interval in which it is occurring.

A variety of interval recording is referred to as *time sampling*. This variation uses the interval method but the observations are conducted for brief periods at different times, rather than in a single block of time.* (p. 107)

Another time-based method of observation is the amount of time, or duration, of a particular response. Kazdin (1981) indicates that

this method is particularly useful for ongoing responses that are continuous rather than discrete acts or responses of extremely short duration. Programs that attempt to increase or decrease the length of time a response is performed might profit from a duration method. For example, duration has been used to assess the amount of time that a claustrophobic patient spent sitting voluntarily in a small room (Leitenberg, Agras, Thompson, & Wright, 1968) and the time delinquent boys spent returning from schools and errands. (Phillips, 1968)

Another measure based upon duration is not how long the response is performed, but how long it takes for the client to begin the response. The amount of elapsed time between a cue and the response is referred to as *latency*. (p. 108)

Situational Observations

Situational observations are used to study the behavior of individuals in structured situations. For example, a group might be given a problem situation but no leader is designated. The group is then observed to see who and how a leader might emerge and also how the different members react. School children might be observed in a study situation in which the instructor observes the individual for an announced period of time. Workers on the job might be observed with and without supervision.

Behavioral Charting

Another form of recording and reviewing observed behavior is behavioral charting, or tallying. In this technique, a particular behavior is observed (e.g., disturbing others, leaves work station, laughs without apparent reason) over specific time periods to determine how frequently it occurs. Figure 9-5 illustrates a reporting format for this technique.

For: Ima Hummer
                                          _____
                                                    (Name of Observed)

Observed by: R. Whiner
Behavior observed: Attracts attention to herself by making disturbing noises
                      during class work period.

                      _____

                      _____

                      _____

                      _____

Date(s) and time: April 6   April 7   April 8   April 9
                      10 A.M.   10 A.M.   10 A.M.   10 A.M.

Place: English Composition Class (2-hour class)

	Times Noted	**Total**
Monday	‖‖ǀ	6
Tuesday	ǀǀǀ	3
Wednesday	‖‖ ǀǀ	7
Thursday	‖‖	5

Figure 9-5 Behavioral Observation Form.

Instrument Selection

The preceding paragraphs have discussed a variety of observation techniques and instruments. In many situations, counselors and other observers will make a decision about which instrument or instruments are most appropriate for the observation task at hand. They may be aided in determining which type of instrument to use by considering the following.

1. Is some direction for recording observation(s) for individual analysis desired? (The answer to this is usually yes—or should be.)
2. Is a descriptive or objective report more appropriate?
3. Will more than one observer be reporting observations of the client (or potential client)?
4. Are assessments or evaluations of what has been observed desired?
5. Are comparisons among different clients or between client and other populations likely to be made?
6. Are opinions or impressions—not necessarily facts or factually based information—desired?
7. Does the instrument avoid complex observations and recording methods?
8. Will the instrument make it relatively easy to complete a report in a short time, even if some accuracy or depth of observation may be sacrificed?
9. Will instruments be used by counselors or others who are experienced or trained in their use?

DSM-IV

The most popular diagnostic system in the United States is the *Diagnostic and Statistical Manual of Mental Disorders IV* (1994), published by the American Psychiatric Association. Although the manual itself presents a standardized system of recording, the judgments on which these entries are often made will be subjective.

According to the *DSM-IV*, a mental disorder is characterized as a clinically significant behavioral or psychological syndrome or pattern that occurs in an individual. Further, according to the *DSM-IV*, one of the following must be present to diagnose a client as having a mental disorder: distress and/or impairment and/or significant risk. Whether or not clients who present themselves for counseling have mental disorders, the multiaxial diagnosis of the *DSM-IV* offers counselors a way to organize the information they have on clients' symptoms, their physical conditions, their levels of coping, and the stressors they are experiencing (Capuzzi & Gross, 1997).

Five categories called AXIS are provided as guidelines for organizing client information, symptoms, physical conditions, levels of coping, and stressors being experienced. The AXIS and their general categories are as follows.

AXIS I	Clinical disorders and other conditions that may be the focus of clinical attention
AXIS II	Personality disorders, mental retardation, borderline intellectual functioning, and other disorders with less severe symptoms
AXIS III	General medical conditions
AXIS IV	Psychological and environmental problems that may be impacting the client
AXIS V	Global assessment of functioning (using a rating scale form)

how well they are functioning in society

The mental disorders and conditions covered in the *DSM-IV* are divided into 17 categories as follows.

- Disorders usually first diagnosed in infancy, childhood, or adolescence
- Delirium, dementia, and amnestic and other cognitive disorders
- Mental disorders due to a general medical condition
- Substance-related disorders
- Schizophrenia and other psychotic disorders
- Mood disorders
- Anxiety disorders
- Somatoform disorders
- Factitious disorders
- Dissociative disorders
- Sexual and gender identity disorders
- Eating disorders
- Sleep disorders
- Impulse-control disorders not elsewhere classified
- Adjustment disorders
- Personality disorders
- Other conditions that may be a focus of clinical attention

Counselors using the *DSM-IV* should have special preparation and supervised experience.

SELF-REPORTING: THE AUTOBIOGRAPHY AND OTHER TECHNIQUES

Up to this point, we have been discussing observation techniques for client assessment. In such techniques, clients may be aware of their being observed, but rarely are they direct participants in the process.

Some of the most valuable techniques for human assessment for counseling purposes are those that call for the active involvement of the client. These techniques not only provide special insights for the counselor but also can be valuable to the clients as they engage in a process of guided self-assessment. The use of such techniques as autobiographies, self-expression essays, questionnaires, and structured interviews can facilitate both counselor and client understanding of the client's strengths, weaknesses, and uniqueness.

The Autobiography: A Popular Genre

The autobiography has been one of the most popular forms of literature throughout the ages. Humankind has consistently been interested in the personal view people have of their own life experiences. Additionally, almost everyone, famous or obscure, has at one time jotted down a personal view of life's experiences. Some hope for publication, whereas others only write for personal satisfaction. For the majority of those feeling compelled to examine and set down in writing life's experiences, it is unlikely that the desire will coincide with a need for counseling. Nonetheless, the autobiography, even when it represents a nonvoluntary effort, can be a useful source of information to the skilled counselor. Let us briefly examine its use as a nonstandardized technique in human assessment.

Autobiography: A Different Approach

At this point, it is probably appropriate to indicate that counselors should avoid using overlapping or similar techniques. For example, there is little to be gained in using both rating scales and observation checklists to report observations of the same type of behavior, or in using three different achievement tests to measure the same area of achievement. A feature of the autobiography is that it is different from any other technique available to the counselor, for it provides clients (or students) with the opportunity to describe their own life as they have experienced it.

The autobiography lets a person express what has been important in his or her life, to emphasize likes and dislikes, identify values, describe interests and aspirations, acknowledge successes and failures, and recall meaningful personal relationships. Such an experience, especially for the mature client, can be thought-provoking, insightful, and a stimulus for action. On occasion, the experience can also relieve tension.

The Autobiography as an Assignment

As previously indicated, there are times in most people's lives when they reach a state of psychological readiness for writing their own life story. However, because this is unlikely to occur at the time such information may be needed by a counselor, the client may be asked to write an autobiography. The counselor should explain the assignment as naturally and straightforwardly as possible, indicating how it will be helpful to both the counselor and the client in the counseling process. The counselor should also emphasize that the contents of the autobiography will at all times (within legal limits) be treated as confidential information. The counselor should indicate possible content and approaches for preparing this assignment as well. Written guidelines may also be prepared for use in such a situation. Example 9-3 is one such set of guidelines that provides the client three possible options for preparing an autobiography.

In a school setting, the autobiography is often collected through a subject-matter classroom. It is most frequently a written assignment in an English class at the secondary school level, and in the elementary school, as a language assignment or an assignment related to the study of famous historic figures. As a classroom assignment, the autobiography should be treated in such a way that the student will regard it as a worthwhile educational experience. This suggests that it is treated as a regular assignment for a grade, although, if grades are assigned, the teacher must emphasize that one is not receiving an A or F for his or her life thus far, but rather, for the technical manner in which he or she described it in relation to the assignment.

Limitations

The autobiography has a number of potential limitations that counselors and other users must take into consideration. For instance, many people may find writing an autobiography a chore; thus, it will become a brief, bleak, and usually boring document that con-

---

EXAMPLE 9–3 GUIDELINES FOR PREPARING AN AUTOBIOGRAPHY

Purpose

1. To provide you with an opportunity to experience the planning, organizing, and writing of your autobiography
2. To provide you, the writer, and me, the reader, with opportunities for increased understanding, insights, and appreciations of you, the writer

Each writer may develop and work to an outline that suits his or her own style. The emphasis and detail that you give any period, event, or person will be whatever you determine as appropriate. The following are *examples only* of outlines and topics that might be appropriate for inclusion in an autobiography. (Note: I will be the only reader of your autobiography and will, of course, regard its contents as confidential.)

Example A

Part I	My preschool years
	My family, where I lived, early memories, friends, likes and dislikes
Part II	My school years
	Elementary, junior, senior high school, college, teachers, friends, subjects liked and disliked, activities, significant events, experiences, travels, concerns, and decisions
Part III	My adult years
	Where I lived, work experience, friends and family, travels, hobbies, continued education, concerns, and decisions
Part IV	The current me
Part V	My future plans

Example B

1. Significant people in my life
2. Significant events and experiences in my life
3. Significant places in my life

Example C

Start your autobiography as far back as you can remember—your earliest childhood memories. Tell about those things that really made an impression on you, that stood out in your memory, whether happy or sad. Try to include those events that you believe have affected your life, such as moving to another city or entering junior high school. As you write about the event, try to show how the event affected you, what people have truly influenced your life the most, and how they affected the way you feel and act today. Mention your hopes and plans for the future—what you hope to be doing 10 years from now, for example.

When a counselor desires that a client emphasize a certain aspect of his or her life's experiences, that should be indicated to the writer.

---

tributes little to a better understanding of the writer. The author's writing ability as well as the conditions under which it is written will influence the autobiography's potential usefulness. Also, as with any recall-based instrument, the ability of the writer to recall past experiences accurately and in considerable detail is important. Self-insight is another important factor. The reader must be aware of distortions that overemphasize insignificant happenings or ignore those that are important, or that inject falsehoods or fantasies, which very often are descriptive of the ideal or hoped-for life experiences of a writer. Current values may also influence how an author views past experiences and associations, and these values may not be consistent with one's present set of values and therefore, could be misleading to the reader.

Interpretation

With both the advantages and limitations of the autobiography in mind, let us note possible analyses by the counselor. The counselor-reader may first of all prepare a checklist or summary form for those items that would be particularly relevant to the counseling needs of the client. In other situations, the counselor may simply summarize at the conclusion of the reading the most relevant aspects or, assuming that the copy will be for the counselor's viewing only, may underline or make appropriate notes in the margins. In a general reading, one might use the format depicted in Figure 9-6 for analyzing an autobiography.

Autobiographical Excerpts

Two brief excerpts exemplify significant statements that are often found in student autobiographies.

> When I moved from East Park High School to Newry High School I guess I had assumed that things would go on as usual. I had been a big wheel at East Park—you know what I mean—member of the Student Council, president of the "Jokers"—most popular boys' club in school; king of the Sophomore Stomp, member of about half a dozen other clubs, invites to all the parties and social activities that were of any importance. But at Newry, many of the clubs I had belonged to before didn't exist. There were no boys' social clubs and, try as I might, I couldn't seem to make friends that moved in the "popular" circles. A lot of the kids spoke to me and were pleasant enough, but they never thought of me at party time. I found as time went on I missed East Park more and more, and I even began cutting school so I could drive back and visit East Park while school was in session. I had been a "B" student before at East Park, but my grades really took a beating at Newry. In fact, some of the kids at Newry began thinking of me as a "dum-dum" and I know many of the teachers did.

The counselor in this instance found a significant clue in this portion of the client's autobiography to explain his poor grades and the subsequent difficulty he was having in securing college admission.

> I guess I felt like a nobody as far back as I can remember. I think maybe my mother resented me because I wasn't a girl, because when I was born she already had five boys. I know as a kid I could never seem to do anything right, and my mother used to say I couldn't do anything right because I was a nobody. I remember that she and my Dad both began calling me "ole nobody." Then my oldest brother, the one with

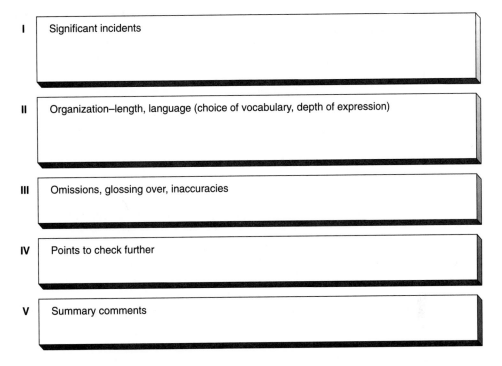

I	Significant incidents
II	Organization–length, language (choice of vocabulary, depth of expression)
III	Omissions, glossing over, inaccuracies
IV	Points to check further
V	Summary comments

Figure 9-6 Analyzing an Autobiography.
Source: From M. A. Kiley, *Personal and Interpersonal Appraisal Techniques,* 1975, p. 66. Courtesy of Charles C. Thomas, Publisher, Springfield, Illinois.

the sense of humor, started calling me "N.B." (for nobody). The rest of the family thought that was real "cute" and so when I started school, and all through school, I have been called "N.B." Actually, my name is James Lucifer Laswich. But I often have to stop to think what my real name is, I'm so used to N.B. I guess one reason I am so used to it is that I just seem to fit the name "Ole Nobody" so well. I sometimes don't think there is a single teacher in this school who remembers me once I leave the class, and I know most of the kids don't. I must be the only kid in school who doesn't have a "best friend."

The case of Ole Nobody is another example of a significant statement in a person's autobiography that provides the counselor with clues to the client's seemingly withdrawn behavior and poor self-concept.

Figure 9-7 is an example of a format which might be used to assess an autobiography.

Autobiographical Tapes

In recent years, counselors have found an innovative deviation from the usual written autobiography—the autobiographical tape—to be useful with some clients. The autobiographical tape presents the client an opportunity orally to describe and discuss one's life. In using this technique, the counselor may first determine whether it is more likely to be useful than the written autobiography. If the tape approach is more appropriate, then the counselor should

Autobiography of _____

When written (date) _____

Required assignment _____   Other _____

Reviewed by (date) _____

Purpose _____

_____

_____

Significant events _____

_____

_____

Periods or topics omitted _____

_____

_____

Periods of topics overemphasized _____

_____

_____

Possible distortion _____

_____

_____

Other comments _____

_____

_____

Figure 9-7   Autobiographical review form.

decide whether to give the client a structured outline to respond to or simply have the client describe her life as it comes to her.

There may be some advantages to the autobiographical tape that will determine the circumstances under which it will be used. For example, some persons can express themselves better orally than in writing. Furthermore, because this method requires less preparation and effort on the part of the client, he or she may more freely present details that would otherwise be omitted. Some clients may feel that there is less likelihood that the contents of a tape will give away one's secrets than a written document. Voice tone on a taped autobiography may reveal the client's feelings and emotions, and, because of the nature of recording, the taped autobiography is less likely to be subject to client editing or censoring. Finally, for some clients, taping an autobiography is a more fascinating or innovative approach than the traditional writing experience.

There are, of course, disadvantages to taping as well. The usual shortcomings of the written autobiography, such as lack of recall, exaggeration, and fantasy, are every bit as probable in this approach. In addition, there are some clients who lack the ability to express themselves clearly orally. Also, for some, the unnaturalness of this approach will be an inhibitor. Nonetheless, the taped autobiography is a tool that the counselor may wish to consider for certain clients under certain circumstances.

Self-Expression Essays

Another useful technique that counselors may want to employ on occasion is the self-expression essay. This technique seeks to solicit the client's response, usually in a short, written essay form, to a particular question or concern. The objective of this technique is to elicit spontaneous, uncensored responses to a topic or topics relevant to the counseling needs of the client. Examples of appropriate topics would include

My biggest concern is . . .

I'll bet you don't know that . . .

I value . . .

My future plans are . . .

My job is . . .

It should be emphasized that such documents can elicit positive responses as well as descriptions of possible problems or concerns. Example 9-4 illustrates a positive response.

EXAMPLE 9–4   A SELF-EXPRESSION ESSAY: MY SCHOOL PROBLEM

My school problem is that I have no problem! Look at us! We have a beautiful school and, just my luck, a great faculty. We can't seem to lose more than once or twice a year in any sport. The greatest gang of kids go here and the crowning blow—even the food in the cafeteria is edible. So I have a problem because I'm a natural born griper—I'm at my best when I can complain—I have a feeling of accomplishment when I can point out the weaknesses of others. I used to have a field day before I came to Lee Street High. Now I'm dejected because I'm not rejected.

To help solve my problem I suggest that:

1. The students get busy and deface the school, mark up the restrooms, pull out the shrubbery, and all the other things that make a school more homelike.
2. The faculty get busy telling us how stupid we are, that they quit treating us like humans (I actually feel superior to my dog now), and that they get back in the old game of teacher versus student to the bitter end.
3. Our teams lose a few more games, and that our coaches get rid of their coats and ties and wear baggy sweatshirts and swear loudly at the officials so they won't be mistaken for ladies and gentlemen, and that our student body do something pronto to get rid of that disgraceful "good sportsmanship" trophy.
4. The students start forming cliques, avoid welcoming newcomers, and in general act more like adolescents than young adults. Oh, yes, we need a few more "kookie" dressers also.
5. Finally, the school cafeteria manager go copy the menus and recipes from some other schools (mashed potatoes should always be served cold, and lumpy gravy should taste like glue, and fried chicken served stringy and dried out).

The Self-Description

The self-description is another client-participation tool that enables the counselor to see the client as he or she sees him- or herself. The client is requested to "paint a picture of yourself in words," in one page, if desired.

Such a portrait may share whatever aspects the client wishes to have the reader know. It is usually desirable to do this in the early stages of counseling to give the counselor an additional means of getting to know the client. This differs from the self-expression essay because the self-description is one's view of one's self, as indicated in Example 9-5, whereas the self-expression essay may describe one's attitudes toward activities, events, and beliefs.

EXAMPLE 9–5   EXCERPTS FROM SELF-DESCRIPTION ESSAYS

Sample 1

I would describe myself as a pleasant and amiable person. Others remark about my easygoing manner and happy-go-lucky personality. Honesty is a virtue I hold very dearly, and I perhaps trust others equally, thinking that they have my virtues.

My mother had always taught me that I should be conscious of others' feelings and do my best to please them. I went for many years applying this philosophy, yet found that others were not as conscious of my feelings. This led me to be hurt and used by others emotionally and mentally. I had to almost retrain myself to believe that thinking of myself was not altogether selfish and at times is the only way to think in order to lead a happy life.

Counselor's Notations: The counselor would no doubt notice the section of this self-description that indicates the client has been hurt and used by others emotionally and mentally. Also of interest to the counselor is the client's statement, "I had to almost retrain myself to believe that thinking of myself was not altogether selfish."

Sample 2

I believe that a person should not be too overtly predictable but should possess a consistency of covert thought and feeling. I do not mean to say that I delight in the misconceptions of those who wish to categorize or predict the responses of others. I am not one to purposely masquerade, or, for some reason, to mislead those I work or come in contact with. But oftentimes an unpredictable action, comment, or response will reveal or trigger a surprising reaction on the part of an eager conversationalist. I do not become close to many and am not always patient enough to seek out the best points of my peers or colleagues. My point of view has been said to be too sensitive at times, but I like to think that my increased sensitivity allows me to take a deeper breath of life and enjoy what beauty I may sense.

I am idealistic, serious, extremely concerned about those who need help, and a good listener.

Counselor's Notations: The counselor reading this self-description might note the fact that the client keeps his or her distance from colleagues and is considered at times to be overly sensitive. This self-description is of interest, too, for the writer's description of interactions with his or her peers.

Self-Awareness Exercises

Many persons pride themselves on their self-control; their ability to put their feelings aside and deal in a practical manner with the situation at hand. Others simply find it difficult to express their feelings openly to others, as, for example, the often dramatized shy young man who never can work up the courage to tell his true love that he cares for her. At the other extreme, we can identify persons who may express their feelings openly in such a way as to be harmful to their personal relationships with others. Even in these extremes, persons are often unaware of how their expressions of feelings and emotions may be handicapping rather than helping their relationships with others.

Self-awareness exercises are designed to help people become more aware of their feelings, emotions, and values as a step toward more effectively expressing them. Egan's (1977) chart of difficulty in expressing emotion (Figure 9-8) says that in many (if not most) cases it

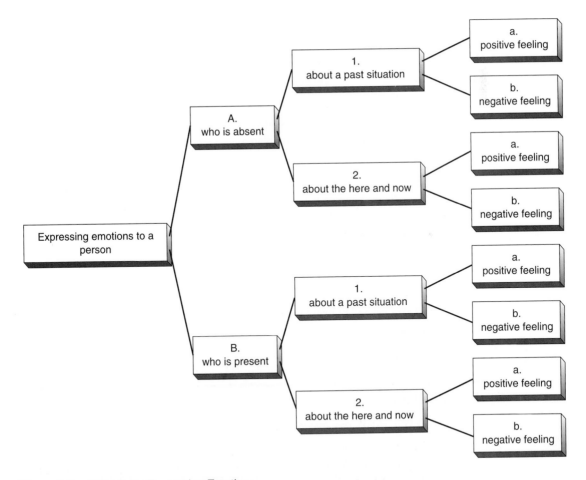

Figure 9-8 Difficulty in Expressing Emotion.
Source: From *You and Me: The Skills of Communicating and Relating to Others,* p. 81, by G. Egan. Copyright © 1977 Brooks/Cole Publishing Company, Pacific Grove, CA. 93950, a division of International Thomson Publishing Inc. By permission of the publisher.

becomes more and more difficult to express feelings and emotions the farther down the chart you go. Therefore, it's relatively easy to express a positive feeling about a past situation when the feeling is directed toward a person who is absent.

Exercises 9-1 and 9-2 are examples of self-awareness exercises.

EXERCISE 9–1

This exercise is designed to help you increase your awareness of how the expression of feelings/emotions affects your relationships with others. There are no right or wrong answers, so you should react to each statement as honestly as you can, recognizing that "who" and circumstances might alter your response in actual situations.

Use the following scale:

> 1 = Very annoying
> 2 = Somewhat bothersome
> 3 = Doesn't usually bother me
> 4 = Feel OK
> 5 = Will probably feel very positive

Indicate in general how you feel about persons who

1. Shout at you in anger
2. Slap you on the back in greeting you _____
3. Cry in your presence when reading a "sad" book or newspaper item _____
4. Talk in a very loud voice when they are frustrated or upset _____
5. Laugh easily and often _____
6. Are silent and moody when they are mad _____
7. Are silent and moody when they are sad _____
8. Are silent when they are disappointed _____
9. Become emotional whenever things go wrong _____
10. Become emotional whenever something nice happens to them _____
11. Never show any emotions _____
12. Are inconsistent in their open displays of emotion _____

EXERCISE 9–2

Indicate how you usually manage your emotions using the following scale:

> 1 = Express my feelings openly
> 2 = May express my feelings openly to close friends or family
> 3 = Would modify my expression of feelings so that they would not convey the real intensity of the emotion I'm feeling
> 4 = Would keep my feelings to myself

1. I think something is funny but I doubt that others may see it that way.
2. I am very disappointed at not achieving a level or a goal I had hoped to.
3. I am very angry as a result of a great inconvenience caused me by the actions of another person.
4. I am frustrated by unnecessary delays and "red tape" in completing an assigned task.
5. I am awarded a great and unexpected honor.
6. I am saddened by a close personal loss.
7. I am a participant in an exciting event or activity.

In reviewing your responses to the items indicated in Exercises 9-1 and 9-2, can you identify circumstances under which emotional expressions directed at you by others or your own emotions affect how you interact with others?

Diaries and Daily Schedules

As with the autobiography, many of us have kept a diary from time to time. We may recall how we bared our soul in those secret pages, often protected with a little tin lock, that if reread today might help us better understand some of our present behavior and attitudes. Probably today's clients are no more willing than their predecessors to share such recordings, but when a client willingly maintains and shares diary entries with the counselor, they can provide valuable insights into understanding the client and his or her concerns. Some clients will find it easier to present some aspects of their behavior and experiences in writing than in oral communication, and, if so, the counselor may decide to suggest keeping a diary for a period of time.

Another technique for systematically recording the client's daily activities is the daily schedule. This is a simple listing, usually an hour-by-hour accounting, of a client's daily activities. This technique can help the counselor and client understand how the latter is organizing her or his time. Whereas the diary is usually a summary of the day's activities, often with feelings and interpretations, the daily schedule is a more objective presentation of the day's activities. Figure 9-9 shows an example of the less familiar of these two instruments, the daily schedule.

Questionnaires

The questionnaire is an extremely popular nonstandardized instrument with which all of us have had many encounters. Questionnaires appear to be a part of the American way of life because they are constantly used to inventory public reactions, solicit opinions, predict needs, and evaluate a wide range of commodities, services, and activities. This popularity does not, however, belittle their importance as an instrument for the economical collection of data from individual clients or groups of clients.

The questionnaire has a variety of uses for the counselor. In a broad way, it obviously provides an easy way to collect a great deal of information that may be useful in further understanding the client. Also, the questionnaire is a client-participation technique that promises opportunities to advance the self-understanding, at least under some circumstances, of those completing it. More specifically, questionnaires may be designed in such a way as to collect specific types of information related to specific needs of the counseling clientele. Questionnaires may also seek information that validates other data already available to the counselor. Additionally, questionnaires can help identify problems of individuals or groups, as well as their

Diary for		Week of
Morning	**Afternoon**	**Evening**
Monday 6:45 Get up 8:00 Leave for school 8:15–12:15 School	12:15–1:00 Lunch in school cafeteria 1:00–3:30 More school 4:00 Get home 4:00–5:00 Loaf around with friends 5:00–5:30 Go to store for Mom 5:30–6:00 Read evening paper, mostly sports	6:00–7:00 Dinner 7:00–8:00 Watch TV 8:00–9:30 Study English and history 9:30–9:45 Take dog for walk 9:45–10:15 Study French 10:45 Bed
Tuesday: Same as Monday	12:15–12:45 Lunch in school cafeteria 12:45–1:00 Talk to Mr. Leonard 1:00–3:30 Classes 3:30–4:30 Work on chemistry experiment 4:45–6:00 Get home, read paper, listen to CDs	6:00–7:00 Dinner 7:00–8:00 Watch TV 8:00–8:30 Study English and chemistry 8:30–9:00 Watch favorite TV program 9:00–9:30 Study English and chemistry 9:30–9:45 Phone call 9:45–10:15 Study French 10:15 Bed
Wednesday: Same as Monday	12:15–1:00 Bring lunch; eat in Mr. Leonard's class and watch experiment 1:00–3:30 Classes 4:00 Get home 4:00–4:45 Study trig 4:45–5:30 Loaf around with guys who come by	6:00–6:30 Dinner 6:30–8:00 Study for history test 8:00–8:30 Watch TV 8:30–9:45 Study for history test 9:45–10:00 Walk dog 10:00–10:30 Study French 10:50 Bed

Figure 9-9 Daily Schedule.

opinions, attitudes, or values. Questionnaires are a good way to collect needs assessment data as a basis for establishing program objectives and evaluation data as a basis for program improvement.

The usefulness of the instrument, however, will be determined, at least in part, by the kind of information it seeks to collect, the appropriateness of the questionnaire's design, and the skill of the person who administers it.

In questionnaire design, there are certain basic considerations to keep in mind.

1. *Directions:* Indicate the purpose of the instrument and give clear, concise directions for its completion.

2. *Item design:* Design items that are clear, concise, and uncomplicated. Items should solicit only one response and should be stated in such a way that the responder will not be

biased or influenced in how she or he responds. Questionnaire items should also reflect the language level of the anticipated respondents.

3. *Item content:* Questions should be designed to collect the kinds of information appropriate to the assessment purpose of the instrument. However, caution must be taken in eliciting socially sensitive, culturally restricted, or personal information. Even a few such items (e.g., "Would you engage in sexual activity outside of marriage?" or "Have you ever thought of committing a crime?") can arouse resentment or suspicions of some respondents that will affect their response to the total questionnaire as well. Although unsigned questionnaires may secure reasonably accurate group responses to a sensitive topic, the counselor will find such unidentified responses of considerably less value in individual counseling.

4. *Length:* A final consideration, obvious but important, is the length of the questionnaire. Often, we receive questionnaires of such length that we are discouraged from even beginning them. Clients and student populations are no exceptions in their reactions to long questionnaires. Such instruments must be of reasonable length if they are to facilitate the data collection for which they are designed.

Structured Interviews

Another basic and popular technique for increasing a counselor's understanding of the client is the structured interview. This approach not only provides opportunities for client observation under certain controlled conditions but, equally important, enables the counselor to obtain specific information and to explore in-depth behavior or responses. Interviews that are structured are usually planned to serve a particular purpose. Once the purpose has been clearly specified, suitable questions are designed to achieve the goal or purpose of the interview. These questions are usually arranged in some sort of a logical sequence, although the interviewer must be flexible to alter both the nature and sequence of the questions as circumstances suggest.

Although the basic principles of counseling apply to the one-to-one interview (see Chapter 5), it is appropriate at this point to note that the interviewing process and setting, to be successful, should be as natural as possible, not anxiety producing. Because the interviewing setting and process may be comfortable to counselors, they may, on occasion, forget that for the interviewee unfamiliar with either, it can be a frightening experience. Perhaps if you recall you own experiences when called in for an income tax audit by the Internal Revenue Service or when interviewed for a first job, you can appreciate a client's wariness. One must also recognize the possible existence of such human qualities as client forgetfulness, exaggeration, or trying too hard to give the right answer as limitations in some structured interviews.

For an example of a structured interview, let us go again to the Beatty-Tingley High School (Example 9-1) and its high school dropout problem. Once potential dropouts had been identified through combining the rating scale with other data, the counseling staff decided to conduct structured interviews with those students who were willing to do so. The purpose of these interviews was to further explore each student's views and attitudes about school in relation to their educational and career planning. They then proceeded to structure the interview as follows.

Structured Interview

1. Give an introduction and explanation of the purpose of the interview, how we will proceed, and answer any questions

2. First, tell me how it has been going for you in school this year.

3. What have been the best things about school this year?
4. What have you disliked the most about school?
5. How do you spend your time when you're not in school?
6. Have you ever thought of dropping out? If so, what would you plan to do then?
7. How could school be made more enjoyable for you?
8. Let's talk a little about your future—what are your job or career plans?
   (Follow up with questions regarding reasons of choice: long-range goals and further education.)
9. Are there any questions you'd like to ask me? Anything else you'd like to say?
10. Conclude.

You will note that an initial explanation is made of the purpose and procedures of the interview. Also, the questions are structured in such a way as to elicit discussion rather than a yes or no response. Of course, the interviewee is given the opportunity to ask questions or make additional comments before the interview is terminated.

In many agency or clinical settings, this process may be referred to as a *diagnostic interview*. In these settings, the large number of individuals served often necessitates some form of diagnostic workup. Many agencies will use a different diagnostic interview, separating the diagnostic from the counseling process. As noted earlier in this chapter, clinical guidelines such as the *Diagnostic and Statistical Manual of Mental Disorders IV* may be used for this purpose.

Intake Interviews

Initial interviews with clients in agencies, and most other counselor settings too, are usually referred to as intake interviews—or sometimes history interviews. (History interviews are designed to collect facts about the client's life in a systematic way.) This, the intake interview, is a part of the assessment process, when the counselor is seeking information regarding the client's concerns, current status, and perhaps certain personal traits. An assumption behind the intake interview, according to Cormier and Hackney (1993)

> is that the client is coming to counseling for more than one interview and intends to address problems or concerns that involve other people, other settings, and the future, as well as the present. Most counselors try to limit intake interviews to an hour. In order to do this, the counselor must assume responsibility and control over the interview. No attempt is made to make it a "therapeutic session" for the client. The second session can begin to meet those needs. . . .
>
> Because the intake session is different from a regular counseling session, it is helpful if the counselor gives the client an explanation about the purpose and nature of the initial session. You might say something like: "Marie, before counseling gets started, it is helpful if I have some preliminary background information about you. So this time, I'd like to spend the hour getting to know you and asking you some questions about your school, work and family background, and so on. Then at the next session, you will be able to start discussing and working on the specific concerns that brought you to counseling. Do you have any questions about this?"* (pp. 80–81)

---

*From Cormier, L. Sherilyn, and Hackney, Harold, *The Professional Counselor*. Copyright © 1993 by Allyn and Bacon. Reprinted by permission.

GROUP ASSESSMENT TECHNIQUES

Group guidance and counseling techniques were discussed in greater detail in Chapter 7, but it is appropriate in this chapter dealing with nonstandardized assessment techniques to review briefly techniques for assessing the roles and relationships of individuals in groups. The understanding of our clients as total beings is heavily dependent on understanding their group associations. Groups are a natural form of human association. In today's world, the hermit is an almost extinct species; persons are no longer rugged individualists, going it alone. Group associations are natural, and all of us belong to many different and diverse groups. For example, some of us may, within a brief period of 24 hours, associate with our family group, our work group, our social recreation group, a civic group, political group, and church group. In each of these settings, the roles and relationships are significant in shaping our behavior, both within and without the group.

Also, in many of these groups, an outsider would find it difficult to assess roles and relationships accurately by only a casual observation of the group. Probably you have experienced going to a party, a class, or some activity where there are in-group jokes, a history of previous group activities that precluded you, and apparent roles and relationships that you did not understand.

Even experienced group observers such as teachers and counselors find it helpful to use structured assessment instruments on occasion to facilitate accurate understandings of persons in the group setting as well as group interactions themselves. The more popular of these techniques include sociograms, Guess Who? questionnaires, communigrams, and social distance scales.

Sociometric Techniques

Sociometric techniques are basic approaches for the study of social relationships, such as degrees of acceptance, roles, and interactions within groups. Sociometric instruments provide a means for assessing and displaying such information as interpersonal choices made by group members.

Although sociometric devices appear to be relatively easy to devise, administer, and interpret, these impressions are deceiving. In fact, extreme caution and careful planning and analysis should be prerequisites to the use of these methods. In determining the appropriateness of conditions for using sociometric analyses, consider the following.

1. *The length of time the group has been together:* The longer the group has existed, the more likely that the data collected will be meaningful.
2. *The age level of the group:* A general rule of thumb is that the older the participants, the more likely that the information provided will be reliable. J. L. Moreno, the acknowledged founder of modern sociometry, hypothesized that social cohesion develops with age (Moreno, 1960). He reports the cohesion of children's groups up to the age of 6 or 7 to be poor and weak; the cohesion of groups formed by children from 7 to 8 years to age 14 to be relatively high; and the cohesion of groups formed by youths between the ages of 14 and 18 to have become stabilized.
3. *The size of the group:* Groups that are too large or too small will provide less valid information. It is also important to remember that all members of a group must be included in any sociometric studies.

4. *The activity provides a natural opportunity to secure responses:* In order for group members to participate willingly and honestly in sociometric analysis, the group activities should appear logical and meaningful to the members. "What gives every sociometrically defined group its momentum is the 'criterion,' the common motive that draws persons together spontaneously, for a certain end" (Moreno, 1960, p. 97).

5. *The group chosen for study is appropriate to the informational needs of the counselor:* For example, if it is a school counselor seeking to identify the causes of behavior problems in a given classroom, the observation of this same group of students in, for example, a recreational setting outside the classroom would not be as appropriate.

Constructing and Administering the Sociometric Test

From a construction standpoint, the sociometric test or inventory is a very simple instrument. The basic and most important aspect of its construction is the nature of the grouping situation, or criterion, on which it is based; unless the criterion is appropriate to the participants' ages, activities, and actual opportunities for association, the elicited responses will have little sociometric value. More specifically, a criterion or situation must be selected to elicit participants' choices that, when applied, will have practical significance; and to maintain the confidence of those participating, as previously noted, the results must be applied. Examples of school situations that lend themselves well to sociometric studies include assigning students to various committees, setting up small study groups, and organizing class projects. In these cases, and in many others, the selection of associates could appropriately be made by the participants themselves.

When the criterion has been determined, attention must next be directed to the number of choices the participant should make. Although the optimum number of choices has not been determined, it would appear that too few choices would not have the practical values of five or six where, for example, group assignments are to follow. It is recommended that sociometric techniques to be used with school groups contain only positive choices.

Much of the success of a sociometric test hinges upon how well it is administered. The person administering it must be respected and be on good terms with the group members. The actual administration of a sociometric test should be kept highly informal; any resemblance to a typical test situation should be avoided. The instrument itself should never be referred to as a test, nor should the group members be forewarned of its administration (in keeping with sociometric theory, which emphasizes spontaneity as an important aspect of response). For example, in a school setting, sociometric studies are more effective when the teacher merely states without prior or subsequent discussion that the class is going to engage in an activity (e.g., forming committees to give special reports) that requires small groups to be established, and that students' choice of associates are to be used as much as possible as a basis for grouping. The teacher then adds a statement about confidentiality and about the impossibility of honoring every choice of every student. Finally, the students are instructed to write their name at the top of the blank paper or card they will be given, number their paper from one to five, and list in order of preference the names of the students with whom they would like to work.

Cautions in Interpretation

The responses to sociometric questions first should be tabulated and then used to construct a *sociogram*—a graphic depiction of the interpersonal relationships existing in a group at the time a sociometric test is given to its members. A sociometric analysis of group structure requires that a sociogram be constructed. However, if each participant's relative degree of social acceptance is all that is desired, a simple count of the total responses each one receives is sufficient.

As previously noted, sociometric data must be interpreted with a great deal of caution. Sociometric techniques do not analyze or provide interpretations in themselves, but rather initiate or contribute to the assessment or understanding of persons. It is also important to remember that in many group settings the choices of group members may say more about the chooser than the chosen. Finally, we should recognize that some group members may not want to be chosen; they may prefer to be alone or with a few friends in certain group settings.

Perhaps the easiest of the different kinds of sociograms to make is that shown in Figure 9-10. This sociogram uses concentric circles in a targetlike pattern, with each student represented by a number. Only mutual positive choices are shown, and preferential rank is not considered. The highly chosen individuals, or sociometric stars, are placed in the small center circle; the sociometric isolates, students not chosen and who choose no one, are placed in the large outer circle; and all other students are placed in the area between the inner and outer circles, those more frequently chosen being placed closer to the inner circle. Sex is indicated by different geometric designs: the males' numbers are placed within a triangle; the females' numbers are encircled. For even clearer differentiation, males are confined to one side of the figure, females to the other.

The Guess Who? Technique

Another useful sociometric technique is the Guess Who? questionnaire. This technique is best used with relatively well established groups in which members have

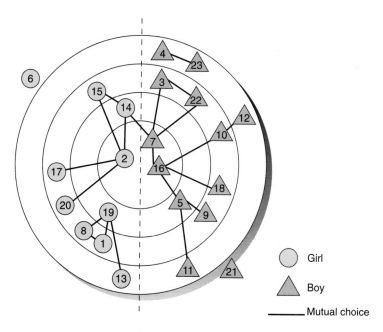

Figure 9-10 Sociogram Depicting Mutual Choices.

had the opportunity to become reasonably well acquainted. It is also most effective when the questions are positive in nature rather than negative. For example, "Who is most friendly?" is a better Guess Who? than "Who is the least friendly?" The Guess Who? questionnaire provides for the association of characteristics or activities with individuals. It can help us understand why some members of the group receive attention, behave in certain ways, or function in certain roles. We may also be able to identify those who are popular with group members and those who receive little, if any, recognition. The Guess Who? instrument is usually designed to collect specific information that counselors, teachers, or other group observers believe would be helpful in working with the group and its individual members. Figure 9-11 presents an example of a short Guess Who? instrument.

The directions for this technique may be altered to permit persons to list all group members they believe are, for example, funny, friendly, helpful, and so on. The teachers or other group observers may use a simple tally system that notes the total number of times each group member was mentioned for each item. A popular variation in school settings is one in which pupils are asked to assume that the class is going to put on a play. They are provided with a list of characters and asked to nominate classmates that could best portray the roles described. Examples of such characters might be as follows.

> This person is known as the arbitrator. He or she is always ready to try and prevent arguments from growing serious by suggesting compromises. He or she usually can see both sides of an argument and as a result rarely takes sides.

Group_____ Date_____

Directions: Write the name of at least one but no more than two persons whom you would identify as most outstanding in your group for the trait or activity listed. Your teacher (counselor, group leader) will use the results from your responses for planning group activities. If you cannot identify a group member for an item, you may leave it blank. It is not necessary to sign your name.

1. Tells the funniest jokes or stories   _____
2. Enjoys funny jokes and stories the most   _____
3. Is the most friendly   _____
4. Is the most helpful   _____
5. Is the most sincere   _____
6. Can always be depended on   _____
7. Has the best imagination   _____
8. Is a good organizer   _____
9. Is optimistic   _____
10. Is a good leader   _____
11. Has special talents   _____
12. Is generous   _____

Figure 9-11   Guess Who? Example.

This person is known as the good humor person. She or he is always pleasant and good-natured. She or he smiles a lot, laughs easily, and rarely shows anger.

One other variation is to tell a story or describe a situation, real or fictional, in which group members are asked to assign to their peers the different characters. Consider Example 9-6.

EXAMPLE 9-6   THE GUESS WHO? TECHNIQUE

Ron Bakersfield is a new student who has just enrolled in Snow Deep High School. In his previous school, Ron was an outstanding and all-round athlete, a good student, and popular with his fellow students. He is a handsome young man who dresses neatly and cleanly, but on this day he is a bit unsure of himself. He wonders whether his new schoolmates will accept him, how long it will take him to get acquainted, who his new friends will be, what his new teachers will be like, and whether he will make the teams.

The school counselor, recognizing Ron as a new student, has called in two of the more popular students in the school to meet Ron and show him around. The first to arrive is Marie Shafer, an attractive, personable girl, who greets Ron with a handshake and a big smile. The counselor suggests to Ron that Marie is known as the sunshine girl in the school because she is always smiling and has a friendly word for everyone. The next arrival is Craig Brewer, whom the counselor introduces as one of the most popular students in the school and whose hobby is photography. Craig appears also to be pleasant but a bit more reserved than Marie. With an assurance that "We'll see that Ron gets around," Craig and Marie usher him out of the counselor's office.

On the way to his first class, Ron is introduced in quick succession to Raquél, whom they refer to as "Miss Energy"; Tom, a serious student who is taking pilot lessons; Rex, who was introduced as the most interesting storyteller in the school; and Denzel, to whom they gave the label, "Mr. Reliable." At this point, Ron is beginning to feel more at home and more welcome in his new school and already sees the prospect of making some good friends with fine qualities.

After reading this brief scenario, to whom would you assign the roles of Ron, Marie, Craig, Raquél, Rex, Denzel, and Tom?

As you may have noted, the Guess Who? technique is relatively easy to use. Scoring is not complicated because a simple counting of the number of individual nominations received for each description will suffice. If both positive and negative descriptors are used, you may subtract the number of negatives from the number of positives received for each characteristic.

Communigrams

Another aspect of group observation and the group process is an assessment of the verbal participation of its members. This is perhaps the easiest communication pattern to observe and record because, in its simplest form, we are recording who talks and how often they talk over a given period. Figure 9-12 charts the number of participations of each member of the group with a tally mark. Each mark represents one communication, usually defined as an uninterrupted statement.

Figure 9-13 is an alternative that uses the same form, but it indicates positions of members within the group to each other and to the group leader. Such reportings not only will identify

Figure 9-12   Communigram:
Participation of Individuals.

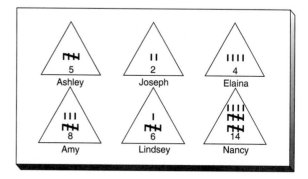

Figure 9-13   Communigram:
Communication of Group Position.
Source: From G. E. Myers and M. T.
Myers, *The Dynamics of Human
Communication,* p. 135. Copyright ©
1973. Used with permission of The
McGraw-Hill Companies.

those who frequently participate versus those who do not but may also, for example, indicate
the amount of discussion generated by certain topics and how members individually react to
one topic and not another; enable comparisons between groups in terms of their frequency of
communication; and, if carried one step further, as noted in Figure 9-14, will also indicate the
direction of communication among members.

Social Distance Scales

Another client participation technique that counselors may find useful is social distance
scales. Most of the existing social distance or social acceptance scales devised for use with
classroom or other school groups are patterned after the scale devised in 1925 by E. S. Bogardus. The Bogardus scale was designed for measuring and comparing attitudes toward different nationalities—specifically, to determine the degree to which various racial and nationality

Figure 9-14   Communigram: Direction of Communication Among
Members.

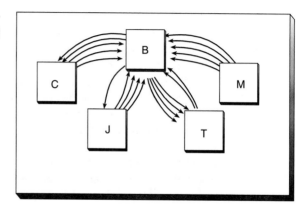

groups were accepted or rejected. Thus, social distance is usually defined by social psychologists as that distance a person indicates exists between other persons and him- or herself. This distance is usually identified through the reaction to statements that measure and compare attitudes of acceptance or rejection of other people. The statements assessing Tommy Rote provide an example of a social distance scale.

Other social distance items may be built around choices such as with whom one would like to take trips, study, or go to a dance. The results from social distance scales may indicate a self social distance and group social distance. The degree of acceptance of the group by a person may be an index of self score and the degree of acceptance of the person by the group would be the group score. Many studies of social distance scales in classrooms have tended to lead to the conclusion that the greatest contribution of social distance scales is in revealing the wide range of acceptance and rejection of any one student in a group. Again, as with many other client participation techniques, there is frequently a tendency to overuse or misinterpret them because of their simplicity of administration. Counselors and other users should be aware that such information does not reveal the why of a person's acceptance or rejection of others. Furthermore, the users of this instrument must determine how they can use negative data, such as indicated group rejection, to the client's advantage.

ECOLOGICAL ASSESSMENT

In recent generations, many people have become environmentally conscious. We are concerned with the preservation of our natural resources, the air we breathe, the water we drink, the fruits and vegetables we eat, and so forth. Too, we note the frequency of publications suggesting the best communities in which to live, the best retirement areas, and the most healthy states. All these examples suggest what we already know: that there is an ongoing relationship between individuals and their environments. As early as 1936 Kurt Lewin, in his *Principles of Topological Psychology*, presented the field of psychology with his mathematical formula of $B = F(PXE)$, or behavior is a result of persons interacting with their environment. Although this formula would seem to be beyond question, it is only in the 1980s and 1990s that we have noted significant attention being given in counseling literature to this concept and the growing importance of ecological psychology.

Thus, although our traditional models of assessment have led us to focus primarily on people, we are now recognizing that people cannot be studied as complete entities outside their environments. As Lewin suggested, behavior always occurs in a specific setting. It is in this context then, and in this chapter discussing nonstandardized assessment, that we examine ecological assessment.

Ecological assessment is concerned with assessing how individuals orient to, operate in, and evaluate their environments. It is interested in how the individual perceives, shapes, is shaped by, and views his or her environments. In this process, counselors would seek to understand the characteristics of such significant settings as the home, school, community, and workplace and their impact on the individual, and, for certain purposes (i. e., prevention programs, minority relationships, etc.), groups of individuals.

All of us seek to optimize our environmental experiences—to find the best environments that fulfill our needs and enable us to achieve our goals. The degree to which we fail to do this will, of course, influence our satisfaction with our lives and mental health. Counselors must become aware of their clients' aspirations and the degree to which their environments are facilitating or handicapping their achievement.

In assessing an environment, counselors should note such ecological variables as the physical, geographic, and meteorological characteristics. They should become aware of the characteristics of the general population as reflected in its norms, values, attitudes, relationships, traditions, and other personal traits.

Counselors should also understand those behavior settings (institutions and agencies) that have control over the behavior occurring within them as well as those that influence external behavior. Ecological assessment would seem to stress the importance of the counselor getting out of the office and into the physical community. This will facilitate an understanding of the environments—the people, agencies, and institutions—with which her or his clients interact.

RECORDS

It has often been suggested that the first slabs of stone that our prehistoric ancestors carved out of the mountains were for the purpose of setting up personnel files. It appears that systems of recording are as old as civilization and that the primary object of much that has been recorded over the ages has been the individual. Record keeping is a reflection of humans' historic curiosity to understand to the fullest extent possible their fellow humans (and just so we will not forget what we have already learned, we record it). Records are important to counselors and other helping professionals in understanding and working effectively with their clients. It is in this context that records are discussed in the following sections.

Basic Considerations

If records or a record system are to serve their potential for client understanding and assistance, certain basic considerations need to be examined before determining the nature and characteristics of the record and its attending system. These include the following.

The Extent of Record Keeping

The ever-increasing and seemingly never-ending preoccupation with record keeping may give all of us cause to wonder how many records we actually have in our name, where they are located, for what purposes, and so on. Extensive records have been maintained by the educational institutions that we attended, for even as students we become aware of the abundant and varied recorded data that the school maintains to understand us better. Figure 9-15 rather accurately (but not too seriously) depicts the varying views to which the many records or types of data might, on occasion, seem to lend themselves.

In a more serious vein, Hummel and Humes (1984) pointed out that

One of the dramatic developments in recent decades was the attention paid to student records. As class action suits developed during the 1960s, there was concern on the part of parents with regard to the use and misuse of pupil records and interpretation. This resulted in legislation in several of the state jurisdictions and culminated in the passage of federal legislation, namely, the Family Rights and Privacy Act (commonly referred to as the Buckley Amendment). Almost immediately the schools had to change their way of doing business. With the passage of this legislation, not only were parents permitted full access to pupil records and the privilege of denying access to them, but

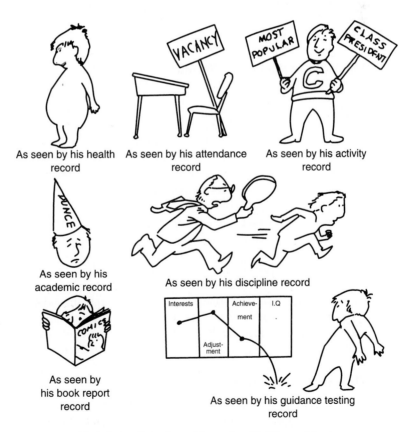

Figure 9-15 "Harry High School" as Seen Through a Multirecord System.

they now had the right to challenge the content of the pupil's record. Accordingly, cumulative records were purged and federal, state, and local guidelines were established for subsequent collection and use.

The new approach to record keeping posed many problems for pupil services. School psychologists, social workers, and school counselors had traditionally been prime contributors to the cumulative record through psychological reports, social case histories, and counselor notations. They now not only had to review the records for appropriateness, but also had to change ways of reporting results and contacts. Perhaps hardest hit were school psychologists who had been accustomed to writing clinical reports designed only for professional view and scrutiny. Reports now had to be written that could be also shared with parents and, at age eighteen, with students. There developed much "tooth gnashing" over watered-down reports that would contribute but little to the presenting problem. This difficulty was finally resolved through the medium of detailed oral reports, usually at team meetings, to be followed by more general written reports. (pp. 358–359)

The advent of the computer and other technological advances have, if anything, seemed to stimulate a challenge to gather and record data in a manner befitting these new developments in data storage, manipulation, and retrieval. Nor can school counselors belittle the importance of the decisions made on the basis of such recorded data—decisions that most frequently influence career directions and educational opportunities. Counselors working with school-aged clients through community agencies and other nonschool settings must also be aware of the extent and impact of school-maintained records.

Who Will Use the Client's Record?

The answer to that question varies across the many places in which counselors function. For example, counselors in private practice may, subject to legal limitations, have exclusive access to a client's records, whereas, at the other end of the continuum, many school counselors may be expected to share client records with school administrative and supervisory personnel, teachers, parents, and, of course, the client. Counselors, ever concerned with client confidentiality, must at the outset determine who legally and ethically will have access to any data recorded in a systematic or institutional manner.

The use of student and client records also raises the question of record security. The increased utilization of computerized record systems requires the exercise of appropriate precautions and restrictions to safeguard client data. Although students and parents may exercise the right to examine their records, that does not lessen the counselor's duty in the school, or in any setting, to provide proper security for those records that are the responsibility of the counseling program. These responsibilities include provisions for the lock-and-key security of client records at all times, instructions and policies for nonprofessional (clerical) handling of data, and stated policies including ethical and legal guidelines for access to and review of data by clients, parents, and others. In determining access to school records, it must be noted that certain records of students are at least quasi-public in nature. The questions that arise are who may inspect such records, for what purposes, and when?

What Are Other Legal and Ethical Considerations?

Practicing counselors, as well as those in preparation, may be confused somewhat by the apparent proliferation of statements by professional organizations providing ethical guidelines for the maintenance and use of client records. However, an examination of statements by the American Counseling Association and the American Psychological Association would indicate little that is in conflict and much in general agreement. These standards are presented in Appendices B and C.

The primary legal concerns of counselors insofar as records and recording are concerned continue to focus on the confidentiality of the counseling records and the right of privileged communications. Although attorneys have possessed this right by common law over the centuries and statutory law has extended this privilege to physicians, clergy, and sometimes psychologists, counselors have limited legal guarantee in terms of statutory provisions.

School counselors must be particularly aware of the provisions of the Family Educational Rights and Privacy Act of 1974. Key statements from this act presented by Flygare (1975) point out the following.

- A student (or his parents) must be given access to his records within 45 days from the time a request is made.
- A student (or his parents) must be granted a hearing by the institution upon request to determine the validity of any document in the student's file.
- Confidential letters or statements placed in the file prior to January 1, 1975, need not be disclosed under the law.
- A student may waive his right of access to confidential letters regarding admissions, honors, or employment.
- An educational institution cannot, with certain exceptions, release personally identifiable information about students.
- Educational institutions must notify students and parents of their rights under the law. (p. 15)

The detailed provisions of this act are presented in Appendix D.

Furthermore, counselors must be aware of the implications of Title IX of the Education Amendments of 1972, effective July 1975, which provides that

no person . . . shall on the basis of sex be excluded from participation in, be denied the benefits of, or be subjected to discrimination under any education program receiving federal financial assistance. (p. 85)

The implications for record keeping are clear; sexual discrimination must not be maintained. That includes standardized test results based on male/female norms, and career exploration activities and counseling that reflect sex-role stereotyping. Counselors must also avoid multicultural discriminations in client record keeping.

School counselors should also be aware of other kinds of unacceptable statements often found in student records. These include statements that may be libelous, slanderous, biased, negative, unverifiable, or confusing.

Counselors must bear in mind that privileged communication is for the benefit of the client. Thus, only clients have the option to waive that right and they may do so if they choose, even if protected legally. It should also be noted that privileged communications are subject to legal limitations.

Privileged communication and confidentiality have often been used interchangeably, even though there is a significant distinction between the two terms. *Privileged communications* refers to the right of the counselor to refuse to divulge confidential information in a course of law. *Confidentiality* represents an ethical guideline in terms of counselor decisions that they should not and will not divulge what has been revealed to them in contacts with their clients.

In this context, we should also note the probability that client and student records will be computerized. As numerous incidents have proven, the confidentiality of so-called secure computerized record and data systems has been violated time and time again. It is obviously a necessity that counselors ensure the security of all client records and record systems.

What Purposes Will the Client's Record Serve?

The use of the client's records will, of course, be determined to a large extent by the answer to the question previously raised—who are the users? There are certain traditional uses appropriate for almost all types of personnel records.

1. They provide an available pool of basic information about the person.
   - Provide a means for recording and preserving meaningful information about the person for later use
   - Assist the users of the information in gaining a better understanding of the person with whom they will be interacting
   - Assist the person on whom the record is maintained to gain new insights and perspectives
2. In addition, counselors use records in
   - Preparation for the counseling interview
   - The development of case studies
   - Client placement or referral
   - Consultation with other therapists, medical personnel, and parents
   - Follow-up and research studies
3. School counselors also use records to identify students who
   - May be in need of counseling assistance
   - Possess special talents or interests
   - May have special needs because of physical disabilities, for example
4. School records assist faculty and parents in gaining a better understanding of the individual student, which, it is hoped, may contribute to positive student-parent and student-teacher relationships.
   - Assist the individual student to gain self-understanding
   - Contribute to school and community needs assessments of school-aged populations
   - Facilitate the orientation of new pupils

These listings are meant to be illustrative only and not exclusive, because any practicing counselor could readily expand on them.

Record Interpretation

The interpretation of any kind of counseling or personnel record will obviously be limited by the data recorded and the skill and understanding of the user. Some guidelines or safeguards include the following.

- Records provide only clues to behavior—no more, and some clues are relevant whereas others are not.
- Does the present (the time at which you are examining the record data) compare to the past (the time when the data were originally recorded)?
- Look for trends or significant changes, but be aware of the fact that many people have unique patterns of growth and development.
- Feelings, attitudes, and intensity of emotions seldom show in recorded information.
- Distinguish between symptoms and causes.
- Determine whether record data are based on substantial facts or merely represent opinions.
- Remember that records present only a small sample of the client's behavior.
- School records, especially, can also provide opportunities to examine certain habitual performance measures, such as attendance, grades, and health.

SUMMARY

This chapter has presented an overview of non-standardized techniques that may be used in human assessment. Although many nonstandardized techniques cannot lay claim to either the validity or reliability of standardized instruments, they nonetheless give the counselor a wide range of data collection options from which to choose, according to the dictates of the counseling situation and the assessment needs of one's clients.

Observation was noted as the most popular of the techniques usually used to assess others; however, in order that it be as accurate and meaningful as possible, we suggested that some forms for recording observation, such as anecdotal records, and forms for further directing observations toward specific characteristics, such as rating scales and checklists, might be used. In this regard, the popularity (and sophistication) of the DSM-IV in clinical settings was noted.

Autobiographies and questionnaires were suggested as techniques in which useful information can be collected. Assessing behavior and roles in groups by techniques such as sociograms, communigrams, social distance scales, and role playing were suggested. The growing interest in ecological assessment was also discussed. There followed an examination of the role of records in human assessment and some of the legal and ethical considerations in record keeping. Assessment, both standardized and nonstandardized, can play an important role in career planning and decision making. Chapter 10 examines this important activity.

DISCUSSION QUESTIONS

1.   If you have taken courses in sociology, anthropology, economics, political science, and the like, have you felt they helped you understand others better? What were these courses? How were they helpful?

2.   Have you ever found your observations of a situation, scene, or person differ from other observers present at the same time? How do you account for these differences?

3.   When you meet someone for the first time, what do you look for or observe that influences your initial impressions?

4.   What autobiographies have you read by famous people? Did any of these provide you with special insights into the writer? Why?

5.   Have you ever kept a diary? What prompted you to keep one? Did it help you understand yourself better in any way? Discuss your responses.

6.   In assessment, would you prefer to have your own traits assessed by standardized tests or rating scales? Why?

7.   What traits or characteristics do you observe when you meet someone for the first time?

8. What are examples of customs, folkways, mores, and laws that influence patterns of normal and abnormal behavior?

9. If you were to write your autobiography for publication, what title would you use?

CLASS ACTIVITIES

1. Identify someone in the class that you are barely acquainted with. Design an observation instrument to guide your observations for the next week. At the end of the week, discuss how your instrument has increased your understanding of the individual.

2. In small groups, develop a checklist that might be used to evaluate candidates applying for admission to a master's-level counselor preparation program. Share and discuss with the class.

3. In small groups, design a rating scale to assess individual personal relationship skills. Share and discuss.

4. In small groups, members are instructed to share learnings from working, living near, and/or contacts with people from different cultures.

SELECTED READINGS

Elliott, T. R. (1993). Training psychology graduate students in assessment for rehabilitation settings. In R. L. Glueckauf, L. B. Sechrest, G. R. Bond, & E. C. McDonel (Eds.), *Improving assessment in rehabilitation and health* (pp. 196–211). Newbury Park, CA: Sage.

Ickes, W. J. (Ed.). (1997). *Empathic accuracy*. New York: Guilford Press.

Ivey, A. (1982). Towards less of the same: Rethinking the assessment process. *Measurement and Evaluation in Guidance, 15* (1), 82–86.

Ponterotto, J. G., & Furlong, M. J. (1985). Evaluating counselor effectiveness: A critical review of rating scale instruments. *Journal of Counseling Psychology, 32* (4), 597–616.

Sodowsky, G. R., Kuo-Jackson, P. Y., & Loya, G. J. (1997). Outcome of training in the philosophy of assessment: Multicultural counseling com-

petencies. In D. B. Pope-Davis & H. L. K. Coleman (Eds.), *Multicultural counseling competencies: Assessment, education and training and supervision* (pp. 3–42). Thousand Oaks, CA: Sage.

Yesseldyke, J., & Marston, D. (1982). Gathering decision-making information through the use of non–test-based methods. *Measurement and Evaluation in Guidance, 15* (1), 58–69.

RESEARCH OF INTEREST

Bernstein, D. P., Kasapis, C., Bergman, A., & Weld, E. (1997). Assessing AXIS II disorders by informant interview. *Journal of Personality Disorders, 11* (2), 158–167.

Abstract

This study determined the diagnostic agreement between the assessment methods of obtaining diagnostic data directly through patients and through interviews with knowledgeable informants, as well as their relative contribution to the formulation of consensus diagnoses. Sixty-two psychiatric subjects were assessed directly with the Structured Interview for *DSM-III* Personality Disorders (SIDP) and were asked to nominate an informant—either a family member or friend—to provide information about the subject in an interview with the same instrument. Diagnostic agreement between subject-based and informant-based personality disorder interviews was poor, confirming the findings of two previous studies. Information obtained from subjects tended to be given greater weight in formulating consensus diagnoses than information provided by informants. However, about one quarter of diagnostic disagreements were resolved in favor of informant-based information. In contrast to a previous study, the inclusion of informant information did not appear to reveal greater psychopathology in subjects. Supplementing direct patient interviews with data provided by a knowledgeable informant appears to enhance the resolution of some personality disorder diagnoses.

Lambert, M. J., Hatch, D. R., Kingston, M. D., & Edwards, B. C. (1986). Zung, Beck, and Hamilton

Rating Scales as measures of treatment outcome: A meta-analytic comparison. *Journal of Consulting and Clinical Psychology, 54* (1), 54–59.

Abstract

Treatment studies using the Zung Self-Rating Scale, the Beck Depression Inventory, and the Hamilton Rating Scale for Depression as dependent measures were viewed to determine whether these scales provide comparable data for assessing treatment effects. Results indicated that the Zung and the Beck showed less change in depression following treatment than did the Hamilton.

Morran, D. K., Kurpius, D .J., Brack, G., & Rozecki, T. G. (1994). Relationship between counselors' clinical hypotheses and client ratings of counselor effectiveness. *Journal of Counseling and Development, 72* (6), 655–660.

Abstract

A total of 27 graduate counseling students participated as counselors and clients. Counselors completed a Clinical Hypotheses Exercise Form. Clients completed the Counselor Rating Form—Short Version following sessions. Counselors able to formulate more multidimensional and comprehensive clinical hypotheses (accounting for a broader spectrum of client data dimensions) and who were able to present multiple options for testing hypotheses were judged more effective. Higher ratings were associated with more hypothesis dimensions within the clinical hypothesis statement, a higher frequency of supportive information units to substantiate the hypothesis, higher quality of the hypothesis and supportive statements, and a higher frequency of questions listed to test the validity of the hypothesis.

Parker, G., Hadzi-Pavlovic, D., Sengoz, A., & Boyce, P. (1994). A brief self-report depression measure assessing mood state and social impairment. *Journal of Affective Disorders, 30* (2), 133–142.

Abstract

A brief self-report measure of depression severity was developed that assesses mood state and functional impairment and is independent of features weighted to any one depressive type. Analyses were undertaken among 360 psychiatric patients. Mood severity and functional impairment scores demonstrated some independence among subjects. Subjects with a melancholic depressive type (categorized by four differing systems) differed from residual non-melancholic depressed patients by having higher impairment scores, but the assigned groups did not differ by mood severity scores. Advantages of the measure were summarized.

Piotrowski, C., & Keller, J. W. (1984). Psychological testing: Trends in master's-level counseling psychology programs. *Teaching of Psychology, 11* (4), 244–245.

Abstract

A survey that investigated the status of psychodiagnostic testing in master's-level counseling (terminal) programs showed that whereas the majority of respondents felt that master's graduates should be familiar with projective techniques such as the Rorschach and TAT, few advocated projective personality assessment as part of the required curriculum.

Spengler, P. M., Strohmer, D. C., Dixon, D. N., & Shivy, V. A. (1995). A scientist-practitioner model of psychological assessment: Implications for training, practice, and research. *Counseling Psychologist, 23* (3), 506–534.

Abstract

This article proposes a prototype for a scientist-practitioner model of psychological assessment that integrates theory and research on human inference, judgment, and decision making; threats to accurate clinical prediction; and counselor characteristics associated with effective judgment processes. Issues related to counseling psychologists' application of research findings and use of scientific reasoning in counseling practice are explored, including implications for training, research, and practice.

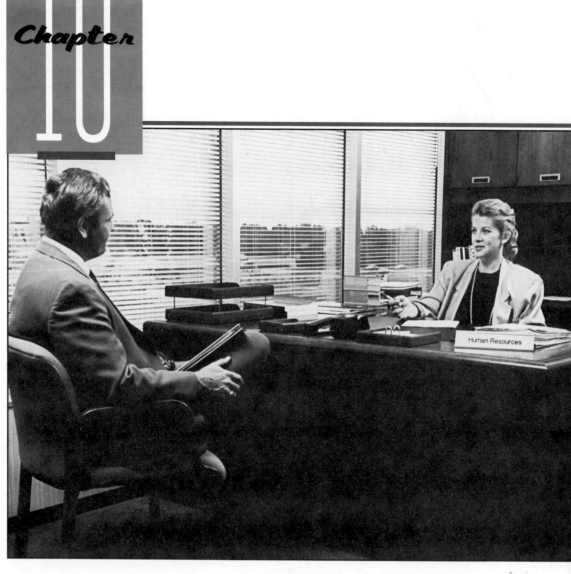

Counseling for Career Planning and Decision Making

As noted in Chapter 1, the counseling movement in the United States has had a long association with and concern for career development and decision making. This chapter will introduce you to this traditional area of counselor activity. The chapter's objectives are to (a) describe specific interests in and influences on career planning, (b) present popular theories of career decision making, and (c) examine career planning and counseling in various settings.

During its early years, organized counseling efforts consisted primarily of vocational guidance. This interest, originating with Parsons, was an outgrowth of a concern for the complexity of the world of work and the resultant difficulty in career planning, a concept that is still viable today. As originally practiced by Parsons and his associates, the concept of matching youths with jobs, based on the characteristics of both, has also had a long and traditional association with the counseling movement.

As this concept was broadened and other basic activities were added in the 1920s and 1930s, vocational guidance became a service activity most frequently identified with the provision of occupational and educational information. In the late 1950s and 1960s, with the original impetus from the National Defense Education Act of 1958, placement and follow-up also became significant activities of the vocational or career guidance phase of counseling programs. Thus, for nearly 60 years the counseling movement had been the caretaker for career planning in U.S. schools and agencies.

In 1971, however, the United States Office of Education, through the Commissioner of Education at that time, Sidney P. Marland, Jr., committed more than $9 million of discretionary funds to research and development projects focusing on the establishment of comprehensive career education models. With this act, the concept of career education as an all-school responsibility was launched, and counselors were no longer the sole designated professionals for providing career counseling and guidance for students in schools.

In the 1990s, a trend has emerged toward once again recognizing counselors as the main professionals in providing career guidance and counseling. This trend has included the development and recognition of career counseling specialists and the establishment of career centers serving special populations such as college students, women, minorities, and retirees. As previously noted, projected changes in the workplace in the immediate future will bring about further demands for career counseling, not just in schools but in nonschool settings as well.

DEFINITIONS AND CLARIFICATIONS

An outgrowth of the increased attention to career needs and the accompanying emphasis on career counseling and guidance has been a proliferation of definitions, with attending confusion, seeking to differentiate among such terms as *career education*, *career development*, *career guidance*, *vocational education*, and *human development*. In this chapter and elsewhere in this text, the following definitions apply.

- *Career:* A career is the sum total of one's work experiences in a general occupational category such as teaching, accounting, medicine, or sales.
- *Occupation:* A specific job or work activity.
- *Career development:* That aspect of one's total development that emphasizes learning about, preparation for, entry into, and progression in the world of work.

- *Career education:* Those planned-for educational experiences that facilitate a person's career development and preparation for the world of work. The totality of experiences through which one learns about and prepares for engaging in work as part of a way of living. A primary responsibility of the school with an emphasis on learning about, planning for, and preparing to enter a career.
- *Career guidance:* Those activities that are carried out by counselors in a variety of settings for the purpose of stimulating and facilitating career development in persons over their working lifetimes. These activities include assistance in career planning, decision making, and adjustment.
- *Occupational information:* Data concerning training and related educational programs, careers, career patterns, and employment trends and opportunities.
- *Vocation:* A trade or occupation.
- *Vocational education:* Education that is preparatory for a career in a vocational or technical field.

These rather limited definitions are perhaps at one end of the continuum. For example, a career is sometimes defined as the sum total of a person's life experiences and lifestyles, whereas career education is frequently viewed as consisting of all activities and experiences, planned or otherwise, that prepare the person for work. However, straightforward and concise—although limited—definitions are most practical in specific planning for programs of career counseling development or education.

It should also be noted, that, though differing in definition, career development, career education, and career counseling are interrelated. One without the other is ineffective and meaningless. As career education stimulates career development, career counseling provides direction for career education and development.

Counselors must also recognize that career education and complementary programs of career counseling should be developmental in nature and thus not limited to a particular age group. Career development across the life span is the appropriate theme for now and the foreseeable future.

CURRENT INTERESTS IN CAREER PLANNING

The present high level of interest in career planning was initiated when Sidney Marland made his plea for "career education now" in a speech to the National Association of Secondary School Principals at its convention in Houston in 1971. Since then, the concept has gained widespread acceptance in the educational establishment in the United States. Educators from every field and discipline have been involved in the movement. Additionally, many state legislatures passed career education legislation, and career education became a mandate of the U.S. Congress when Public Law 93-380 was signed by former President Ford in August 1974. In less than a decade, more than ten major national associations endorsed career education, hundreds of publications on career education were published and distributed, and an astounding array of proponents and interpreters of the career education concept emerged.

Continued interest in career guidance and counseling programs was reflected in the Carl D. Perkins Vocational Education Act (Public Law 98-524) of 1984, which mandated programs designed to assist individuals in developing self-assessment, career-planning, career decision-making, and employability skills. Two federal acts indicate the government's continuing interest in providing career assistance to youth preparing to enter the labor force: (a) the amendments in 1992 to the Job Training Partnerships Act, a partnership of federal, state, and local agencies, with school systems, employers and their communities to help youth acquire the skills and knowledge they need to assume full participation in society; and (b) the School-to-Work Transition Act of 1994, which provided funding to bring together schools and their pupils, parents, and communities and their businesses to fashion America's future workforce. The latter act includes career counseling and a mandate for career exploration in schools to make the connection from school to work a realistic one. The major purpose of the act is to link what students learn in school to what they will need to know to succeed in the world of work.

In 1990, the U.S. Congress passed the Americans with Disabilities Act, which extended the prohibition of job-related discrimination (initially in the Rehabilitation Act of 1973) to all firms that employ 15 or more people. Also, the act appears to encourage equal access to counseling services by workers with disabilities.

Significant national conferences attracted professional counselors such as the 20/20 Conference: Building Strong School Counseling Programs, held in Washington, DC, in 1987; The National Career Development Association's Diamond Jubilee Conference, Orlando, Florida, in January 1988; the first Association for Counselor Education and Supervision national conference in St. Louis in October 1988, which established three national task forces, including one chaired by Dr. Kenneth Hoyt, to examine national concerns in the world of work; and a series of national conferences sponsored or cosponsored by the National Career Development Association, including the Daytona Beach Conference of 1997 examining "Careers and Technology." These conferences reflect the interest and commitment of the counseling profession in a continued and major involvement in career development, counseling, and guidance.

In addition, the need for this assistance became increasingly apparent in the late 1980s and early 1990s as career-related problems such as youth unemployment, underemployment, midlife career changes, discrimination in the workplace, and so forth, became major societal issues. Further reflecting the need for planned career assistance programs for all ages has been the establishment of career counseling centers on many campuses, women's (career) centers, and other community centers focusing on the special career needs of individuals as we move toward a new century.

Too, career development has moved from the stage theories of the 1940s, 1950s, 1960s, and early 1970s in which individuals explored, made decisions about, prepared for, and entered into careers by early adulthood and stayed until retirement, to the concept of recent decades: career development across the life span. The current and projected demands of the workplace, plus the lifelong working potential of the individual, have established new career variables that include workers experiencing a variety of jobs and related educational experiences, across an increasingly healthier and longer lifetime. The career development of the individual promises to be continuous and ongoing; thus, career counseling and assistance programs must be available to all ages from elementary school children to the elderly. By the same token, counselors may assist client populations in settings ranging from elementary schools to senior citizen centers to meet the needs of career development across the life span.

THE CHANGING NATURE OF THE WORLD OF WORK

In addition to the needs that prompted the career education movement and have more recently created a renewed interest in career counseling and guidance, other needs also have been generated by significant changes in some of our traditional concepts of careers and work. Symptomatic of these changes are the following points.

1. No longer one career—one's lifetime work

Whereas our ancestors, perhaps even our parents, could, on identifying their life's work, enter into their career for life, more and more persons entering the workforce in the late 1990s and early generations of the 21st century will have, at the very least, three to seven significant careers over the span of their life's work. From a career standpoint, we are now living in an age in which the rapidity of technological development can affect what we do and how we do it almost overnight. Counselors are being more frequently reminded that such changes can result in increasing numbers of adults who, either by choice or necessity, will be making career decisions throughout their working life span.

2. Going, going, gone! Men-only, women-only, White-only careers

The influx of women into the workplace since World War II has changed "who" is working. "Where" they are working has also changed as recent generations have witnessed the elimination of many barriers which in the past limited certain professions and occupations to certain populations or sexes. Career exclusiveness, for example, excluded women from traditional male occupations such as engineering, airline piloting, and taxicab and truck driving, to mention but a few. These once male-dominated careers (and some for women, such as nursing) have been effectively challenged not only in the courts, but, more importantly, in the world of work.

Additionally, the antidiscrimination and antipoverty movements have further challenged the exclusiveness of certain careers that were once limited to only racial majority members or upper-socioeconomic income populations.

All projections point to the early years of the new century as a time when the percentage of adult women in the workforce will equal that of the male population. Further, although the invisible glass ceiling restricting the advancement of women and minorities into managerial and supervisory positions still subtly exists, progress has and will continue to be made, especially in the new and emerging industries.

Youth unemployment among minorities continues to be of national concern, and the projected immigration influx from Central and South America could further inflate these numbers in the years ahead. It should also be noted that immigrants, along with women and minorities, are underrepresented in those career areas experiencing the greatest growth. Too, minority youth and women single parents are often handicapped in the job market by their poverty status.

So, although progress has and will continue to be made, much remains to be done to ensure equality of career opportunity for all regardless of gender, race, or socioeconomic status. This presents a major challenge to counselors and the counseling profession.

3. No longer the old college try and tie

Much has also been written in recent years regarding the decrease of demand in the job market for the college graduate. Although this is not necessarily a rationale for declining college enrollments in some fields, as some claim, it indicates that career opportunities are no longer tied directly to the level and locale of educational preparation, but may be more appropriately linked to the career relevancy of one's educational preparation and the opportunities available in a constantly shifting job market.

Further, although we anticipate the future workplaces will need more workers with post–high school education, this growth will probably occur in occupations taught primarily in vocational and technical schools and colleges. Here again, the underrepresentation of minorities in all postsecondary educational institutions, including four-year colleges and universities, must be an active concern of counselors, especially in educational settings.

4. No longer can the future be totally predicted by the present
In other times, people interested in charting their future could make many appropriate preparations and predictions based on their knowledge of the present or even the past. However, changing technology affecting the workplace, plus drastic changes in the international marketplace, and changes in the makeup of our workforce have made it increasingly difficult, if not almost impossible, in recent years to adequately predict the future by examining only the present and the past.

As a matter of fact, the last half of the 20th century has witnessed the virtual disappearance of the small mom-and-pop family-run business, the locally owned corner service station, the owner-on-the-premises "we deliver" grocery store, and the neighborhood drug store—soda fountain and all! All are now a part of the nostalgia for our older generation, replaced by the corporate-run supermarket, chain drug store, and mega-corporate oil company. Too, many workers now work for distant owners or corporate boards with declining input into the business or industry of which they are a part. All of this serves as a reminder that changes in the way America earns its living brings about changes in how Americans live. We live in an interactive society where work influences not only how we earn our living but also how we live our life.

This accelerated rate of change in modern society prevents us from assuming, as we might have in the past, that the future will be similar to the present. In fact, we must recognize that much present planning is being based on what is anticipated in the future. Furthermore, this science of future predicting has become an increasingly precise and accurate one. Even without the scientific evidence, the one certainty we can predict for the future is that it will be different.

5. No longer is one in charge of one's own destiny
It is clear that the day of the rugged individualist—one who would achieve his or her own destiny—is but a memory. In today's complicated society with its numerous interacting forces, many variables affect the destiny of people over which they have little or no control and of which many are unaware. Although people can plan their futures, they must also consider alternatives. Not the least of these is the reality of the international marketplace which has resulted in the replacement of a national labor market by a global one. International competition has severe implications for the American worker in terms of wages and benefits, job security, and where they work. With these changes has come a dramatic increase in the employment of temps (workers employed for temporary periods, usually without benefits) and a transitory workforce moving from geographic locale to locale. Because these and other factors will lessen the individual's control over career destiny, it is clear that the need for qualified career counselors will be unprecedented.

THEORIES OF CAREER DEVELOPMENT AND DECISION MAKING

One of the more fascinating aspects of the study of careers, both formally and informally, is the never-ending attempt to identify why people end up in certain careers. In history we may read about the factors that resulted in a lifetime of politics for Franklin D. Roosevelt; the multi-career talents of Benjamin Franklin, Thomas Jefferson, or George Washington Carver; the cowboy who became O. Henry, the famous author; a 19th-century suffragist, Elizabeth Cady Stanton, who became a dazzling patriot and activist; and more recently, the actor who became president of the United States, Ronald Reagan. At one time or another, we have probably been curious about the career decisions of friends and acquaintances. But to become more personal, why are you in your present career? What influenced your career planning and decision making?

You probably have been asked this question before, and as you responded, you may have analyzed a set of facts that appeared relevant to your decisions. You presented some plausible explanation. Many of us have also offered career advice to others, based on our own personal career experiences or personal theory of career development. Even so, one must recognize the biases and limitations of one's own experiences. To develop a theory to a usable state, it is necessary to gather data that are relevant, study the relationships between the data, and finally, speculate on what these mean. One's speculations are stated as hypotheses, explanations, or predictions, which can be tested. If a theory proves to have some validity, it will be built on and developed further through research and application activities.

Counselors and others who work as helping professionals with youth and adults for their career development, planning, and adjustment must have some understanding of the better recognized and researched theories of career development that have emerged in the last half of the 20th century. An understanding of such theories gives the practicing counselor a knowledge of the studies of others, usually specialists in the field. They provide a rationale for counselor action that goes beyond personal experience and intuition.

Because many disciplines (education, economics, psychology, sociology) are actively engaged in investigating various career questions, a multitude of theories have emerged. Both the numbers of theories and the extensiveness of investigation of some preclude any attempt here to analyze the various major theories in detail. Also, it is appropriate to point out that the diversity which exists among human beings and the constantly changing nature of work, life, and our environments, make theoretical conception difficult and less than absolute to say the least.

In this regard, we would further note that in recent years the relevancy of many of the traditional theories of career choice have been examined for their appropriateness for the high-tech information-processing work world of the 1990s and 2000s and for a workforce with a significant female and minority population. Further, as noted earlier, the drastic changes in career stability for the future generations will continually challenge the traditional career theories. However, we suggest that proven theories, though in need of ongoing updating, can still provide us with some appropriate guidelines. With these limitations in mind, let us explore several of the more popular categories for illustrative purposes only, without any intent to suggest or recommend a particular theoretical approach.

The Process Theories

The process theories state, in effect, that occupational choice and eventual entry is a process consisting of stages or steps that the individual will go through. For example, more then 40 years ago Ginzberg, Ginsburg, Axelrad, and Herma (1951) analyzed the process of occupational decision making in terms of three periods: fantasy choices, tentative choices, and realistic choices. This theory suggests a process that moves increasingly toward realism in career decision making as one becomes older.

In 1972, Ginzberg modified the original theory to suggest that the process of vocational choice and development is lifelong and open-ended. In the process, achieving the optimum is more appropriate to describe the ongoing efforts of persons as they seek to find the most suitable job. Originally, Ginzberg and colleagues suggested that the crystallization of occupational choice inevitably had the quality of compromise. Ginzberg's revised theory also places considerable weight on constraints such as family income and situation, parental attitudes and values, opportunities in the world of work, and value orientations. Both the early theory and Ginzberg's later revision suggest the importance of the early school years in influencing later career planning.

Blau, Gustad, Jessor, Parnes, and Wilcock (1956) conceived of occupational choice as a process of compromise, continually modified, between preferences for and expectations of being able to get into various occupations. They identify eight factors determining entry into an occupation. Four of these characterize the occupation: demand, technical (functional) qualifications, personal (nonfunctional) qualifications, and rewards. Those characterizing the person were information about an occupation, technical skills, social characteristics, and value orientations.

Ginzberg's revisions seem cognizant of the changes emerging in the world of work (i.e., career decision making across the life span and repeatedly assessing their career goals in light of the changing world of work).

The Developmental Theories

The developmental theories relevant to career planning view career development as one aspect of a person's total development. Donald Super, a leading researcher in career or vocational development theory since the 1950s, formulated a theory of vocational development in 1953 that became a basis for later research and theory.

Super (1975) states that like other aspects of development, vocational development may be conceived of as beginning early in life and proceeding along a continuum until late in life, passing through the stages of growth, exploration, establishment, maintenance, and decline. At each of these stages, the person must master increasingly difficult tasks. Such a concept of vocational development leads logically, according to Super, to that of vocational maturity as denoting the degree of development reached on such a continuum.

In revisions to Super's original theory, Super, Starishevsky, Matlin, and Jordaan (1963) point out that one's occupation makes possible the playing of a role appropriate to the self-concept of the person. Role playing, stimulated by the process of identification, further facilitates the development of the vocational self-concept among youth. This does not suggest, however, that a person's characteristics or traits are so unique that only a specific type of person would qualify. To the contrary, Super suggests that the range of individual abilities and the latitude within occupational areas result in a multipotential of appropriate opportunities for most people.

More recently, Super (1990) has presented a life-span development theory based on 14 propositions, as follows.

1. People differ in their abilities and personalities, needs, values, interests, traits, and self-concepts.
2. People are qualified, by virtue of these characteristics, each for a number of occupations.

3. Each occupation requires a characteristic pattern of abilities and personality traits—with tolerances wide enough to allow both some variety of occupations for each individual and some variety of individuals in each occupation.

4. Vocational preferences and competencies, the situations in which people live and work, and, hence, their self-concepts, change with time and experience, although self-concepts, as products of social learning, are increasingly stable from late adolescence until late maturity, providing some continuity in choice and adjustment.

5. This process of change may be summed up in a series of life stages (a "maxicycle") characterized as a sequence of growth, exploration, establishment, maintenance, and decline, and these stages may in turn be subdivided into (a) the fantasy, tentative, and realistic phases of the exploratory stage and (b) the trial and stable phases of the establishment stage. A small (mini) cycle takes place in transitions from one stage to the next or each time an individual is destabilized by a reduction in force, changes in type of personnel needs, illness or injury, or other socioeconomic or personal events. Such unstable or multiple-trial careers involve new growth, re-exploration, and reestablishment (recycling).

6. The nature of the career pattern—that is, the occupational level attained and the sequence, frequency, and duration of trial and stable jobs—is determined by the individual's parental socioeconomic level, mental ability, education, skills, personality characteristics (needs, values, interests, traits, and self-concepts), and career maturity and by the opportunities to which he or she is exposed.

7. Success in coping with the demands of the environment and of the organism in that context at any given life-career stage depends on the readiness of the individual to cope with these demands (that is, on his or her career maturity).

8. Career maturity is a hypothetical construct. Its operational definition is perhaps as difficult to formulate as is that of intelligence, but its history is much briefer and its achievements even less definite.

9. Development through the life stages can be guided partly by facilitating the maturing of abilities and interests and partly by aiding in reality testing and in the development of self-concepts.

10. The process of career development is essentially that of developing and implementing occupational self-concepts. It is a synthesizing and compromising process in which the self-concept is a product of the interaction of inherited aptitudes, physical makeup, opportunity to observe and play various roles, and evaluations of the extent to which the results of role playing meet the approval of superiors and fellows (interactive learning).

11. The process of synthesis of or compromise between individual and social factors, between self-concepts and reality, is one of role playing and of learning from feedback, whether the role is played in fantasy, in the counseling interview, or in such real-life activities as classes, clubs, part-time work, and entry jobs.

12. Work satisfactions and life satisfactions depend on the extent to which the individual finds adequate outlets for abilities, needs, values, interests, personality traits, and self-concepts. They depend on establishment in a type of work, a work situation, and a way of life in which one can play the kind of role that growth and exploratory experiences have led one to consider congenial and appropriate.

13. The degree of satisfaction people attain from work is proportional to the degree to which they have been able to implement self-concepts.

14. Work and occupation provide a focus for personality organization for most men and women, although for some persons this focus is peripheral, incidental, or even nonexistent. Then other foci, such as leisure activities and homemaking, may be central. (Social traditions, such as gender-role stereotyping and modeling, racial and ethnic biases, and the opportunity structure,

as well as individual differences, are important determinants of preferences for such roles as worker, student, leisurite, homemaker, and citizen.) (pp. 206–208)

Another popular theory, very often referred to as classic, was Havighurst's developmental tasks theory. Havighurst (1964) discusses vocational development as a lifelong process consisting of six stages from childhood to old age. Each age period has characteristic tasks that must be successfully achieved if a person is to attain happiness and success with tasks appropriate to the vocational stages that follow. The developmental stages are outlined in Table 10-1.

Another classic theory, developed by E. H. Erikson, identified eight psychosocial stages from birth through death. Each of these stages consists of a developmental crisis that must be resolved. Depending on the reactions of individuals, a conflict is involved with each crisis that will be resolved in a positive or negative way. The successful accomplishments in early stages will contribute to the individual's ability to resolve future crises thus creating an interdependence

TABLE 10-1 Vocational Development: A Lifelong Process

Stages of vocational development	Age
I. Identification with a worker Father, mother, other significant persons. The concept of Working becomes an essential part of the ego-ideal.	5–10
II. Acquiring the basic habits of industry Learning to organize one's time and energy to get a piece of work done. School work, chores. Learning to put work ahead of play in appropriate situations.	10–15
III. Acquiring identity as a worker in the occupational structure Choosing and preparing for an occupation. Getting work experience as a basis for occupational choice and for assurance of economic independence.	15–25
IV. Becoming a productive person Mastering the skills of one's occupation. Moving up the ladder with one's occupation.	25–40
V. Maintaining a productive society Emphasis shifts toward the societal and away from the individual aspect of the worker's role. The individual sees himself as a responsible citizen in a productive society. He pays attention to the civic responsibility attached to his job. The individual is at the peak of his occupational career and has time and energy to adorn it with broader types of activity. He pays attention to inducting younger people into stages III and IV.	40–70
VI. Contemplating a productive and responsible life This person is retired from work or is in the process of withdrawing from the worker's role. He looks back over his work life with satisfaction, sees that a personal social contribution has been made, and is pleased with it. While he may not have achieved all of his ambitions, he accepts life and believes in himself as a productive person.	70–+

Source: Reprinted from R. J. Havighurst, *Youth in Exploration and Man Emergent* (1964), p. 216. © American Counseling Association. No further reproduction authorized without written permission of the American Counseling Association.

among the stages. However, an undesirable or unhealthy resolution of a psychosocial crisis can result in difficulties throughout one's later life. It is possible, however, that an unsatisfactory resolution may later be altered to satisfactory outcomes when proper conditions present themselves. The importance of meeting the personal, cultural, cognitive, and social- emotional needs of individuals as they develop has obvious implications for the individual's career development and later adjustments. Erikson's stages are presented in Table 10-2.

Personality Theories

Personality theories view vocational preferences as expressions of personality. They suggest that much career-seeking behavior is an outgrowth of efforts to, in effect, match one's individual characteristics with those of a specific occupational field. The original personality the-

TABLE 10-2 Erikson's Stages of Personal and Social Development

As people grow, they face a series of psychosocial crises that shape personality, according to Erik Erikson. Each crisis focuses on a particular aspect of personality and each involves the person's relationship with other people.

	Approximate ages	Psychosocial crises	Significant relationships	Psychosocial emphasis
I	Birth to 18 mo.	Trust vs. mistrust	Maternal person	To get To give in return
II	18 mo. to 3 yr.	Autonomy vs. doubt	Parental persons	To hold on To let go
III	3 to 6 yr.	Initiative vs. guilt	Basic family	To make (= going after) To "make like" (= playing)
IV	6 to 12 yr.	Industry vs. inferiority	Neighborhood, school	To make things To make things together
V	12 to 18 yr.	Identity vs. role confusion	Peer groups and models of leadership	To be oneself (or not to be) To share being oneself
VI	Young adulthood	Intimacy vs. isolation	Partners in friendship, sex, competition, cooperation	To lose and find oneself in another
VII	Middle adulthood	Generativity vs. self-absorption	Divided labor and shared household	To take care of
VIII	Late adulthood	Integrity vs. despair	"Mankind" "My kind"	To be, through having been To face not being

Source: From Educational Psychology, 3rd ed. (p. 40) by R. E. Slavin. Reprinted with permission as adapted from Identity and the Life Cycle (2nd ed.) (p. 178) by Erik H. Erikson. Copyright © 1980 by W. W. Norton & Co., Inc. Copyright © 1959 by International Universities Press, Inc. Reprinted by permission of W. W. Norton & Company, Inc.

ory was the trait-factor theory pioneered by Frank Parsons. This theory assumed that by assessing such traits of the client as interests, abilities, achievements, and so forth, through objective measures and matching results to those factors required for successful performance in a given occupation, predictions could be made which would enable the client, with the counselor's guidance, to make an appropriate career decision. The basic premise of the trait-factor approach is still a dominant one, especially in the use of the psychological measures for career assessment and planning.

A more current and popular approach is represented by Holland's theory of personality types and environmental models. This theory is based on major assumptions regarding personality types, their determination, and relation to various outcomes and vocational choices. In other words, individuals express themselves, their values and interests, and so forth, through their career choices—their work environments. The concepts and assumptions that underlie the theory are as follows.

- The choice of vocation is an expression of personality.
- Interest inventories are personality inventories.
- Vocational stereotypes have reliable and important psychological and sociological meanings.
- The members of a vocation have similar personalities and similar histories of personal development.
- Because people in a vocational group have similar personalities, they will respond to many situations and problems in similar ways, and they will create characteristic interpersonal environments.
- Vocational satisfaction, stability, and achievement depend on the congruence between one's personality and environment (composed largely of other people) in which one works.

The following statements summarize the major assumptions of Holland's (1966, 1973, 1985a) theory.

- In our culture, most persons can be categorized as one of six types: realistic, intellectual, social, conventional, enterprising, and artistic.
- There are six kinds of environments: realistic, intellectual, social, conventional, enterprising, and artistic.
- People search for environments and vocations that will permit them to exercise their skills and abilities, to express their attitudes and values, to take on agreeable problems and roles, and to avoid disagreeable ones.
- A person's behavior can be explained by the interaction of his personality and his environment. (1966, pp. 8–12)

Table 10-3 summarizes Holland's (1985b) theory, describing the personality characteristics of the six categories and the work environments related to each. Holland has developed a popular assessment instrument based on his theory, *The Self-Directed Search*, accompanied by an *Occupational Finder*. Holland does not suggest his categories as mutually exclusive, as noted in the *Occupational Finder*, which suggests a work setting would be a combination of three environments. It is also equally rare for an individual to fit into only one of the six psychological types.

TABLE 10-3   Holland's Personality Types

The **Realistic** type likes realistic jobs such as automobile mechanic, aircraft controller, surveyor, farmer, electrician. Has mechanical abilities but may lack social skills. Is described as

Asocial	Inflexible	Practical
Conforming	Materialistic	Self-effacing
Frank	Natural	Thrifty
Genuine	Normal	Uninsightful
Hardheaded	Persistent	Uninvolved

The **Investigative** type likes investigative jobs such as biologist, chemist, physicist, anthropologist, geologist, medical technologist. Has mathematical and scientific ability but often lacks leadership ability. Is described as

Analytical	Independent	Rational
Cautious	Intellectual	Reserved
Complex	Introspective	Retiring
Critical	Pessimistic	Unassuming
Curious	Precise	Unpopular

The **Artistic** type likes artistic jobs such as composer, musician, stage director, writer, interior decorator, actor/actress. Artistic abilities: writing, musical, or artistic, but often lacks clerical skills. Is described as

Complicated	Imaginative	Intuitive
Disorderly	Impractical	Nonconforming
Emotional	Impulsive	Open
Expressive	Independent	Original
Idealistic	Introspective	Sensitive

The **Social** type likes social jobs such as teacher, religious worker, counselor, clinical psychiatric case worker, speech therapist. Has social skills and talents but often lacks mechanical and scientific ability. Is described as

Ascendant	Helpful	Responsible
Cooperative	Idealistic	Sociable
Empathic	Kind	Tactful
Friendly	Patient	Understanding
Generous	Persuasive	Warm

The **Enterprising** type likes enterprising jobs such as salesperson, manager, business executive, television producer, sports promoter, buyer. Has leadership and speaking abilities but often lacks scientific ability. Is described as

Acquisitive	Energetic	Flirtatious
Adventurous	Excitement-	Optimistic
Agreeable	seeking	Self-confident
Ambitious	Exhibitionistic	Sociable
Domineering	Extroverted	Talkative

The **Conventional** type likes conventional jobs such as bookkeeper, stenographer, financial analyst, banker, cost estimator, tax expert. Has clerical and arithmetic ability but often lacks artistic abilities. Is described as

Careful	Inflexible	Persistent
Conforming	Inhibited	Practical
Conscientious	Methodical	Prudish
Defensive	Obedient	Thrifty
Efficient	Orderly	Unimaginative

Source: Adapted and reproduced by special permission of the Publisher, Psychological Assessment Resources, Inc., 16204 North Florida Avenue, Lutz, FL 33549, from *The Self-Directed Search Professional Manual,* by John L. Holland, Ph.D. Copyright 1985, 1987, 1994 by PAR, Inc. Further reproduction is prohibited without permission from PAR, Inc.

Another popular personality theory, developed by Anne Roe (1956), was based on Maslow's classic theory of basic needs. These needs, in order of their importance from high to low, were stated as follows.

- Physiological needs
- Safety needs
- Need for belongingness and love
- Need for self-esteem and respect
- Need for information
- Need for understanding
- Need for beauty
- Need for self-actualization

This concept suggests that until the higher needs are met, the need or needs which follow will not be attended to. For example, those needs for maintaining life (i.e., the first two indicated above) must be satisfied before addressing needs for love and respect (the third and fourth indicated above).

Roe's research led her to believe that the needs structure of the individual would be greatly influenced by early childhood experiences. This needs structure would in turn influence occupational categories the individual would select. Roe's extensive research into occupations led her to develop eight occupational groups (Roe & Klos, 1972).

- Service
- Business contact
- Organization
- Technology
- Outdoors
- Science
- Culture
- Arts and entertainment

These eight occupational categories were then subdivided into six classification levels as determined by degree of responsibility and abilities needed.

- Professional and managerial (1), independent responsibility
- Professional and managerial (2), less independence of important responsibility
- Semi-professional and small business
- Skilled
- Semi-skilled
- Unskilled

Roe's system of classification and categorization has proved useful as a framework for organizing in a meaningful way a multitude of occupations, and her work has had an impact on interest test development and career research.

Sociological Theories

Popular among the sociological views of careers is one that suggests that people arrive at a particular occupation destiny more by chance than through deliberate planning or steady progress toward an earlier defined goal. Newspapers and television reports constantly remind us of persons who seem to be in the right place at the right time and for no other reason end up in an unanticipated career. In a broad sense, we might include the chance one has for career choice as influenced by the environment, social class, culture, and other conditions one is born into or raised in; opportunities for education; observation of role models; and so forth. More narrowly, we may note that chance factors result in occupational choice by an impulse or sudden emotional reaction in which unconscious forces appear to determine a person's behavior and occupation choice. Consider, for example, the person who on apparent impulse walks out of a good office job to work as a missionary in an African jungle. Perhaps you have decided to enter the counseling field based at least in part on chance or unanticipated influences. In any event, accident theory contends that because people may make decisions or be influenced by unforeseen or accidental circumstances, it is not possible to evaluate all the decisive factors in their choices.

Bandura (1982) has expressed the view that chance encounters play a prominent role in changing the course of the lives of many of us. Herr and Cramer (1996) synthesize Bandura's perspectives (see Table 10-4).

Sociological theory also notes the influences of home, school, social class, communities, and peer groups.

Economic Theories

Economic theories suggest the importance of economic factors in career choice. Prominent among these are the availability of types of jobs versus the availability of qualified workers for these jobs. Too, as many studies have indicated, a major factor in career choice is "What kind of job can I get?" In these instances, the most important consideration is being able to provide at least the basic necessities for oneself and family. Job security has also become an important consideration in career choice in the 1990s and beyond, and worker benefits, especially medical insurance and retirement plans, can also be factors in where one seeks employment.

Decision-making theory has its origins in the field of economics and implies that careers are selected from alternatives on the basis of which choice promises to be the most rewarding or of value to the individual (and not necessarily in a monetary sense).

Other Theories

A number of other perspectives further broaden the concepts of influences on career development and decision making. For example,

A social-learning theory approach to career decision making was first proposed by Krumboltz, Mitchell, and Gelatt (1975), and then several years later by Mitchell and Krumboltz (1990). More recently, Mitchell and Krumboltz (1996) have extended the earlier social-learning theory approach to include Krumboltz's learning theory of career counseling, and they now suggest that the entire theory be referred to as learning theory of career counseling (LTCC).

The theory is an attempt to simplify the process of career selection and is based primarily on life events that are influential in determining career selection. In this theory, the process of career de-

TABLE 10-4   A Synthesis of Bandura's Perspectives of Factors Influencing Chance Encounters

Personal determinants of the effect of chance encounters	Social determinants of the effect of chance encounters

Entry Skills
  Interest, skills, personal knowledge likely to gain acceptance or sustain contact with another
	Milieu Rewards
	  The types of rewards and sanctions an individual or group provides if a chance encounter alters a life path

Emotional Ties
  Interpersonal attractiveness tending to sustain chance encounters so that certain social determinants might operate
	Symbolic Environment and Information
	  Images of reality provided by other than direct experience; different individuals or groups furnish different symbolic environments

Values and Personal Standards
  Unintended influences more likely to be important if persons involved share similar standards and value systems
	Milieu Reach and Closedness
	  Chance encounters with a relatively closed milieu—e.g., cults, communal groups—have the greatest potential for abruptly reordering life paths

	Psychological Closedness Belief systems provide structure, directions, and purpose in life. Once persons, through chance encounter, get caught up in the belief system of a particular group, it can exert selective influence on the course of development and erect a psychological closedness to outside influence. Beliefs channel social interactions in ways that create their own validating realities

Source: From E. L. Herr and S. H. Cramer (1996), *Career Guidance and Counseling Through the Lifespan: Systematic Approaches* (5th ed.), p. 208. Copyright © 1996. Reprinted by permission of Harper-Collins College Publishers.

velopment involves four factors: (1) genetic endowments and special abilities, (2) environmental conditions and events, (3) learning experiences, and (4) task approach skills. (Zunker, 1998, p. 58)

Learning theory suggests that career development is a learning process in which academic experiences influence career decisions. Isaacson (1985) suggests an eclectic theory, drawing from the prominent theories of occupational choice. The eight major points of his summary are as follows.

1. The career development process is an ongoing, lifelong aspect of human existence.
2. Since the process is essentially developmental in nature, it is generally predictable but also can be modified by changing circumstances, even to the point of being reversible as the individual attempts to optimize the benefits and satisfactions derived from the worker-job relationship.
3. Individuals have differing patterns of abilities, interests, and personality as a result of the interaction of genetic inheritance and environmental factors.

4. Occupations also have differing patterns of characteristics required or expected of successful workers.

5. The extent to which a person develops and applies his or her unique pattern of individual characteristics depends on attitudes, motivations, and values. These patterns can be approached from either the basis of psychological need or the development of self-concept.

6. The individual learns about jobs and their relationship to the individual specifically and to society generally from many sources, including the family, peer groups, community, school, media, and the planned and unplanned experiences of everyday life. The attitudes toward and knowledge of work developed in the growth, exploration, and crystallization periods of childhood and adolescence will have lasting influence on the worker-job relationship of the adult years.

7. The optimization that the individual seeks in the worker-job relationship is the product of the interaction between the individual and the realities of his or her situation. The ability and desire of the individual to capitalize on these interactions influence the level of optimization.

8. The degree of satisfaction experienced by the worker is largely determined by the extent to which the potential for optimization is apparent to the individual and is viewed as agreeable and acceptable.* (pp. 76–77)

IMPLICATIONS OF CAREER THEORIES FOR COUNSELORS

A review of the various theories can lead to the conclusions that career development is a process that leads to a decision; there are stages through which one passes en route to vocational maturity and decision making; one must accomplish certain tasks at each stage; and personality traits are related to career decision making. Furthermore, there are environmental constraints on the careers to which one may aspire or recognize, and the best-laid career plans may be altered by chance or accident.

The characteristics of these theories have certain implications for counseling clients with career development or adjustment needs.

- Counselors must understand the process and characteristics of human development, including readiness to learn and successfully complete particular tasks at certain developmental stages.

- Counselors must understand the basic human needs as well as the special needs of persons and their relationship to career development and decision making.

- Counselors must be able to assess and interpret individual traits and characteristics and to apply these assessments to a variety of counselee career-related needs.

- Counselors must assist clients to recognize that unforeseen or chance factors may, on occasion, alter career planning.

- Counselors must recognize that the rapid changes in the way people work and live in this high-tech era require a constant examination and updating of the theory and research we use as a basis for our career counseling efforts.

---

*From Isaacson, Lee E., *Basics of Career Counseling.* Copyright © 1985 by Allyn and Bacon. Reprinted by permission.

In recent years, there have been efforts to bring the different major theoretical perspectives together in what has been labeled a convergence theory. This would not be an eclectic theory, but rather one in which commonalities shared by major theories would be examined with a view toward the converging of these shared assumptions into one global theory. At this writing, no significant progress has been made.

CAREER COUNSELING AND THE DEVELOPMENT OF HUMAN POTENTIAL

Beyond the various career choice theories is the recognition that all aspects of human development, whether they be social, physical, emotional, or educational, are but parts of one's total development—parts that are usually interwoven and often difficult to distinguish from the other aspects of human development. Career development is, of course, no exception. A recognition of these relationships and the application of certain basic principles of human development are significant in the design and implementation of programs providing counseling over the life span for the development of human potential. Seven of these developmental dimensions were discussed in a publication of the National Vocational Guidance Association (1973) (which is now the National Career Development Association).

1. Development occurs during the lifetime of an individual. It can be described in maturational terms denoting progression through life stages and the mastery of developmental tasks at each stage. Although research evidence is lacking, it seems unlikely that intervention can substantially shorten this maturational process.

2. Individual development is influenced by both heredity and environment. Psychological, sociological, educational, political, economic, and physical factors affect development. Appropriate intervention strategies which focus upon these factors can influence the quality of individual development.

3. Development is a continuous process. Individual development can best be facilitated by intervention strategies that begin in the early years and continue throughout the life of the person. Programs which focus only at certain points or at certain stages in the individual's life will have limited effectiveness.

4. Although development is continuous, certain aspects are dominant at various periods of the life span. Programs designed to facilitate career development should account for the dominant aspects at given stages.

5. Individual development involves a progressive differentiation and integration of the person's self and his perceived world. Intervention strategies need to be designed to assist individuals during normal maturational stages of career development rather than to provide remedial assistance to individuals whose development has been damaged or retarded.

6. While common developmental stages can be observed and described during childhood and adult life, individual differences in progressing through these stages can be expected. Intervention programs should provide for these differences, making no assumption that something is wrong with those who progress at atypical rates.

7. Excessive deprivation with respect to any single aspect of human development can retard optimal development in other areas. Optimal human development programs are comprehensive in nature, not limited to any single facet. It is recognized that those who suffer from deprivation may require special and intensive assistance. Where deprivation is long term, short-term intervention is not likely to be sufficient. (pp. 3–4)

Of course, we do not have to examine developmental theory to understand the potential that exists within the human being. The achievements of humankind from the discovery of fire to walking on the moon are testimony to the ever-present undetermined potential of human beings. Although we must presume that the multiple potentials of most people will never be fully exploited, the challenge nonetheless remains to achieve and develop to the optimum possible.

As countries prepare to compete in the global marketplace, a resource that will be examined more and more with a view to promoting the advancement and well-being of societies will be the most valuable of all resources, the human potential. Too, as disadvantaged populations seek to overcome their inequalities, they will continue to call, with public support, for increased equal opportunities to develop their potential.

Although we have historical examples of counselors being called upon to assist in the identification and development of human potential in limited ways (e.g., science and math, the gifted, etc.), we are now moving into an era where the development of every individual's potential becomes their right and society's hope. Three phases for a human resource development program are

1. Assessment for the identification of the individual's potential aptitudes and interests
2. Planning for appropriate experiences to assist the individual's development and enhancement of their potentials
3. Placement in those educational and/or career settings where the individual's developed potential can be realized for the benefits of the individual and society

Although the identification and development of individual human potential should be initiated in their early years of schooling, it is appropriate to continue to assess, monitor, and assist individuals across their life span. Postsecondary educational institutions, adult education programs, career centers and employment offices, community mental health agencies, and private practitioners can all play significant roles in this process. They cannot afford to do less. Society cannot afford to let them do less.

A career may offer the greatest opportunity for a person to achieve much of his or her potential. Career counseling for the development of human potential may include a focus on encouraging clients to challenge the limitations of their present self-concept; to, in a manner of speaking, redefine their potential and stimulate their vitality. Let us next examine groups that traditionally represent populations in our society with underdeveloped human potential: women, minorities, the poor, people with disabilities, and dual-career couples.

Women

A prime example of the development of human potential through the world of work is the large-scale movement of women into the workforce during and since World War II. Not only are more women entering the workforce, but they are entering a wide range of occupations far beyond such traditional women's careers as nursing, teaching, waitressing, and clerical work that represented the limits of their realistic aspirations in the first generation of the 20th century. Today, women seek careers in the medical, legal, law enforcement, military, construction, sales, and transportation fields, to name but a few heretofore bastions of male employment. Further, women are being increasingly appointed to managerial and supervisory positions and high judicial offices, elected to governorships and legislative bodies, and, in general, are making significant advances up the career ladder in all areas. All this is happening as we note projections that anticipate nearly as high a percentage of adult women in the workforce as adult men by the early 2000s.

Despite the previous optimistic note on progress in developing women's career potential, we must recognize that many barriers to women achieving their full potential still persist. High among these restrictors is the age-old problem of prejudice. Prejudice is reflected in numerous ways, but two specific examples might be salaries and opportunities.

Additionally, we have noted increased media attention in recent years to the old problem of sexual harassment of the female worker; home and workplace demands on the dual-career couple's working females when males fail to be equal partners at home; and increasing numbers of female single parents. The majority of women in today's workforce work because of economic necessity—and this includes the nearly 60% of single-parent families headed by women. Because of these and other circumstances, women often accept lower wages than their male counterparts. There are serious salary discrepancies at every career level, and women are far more frequently underemployed in low-wage jobs than men of comparable qualifications.

Thus, although laudable progress has been made in developing women's potential, much remains to be done. Career counselors have the opportunity to facilitate this development. The female client must be aided in looking beyond stereotypes and other restrictions. Some may need assistance in appropriately balancing family life and work and accepting their rights to be both a mother and a worker.

A 1994 U.S. Department of Labor survey of 250,000 working women cited the demands of balancing family life and work as their primary concern. Where corporate America has failed to be more responsive to the needs of their female workers, mothers are beginning to seek or develop opportunities to work out of their homes, do contract jobs, or opt for employment as temporaries. Counselors must also help female clients identify alternatives to traditional work opportunities as well as recognize educational opportunities that may increase their opportunities and enhance their earning power. With some, assertiveness training, job search skills, and positive self-concept development may also be helpful.

Minorities

Minorities in the United States have, throughout the country's history, represented a tragic loss of human potential. Although progress has been made in recent generations to eliminate barriers and open opportunities to minority populations, much remains to be done. The nation's shortcomings are recognizable in the underrepresentation of minorities in professions, managerial and super-visory positions, government offices of leadership, and preparatory programs in higher education. At the opposite end of the career ladder, minorities are over represented in lower-paying and lower-prestige jobs, underemployment and unemployment, and school attrition. As we look to our future, it is especially disturbing to note that more of our African/American youth are in the criminal justice system than gainfully employed and that high percentages of minority girls are single parents, heads of households, and living in poverty. Obviously, our societal future is not a healthy one if tomorrow's minority adults are already seriously disadvantaged in developing their human potential. They truly have been neglected and underserved.

Looking to the turn of the century, Sue and Sue (1989) comment that

in California, nonwhite youths now account for over half of the student population in the schools. By the year 2000, half of the working-age population in the state will be Hispanic, Asian, Native

American or Black. By the year 2003, it is estimated that minorities will constitute the majority population in California. And the rapid increase in minority population is not just a one-state phenomenon. The United States is becoming increasingly heterogeneous in ethnic characteristics. Twenty percent of children in the United States are nonwhite, and by 2020, this will increase to 38 percent (U.S. Bureau of Census, 1980). The rapid increase in the nonwhite population increases the urgency for counselors to develop the multicultural knowledge and skills necessary to deal with a much more diverse clientele. (p. 1)

Counselors and counseling programs clearly have both a significant challenge and a significant opportunity to assist minority populations in achieving career equity and developing their individual human potential. To even entertain the promise of effectiveness in this regard, counselors must be sure that they themselves do not hold or reinforce educational or career stereotypes for minorities, do not use biased assessment instruments, and are at all times culturally aware and sensitive.

What do counselors need to consider when designing career interventions for ethnic minorities? From a sociological perspective, Hotchkiss and Borow (1990) noted that the counselor should be involved in the following tasks. First, they must inform clients about potential barriers to ethnic minorities in the labor market, and help them develop strategies to meet them. Second, counselors must provide direct advocacy (e.g., help in completing applications for programs or jobs). Third, they should work to reduce racial and ethnic barriers to success whenever possible (e. g., by assisting in school-to-work transitions). Finally, they should help raise clients' educational aspirations as a way of expanding vocational opportunities. Hawks and Muha (1991) added that counselors should emphasize student-generated versus counselor-generated knowledge, and should incorporate the student's language and culture into programs. They also stated that the minority community, especially parents, should be included in career programs. Finally, they suggest that counselors view problems as external or systemic problems instead of flaws within the student, then use that viewpoint to challenge students to overcome those problems. (Bowman, 1993, p. 18)

The Poor

Although we are frequently reminded that the United States is the richest country on earth, not all of our population shares the wealth. Certainly, a glaring tarnish on our image is the significant numbers of our population who exist in poverty. Of all Americans, it is estimated that approximately 14% live below the poverty line and 11% of all families live below the poverty line. The figures are even more despairing for minority populations, and when we consider that children represent the largest population living in poverty, we must ask how can this happen in North America? Often overlooked or uncountable are the estimated one million plus homeless, a group that represents the ultimate in underdeveloped human potential. The challenges presented to counseling and the other helping professions are complex and difficult.

Here again, we have high numbers of children from preschool through adolescence. In San Francisco, for example, there were an estimated 5,000 homeless youth in the mid-1990s. Although the Homeless Assistance Act (1987) was designed to aid school systems to develop programs that reconnect homeless children with schools, the results have been slow and often discouraging as schools often fail to understand how life on the streets can affect homeless youth. Gracenin (1993) notes that programs in schools . . . have to work to keep homeless children from being set apart and stigmatized. And programs that concentrate on remedial or basic skills run the risk of boring—and thus losing—intelligent youngsters who just happen to be homeless.

But such programs are a start—a start today's cast-off youth deserve. (p. 28)

From a programmatic standpoint, three concerns must be addressed. First, schools in poverty areas must have good counseling programs, staffed by competent, caring, and environmentally aware counselors. Second, community career assistance programs must be located in those areas where the need is greatest—where the poor reside. Finally, adult education programs with strong counseling components must be made much more accessible to these populations.

In terms of individual counseling, Isaacson and Brown (1993) point out that

personal counseling may be needed by disadvantaged individuals to clarify self-concept as well as to understand their circumstances. Several authors have emphasized the devastating impact that job loss has on feelings of self-worth. The chronically poor are likely to carry an even heavier feeling of worthlessness. The so-called American dream suggests that one's success in life is the product of hard work—the harder one works, the more one reaps in material rewards, status, and self-satisfaction. One frequent product is the feeling of guilt and failure by those without jobs or with only marginal jobs. Marshall (1983) and Shifron, Dye, and Shifron (1983) describe ways to help such clients deal with feelings and values that may interfere with everyday life and often result from forces outside the individual's control.

Realistic and practical information about the world of work can be used to help the disadvantaged to see potential opportunities to break out of what is frequently viewed as a hopeless morass. Interviews with workers, work samples, plant visits, and synthetic work situation may help the person to understand the job, to relate that job to self, to see attainable goals, and perhaps to acquire usable role models. (pp. 314–315)

The homeless poor are the most challenging of all. Responding to the diverse needs of homeless people calls for the emergence of a counseling professional who is both client sensitive and a skilled enabling model of helping. Therefore, the helping professional's intervention strategies should begin with focusing on the immediate needs and concerns of the homeless client: providing transportation, locating a safe place to sleep for the night, completing forms, arranging a meeting with school officials, providing support by going to a scheduled appointment with the client, and identifying the local soup kitchens and facilities for taking a shower. In addition, case management is highlighted as perhaps the most effective intervention for providing comprehensive, continuous, and coordinated services for homeless people. The basic functions of the case management system include client identification and outreach, individual assessment, service planning, linkage with requisite services, monitoring of service delivery, and client advocacy. (Solomon & Jackson-Jobe, 1992, p. 104)

People with Disabilities

Another population whose human potential is often underdeveloped is individuals with disabilities. The Americans with Disabilities Act (ADA) is a comprehensive law. The ADA identifies individuals with disabilities as follows.

- An individual with a disability is a person who has a physical or mental impairment that substantially limits one or more "major life activities," or has a record of such an impairment, or is regarded as having such an impairment.

- Examples of physical or mental impairments include, but are not limited to, such contagious and noncontagious diseases and conditions as orthopedic, visual, speech, and hearing impairments;

cerebral palsy, epilepsy, muscular dystrophy, multiple sclerosis, cancer, heart disease, diabetes, mental retardation, emotional illness, specific learning disabilities, HIV disease (whether symptomatic or asymptomatic), tuberculosis, drug addiction, and alcoholism. Homosexuality and bisexuality are not physical or mental impairments under the ADA.

- "Major life activities" include functions such as caring for oneself, performing manual tasks, walking, seeing, hearing, speaking, breathing, learning, and working.
- Individuals who currently engage in the illegal use of drugs are not protected by the ADA when an action is taken on the basis of their current illegal use of drugs. (*Americans with Disabilities Act Handbook*, 1991, pp. 3–4)

Herr and Cramer (1996) define *the disabled* as

a population that has a disability or several disabilities that may or may not be a vocational handicap. The disability may be *physical* (such as amputations, birth defects, cancer, heart problems, burns, deafness, blindness, multiple sclerosis, muscular dystrophy, orthopedic, spinal injury), *intellectual* (mental retardation, learning disability, brain damage, speech and language disorders), *emotional* (mental illness, substance abuse, alcoholism, obesity and other eating disorders), or *sociocultural*. In any case, best estimates are that in the United States over ten percent of the population have chronic physical, mental, or emotional conditions that limit their activity sufficiently to make a substantial career difference. (p. 294)

State rehabilitation agencies provide individual counseling and other services to individuals who meet two eligibility requirements: (a) the person must have a disability that results in a substantial handicap to employment, and (b) vocational rehabilitation services must reasonably be expected to benefit the person in terms of employability (Texas Rehabilitation Commission, 1984).

In counseling clients with disabilities for career assistance, counselors must (a) have an understanding of various disabilities and their career implications; (b) be knowledgeable regarding appropriate resources, training, and career opportunities; and (c) be sensitive, supportive, and, at the same time, realistic. Counselors must be prepared to assist clients with disabilities in personal adjustment, self-concept development, career development, and job placement. Counselors may also play the role of advocates for such clients seeking access to education or other training or the workplace itself. In other instances, counselors may find themselves facilitating family support for the efforts of people with disabilities. The family support system is important at all ages, of course, and with children it is important in many ways, not the least of which is the influencing of how they feel about themselves. Gilbride (1993, p. 149) reports the results of a study that suggests that parents' attitudes, apart from their actual instrumental capacity, may influence attitudes and expectations of their child's success.

Counselors also assist these clients' placement in peer support groups with other individuals with disabilities. As with so many other services, minorities have not proportionally availed themselves of rehabilitation counseling. Dziekan and Okocha (1993) comment that

it is only possible to speculate about reasons for lower acceptance rates for minority clients, and a number of factors might have contributed. Lower proportions of minority individuals applying for services may have actually met agency eligibility criteria. Lower proportions of minority clients may have chosen not to follow through with the acceptance process because of their frustrations with the steps and delays involved. Alternatively, biases in the perceptions of rehabilitation counselors determining eligibility for services may have resulted in inaccurate assessments and underestimations of rehabilitation potential. (p. 187)

Although much progress has been made through legislative enactments and increased public awareness, counselors can play a vital role in the still-needed advancements of people with disabilities toward the development of their potential.

Dual-Career Couples

Dual-career couples are becoming the norm rather than the exception. This development is already affecting both family life and corporate life and is leading to reexamination of models of family functioning and corporate policies. Certainly, the issue of human potential development will be a challenging one. Will one partner have priority? Can both be equally developed? And what about children? How will they be cared for and by whom? These and other issues loom large as we approach a dramatically changing world of work, with its new challenges as well.

Stoltz-Loike (1992) presents

> five major career dilemmas (Rapoport & Rapoport, 1976; Sekaran, 1986): (1) role overload from multiple roles, (2) identity confusion between socially learned roles, (3) role-cycling dilemmas between family and career roles, each receiving priority at different points in time, (4) social network dilemmas because of limited discretionary time, and (5) normative dilemmas that result from environmental sanctions. (p. 14)

The continued growth of dual-career couples has presented counselors with relatively new and unexplored challenges in career and marriage and family counseling. Certainly, the traditional theories of career counseling were not developed with the dual-career couple in mind. New conceptual frameworks must be researched and developed. Individual counseling must be interspersed with cojoint counseling. Too, open communications and compromise must be encouraged. A multitude of issues regarding the shared responsibilities of child rearing should be explored before they become major issues.

A code or credo of couple equity, either written or verbally discussed, is suggested by Stoltz-Loike (1992) consisting of six elements.

> (1) personal needs, (2) preferences for balance, (3) gender issues, (4) life-span issues, (5) balance of career concerns, and (6) commitment to redeveloping the credo. This credo will direct individual performance and couple balance, and result in greater satisfaction with the couple relationship. Moreover, it can specify functional ways to deal with the normal stresses and strains of the relationship over time.
>
> The rewards of couple growth associated with negotiated equity will enhance both individual and family functioning and lead to richer dimensions in the couple relationship. Moreover, equitable couples will be able to pursue a greater variety of challenging business and personal roles. This balance will be attained through discussion of, commitment to, and concern with family and career achievements. Family and career equity may be quite difficult to negotiate, but when it exists, it represents life-span success. (p. 245)

Because society looks at schools as an agency for developing the potential of youth, let us examine in the next section how career-planning and decision-making programs in schools contribute to the development of human potential.

CAREER PLANNING AND DECISION MAKING
IN SCHOOLS

Nearly all human beings can anticipate three common experiences. The first of these, development or growth, begins at birth and is especially attended to through much of one's youth. Second is education, which, in an informal sense, also starts at birth and continues throughout life, with a special societal emphasis during most of one's youth when formal schooling is provided. The third common experience is work, beginning in one's youth and continuing through most of adulthood.

These three experiences are significantly shaped by one common setting—the school. It is here that a person's development is stimulated and shaped for the three great experiences of her or his life: learning, living with others, and working. Thus, the role of the school in what the person may become and, in turn, what society itself may become is critical. Counselors in any setting have an interest in the impact the school experience has on their clients.

The counseling program's role in the school setting must be one of facilitating and enhancing the school's contributions to the learning, growth and development, and preparation for work by youths. In this chapter, we are particularly concerned with the latter—preparation for the world of work, including attending to a person's career development, planning, and decision making within the educational context.

In order to emphasize the opportunities for the student's career development, certain guiding principles are suggested as appropriate objectives for the school counseling program in general and the career guidance phase in particular. The following principles are stated within a developmental framework.

1. *All students should be provided with an opportunity to develop an unbiased base from which they can make their career decisions.* The shrinking of the pupil's occupational choices as one proceeds through the school years is an educational tragedy. The first-grader seems to regard most familiar occupations in a positive light. By the time they reach the seventh or eighth grade, pupils have begun to make decisions based on at least some general occupational considerations. Many have developed or have been educated toward biases that automatically eliminate many possibilities from further consideration. The large percentage of students who enter college preparatory courses at the ninth-grade level and never enter college or even fail to complete their secondary schooling is but one evidence of this fact. In this regard, then, the school counseling program seeks, in effective cooperation with the classroom teacher, to develop in each pupil positive attitudes and respect for all honest work. This is a formidable task, for many students are almost constantly bombarded with the biases of the adult world surrounding them. If these students are to benefit from a true freedom of choice, the career counseling and guidance programs have a vital mission in the schools.

2. *The early and continuous development of positive pupil attitudes toward education is critical.* The deterioration of the elementary pupil's occupational choices is unfortunate, but the failure to maintain the pupil's continuing interest in an optimum educational development is disastrous. For objective evidence, one need only turn to the various dropout studies and the equally countless studies concerning the lack of pupil motivation and achievement commensurate with ability. In short, career development has limited meaning without parallel educational development. Any program of pupil career counseling and guidance must have as a major objective the stimulation of the student's educational development.

3. *As a corollary to these previous points, the student must be taught to view a career as a way of life and an education as a preparation for life.* Frequently, pupils arrive at the educational decision-making stage of life viewing careers only in terms of job descriptions. At all educational levels, the opportunity exists to develop, not only widen, occupational horizons. This broader approach to the eventual career choice is based on the realization that one's way of work is one's way of life. Similarly, there must be attention to the concept of education itself, keeping in mind the idea of education for life rather than education only for one's eventual career. This approach—one of education for the fuller life—also has obvious implications for education's continuing efforts to reduce the percentage of school dropouts.

4. *Students must be assisted in developing adequate understanding of themselves and must be prepared to relate this understanding to both social-personal development and career-educational planning.* These understandings are significant in the fulfillment of the individual's need for self-actualization. In this context, both career guidance and pupil appraisal seek to further enrich their meaning and value to students by preparing them to look at themselves realistically in terms of continuing educational opportunities, career requirements, and the demands and relationships of society.

5. *Students at all levels must be provided with an understanding of the relationship between education and careers.* If pupils are to develop an attitude and belief that education is relevant, they must understand how it is relevant. Pupils need an awareness of the relationships between levels of education and related career possibilities. They should also be made aware of both the vocations and avocations that stem directly from certain subjects.

6. *Pupils need an understanding of both where and why they are at a given point on the educational continuum at a given time.* It is not enough for pupils to know they will be in the third grade this year and in the fourth grade next year if all goes well. If they are to gain an increased appreciation of current educational programs as well as future educational possibilities, pupils must be provided specific opportunities to gain insights into the educational process, its sequence, and its integrating of knowledge.

7. *Pupils at every stage of their educational program should have career-oriented experiences that are appropriate for their levels of readiness and simultaneously meaningful and realistic.* This means that opportunities for participation and observation will frequently take precedence over discussions and teacher or counselor lectures.

8. *Students must have opportunities to test concepts, skills, and roles to develop values that may have future career application.* The school career counseling and guidance program takes advantage of natural school groupings in providing secure opportunities for the pupil to experience and develop human relationships and other skills, a variety of roles, and a system of values and concepts that are related to everyday living.

9. *The school career counseling and guidance program is centered in the classroom, with coordination and consultation by the school counselor, participation by parents, and resource contributions from the community.* The pupil's career counseling and guidance team needs the involvement of all those concerned with her or his development, with the teacher, counselor, and parent playing key roles.

10. *The school's program of career counseling and guidance is integrated into the functioning counseling and guidance and total educational programs of the institution.* The complete development of the individual is vital; therefore, the career aspects should not be separated from the whole.

In fact, it is only within the total educational program framework that each segment can be strengthened by and in turn strengthen every other segment.

The School Counselor's Role in Student Career Development

As has been noted, the need for career guidance and counseling is increasingly evident in the mass of data pointing to difficulties in career decision making, the underutilization of human resources, dissatisfaction with chosen careers, and such perennial problems as the hard-core unemployed. Career guidance programs are designed, in cooperation with programs of career education, to cope with such needs. To satisfactorily plan such programs, which will increase students' planning and decision-making skills, counselors must understand how career decisions are made and the possible consequences of certain kinds of decisions. This approach implies an understanding of theories and related research in career decision making and the counselor's potential role in the career development of youth.

Because the career movement in schools has been viewed as primarily a developmental and educational process, the school counselor has, at last, the opportunity to function in a developmental and, in a sense, preventive capacity. Although the teacher is clearly the key person on the career education team, the school counselor, by virtue of special understandings and skills, can make a valuable contribution to the school's total effort. These contributions may be categorized under the following activities.

Career Counseling

Programs of career education are designed to prepare persons for the eventual selection of a career, but many adolescents and young adults will be unable to adequately cope with this critical decision making without the assistance of a professional counselor. Parental counseling, group counseling, and group guidance activities represent contributions of the counselor to the career development of the individual and the school's career education program.

Career Assessment

An important aspect of the career education program provides students the opportunities to assess their personal characteristics in relation to career planning and decision making. The counselor can make a significant contribution to the development of appropriate self-understandings of youth through the employment of both standardized and nonstandardized assessment techniques. However, it is important that these instruments are free of gender or cultural biases.

Resource Person and Consultant

The school counselor has been traditionally active in acquiring materials appropriate to career decision making and planning. The counselor is also aware of computerized information programs and media aids such as films, filmstrips, and audio- and videotapes. Although the counselor cannot collect all materials, it is reasonable to expect that the counselor will be aware of the sources from which such materials may be obtained. In this capacity, the counselor serves as a resource person to the individual teachers involved in the career education program.

The counselor also serves in a consulting capacity, utilizing her or his understanding of the pupil population and career development resources and opportunities to complement the career education program.

Linkage Agent

Increasingly, the counselor will be active in collaborative efforts, not only with teachers and others in the school setting, but with community agencies and employers. Local government employment counselors and their agencies are especially important contacts.

The counselor has an important role to play in implementing and strengthening career education programs. This role does not, however, diminish the importance of the career guidance function in career planning and decision making. Let us, therefore, move on to examine some techniques for this activity.

Techniques for Career Planning and Decision Making

In counseling youths for their career development and eventual placement, counselors may employ a variety of facilitative techniques to assist persons in self-awareness, educational and career awareness, career exploration, and planning and decision making.

Self-Awareness

From a very early age onward, people must become aware of and respect their uniqueness as human beings. Learning about one's aptitudes, interests, values, personality traits, and so forth, is important in the development of concepts related to self and the utilization of these concepts in career exploration. Counselors may use such techniques as values clarification exercises, group guidance activities, written assignments (such as autobiographies), films and videotapes, and standardized tests. Individual or group counseling should follow if circumstances warrant.

Educational Awareness

Awareness of the relationships between self, educational opportunities, and the world of work is an important aspect of career planning. Counselors may use films as well as printed materials for this purpose. Group guidance activities (such as orientation days), presentations by school alumni, and the use of educational awareness inventories can be useful. Games that relate hobbies and recreational activities to courses and careers can be stimulating for grade school and middle school pupils. Guided activities can also educate school-aged youth to the relationships between desirable school habits (i.e., responsibility, punctuality, effort, positive human relationships) and good worker traits.

Career Awareness

Counselors and counseling programs in schools should, at all educational levels, assist the pupil in the continuous expansion of knowledge and awareness of the world of work. This must include a developing recognition of the relationships between values, lifestyles, and careers. Many excellent films and printed materials are available for this purpose, but of course these must be integrated into a planned, developmental program appropriate to the student's age or grade level. Specialized programs (i.e., career days, career shadowing, junior partners, closed circuit television "trips," and actual field trips) are useful if well planned. Excellent computer programs (noted later in this chapter) are available, and with secondary school students, standardized interest inventories can increase a student's career awareness.

Career Exploration

Career exploration represents a movement toward a systematic, planned inquiry and analysis of careers that are of interest. Comparisons, reality testing, and, again, standardized testing may be useful. Computerized programs, to be discussed later, can also be helpful. Classes in career exploration and decision making are not uncommon.

A variety of techniques are available for career exploration in schools. Integrating career information into classroom instruction enhances the meaning of both as the relationship between learning in school and living out of school becomes more evident to the pupil. The relation of subject matter to careers, hobbies, and everyday living needs and the accomplishments of well-known personalities exemplifies this integration. Many excellent published materials are also available for facilitating career exploration.

Career Planning and Decision Making

Students eventually need to narrow their career possibilities and then proceed to examine and test these options as critically as possible. Here again, such established techniques as values clarification activities, standardized testing, job shadowing, career days, and other group guidance activities are helpful. Many students will need to learn the process of decision making, including choosing between competing alternatives, examining the consequences of specific choices, the value of compromise, and implementing a decision. At this point, students must recognize the impact of their current planning and decision making on their future life. It should also be a time when students are assisted to take control of their life and become an active agent for the shaping of their own future.

Placement and Follow-Up

Career placement and follow-up services are significant to the success of career counseling programs. The high rate of youth unemployment has highlighted the need for a greater emphasis on career placement for youth. Assistance to young people by both school and employment counselors is important if they are to avoid unnecessary difficulties and frustrations in their career search activities. Also, counselors are aware that unsatisfactory career entry can have long-term effects for youth. In this regard, it must be recognized that the current TV generations are often unrealistic in their expectations of career opportunities and their viewpoints of specific careers. Preemployment counseling may be necessary to assist these young people in obtaining a more realistic understanding of the world of work.

As we examine an increasingly complex and changing career world, it is clear that the career placement service has the potential for assisting many, perhaps most, youth in the school setting. Such programs should be designed to assist both in-school and out-of-school youth, both school dropouts and school graduates. Such programs are typically involved in

1. Assessing the needs of students regarding part-time and full-time employment, training, employability skills, and further educational desires
2. Establishing a working relationship with business, industry, and labor representatives in order to facilitate effective cooperation and communication between these groups and educators
3. Providing avenues and assistance to students seeking part-time or full-time employment that are compatible with their abilities and interests
4. Establishing an efficient, participatory communication-feedback network among all involved—students, business, industry, and labor personnel, community leaders, parents, media, and school personnel (Gibson & Mitchell, 1976, p. 1)

In considering placement program development, the existence in many communities of well-established local governmental employment programs that often give special attention to the needs of local youth should be recognized. In such settings, the school guidance program seeks to work cooperatively and in a complementary manner with local government employment personnel to provide the best possible assistance for youthful job seekers. Even under such ideal conditions, however, it must be remembered that the important developmental aspects of school placement programs are not the responsibility of other agencies or institutions. School placement programs, therefore, must include activities that develop or enhance the student's skills, attitudes, and knowledge needed for job acquisition and retention. Programs developed under the School-to-Work Transition Act of 1994 would be expected to include many of these elements.

Placement program activities may be viewed as three-dimensional. The primary activity, of course, is student development; however, this will obviously be handicapped if job development is not also a planned program activity, and both of these activities will be less than effective without plans for program maintenance and operation. Because placement in its broader context includes the placement of clients in a variety of settings (i.e., work, educational, environmental) for a variety of reasons and benefits, let us now proceed to examine educational and environmental placement.

Educational Placement

In general, educational placement differs little from other forms of placement inasmuch as it represents an organized effort to match the qualifications of individuals plus personal interests and resources with the requirements of institutions and programs. Typically, school counselors, with responsibilities for college and other postsecondary educational placement, provide students information regarding institutional entrance requirements, expenses, characteristics of the institution, and program content. They also frequently assist students in completing the necessary application forms. An example of a form that counselors may use with high school students interested in college placement is the college checklist (see Figure 10-1).

Many school counselors are also involved in educational placement within their schools. In this capacity, they are concerned with placing students in appropriate curricula and specific courses. However, scheduling activities that consist largely of a mechanical process designed to get all pupils into all slots at a given time, with a total disregard of individual differences, is not considered a guidance responsibility, even though counselors report that they spend many hours doing such tasks.

	Name of College		Name of College		Name of College	
I. Entrance Requirements and General Information						
1. Does this college offer major preparation in the field of _____ (student's planned major)?	Yes	No	Yes	No	Yes	No
2. Will I be eligible for admission upon completion of my currently planned program for high school graduation?						
3. Are entrance examinations required?						
4. Must I take a physical examination?						
5. Are there other entrance requirements? (If so, list in Section VII, under Notes and Comments.)						
6. Is this a coeducational college?						
7. Is this a state- or city-supported college?						
8. Are the offerings of this college accredited by the accrediting association?						
9. Does this college have an ROTC program?						
10. What is the average enrollment?						
II. Expenses (per school year)						
11. Room						
12. Board						
13. Tuition						
14. Activity fees						
15. Any other special expenses: (item) _____ (item) _____						
16. Total basic cost per year	$		$		$	
III. Room and Board						
17. Are dormitory facilities available for men and women?						
18. Are noncommuting freshmen required to live in the dormitory?						
19. May you select your own roommate if you desire?						
20. Are dining facilities available (three meals per day) for students?						

Figure 10-1   College Checklist.

In the literature, at least, if not always in practice, placement within educational institutions has been viewed as more than just career, college, and educational placement. In its broadest sense, placement is an activity that places or facilitates the self-placement of persons in situations or settings that will enable them to benefit from needed experiences, make satisfactory adjustments, gain useful information, and, in general, contribute to their total development. As an example of this broader concept of placement, let us look at placement that focuses on giving a person experiences in different roles and environments.

Role placement assumes that experiencing different and significant roles is important for all developing pupils. Although many will experience some of these roles natu-

	Name of College		Name of College		Name of College	
	Yes	No	Yes	No	Yes	No
IV. *Student Services and Aids*						
21. Are scholarships available?	——	——	——	——	——	——
22. Are part-time jobs available?	——	——	——	——	——	——
23. Are guidance services provided?	——	——	——	——	——	——
24. Is there a freshman orientation program?	——	——	——	——	——	——
25. Are placement services available for						
(a) graduating seniors?	——	——	——	——	——	——
(b) summertime jobs?	——	——	——	——	——	——
26. Are health services provided?						
(a) Dispensary care?	——	——	——	——	——	——
(b) Dental care?	——	——	——	——	——	——
(c) Hospitalization plan?	——	——	——	——	——	——
27. Can I get special scholastic help (such as tutoring) if I need it?	——	——	——	——	——	——
V. *Student Activities*						
28. Fraternities and sororities?	——	——	——	——	——	——
29. Honorary organizations?	——	——	——	——	——	——
30. Social dancing permitted?	——	——	——	——	——	——
31. Are campus recreational facilities available?	——	——	——	——	——	——
32. Is there an intramural program?	——	——	——	——	——	——
33. Major varsity sports?	——	——	——	——	——	——
34. A convocation series?	——	——	——	——	——	——
35. Dramatic opportunities?	——	——	——	——	——	——
36. Music (band and glee club)?	——	——	——	——	——	——
37. Any others you are particularly interested in: (item) _____	——	——	——	——	——	——

VI. Any special questions you want to ask? _____

_____

VII. Notes and comments _____

_____

(Student's name)_____

Figure 10-1   (*Continued*)

rally and without planning, for the majority these developmental opportunities would be missed unless specific provisions are made. This is another opportunity for the school counselor and classroom teacher to work cooperatively in planning meaningful experiences that enhance both the instructional programs and the student's personal development. Significant role experiences would include opportunities to function periodically as a leader, a team member, an individual (isolated) worker, a teacher, an achiever, a responsible person, a social being, a person of authority and decision making, or one who serves others. A role assignment sheet, as illustrated in Figure 10-2, is a method of recording these experiences.

_____ Grade   Class of _____ Period _____ to _____

B. D. Lewis Elementary School

Role Assignments	Leader	Team Member	Individual Worker	Achiever	Responsibility	Social Leader	Decision Maker	Server
Pupils' Names								
1. Marie Adams								
2. Alyssa Debrovitz								
3. Marc Collins								
4. Chester Dent								
5. Charles James								
6. Kathryn James								
7. Liona Chan								
8. Archie Leedy								
9. Paul Lewis								
10. Katherine Louise								
11. Daniel Kim								
12. Matt Nuzrem								
13. Jack Smith								
14. Alex Wagner								
15. Heather Watson								

* Dates are entered where role is assigned.

√ indicates student has assumed or experienced this role and further assignment is not needed at this time.

Figure 10-2   Role Assignments.

Source: Gibson (1972). *Career development in the elementary school.* Merrill: Columbus, OH.

Environmental Assessment

Environmental placement can be another developmental activity. The major focus of this type of placement is to provide students with the opportunities to experience other significant, yet distinctly different, environments from their own. An example is giving city youth opportunities to spend time in rural areas as part of farm days or country cousins programs. Urban youth may exchange places with farm youth for several days or weeks. Another example is a blend of educational preparation and environmental placement in which students spend some time in diverse collegiate settings.

Regardless of the nature of client placement, follow-up should also be planned. In the following section, reasons that clients are not placed and forgotten are set forth.

Follow-Up

Programs of placement activities, regardless of setting, must provide evidence of the effectiveness of their practices for both accountability and program improvement purposes. A large measure of supporting evidence for these purposes may be secured through carefully planned follow-up activities. As a complement to the guidance placement program, follow-up activities focus on effectiveness in placing persons for a variety of purposes and settings, as viewed not only by the clients but also by those to whom the client is responsible in such settings as job placement.

Follow-up data may be obtained through questionnaires, checklists, interviews, and phone calls. Placement follow-up usually focuses on how satisfied the persons are with their placement and the process; progress they believe they are making in their situation; adequacy of their previous preparation experience; and future plans and recommendations. Employers may be asked to respond concerning the adequacy of preparation and experience of the employee, adaptation to work, ability to work with others, progress anticipated by employee, and recommendations for improving the placement process.

In college placement, follow-up may seek to identify how adequately prepared for college the entering student is and areas of strength and weakness, the degree to which the student appears to be adjusting to college, and recommendations for improving the placement process. As follow-up data are collected, it is equally important to anticipate and plan for systematic utilization of the data.

In recognizing the importance of planning for career placement and follow-up, we would also be cognizant of the complexities and variables involved. In an effort to assist counselors and their clients to deal more effectively with those complexities and variables, computerized assistance systems have been and continue to be developed. Several of these systems will be described in a later section in this chapter.

CAREER COUNSELING IN NONSCHOOL SETTINGS

The initial out-of-school career contacts of many youths will be made through the assistance of their state employment services. In these offices, career guidance activities may be based on a review and discussion of the applicant's qualifications and interests in relation to available employment opportunities. Appraisal instruments, such as the General Aptitude Test Battery, may be used to further assist the client and the counselor in career planning. Counselors in these settings are usually especially well versed in their knowledge of local job opportunities and characteristics and usually have access to computerized job bank systems. These employment office counselors often work closely with high school counselors in facilitating the career planning and transitions of youths from school to work.

The young adult entering the workforce for the first time can encounter a number of challenges including the following.

- The individual discovers discrepancies between what he or she anticipated upon entry into the workplace and what is actually encountered. This initial let down or disillusionment can affect the individual's initial attitude and achievements.
- Adjusting to supervision and direction from superiors as well as adhering to company policies can be frustrating to those who were recently free spirited students.

- The assumption of complete responsibility, especially financially, for their life and lifestyle can be a burden if the individual is unprepared.
- The possibility of marriage brings another major responsibility and dramatic change in the individual's lifestyle to mesh with their initial career entry.
- The individual may suddenly have less free time as well as encounter possible changes in the types of leisure activities.

Career counseling can function at the pre-entry level to assist the individual in realistically entering the workplace as well as locating a first job commensurate, to the degree possible, with the client's interests and expectations. Counselors can also assist clients in their initial adjustments to the demands of the workplace, marriage, and changing lifestyle. Counselors in community mental health agencies, community career centers, employment offices, EAPs (employee assistance programs), and private practice may be called upon to provide young clients with career assistance.

Career counseling and placement, however, can no longer be considered an activity that focuses on youth alone. A variety of factors have resulted in significant changes in the career habitats of adult populations. Those changes, some of which were noted earlier in this chapter, in turn, have influenced the career counseling and placement efforts in governmental and business settings. Contributing factors include the impact of technological and social change, shifts in societal and consumer values, a population that is growing older and capable of working longer, economic necessity, and international market influences.

Moreover, technological change has resulted in related societal changes such as population shifts, altered consumer demands, and major new government policies regarding health, education, and welfare. These changes have had an impact on other occupations not directly affected by changing technologies. Human service occupations are a good example. Thousands of young adults entered educational programs in these fields. When they graduated several years later, they frequently found the labor market quite different from what it was when they began their schooling. Many could not find jobs in their career areas; others took jobs for which they were overqualified and underpaid.

Americans preparing for jobs in several other occupations have encountered similar difficulties. As technological and social changes become more rapid, predicting the state of the workforce becomes increasingly difficult.

During recent generations, social and cultural changes have also altered traditional concepts and expectations that resulted in sex-role stereotyping in the world of work. As noted earlier in this chapter, this situation has led to not only more female engineers, construction workers, airplane pilots (and more male nurses and elementary school teachers) but also increasing numbers of women who, in the process of combining careers and marriage, interrupt their careers for child rearing before returning to the labor force.

In short, midlife career changes and entries are becoming commonplace for both men and women.

Every occupation is represented, but some are more visible than others. Classic cases of midlife career change can be found in the ranks of those who put in twenty years or so in the military or in municipal activities, such as fire and police protection and then retire at a relatively young age, free to pursue a second career. In the 1970s, thousands of engineers and scientists became unemployed because of substantial cuts in space and defense spending; these workers in declining industries were often forced to seek unrelated types of employment, or to take lesser paying jobs in the same occupation. More recently, the field of education has experienced cutbacks, causing teachers and other educational personnel to switch career paths. Whether voluntary or involuntary, it is clear that midlife career change is a visible phenomenon and that a significant proportion of workers will not fit the one life—one occupation mode. (Herr and Cramer, 1996, pp. 535–536)

Though midlife career changes may be commonplace, even anticipated by many workers, such changes can prompt adjustment as well as decision-making difficulties. Some adjustments will be the result of adapting to a new work routine with new skills, new work associates, and possible movement to a new environment and new way of life. Also, some will view the necessity or desirability of career change as a reflection on their status as valued workers and an indication that they have erred in their earlier career planning. Marital relationships can be threatened, even when one of the spouses is not facing career change, and existing problems are often agitated further.

In counseling this more mature and work-experienced group, the career counselor will want to consider the following counseling goals (many of which involve reassurance and immediate assistance) outlined by Herr and Cramer (1996).

1. Provide support in building and maintaining positive attitudes toward one's worth and dignity. Is the individual confusing temporary rejection as a worker with rejection as a human being? Does the individual have a work history of rejection? Does the person express feelings of hopelessness, worthlessness, obsolescence, despair? Is confidence shattered?
2. Explore possible retraining and other avenues for improving employment opportunities.
3. Provide any and all geographic information. Does the individual know where the best markets for employment are? Is mobility a problem?
4. Assess the actual reasons for employment difficulties. For example, is the person coming for assistance because of layoff, resignation, sickness, retirement, or firing?
5. Assist individuals in accurately gauging their present state of motivation, the expectations they hold for future employment, and their perceptions of themselves as workers.
6. Especially with managerial, professional, and technical occupations, help the individual to consider the relative importance of such factors as salary, use of abilities, status, amount of responsibility, security, opportunities for advancement, chance to make a contribution, and so on. Also important is the need to explore the possibilities and consequences of occupational downgrading and salary decrease.
7. Assist in developing job-seeking behaviors, if necessary.
8. Provide placement and follow-up services if no other opportunities exist in the area served; refer to appropriate agencies and institutions if placement services are available. (p. 546)

Many of those seeking new careers will probably again seek the assistance of counselors in the Employment Security Division of the U.S. Department of Labor. The Comprehensive Employment and Training Act of 1982 is an example of federal assistance to state and local governments for the purpose of developing training programs to meet local job needs. This program has a wide range of training activities aimed at economically disadvantaged youth and adults.

More recently, the School-to-Work Opportunities Act was passed by Congress and was enacted into law in May 1994. This act is administered by the National School-to-Work Office under the joint direction of the U.S. Departments of Labor and Education. The act encourages educational and career opportunities for all students by creating a framework for business and educational partnerships at the state and local levels. It is anticipated that these partnerships help students make the vital connection between what they learn in school and in the workplace and prepare them for good careers and advanced education and training.

Other state and/or federal government programs include provisions for school-to-work transition programs, senior community service employment, job corps, and work incentive programs. State rehabilitation agencies provide career counseling and other services to those eligible.

Although ideally much midlife career change and career retirement counseling would take place in the workplace, some obstacles still impede this development. However, career development programs that provide supporting counseling services are also beginning to emerge in business and industry.

Moving along the maturity continuum, the aging of America is another phenomenon that is increasingly challenging those responsible for providing career counseling in institutional and agency settings. As people marvel at the artistic accomplishments of Grandma Moses at 100 and Pablo Picasso at 90, or George Burns's Academy Award–winning performance in *The Sunshine Boys*, one must be aware that age is not an inevitable barrier to career accomplishments. Coupled with this is also an awareness that life expectancy is increasing at the same time that human physical well-being and vigor are steadily improving for all age groups. It can be anticipated that increasing numbers of older and healthier citizens will be capable and desirous of work.

As with other age groups, the older American worker is entering a changing era highlighted by the virtual abolition of mandatory retirement. Age-based mandatory retirement was eliminated for all but a few special circumstances by the 1986 amendments to the 1967 Age Discrimination in Employment Act. Although on the surface this would appear to ensure that older workers could work as long as they wish, the restructuring of the world of work and its labor economy has resulted in older workers being prematurely forced into early retirement. This, at a time when more and more of the elderly are living longer, healthier lives is a source of concern to workers and employers alike. As a result, counselors in corporate employee assistance programs are being called upon with increasing frequency to assist older employees to prepare psychologically as well as economically for retirement and/or alternate career possibilities. Too, counselors in other nonschool settings, including older American Centers, churches, YWCAs and YMCAs, and elderhostels, are noting that many older retirees want to continue in or return to the workforce. Although some wish to do so for economic reasons, for others there may be the feeling of a loss of worth or status; loneliness and the lack of opportunity to associate with others, including feelings of belonging; and some retirees report boredom or the lack of any meaningful leisure time activities.

In assisting this client population, counselors must identify the expectancies and desires of the individual. In some instances, clients may be assisted in examining part-time or full-time reemployment options, or they may be given a more realistic view of retirement and retirement living.

In some situations, the exploration of meaningful leisure time and volunteer activities may be helpful. Elderly support groups may assist in coping with the loss of a spouse, a close friend's changing lifestyle associated with aging and retirement, or leisure planning and reentry into the job market.

COMPUTERIZED CAREER ASSISTANCE SYSTEMS

The 1990s have witnessed the continued rapid development and public acceptance of the computer. Computers, already popular in business, industry, and higher education, are now becoming commonplace in schools at all levels, and the current boom in home computers appears likely to continue. Young people's fascination with this technological marvel is reflected not only in their patronage of video arcades and purchase of computerized video games but also in their quest for knowledge and use of even the most sophisticated of computers. In fact, it may be that youth have become one of the most computer-literate groups.

The attraction of students at all age levels to the computer has given schools unprecedented opportunities for its utilization in motivation and learning. This potential exists for school counseling programs as well, especially in providing career information and assistance.

Although computer usage in counseling programs in educational settings is not new, having been around since the 1960s, the introduction of the microcomputer in the 1970s promoted major changes as well as opportunities for the utilization of computer-assisted career guidance systems. The economic and technical advantages of the microcomputer continue to be a major stimulus to their use in school settings for career counseling and guidance purposes.

Types of Systems

In this section, two types of systems will be briefly described: (a) information systems and (b) guidance systems.

Information Systems

Information systems are generally designed to provide a structured search scheme for occupations and to disseminate occupational and educational information to users. These procedural steps may be used separately or in sequence. In the former, the user may complete exercises or provide ratings or test scores, indicating interests and aptitudes as a basis for the computer's search for compatible occupations. In the latter, the user can access general information regarding specific occupations. The computer may also be programmed to respond to certain specific questions the user may ask about the occupation.

The development of information systems was greatly stimulated by grants provided by the Department of Labor and the National Occupational Information Coordinating Committee, which enabled states to develop statewide career information systems. Many of these, labeled career information systems (CIS), emphasize local and regional information. The components of the CIS includes an initial questionnaire, labeled QUEST, for providing self-estimates of various areas including aptitudes, interests, physical limitations, and so forth. Users then receive a printout briefly describing occupations related to their QUEST's responses. Many career information systems also use a file identifying ways to prepare for an occupation and a file identifying sources for additional information on each occupation.

Another information system, identified as the guidance information system (GIS), provides access to various kinds of national data regarding careers, educational opportunities, and the armed services. Several interest inventory systems are available as options. This system is marketed through the Educational Software Division of Houghton Mifflin Company, which reported use in 1990 at more than 4,500 locations. Information in this system is arranged according to groups of characteristics related to occupations and four-year colleges.

Another popular system, the C-LECT, offers three modules: an occupational module, an educational module, and a financial aids–apprenticeship module. In addition, the system provides a report writer that allows the user to get a report on his or her inputs at any time during the session. C-LECT is marketed by Chronicle Guidance Publications, Inc.

Guidance Systems

Guidance systems are broader in scope and more instructional than information systems, providing in addition to the organized search and dissemination functions of information systems modules such as self-assessment, instruction in decision making, future planning, and so forth. The two most popular of these systems are the System of Interactive Guidance and Information (SIGI), now updated as SIGI PLUS, developed and marketed through the Educational Testing Service, Princeton, New Jersey, and the Discover System, developed by JoAnn Harris-Bowlsbey and marketed through Discover, Inc., Hunt Valley, Maryland, and the American College Testing Program.

SIGI was designed originally to assist college and college-bound students and out-of-school adults. It is now applied to four-year schools and adults in a wide range of settings as well. SIGI PLUS consists of nine modules: (a) Introduction (orientation to the process), (b) Self-assessment, (c) Search (of possible preferred occupations), (d) Information (regarding possible occupations), (e) Skills, (f) Preparation, (g) Coping (can the individual do what is required), (h) Deciding (decision making), and (i) Next Steps (putting a plan into action).

The Discover system offers different programs for junior/middle school, high school, adults in transition, employees and organizations, and those approaching retirement. The junior/middle school version consists of three modules: (a) You and the World of Work, (b) Exploratory Occupations, and (c) Planning for High School. The popular high school version has seven modules.

Module 1
Beginning the Career Journey
Administers and scores a career maturity inventory and suggests parts of Discover to be used

Module 2
Learning About the World of Work
Helps users understand American College Testing's World-of-Work Map

Module 3
Learning About Yourself
Administers and scores online assessment and inventories and accepts results of paper-and-pencil versions

Module 4
Finding Occupations
Generates occupation lists from the results of Module 3

Module 5
Learning About Occupations
Provides national details about hundreds of occupations and includes local or state information if customized

Module 6
Making Educational Choices
Helps users select a training pathway

Module 7
Planning Next Steps
Provides details about educational opportunities and develops job-seeking skills (published by American College Testing)

The college versions add modules in career planning and transitions. The organizational and retirement versions consist of four modules, each unique to organizational settings or retirement planning.

In the mid-1990s, the downsizing of the military and many of the industries supplying the military, the conversion of industries to new products and production methods, and the creation of large pools of temporary or transitional employees have increased the need for adult career counseling and placement services.

Ethical Considerations

The rapid growth of computer use in the field of counseling, which is expected to increase in the future, has raised certain ethical questions. Potential problems in client confidentiality, misinterpretation of tests results and other data by clients, and lack of appropriate counselor interaction with clients are but a few examples. Sampson and Pyle (1983) suggest 14 principles in response to ethical issues involved with the use of computer-assisted counseling, testing, and guidance systems.

1. Ensure that confidential data maintained on a computer are limited to information that is appropriate and necessary for the services being provided.
2. Ensure that confidential data maintained on a computer are destroyed after it is determined that the information is no longer of any value in providing services.
3. Ensure that confidential data maintained on a computer are accurate and complete.
4. Ensure that access to confidential data is restricted to appropriate professionals by using the best computer security methods available.
5. Ensure that it is not possible to identify, with any particular individual, confidential data maintained in a computerized data bank that is accessible through a computer network.
6. Ensure that research participation release forms are completed by an individual who has automatically collected individually identifiable data as a result of using a computer-assisted counseling, testing, or guidance system.
7. Ensure that computer-controlled test scoring equipment and programs function properly thereby providing individuals with accurate test results.
8. Ensure that generalized interpretations of test results presented by microcomputer-controlled audiovisual devices accurately reflect the intention of the test author.
9. Ensure that a client's needs are assessed to determine if using a particular system is appropriate before using a computer-assisted counseling, testing, or guidance system.

10. Ensure that an introduction to using a computer-assisted counseling, testing, and guidance system is available to reduce possible anxiety concerning the system, misconceptions about the role of the computer, and misunderstandings about basic concepts or the operation of the system.

11. Ensure that a follow-up activity to using a computer-assisted counseling, testing, and guidance system is available to correct possible misconceptions, misunderstandings, or inappropriate use as well as assess subsequent needs of the client.

12. Ensure that the information contained in a computer-assisted career counseling and guidance system is accurate and up to date.

13. Ensure that the equipment and programs that operate a computer-assisted counseling, testing, and guidance system function properly.

14. Determining the need for counselor intervention depends on the likelihood that the client would experience difficulties that would in turn limit the effectiveness of the system or otherwise exacerbate the client's problem. It is the counselor's responsibility to decide whether the best approach to avoiding the above problems for a specific client population is direct intervention or indirect intervention through the use of workbooks, self-help guides, or other exercises. (pp. 285–286)

Sampson and colleagues (1997) indicate that

A better understanding of counseling applications available on existing computer networks (the Internet), combined with an understanding of evolving computer capabilities, can help counselors be better prepared to design and use applications to effectively serve clients when the future information highway becomes fully operational. (p. 203)

Certainly, we must hope that rapid developments in computer technology will not outrun careful consideration of the ethical issues involved.

SUMMARY

Dramatic changes in the world of work and the increased need for career assistance among all ages has resulted in career counseling and placement receiving a new impetus in both school and agency settings in recent decades. In the past, career counseling was a recognized activity of most school counseling programs, but it received little curricular emphasis and, as a result, was less than effective in many settings. The career education movement of the 1970s, however, led schools to recognize the inseparability of career education and career counseling and guidance. Career counseling programs were also encouraged to provide increased attention to placement and follow-up as a planned program activity. This emphasis has been prompted by legislative funding and recognition that career development without placement is an incomplete process. In this area, significant developments in computerized career assistance programs have been noted.

The concern over career planning and decision making has focused attention on why people make the decisions they do and with what results. To help develop an understanding of these issues, a number of the traditional theories were reviewed in this chapter. Some investigators are challenging these theories as inappropriate for today's populations and careers.

Agencies and other noneducational institutions that, in the past, were primarily concerned with career placement of first-time job seekers are now recognizing the probability and importance of midlife career changes, the possibility of employment in a new field after retirement, and the elimination of many traditional barriers to the employment of women, minorities, and older adults. Additionally, attention is being focused on increased recognition of the career needs of workers with disabilities and the career concerns of dual-career couples. These and other factors have led to a renewed interest in and examination of influences on career planning and decision making of adults. Also, the unique career assistance needs of older, retiring Americans is receiving increased attention.

Career counseling across the lifetime is becoming a reality.

Although, as previously noted, career counseling has been a historic traditional concern and activity of counselors, the next chapter will discuss a comparatively recent development in our profession—the counselor's role as a developmental and educational consultant.

DISCUSSION QUESTIONS

1.   What are the differences among career education, vocational education, and business education?

2.   If we anticipate that most adults will have as many as five major career changes during their working lifetimes, what are the implications for counseling in all settings? Identify five different careers you might consider.

3.   Discuss this multipotentiality of individuals and the implications of numerous career changes for career planning and decision making.

4.   What significant changes have occurred in careers and the world of work as you have observed it in recent generations? What changes may be anticipated in the beginning of the 21st century?

5.   Discuss a career in counseling as a way of life.

6.   Why have you decided to enter the career that you are in? What do you expect to give to this career? What do you anticipate that you will receive from it?

7.   Discuss the impact of significant career development experiences in your life.

8.   How are technological developments affecting the way we work?

9.   Discuss relationships between leisure time and work time.

10.   Identify and discuss the relationship between basic needs and career decisions.

CLASS ACTIVITIES

1.   Each member of the class identifies the significant influences on his or her career planning and decision making. Following a discussion of these with other members (in small groups), each individual identifies the theory of career choice that seems most appropriate for her or his career development and choice. Individuals form groups according to the theories they have identified and allow time for comparison of influencing factors among group members.

2.   Draw a career map (using newsprint and felt pens, with stick figures and simple drawings going from lower left to upper right) that depicts significant events and influencing factors in your career development and experiences.

3.   Organize small groups to investigate societal problems of a career nature and recommend national and/or local solutions. Problems might include concerns such as unemployment or underemployment for a special population (i.e., minorities, youth, women), substance abuse in the workplace, dual-career families and latchkey children, and school dropouts and career failures.

4.   Discuss your personal experiences with career assessment instruments and/or take a career interest or aptitude test and report your impressions of the results.

5.   Interview individuals either entering the workforce for the first time or those approaching retirement regarding their experiences for the coming year.

6.   If you had to identify an alternate career, indicate what that career might be and why.

7.   Discuss the implications of the suggestion that a career is a way of life as it applies to a career in counseling.

SELECTED READINGS

Borders, L. D., & Archadel, K. A. (1987). Self-beliefs and career counseling. *Journal of Career Development, 14* (2), 69–79.

Borgen, F. H., Layton, W. L., Veenhuizen, D. L. & Johnson, D. J. (1985). Vocational behavior and career development. *Journal of Vocational Behavior, 27* (2), 218–269.

Brown, D. (1987). The status of Holland's theory of vocational choice. *The Career Development Quarterly, 36* (1), 13–23.

Bundy, M., & Boser, J. (1987). Helping latchkey children: A group guidance approach. *The School Counselor, 35* (1), 58–65.

Cochran, L. (1997). *Career counseling: A narrative approach.* Thousand Oaks, CA: Sage.

Feller, R., & Gluckman, N. (1986). The unemployed and counselors: An analysis of responses to a complex social issue. *Counseling and Human Development, 18* (6), 1–11.

Gerstein, L., & Bayer, G. (1988). Employee assistance programs: A system's investigation of their use. *Journal of Counseling and Development, 66* (6), 294–297.

Gilbert, L. A. (Ed.). (1987). Dual-career families in perspective [Special edition]. *The Counseling Psychologist, 15* (1), 3–145.

Herr, E. (1987). Comprehensive career guidance and vocational education: Natural allies. *Vocational Education Journal, 62* (6), 30–33.

Holland, J. (1987). Current status of Holland's theory of careers: Another perspective. *The Career Development Quarterly, 36* (1), 24–30.

Holland, J. L. (1996). Integrating career theory and practice: The current situation and some potential remedies. In M. L. Savickas & W. B. Walsh (Eds.), *Handbook of career counseling theory and practice* (pp. 1–11). Palo Alto, CA: Davies-Black.

Johnson, R. (1985). Microcomputer-assisted career exploration. *The Vocational Guidance Quarterly, 33* (4), 296–304.

Levinson, E. (1987). Vocational assessment and programming of students with handicaps: A need for school counselor involvement. *The School Counselor, 35* (1), 6–8.

Lopez, F., & Andrews, S. (1987). Career indecision: A family systems perspective. *Journal of Counseling and Development, 65* (6), 304–307.

Myers, S. L., Jr. (1986). Black unemployment and its link to crime. *Urban League Review, 10* (1), 98–105.

Patterson, J. (1985). Career development: Revolution, reform, and renaissance. *Journal of Career Development, 12* (2), 129–144.

Perosa, S. L., & Perosa, L. M. (1987). Strategies for counseling midcareer changers: A conceptual framework. *Journal of Counseling and Development, 65* (10), 558–561.

Phillips, S. D., & Imhoff, A. R. (1997). Women and career development: A decade of research. *Annual Review of Psychology, 48,* 31–59.

Prediger, D. J., & Sawyer, R. L. (1986). Ten years of career development: A nationwide study of high school students. *Journal of Counseling and Development, 65* (1), 45–49.

Raskin, P. M. (1994). Identity and the career counseling of adolescents: The development of vocational identity. In S. L. Archer (Ed.), *Interventions for adolescent identity development* (pp. 155–173). Thousand Oaks, CA: Sage.

Repp, A. C., Favell, J., & Munk, D. (1996). Cognitive and vocational interventions for school-age children and adolescents with mental retardation. In J. W. Jacobson & J. A. Mulick (Eds.), *Manual of diagnosis and professional practice in mental retardation* (pp. 265–276). Washington, DC: American Psychological Association.

Wrenn, C. G. (1988). The person in career counseling. *The Career Development Quarterly, 36* (4), 337–342.

RESEARCH OF INTEREST

Apostal, R. A. (1985). Expressed inventoried interest agreement and type of Strong/Campbell Interest Inventory Scale. *Journal of Counseling Psychology, 32* (4), 634–636.

Abstract

This study examined expressed inventoried interest agreement for each type of Strong-Campbell Interest Inventory Scale in a sample of female college students. Three levels of agreement were established: low, statistical, and high. Findings revealed statistical and high levels of agreement across occupations in addition to differences in agreement level across scale types.

Baker, S. B., & Popowicz, C. L. (1983). Meta-analysis as a strategy for evaluating effects of career education interventions. *Vocational Guidance Quarterly, 31* (3), 178–186.

Abstract

Meta-analysis techniques, which allowed research from numerous empirical studies to be synthesized, was used to analyze the effects of career education. Data were obtained from 18 published empirical studies. The experimental treatment group post-test results were compared with control group post-test outcomes to determine the effect sizes in each study. The accumulated effect sizes were then averaged and are reported in terms of average standard deviations across the 18 studies: 17% were negative and 83% positive. Career education interventions resulted in respectable effects on students, and similar results may be expected in the future. It is suggested that for career education planners, this synthesis offers evidence that career education works.

Best, S., & Knapp, L. L. (1982). Relationship of interest measurement derived from the COPSystem Interest Inventory and the Kuder General Interest Survey: Construct validation of two measures of occupational activity preferences. *Educational and Psychological Measurement, 42* (4), 1289–1293.

Abstract

Similar scales on the California Occupational Preference System (COPSystem Interest Inventory) and the Kuder General Interest Survey were compared in terms of correlations between the scales. The results of comparing the three highest interest areas are interpreted as supporting the construct validity of the two instruments.

Brown, D., Wase, W. B., & Brown, S. T. (1985). A predictive validation of the Career Decision-Making System. *Measurement and Evaluation in Counseling and Development, 18* (2), 81–85.

Abstract

A predictive validation study of the Career Decision-Making System (CDM), using as criteria the stated career choices and expected postsecondary majors of high school seniors ($N = 164$), yielded support for the instrument.

Cooper, S. E. (1986). The effects of group and individual vocational counseling on career indecision and personal indecisiveness. *Journal of College Student Personnel, 27* (1), 39–42.

Abstract

A sample of 24 students, in both group and individual vocational counseling, showed decreases in career indecision and personal indecision.

Emmett, J. D. (1997). The preparation of elementary school counselors for career development: What exists—what is needed? *Journal of Career Development, 23* (3), 177–187.

Abstract

Forty directors of accredited programs in school counseling responded to a survey. Participants were asked whether or not they had modified the requirements of their career development courses for students preparing to work in career development at the elementary school level. Those answering in the affirmative were asked which of six course areas they had modified and to describe the modifications made. The six course areas were career development theories, career assessment, career information resources, career development programming, field experiences, and career interviewing/career counseling competencies. Participants were also asked to describe those modifications to their career development courses that they believed to be most successful. Eighteen of the respondents reported modifying their career courses for elementary school counselors-in-training. Many of the modifications occurred in the areas of career theory, information resources, and development programming.

Fleenor, J. (1986). The personal career development profile: Using the 16 PF for vocational
exploration. *Measurement and Evaluation in
Counseling Development, 18* (4), 185–189.

Abstract

This article reviews the Sixteen Personality Factor Questionnaire and the Personal Career Development Profile as tools for vocational
exploration and career development. Reliability and validity problems are reported, followed
by a recommendation to use the Strong-Campbell Interest Inventory instead.

Glaize, D. L., & Myrick, R. D. (1984). Interpersonal groups or computers? A study of career
maturity and career decidedness. *Vocational
Guidance Quarterly, 32* (3), 168–176.

Abstract

This article compares the effectiveness of a
computer-assisted guidance program (Discover),
a small group guidance intervention (Vocational
Exploration Group), and a combined approach
on career maturity and decidedness in 120 high
school students. All three interventions were significantly helpful to students.

Haviland, M. G., & Hansen, J. I. C. (1987). Criterion Validity of the Strong-Campbell Interest
Inventory for American Indian college students. *Measurement and Evaluation in Counseling and Development, 19* (4), 196–201.

Abstract

This study assessed criterion validity of the
Strong Vocational Interest Blank–Strong-
Campbell Interest Inventory for a heterogeneous
sample of American Indian college students
(N = 49). For the analysis of the concurrent validity between major and Occupational Scale
score, the excellent and moderate concurrent hit
rate for women in the direct relationship category was 64%; for men it was 44%.

Juntunen, C. (1996). Relationship between a feminist approach to career counseling and career
self-efficacy beliefs. *Journal of Employment
Counseling, 33* (3), 130–143.

Abstract

To determine whether liberal feminist and
conventional approaches to career counseling
might differentially affect women's career self-
efficacy beliefs, 40 college women heard audio-
tapes of career counseling and provided ratings
of their own career self-efficacy. Results show
that a feminist approach to career counseling
can have a significantly more positive effect on
career self-efficacy than a conventional approach. This was true for ratings on the category of nontraditional careers as well as for
overall career self-efficacy ratings.

Kivlighan, D. M., Jr., & Shapiro, R. M. (1987).
Holland Type as a predictor of benefit from
self-help career counseling. *Journal of Counseling Psychology, 34* (3), 326–329.

Abstract

Holland high-point code and Self-Directed
search scale scores were used to predict benefit
from a self-help career counseling intervention
for 52 students undecided as to career. Participants with realistic, investigative, or conventional high-point codes showed greater changes
in vocational identity when compared with participants with artistic, social, or enterprising
high-point codes.

Luzzo, D. A., James, T., & Luna, M. (1996). Effects
of attributional retraining on the career beliefs and career exploration behavior of college students. *Journal of Counseling Psychology,
43* (4), 415–422.

Abstract

Two studies were conducted to evaluate
the efficacy of attributional retraining as a ca-

reer counseling technique for college students. Participants who received the attributional retraining treatment viewed an eight-minute videotape designed to foster internal, controllable, and unstable attributions for career decision making. Participants in the control groups viewed a similar videotape that lacked any reference to career-related attributions. Results revealed that participants who received attributional retraining exhibited significant changes in career beliefs and attributional style and engaged in significantly more career exploration behavior than the participants in the control groups. An evaluation of attributional retraining as a career-counseling technique for college students is provided, and ideas for further research are suggested.

Marshall, E. (1985). Relationship between client-learning style and preference for counselor approach. *Counselor Education and Supervision, 24* (4), 353–359.

Abstract

A client-counselor matching model based on Kolb's experiential learning theory was examined. A questionnaire, which included Kolb's Learning Style Inventory (LSI) and four counselor approach profiles, was completed by 205 counseling clients. The clients indicated which counselor they preferred. The following four preference patterns were predicted: concrete learners—experiential approach, abstract learners—rational approach, active learners—behavioral approach, and reflective learners—client-centered approach. The results did not confirm the hypothesized four-way model, although limited support for the matching concept was evident when only two counselors were considered. Clients preferring directive counselors were more abstract learners. Clients preferring nondirective counselors were more concrete learners. Overall, clients preferred the rational counselor approach. A nonclient comparison group ($N = 75$) preferred the client-centered approach.

Mitchell, L. K., & Krumboltz, J. D. (1987). The effects of cognitive restructuring and decision-making training on career indecision. *Journal of Counseling and Development, 66* (4), 171–174.

Abstract

These researchers designed a cognitive restructuring intervention for individuals having difficulty with career decision making, which proved more effective than decision-making training and a nontreatment control condition in reducing anxiety about career decision making and in encouraging vocational exploratory behavior. Cognitive restructuring clients used skills, learned more, and were more satisfied with their decisions.

Olson, T. F., & Matkin, R. E. (1992). Student and counselor perceptions of career counselor work activities in a community college. *The Career Development Quarterly, 40* (4), 324–333.

Abstract

This study examined whether differences exist between student and counselor perceptions of work activities performed by counselors in a community college. Three hundred and twenty-two students and eleven counselors responded to a 40-item questionnaire indicating whether tasks were actually performed and whether they ought to be performed by counselors when providing career guidance. Students indicated they did not believe counselors were actually performing the majority of tasks commonly and ideally associated with career counseling services. Although students and counselors agreed on ideal career counselor work activities, counselor responses revealed no differences between their actual and ideal duties.

Smith, M., & Glass, G. (1977). Meta-analysis of psychotherapy outcome studies. *American Psychologist, 32* (9), 752–760.

Abstract

Results of nearly 400 controlled evaluations of psychotherapy and counseling were coded and integrated statistically. The findings provide convincing evidence of the efficacy of psychotherapy. Few important differences in effectiveness could be established among many quite different types of psychotherapy. More generally, virtually no difference in effectiveness was observed between the class of all behavioral therapies (systematic desensitization, behavior modification) and the nonbehavioral therapies (Rogerian, psychodynamic, rational emotive, transactional analysis, etc.).

Sumerel, M. B., & Borders, L. D. (1995). Supervision of career counseling interns. *Clinical Supervisor, 13* (1), 91–100.

Abstract

This study examined data concerning career counseling internships and compared supervision practices in various internship sites. Thirty-four supervisors of career counseling interns in three settings (college/university career planning centers, college/university counseling centers, and community colleges) described their supervisory approach, format, and focus, and indicated which career counseling competencies they emphasized. Results indicate that supervision practices were similar in the three settings: supervision occurred weekly and was based on self-report given by the intern in individual sessions. Supervisors emphasized the career counseling competencies of counseling skills and career information most often and consultation least often.

The Counselor as Developmental and Educational Consultant

A network television news program recently carried a report that a group of big business executives were going to offer their consulting services to small businesses to aid their survival chances. These businesspeople were referred to as consultants—a term so common that the newscaster did not bother to define it. Consultation as an activity and consultant as a career label became increasingly prevalent in the last generations of the 20th century. Although generally recognized as originating in the medical profession in the 19th century, today the professions themselves only number among the many career areas using the label *consultant*. This includes such common examples as loan consultant, landscape consultant, travel consultant, tax consultant, automotive sales consultant, and on and on.

A *consultant* is usually an expert in a field who consults with or offers her or his expertise to others both within and outside the career area. In fact, the activity is so common in the business world that we frequently hear humorous definitions of a consultant, such as "anyone 50 miles from home with a briefcase," or "one who pulls in, pops off, and pulls out."

Consultation as a mental health and educational activity is less well recognized and understood, although mental health consultation has a long tradition in the healing arts. This chapter's objective is to introduce and describe the activity of consulting and the counselor's role as a consultant.

The label *consultant* usually refers to an individual possessing extra expertise, knowledge, and/or skill in a specific field. The individual engages in consultation when her or his expertise is requested by another party or organization, usually to enable the requesting party or organization to assist another—a third party or organization.

The consultant is the helper in a triad that includes a consultee and the object of the consultation. For example, a mental health counselor may serve as a consultant to parents who want to improve their children's social skills; unlike counseling, this is not a therapeutic relationship. It is also important to keep in mind that the consultant's role is an advising or enhancing one, not a supervisory one. Remember too, that these distinctive roles are maintained throughout the consultation experience and that their identities are not blurred or distorted in any way.

Consultation in its application to counseling as a mental health activity in schools has been even less widely recognized and defined. Most of the attention given to consultation as a school counseling activity before the 1970s seemed to suggest that it was primarily appropriate for the elementary school only. Articles such as Abbe (1961), "Consultation to a School Guidance Program," Crocker (1964), "Depth Consultation with Parents," Eckerson and Smith (1962), "Elementary School Guidance: The Consultant," and Faust (1967), "The Counselor as a Consultant to Teachers" dealt with consultation in elementary school guidance programs. Some of the popular basic guidance texts of the 1950s and 1960s such as Jones (1963), *Principles of Guidance*, Hutson (1958), *The Guidance Function in Education*, Crow and Crow (1960), *An Introduction to Guidance*, Ohlsen (1955), *Guidance: An Introduction*, and Froehlich (1958), *Guidance Services in Schools* made no mention of consultation as a school counseling activity.

In discussing consultation in his early landmark publication, *The Counselor-Consultant in the Elementary School*, Faust (1967) notes that

> although counseling has been described and researched for many years, this is not true of consultation. The latter has been practiced for as many years as counseling, if not longer, but the literature is strangely sparse in its treatment of this role. (p. 32)

Although these early discussions focused on mental health consultation in community agencies, industrial settings, and the elementary school, in the past decade consultation as an appropriate counselor activity in any setting, including secondary schools and higher education institutions, has developed rapidly. For example, two consecutive special issues of the American Counseling Association's (then called the American Personnel and Guidance Association) journal, the *Personnel and Guidance Journal* (February and March, 1978: Kurpius & Robinson, 1978; Kurpius, 1978) and the special issue of *The Counseling Psychologist* [Volume 13 (3), July 1985: Brown & Kurpius, 1985] consider the counselor's role and function as a consultant at all educational levels as well as in community and other mental health settings. An increasing number of textbooks also deal with the topic. The Association for Counselor Education and Supervision published two monographs in 1988 (Kurpius & Brown, 1988; Brown, Kurpius, & Morris, 1988) focusing on consultation, and then, in 1993, the American Counseling Association (formerly named the American Association for Counseling and Development) again devoted two special issues of its journal, *Journal of Counseling and Development* (July–August: Kurpius & Fuqua, 1993a, Volume 71 (6); and November–December (Kurpius & Fuqua, 1993b, Volume 72 (2)] to consultation. Let us, therefore, proceed to examine the consultation process and some of the roles and models for consultation.

THE CONSULTATION PROCESS

When the counselor functions as a consultant, one must keep in mind certain assumptions that are basic to the consultation process.

- The need that exists cannot be adequately met by the individual or organization requesting consultation.
- The consultant possesses the special expertise to appropriately assist the requestor.
- The requesting party (the consultee) has the capacity to implement the consultant's recommendations.
- The consultant understands the organizational and environmental context within which his or her suggestions will be applied and their possible consequences beyond problem solutions.

Woody, Hansen, and Rossberg (1989), after reviewing several writers, consolidated their conceptualizations of the consultation process into five stages: "(1) pre-entry, (2) initial contact and establishment of a relationship, (3) assessment and diagnosis, (4) intervention, and (5) termination" (p. 179).

Even though the process of consultation is initiated by the consultee in need of assistance, the consultant must keep in mind that consultation is not primarily therapeutic in nature. In other words, those seeking consultative assistance do not usually come to the counselor-consultant for personal counseling; rather, they come for assistance with a well-defined professional problem.

CONSULTATION MODELS

The increased demand for consultation services has resulted in the development of a variety of models appropriate to the consultation process. Although differences exist among authorities in the area of consultation in terms of the organization or categorization of theories or systems for providing consultation services, similarities are far more prevalent than differences.

The traditional historic model that highlights the basic consultation process is a triadic model, as suggested by Tharp and Wetzel (1969). In this model, consultation services are offered indirectly through an intermediary to a target client or clients. The model illustrated in Figure 11-1 is described as a consultative triad, in which all effects proceed to the target via the mediator, none directly from consultant to target. This analysis describes functional positions, not the people who occupy those positions.

Four popular consultation models suggest the counselor-consultant can function effectively by providing a direct service to a client identified by another party, prescribing a solution to a specific problem identified by a consultee, assisting others in developing a plan for problem solution, and taking direct responsibility for defining a problem and proposing a solution. Kurpius (1978) and Kurpius and Fuqua (1993b) organize these functions into four consulting modalities as follows.

Provision Mode

The provision mode of consultation is commonly used when a potential consultee finds himself confronted with a problem for which he or she may not have the time, interest, or competence to define objectively, to identify possible solutions, or to implement and evaluate the problem-solving strategy. Consequently, a consultant is requested to provide a direct service to the client, with little or no intervention by the consultee after the referral is accepted.

Prescriptive Mode

Sometimes consultees experience unusual work-related problems for which they request special help. Even though competent and motivated to solve the problem directly, the consultees may lack confidence in their own intervention strategy or may lack certain specific knowledge and skills for carrying out a given problem-solving plan.

In these situations, the consultee is often in need of a resource person (consultant) to support the diagnosis and treatment plan already developed by the consultee or to explore additional alternatives for defining and solving a specific problem.

There are other times, however, when a consultee is looking for an exact "prescription" to ameliorate a specific problem. While the prescriptive mode is quite appropriate for many situations, there are four questions that should be answered jointly by the consultant and consultee: (a) Has all the information needed to define and solve the problem been shared and is [it] accurate? (b) Has the plan prescribed by the consultant been accepted by the consultee and will it be implemented as designed? (c) Who will evaluate the "process" and "outcomes" associated with the prescriptive plan—the consultant, the consultee, or both? (d) Will adjustments in the prescription, if needed, be requested by the consultee?

Collaboration Mode

When following the collaboration mode the consultant's goal is to facilitate the consultee's self-direction and innate capacity to solve problems. As a result, the consultant serves more as a

Figure 11-1 The Consultative Triad.
Source: From R. G. Tharp and R. Wetzel, *Behavioral Modification in the Natural Environment* (1969), p. 47. Copyright © 1969. Used with permission of Academic Press and Ralph J. Wetzel.

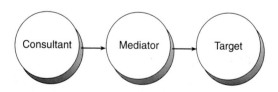

generalist than a technical expert. His major efforts are directed toward helping people develop a plan for solving problems. Hence he acts as a catalyst and "reality tapper," helping consultees to share observations, concepts, and proven practices. He also helps consultees examine forces that are facilitative or debilitative in both the immediate and larger environments.

Mediation Mode

Mediation is uniquely different from the other three modes of consultation in which the consultee initiates the contact and requests help for solving a problem. In mediation, it is the consultant who recognizes a persisting problem, gathers, analyzes, and synthesizes existing information, defines the problem, decides on the most appropriate intervention, and then calls together the persons who have direct contact with the problem and have the greatest potential to influence a desired change. (Kurpius, 1978, p. 335)

Schein (1978, 1991) organizes the consultation process into three models. The assumptions of these models are as follows.

Model 1: Purchase of Expertise

The core characteristic of this model is that the client has made up his or her mind on what the problem is, what kinds of help are needed, and to whom to go for this help. The client expects expert help and expects to pay for it, but not to get involved in the process of consultation itself.

In order for this model to work successfully, the following assumptions have to be met, however.

1. That the client has made a correct diagnosis of his or her own problem.
2. That the client has correctly identified the consultant's capabilities to solve the problem.
3. That the client has correctly communicated the problem.
4. That the client has thought through and accepted the potential consequences of the help that will be received.

In summary, this model of consultation is appropriate when clients have diagnosed their needs correctly, have correctly identified consultant capabilities, have done a good job of communicating what problem they are actually trying to solve, and have thought through the consequences of the help they have sought. As can be seen, this model is "client intensive," in that it puts a tremendous load on the client to do things correctly if the problem is to be solved. If problems are complex and difficult to diagnose, it is highly likely that this model will not prove helpful.

Model 2: Doctor-Patient

The core of this model is that the client experiences some symptoms that something is wrong but does not have a clue as to how to go about figuring out what is wrong or how to fix it. The diagnostic process itself is delegated completely to the consultant along with the obligation to come up with a remedy. The client becomes dependent upon the consultant until such time as the consultant makes a prescription, unless the consultant engages the client in becoming more active on his or her own behalf. Several implicit assumptions are the key to whether or not the doctor-patient model will in fact provide help to the client.

1. That the client has correctly interpreted the symptoms and the sick "area."
2. That the client can trust the diagnostic information that is provided by the consultant.
3. That the "sick" person or group will reveal the correct information necessary to arrive at a diagnosis and cure, i.e., will trust the doctor enough to "level" with him or her.
4. That the client has thought through the consequences, i.e., is willing to accept and implement whatever prescription is given.
5. That the patient/client will be able to remain healthy after the doctor/consultant leaves.

In summary, the doctor-patient model of consultation highlights the dependence of the client on the consultant both for diagnosis and prescription and thus puts a great burden on the client to correctly identify sick areas, accurately communicate symptoms, and think through the consequences of being given a prescription.

Model 3: Process Consultation

The core of this model is the assumption that for many kinds of problems that clients face, the only way to locate a workable solution, one that the client will accept and implement, is to involve the client in the diagnosis of the problem and the generating of that solution. The focus shifts from the content of the problem to the process by which problems are solved, and the consultant offers "process expertise" in how to help and how to solve problems, not expertise on the particular content of the client's problem. The consultant does not take the problem onto his or her own shoulders in this model. The "monkey always remains on the client's back," but the consultant offers to become jointly involved with the client in figuring out what is the problem, why it is a problem, why it is a problem right now, and what might be done about it. This consulting model is not a panacea appropriate to all problems and all situations. It also rests on some specific assumptions that have to be met if the model is to be viewed as the appropriate way to work with a client.

1. That the nature of the problem is such that the client not only needs help in making an initial diagnosis but would benefit from participation in the process of making that diagnosis.
2. That the client has constructive intent and some problem-solving ability.
3. That the client is ultimately the only one who knows what form of solution or intervention will work in his or her own situation.
4. That if the client selects and implements his or her own solution, the client's problem-solving skills for future problems will increase.

How does the consultant implement the process consultation model? The basic principle is to get into the client's world and see it initially from the client's perspective. This usually means paying attention to the "task process"—and how the problem is defined, how the agenda is set, how information is gathered, how decisions are made, all the activities that make up the "problem-solving process." (Schein, 1978, pp. 340–342)

It has become a principle in education and psychology that it is far better in the long run to teach others to be effective problem solvers than it is merely to solve a given problem for them. Thus, the more effective organizational consultants will leave the organization with a model that has been learned and can be independently implemented. (Fuqua & Kurpius, 1993, p. 607)

Fuqua and Kurpius (1993) then go on to discuss five conceptual models and conclude by presenting them in a table (see Table 11-1).

Blocher (1987) identifies seven models of consultation as follows.

1. *Triadic consultation*—three distinct roles characterize this model. They are the consultant who provides the expertise, the mediator who applies what he or she receives from the consultant and the client who is the object or recipient of the service.
2. *Technical consultation*—a more narrow and focused intervention in which a consultant's expertise is sought in relation to a specific situation or problem.
3. *Collaborative consultation*—suggests a cooperative relationship in which information and resources are pooled and the consultant and consultee work together as equal partners in the process.
4. *Facilitative consultation*—the consultant facilitates the consultee's access to a variety of new resources. In this model both parties recognize the consultant's legitimate interest in the broad aspects of the functioning of the consultee system.

TABLE 11-1 Integrating Conceptual Models

Conceptual model	Operating frames			
	Reactive	Responsive	Proactive	High performing
Systems Theory	Where is the breakdown? What subsystem is causing the problem?	Who's responsible for what?	How do we refine our system for the long term?	How does a system achieve flexibility?
Organizational Culture	Who is causing us pain and why?	How do we resolve conflict?	How is our culture affecting us?	How do we manage our culture for improving the quality of life?
Strategic Planning	How do we alleviate the pain in the short term?	What needs to work better? How do we correct it?	How do we develop a plan for moving forward?	How does strategic planning become part of our system?
Organizational Change Cycles	How did we "bottom out" developmentally?	How do we cope with these circumstances?	How do we get to the developmental phase?	How do we monitor and influence normal developmental cycles?
Paradigm Shift Thinking	How can we relieve stress without changing our thinking?	What thoughts need to be adjusted?	Is our thinking congruent with our purposes?	How can we continually update our knowledge and our thinking in a changing world?

Source: Reprinted from D. R. Fuqua & D. K. Kurpius, "Conceptual Models in Organizational Consultation," *Journal of Counseling and Development, 71,* 1993, p. 617. © American Counseling Association. Reprinted with permission. No further reproduction authorized without written permission of the American Counseling Association.

5. *Mental health consultation*—the consultant assists a consultee (therapist) to gain a better understanding of one's interaction with a client through such means as analyzing the treatment approach, consideration of their (consultee's) responses to their client and in general, providing support to the consultee.

6. *Behavioral consultation*—focused on the use of behavioral management techniques as suggested or taught by the consultant to a consultee in order to influence or shape the behavior of the consultee's clients in a systematic way.

7. *Process consultation*—the consultant delivers services to an organization in order to increase the effectiveness of a work group in reaching its goals. This consultation addresses the interactions among groups of individuals who work with each other in face-to-face relationships. (pp. 264–270)

CONSULTATION SKILLS

As with all counseling and guidance activities, certain special skills are needed if the counselor is to function effectively as a consultant in either agency or school settings. These skills include

- The special expertise needed to provide effective consultation for the identified need
- Knowledge of and experience in the consultation process
- The recognition and understanding of differing environments and their impacts on populations and organizations

Of course, the counselor who is functioning in a consultation role should possess and employ those skills essential in the counseling process. Certainly communication and other interpersonal skills such as attending, listening, questioning, and feedback are critical. Respect and understanding should be exhibited. Consultants should possess expertise in systematic problem-solving techniques and evaluation procedures as well. The counselor's skills in facilitating groups can be very helpful. Counselors must also possess the ability to effectively assume different roles as needed during the consultation process. These include roles as facilitators, coordinators, mediators, planners, educators, and motivators.

CONSULTATION IN SCHOOL SETTINGS

In school settings, counselors who function in a consulting role are, in effect, giving their special expertise to teachers, school administrators, and other appropriate personnel. In this role, they become a resource professional for the developmental or adjustment needs involving third parties, usually students. For the counselor to function effectively as a consultant in the educational setting, one must possess, as noted earlier in this chapter, special knowledge or skills appropriate to the consulting need. Among the relevant skills the counselor can bring to consulting with teachers and other educational providers and planners are the following.

1. An understanding of human growth and development, the problems and processes of adjustment, and the needs of the individual as one goes through those processes.

2. An understanding of psychological or affective education in the classroom, and a concern for its importance.

3. An understanding of and skills in promoting communications and other desirable human relationship skills.

4. Training in the assessment of individual characteristics and skills in relating these assessments
to the development of the individual's potential.

5. Special knowledge of educational and career development and opportunities.

6. An ability to communicate, counsel, and consult with parents, fellow educators, and the community.

7. An understanding of group processes and skills useful in facilitating group motivation and
change. (Gibson, 1973, p. 51)

In addition, to function effectively as a consultant, the counselor must have a background of understanding of the person or group with whom she or he is consulting, the target
population for the consulting, and the characteristics of the school in which the consulting is
taking place. The counselor-consultant should also be knowledgeable regarding contributing
external environmental factors.

As a consultant, the school counselor has the potential to engage in a wide range of activities or roles, which we will look at next.

Consulting with Teachers

As mentioned previously, the teacher is the key person in school settings at any level. In consultation in schools, then, the counselor must assume that he or she will most frequently consult with teachers individually or in groups. This probability is further highlighted by the fact
that teachers have the most frequent contacts with pupils and that the developmental and adjustment needs of their pupils are often expressed in classroom groups. Counselors may effectively assist teachers as consultants to individualize classroom instruction.

School counselors are also experienced in collecting, organizing, and synthesizing data
on individual students and in interpreting this information to identify individual differences.
Through these activities, they sharpen their own understanding of the individual and share
these insights in consultation with the classroom teacher.

Additionally, the counselor's expertise in human behavior and development theory
combined with the teacher's knowledge of instructional methods and materials is the basis for
an excellent team effort in the crucial task of planning and establishing a productive learning
environment.

The classroom teacher is obviously the most knowledgeable about resources appropriate to his or her subject matter, but the counselor can nonetheless be profitably consulted on
those occasions when specialized career and educational information is needed to make a class
more meaningful. He or she can also be consulted to identify out-of-school resources and experiences relevant to students' learning needs. The counselor's insights can be helpful in the
development of materials and methodologies that will enable counselors and teachers to work
together in special educational activities with vocational students.

Further, the effects of Public Law 94-142, requiring all children categorized as disabled to be placed in regular educational programs to the fullest extent possible, has
resulted in a wider diversity in the characteristics and abilities of classroom groups. Too, the
counselor has an important role to function as a guidance curriculum consultant. Schmidt
(1993) suggests that

guidance is the responsibility of everyone and is best implemented when it is integrated as an essential part of the school curriculum. Guidance does not occur at a single moment or as a solitary event with a teacher saying "Students put your books away; it is time for guidance!" Rather, it is infused with all subjects, and in all daily instruction. For this infusion to happen successfully, teachers and counselors plan appropriate activities for classroom instruction.

In elementary and middle schools where teachers team by grade levels or subject areas to plan instructional programs, counselors consult with these groups to share guidance objectives and offer suggestions of activities to use in classroom instruction. In high schools, counselors meet with departments to achieve a similar purpose. This process of planning together allows teachers to use counselors as resources while maintaining their leadership role in the instructional program. These consultations also allow counselors and teachers to share information about particular students who are struggling and in need of additional services beyond classroom guidance. (p. 85)

Counselors will continue to play a significant consultant role in assisting teachers specifically and the educational system generally in implementing this act.

Again, a basic principle of effective consultation is that the recipients must believe that they need it. Teachers and others will neither seek out nor be receptive to the counselor as a consultant if they see no value or rationale for such assistance. In each situation, therefore, the counselor must communicate and demonstrate her or his role as an effective consultant.

Consulting with the School Administrator

The school counselor can also make significant contributions to the educational leadership of the school and the school system. The counselor has the capacity to gather data descriptive of the characteristics of the student population and their needs, which, in turn, can provide useful information for educational planning and management.

The counselor's understanding of the process and characteristics of human growth and development enables him or her to relate and provide counsel regarding the special needs of individuals and groups of pupils.

The counselor can also provide valuable consulting experience to the school administrator on the school climate or environment. A mentally healthy school environment facilitates not only learning but also positive social interactions and good citizenship. Because this aspect of school life seems often overlooked (or ignored, as accountability models stress standardized measured academic achievements), counselors may have to become advocates for a healthy school environment with their school administrators. In this capacity, counselors may help administrators understand the counselor's role in planning and implementing schoolwide programs that have a good impact on the school's psychological environment. Finally, the counselor does not overlook the morale needs of his or her colleagues—the teachers. Stress management workshops, working to establish better and more open communications between teachers and administrators, and jelly bean days (i.e., special compliment-giving times) are all helpful ways counselors can, through consultation, assist school administrators and the school environment.

Consulting with Parents

The counselor can effectively consult with parents on various occasions to promote understanding of pupil characteristics and their relationships to pupil behavior. Consultation can assist parents in coping with or modifying student behaviors, improving interpersonal relationship skills, and adjusting attitudes. Parents may also consult with the school counselor in regard to their children's academic planning, progress, or problems. High school parents will frequently consult with school counselors about their child's career-planning needs. The counselor may also serve as a consultant to interpret school programs to parents and in the mainstreaming of students with disabilities.

Most parents expect and want to be informed by the school regarding their child's needs and accomplishments. The school's public relations program in general and their counseling program in particular will be enhanced by an active program of consultation with parents.

It should be noted that when consulting with parents

> regarding maladaptive behavior, first and foremost the counselor must communicate concern for the child and for his or her success in school. It is critically important that the counselor and teacher both communicate explicitly to the parents that they are not blaming them or their child-raising techniques for any problem behaviors their child may be exhibiting. Simply stating an awareness of the presence of difficulties and that they are interfering with the child's success in school may be sufficient. At this point the counselor may go on to inform parents of specific behaviors or attitudes that may be thwarting their child's success. Parents are usually aware that a problem exists prior to their coming in for the consultation process. With encouragement and a positive attitude from the counselor, parents typically contribute background knowledge and are helpful. (Gibson, Mitchell, & Basile, 1993, pp. 244–245)

The school counselor-consultant must keep in mind that many behavioral issues in the school may be a product of other environments, including the home.

The Counselor as a Curriculum Consultant

As noted when discussing the counselor's consulting role with the classroom teacher, the counselor can play an important role in curriculum consultation. Additionally, federal legislation specifies the counselor's importance in implementing programs of career education and education of children with disabilities. In an instructional sense, the school counselor is not, of course, a curriculum specialist. However, when the curriculum is viewed as the sum of educational experiences the school proposes to provide, it follows that the counselor, because of her or his professional commitment to each student's total development, should be actively involved, regardless of legislative mandates, in curriculum planning.

As a consultant in matters related to the career interests and concerns of students, a counselor may conduct comprehensive assessments of student career interests to provide a basis for expanded and relevant curriculum offerings. Nor should the important area of avocational interests be overlooked. A combination of educational and avocational opportunities often serves to maintain student interest and motivation. The counselor should assume major responsibility to identify and interpret these interests and concerns to all educators involved. Assessment of student interest must be translated into action, however, and it is at that point that many opportunities for curriculum development are left to flounder in the sea of academic indifference.

School counselors and curriculum planners have a joint responsibility to see that these important aspects of the student's total development are not left to chance. In this regard, it should be noted that curricular consultation frequently points out the need for curricular change. Because the school counselor's responsibilities involve him or her with both teachers and administrators, the counselor is in a position to facilitate their cooperation and interaction in promoting curricular change. Such change usually involves the prerequisites of

(a) identification of the need for change, (b) a willingness on the part of those involved to consider change, and (c) the development and acceptance of a plan for change.

CONSULTATION IN COMMUNITY MENTAL HEALTH SETTINGS

Consultation has emerged, since the 1970s, as a well-established activity and specialty in mental health agencies. The general purpose

> of the consultation mandate in community mental health is for professionals to provide "indirect" services that will expand mental health personpower. In general, consultation efforts are directed to schools, clergy, criminal justice settings, industry, and other human service agencies. . . . The classic typology of so-called mental health consultation was offered by one of its founders, Gerald Caplan (1963, 1970). He divides consultation activities in community agencies into four major categories: (1) client-centered case consultation, in which the focus is on helping the consultee deal with a particular case or client; (2) program-centered administrative consultation, in which the major aim is to help the consultee in administering a treatment or prevention program; (3) consultee-centered case consultation, in which the primary goal is to help the consultees with problems in working with clients in general; and (4) consultee-centered administrative consultation, in which the goal of the consultant is to aid the consultee or consultee agency in planning, implementing, and maintaining mental health programs. (Jeger & Slotnick, 1982, p. 141)

Bloom (1984) believes, "Mental health consultation is the major form of indirect service associated with the community mental health movement" (p. 155). He distinguishes consultation

> from other mental health activities with which it is sometimes confused and with which it has some overlapping characteristics. Consultation can be distinguished from supervision on the grounds that (1) the consultant may not be of the same professional specialty as the consultee, (2) the consultant has no administrative responsibility for the work of the consultee. Consultation can be distinguished from education on the basis of (1) the relative freedom of the consultee to accept or reject the consultant's ideas, (2) the lack of a planned curriculum, and (3) the absence of any evaluation or assessment of the consultee's progress by the consultant. Consultation also needs to be differentiated from psychotherapy. In psychotherapy, there is a clear contractual relationship between an individual designated as a patient and another individual designated as a therapist. In this relationship, the patient acknowledges the existence of personal problems and allows the invasion of his or her privacy in order to resolve these problems. No such contractual relationship exists between consultant and consultee. The goal of consultation is improved work performance rather than improved personal adjustment. The consultant and consultee are in a peer relationship, and each expects his or her privacy to be honored. Consultation should, finally, be distinguished from collaboration. Consultation carries no implication that the consultant will participate with the consultee in the implementation of any plans. The task of the consultant is to assist the consultee in meeting his or her work responsibilities more effectively. (p. 156)

Bloom (1984) also notes that

> To assist community mental health centers in evaluating their consultation programs, Mannino and MacLennan (1978) reviewed how consultation services were monitored and evaluated in nearly 80 settings. They found that information being collected could be grouped into three categories: (1) information on the community being served, such as assessment of needs, survey of

available resources, or characteristics of the population, (2) characteristics of the consultation program, such as target groups, frequency of contacts, financing, program descriptions, progress reports or use of staff, and (3) outcome data, such as measures of consultee satisfaction, subjective judgments by consultants, or goal attainment measures. (p. 177)

Bloom (1984) concluded that

the usefulness of consultation as a community mental health technique is being increasingly supported. Consultation has enormous appeal among mental health professionals, and substantial time is currently allocated to the activity by mental health professionals working in community health centers. (pp. 186–187)

Blocher (1987) draws attention to the suggestion that

Like other forms of consultation, mental health consultation is not seen as the taking over of a case by a more highly trained or specialized professional. The primary purpose of such consultation is to help the consultee or therapist to understand better his or her own interaction with the client. The consultant helps the consultee analyze the approach to treatment, consider his or her own responses to the client, and also provides a supporting relationship to the consultee in coping with stress and tension. The nature of the consultant/consultee interaction in mental health consultation is heavily dependent on the theoretical orientation of the consultant. (p. 268)

In discussing community-based interventions, Werner and Tyler (1993) project that

community mental health centers can play a large role in helping communities solve their social problems by working to create an interdependent service delivery system through consultation and education. Jemerin and Philips (1988) note that this coordination effort is essential for the success of our interventions with children. Furthermore, it is recommended that this coordination emanate from a single, central location, which can ensure both vertical integration, moving the child into the least restrictive therapeutic environment, as well as horizontal integration, allowing the breadth of services the child is entitled to.

In the role of community consultant, the community mental health center can have a broader impact on the community structure than would be possible through direct services alone. (p. 690)

Contracts between consultants and consultees have become increasingly popular in recent years. Such agreements can benefit both the consultant and the consultee. Remley (1993) notes that

consultants enter into legal contracts each time they agree to a consultation arrangement outside of their regular work setting. They need to understand the legal context of contracts within which they perform their services and recognize the benefits a written agreement provides. Counselors often provide consultation services as a regular part of their job responsibilities. In such situations, a separate legal contract is not formed when a consultation relationship is created. A written understanding of the consultation arrangement, however, can be beneficial to the consultant and consultee even though a legal contract does not exist. (p. 157)

CONSULTATION IN BUSINESS AND INDUSTRIAL SETTINGS

Counselors in such business and industrial settings as employee assistance programs may be called upon as the resident expert to provide consultation to management and other executive decision makers in such areas as employee relationships, stress management, environment manipulation, employee absenteeism, and so forth. Counselors may use their group skills to help management and supervisors lead total quality groups (TQG). Such groups are site-based management groups or councils seeking the solution or prevention of certain specific problems that are related to the quality of their product or services and customer satisfaction. In some instances, especially with smaller organizations, counselors may be hired from outside the organization to provide the needed consultation assistance whether within or without the organization. The counselor should follow a process of assessing and defining the problem, setting goals, identifying the process, applying the process, and evaluating the results.

SUMMARY

In almost any Sunday issue of a major metropolitan newspaper, such as the *New York Times* or the *Chicago Tribune*, the classified business section advertises either to employ consultants or utilize their consulting services. Usually, these consulting services focus on planning and strategies, economic and technical reviews, marketing assistance, material development, and evaluations. Certainly the business and industrial world has used consulting services for generations.

Consultation has also been a recognized mental health activity for a number of years, although not nearly as well publicized as its business counterpart. There are consulting firms that specialize in educational matters, and consultation contracts are also becoming increasingly popular.

However, consultation as an activity of counselors has led to an examination of various models appropriate to the consultation process and their adaptation to counselor use. Kurpius (1978) describes these four modalities as provision, prescription, collaboration, and remediation. Schein (1978) organizes the process into three models: purchase of expertise, doctor-patient, and process consultation. Werner (1978) describes six possible agency models as client-centered case consultation, consultee-centered case consultation, program-centered administration consultation, consultee-centered administrative consultation, community-centered ad hoc consultation, and consultee-centered ad hoc consultation.

Regardless of model choice, counselor-consultants must recognize that they are involved in a process that provides structure and direction for their consultation efforts. It is naive to think that knowledge or experience in itself qualifies one to consult. An understanding of the process of consultation and the acquisition of the skills for consultation are prerequisites to success as a consultant. These are usually acquired through special courses in consultation.

The qualified counselor will have opportunities to consult. It is important to keep in mind, however, that consultation must be wanted—must be requested—if it is to take place. Even when requested, the counselor-consultant should proceed with tact and understanding. After all, no one likes to be told off, even by experts!

Counselors have used consultation more and more to enhance the delivery of their services. The 1990s saw yet another trend increasingly emphasized in our profession. Prevention and wellness have caught the public's fancy, and serious efforts to prevent many of the disorders that have handicapped individuals and society are under way. The helping professions are responding, and the next chapter discusses how the counseling profession is doing just that.

DISCUSSION QUESTIONS

1. In your opinion, how is the title *consultant* generally viewed by the public?

2. Discuss any experience that you, your family, or a close friend has had involving a consultant. What were the circumstances leading to the use of the consultant? What were his or her special skills

or knowledge? How had he or she acquired these special skills or knowledge? Describe the consultation process.

3.   Describe circumstances in which you as a practitioner-counselor might call on the services of a consultant. Describe the setting of your envisioned employment and how you might use consultation assistance.

4.   What is the consultation expertise that a counselor can offer to

    a. Schools

    b. Business or industry

    c. Other settings

5.   Give examples in which each of the following models of consultation might be used.

    a. Purchase of expertise

    b. Doctor-patient

    c. Process consultation

CLASS ACTIVITIES

1.   Organize the class into small groups of three or four people. Groups are to discuss the following situation. Assume that you are the newly hired counseling staff of North Rogerian High School. Your predecessors were terminated, in the words of the school principal, because "they were too much into therapy—spent all their time in one-to-one!" You have been advised to avoid even a hint of this image in your first year on the job. The director of pupil services for the school system has suggested the consultation approach for this coming year. Discuss and outline a consultation approach for this three-year high school of 57 teachers and 1,400 students in an affluent midwestern setting. How and what would be your rationale, and how would you describe your model in a presentation to the school's faculty meeting? And later to the school's parents' association? Compare and discuss the differing approaches among the small groups.

2.   Organize the class into three groups (one group per each of three topics). Groups are to develop a rationale for one of the following topics they are assigned.

    a. A major role for consultation in community mental health agencies

    b. Consultation on the college campus

    c. A private practice mental health consulting firm

3.   Organize into groups of three or four. Assess the strengths of your group from the perspective of a consultation team. Report to the class the special consultation expertise (counseling or noncounseling) of your group.

4.   Identify several consultants or consulting firms in your community and invite them to participate on a class panel discussing their qualifications, role, and function as consultants.

SELECTED READINGS

Aplin, J. (1985). Business realities and organizational consultation. *The Counseling Psychologist, 13* (3), 396–402.

Fuqua, D., & Newman, J. (1985). Individual consultation. *The Counseling Psychologist, 13* (3), 390–395.

Goodman, R., & Sonaas, D. (1984). Elementary school family counseling: A pilot project. *Journal of Counseling and Development, 63,* 255.

Heller, K. (1985). Consultation to community groups: Some useful discussions between social regulators and indigenous citizen groups. *The Counseling Psychologist, 13* (3), 403–409.

Henning-Stout, M. (1993). Theoretical and empirical bases of consultation. In J. E. Zins, T. R. Kratochwill, & S. N. Elliott (Eds.), *Handbook of consultation services for children: Applications in educational and clinical settings* (pp. 15–45). San Francisco: Jossey-Bass.

Kurpius, D., & Brown, D. (Eds.). (1985). Consultation [Special issue]. *The Counseling Psychologist, 13* (3), 333–476.

Martin, R. (1983). Consultant, consultee, and client explanations of each other's behavior in consultation. *School Psychology Review, 12* (1), 35–41.

Meyer, E. C., DeMasso, D. R., & Koocher, G. P. (1996). Mental health consultation in the pediatric intensive care unit. *Professional Psychology: Research and Practice, 27*, 130–136.

Schmidt, J. J., & Medl, W. A. (1983). Six magic steps of consulting. *The School Counselor, 30* (3), 212–216.

Turner, A. (1982). Consulting is more than advice giving. *Harvard Business Review*, Sept.-Oct., 120–129.

Ulmansky, D. L., & Holloway, E. L. (1984). The counselor as consultant: From model to practice. *The School Counselor, 31* (4), 329–338.

RESEARCH OF INTEREST

Buetens, K. K., & Sullivan, E. (1996). Team consultation model: Alcoholism and drug abuse training for Head Start staff. *Child and Youth Care Forum, 25* (6), 393–402.

Abstract

This study presents two training approaches used in assisting Head Start staff to increase their knowledge and skills in identification and intervention with substance abuse issues among families. The first phase of the project, the Workshop Model, provided formalized education of substance abuse to all staff that was essential to developing a solid foundation and common framework in substance abuse and related issues. The second phase of the project, the Team Consultation Model, used a case consultation format. This model was successful in creating a more collaborative and interactive approach to training staff in substance abuse identification and intervention; sample cases are provided. The process by which the training approaches evolve and the willingness of consultant and staff to find a solution to training needs are discussed.

Buysse, V., Shulte, A. C., Pierce, P. P., & Terry, D. (1994). Models and styles of consultation: Preferences of professionals in early intervention. *Journal of Early Intervention, 18* (3), 302–310.

Abstract

This study examined the consultation model and style preferences of 67 professionals from Colorado early intervention programs. Subjects viewed two simulated consultations and rated each in terms of the consultant's perceived effectiveness. Results show that a collaborative approach involving shared responsibility across all stages of the consultation process was preferred. Results also indicate a marked preference for a directive style that involved sharing specific strategies to address the concerns of a consultee over a nondirective style that consisted merely of facilitating the consultee's own problem-solving abilities. These results are consistent with the findings of consumer preference studies.

Gresham, F. M., & Kendell, G. K. (1987). School consultation research: Methodological critique and future research. *School Psychology Review, 16* (3), 306–316.

Abstract

This article reviews the current status of school consultation research and critiques the research methodologies used in consultation research. Major theoretical models in which consultation research has been conducted are briefly described. Consultation research is reviewed in three primary areas of investigation: (1) outcome research; (2) process research; and (3) practitioner utilization research.

Henning-Stout, M. (1994). Consultation and connected knowing: What we know is determined by the questions we ask. *Journal of Educational and Psychological Consultation, 5* (1), 5–21.

Abstract

This article explores an alternative epistemology from which the practice of consultation can be considered. The alternative, described as connected knowing, characterizes the ways that many women make sense of the world. Connected knowers explore academic and practical questions in the context of the human relationships involved. They ask questions and attempt to understand the positions and interests of the other people whose lives are touched by those questions. This way of knowing, available both to women and men, has immediate relevance for consultation research, practice, and training.

Ikeda, M. J., Tilly, W. D., Stumme, J., & Volmer, L. (1996). Agency-wide implementation of problem-solving consultation: Foundations, current implementation, and future directions. *School Psychology Quarterly, 11* (3), 228–243.

Abstract
    This article describes steps taken and the support needed for large-scale implementation of a consultative service delivery model. The foundation of a problem-solving consultation model used at Heartland Area Educational Agency 11 in Iowa is presented. Case examples are used to illustrate various components within problem-solving consultation. Efforts to evaluate perceptions of problem-solving consultation and to guide further implementation of consultation at the systems level are summarized. Areas in which additional resources would enhance problem-solving consultation are discussed. Shifts in the philosophy of service delivery that are fundamental for successful implementation of problem-solving consultation are described.

Pryzwansky, W. B. (1986). Indirect service delivery: Considerations for future research in consultation. *School Psychology Review, 15* (40), 479–488.

Abstract
    This article considers trends in recent consultation research from the standpoint of themes or emphases that are emerging rather than from a methodological perspective. The

effect of those patterns is considered on future research and practice. Some directions for enhancing the database of consultation are presented for trainers and practitioners.

Taylor, I., O'Reilly, M., & Lancioni, G. (1996). An evaluation of an ongoing consultation model to train teachers to treat challenging behavior. *International Journal of Disability, Development and Education, 43* (3), 203–218.

Abstract
    This study investigated the use of functional assessment techniques to develop a multicomponent intervention for a male primary school student with high levels of self-injury and aggression. An in-depth functional assessment, as outlined by the *Diagnostic and Statistical Manual of Mental Disorders IV*, identified the operant function of these behaviors. This information allowed for the development of an extensive behavior support plan. The classroom teacher was then trained to implement the support plan and received ongoing consultation from a psychologist regarding her adherence to the behavioral techniques. The intervention resulted in significant decreases in challenging behavior.

White, G. W., & Pryzwansky, W. B. (1982). Consultation outcome as a result of inservice resource teacher training. *Psychology in the Schools, 19* (4), 495–502.

Abstract
    The effects of training learning disabilities teachers for consultation with classroom teachers was investigated. Learning disabilities resource teachers ($N = 4$) receiving communication skills training and resource teachers ($N = 4$) receiving communications skills resulted in significantly higher classroom teacher ratings of resource teacher empathy.

Chapter 12

Prevention and Wellness

Although the old saying "an ounce of prevention is worth a pound of cure" would seem to be particularly appropriate to the health professions, the fact is that until recently, these professions, including the mental health professions, have given little more than lip service to prevention. However, recent generations have witnessed the pursuit of wellness by millions of Americans with near revolutionary zeal. At times, our whole country seems to be waking up to Jazzercize, washing down vitamin pills with instant stay-trim breakfasts, practicing relaxation techniques on the job, jogging after work, attending stress management workshops, following the Pritikin diet, and so forth. These signs of the times point to our growing concern with the prevention of health disorders, including mental health. It represents, if not a shift in emphases, a sharing of emphasis between remediation and prevention. This chapter's objectives are, therefore, to (a) present the role of prevention in counseling programs and (b) introduce prevention through stress management, attention to nutrition, and the wise use of recreation and leisure time.

PREVENTION

In the mental health field, a substantial increase in reported prevention activities, research, and professional literature appropriate for counselors is evident. These include a broad range of studies reported in various publications such as *Preventive Psychology* (Felner, Jason, Moritsugu, & Farber, 1983); special issues of the *Personnel and Guidance Journal* (Barclay, 1984a, 1984b), now entitled the *Journal of Counseling and Development*, focusing on primary prevention in schools, on college campuses, and in the community; more recent special issues of the *Journal of Counseling and Development* (November/December 1992), focusing on wellness throughout the life span, and the *Journal of Mental Health Counseling* (Robinson & Roth, 1992) special issue on women and health; and the *American Psychologist* [Volume 51 (11), 1996], with five excellent articles on prevention. Also of interest is the April 1997 issue of the *American Journal of Community Psychology* [Volume 25 (2)], which contains five articles on prevention.

The prevention model adopted by counselors and other mental health workers is in large part the prevention model adopted by psychology, which in turn was borrowed from the field of public health. Prevention may be viewed as an effort that seeks to avoid the occurrence of something undesirable. Within this definition, three levels of prevention are identified as primary, secondary, and tertiary. *Primary prevention* generally refers to programs designed to impact specific and sizeable populations who are not presently affected by a disorder for the purpose of keeping them free of the disorder. It is similar to the medical profession's immunization of populations to prevent a disease often with epidemic possibilities. *Secondary prevention* represents efforts to identify and intervene with individuals affected at the early onset of the disorder, because treatment is clearly more effective at the early stages than later when the disorder is more firmly established. *Tertiary prevention* is preventative only in the sense that it is seeking to prevent the growth of the disorder, reduce the effects, and rehabilitate the individual.

Acknowledging that prevention is the effort to avoid the undesirable, we would recognize that the priority prevention activities of societies have been on (a) prevention of that which threatens life and/or healthy living—hence immunizations against killing or disabling diseases, treaties to avoid war, diets and exercise, and so forth, to promote our health; and

(b) prevention of that which threatens our security—hence insurance against financial loss, contracts for job security, concern about law enforcement to prevent crime, and so forth.

In these instances, individuals do not want to spend time in the best hospital or the best jail or have the best artificial tooth. Prevention is clearly preferred when the alternative is undesirable; hence, we work at it and are willing to pay for it. Thus, prevention programs are in demand when life or security is threatened. These demands are further underlined when large numbers are victims or potential victims of the threat. Such current social problems as substance abuse, people abuse, AIDS, crime and delinquency, teen pregnancies, and school dropouts clearly meet the criteria of affecting or threatening large numbers.

The counseling profession, with counselors strategically positioned in schools and influentially located in community, health, business and industry, religious, and armed services settings, to mention but a few, must respond with prevention programs. Here too is another area of opportunity to develop our uniqueness as a helping profession, as a profession distinct from other helping professions.

Schmolling, Youkeles, and Burger (1989) give four reasons why an emphasis on primary prevention is critical.

- There has never been a major disease or disorder eliminated through treatment alone.
- There are not enough human services personnel to treat or rehabilitate all those in need.
- Society pays a high financial cost for disorders that are not prevented.
- Emotional and behavioral disorders exact an enormous human cost in terms of personal pain and suffering. (pp. 235–237)

Of course, conditions must be met for programs to be effective. These include the following.

1. It must occur before the onset of the advance indicators or symptoms of the disorder.
2. It must be aimed at populations rather than individuals.
3. The design of the program must recognize the uniqueness of the population and their environments. This includes an assessment of the wide range of forces that influence the lives of the target population.
4. Program planners should review appropriate research to identify proven or promising prevention procedures.
5. Organizational support for the program must be strong. This includes a willingness to support long-term goals (even though the quick fix approach is easier to sell).

In planning for prevention, some obvious needs may exist. Preventive programs in substance abuse are popular in schools. Premarital counseling is commonplace. Also, many counseling agencies have programs to help married couples avoid some of the anticipated problems and adjustments of marriage. In general, however, prevention has not reached the level of sophistication or popularity attained by remediation.

In the area of physical health, prevention has always been recognized by the public and the medical professions as the most valued approach. Millions of dollars have been spent to develop vaccines and other preventive measures. In the field of mental health, however, the public (and often the profession itself) has, until recently, appeared to give a higher priority to remediation and treatment. For example, the public seems to consistently support the building of bigger and better jails, substance abuse treatment programs, and rape crisis centers; and at the same time, in many locales, it has opposed such preventive efforts by schools as sex education and values clarification techniques.

Despite the obstacles, counselors and other mental health professionals are being urged, even mandated by legislation in some instances, to broaden the scope of their prevention activities in order to identify and thus intervene with even larger populations at risk. This approach recognizes the importance of significant settings and experiences that influence individual adjustment and development. The home, school, workplace, church, and community are obviously relatively stable settings over periods of time that have a significant impact on large numbers of people. It is in these settings that prevention programs should flourish.

Of course, prevention planning must be based on some systematic approach for identifying the needs of specific client populations. This involves the study of factors associated with adjustments, characteristics of particularly susceptible people, interrelationships between the first two items, examination of how people adapt in a given environment, and identification of significant events in the environment that signify success or growth outcomes.

It is important at this point to note the significance of environment. Environment is a major factor influencing the development of behaviors that put populations at risk or inhibits the development of undesirable behaviors. As a major influence on behavior, counselors and other helping professionals engaged in preventive efforts must understand it in order to predict, control, modify, or prevent human behaviors that occur within a given environment. Significant environments such as the home, school, workplace, and community are behavioral settings that not only influence and control behavior within them but also condition behavior beyond these settings. This includes the setting of limits on deviant behaviors and coping styles.

Environments are also assessed to determine what specific characteristics are present that place populations at risk for certain disorders. Environments are not just physical in nature, but they also have a psychological dimension. Although the latter may be more complex and difficult to clearly identify, its impact must not be underestimated, and its significance must be addressed in successful prevention programs.

In prevention, individuals' transactions with their environments may provide critical clues for successful programs. The consensus of experts seems to suggest that environmental assessment using the field survey method is the most reliable technique, and Public Law 88-169 has mandated needs assessments for community mental health centers. In examining environments and their impacts on populations, special attention should be given to (a) high-impact environments such as the home, school, and workplace; (b) how normal developmental tasks are facilitated or impeded by the environment; (c) what is important?—significant life events in the environment; and (d) the quality of everyday life for the inhabitants of the environment. An environmental needs assessment also gives counselors the opportunity to assess the readiness of a population for a given type or types of prevention programs.

Prevention programs are usually complex because they must be designed to deal with multiple factors. Some disorders are associated with many risk factors, and some risk factors are also selected with many disorders. Additionally, some risk factors appear to vary in their impact at different stages of the individual's development. Too, certain disorders may result from a specific chain of events. All of these factors may heighten the public's wariness of prevention programs.

Although prevention programs are receiving increasing public acceptance today, there are factors that increase the public's support of such programs.

- The more serious the public threat, the greater the readiness to support preventive efforts.
- The greater the number affected or potentially affected, the greater the support.
- The likelihood of program success as perceived by the public will increase their support.

Although the last criterion cannot be guaranteed, factors such as successes of similar programs in comparable settings, the program director's reputation for succeeding, and an effective public communications program can all be helpful.

As an obvious and crucial starting point, the elementary school can play a significant role in any community or school system's preventive efforts, and evidence indicates that schools are responding to this challenge. A study by Gibson (1989) indicates that prevention was a major emphasis of elementary school counseling and guidance programs in 85% of the 114 elementary programs surveyed. The primary objectives of these programs are noted in Table 12-1.

Among the popular activities used in elementary school prevention programs were group counseling for self-concept improvement, a guidance curriculum for the classroom to develop interpersonal and social relationship skills and avoid personal conflicts, and facilitation of problem solving and decision making. Self-concept development was also facilitated through consultation and training with parents. Attendance was improved and dropouts prevented through tutoring, career guidance, and group guidance activities. Substance abuse prevention was initiated through a wide range of activities including Just Say No clubs, peer intervention, behavioral self-management groups, drug education, and use of local celebrities as advisers.

Many schools have successfully initiated comprehensive safety programs for the prevention of sexual abuse and child abuse and the promotion of personal safety using drama, games, films, and classroom guidance programs.

In recent decades, a variety of studies have reported successful prevention programs in schools. Successful programs appear to share a number of common features.

Table 12-1   Prevention Objectives of Elementary School Counseling and Guidance Programs

Prevention objectives	Percentage
1. To prevent child and/or sexual abuse	69.7
2. To prevent substance abuse	64.9
3. To promote self-concept development	35.8
4. To promote personal safety	17.6
5. To promote social-skills development	15.0
6. To prevent teenage pregnancy	6.3
7. To prevent premature school leaving	4.4
8. To prevent school vandalism	2.1

Source: From R. L. Gibson (1989), "Prevention and the Elementary School Counselor," *Journal of Elementary School Guidance and Counseling, 24,* p. 34. © 1989 by the American Counseling Association. Reprinted by permission. No further reproduction authorized without written permission of the American Counseling Association.

- Assistance in developing coping skills
- Self-esteem and values development
- The building of support groups
- Parental involvement
- The involvement of older peers as role models and mentors
- Environmental assessment and, to the extent possible, environmental manipulation
- Elements that reflect the uniqueness of the target population, the setting, and the problem
- Instruction in basic life skills aimed at helping individuals resist peer and social pressures
- Subtle education
- A futures element, including a commitment to the time necessary to obtain results
- An evaluation component
- Program planning involving counselors and other helping professionals, parents, students, teachers, and community leaders
- Group counseling
- Behavior and attitude modification education
- Individual counseling
- Training programs for teachers, parents, counselors, and school administrators.

Gelso and Fretz (1992) report some evaluative studies of selected prevention programs. Sprinthall (1990) notes

> the evidence for both primary prevention and developmental interventions has been remarkable. Baker, Swisher, Nadenichek, and Popowicz (1984) reviewed a large number of empirical evaluations of prevention strategies and, using meta-analytic techniques to combine the results of these studies, concluded that the treatment effect size was larger for such interventions than that found in meta-analytic analyses of the results of psychotherapy. In addition to such research on primary prevention strategies, there are now an ever increasing number of studies of all sorts of outreach endeavors which continue to yield significant results for their target populations. For two very different examples, consider the work of Taylor and colleagues (1986) showing that social support groups for persons suffering from cancer led to significantly decreased depression and the work of Burnette, Williams, and Law (1987) suggesting that, for Vietnam veterans who participated in discussion groups, self-management effectiveness increased and expression of anger scores decreased. (p. 506)

Whereas the focus of prevention programs through much of the 1990s has been on substance (especially drug) abuse, recent years have shown a rapidly escalating interest in smoking prevention, as statistics indicate a continuing increase in preteen and teenage use of tobacco products. The prevention of teen pregnancies and sexually transmitted diseases have also increasingly become the subject of school prevention programs.

Prevention in Nonschool Settings

Although prevention activities are logically and justifiably present in school settings due to their before-the-onset nature and also due to the fact that near-total pre-adolescent populations can be impacted, they are not by any means limited to these settings. Many of the prevention programs in nonschool settings are classified as secondary or tertiary prevention efforts, but there are some examples of primary prevention programs as well. For example, in many communities programs such as those represented by Alcoholics Anonymous and Koala are not only engaged in treatment at secondary and tertiary levels, but at the primary level as well with youth preventive programs. Community mental health agencies, private practitioners, and residential and daytime treatment centers are very active in the prevention arena. Many employee assistance programs (EAPs) are also involved in prevention programs. Here again, drug abuse, alcohol abuse, and tobacco are the focus of many of these programs. In addition, however, programs dealing with spouse abuse, sexual abuse, and stress management and wellness have become increasingly popular.

Of course, prevention of the undesirable in both mental and physical health must include a commitment and effort to total wellness. The sections which conclude this chapter will briefly examine wellness and two important contributors to wellness, stress management and the enjoyable and prudent use of leisure time.

WELLNESS

Nowhere has the craze for wellness and prevention manifested itself more than in the growth in popularity of health foods and healthy eating plans, exercise books, fitness equipment, and clubs. The United States has jogged its way through the 1990s munching alfalfa sprouts and drinking mineral water. The individual's concern for his or her well-being cannot and should not be ignored by today's counselor. Counselors must be aware of the relationship between individual experiences and individual health, both mental and physical. Counselors need to understand the psychological consequences of illness and accidents.

A special issue of the *Journal of Counseling and Development* (Myers, Emmerling, & Leafgren, 1992) focused on the theme of "Wellness Throughout the Lifespan." In this issue, one of the editors, Myers (1992), indicates that

> Remley (1991) noted that the counseling profession has rejected the medical-illness-oriented model as the basis for our services. In defining what differentiates us as a separate and distinct mental health profession, he stated, "We do not believe that people must first be diagnosed with an illness before they can be treated with counseling services. Instead, we believe that all people can benefit from counseling. . . . Fully functioning people who experience everyday stress in their lives and those who are seriously mentally ill can benefit from a counseling philosophy that offers help for a better tomorrow." The philosophy described by Remley is grounded in a developmental approach that focuses on prevention and wellness. (p. 138)

Counselors in community, school, business, and industrial settings are being increasingly involved in programs promoting lifestyle change for healthy living. These efforts have focused on health concerns such as smoking, alcohol and drug abuse, eating disorders, and sexually transmitted diseases. Nor should this concern be limited to our clients. As fully functioning counselors, we must also be concerned with our own physical well-being.

A popular phrase is that "you are what you eat." Now, scientific inquiry seems to be further emphasizing this point as research has increasingly highlighted the relationships between nutrition and behavior, between our emotions and our diet. Although counselors are not expected to be experts in nutrition, dieting, and exercise, they should be aware of basic factors and their possible link with the client's mental health. own physical well being

Promoting concepts of wellness cannot begin too early. For example, Omizo, Omizo, and D'Andrea (1992) report a program promoting wellness among elementary school children. The results of the study

seem to support the use of classroom guidance activities in promoting wellness among elementary school children. Children who participated in the guidance activities had significantly higher levels of self-esteem and knowledge of wellness information than did children who did not participate in the guidance activities. Although the anxiety measure did not reach a level of significance, children in the experimental group had lower levels of stress subsequent to the treatment. The class allowed the children to participate in the activities that focused on prevention as opposed to remediation. They had opportunities to share, receive and give feedback, receive guidance and information, and apply what they had learned. The teacher was an excellent role model and practiced good health habits. She also incorporated the material into other areas of the curricula. (p. 197)

Nelson (1992), a choice-awareness counseling theorist, suggests that there are three levels of counseling: spa, learning, and relearning.

A place may be made in nearly every counseling session for *spa*; uplifting, positive experiences in which the focus is placed directly on helping clients feel good about themselves. With many clients, a few minutes at the end of each interview may be saved for these positive experiences; with some clients the entire effort of an individual session may be that of spa. The simplest of the several examples of spa in counseling offered in Nelson's article is the activity "Things I Can Do," in which the counselor helps the client focus on and savor some of the most often-repeated actions of which he or she is capable: breathe, walk, talk, eat, sleep, think, and so on. All counseling clients can benefit from the emerging sense of wellness that can come from spa in counseling. (p. 214)

As we consider counseling across the life span, Ponzo (1992), among others, encourages counselors to become more active in promoting successful aging. He stresses that

prime-time living is possible to the end. People need to know and believe this. So imbued, and given the skills to translate vision into reality, we should find larger numbers of people dying at the prime of their life. Consequently, there will be reductions in health care costs and increases in the productivity of elderly persons. Accomplishing this, the huge waves of people soon to be old need not be seen as a potentially destructive force, but as a dynamically productive opportunity for society. These people can view their elder years as a time for continued growth and fulfillment. Counselors can play a key role in helping people better prepare for living out a long and vital life. As many have said, "If I knew I was going to live this long, I would have prepared better." Regardless of how good the preparation, it will not restore Woody Allen's desired immortality, but it will assure mortal beings of more prime-time living. Promoting successful aging is a lifetime process. The time to start is now. (p. 213)

Appropriate exercise, a good diet, and a stress-free lifestyle are recognized important considerations in any program of client wellness. Perhaps not so well recognized is the importance of managing the daily stressors of today's living by wise and enjoyable leisure and recreational activities in prevention and wellness.

STRESS MANAGEMENT

The U.S. workforce has become aware that millions of its members are "going up in smoke"— that their effectiveness is handicapped by the psychological symptom labeled *burnout*. Although we must assume that many workers across all careers have, over the centuries, felt that their job is getting them down, the pressures are getting to them, the boss is driving them to drink, and so forth, it was not until the 1970s that a popular label, *burnout,* was commonly used to describe various psychological conditions associated with stress and adjustment needs. In fact, today, we recognize that the term *burnout* can refer to one or a combination of factors that psychologists say contribute to a person's inability to cope with the expectancies and demands of everyday living. Counselors in all settings must be prepared to prevent or intervene with clients threatened by or actually under stress.

Synonymous with the labeling of the disorder was the increasing awareness at management and supervisory levels that employee health is as important as other job-related concerns to the effectiveness of the organization and a further recognition that employee illness can be psychological as well as physical. As a result, one of the large-scale preventive efforts of the 1980s and 1990s was the stress management movement. Not unexpectedly, counselors have been increasingly called on to develop prevention and early intervention programs in stress prevention and management. Counselors involved in these efforts have been quick to recognize the value of such prevention efforts because of the dangerously cumulative phenomenon of psychosocial stress.

Although the causes for burnout or stress may vary significantly from person to person, counselors need to be cognizant of the more common factors, such as the following.

- Too many demanding, frustrating, or otherwise stressful situations
- Constant pressure to do more than can be done
- Too much time-consuming yet unrewarding work (i.e., paperwork)
- Constant conflicts between competing alternatives for time and effort (i.e., home and work)
- Persistent demands for skills or knowledge that appears beyond that possessed by the individual
- Constant interference or interruptions of planned or anticipated activities
- Lack of positive feedback, recognition, reward, or notice of efforts or accomplishments
- Lack of clarity or direction regarding work expectancies
- Depressing work environment
- Poor interpersonal relationships
- Constant disillusions or disappointments
- All work and no play, failure to lead a balanced lifestyle

Counselors may also recognize that candidates for burnout may be identified by the level, stage, or degree of burnout. For example, Veninga and Spradley (1981) identify five stages of job burnout.

Stage 1: The Honeymoon: A period of enthusiasm and job satisfaction that nevertheless begins to use up valuable energy reserves.

Stage 2: Fuel Shortage: Job dissatisfaction and inefficiency; fatigue coupled with sleep disturbances; escape activities such as smoking, drinking, drugs, shopping sprees.

Stage 3: Chronic Symptoms: Chronic exhaustion, physical illness; acute anger and depression.

Stage 4: Crisis: Deep pessimism and self-doubt; obsession with problems; physical illness grows from discomfort to incapacity; development of an escape mentality: the "flight response."

Stage 5: Hitting the Wall: Career, and life, are endangered. (pp. 33–73)

Here is another view of this sequence to burnout:

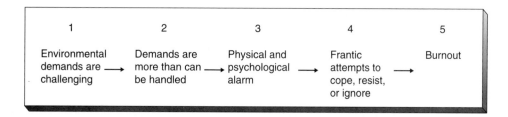

Counselors working in business and industrial settings should be aware of the extent and impact of stress in these settings.

A study by Tableman, Marceniak, Johnson, and Rodgers (1982) describes a pilot program of stress management training involving women on public assistance who were generally isolated and subjected to more than average stress in their lives.

> None of the women were in crisis, nor did they display maladaptive behaviors that required treatment. The women took part in ten sessions during which they learned skills and methods of reducing stress that helped them change their perceptions of their situations. The program resulted in significant change in the lives of the participants. They were no longer isolated and were able to function more effectively with stress, thus preventing the kinds of behavioral disorders discussed earlier. The program has been further tested and used with different populations living under stressful conditions. (Schmolling et al., 1989, pp. 242–243)

Fong and Amatea (1992) discuss stress and the single professional woman. They report that

> studies of the work stress of women have conceptualized stress as stemming from multiple role issues, ignoring other potential stressors and the fact that many women are single. This study of 141 academic women explored levels of stress, career satisfaction, career commitment, personal resources, and coping strategies among four role groups: single, single-parent, married, and married-parent women. Although all groups of women had high levels of career commitment, career satisfaction, and personal resources, the single women had significantly higher ($p = .01$) levels of stress symptoms than did the married-parent women. A near significant association ($p = .07$) was found between typical coping strategy and role group, with single women using passive coping strategies more often. (p. 20)

In working for stress prevention or reduction, initially the counselor and client need to identify the stressors in the client's situation, their relative significance, whether they can be dealt with or not, and possible preventive or coping strategies. Among the general strategies that may be helpful to clients (and even yourself on occasion) are the following.

1. Bring burnout into the open—talk about it, especially with others sharing the same situation and concerns.
2. Build a support system with a small group of colleagues (including at least one optimist); help others in stress, be positive, be mutually supportive.
3. Practice time management; organize your time and stick with it. This includes planning for and protection of your free time on and off the job.
4. Develop leisure time pursuits or hobbies.
5. Get away from it all, especially when you feel the pressure beginning to build. Take real vacations regularly.

6. Shape up, both physically and psychologically; feel good about yourself!

A prime candidate for burnout and prognosis for stress management is the workaholic—a "species" who has become all too commonplace in today's often stressful and uncertain workplace. To the casual observer, the workaholics seem addicted to their jobs. Their work profile usually reflects a number of the following characteristics.

1. Get to work early and leave late.
2. Work at workstation while eating lunch.
3. Work during the commute to and from the office, and have a car phone for business purposes.
4. Take work home most evenings and weekends.
5. Rarely take vacations, and when one does, take work along and keep in touch with the office.
6. Recreational pursuits, if any, usually are for business purposes (i.e., golf with a client, dinner with clients, a trip to Florida to attend a convention, etc.).
7. Time for children and family is strictly rationed. (Rationale: I'm doing what I must to be a good provider!)
8. Eating and sleeping habits are irregular. Personal health becomes a concern only when it threatens work schedule.
9. Unable to say no when asked to do a job; often tending to volunteer for extra duties.

When counselors encounter burned out or nearly burned out workaholics as their clients, it is important to understand the reasons for the behavior. Among those commonly encountered are fear of job loss, failure to advance, an effort to gain control of their lives, or as compensation for their shortcomings. In addition to stress and time management, more enjoyable use of leisure time, assertiveness training, and social growth groups may help.

RECREATION AND LEISURE

If you could spend three days doing whatever you wished, how would you choose to spend your time? What do you plan to do with your vacation time this year? Chances are, your answers to these questions indicate what recreational and leisure time activities are important to you. We may also be reminded of how important this time is to us and that recreation and leisure are important activities in American society. We need but pause to consider the amount of time, money, and effort we expend in these pursuits to recognize their significance in our lives. The interrelationships between a career and a way of life cannot ignore the role of recreation and leisure in the latter. Counselors concerned with the total well-being of their clients must, therefore, become more sensitive to the role and potential of leisure time activities for enhancing their clients' quality of life and meeting their unmet or partially fulfilled needs.

Tinsley, Hinson, Tinsley, and Holt (1993) report an earlier (Tinsley & Tinsley, 1986, 1988) proposed theory of leisure that

> focuses on the individual's subjective experience. They viewed leisure experiences as characterized by both cognitive (i.e., concentration on the ongoing experience, forgetting of self, and decreased awareness of time) and affective (i.e., feelings of freedom, enriched perception of objects and events, and increased intensity of emotions and sensitivity to bodily sensations) attributes. Leisure can vary in intensity, but four conditions are necessary for this experience to occur. The individual must perceive the activity as (a) freely chosen, (b) intrinsically satisfying, (c) optimally arousing, and (d) requiring a sense of commitment. Leisure experiences are thought to occur in all aspects of life, including work, but they are most likely to occur during leisure activity because of the importance of the perception of freedom of choice. (p. 447)

At this point, it may be helpful to distinguish between free time and leisure time. We might define free time as unencumbered time that the individual can use or not use in any way he or she may decide. Leisure time is that time spent in the pursuit of specific activities anticipated to be enjoyable. Although some free or unencumbered time is desirable, large amounts of free time can result in boredom, frustration, anger, low self-esteem, anxiety, and stress. Enjoyable leisure time, however, has a number of potential benefits such as stimulation and motivation (which often carries over into work), feelings of rejuvenation (also important to work), relaxation and stress reduction, personal growth, opportunities for exploration, and the development of new horizons.

A rationale for leisure counseling may be based on the following.

1. The amount of time available for leisure pursuits for many individuals is increasing.
2. The interactions between an individual's work experiences and his or her leisure and recreational experiences clearly impact his or her mental health.
3. Self-fulfillment includes the development of all the individual's potentials, including those that might be labeled avocational or recreational.
4. Therefore, planning for the wise and fulfilling use of leisure time is essential if the individual is to use her or his time in rewarding, enriching, and stress-reducing ways.
5. Leisure counseling can facilitate this planning by assisting individuals in identifying possible options consistent with their lifestyles and interests, making appropriate choices, and, when needed, securing the necessary education.

We have become increasingly aware of the lack of recreational facilities and positive leisure time activities for large segments of our youth population today, especially among the poor, inner-city, and rural youth. We are also aware that the resulting time on their hands frequently leads to youth gangs, substance abuse, delinquency, and crime. Perhaps school counselors should develop programs to assist youth in exploring and developing avocational interests as well as vocational interests.

Much of the adult population also needs assistance in expanding their leisure time activities beyond visiting relatives and watching television. Growth groups focusing on the discovery of meaningful recreational pursuits can be helpful. Special-interest groups in which individuals can explore and learn more about specific leisure activities (e.g., travel, ballroom dancing, square dancing, eating out, bowling, playing tennis, swimming, etc.) can arouse interests, as can "play" fairs.

Counselors who provide counseling and guidance services to our senior citizens must be aware that many preparing to enter retirement have no adequate alternative to their work to fill this void when retirement occurs. This involuntary isolation from their working colleagues leaves many an individual lonely, depressed, and physically as well as mentally stagnated. This population must be assisted in identifying enjoyable, meaningful and doable leisure time activities. In this process, counselors may use assessment techniques, including standardized interest inventories, values clarification techniques, exploratory and growth groups, and special educational programs.

As counselors we are seeking to assist our clients in improving their quality of life—to live life to the fullest—to optimize their human potential. In this context, then, the professional counselor is sensitive to the potential contributions that leisure counseling may make to their clientele in achieving these outcomes. In so doing, we are, once again, seeking to help clients become the best they've ever been; to view counseling not as just a restorative process, but an experience that advances the individual toward his or her true human potential.

In concluding this brief examination of leisure counseling, we suggest that the demands for counseling in this area will increase rapidly in the years ahead. We also believe that continued research into the role of leisure and its relationship to work will increase our knowledge and skills not only for life adjustment counseling but, perhaps more importantly, for preventive and developmental purposes as well.

SUMMARY

This chapter has presented, in a sense, a beginning to important new directions for counselors and the counseling profession that promise to raise the profession to heretofore unanticipated heights of societal service. To what more lofty goals can counselors aspire than the prevention of mental illness and the promotion of a happy, productive life through wellness and wise, enjoyable use of leisure time?

Whereas other helping professions may concentrate on the remedial or, at best, the restoration of the client to a previous status quo, counseling, of all the helping professions, has the prospects to advance clients to the level of the best they can become! This potential does not mean a deemphasis on our traditional skills and knowledge discussed in earlier chapters (i.e., counseling, assessment, career development, and so forth) but rather suggests applying these skills to new opportunities that optimistically view the positive, the possible.

The success of prevention and the other activities of counseling programs will be influenced to a large degree by how effectively programs are planned, managed, and led. The next chapter will

discuss this important contribution to the delivery of counseling services.

DISCUSSION QUESTIONS

1. What major societal/mental health concerns would appear to be most effectively treatable by prevention programs?

2. What can be done nationally, that may not be currently undertaken, to more effectively prevent such social ills as substance abuse, child/spouse abuse, AIDS, homelessness, and teen pregnancies? What can counselors do at the local community level?

3. What are the implications of the current interest in health and wellness for the counseling profession?

4. How important is leisure time in your life? Explain. How do you like to spend your leisure time? (Discuss and compare with your classmates.)

5. Discuss the relationship between nutrition and mental health.

6. Discuss ways in which you have personally adapted to your environment.

CLASS ACTIVITIES

1. In small groups, discuss and compare the healthy living efforts of class members. Each group will identify a member to briefly report their discussion to the class.

2. Each class member shares (a) two or three favorite recreational or leisure time activities with the class, (b) their favorite vacation, and/or (c) a new leisure activity they would like to explore.

3. In small groups, identify a mental health problem and design a prevention program or activity for a specific organizational setting. Share with the group.

4. Read one prevention article in a professional journal. Summarize this article in an oral presentation to the class.

SELECTED READINGS

Backer, C. (1988). Health professionals and mass media's campaigns to prevent AIDS and drug abuse. *Counseling and Human Development, 20* (7), 1–10.

Backer, T., Batchelor, W., Jones, J., & Mays, V. (1988). Psychology and AIDS [Special issue]. *American Psychologist, 43,* 835–987.

Corney, R. (1996). Counselling psychology in the context of health and illness. In R. Woolfe & W. Dryden (Eds.), *Handbook of counselling psychology* (pp. 401–418). London: Sage.

Hubbard, G. (1984). Nutrition: A counselor's guide through the maze. *The School Counselor, 31* (5), 422–427.

Kagan, D., & Squires, R. (1984). Compulsive eating, dieting, stress and hostility among college students. *Journal of College Student Personnel, 25* (3), 213–220.

Lightsey, O. R. (1996). What leads to wellness? The role of psychological resources in well-being. *Counseling Psychologist, 24,* 689–759.

Nicholson, J. (1986). Risk recreation: A context for developing client potential. *Journal of Counseling and Development, 64* (8), 528–530.

Paisley, P. (1987). Prevention of child abuse and neglect: A legislative response. *The School Counselor, 24* (3), 226–228.

Panterotto, J. (1985). A counselor's guide to psychopharmacology. *Journal of Counseling and Development, 64* (2), 109–115.

School, M., & Johnson, J. (1988). Keeping pregnant teens in school. *Vocational Education Journal, 63* (6), 42–43.

Shaw, M. (1986). The prevention of learning and interpersonal problems. *Journal of Counseling and Development, 64* (10), 624–627.

Weber, J. (1988). The relevance of vocational education to dropout prevention. *Vocational Education Journal, 63* (6), 36–38.

Zarski, J., Bubeuzer, D., & West, J. (1986). Social interest, stress, and the prediction of health status. *Journal of Counseling and Development, 64* (6), 386–389.

RESEARCH OF INTEREST

Baker, S. B., Swisher, J. D., Nadenichek, R. E., & Popowicz, C. L. (1984). Measured effects of primary prevention strategies. *Personnel and Guidance Journal, 62* (8), 459–464.

Abstract

These researchers conducted a meta-analysis of more than 40 primary prevention studies to investigate the measured effects of primary prevention strategies. Studies selected were those that were controlled experiments with empirical comparisons between treatment and controlled conditions and studies in which the treatment conditions had goals and involved participants; this allowed the studies to be classified as primary prevention. Fifteen of the studies utilized or included elementary school populations. It concludes that, considering the difficulties that limit opportunities to conduct successful primary prevention programs in the school, the results are encouraging.

Blount, W. R., & Dembo, R. (1984). Personal drug use and attitudes toward prevention among youth living in a high risk environment. *Journal of Drug Use, 14* (3), 207–224.

Abstract

Nonusers, users of alcohol, and users of both alcohol and marijuana were identified co-existing in the same neighborhoods. (Sample selection also included a procedure which guaranteed that at least part of each group saw themselves at risk.) Separate subcultures for each of the three populations were strongly indicated. Differences were found in terms of behavior, attitudes, peer groups (including a distinct rejection of hard drug users), and significant adults in the environment; especially those felt to possess accurate information about drugs and to whom they would go for help with a drug problem. Almost any activity was seen as appropriate for a drug-use prevention program, although there were strong differences in terms of desirability. How users can be differentiated from nonusers in the same population is discussed along with additional implications of prevention programming.

Bunce, D. (1997). What factors are associated with the outcome of individual-focused worksite stress management interventions? *Journal of Occupational and Organizational Psychology, 70* (1), 1–17.

Abstract

This article examines research contrasting different approaches to individual-focused stress management interventions (SMIs). SMIs target individual workers and generally seek to enhance their ability to cope with occupational strain. Several issues regarding SMIs are addressed including the efficacy of SMIs relative to one another, the active ingredients of SMI's, and the extent to which research has considered individual differences including their impact on outcome variance. General conclusions discussed include the finding of many comparative studies that SMIs are outcome equivalent and the finding that both nonspecific factors and factors related to the technical content of the intervention are associated with outcome. Very little research was available regarding individual differences, and none was located which examined potential mediators of change. It is argued that due to design and methodological limitations in the majority of studies, a new generation of research is required which, among other things, clearly delineates between interventions of differing technical content and includes session process measures to help distinguish the degree of outcome variance associated with specific and nonspecific factors.

Carlson, K. A. (1994). Prevention in its social context: Student views. *Journal of Alcohol and Drug Education, 40* (1), 26–35.

Abstract

This study surveyed 2,791 students in 4th through 12th grade concerning prevention programming and substance use. Subjects evaluated the helpfulness of their school's prevention programs, including punitive sanctions, and gave their views on the adequacy and fairness of school and legal punishments for common drug and alcohol offenses. The most favorable evaluated prevention activities were those providing support and skills for nonuse. Punitive sanctions delivered at the school or through external legal authorities received more variable responses; those directed at the most serious drug offenses were strongly supported, whereas punishments for common alcohol violations were seen as inappropriate. As grade level increased, the attitude toward such sanctions shifted from a judgment of these as helpful to the view that they were not helpful.

Chandler, C. L., Weissberg, R. P., Cowen, E. L., & Guare, J. (1984). Long-term effects of a school-based secondary prevention program for maladapting children. *Journal of Consulting and Clinical Psychology, 52* (2), 165–170.

Abstract

This study assessed the current status of 61 fourth through sixth graders, seen two to five years earlier in an intervention program for children experiencing school adjustment problems. Based on comparisons of teacher ratings of children's problems and competencies at three time points (referral, termination, and follow-up), program children were found to have maintained initial intervention gains. At follow-up, they were significantly better adjusted than a demographically comparable, teacher-identified group of current problem children, but not as well adjusted as a randomly selected, demographically matched never-seen group. The three groups did not differ systematically on measures of self-esteem or academic achievement. The absolute placement of the seen sample on those measures was at the midpoint of normal range. Thus, the immediate gains shown by young, maladjusted children seen through the early intervention program endured over time.

Elliott, T. R., & Marmarosh, C. L. (1994). Problem-solving appraisal, health complaints, and health-related expectancies. *Journal of Counseling and Development, 72* (5), 531–537.

Abstract

This study examined the relation of problem-solving appraisal to health complaints and health-related expectancies among 251 undergraduates. Subjects completed measures of problem-solving ability, health expectancies, and health complaints. Self-appraised effective problem solvers (EPSs) reported fewer physical symptoms three weeks before, during, and three months after assessment than did ineffective problem solvers (IPSs). EPSs also had greater internal and lower chance expectancies for health outcomes than did IPSs. Self-appraised personal control over emotional experiences when engaging in problem solving was significantly predictive of health perceptions. Behavioral health and wellness interventions with college students may be improved by incorporating problem-solving perspectives.

Foster, G. D., Wadden, T. A., & Brownell, K. D. (1985). Peer-led program for the treatment and prevention of obesity in the schools. *Journal of Consulting and Clinical Psychology, 53* (4), 538–540.

Abstract

Eighty-nine overweight children in grades two to five in one experimental and one control school participated in a 12-week weight reduction program conducted by older children trained as peer counselors. Children in the experimental school lost weight and reduced their percentage overweight, whereas those in the control school gained weight and increased their percentage overweight.

Glasgow, R. E., Terborg, J. R., Hollis, J. F., & Severson, H. H. (1995). Take heart: Results from the initial phase of a worksite wellness program. *American Journal of Public Health, 85* (2), 209–216.

Abstract

This study evaluated the short-term effects of a low-intensity worksite (WS) heart disease risk reduction program using a matched pair design in 26 heterogeneous WSs assigned to early intervention and delayed intervention conditions. WSs did not differ on changes in smoking prevalence, dietary fat intake, and serum cholesterol. The intervention did not produce improvements beyond secular trends observed in control WSs and did not improve employee health behaviors related to nutrition and tobacco use more than repeated assessments alone. Six potential explanations for the lack of effects are offered.

Smith, M. U., & Katner, H. P. (1995). Quasi-experimental evaluation of three AIDS prevention activities for maintaining knowledge, improving attitudes, and changing risk behaviors of high school seniors. *AIDS Education and Prevention, 7* (5), 391–402.

Abstract

Seven hundred and twenty-eight 12th-grade students participated in one of three AIDS interventions: a question and answer (QA) session, a presentation by a person with AIDS (PWA), or a role-play activity (RP). A pre-intervention questionnaire assessed AIDS-related knowledge and attitudes. Immediate post-intervention questionnaires assessed knowledge and the intervention, and, five weeks later, a questionnaire reassessed knowledge and attitudes in addition to changes in risk behaviors. Knowledge gains were similar in the three groups; forgetting was greatest among PWA students. The attitudes of the RP group toward persons with AIDS tended to be the most positive, but differences among the groups were not statistically significant. The proportion of RP students who reported changing their sexual activities after the intervention was significantly greater than that proportion of the other groups.

Stevens, R., & Pihl, R. O. (1982). The remediation of the student at risk for failure. *Journal of Clinical Psychology, 38* (2), 298–301.

Abstract

The efficacy of teaching students at risk for academic failure to deal with school related stress was investigated. The high school students given coping skills training showed significantly improved social problem-solving ability.

Thomson-Rountree, P., & Woodruff, A. E. (1982). An examination of Project AWARE: The effects on children's attitudes toward themselves, others, and school. *Journal of School Psychology, 20* (1), 20–31.

Abstract

Findings indicated that children involved in the program achieved greater personal adjustment and accepted responsibility for negative outcomes in social situations.

Chapter

13

Program Management, Development, and Leadership

Through the centuries, a great deal has been written about the importance of management, development, and leadership to success in the worlds of business and government. The business world has long studied the successes and failures of corporations large and small and the styles of management that have accounted for their achievements or lack of them. Management is also important in government effectiveness and fiscal soundness. Development is crucial to many countries, geographic areas, and companies, the success or failure of armies, the winning of athletic championships, and so forth. Leadership has played a major role in the rise and fall of nations. Management is important to government effectiveness and fiscal soundness, and development is crucial in many countries, even in these modern times.

In this century, school administration in education, hospital administration in medicine, and personnel administration in business and the armed services have become areas for specialization. Beginning in the 1980s, business books such as *In Search of Excellence* by Peters and Waterman (1982), *The One Minute Manager* by Blanchard (1982), *A Passion for Success* by Inamori (1995), and *Iacocca: An Autobiography* by Iacocca and Novack (1984) are examples of publications in this area that appeared with regularity on the best-seller lists.

Additionally, by the 1990s, the taxpaying public became increasingly interested in how efficiently and effectively human service organizations are serving their designated publics. As inflation deflated personal incomes—as well as real dollars available to tax-supported organizations, including school systems and mental health agencies—these organizations were called upon to give good value. This good value in turn meant that counseling programs were expected to be responding to client needs in an effective (proven results) and efficient (maximizing services, minimizing costs) manner. Thus, prospective counselors should know how to develop, manage, and lead counseling and guidance programs. This chapter's objective is to provide an introduction to some guiding principles and practices of counseling program development, management, and leadership.

Lewis, Lewis, and Souflee, Jr. (1993), state that

> given the turbulent environments in which most of today's human service organizations find themselves—environments characterized by scarcity, ambiguity, and uncertainty—one of the issues revealed to the manager in the move up the managerial tiers is that of organizational survival. Demands for accountability, demands to do more with less, shifting political and economic priorities—all of these factors constitute an additional challenge to management and to contemporary human service organizations. (p. 21)

Thus, despite a general recognition of the importance of management, development, and leadership to organized enterprise, little attention has been given (in terms of formal preparation, at least) to the art of developing and managing counseling programs in various settings. Today, the complex, multiple goals required of most public agencies, institutions, and schools and school systems emphasize the need for development and management of counselor programs and accountability to the public. From a program management standpoint, *accountability* means the provision of objective evidence to prove that counselors are successfully responding to identified needs. Such evidence can be records, written reports, and perhaps computations and tables. All too often those preparing to enter the profession naively assume that the practice of therapy precludes any involvement with mundane matters such as program management, including administration. This is not to suggest that paperwork should replace people work or that it should be an equal priority. However, prospective counselors should be aware of the significance of their other responsibilities as well. Let us first define these terms.

- *Management:* Those activities that facilitate and complement the daily, ongoing functions of the counseling staff. These include such administrative activities as recording and reporting, budgetary planning and control, facility management, and provisions for support personnel resources.
- *Development:* Includes needs assessment for program planning, research, evaluation, and the establishment of program accountability. Also presumes planning for program improvement.
- *Leadership:* The providing of positive direction and motivation for personnel and program improvement. Primarily, but not exclusively, the responsibility of the professional designated as the chief management person for a specified unit (program, office, department, clinic).

UNDERSTANDING PROGRAM MANAGEMENT AND DEVELOPMENT

Beginning counselors might view the prospects of program management and development responsibilities and the likelihood of being involved in administering an ongoing program as not only remote but also as potentially undesirable. Let us therefore advance some of the reasons that counselors should possess a minimal understanding of management, development, and leadership.

Administration and Your Job

A common complaint throughout all organizations today and perhaps throughout history concerns the inroads made upon professional time by nonprofessional or administrative activities. Administrative obligations, however, are a fact of life for all functioning professionals, including counselors in all settings. Because one cannot avoid all responsibilities for program administration, management, and development at any level, it will be beneficial if, from the beginning of your professional activities as a counselor, you have some minimal understandings of these matters and how you may best respond.

Recognizing the inevitability of administrative responsibilities, what can one do to discharge these duties as expeditiously and effectively as possible? The following are suggestions gleaned from informal interviews with successful program managers and administrators in various settings.

1. *Be organized.* To be organized means, among other things, having a place for everything and everything in its place. This keeps you from wasting time in search-and-find operations. Being organized also means planning the use of your time. This includes maintaining a daily calendar that allows sufficient time for each task for which you are responsible. Because it is not always possible to estimate the exact amount of time a counseling interview may consume, it is better to allocate too much rather than too little time on one's calendar. Implicit in organization is an efficient filing and record-keeping system that allows ready access to items as needed. Files should contain all necessary and relevant information but should be periodically purged

of outdated and nonuseful materials. Although neatness is not necessarily a guarantee of organization, there appears to be a relationship between a neat office and a well-organized one.

2. *Do it right the first time*. Much administration seems to focus on preparing reports, maintaining records, and organizing data. As previously indicated, increasing emphasis on accountability, plus requirements mandated by state or federal statutes, has further accentuated the necessity of gathering objective data supporting the counseling enterprise. It is important to take time to understand exactly what it is you have to report and how it is to be reported. If you do not understand it, do not hesitate to ask for help if you need it. Do not waste your time and someone else's by doing it wrong the first time. You must also demand accuracy of yourself in the completing of any report or record and in the organizing of data. Long, cumbersome documents encourage guessing on the part of respondents. Other reports, especially those of an evaluative nature, may tempt one to fake or fudge a bit on the responses. The single word of advice is *don't*. In addition to the risk of being embarrassed by someone noting your inaccuracies, you risk the more dangerous possibility of important decisions being made on the basis of inaccurate and irresponsible data.

3. *Do it on time*. Assuming that you have been convinced to do your reporting and recording accurately, do not detract from your administrative responsibilities by being late. Usually, there is a reason that certain data are required at certain times for certain decisions. Your delays can handicap this process, especially when your colleagues have all responded on time. On those rare occasions when an emergency prevents you from discharging a responsibility on time, you must give it the highest priority and comlete it at the earliest opportunity to avoid a domino effect in which every activity down the line will also be subject to tardiness.

4. *Plan your own time*. All of us on occasion will come up against constraints on our time. Walking down the halls in almost any setting, we can hear comments such as "All I ever do is go to meetings," or "All I get done is answer the phone," or "If people would just stop dropping in unannounced," or "I don't seem to have any time to myself any more." Time frustration seems to occur with all of us. Thus, the use and control of time are critical in one's efficient functioning, in both administration and in counseling; they also have an impact on one's morale. The objective of planning your time is to make the most of it and, at the same time, leave you enough freedom and flexibility so you do not feel that the clock is your boss. In order to do this, there are several considerations. One is to do the things you do at the times when you do them best. For example, some may find they prepare reports most efficiently if they do so first thing in the morning. Others may find it desirable to use the first hour or so at work to complete the waking-up process with a second cup of coffee. It is also important to do the things we do where we do them best, perhaps getting away to some private little corner where we are uninterrupted for certain administrative responsibilities. We may also wish an informal setting for conferences with colleagues. In planning the use of time, it is important that we understand ourselves in relationship to where and how we function best. We adapt our time commitment to our working style.

5. *Do it neatly*. The effects of doing it right and doing it on time may still be lost if an interpreter is needed to translate what you have done. If your handwriting is sloppy, try typing or printing reports for others. Lack of neatness can also detract from the impact of reports. A report that looks as if it had been done and redone a dozen times may also be more subject to scrutiny and questions by superiors.

Suggestions for functioning effectively also include the following don'ts:

1. *Don't let it spoil your day.* Although not everyone may enjoy the challenges of recording and reporting, such tasks should be accepted as inevitable responsibilities that will not be facilitated by constant complaints. The frequent suggestions of many administrators is that you do it and forget it.

2. *Don't expect to understand the need for every report.* Frustrations frequently occur when one fails to see a rationale for the kind of data that are needed. Allied with this is the fact that we may also not understand why it has to be done "their" way instead of our "better" way. When something is requested by your immediate supervisor, you are more likely to understand the need than if it is requested by the upper management, several layers removed. However, inevitably there will be occasions when reports are requested from afar that will challenge all that is rational. Again, do it and forget it.

3. *Don't be tempted to become an administrator.* In some settings, counselors appear to receive their largest number of "brownie points" from their superiors by meeting their administrative responsibilities. It therefore becomes a natural temptation to overemphasize that aspect of the job. Many counselors commonly complain that they spend too much time in administrative activities; even many program administrators agree. A counselor's major responsibility in any setting, with the possible exception of a program director, is to counsel. This should be the counselor's primary, time-consuming activity. Although it is important to meet one's administrative responsibilities efficiently and effectively, that does not imply they overshadow in importance or time the main reason for which one is hired as a counselor.

As an aid to help those who may be reluctant to move from disorganization to organization, the following score pad (Table 13-1) will enable you to play the time game. It may help persons develop an awareness of their personal time management styles.

Program Management

Kotter (1988), writing from a business school perspective, states

> Modern management, as it has evolved over the past five decades, can be described in any number of different ways. But at the heart of virtually all such descriptions, one always finds four or five key processes:
>
> 1. *Planning.* Planning is the science of logically deducing means to achieve given ends. A variety of techniques have been developed to aid in this process.
> 2. *Budgeting.* Budgeting is that part of the planning process associated with an organization's finances.
> 3. *Organizing.* Organizing means creating a formal structure that can accomplish the plans, staffing it with qualified people, defining clearly what each person's role is, providing them with appropriate financial and career incentives, and then delegating appropriate authority to those people. Again, a variety of techniques have been created to aid these processes.
> 4. *Controlling.* Controlling involves looking constantly for deviations from plan ("Problems"), and then using formal authority to "solve" them. This often takes place via "review" meetings. For the financial part of plans, this means using management control systems and the like. (pp. 21–22)

Program management as a process seeks to provide structure, order, and coordination of those activities for which it is responsible. This information, of course, will function at varying levels. For example, in educational systems, the Board of Education, the school

TABLE 13-1 The Time Game Score Pad (Object: To Improve Your Score on a Daily, Weekly, or Monthly Basis)

Hour	What did I do?	Had I planned to do it?[a]	How well did I do it?[b]	Did I do it with a positive attitude?[c]	Comments to self[d]
8 A.M.					
9 A.M.					
10 A.M.					
11 A.M.					
12 noon					
1 P.M.					
2 P.M.					
3 P.M.					
4 P.M.					
5 P.M.					

[a]5 points if you had planned to do it.
3 points if you had planned to do it because it was overdue.
0 points if you hadn't planned to do it.
−3 points if you hadn't planned to do it but it was an unexpected requirement that had a higher priority than what you had planned.

[b]Score yourself on a scale of 0 to 5.

[c]3 points if you did it with enthusiasm.
2 points if you did it with a positive attitude.
1 point if you did it and then forgot about it.
0 points if you did it and then worried about it.
−1 point if you did it with frustration and/or anger.
−5 points if you did it and it drove you to distraction.

[d]1 point for each constructive suggestion.
−1 point for statements using profanity.

Totals:

1. Subtotal A + B + C + D.
2. Subtract 5 points if you didn't take a lunch break.
3. Subtract 10 points if you didn't take a lunch break for a second day in a row.

399

superintendent, and the assistant principals can be viewed as middle management, and program directors, such as the director of counseling, represent component or lower management. Figure 13-1 depicts this concept.

Regardless of the levels of management, however, the overall objective remains the same: to help organizations achieve their goals. It is important for counselors in various settings to note that the objectives of the counseling program must be consistent with and contribute to the achievement of the objectives of the institution of which it is a part. For example, in recent years, counselors working in school settings have been called upon to indicate the contributions they are making to the education of school-aged youth. Although education may be viewed broadly as all growth and development, it may be more difficult for counselors to respond in those settings when education is viewed as a learning activity only.

In this era of accountability in schools, counseling programs must be able to provide evidence that they are, in fact, meeting the needs of their student clients, which, in turn, is facilitating their educational progress. Similarly, in the corporate world, counselors in employee assistance programs must be able to document that serving the personal adjustment and development needs of employees has a dollars-and-cents payoff for the corporation.

Figure 13-1 Levels of Educational Management.

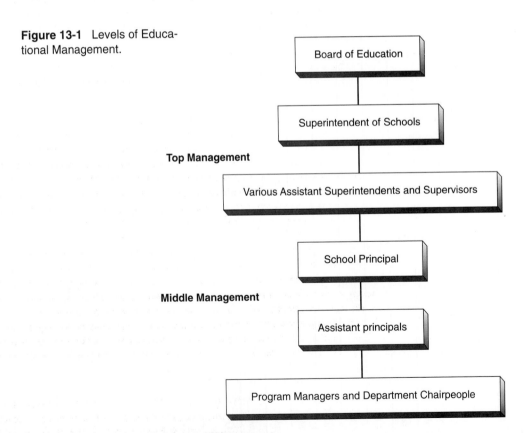

Board of Education

Superintendent of Schools

Top Management

Various Assistant Superintendents and Supervisors

School Principal

Middle Management

Assistant principals

Program Managers and Department Chairpeople

Component Management

The responsibilities and activities of program management may vary according to levels and settings, but it is possible to identify two basic areas of functioning. The first deals with the managing of basic resources, such as personnel, budget, and facilities. The second focuses on organizing and facilitating such basic activities as coordination, communication, cooperation, decision making, and evaluation. The emphasis of discussions here will be on what is involved rather than on how one should do it. Following are some suggestions appropriate for entry-level counselors, who should also be aware that as one moves into management responsibilities, one's own style and techniques tend to emerge.

MANAGING RESOURCES

Of all the resources that a program manager is called upon to use, the human resource is by far the most important. The manner in which this resource is managed will largely determine the success or failure of the program and also whether the manager is a program leader or simply a program administrator. Program managers, on the one hand, view themselves as facilitators—leaders who function in such a manner that it enables their staff to function more effectively, and yes, more easily, in meeting their assigned responsibilities. Program administrators, on the other hand, often view themselves as overseers—policy enforcers and performance evaluators—hardly ones to inspire performance. The program manager's initial responsibility in many instances will begin with staffing, which will be a consistent consideration as long as there is staff turnover. Staff selection should minimally involve three factors, which are discussed next.

Qualifications

These are primarily but not exclusively based on training and experience in relation to the expectancies of the position. In viewing one's training background, consideration should be given not only to the content of the training program but also to when, where, and areas of specialization. Although academic achievements in themselves are not the sole criterion for performance on the job, one's academic achievements should not be completely ignored. There may be little difference in performance between the A and B student, but one should not anticipate that the C student will perform as well on the job as the A student.

When examining experience, program managers usually compare the type, amount, and success of previous experiences. Experience may not always be a factor, for many program managers are anxious to hire recent graduates who can bring new ideas, more up-to-date concepts, and, perhaps, needed youthful enthusiasm to their programs.

In school settings, Gysbers and Henderson (1994) note

> Effective performance in a position is a shared responsibility of the position holder and the school district. Counselor applicants have a responsibility to define themselves adequately so that prospective employers can evaluate whether they are "right" for the jobs available. Employers have the responsibility for clearly and specifically defining the positions available. Counselors have a professional responsibility to be competent in what the district has the right to expect—that is, the educational areas defined as minimum standards for certification by the state and the ethical standards defined by the profession. (p. 293)

Staff Versatility

When the program manager has a staff of at least one to manage, providing for program versatility enters into staff selection. Differing backgrounds should provide a wider range of specialty skills. Also, it has frequently been noted that staffs of two or more should include one member of each sex and minority or cultural representation, as appropriate. Some range in age representation is important, especially in institutional and community settings, and the old schoolboy network (hire all graduates from the same school) should not be perpetuated at the expense of program versatility.

Adaptability

Another consideration that is often overlooked in staffing is the adaptability of a staff member to both the job setting and the community or area environment. The person must not only like the job, but the job must like the person. A staff member will function more effectively when there are congenial relationships among the staff as well as those with whom they come in frequent contact. This, of course, would include the clients that the staff is serving. It is not suggested that one form friendships with clients, but it is important to be able to relate to the client population, whether it is inner-city, suburban society, Appalachian poor, or Alaskan Eskimo.

Staff members must also be able to adapt to the community or area environment that supports the job setting. It is highly unlikely that people can be unhappy in their community-home life and happy in their work life. The inability to adapt to a community environment can also have adverse effects on the public relations aspect of the counseling program.

Staff Management

Once staffing decisions have been made and personnel are functioning on a job, management's responsibilities continue to be important. These include the following.

1. *The assignment of responsibility.* Staff members should have specific activities for which they are responsible and for which each staff member knows she or he is answerable. In assigning these responsibilities, the program manager seeks to capitalize upon the special skills, experience, and personal characteristics of the staff member. It must be recognized that in some instances this will involve the delegation of some undesirable or less-favored tasks. Staff members must anticipate these as well as their share of the more rewarding activities. A good program manager will not delegate all the "donkey work" and keep only the "goodies" for himself or herself. It is of utmost importance that every staff member have some duties that are enjoyable, challenging, and motivating. To paraphrase an old saying "All dull work and no fun work, makes Jack or Jill an unmotivated professional!"

2. *Provisions for staff support.* The fact that counselors are providing helping services and human support to others does not mean that counselors should or can function without the support of others. A program manager must see that staff members help and support each other and, additionally, receive help and support from beyond the counseling offices. Ways in which this may be accomplished include meaningful group work or committee assignments in which members share interest in a common problem or topic with other personnel outside the counseling staff. Obviously, part of this human support system is the program manager's personal interaction with each staff member.

3. *Provisions for staff development.* The effective program manager is ever alert to the ongoing need for the professional development of all staff members. Completing a degree provides entry into the professional workforce, but it does not signify an end to the development of a counselor's professional competencies. In fact, it should signal the beginning of such development. Clients have the right to expect that their counselors will be up to date—aware of the latest advancements, significant research, and promising practices in the field. Thus, professional development is to be anticipated and sought after by the professional counselor throughout his or her active career. Program leaders have the responsibility of providing opportunities, motivation, and, hopefully, resources. This topic is discussed further later in this chapter in the section entitled "The Counselor's Professional Development."

Budget

The importance of budget and budget management in any setting can hardly be overemphasized. A budget's significance in any system of accountability is paramount. In effect, it enables the supporting public, whether they are taxpayers or donators, to see what they are paying for or whether they are getting their money's worth. To the individual staff member, budgeting is often a mysterious, misunderstood, maddening, and far-removed process that has a direct and undeniable relationship to staff morale. It is therefore important that staff members recognize the level at which their immediate program manager is involved and the extent of that involvement.

It is also helpful to understand the level at which budgeting decisions, especially those affecting staff members, are made. In many settings, lower-level managers may be limited in their budget responsibilities to recommending or requisitioning from budgets established elsewhere. Crucial budget decisions, such as salaries and salary increments, staffing additions, and equipment purchases, tend to be made at middle- and upper-management levels. These real budget managers are usually involved in budgeting for personnel, including both professional and support staff; and services, such as consultants, communications, supplies, equipment, and travel. Budget decisions for capital improvements, such as new buildings or significant remodeling, are usually made at only the highest level of management.

One form of budgeting that has become increasingly prevalent at even the lower levels of management involves program activities supported by federal or state grants. These are usually developed in response to mandated federal or state programs. These programs have specific objectives and procedures and a budget that is directly related and accountable to those procedures and objectives.

Beginning counselors are unlikely to be involved in budget management, but they probably will be involved in budget expenditures. Because mismanagement or misspent monies may become your personal expense, the following suggestions are pertinent.

1. Each budget item is related to an activity, which in turn is related to a specific goal or objective of the organization. It is important to understand the reason for an expenditure, which also suggests spending only for those categories that are budgeted; for example, if professional travel is not provided for in a budget, you do not travel to a professional meeting by taking $500 from the supply item in the budget, even if it is not being spent elsewhere.

2. Spend only what you have. Although you may occasionally overdraw a bank account, you are usually reminded quickly and make amends before it becomes a bankruptcy disaster. However, all too frequently, when spending someone else's money, there is an inclination to be less

concerned until it is too late. Remember, any spending you do that is beyond the available budget will probably end up being your own personal expense.

3. Spend economically. The fact that you have a budget does not mean that the sky is the limit as long as you spend it for items in the budget and as long as you do not exceed the budget. Budget managers are expected to be good shoppers. This does not mean that you sacrifice quality for economy but that you get the most for your budgetary dollar. For example, on major purchases, such as computers, typewriters, video equipment, and tape recorders, it is customary to obtain two or three estimates including those provided by traditional discount houses before determining the place of purchase. If the expenditure is for travel, recipients are usually expected to be aware of the various bargain travel fares and travel regular or tourist class on common carriers. If private vehicles are used, mileage rates are usually established by federal, state, or local agencies.

4. Secure receipts. If you spend budgeted funds in any amount, you will be reimbursed only when there is proof of purchase. The only acceptable proof of purchase is a receipt for the goods or service obtained (showing the item, even if it is an elephant, is not considered proof of purchase).

5. Keep a running account. Anyone who has responsibility for any budget or segment of one must know exactly what has been expended and what remains at any given point during the duration of the budget. This means keeping a daily, if necessary, running account of debits, credits, and balances.

6. Be aware of any unusual (or usual) legal or contract restraints. This point is perhaps most appropriate when persons have budgetary responsibilities emanating from special contracts or grants. In such instances, budget managers, when in doubt, should consult the appropriate legal or contract authority before authorizing an expenditure.

Managing Facilities

The management of facilities takes on appropriate importance when one considers that persons spend more of their waking hours in their place of work than in their home or anywhere else. Facilities are important in determining whether persons will have the opportunity to do their job in a manner in which they are capable of doing it. In large, complex institutions, facilities are often viewed as symbols that reflect the importance with which the operation is viewed. (It is thus inevitable that a school principal's office will always be a shade larger, at least, than the school counselor's; that the college president's office and decor will be considerably larger and more luxurious than that of the institution's most distinguished professor, etc.) Facility concerns of program managers include the following.

- *Adequacy*. Size, furnishings, general decor, cleanliness, and, above all for counselors, privacy are determinants of the adequacy of one's work space. These factors tend to determine the atmosphere in which one works. During a recent university visitation, a dean of students, showing the offices of the university counseling center, remarked that he had $30,000-a-year counselors in $10,000 offices turning in $5,000-a-year performances. Those who have ever worked in dingy, dreary, ill-equipped, or dirty facilities can recall the impact of these on one's morale and subsequent performance. Yet, from time to time, high-level program managers seem to expect that as long as they are comfortable and their morale is good, it will spread to all levels regardless of working conditions.

- *Accessibility.* A person should not feel that she or he has already done a half day's work just by getting to the office. Accessibility is also important in terms of clients. Countless studies have noted that when university counseling centers or community agencies are situated in locations far from the main populations they are intended to serve, their clientele does not materialize.
- *Individuality.* Have you ever viewed the administrative offices of large-scale enterprises or business corporations, where dozens of employees have been provided identical cubicles and furnishings as so many similar mechanical parts in a precision machine? Such facilities provide little opportunity for the individual worker to assert any individuality. It would, therefore, seem inconsistent with that theoretical framework to suggest that individual counselors would not have enough flexibility in their personal office facilities to express this individuality.
- *Supplementary space.* Program managers also are responsible for securing and managing supplementary facilities, such as conference rooms, resource or staff rooms, filing areas (security can be important here), storage and supply areas, reception areas, and support staff facilities.

Organizing and Facilitating Basic Activities

The program manager must also guide the organization through the basic activities of the counseling program. This does not mean the professional activities but rather the basic supporting activities that complement the professional services of the organization. These include the following.

- *Coordination.* In even less-than-complex organizations, some degree of coordination is necessary to prevent overlapping, conflicting, or duplicating of activities. Coordination is necessary among activities and programs, both internally and externally.
- *Cooperation.* Cooperation is a vital ingredient in both coordination and public relations. Program managers must encourage and demonstrate a willingness to work with others in such vital counselor activities as case studies, conferences, referrals, and consultation. As suggested previously, counselors should be willing to give help when called upon by fellow professional colleagues or support personnel in other fields as well. Cooperation is one of the basic functions in establishing and maintaining positive professional connections.
- *Effective communications.* Communications often determine whether a program is managed efficiently. Counselors are usually well trained in the art of personal communication, but it is surprising how frequently the communication process breaks down within a program as well as with higher-level management and external agencies and organizations. Guidelines for effective communication in management suggest care must be taken that the personal touch is not lost as a result of using impersonal means to communicate, such as memos, policy statements, and directives. When such impersonal means are necessary, there must be adequate personal follow-up to ensure that such communications are understood. In addition, communication must provide for some sort of feedback. Oral communication to large groups such as staff or faculty meetings must justify the time it consumes for the number of people present.

- *Evaluation.* A program manager is responsible for ensuring the gathering of data that provide for systematic, ongoing evaluation of the program's activities. A program manager also coordinates periodic and accreditation types of planning. At the individual staff member level, a program manager is responsible for evaluating each member of the organization and communicating this evaluation to both the individual staff member and higher management.
- *Decision making.* Effective program management requires that someone be in charge. As the one in charge, a program manager must have decision-making authority commensurate with the responsibilities of the decision. Program managers can share the decision thinking, but they cannot be expected to share all the decision making.

Berk and Berk (1991) describe program management as

simultaneously an art and a science. The scientific aspects of the management discipline are fairly straightforward, and anyone with a reasonable degree of intelligence can learn the mechanics. You can't be successful as a manager if you are equipped only with the rules and procedures of the managerial business. You have to be adept at the artistic side of the managerial discipline. This is the part that requires an appreciation of the essence of the manager's job: understanding what it is you are responsible for doing, determining the best way to do it, recruiting and cultivating the right people, and helping these people to realize their full potential. (p. 9)

CONTRIBUTING TO PROGRAM DEVELOPMENT AND IMPROVEMENT

All of us like to be members of winning teams. We would also probably agree that talent alone is not enough; that winning teams require teamwork and a winning game plan. On joining a counseling staff, a counselor becomes not only a team member but also committed to and involved in the continuous process of program development and improvement—the implementation of a game plan. The effective development of any counseling program, regardless of setting, depends first on an accurate and continuous assessment of the needs of the target population to be served. Such needs assessment is the key to successful planning for goals and objectives. The accurate assessment of potential client needs is critical in establishing and maintaining program relevance and fostering program accountability and evaluation. The needs assessment activity, which can range from a simple to a complex process, is concerned with two databases, as follows.

1. *Target population assessment:* This data gathering seeks to establish factually the needs of the target population that the counseling program has been created to serve. These data will also influence priorities among these needs.
2. *Environmental assessment:* This is the gathering of factual data that facilitate the counseling program's understanding of the setting from which the target population comes and within which the program functions. Also, it is important that counselors understand the environment in which behavior occurs.

Target population assessment provides a factual basis for a program's goals and objectives, and environmental assessment provides a factual basis for the procedures by which a program achieves its goals and objectives. The personal needs are the internal factors that initiate, direct, and sustain the program's activities, whereas the environmental characteristics provide the depth of understanding for more effectively responding to the needs.

Lewis and Lewis (1991), writing from a community agency perspective, identify the generic planning process as one using the following basic steps: (a) needs assessment, (b) definition of goals and objectives, (c) identification of alternative methods for meeting goals, (d) decision making, and (e) development of plans for implementation and evaluation. "Each of these steps involves a major commitment both from agency personnel and from community members. Each step also depends on the effective completion of the previous task, beginning with the all-important process of needs assessment" (p. 35).

The Needs Assessment Survey

As we mentioned, the development of accountable and relevant programs begins with the assessment of the needs of the target population (see Figure 13-2). In this process, developmental, preventive, and enhancement needs of the population are considered as well as those that have intervention and remediation implications. This is a technique for factually establishing program goals and objectives. Such an assessment directly involves the target population or a sampling of it, as well as critical support populations. For example, a school guidance program would not only gather data from students but would also survey parents, teachers, and others who had frequent and direct contact with the student population.

The direct involvement of these populations is usually secured through questionnaires or structured interviews. Figure 13-3 presents an example of a simple questionnaire used in student needs assessment and completed by not only students but support populations as well.

In addition to questionnaire and interview data, other sources such as school and community records will provide data that substantiate or identify the needs of potential clients. Environmental assessment seeks to establish the characteristics of program and population setting through identifying the characteristics of the environment's population, economics, and geography. Community assessment may be facilitated through the use and development

Step 1	Step 2	Step 3	Step 4	Step 5	Step 6
Assessment of Needs through Data Collection	Interpretation of Data	Priority Needs	Program Objectives	Program Procedures (activities developed based on program resources available)	Planning for Program Improvement (based on evaluation of outcomes and procedures)

Figure 13-2 Sequence of Procedures for Developing an Accountable Program of Counseling and Guidance.
Source: From Gibson, Robert L., Mitchell, Marianne H., and Basile, Sherry K., *Counseling in the Elementary School: A Comprehensive Approach*, p. 272. Copyright © 1993 by Allyn and Bacon. Reprinted by permission.

Person filling out form:	Very Important	Quite Important	Moderately Important	Somewhat Important	Not Important At All	In your opinion is this service being provided? (check one)
____ Student ____ Parent ____ Teacher ____ Businessperson						**Rankings: Check one for each question below** / **Additional Response**
1. How important is it for students to be able to discuss personal problems with the school counselor?						yes____ no ____
2. How important is it for the school counselor to provide career information?						yes____ no ____
3. How important is it for the school counselor to provide information concerning colleges, trade schools, or the armed services?						yes____ no ____
4. How important is it for the counselor to show the relationship between education and careers?						yes____ no ____
5. How important is it for the counselor to provide assistance to the student in job placement upon graduation?						yes____ no ____
6. How important is it for the counselor to discuss with students which courses they will take in school?						yes____ no ____
7. How important is it for the counselor to work with students who are failing or dropping out?						yes____ no ____
8. How important is it for the counselor to lead small-group discussions on current student problems?						yes____ no ____
9. How important is a counseling and guidance program in a high school?						yes____ no ____
10. What other services for students do you think the school counselor should provide? (Please write in the space below and on the back.)						yes____ no ____

Figure 13-3   Needs Identification Questionnaire.

of certain data planning instruments, as noted in Figures 13-4 and 13-5. Typical sources from which the previously suggested data may be gathered are noted in Figure 13-4. Figure 13-5 is a checklist designed to guide the information seeker to common sources of community information. The form is not intended to record data but only to provide a guide to possible sources.

Community: _____

Survey dates: _____

Survey team: _____

_____

_____

_____   1.   Political leadership

_____

_____

_____   2.   Governmental (nonpolitical) leadership

_____

_____

_____   3.   Educational leadership
                        (School board members, superintendents, principals,
_____   education association or union officials)

_____   4.   Major religious denominations
                        (ministers, priests, rabbis)
_____

_____   5.   Minority group (or groups) leadership

_____

_____   6.   Judicial system
                        (Chief of police, juvenile judge, lawyers,
_____   county sheriff, probationary officials)

_____   7.   Business/commercial/industrial leadership
                        (Presidents [in residence] of local corporations,
_____   plant managers, owners of prominent local businesses)

_____   8.   Labor organization leadership

_____

_____   9.   Youth leadership
                        (Student council members, athletic standouts,
_____   social club or gang leadership)

_____ 10.   Civic leadership
                        (Officials of civic clubs, volunteer organizations)

_____

_____ 11.   Other (indicate status and representation)

_____   _____

_____   _____

Note: Be sure all interviewees meet the criteria for "significant contributors"
as indicated in interviewing instructions. Structured interview guides
should be adhered to insofar as possible. Exceptions should be noted
and reasons for deviations explained.

Figure 13-4   Community Survey Checklist: Interview Schedule.

Community: _____

Survey dates: _____

Survey team: _____

_____

_____

_____	1. Census data
_____	2. News media analysis
_____	3. Board of education (minutes of) meetings
_____	4. Annual reports of schools
_____	5. County government data
_____	6. City government data
_____	7. Employment agencies
_____	8. Church board reports
_____	9. Chamber of Commerce data
_____	10. Geographic data
_____	11. Ecological-environmental data
_____	12. Other significant data (list sources)

_____

_____

_____

_____

_____

Note: If data are not available, place notation "NA" in blank at left of item. Otherwise, when data are collected, place a "✓".

Figure 13-5   Community Survey Checklist: Data Collection.

Braucht and Weime (1990) describe a multi-agency needs assessment in a rural setting with very limited financial resources. The school system networked with the Youth Services Planning Board established by the Illinois State Department of Children and Family Services in conducting a needs assessment using the key informant approach. This approach involves selecting community or area leaders to provide estimates of the needs and required services of a specific population. The result is a broad picture of these needs and services as perceived by community leaders. In Braucht and Weime's needs assessment, a questionnaire was sent to the key informants to determine the problems they encountered in their contacts with youth. The questionnaire consisted of five items:

1. What problems or issues do adolescents face in your community?
2. If money were growing on trees, what services for adolescents would you like to see begun or improved in your community?

3. To which of the following sources have you referred adolescents in the past year? (Choices were churches, counseling agencies, investigating agencies, parents, school staff, self-help groups, significant adults, other—please specify.)

4. Please rank the top five referral sources from Question 3 according to frequency of referral, with 1 designating the most frequent and 5 the least.

5. Please feel free to share comments, concerns, or suggestions.

Follow-up telephone calls were made to encourage a higher response rate. (p. 179)

Identifying Priorities and Developing Program Relevancy

Once gathered, the needs assessment data provide direction for determining goals and priorities and for developing counseling program objectives that are relevant and meaningful to the target population and setting. The initial procedure is a simple listing of goals and priorities, first as perceived by the target population. These then may be slightly reordered, as verified by immediate support population, and then slightly reordered again, once these base data are supplemented by secondary populations and sources. In the school setting, the students would represent the target population, and teachers and parents, the immediate support population. Supplementary or secondary population would include community personnel and data from student and other relevant records. This process leads to a tentative prioritizing of needs. A final reordering is established by eliminating any needs that may not be the professional responsibility of the counseling program or may require resources beyond those available to the counseling program. The outcome of this process is the establishment of working priorities in a hierarchical order, which are then translated into goals and objectives.

The translation of priorities into goals and objectives requires their being stated in writing. The program goals are typically described in broad, general terms that may not be tied to specific time constraints. The program objectives must be stated in objective, measurable terms and related to a time frame. Objectives are designed to describe desired performances and should contribute to the achievement of a program goal and the meeting of one or more specifically identified needs. Of course, the assessment of needs and the establishment of related goals and objectives are not in themselves a guarantee of program relevancy. A needs assessment only establishes an awareness of what a counseling program should consider in planning the utilization of its resources. The real criteria of program relevancy will result from the degree of understanding and concern and the appropriateness of the plan of action developed and executed by the counseling staff. An effective plan of action will reflect many, if not all, of the following characteristics.

1. *It should be developmental.* Program planning should be developmental, indicating immediate, intermediate, and long-range program goals. As a starting point, it may be appropriate to envision an ultimate, utopian program for the setting for which it will be designed and, once having established these long-range goals, determine those priorities that should be given immediate attention, those that may need attention within the next several years, and those that the program ultimately hopes to accomplish. Programs should at all times be developmental, for development implies continuous growth and improvement.

2. *It should have a logical, sequential plan of development.* The development of any program usually proceeds from a foundation which seems appropriate to subsequent development. As previously suggested, the appropriate foundation from which planning proceeds are its needs and readiness assessment and their relationship to the resources at hand.

3. *It should be flexible.* Counseling programs must be flexible in order to meet the changing needs of youth and other client populations. This suggests also that initial planning for program development must be limited to that which can be reasonably achieved. Programs that are overly ambitious in their design allow little room for unexpected opportunities. A part of flexibility in planning should be the identification of possible problems and alternate procedures for goal achievement.

4. *It should give a high priority to communication, coordination, and cooperation.* Like the other components of program development, these activities should not be left to chance. It is important, for example, that there be a plan for communicating the development of the school guidance program to faculty members individually and in groups, as well as to students, parents, and others. Cooperation with other programs and persons is important if the program is to receive reciprocal cooperation. In communicating with the various relevant groups and people in the community, different approaches must be used that recognize the uniqueness and differences of these individuals and groups. For example, techniques for communicating with youths would certainly be different in many ways than those that are effective with adults and related professionals. Often, counseling programs increasingly fail to communicate their mission clearly and effectively to others, which results in many questioning the need for such programs. Coordination and cooperation failures have also adversely affected the positive image that counseling programs seek to portray.

5. *It should provide a basis for resource employment.* An adequate plan for program development provides a logical basis for personnel assignment, budget development, and resource allocation and utilization. This means that the plan must be a clear and concise one in which the relationships between program goals, the activities for achieving these goals, and the personnel and other resources needed to accomplish them can be readily recognized. The program director must be a resource coordinator. Program planning must, therefore, take into account those resources that may be available for program development and goal accomplishment. An inventory of possible resources becomes an important activity in planning for program development.

Any plan for program initiation and development must include provisions for program accountability or evaluation. The evaluation component of a developmental plan provides a built-in mechanism for program accountability, development, and improvement. Gysbers and Henderson (1994) suggest four phases for program improvement and development with modified descriptors as follows.

1. *Planning:* This stage assumes the services provided must be organized into a program and that these services will be both developmental and comprehensive. It also includes planning to move from where the program is currently to the desired program plan.

2. *Designing:* "Once a comprehensive program model has been selected and data have been gathered that describe the current guidance program, the next phase of the program improvement process is to design the specific program that is desired for your school district or school building." (p. 135)

3. *Implementing:* "Having organized for change, adopted a comprehensive program model, assessed the current program, established the design for the desired program, and planned the transition, you, as the guidance program leader, are now ready to make the transition to an improved program. You also are ready to develop mechanisms to main-

tain the program once it is in operation. This is one of the most critical phases of the entire program improvement process. The questions to be answered include: How is the transition to a comprehensive program to be made? What new resources are needed to enhance the effectiveness and efficiency of the program? Are there special projects that will provide impetus to the needed changes in direction? How can we assist each building to improve its program?" (p. 209)

4. *Evaluating*: This process is described as ongoing, using specific and relevant criteria and as essential to continuous program improvement.

Gysbers and Henderson (1994) go on to say

> Three kinds of systematic evaluation are required to achieve accountability for your guidance program. The first kind of evaluation—personnel evaluation—describes the procedures used by your district to evaluate school counselors and other personnel who may be assisting them in implementing the district's guidance program. Program evaluation, the second kind, examines your district's written guidance program using a process called an audit, to see if it is the district's implemented program. The third kind of evaluation, called results of evaluation, focuses on the impact that the guidance and counseling activities in your district's program are having on students, the school, and the community (Gysbers, Hughey, Starr, & Lapan, 1992). (pp. 325–326)

Program relevance and, hence, development and improvement must, of course, consider previously mentioned priorities, including the following as appropriate.

- Career development and assistance needs of the population to be served
- Attention to preventive and developmental opportunities and needs of the target population
- Recognition of special populations (i.e., minorities, poor and homeless, people with disabilities, etc.)

The Counselor's Professional Development

Much has been written in recent years regarding staff development, yet, it is our observation that few counseling organizations have planned active programs for this purpose. However, it seems reasonable to assume that more programs will recognize the benefits that accrue, not only to the programs themselves, but to their professional staffs as well, from active staff development programs that increase the skills and knowledge of their counselors.

Professional development can be facilitated by attending professional conventions, conferences, and workshops. Participating in Internet exchange networks is an innovative and growing approach to professional growth; visiting other programs is a more traditional, but still popular one.

Other activities may include quality circles, research involvement, exchange programs, sabbatical leaves, and reviews of professional literature. Of course, practicing counselors must assume the primary responsibility for their own professional development, even when benefiting from well-planned organizational staff development programs. This means your career will be in your own hands, so to speak, and therefore you will be largely responsible for determining your professional goals, the accomplishments or procedures needed to achieve these goals, and the resources that must be used in the process. Your professional development, of course, can contribute to the further development of your organization and the counseling profession as well.

One of the first steps beginning counselors can take to ensure their professional development is to join their appropriate professional organizations. Such organizations as the American Counseling Association and the American Psychological Association and their divisions provide excellent professional journals, newsletters, workshops, and conventions for the professional development of their members.

Beyond joining the appropriate professional organizations, counselors should be active participants in the development of the profession as well. This means participating and sharing through attendance at professional meetings and conference presentations and sharing one's ideas and findings through writing and research.

Finally, we would note that the counselor's professional development is not just about self-enhancement, although that is certainly one of the goals of professionalization. Nor is it just about contributing more to your organization and the profession of counseling, although these, too, are desirable outcomes. It is first and foremost being the best, the most up to date, the most relevant you can be for the benefit of your clients. Your clients have the right to expect this from you—as you in turn expect it of your physician, dentist, lawyer, and so forth. Thus, the true professional is one whose learning is continuous and ongoing, who steadily grows across his or her professional life span.

PROGRAM LEADERSHIP

Although discussed in brief earlier, we would once again emphasize that perhaps no single characteristic beyond the professional qualifications of the counseling staff is more significant to the success of the counseling operation than the quality of program leadership. It is desirable that counselors at least recognize those characteristics that tend to identify leaders and distinguish them from program administrators or managers. Most persons recognize the individual who is a true leader. A real leader is one who leads, not directs; real leadership gives priority to the benefit of the program and those who are led, rather than to the leader. Some of the characteristics of program leadership include the following.

- *Is successful:* Program leaders have good track records. They justify the old concept that success breeds success. Included in the program leader's win column is previous recognition as a successful and resourceful counselor. Also, the program leader is an extra competent professional. Program leadership for counseling programs can be provided only by professional counselors. Program leaders will contribute their competence and expert knowledge to the successful functioning of the counseling program, including an awareness of professional, ethical, and legal guidelines for the profession.
- *Inspires confidence:* A program leader inspires confidence in herself and individual staff members. She does this by being supportive and also realistic. She expects the possible, but not the impossible. She gives and shares credit publicly so that others know of the successes of individual staff members.
- *Shares:* The program leader shares the ownership of the operation and develops a feeling of us rather than me and you. Active ownership does not mean that the staff runs the operation. It means that the staff shares in the running of it. Sharing the ownership of the operation creates a feeling of belonging, of being on the team. Real leadership sees that no one feels left out. There are no in-groups and out-groups.

- *Motivates:* All studies of leadership indicate that a common ingredient of leaders in nearly every setting is an ability to motivate others to achieve their potential, and, perhaps at times, even exceed it. Although each leader has a different and unique style, the evidence is present when one observes hardworking, achieving staff members.
- *Creates a positive atmosphere:* A leader understands what makes life at the office liveable or one happy in one's work by creating professional atmospheres conducive to accomplishment. This includes effective program organization, management, and administration. As Ailes (1988) points out, one of the secrets of successful leaders is being likeable.
- *Is visible:* One cannot lead in absentia. Successful program leaders at all levels are those who are frequently and clearly visible to and available for interaction with their supporting staff.
- *Is forward-looking:* Leadership demands planning for the future. Program leaders are insightful and future oriented in their planning.
- *Is a decision maker:* Effective leadership not only accepts the decision-making responsibility and will make the hard decisions but will also make the appropriate decisions.

These characteristics can provide a checklist to identify potential counseling program leaders. As noted in Gibson, Mitchell, and Higgins (1983), program leaders are not likely to be chosen when the top management position is viewed as a consolation prize, a stepping stone for someone tagged to proceed up the organization, a political position to shore up support for top management, or proof that the Peter Principle (Peter & Hull, 1959) really operates. (This principle suggests that one is eventually promoted to his or her level of incompetence.)

SUMMARY

Much of the success of any counseling program will depend on how the program is managed, developed, and led. As educational and community institutions have become more complex in their organizational and operational structure, the necessity for special preparation of program leaders in terms of managing resources, coordinating and facilitating activities, and providing personnel motivation has become increasingly self-evident. Counselors, as organizational staff members, must also be aware of their responsibilities and be knowledgeable enough to carry them out.

The next chapter discusses an area to which counseling program leaders and their staffs are giving increased attention. Accountability and evaluation are being demanded of all programs, and counselors are being called on to advance the frontiers of knowledge of our profession.

DISCUSSION QUESTIONS

1.   Do you find such activities as writing letters, managing your finances, and handling personal management items—such as insurance, food planning, and study planning—challenging, boring, or something you put off?

2.   What differences do you see between the manager of a business (e.g., auto dealer, grocer, insurance agent) and the manager of a counseling program?

3.   Identify some well-known leaders (past or present) that you have admired. What is it that you've admired about them?

4.   What kind of a program leader would you like to work for?

5.   What is the relationship between needs assessment and program relevancy?

6.   Comment on the suggestions given when budgeting is of concern in program management.

CLASS ACTIVITIES

1.   Examine the leadership characteristics offered as being significant to the success of counseling and compare those to your personal characteristics. How do you size up?

2.   Compare the leadership qualities desired in counselors to leadership qualities typically identified with other fields of endeavor (e.g., the military, business and industry, and politics). Discuss in small groups and compare answers.

SELECTED READINGS

Cunningham, G. (1994). *Effective employee assistance programs: A guide for EAP counselors and managers.* Thousand Oaks, CA: Sage.

Ebert, M. K., Richardson, W. M., & Stevenson, J. W. (1985). *A study of the guidance program and its management in the Montgomery County Public Schools.* Rockville, MD: Montgomery County Public Schools, Dept. of Educational Accountability.

Hadley, R. G., & Mitchell, L. K. (1995). *Counseling research and program evaluation.* Pacific Grove, CA: Brooks/Cole.

Hannaford, M. J. (1987). Balancing the counseling program to meet school needs. *National Association of Secondary School Principals Bulletin, 71* (499), 34, 69.

Kelly, F., & Ferguson, D. (1984). Elementary school guidance needs assessment: A field tested model. *Elementary School Guidance and Counseling, 18* (3), 176–180.

Lampe, R. E. (1985). Principals' training in counseling and development: A national survey. *Counselor Education and Supervision, 25,* 44–47.

MacDevitt, M., & MacDevitt, J. (1987). Low cost needs assessment for a rural mental health center. *Journal of Counseling and Development, 65* (9), 505–507.

Orzek, A. (1987). Innovations in ecological psychology: Conversations with Roger and Louise Baker. *Journal of Counseling and Development, 65* (5), 233–237.

Terril, J. L. (1987). Positive approaches strengthen school and counseling programs. *National Association of Secondary School Principals Bulletin, 71* (499), 19–22.

Wampold, B. E. (1997). Methodological problems in identifying efficacious psychotherapies. *Psychotherapy Research, 7* (1), 21–43.

Wilson, N. S., & Remley, T. P., Jr. (1987). Leadership in guidance: A survey of school counseling supervisors. *Counselor Education and Supervision, 26* (3), 213–230.

Wysong, H. E. (1983). *Needs assessment in counseling, guidance, and personnel services. Searchlight plus: Relevant resources in high interest areas.* (Tech. Rep. No. 21+). Ann Arbor: University of Michigan.

RESEARCH OF INTEREST

Carter, M. F., Crosby, C., Geertshuis, S., & Startup, M. (1996). Developing reliability in client-centered mental health needs assessment. *Journal of Mental Health UK, 5* (3), 233–243.

Abstract

This article provides a method for conceptualizing and assessing the expressed needs of people with a long-term mental illness. Based on a study involving 57 patients with long-term mental illness, client-key informant agreement and test-retest reliability are reported for the Bangor Assessment of Need Profile. The results suggest poor client-key worker agreement and fair to very good test-retest reliability. The paper discusses the meaning and objective of indices of agreement in relation to the presence or absence of need. It concludes that a clearer understanding of what the mental health service user has to say concerning her or his own needs is required in relation to individual client mental state and quality of life outcome measures.

Delaney, J. T., & Huselid, M. A. (1996). The impact of human resource management practices on perceptions of organizational performance. *Academy of Management Journal, 39* (4), 949–969.

Abstract

This study examined 727 for-profit and nonprofit firms from the National Organizations Survey to determine if human resource management practices affect firms' perceptual measures of organizational performance. Results show positive associations between human resource management (HRM) practices, such as training and staffing selectivity, and perceptual firm performance measures. Results also suggest methodological issues for consideration in examinations of the relationship between HRM systems and firm performance.

Huselid, M. A., Jackson, S. E., & Schuler, R. S. (1997). Technical and strategic human resource management effectiveness as determinants of firm performance. *Academy of Management Journal, 40* (1), 171–188.

Abstract

This study evaluated the impact of human resource (HR) managers' capabilities on HR management effectiveness and the latter's impact on corporate financial performance. For 293 U.S. firms, effectiveness was associated with capabilities and attributes of HR staff. Also found were relationships between HR management effectiveness and productivity, cash flow, and market value.

Mayes, A. N., & McConatha, J. (1982). Surveying student needs: A means of evaluating student services. *Journal of College Student Personnel, 23* (6), 473–476.

Abstract

To obtain information about problems and concerns of incoming students and to compare results with previous studies, these researchers had students ($N = 248$) complete the Mooney Problem Check List. Results emphasized the need for institutions to continuously review and revise existing counseling programs based on students' expressed needs.

Peterson, S., & DeGracie, J. S. (1983). *Secondary counseling services as perceived by selected publics.* (Tech. Rep. No. RR-49). Mesa, AZ: Mesa Public Schools, Dept. of Research and Evaluation.

Abstract

In the spring of 1983, an evaluation of the junior and senior high guidance programs in the Mesa Public Schools was conducted. Surveys were developed to solicit opinions from parents, teachers, counselors, administrators, career specialists, and students as to how counselors actually spend their time versus how they should spend their time. Results were analyzed separately for each group of respondents and for the junior high and high school programs. Parents, teachers, counselors, career specialists, and students believed that junior high counselors devote the greatest amount of time on student registration, followed by registration and consultation with parents. All groups believed that counselors should spend most of their time on individual personal or academic/vocational counseling. Overall ratings of the junior high program varied by group; parent and student ratings were lowest. Results from the high school program evaluation were very similar, and recommendations cover both levels. Survey instruments and responses are included in the report's appendix.

Priest, S. (1984). Effective outdoor leadership: A survey. *Journal of Experiential Education, 7* (3), 34–36.

Abstract

A survey completed by 189 persons attending the 1983 National Association for Experimental Education Conference resulted in a rank ordered list of 39 competency areas considered essential to the effective outdoor leader. Respondents placed greatest importance on items related to safety, group counseling, and interaction.

Prout, H. T., & DeMartino, R. A. (1986). A meta-analysis technique to school-based studies of psychotherapy. *Journal of School Psychology, 24* (3), 285–292.

Abstract

The results indicate that psychotherapy in the schools is moderately effective. Evidence was also found of the greater efficacy of group and behavioral theory interventions that target observed behaviors and problem-solving abilities.

Spreitzer, G. M., & Quinn, R. E. (1996). Empowering middle managers to be transformational leaders. *Journal of Applied Behavioral Science, 32* (3), 237–261.

Abstract

This article describes a field study of a large-scale management development program in a manufacturing corporation, designed to stimulate middle managerial change. Three thousand middle managers participated in the program, entailing a one-week core session and a six-month follow-up. Subjects with low levels of self-esteem, job affect, and social support tended to limit their efforts to changing themselves and thus had little impact on the organization. Subjects with high levels of self-esteem, job affect, and social support were more likely to make transformational changes. Thus, results suggest that individual mind-set before attending the program moderates the type of change undertaken by the middle managers. Middle managers who were plateaued were most likely to make the most radical changes. Implications for change mastery and resistance to change are discussed.

Stavros, D., & Moore, J. E. (1985, March 31–April 4). *Two perspectives on school climate: Do staff and students see a school the same way?* Paper presented at the Annual Meeting of the American Educational Research Association, Chicago, IL.

Abstract

Two studies of school climate were conducted at Detroit's Boulevard High School in 1984, three years after the institution of a school improvement program. One study measured students' perceptions, the other assessed staff perceptions. Based upon the findings of this research, it became clear that in order to get a good picture of the school climate, data from both students and staff were needed. Staff and students had convergent opinions in many areas. The school's academic program was viewed positively by both groups. Students were positive about guidance and counseling, the curriculum, and the instruction. The staff were positive about related areas: frequent monitoring of student progress and opportunity to learn and time-on-task. They viewed the department head, especially in the role of instructional leader, in a positive light. The staff did not feel safe in the school (and students did not participate in activities that would cause them to remain at school after hours). Both students and staff were generally satisfied with the school but had negative perceptions concerning Boulevard's administration. The staff viewed the principal as accessible but as a poor instructional leader. Students felt that the administration was not accessible, and they were not involved in the decision-making process. And finally, although staff tended

to have low expectations of student performance, students felt they were learning almost all they could and learning a lot in
most or all classes.

Warchal, P., & Southern, S. (1986). Perceived importance of counseling needs among adult students. *Journal of College Student Personnel, 27*
(1), 43–48.

Abstract
    This study failed to confirm the existence of
major differences in the perceptions of counseling
needs attributable to developmental period (age)
and sex. Existing data on the nature of counseling
needs of adult students was confirmed.

Accountability, Evaluation, and Research

It is important for the beginning counselor to recognize that he or she alone is responsible—accountable—for being an effective and efficient counselor. The newcomer must also anticipate being the subject of professional evaluation as well as participating in organizational evaluation. Also, because both accountability and evaluation frequently imply research needs, it is important to understand basic research design and sources of research reports that may provide insights into local concerns or issues. Therefore, this chapter's objective is to introduce concepts and guidelines for the beginning counselor's involvement in program accountability, evaluation, and research.

The mere mention of the activities of accountability, evaluation, and research is said frequently to strike fear into the hearts of many honest practitioners. Such concern includes the fear of being (a) held responsible, regardless of intervening variables, for one's activities; (b) judged by criteria determined externally, over which one has no control; (c) judged by unrealistic standards and expectancies; (d) required, in the case of research, to master difficult mathematical formulas that one feels will never be used again; and (e) expected to understand and possibly even apply the results of research studies written by researchers to impress other researchers. Then, of course, there is the fear, or assumption, that evaluation is never intended to be positive. Many of these fears will diminish to mere myths when one learns to appreciate the values and advantages of accountability, evaluation, and research for the practicing counselor.

DEFINITIONS

Although textbooks and many periodical articles have been published dealing with the separate topics of accountability, evaluation, and research, this chapter will present an overview that, while giving each area its just due, stresses the relationships among accountability, evaluation, and research. Let us then distinguish among these terms.

Leon Lessinger, who is often referred to as the father of accountability for the impetus given this movement during his tenure as Commissioner of Education, defines *accountability* as responsibility for something, to someone, with predictable consequences for the desirable and understandable performance of the responsibility (Lessinger, Cunningham, & Sabine, 1973). In effect, accountability is the holding of some one, group, or organization responsible for their planning, actions, and outcomes.

The term *evaluation* seems to take on many meanings depending on the definer. Certainly evaluation is both a term and a process, each suggesting a determination of the value or worth of the object of the process. Evaluations can be made of individual, group, organizational, or institutional performances. Evaluation is also commonly viewed as the degree to which an individual or organization has achieved, usually within a time frame, predetermined goals.

In this regard, we suggest that the process of evaluation seeks to provide objective evidence of a program's performance through an assessment of progress toward program objectives. The evidence collected through this process then becomes valuable as a basis for future program planning and decision making. As such, a planned and conscientious program evaluation is essential to the continuous improvement of counseling programs in any setting.

A long-standing definition of *evaluation* from the National Institute of Mental Health suggests as a working definition the following.

Program evaluation is a systematic set of data collection and analysis activities undertaken to determine the value of a program to aid management, program planning, staff training, public accountability, and promotion. Evaluation activities make reasonable judgments possible about the efforts, effectiveness, adequacy, efficiency, and comparative value of program options. (Hagedorn, Beck, Neubert, & Werlin, 1976, p. 3)

A common definition views *research* as organized scientific efforts for the advancement of knowledge. Research represents an effort and a way of establishing truths. It is a process for validating—or rejecting—theoretical assumptions and/or unsubstantiated claims or practices. Of course, for research to have value and validity requires a systematic study of the interrelationships among variables as they relate to the objectives of the inquiry.

ACCOUNTABILITY

In the 1990s, taxpayers, consumers, and organizational managements have demanded more and more that those offering goods and services provide some concrete evidence of their worthwhileness in return for the public's expenditures of monies, whether through taxation or purchases of goods or services. These demands have resulted from not only increased costs but also frequent failures to meet the public's expectations and/or lack of proof of accomplishments. The November 1993 issue of *Guidepost* (currently entitled *Counseling Today*), the official newspaper of the American Counseling Association, is headlined "Many school counseling programs cut when finances run low!" The article goes on to state that cuts are often made when school boards and the public perceive counseling as auxiliary services. Some examples are also noted of school systems retaining their counseling staffs thanks to public support. It might be concluded that accountability is an opportunity for counseling programs to prove themselves. It must not be neglected!

Although accountability first became a byword in education, its popularity has also spread to other tax-supported governmental institutions and agencies, including mental health agencies. As a result, community as well as many privately financed counseling agencies are also being subject to review, often resulting in staff downsizing and budget reductions.

Counselors in many tax-supported health care settings must be aware of the possible impact of HMOs (which provide managed care) on their practice. Managed care case managers are nearly always businesspeople with the primary mission of saving money. Trimming counseling staff and counselor availability can, of course, have highly undesirable effects on clients and those in need of access to counselors. This possibility simply underscores the need for counselor accountability and the evidence to support it.

Thus, with the possible and rare exception of private practice, the likelihood is great that counselors will be employed in settings in which they will be expected to be accountable—to provide factual evidence of their accomplishments related to their costs.

A Positive View of Accountability

Recognizing that many helping professionals have negative attitudes or, at the least, uneasy feelings about accountability, let us accentuate the positive. More than 20 years ago, in his "An Argument for Constructive Accountability," Baker (1977) presented five positive aspects of accountability.

1. *Skill acquisition:* Whatever accountability system one uses, certain specific skills are required of the participants. Acquisition of such skills may increase one's satisfaction and confidence. Satisfaction with one's level of competence is associated with knowledge of specific skills possessed. Confidence in one's capacity to encounter new tasks, such as those related to an accountability system, increases with acquisition of new skills. Among those skills that may be acquired or improved through attention to an accountability system are the ability to envision and develop a system; developing data collection instruments; analyzing data; reporting results; making decisions based on acquired results; making plans for future actions based upon acquired results; and applying those plans to a real life setting.

2. *Program improvement:* Conscientious counselors are constantly searching for ways to improve their services. Finding useful sources of evaluative information about the existing services is a universal problem for these people. An accountability system offers the solution of this universal need because data acquired from the accountability activities may be used as the basis for program improvement. As a result, data are used constructively.

3. *Positive results:* Results acquired through an accountability system may be complimentary. Prospects of acquiring complimentary outcomes from accountability studies need to be emphasized more than is presently the case. . . . Such results provide intrinsic rewards for the counselor because awareness of consumer's satisfaction or of successful program outcomes provides the counselor with a feeling of satisfaction and accomplishment.

4. *A process rather than an event:* A systematic ongoing model incorporates the accountability activities and other planned enterprises with a minimum amount of drudgery and maximum efficiency.

5. *Rewards for a job well done:* The ultimate outcome for an accountability system, it seems, is to reward intrinsically those who have demonstrated that their accomplishments are extraordinary. . . . The reward system is viewed as the ultimate outcome because it completes the unfinished accountability model. (pp. 53–55)

It is clear from the statements of Baker and others that conscientious counselors, dedicated to improving their skills and serving their clientele as effectively and efficiently as possible, have little to fear and much to gain from a system that will be their ally. Accountability may, at last, provide the ultimate proof that counseling programs can make a positive difference.

Developing Accountability in Counseling Programs

Although there is no best approach to developing an accountability model, most programs seem to focus on some form of needs assessment out of which program objectives are identified and perhaps prioritized and that, in turn, lead to program activity planning and an accounting for and evaluation of the outcomes. The development of this type of accountable counseling program has already been implied in the previous chapter in discussions regarding the development of effective programs. Now let us reexamine these concepts as they apply to accountability.

The first step in developing an accountable program is to obtain the facts needed to establish or reorient a viable program. This involves the collection of factual data about the target population, their needs, and other characteristics. Factual data on the environment that may contribute to client understanding and organizational functioning are also collected. Techniques for this process were noted in the previous chapter. The second step involves interpreting data followed by the third step, identifying program priorities and related objectives. Fourth, procedures are developed that promise to achieve the program objectives. As may be noted, each phase of the process depends on the preceding steps being accomplished, all leading back to the first step—the establishment of a factual base for being accountable—and, of course, relevant! The four steps of (1) assessment, (2) data interpretation, (3) goal setting, and (4) procedures for goals attainment form the basis (still a factual one) for program resources, including budget, and, finally, program evaluation and accountability.

It is important for counseling to keep in mind that accountability means responsibility, not only for *what* you do, but *why*, and *how well* you do it. As we proceed to the next section discussing evaluation, we should note the relationship of evaluation to accountability. As Lewis and Lewis (1991) explain

> Most human service programs are required to submit yearly evaluation reports for the scrutiny of funding sources or public agencies and many specially funded projects are required to spend set percentages of their total budgets on evaluation. Beyond this, however, agencies are also accountable to their communities. The "accountability model" Windle and Neigher (1978, p. 97) describe stresses this component of evaluation. The accountability model takes the position that a program should be evaluated by the public and/or those who support it. Such evaluation can have at least three purposes: (1) to let the public or other supporters make wise decisions concerning support, (2) to motivate the public and other supporters to greater program support by involving them in the goals and activities of the program, and (3) to motivate the program staff to greater public service and efficiency by their awareness that their activities are being monitored.
>
> Dissemination of evaluation reports describing the agency's activities and their effects can help reinforce program accountability. People concerned with agency performance can gain knowledge about the results of services, and this information undoubtedly increases community members' impact on policies and programs. (p. 235)

EVALUATION

Everyone constantly seeks ways to improve many routine chores, whether it is trying a new toothpaste or a different breakfast cereal or taking a new route to work. In a sense, people constantly evaluate many daily decisions and activities. People are also involved, usually unofficially, in many external evaluations such as of the local newspaper; a current TV program; the decisions of Congress; and the teachers, courses, and textbooks with which children come in contact. Just as these evaluations are a part of the process of improving daily living or exercising a right to express one's opinions, the more formal, structured evaluations of one's professional activities and organizations should also receive daily attention.

As the critics of counseling have constantly pointed out in recent years, justifiably or not, evaluative evidence and activities appear, all too frequently, to be either missing or often misleading at best. Certainly, counseling programs are under closer scrutiny and increased accountability from a variety of sources as demands for counseling services and programs have expanded.

A Process for Professional and Program Improvement

One often reads or hears about a public office holder, a salesperson, or a teacher with 30 years of experience but with no mention of the quality of that experience. Experience does not, in and of itself, guarantee improvement and quality. Professionals must have as their own personal-ethical goal the constant and critical evaluation of their professional performance. A lack of evaluation often leads to mediocrity or failure to reach one's full potential in terms of what professionals might accomplish for the clients they serve. Evaluation, then, for counselors in a variety of settings and for other professionals, is first and foremost a process for professional improvement, a process in which one gathers objective, performance-oriented data on a systematic and nonbiased basis. These data are then used to constantly improve, upgrade, and update one's professional performance.

Amid the changing concepts of evaluation in recent decades, one of the most popular among evaluation experts is the view of evaluation as a process for providing information for decision makers. Evaluation is seen as a process that can provide decision makers at all levels with objective data that will assist them in determining the relative value of competing alternatives and that will immeasurably improve their probability of making the right decisions for program improvement.

In this context of evaluation as a process for program improvement, two distinctions in evaluation are important. The first—*formative evaluation*—focuses on the major purposes evaluation can serve. The second—*summative evaluation*—is concerned with the locus of the evaluator.

Worthen, White, and Borg (1993) note that

> formal evaluation studies can serve either a *formative* purpose (such as helping to improve a mathematics curriculum) or a *summative* purpose (such as deciding whether that curriculum should be continued). Although these distinctions may blur somewhat in practice, they are useful nonetheless.
>
> *Formative evaluation* is conducted during the planning and operation of a school program to provide those involved with evaluative information they can use in improving the program. For example, assume a school district is attempting to develop a local curriculum package on the history of their particular county. During development of the new curriculum unit, formative evaluation might involve content inspection by history experts' early tryouts with small numbers of children in one school in the district, and so forth. Each step would provide immediate feedback to the curriculum developers, who could use such information to make necessary revisions.
>
> *Summative evaluation* occurs after a curriculum or program is considered ready for regular use, and provides potential consumers evidence about the program's worth. In our example, after the local history program was developed, a summative evaluation might determine how effective the program was in teaching local history, using a broad sample of the schools, teachers, and students in the district for which it was developed. The findings of that summative evaluation could be made available to all schools in the district who could then better determine whether to use the history unit in their schools. Summative evaluation is also used to make "go/no go" decisions, such as whether to continue or terminate a particular curriculum.
>
> Formative and summative evaluation are both essential because decisions are needed early in the development of a program, to improve it, as well as when it has stabilized, to judge its final worth. (p. 625)

Other Functions of Evaluation

The wide range of evaluation purposes may seem to rival that of the political party platforms of promising something for everybody. Although that is not the intent, it is important to recognize some of the values of this activity. Examples of these additional functions of evaluation are as follows.

- Verifies or rejects practices by providing evidence for what works and what does not, or the degree to which an activity seems to be effective. This also tends to lead to the avoidance of meaningless innovations and unproven fads.
- Measures improvement by providing evidence on a continuous basis so that both rate and level of progress may be ascertained.
- Enhances probability of growth by providing a basis for improvements in the operation and its activities.
- Builds credibility. By the very nature of the activity, evaluation suggests a continuous search for better ways of doing things; a constant quest for improvement; a willingness to put efforts on the line and take a look at how we're doing.
- Provides for increased insights. By the fact of examining our own or an organization's functioning, we become more knowledgeable and understanding about this functioning; more aware of influencing factors and potential consequences.
- Increases and improves participation in decision making. Because evaluation involves everyone within the organizational structure, the process, by necessity, involves them in the outcomes, which in turn should bring about the participation of all such personnel in the planning of new directions and implementing the findings.
- Places responsibilities. By identifying who is responsible for what and when, evaluation stimulates links between specific persons and specific activities. It decreases the probability of everyone claiming responsibility for the successes and no one claiming the failures.
- Provides a rationality for the enterprise by improving overall accountability, including evidence of accomplishments and growth.

Lewis, Lewis, and Souflee (1993) state that evaluators may use

research techniques, but they apply them to the needs of specific agencies. Evaluation can be used to aid in administrative decision making, to improve currently operating programs, to provide for accountability, to build increased support for effective programs, and, in some instances, to make generalizations about the connections between specific activities and their effects. (p. 234)

Principles of Evaluation

Because evaluation is a process for appraising the effectiveness of a program or activity, it is most beneficial when conducted within a framework of guiding principles. Seven of these, as presented by Gibson (1977, pp. 70–72), are discussed in the following list.

1. *Effective evaluation requires a recognition of program goals.* Before any meaningful program of evaluation can be undertaken, it is essential that the goals of that program be clearly identified. These objectives provide indications of program intent, which form the basis for subsequent planning and procedures. The objectives of the program should be stated in clear and measurable terminology. This principle suggests that counseling programs be evaluated on the basis of how well they are doing what they set out to do.

2. *Effective evaluation requires valid measuring criteria.* Once program goals are clearly defined, valid criteria for measuring progress toward those goals must be identified. The development of such criteria is crucial if the evaluation is to be both valid and meaningful. For example, if an annual program goal for a junior community college counseling program would be to

provide each entering student with a series of three career interviews with a counselor, the measuring criteria could be a simple count indicating the percentage of students who did, in fact, have such an opportunity. If, however, the program goal was to provide each student with a broadening of his or her career understanding, the measuring criteria would be less obvious and might depend on a further refinement of what is meant by career understanding. In other words, vaguely stated goals and vaguely stated criteria lessen the effectiveness of program evaluation.

3. *Effective program evaluation depends on valid application of the measuring criteria.* As discussed in the previous paragraph, valid criteria for measuring progress toward the program's stated goals must be established. It is not sufficient, however, to merely establish criteria. Their ultimate validity will depend on their valid application. This implies that effective evaluation of all counseling programs should involve, in each instance, persons who are professionally competent in both evaluation techniques and understandings of such counseling programs. Too often, effective evaluation criteria are dissipated in the hands of evaluators who have, at best, only a superficial knowledge of the appropriate role and functions of counseling programs.

4. *Program evaluation should involve all who are affected.* Evaluation of a school counseling program, for example, should involve those who are participants in or who are affected by the program. This would include, in addition to the counseling staff, faculty members, and administrators, students and their parents and, on appropriate occasions, members of the community or supporting agencies. The major contribution to effective evaluation must come from those who have a firsthand knowledge or involvement in the program. External evaluators from governmental agencies, accrediting associations, or other educational institutions can, of course, be helpful, but those should not be the sole bases of evaluation.

5. *Meaningful evaluation requires feedback and follow-through.* The evaluation process and the evaluation report are not in and of themselves of great value. Only when the results are used for program improvement and development does the evaluation process take on meaning. This presumes, then, that the results of any program evaluation are made available to those concerned with program management and development. It also presumes that the program manager and his or her staff will use these results for future program planning, development, and decision making.

6. *Evaluation is most effective as a planned, continuous process.* This approach may enable the program staff to identify at any point in time weaknesses that need correcting immediately or accomplishments that should be capitalized on. This means that there are specific plans and designated responsibilities for both the ongoing evaluation of a program's progress and the more extensive annual or semiannual reviews.

7. *Evaluation emphasizes the positive.* Frequently, evaluation is viewed as a threatening process aimed at ferreting out hidden weaknesses and spotlighting goofs. If program evaluation is to produce the most meaningful results possible, it must be conducted in a spirit that is positive, is aimed at facilitating program improvement, and emphasizes strengths as well as weaknesses.

Methods of Evaluation

Before-and-After Method

This method of evaluation seeks to identify the progress that takes place in a program's development as a result of specific program activities over a given period. For example, a school counseling program's objective might be to provide each student with a weekend work experience during her or his junior year. At the beginning of the school year, before the program, it could be presumed that none had had this experience. At the end of the year, after the program, the number who actually participated would give some indication of goal achievement.

Comparison Methods

The how-do-we-compare process makes evaluations on the basis of comparing one group against another or against the norm of a number of groups. Different techniques for achieving the same goal can also be evaluated by this comparative method. For example, a secondary school in Bloomington, Indiana, might note that it has a counselor/pupil ratio of 1 to 258, compared with the norm for 200 midwestern secondary schools of 1 to 418. Such a comparison would indicate, of course, that the Bloomington school system is making more adequate provisions for high school counseling personnel than most other school systems in the Midwest.

The How-Do-We-Stand Method

This method is based on identifying desirable program outcomes and related characteristics and criteria. From these criteria, rating scales, checklists, and questionnaires may be developed and used to indicate the degree to which a program measures up. For example, evaluative criteria or checklists used by most accrediting associations and many state governmental agencies and departments reflect this approach. Although this evaluation method may ignore appropriate objectives and sometimes unique and innovative practices on a local level, it does provide guidelines that enable programs to be compared with generally accepted standards.

Procedures for Evaluation

The evaluation process usually involves a series of activities in a sequence, which approximates the following.

1. *Identifying goals to be assessed.* The first step establishes the variables, or limits, for the evaluation. Evaluation can focus on the total counseling program or on only one or several particular objectives. These program objectives should be stated in clear, concise, specific, and measurable terms. Broadly stated goals (e.g., "to facilitate the adjustment of the student body of J. J. Jenkins High School") are much more difficult to measure than a specifically stated goal, such as "to provide each student in J. J. Jenkins High School with a yearly scheduled opportunity to discuss his or her career planning with a school counselor."

2. *Developing an evaluation plan.* Once the objectives for evaluation have been established, the identification and validation of criteria appropriate for measuring the program's progress toward these objectives follow. In the previous example, a simple yet valid criterion would be an indication of the percentage of the J. J. Jenkins High School students who actually did have a scheduled career-planning interview with a school counselor. This example illustrates the principle that measuring criteria should also be stated in specific and objective terms. The overall evaluation plan, in addition to specifying the kinds of data to be collected, should also specify how it will be collected, when, and by whom. This plan must also give attention to how the data will be organized and reported and to whom. Finally, such a plan should conclude with provisions for using the findings for future program development.

3. *Applying the evaluation plan*. After an acceptable evaluation plan has been designed, its validity is then dependent on the manner in which it is carried out. Once again, we stress the importance of adequate planning and a positive approach, utilizing evaluators who possess the necessary understanding and competency. Timing is also important because some aspects of a program can only be appropriately evaluated in a "longitudinal" sense, whereas other specific activities need an "immediately after" assessment.

4. *Using the findings*. Evaluation as an activity is in itself of little value. It is in the application of the findings that the real worth of evaluation lies. Through the process of evaluation, programs can ascertain their strengths and weaknesses. The resulting insights may then provide directions for future program improvement. The utilization of these findings, however, cannot be left to mere chance. There must be planning, with specific responsibilities for the utilization of the findings, and subsequent follow-up to establish the degree to which the evaluation recommendations have been fulfilled.

Worthen, White, and Borg (1993) state that

evaluations of school programs would improve if more people knew the importance of

- deciding *when* to evaluate
- deciding *what* precisely to evaluate
- deciding *whom* the evaluation is intended to serve
- deciding *who* should conduct the evaluation
- deciding *what* questions the evaluation should address
- planning the evaluation study
- deciding *how* to report the evaluation study
- dealing effectively with the political, ethical, and interpersonal issues in evaluation (p. 628)

Evaluation for Community Mental Health Counseling Programs

Community mental health center programs have also felt increased pressures to conduct systematic program evaluations, partly as the result of the increasing demands of the federal government to verify program efficiency and effectiveness in community mental health centers. In this regard, Public Law 94-63, the Community Mental Health Centers Amendments of 1975, requires community mental health centers to allocate not less than 2% of their previous year's operating budgets to conducting program evaluation. The law mandates three general types of evaluation, as follows.

1. *Quality assurance of clinical services*. Each center is to establish an ongoing quality assurance of its clinical services.
2. *Self-evaluation*. Each center will collect data and evaluate its services in relation to program goals and values and to catchment area needs and resources. The data shall consist of (a) Cost of center operations; (b) Patterns of use of services; (c) Availability, awareness, acceptability, and accessibility of services; (d) Impact of services upon the mental health of residents of the catchment area; (e) Effectiveness of consultation and education services; (f) The impact of the Center on reducing inappropriate institutionalization.
3. *Residents' review*. Each center will at least annually publicize and make available all evaluation data of the type listed above to residents of the catchment area. In addition, it will organize and

publicize an opportunity for citizens to review the Center's program of services in order to assure that services are responsive to the needs of residents of the catchment area. (Hagedorn, Beck, Neubert, & Werlin, 1976, pp. 6–7)

RESEARCH

Research does not always project a popular image for some of the reasons listed here.

- Most research seems to ignore the common problems and everyday needs of practitioners.
- Most research reports are written in a manner that limits their interpretation and hence their application by practitioners.
- Research activities and resulting research reports rarely excite the imagination.
- The research monies made available by federal and state agencies are cornered by universities and private research and development corporations.
- Research is too time-consuming and has very few rewards for most practitioners.

Not withstanding the usually exaggerated misconceptions about research, the helping profession of counseling and its membership have a responsibility to advance the knowledge and practice of the profession by, at the very least, the utilization of research findings, and, hopefully, involvement in such studies as well. Research becomes another valuable tool that counselors can use in this era of accountability to prove that what they do can make a positive difference in the lives of individuals, groups, and the function of organizations. Let us now examine some of the positive outcomes you can anticipate from research.

Positive Outcomes of Research

For general practitioners in counseling and other helping professions, the most positive general outcome of practitioner research is the improvement of one's professional skills and understanding. Research can answer professional questions, dilemmas, and failures. Research enables practitioners to become better at their art. It can enable us to verify what works and what does not and, if pursued, why. It can eliminate much of the guesswork and uncertainty from practice. Engaging in practical research can increase our insights and deepen understandings of ourselves, the counseling profession, and the relationships between the two. Our own research can help us as individual professionals become better at what we do.

Also, practitioners' research tends to focus on local problems or concerns and may, therefore, have opportunities to provide results that are immediately applicable. The occasion to make a positive difference in one's job environment can be challenging. Furthermore, even if practitioners tend to focus on local concerns in their research activities, that still gives them opportunities to make contributions to their profession; to exchange their ideas and findings with other similar local settings and other interested professionals. Presentations and discussions at local, state, and national conferences give the researcher further chances to share findings, explore with other professionals the implications of the results, and possibly expand the interpretation of the research findings.

Finally, research can be interesting. Any new experience, learning of new knowledge, or finding an answer to an old problem can be stimulating. Research only becomes dull and meaningless to researchers when they investigate topics or problems that are to them dull and meaningless. Identify a professional question (problem or concern) that you would personally like answered and set out to find the answer. You may find it a surprisingly exciting quest, and you may then agree that research can be one of the most rewarding professional activities.

Some Definitions

Basic Research

Basic research is concerned with or conducted solely for the purpose of developing theories or establishing general principles. In educational and other settings, basic research provides the theory that, in turn, produces implications for solving problems.

Applied Research

Applied research provides data to support a theory through applying or testing the theory and evaluating its usefulness in problem solving.

Action Research

Action research is designed to solve problems through the application of scientific method. For example, a counselor may utilize a systematic and scientifically appropriate process to determine if a new approach is effective in decreasing cigarette smoking among adolescents.

Historical Research

As the label implies, historical research involves studying, understanding, and explaining events which occurred in the past. The purpose of historical research is to investigate causes, effects, or trends of past occurrences which may, in turn, help to explain present events and predict future events. By necessity, most historical studies rely on documentary resources and, in some instances, personal recall.

Descriptive Research

Descriptive research seeks to test hypotheses or answer questions concerning the present. There are two major classifications of descriptive research: qualitative and quantitative. In quantitative research the investigator

> either directly or through coding schemes observes events and then makes inductive inferences based on these observations. The qualitative researcher, rather than rely on outside observational schemes, tries to retain the perspective of the people being studied. This usually involves an analysis of field or observational notes or a study of audio or video recordings. Finally, quantitative and qualitative researchers usually address different research questions. According to Patton, the goal of quantitative research is to describe cause-and-effect relationships in the physical world. Qualitative researchers, on the other hand, attempt to describe and understand the ways that people give meaning to their own and others' behavior. (Patton, 1984, as cited in Heppner, Kivlighan, & Wampold, 1992, p. 195)

Experimental Research

This sort of research experiments with different variables in order to predict what will occur in the future under a given set of conditions.

> Experimental research provides stronger support for inferences about causal relationships among variables than does any other research approach. Four essential features of experiments follow:
>
> - The mission includes the idea of cause.
> - The researcher manages or manipulates one or more independent variables.
> - Measures are taken of one or more dependent variables.
> - The research plan controls extraneous factors that might contaminate the results to minimize unwanted influences of such factors and strengthen the inferences made about causal relationships between independent and dependent variables.
>
> Experimental approaches frequently used in counseling research include analogue research, traditional group experiments, and time series experiments. Sometimes circumstances do not permit controlling extraneous factors to the degree that true experiments require. Quasi-experiments represent a compromise in such instances. (Hadley & Mitchell, 1995, p. 43)

Pilot Study

A pilot study is a preliminary trial of research methods and instruments before the development of the final research plan.

Hypotheses

Hypotheses are predictions regarding the probable outcome of a research study that, in turn, form a basis for goals and procedures to achieve these goals.

Sampling

Sampling is a research technique for selecting a specified number of people from a defined population as representative of that specific population.

The Research Process

Some research undoubtedly requires complex, sophisticated research skills. However, much valuable information can be obtained through research that meets the requirements of scientific inquiry but does not require a high level of research skill. Thus, the following examination of research procedures is not intended to provide a basis for undertaking research but rather to provide a better understanding of the basic factors involved in conducting research. It is hoped it will encourage practitioners to consider and become involved in relatively unsophisticated research investigations.

The first step in undertaking research is to identify a researchable problem—a need for information. Whatever stimulates your interest or curiosity or arouses doubts in you may be the basis for a research problem. Most of us experience a constant and continuing need for information in our daily jobs. We wonder about the adequacy or effectiveness of our techniques, the various characteristics of our clients, and the nature of client needs. If we decide to initiate research in the area of techniques, we might simply seek to determine the kinds of information needed for justifying present practices or developing more effective and functional ones.

A second step in most research is to review or survey previous research and writings relevant to the possible research topic. The purposes of this review are to (a) see if adequate answers have already been found to the questions the researcher has in mind; (b) gain a better understanding of the nature of the problem; and (c) gain insights regarding approaches that might be used to efficiently attain the outcomes desired. Although in the past this particular step may have been one that discouraged many from considering research activities, the computer capacities of libraries with their various information retrieval systems enable even the neophyte researcher to have in hand, quickly, a computerized printout of relevant research and writings, usually summarized for convenience.

The third step is to identify specifically the nature of the information desired or formulate the specific research problem. The problem should be stated fully and precisely in objective terminology in a complete grammatical sentence. It should be written so that others can understand it without the prompting of the researcher. The beginning researcher should also be aware that within the main problem there may be logical subcomponents, identified as subproblems.

The fourth step in the research process is to determine the kinds of information needed to permit sound conclusions about the issue (or issues) in question. In this step, the previously stated problem and related subproblems are now viewed through questions or logical constructs, called *hypotheses*. Hypotheses are assumptions made regarding the problem or its solution that steer the researcher in some direction for the gathering of facts that will provide the most valid answers. For example, a research investigation may be attempting to determine why a school has an unusually high dropout rate. Several possibilities for this dropout rate could be hypothesized: (a) students are not interested in school; (b) students lack the ability to continue in school; (c) students are under economic pressure to leave school and obtain a job. Each of these assumptions or hypotheses provides some direction or basis for identifying facts, which would enable the investigator to determine factually why the majority of students are leaving school.

Having identified the kinds of information needed, the researcher determines what procedures are most appropriate for collecting and analyzing the data. In this fifth step, the population or sample to be used and the means by which it is to be selected are determined, as are instruments and other data-collecting tools appropriate for the questions or hypotheses that have been stated. In this stage, the researcher seeks to determine the most appropriate sampling procedures and the most efficient, effective instruments or techniques for gathering the data needed in order to respond to the hypotheses as completely and as validly as possible.

Once the types of information and the procedures and instruments needed for collecting this information have been determined, the sixth step is the actual collection of the data. A data collection plan should be developed indicating the data needed, probable source of the data, how it is to be collected (i.e., questionnaires, surveys, interviews, reading of reports), who is to collect the data, and deadlines for collection.

In the seventh step, the collected data are systematically organized and analyzed. The method of data analysis should be determined before collecting data in order to ensure that the suggested treatment is appropriate to the data collected and the manner in which it is organized. Depending on the research design developed in step five of this sequence, the analysis may be no more than a simple mathematical or elementary statistical one.

Beginning practitioners can still engage profitably in research activities by simply recognizing their limitations in the design of their study. In the final step, the research findings are interpreted and conclusions drawn, which may lead to resolving or answering the problems. Here the previously stated hypotheses are either confirmed or rejected and answers are provided to the questions that initiated the research activity. Figure 14-1 depicts the research process.

Utilizing Research Reports

Findings from research studies can be important to counselors in all settings. Research findings can provide factual data to reinforce or guide their professional judgment and improve their practice. Whether one is an active researcher or not, a counseling professional cannot afford to gloss over the important research in the field. We must, for example, be aware of both the reservoir of accumulated knowledge dealing with human behavior and the results of current research studies that broaden, deepen, or perhaps alter our understanding of this behavior. As research technology continues to improve, we can anticipate an increase in research studies, more sophistication in their methodology and validity in their outcomes, as well as more relevance and application of the findings. Thus, all practicing counselors must not only recognize the importance of research but also be cognizant of what we might label guidelines for identifying research of potential significance. Gibson, Mitchell, and Higgins (1983) identify these as follows.

Be Aware of Common Sources of Research Reporting in Your Field
Some common indices and abstracts such as the *Review of Educational Research*, the *Education Index*, *Social Science Index*, *Sociology Index*, *Index Medicus*, *Psychological Abstracts*, and *Dissertation Abstracts* are good starting points to broadly identify reports of recent research investigations. Publications representing the professional organizations in counseling and related fields are rich sources of recent research studies in the field.

Identify Research Studies Which Appear to Be Relevant to Your Own Professional Needs
The abundance of reported research, past and present, is enough to overwhelm the most conscientious researcher. Any user of research findings must learn to be selective lest she or he drown in the ever growing tidal waves of research reporting. Therefore, it is important that we identify as specifically as possible the kind of knowledge we are seeking and focus our search on this topic.

Review the Studies You Have Selected in Terms of the Following:
1. The design of the study: (You may need the assistance of a competent researcher at this point. They are not too difficult to locate if you are close to a large school system, institution of higher education, large mental health agency, or state government office.) This is important in determining the probable accuracy of the findings, their generalizability to your situation, and the conclusions or implications which can be drawn from them.
2. Readability: Some research reports are technical reports written primarily for other researchers. Both the vocabulary and the statistical methods through which the data are presented may confuse, mislead, or simply confound the reader. Unsophisticated attempts to "figure out" what the report is saying should not be undertaken. If you cannot understand the report you should select a different report to study or you may again seek the help of a competent researcher who can interpret the study to you.
3. Originality of the research: A firsthand report of a study by the researcher(s) who was the principal investigator is more desirable than "secondhand" reporting, summaries, or citations by oth-

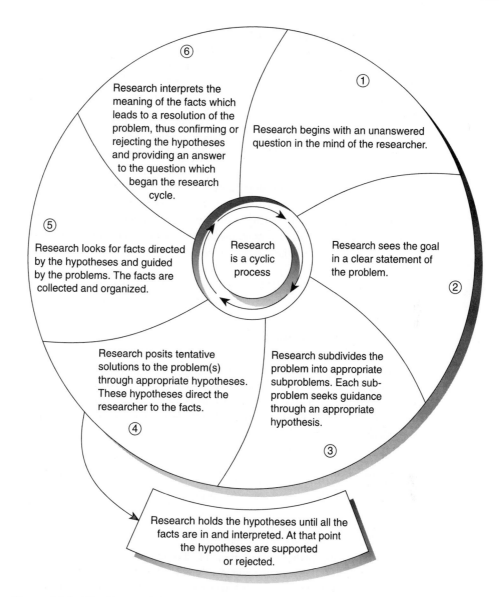

Within the figure:

⑥ Research interprets the meaning of the facts which leads to a resolution of the problem, thus confirming or rejecting the hypotheses and providing an answer to the question which began the research cycle.

① Research begins with an unanswered question in the mind of the researcher.

Research is a cyclic process

② Research sees the goal in a clear statement of the problem.

⑤ Research looks for facts directed by the hypotheses and guided by the problems. The facts are collected and organized.

④ Research posits tentative solutions to the problem(s) through appropriate hypotheses. These hypotheses direct the researcher to the facts.

③ Research subdivides the problem into appropriate subproblems. Each sub-problem seeks guidance through an appropriate hypothesis.

Research holds the hypotheses until all the facts are in and interpreted. At that point the hypotheses are supported or rejected.

Figure 14-1 The Research Process.
Source: From Leedy, Paul D. *Practical Research: Planning & Design* 6/e, ©1997. Reprinted by permission of Prentice-Hall, Inc., Upper Saddle River, N.J.

ers. Whereas secondary sources can be useful, they are usually more brief than the original source and may inadvertently misrepresent the findings.

4. Reputation of the author/researcher may also be considered. Established researchers/authors have achieved their preeminence through previous studies that have been endorsed by their peers as sound in design, addressing important needs, and significant in their findings. (pp. 330–331)

Writing Research Grant Applications

Millions of dollars are made available to agencies, institutions, and school systems annually from federal and state agencies and private foundations. These monies, usually earmarked for specific purposes, are most frequently allocated or awarded on the basis of a competitive review of proposals or grant applications received. Because many of the funding opportunities are in the areas of counseling interest and expertise, counselors must possess the necessary application skills to competitively pursue such funding as may be of interest and appropriate for their organizations. The following general guidelines are suggested.

1. Read thoroughly the published announcements and/or other information that describes the guidelines to follow in preparing and submitting a grant application. This will, among other things, help you to determine your organization's eligibility.
2. Follow to the letter the guidelines for the preparation and submission of the grant proposal. The appropriate format is expected, and the dates or submission deadlines must be met.
3. Know, to the extent possible, the funding agency or foundation.

Personal contacts by visit or phone are, of course, very useful in clarifying, explaining, or elaborating on purposes, procedures, and guidelines. Some agencies will provide, on request, examples of exemplary projects and lists of previous recipients. Foundations will send you their annual reports and publications such as the *Commerce Business Daily*, *Federal Register*, *The Education Daily*, and *Federal Grants and Contracts Weekly*. Descriptions of private foundations and their research priorities are indicated in *The Taft Foundation Reporter* (published by the Taft Group in Washington, DC) and *The Foundation Directory* (published by the Foundation Center, New York).

As Gibson et al. (1983) note

All specified sections of a proposal format are important, but the four that are briefly explained in the following discussion require special attention.

Statement of the Problem

This section of the proposal should contain a well-defined, specific statement of the problem; the need for such a study (its educational significance); and concisely stated, measurable objectives. Conceptual and research literature should be cited to stress the significance of, or the need for, the study, but the literature cited should be specifically relevant to the proposed study.

Procedures

This section of the proposal must present the design of the study and a fully detailed description of the procedures to be utilized. It should be apparent to a reader that the stipulated procedures will enable the achievement of the project's stated objectives. It should describe the sample to be used and how the sample is to be selected, the instruments and other data-collecting tools or approaches to be utilized, the statistical treatments to be applied, and the evaluational procedures to be employed. If the objectives were definitely stated—as they should be—the evaluational procedures should evolve from them. Although this section must be concise, it must also be complete. A basic criterion for evaluating most proposals is the soundness of the methodology employed.

Personnel and Facilities

This, too, is a most important section, especially in proposals for federal funding. As the purpose of this section is to enable a determination of the research capabilities, care must be taken to identify the personnel involved and to show that by training and experience, these individuals have the research competencies required for the implementation of the proposed study. Similarly, the facilities required for the research endeavor should be described and their availability assured.

Budget

The cost estimates for the proposed project must be accurate, detailed, justifiable, and reasonable. It must be clearly evident how the anticipated expenditures relate to each of the specific procedural steps. (pp. 333–334)

Reporting Research Results

Obviously, conducting research is not enough—unless you intend to keep the results selfishly to yourself! Reporting your study enables you to advance not only yourself professionally but the profession as well. This can either be an oral report—through presentations at professional conferences, workshops, and such—or a written report—in professional journals, newsletters, monographs, and so forth. Oral reports have the advantage of enabling the audience to directly question and interact with the presenter. Written reports have the advantage of reaching a wider audience. Heppner, Kivlighan, and Wampold (1992) present some general principles for writing research reports: "(1) be informative, (2) be forthright, (3) do not overstate or exaggerate, (4) be logical and organized, (5) have some style, (6) write and rewrite, and (7) if all else fails, just write!" (p. 376).

These authors go on to note that in writing for publication, the exact organization

of a research report varies depending on the publication for which it is intended and the nature of the study. Nevertheless, a perusal of counseling journals reveals a modal organization, roughly as follows:

Title

Abstract

Introduction

Method

- Subjects
- Measures (or Variables or Instruments)
- Materials
- Design (or Design and Analysis)
- Procedures

Results

Discussion (or Conclusions)

References

Tables

Figures

The nature of each of these components depends on the publication and the readership. Nevertheless, there are some aspects of each of these components that are critical to a well-written research report. (p. 376)

Ethical Issues in Human Research

By its very nature, counseling research, with rare exceptions, must involve human beings. Growing concern for the rights of human subjects has resulted in increased efforts on the part of professional organizations and research institutions and agencies, including the U.S. government, to safeguard the rights and dignity of individuals who are involved as subjects of research.

In this regard, attention must be given to protecting subjects' right to privacy, determining whether the research puts subjects at risk in any way, obtaining informed consent of subjects, and not involving subjects in research that challenges or threatens their morals or values.

SUMMARY

Accountability, evaluation, and research are all responsibilities of counseling programs and counselors in any setting. Although each is a distinct activity in its own right, the interrelationships are evident, because all can improve a program. Furthermore, all three activities hold promise for the advancement of the professional and the profession. Accountability provides a model or method for the assessment of professional achievements. Evaluation enables one to gather evidence regarding the quality of a program's performance. Research allows one to advance the scientific knowledge in a field. Counselors should, therefore, understand the research process, how to locate and read research reports, and to compete for research monies. Accountability and evaluation, as well as research are often influenced by legal or ethical guidelines. These will be discussed in the next chapter.

DISCUSSION QUESTIONS

1. What is meant by the term *accountability?* Why has it become so popular in education in recent years?

2. How can counselors become more accountable?

3. What are the differences between accountability and evaluation?

4. Have you ever had an idea that you would have liked to research? If so, what did you do about it?

5. What are some of the relationships between evaluation and research?

6. What objective evidence could you provide a potential employer as to your excellence in counseling?

7. What difficulties do you envision in providing objective evidence that your counseling is effective?

CLASS ACTIVITIES

1. In small groups, discuss the pros and cons of your experiences of being evaluated as a student over the years of your schooling.

2. Students are currently evaluated (graded) on certain performance criteria (i.e., tests, papers, projects, etc.). How might this change if students were asked to become accountable? Discuss in small groups.

3. Read a recent research report (periodical article) in the field of counseling and present this research to the class. Discuss its implications for practice.

4. In dyads, share your professional and personal ethical standards in the counseling practice you intend to make your career.

SELECTED READINGS

Anderson, W., & Heppner, P. (1986). Counselor application of research findings to practice: Learning to stay current. *Journal of Counseling and Development*, 65 (3), 152–155.

Barker, C., Pistrang, N., & Elliot, R. (1994). *Research methods in clinical and counselling psychology*. Chichester, England: John Wiley & Sons.

Barkham, M., & Barker, C. (1996). Evaluating counselling psychology practice. In R. Woolfe & W. Dryden (Eds.), *Handbook of counselling psychology* (pp. 87–110). London: Sage.

Brown, M. (1988). The mental health counselor and research: And never the twain shall meet? *Journal of Mental Health Counseling, 10*, 9–15.

Chamberlain, K., & Borrough, S. (1985). Techniques for teaching critical reading. *Teaching of Psychology, 12* (40), 213–215.

Conley, D. (1988). Critical attributes of effective evaluation systems. *Chronicle Guidance* (pp. 88–122). Monrovia, NY: CGP Professional.

Drott, M. C. (1984). How to read research: An approach to the literature for the practitioner. *School Library Media Quarterly, 12*, 445–449.

Fairchild, T. N. (1986). Time analysis: Accountability tool for counselors. *The School Counselor, 34* (1), 36–43.

Fish, L. (1988). Why multivariate methods are unusually vital. *Measurement and Evaluation in Counseling and Development, 21*, 130–137.

Gelso, C. J. (1996). Applying theories in research: The interplay of theory and research in science. In F. T. L. Leong & J. T. Austin (Eds.), *The psychology research handbook: A guide for graduate students and research assistants* (pp. 359–368). Thousand Oaks, CA: Sage.

Heaney, R. P., & Barger-Lux, M. J. (1986). Priming students to research critically. *Nursing and Health Care, 7* (8), 421–424.

Heppner, P. P., Gelso, C. J., & Dolliver, R. H. (1987). Three approaches to research training in counseling. *Journal of Counseling and Development, 66* (1), 45–49.

Heppner, P. P., & Neal, G. W. (1983). Holding up the mirror: Research on the roles and functions of counseling centers in higher education. *Counseling Psychologist, 11* (1), 81–98.

Mancall, J. C. (1985). Evaluating research: A critical consumer approach. *Top of the News, 42* (1), 101–104.

Matthews, B., & Paradise, L. (1988). Toward methodological diversity: Qualitative research

approaches. *Journal of Mental Health Counseling, 10* (4), 225–234.

Myrick, R. D. (1984). Beyond the issues of school counselor accountability. *Measurement and Evaluation in Guidance, 16* (4), 218–222.

Newman, J. & Scott, T. (1988). The construct problem in measuring counseling performance. *Counselor Education and Supervision, 28*, 71–79.

Ponterotta, J. (1988). Racial/ethnic minority research in the *Journal of Counseling Psychology*: A content analysis and methodological critique. *Journal of Counseling and Development, 35* (4), 410–418.

Robinson, S. E. (1986). Counseling research: Ethics and issues. *Journal of Counseling and Development, 64* (5), 331–333.

Sapp, M. (1997). *Counseling and psychotherapy: Theories, associated research, and issues.* Lanham, MD: University Press.

Stockton, R., & Hulse, D. (1983). The use of research teams to enhance competence in counseling research. *Counselor Education and Supervision, 22* (4), 303–310.

Tait, P. E. (1984). Do-it-yourself evaluation of experimental research. *Journal of Visual Impairment and Blindness, 78* (8), 356–363.

Tracey, T. J. (1983). Single case research: An added tool for counselors and supervisors. *Counselor Education and Supervision, 22* (3), 185–196.

Vacc, N., & Loesch, C. (1984). Research as an instrument for professional change. *Measurement and Evaluation in Counseling and Development, 17* (3), 124–131.

Wampold, B. E. (1996). Designing a research study. In F. T. L. Leong & J. T. Austin (Eds.), *The psychology research handbook: A guide for graduate students and research assistants* (pp. 59–72). Thousand Oaks, CA: Sage.

RESEARCH OF INTEREST

Aspenson, D. O., Gersh, T. L., Perot, A. R., & Galassi, J. P. (1993). Graduate psychology students' perceptions of the scientist-practitioner model of training. *Counseling Psychology Quarterly, 6* (3), 201–215.

Abstract

Ten clinical, nine counseling, and five school psychology graduate students participated in a qualitative and quantitative study to assess perceptions of the scientist-practitioner model for training professional psychologists. Subjects participated in semistructured interviews and were administered the Vocational Preference Inventory and a scientist-practitioner inventory. Data were analyzed using a combination of grounded theory and additional qualitative data analytic approaches. Reported experiences ranged from subjects with a zeal for the model to those who considered it impractical, unnecessary, and irrelevant to their career goals. Most interpreted the model to mean that psychologists are trained as producers/consumers of research and as practicing clinicians.

Boser, J. A., Poppen, W. A., & Thompson, C. L. (1988). Elementary school guidance program evaluation: A reflection of student-counselor ratio. *The School Counselor, 36,* 125–135.

Abstract

This article examines the perceived effectiveness of guidance programs in Tennessee public schools representing the following three distinct student-to-counselor ratios: (a) one school, one counselor, fewer than 600 students; (b) one school, one counselor, 750 to 1,000 students; and (c) three to four schools, one counselor, 1,000 to more than 2,000 students per counselor. It was found that as the student-to-counselor ratios increase, the number of students who cannot be adequately served by the counselor also increases, which thus reduces the overall effectiveness of the counselor as perceived by students, parents, and school staff.

Gerler, E. R. (1985). Elementary school counseling research and the classroom learning environ-

ment. *Journal of Elementary School Guidance and Counseling, 20,* 39–48.

Abstract

This author studied research evidence of elementary school counselors' effectiveness in helping children improve classroom behavior, explore feelings, improve socially, and enhance sensory awareness and mental imagery. The article concludes that counselors should be able to use this evidence for demonstrating the importance of their work to school policymakers.

Hillenbrand, E., & Claiborn, C. D. (1990). Examining reasoning skill differences between expert and novice counselors. *Journal of Counseling and Development, 68,* 684–691.

Abstract

The cognitive reasoning of expert and novice counselors involved in a diagnostic activity is examined. Cases experienced variation according to the extent to which problem-relevant information was clear and apparent. The conclusion is that the structure of the problem being diagnosed is likely to be a significant variable influencing reasoning.

Hinkle, J. S. (1992). Computer-assisted career guidance and single-subject research: A scientist-practitioner approach to accountability. *Journal of Counseling and Development, 70,* 391–395.

Abstract

An overview of computer-assisted career guidance is presented. The author describes how use of intensive research designs can promote further accountability among computer-assisted career counselors. Applicable single-subject research, alternating treatment designs, and replication information is described.

McLennan, J. (1996). Improving our understanding of therapeutic failure: A review. *Counseling Psychology Quarterly, 9* (4), 379–391

Abstract

This article reviews the literature concerning therapeutic failure and offers a general conceptual account of therapeutic failure in individual counseling and psychotherapy. The literature suggests that there are large individual differences in therapists' overall effectiveness. A conceptual model of therapeutic failure is proposed, organized around the assumption that failure results from a therapist's inability to meet the needs of a particular client. Suggestions aimed at reducing the likelihood of therapeutic failure are offered, and implications for training and practice are presented.

Plake, B. S., Conoley, J. C., Kramer, J. J., & Murphy, L. U. (1991). The Buros Institute of Mental Measurements: Commitment to the tradition of excellence. *Journal of Counseling and Development, 69*, 449–455.

Abstract

This article reviews the history of the Buros Institute of Mental Measurement by highlighting origins of the *Mental Measurements Yearbook*. Bibliographic reference series, Tests in Print, and specialized monographed series are described through a historic perspective. Plans for the 1990s are discussed.

Sedlacek, W. E., & Adams-Gaston, J. (1992). Predicting the academic success of student-athletes using SAT and noncognitive variables. *Journal of Counseling and Development, 70*, 724–727.

Abstract

This study compares the reliability of the Noncognitive Questionnaire (NCQ) and the Scholastic Aptitude Test (SAT) in predicting academic success for student-athletes at the collegiate level. It suggests that noncognitive variables are better predictors of grades and academic success for athletes than are SAT scores. It concludes that athletes need to be considered nontraditional student-athletes rather than student-athletes.

Segal, N. L. (1990). The importance of twin studies for individual differences research. *Journal of Counseling and Development, 68*, 612–622.

Abstract

Ten research methodology designs related to twin research are described. Findings focus on personality and temperament issues, learning disabilities, attitudes, behavior disorders, and social behavior. Implications for mental health practitioners and counselors are discussed.

Seligman, L., & Kelly, S. C. (1990). Writing and publishing books in counseling: A survey of authors. *Journal of Counseling and Development, 68*, 42–45.

Abstract

This article provides data from 74 authors of books published in the field of counseling. It reviews the process of writing and publishing books and presents information regarding timetables, choosing publishers, and obtaining and negotiating contracts. Authors' suggestions for prospective authors are provided.

Whiston, S. C. (1996). Accountability through action research: Research methods for practitioners. *Journal of Counseling and Development, 74* (6), 616–623.

Abstract

This article summarizes how outcome research methodologies can be incorporated into counseling practice in many settings. Findings reveal that performing an outcome study can assist counselors in evaluating their own effectiveness. In addition, more field-based studies can contribute to the empiricial knowledge base. An overview of the steps involved in an outcome or evaluative study is discussed, and a summary of the instruments and techniques for research in mental health counseling, career counseling, and school counseling is provided.

White, A., & Hernandez, N. R. (1991). Trends in article citations in three counseling journals, 1952–1988. *Journal of Counseling and Development, 69,* 419–422.

Abstract

    These authors examine article citations in the *Personnel and Guidance Journal, Journal of Counseling and Development, Journal of Counseling Psychology,* and *Counselor Education and Supervision Journal.* Results demonstrate that citations gradually became more numerous while also coming from increasingly distinct sources. The authors conclude that the focus of each journal fills a special function while also contributing to the field of research as a whole.

Chapter 15

Ethical and Legal Guidelines

This final chapter focuses on the responsibilities that you incur as you enter the career world of the professional counselor. It emphasizes the importance of practicing within the ethical guidelines established by your professional associations and those legal guidelines established by law. In fact, the very labeling of counseling as a helping profession suggests that we have assumed the responsibilities of all professions in providing for our clientele and serving the public. These responsibilities include acceptable standards of performance or competence, an accepted code of personal conduct in relationships with clients and the public, and a commitment to contribute to the public well-being that transcends monetary gain for the counselor.

A profession also takes responsibility for regulating or policing its membership to ensure that ethical and legal guidelines are adhered to and that legal enactments are sought where desirable to protect the public. A profession's commitment to appropriate ethical and legal standards is critical to the profession earning, maintaining, and deserving the public's trust. Without this trust, a profession ceases to be a profession. In addressing this point, Biggs and Blocher (1987) state

> Ethical questions are rooted in the public trust that defines any profession, and that is the major reason that they are of central concern to all of the members of a professional group. Whenever the perceptions of the public are changed by the unethical, unprofessional, or irresponsible behavior of a member of the profession, all other members are harmed, and indeed their ability to function in professional ways is diminished or impaired.
>
> Professionals who deliver counseling services must be especially concerned with ethical problems because their clients are often very vulnerable to manipulation and exploitation. Clients disclose very intimate issues in their lives and should be assured that such risk-taking will be respected and dealt with in a professional manner. We believe that ethical counseling should involve an awareness of and a commitment to maintain this important responsibility to protect client trust. The ethical counselor must be keenly aware of the possible impact of his or her actions on a client's present and future status and must be able to make complex moral/ethical judgments. (pp. 4–5)

THE NATURE OF ETHICS

A code of ethics represents the professional values of a profession translated into standards of conduct for the membership. Codes of ethics provide structure or guidelines for its membership to follow in their professional practice and also for the public to anticipate in their interactions with the profession and its membership.

For counselors at least two basic statements of ethical practice and behavior apply to work in the profession: (a) *Code of Ethics and Standards of Practice* of the American Counseling Association (see Appendix B), and (b) *Ethical Principles of Psychologists and Code of Conduct* of the American Psychological Association (1992) (see Appendix C). The members of these associations are expected to follow these codes of ethics and professional standards. Failure to abide by these standards may result in expulsion.

ETHICAL ISSUES

Competence

The ethical issue of competence begins when the counselor accepts a position as a professional counselor. The counselor must determine, along with the potential employer, whether she or he is qualified by virtue of training and, where appropriate, experience for the position. The counselor-applicant must indicate qualifications for licensure or certification where appropriate and also special interests and/or values that might influence on-the-job functioning. Obviously, from the outset, counselors should not apply for positions in which they are not interested or not competently qualified to fill.

On the job, the counselor is professionally responsible to practice within his or her limitations. Although competence is often difficult to determine, training and experience can provide useful guidelines for determining what we are qualified to do. Consultation with supervisors and/or more experienced professional colleagues can help identify the limits of one's professional competence.

Degrees, licenses, and certificates may convey to the public levels of competence, yet, in actuality, we must recognize variations in the competencies among practitioners with the same credentials. We would also again note the responsibility of the professional counselor to continuously update his or her competence through participation in various professional educational opportunities, reading the professional literature, and so forth.

When a counselor determines that a client's needs may be beyond his or her competencies, arrangements should be promptly made for an appropriate referral. This responsibility includes assisting the client in identifying and arranging a suitable professional referral.

Confidentiality and Privileged Communication

Trust is an important cornerstone in the counseling relationship, and central to the development and maintenance of trust is the principle of confidentiality. The obligation of counselors to maintain confidentiality in their relationships with their clients is not absolute, however, and counselors need to be aware of both the ethical and legal guidelines that apply.

In distinguishing between confidentiality and privileged communication, it is important to keep in mind that confidentiality is an *ethical* concept, whereas privileged communication is a *legal* concept.

Confidentiality is defined as

> an ethical responsibility and a professional duty that demands that information learned in private interaction with a client not be revealed to others. Professional ethical standards mandate this behavior except when the counselor's commitment to uphold client confidences must be set aside due to special and compelling circumstances or legal mandate. (Arthur & Swanson, 1993, p. 3)

Sometimes counselors may be working with life-endangering clients involving child abuse, possible homicide, or suicide threats. State laws require that suspected cases of child abuse be reported. Legally, counselors are also required to breach confidentiality to protect the life of a third party. The ethical codes of both the American Psychological Association and the American Counseling Association allow counselors to breach confidentiality if necessary to protect the life of a suicidal client. More on the legal aspects of privileged communication will be presented in the section entitled "Legal Concerns of Counselors."

Arthur and Swanson (1993) note exemptions cited by Bissell and Royce (1992) to the ethical principle of confidentiality.

1. The client is a danger to self or others. The law places physical safety above considerations of confidentiality or the right of privacy. Protection of the person takes precedence and includes the duty to warn.

2. The client requests the release of information. Privacy belongs to the client and may be waived. The counselor should release information as requested by the client.

3. A court orders release of information. The responsibility under the law for the counselor to maintain confidentiality is overridden when the court determines that the information is needed to serve the cause of justice.

4. The counselor is receiving systematic clinical supervision. The client gives up the right to confidentiality when it is known that session material will be used during supervision.

5. Clerical assistants process information and papers relating to the client. The client should be informed that office personnel will have access to the records for routine matters such as billing and record keeping.

6. Legal and clinical consultation are needed. Again, the client should be informed of the (ethical) right of the counselor to obtain other professional opinions about progress and the name(s) of those used as a consultant(s).

7. Clients raise the issue of their mental health in a legal proceeding. In a custody suit, for example, parents introduce their mental condition into the suit, whereupon they authorize release of the counselor's records.

8. A third party is present in the room. Clients are (presumably) aware a person other than the counselor is present and therefore waive their right of privacy in permitting the third person to be present.

9. Clients are below the age of 18. Parents or guardians have the legal right to communication between the minor and the counselor.

10. Intra-agency or institutional sharing of information is part of the treatment process. Otherwise confidential material may be shared among professional staff when it is in the interest of the client to do so. However, the client must be aware that this is being done.

11. Sharing of information is required within a penal system. Information obtained from prisoners that may otherwise be considered confidential may be shared within the system in the interest of the operation of the system and disposition of the case.

12. The client's purpose in disclosing information was to seek advice in the furtherance of a crime or fraud. The obligation here changes from one of maintaining confidentiality to one of protecting society from further criminal activity.

13. The counselor has reason to suspect child abuse. All states now legally require the reporting of suspected abuse. (pp. 20–21)

Personal Relationships with Clients

In examining the personal relationships between counselors and their clients, professional organizations have sought to define the ethical limits of the professional relationship. A major concern of the mental health professions, in this regard, has been the sexual exploitation of clients by their therapists. Although the code of ethics of all major professional organizations unequivocally condemn such activities, Herlihy, Healy, Cook, and Hudson (1987), among others, have specifically discussed the extent of this ethical violation. In this study, the authors state

> The second most frequently claimed type of violation involved sexual relationships with clients. Although similar claims against psychiatrists and psychologists have received considerable publicity in the popular press, it is disturbing to learn that claims of sexual exploitation of clients by licensed counselors are reported with this frequency. (p. 75)

In their relationships with clients, the counselor must, at all times, avoid exploiting the trust of the client. This exploitation might be for financial gain, social status, research data, or other motives, as well as sexual favors. Hopkins and Anderson (1990) warn that

> a sexual relationship between a counselor and a client is clearly unethical, and may form the basis of an action for professional malpractice or negligence. In many states such conduct also constitutes a criminal offense, although a separate criminal suit must be prosecuted. The laws vary among the states in the requirements of this offense as well. In Minnesota, for example, sexual conduct with a patient is prohibited regardless of the client's consent. Some states also prosecute such relations as rape, or statutory rape in the case of a minor client. In each case specific penalties are prescribed as punishment, and in some states victim compensation may also be required. (p. 52)

In addition, relationships with clients that may impair the counselor's professional judgments or the client's responses must be avoided. This means avoiding counseling relationships with relatives, close friends, and employers, among others.

Finally, the counselor must at all times be aware of the human rights of clients. Even the severely mentally ill have legal and ethical rights that the counselor must be guided by in practice. This includes their right to participate in the decision making regarding their treatment, the use of psychological tests, and any participation in research studies.

THE COUNSELOR AND THE LAW

During recent decades, few aspects of the counselor's role and function in any setting have remained untouched by judicial and legislative activities. For example, the Community Mental Health Centers Act of 1980 defined community to be served in terms of geographic and topographic characteristics. Of even greater consequence, however, is the effort

> to integrate mental health and general health services. In associating the community mental health center with physicians and hospitals, the current policy seems to assert that emotional disorders are primarily biological and require, among other responses, medical treatment, often including hospitalization. This assertion would seem inconsistent with the bulk of the evidence. At the same time, however, the policy recognizes the special role of the general hospital as the locus of what is ordinarily the highest quality community health care and serves to induce the general hospital to concern itself more with the treatment of emotionally disordered persons, even when such treatment is not medical in nature. In other words, the policy implied in the Act encourages the general hospital to broaden its view of its role in the community. (Bloom, 1984, p. 33)

Many other services that counselors and their fellow helping professionals must provide in community agency settings are specified by law. These include drug abuse treatment as well as treatment for the chronically mentally ill and severely disturbed children and adolescents. Most states have enacted legislation that provides a legal basis for those who may practice or designate themselves as counselors and social workers.

Increasingly, managers of counseling programs and counselors themselves have become aware of the legal implications of their activities, the legal restrictions, and even legal conflicts with their professional conscience. This increased legal intervention is an outgrowth of a dramatic increase in litigation and attending legislation during the past 25 years.

In performing their professional duties, counselors must not put themselves in jeopardy for either civil or criminal liability. Thus, counselors must exercise due care or face liability in a civil suit for failing to perform their duties as required by law. Civil liability, stated simply, means that one can be sued for acting wrongly toward another, or for failing to act when there was a recognized duty to do so. Judicial relief is usually in the form of money damages awarded to the injured party. (Hopkins & Anderson, 1990, p. 23)

Certainly few counselors ever anticipate that they might become defendants in a criminal action simply by practicing their profession. Fortunately, very few ever do. But counselors should be aware of certain occupational hazards that could lead to criminal liability. The ideal for professional counselors is to maintain a certain distance between themselves and their clients so they may advise the clients in a professional way. Occasionally, however, situations arise that might lead counselors to go much further in protecting their clients, or to provide emotional support and comfort, than the law literally allows. In such cases, the counselor may unwittingly risk criminal liability.

Criminal liability resulting from the professional practice of counseling might result in a variety of criminal charges such as:

- accessory to a crime;
- failure to report suspected child abuse;
- contributing to the delinquency of a minor;
- sexual misconduct. (Hopkins & Anderson, 1990, p. 49)

Contributing to the delinquency of a minor is of special concern to school counselors and those whose practice includes children and families. However, counselors in all settings where the potential exists for juvenile clients should be aware of actions that could lead to prosecution for contributing to the delinquency of a minor. All states have enacted legislation designed to protect children from acts or relationships deemed injurious. However, as Hopkins and Anderson (1990) point out,

> Unfortunately, most state legislatures have not defined the specific conduct that constitutes the crime, and many jurisdictions leave it to the jury to determine whether a defendant's conduct was criminal. A broad definition of the offense might include any actions that tend to injure the health, morals, or welfare of juveniles, or that encourage juveniles to participate in such actions. There is no certainty as to what constitutes this immoral conduct from state to state, however. (p. 52)

Counselors in all settings cannot afford to be legally ignorant. They must understand the law and its implications in arenas of counselor concern and function. These include acts or practices that might be viewed as discriminatory, compromising the constitutional and other legal rights of, and prejudicing the opportunities of individuals. In this regard, note some of the legal implications for counselors of Title IX, the Buckley Amendment, and the Education for All Handicapped Children Act.

The Counselor and Title IX

Title IX of the Education Amendments of 1972, which took effect in July 1975, provides that

> no person . . . shall on the basis of sex, be excluded from participation in, be denied the benefits of, or be subjected to discrimination under any education program receiving federal financial assistance.

Some implications of this act for practicing counselors are as follows. First, adequate counseling services must not only provide for the needs, interests, and abilities of clients but also must consider the changing nature of society and how such changes affect working with clients. Counselors must help clients in self-understanding and sorting through varying options and what their decisions may imply.

⤙   Second, counselors must be aware that differential sex socialization is often subtly perpetuated in the language and impressions of the media (e.g., textbooks, newspapers, magazines, television). Although not justifiable, it is not surprising that such biases appear in career and other counseling materials.

The Counselor and the Buckley Amendment

Few legislative actions have had a greater impact upon the practice of counseling and attendant record keeping than the Buckley Amendment. Before the passage in 1974 of the Family Educational Rights and Privacy Act (FERPA) as it is titled (or the Buckley Amendment as it is commonly called), counselors derived most of their directions for their professional functioning from the ethical guidelines provided by their professional associations. In this regard, the *Code of Ethics and Standards of Practice* (1995) of the American Counseling Association has an entire section devoted to confidentiality (Section B) and a subsection regarding records (Section B.4). (See Appendix B.)

Although ethical standards are not, in themselves, legally binding, there are numerous instances, beginning with the case of *Cherry v. the Board of Regents of the State of New York* in 1942, that suggested courts might use professional ethical codes as guidelines for making judicial decisions. In the case of record keeping and confidentiality, however, the passage of the Buckley Amendment became the single most important guideline for professional conduct with regard to student records and related activities.

> ⸌The FERPA stipulates that the parents of unemancipated minor students have . . . the right to inspect and review any and all official records, files, and data directly related to their children, including all material that is incorporated into each student's cumulative record folder and intended for school use or to be available to parties outside the school or school system, and specifically including but not necessarily limited to identifying data, academic work completed, level of achievement (grades, standardized achievement scores), attendance data, scores of standardized intelligence, aptitude, and psychological tests, interest inventory results, health data, family background information, teacher or counselor ratings and observations, and verified reports of serious recurrent behavior patterns. (Getson & Schweid, 1976, p. 57)

Recognizing the conflict or, as they put it, ethical standards squeeze, Getson and Schweid (1976) suggest the following steps for school counselors to protect their counselees and students.

> First, review all existing records to assure that there is not material that predates FERPA that would violate implied to stated guarantees of privacy to the child. Second, remove all material that, because of its technical nature or vocabulary, may be inappropriate for use by lay persons. Retain only materials that can be expressed in a form unlikely to be misinterpreted. Third, initiate a policy of maintaining only records that can be reviewed with parents without threat to the welfare of a counselee. Fourth, be sure that counselees understand the legal limitation of the privacy afforded the counseling relationship relative to the rights of parents to inspect official records. Fifth, initiate a study of the full implications of the conflict between the FERPA and AACD's Ethical Standards [now the American Counseling Association's *Code of Ethics and Standards of Practice*, 1995]. There may be safeguards to the right to privacy of the student implicit in FERPA of which we who are not lawyers are not aware. Sixth, if there is a clear or probable conflict between the FERPA and

AACD's Ethical Standards [now the American Counseling Association's *Code of Ethics and Standards of Practice*, 1995], initiate action to change the act, the standards, or both. It would seem that, as a minimum a provision should exist within the act that withholds from anyone except public authorized investigative bodies information under study. (pp. 57–58)

Because school counselors as well as counselors in other educational settings are frequently called on to write letters of recommendation for college admissions or employment, it should be noted that the Buckley Amendment implications are clear that

unless the educator is specifically informed otherwise, he or she should assume that the student may have access to letters of recommendation. The student can be requested to sign a waiver, so that he or she will not have such access. However, unless such a waiver is signed, the student can be defended, both factually and professionally. In general educators are on relatively safe ground when writing letters of recommendation if the following conditions are met:

1. Letters of recommendation are an expected, normal, and integral part of one's duties and responsibilities.
2. Letters are sent only to second parties (not published), who can be expected to have a reasonable interest in and concern for the person in question.
3. Letters are factual, free of malice, and reasonably objective.
4. Letters are in response to a request. (St. John & Walden, 1976, p. 683)

St. John and Walden (1976) make three recommendations.

First it is recommended that professional educators consult with an attorney, preferably one conversant with educational matters, or with the school district's legal counsel, on all matters regarding confidential communications. Second, it is recommended that school districts and state departments of education cooperatively develop detailed guidelines to assist all school personnel in protecting student confidences and to respect the confidentiality of communications consistent with state and federal statutes. Third, it is recommended that the various professional organizations develop specific and up-dated codes of ethics related to this area. (p. 683)

School Counselors and Public Law 94-142

Another act of importance to school counselors is the Education for All Handicapped Children Act (PL 94-142) of November 1975. This law guarantees the rights of all children, regardless of the severity of the disability, to a free, appropriate education. The law further establishes a formula for providing financial aid to states and local school districts, based on the number of children with disabilities receiving special education plus related services. It is this latter activity—related services—that provides for counseling by a certified counselor. In noting the implications of this act for counselors, Humes (1978) states that

while the role of the counselor in the implementation of PL 94-142 will vary from district to district and in part will be contingent on the availability of other specialized personnel and whether the counselor has an elemental or secondary assignment, it is difficult to conceive of any situation in which a counselor will have no role to play. Some of the possible ranges of responsibility are

1. participation in team meetings.
2. development of the IEP [Individual Education Plan].
   (IEP—The core of the law is the concept of the IEP. An IEP, which is to be reviewed annually, must be developed for each handicapped child. The content of the IEP must include the

present level of functioning, annual goals, short-term measurable objectives, and specific educational services required by the child.)

3. monitoring progress.
4. parental counseling.
   (A section of the law that is overlooked, partly because of its traditional neglect in American public education and partly because of the ambiguous nature of the language in the statute, is the requirement for parent counseling. Parent counseling may have a variety of meanings. Parent counseling suggests a possible range of services from psychiatric assistance to advice about academic offerings and may occur in an outside agency or within the school. A conservative approach would suggest that parent counseling should occur in the school setting and satisfy the definition of counseling as opposed to therapy. If we accept this assumption, the logical person to satisfy this need would be the counselor.)
5. extracurricular planning.
6. classroom consulting.
7. In-service training.
   (While it is reasonable to assume that in the early stages counselors will be the recipients of in-service training along with other pupil personnel services workers, it would be a reasonable assumption that in the middle-to-later stages of implementation the counselor will become one of the providers of in-service training.)
8. record keeping. (pp. 193–195)

Jenkins (1985) specifies skills for elementary school counselors involved in mainstreaming as follows.

1. Working with nonhandicapped elementary school children to encourage acceptance of individual differences.
2. Helping handicapped children understand their strengths and weaknesses and make use of existing skills to function in an environment not equipped for handicapped persons.
3. Developing counseling activities for all elementary school children, including those with special needs.
4. Developing activities to assist the development of a positive self-concept in the child with special needs.
5. Formulating teacher, parent, and administrator counseling groups to discuss attitudes and feelings toward the student with special needs. (p. 203)

The Counselor and the Americans with Disabilities Act

Although noted previously in Chapter 10, it is appropriate to discuss the Americans with Disabilities Act, which became law in 1990, further in this chapter. This act prohibits discrimination on the basis of disabilities. Its provisions cover discrimination under titles dealing with (1) employment, (2) accessibility, (3) accommodations in public facilities, (4) telecommunications, and (5) miscellaneous provisions. This act has implications for counselors assisting clients with disabilities. These include the following.

- Counselors at all levels and in all settings must become familiar with the provisions of the act.
- In many settings, counselors should work with local businesses and industries to facilitate the employment of disabled individuals.
- Counselors should help disabled clients understand their rights as specified by the act.

- In counseling the disabled, the focus is on what the client can do, on the client's potential, not one's limitations. In this regard, counselors must examine and ensure that their own attitudes are not discriminatory.
- The counselor's office and organization must be physically accessible to disabled clients.

LEGAL CONCERNS OF COUNSELORS

Confidentiality

Earlier in this chapter, we discussed the issue of confidentiality and privileged communication for counselors. This remains a paramount legal as well as ethical issue confronting the counseling profession. In a survey of existing privileged communication statutes and rules of evidence in the 50 states and the District of Columbia, Herlihy and Sheeley (1987) note (see Table 15-1) that among helping professionals, psychologists are most frequently protected, followed by social workers. School counselors were granted the right to privileged communication, sometimes limited, in 27 states.

In a personal communication with us, Herlihy and Glosoff (1998) indicate the following.

At the present time, 44 states and Washington, DC, have some form of licensure, registration, or certification for counselors. A *preliminary* examination of the data from these states reveals that:

1. Some statutory provision that establishes privileged communication between credentialed counselors and their clients exists in 42 states and the District of Columbia (AL, AR, AZ, CO, DE, DC, FL, GA, ID, IL, IN, IA, KS, KY, LA, ME, MD, MA, MI, MS, MO, MT, NE, NH, NJ, NM, NC, ND, OH, OK, OR, RI, SC, SD, TN, TX, UT, VA, VT, WA, WI, WV, WY). No privileged communication statute that included credentialed counselors and their clients was found in 8 states (AK, CA, CT, HI, MN, NV, NY, PA).
(NOTE: These states do have priviledged communication statues. These statutes do not, however, mention communications between professional counselors and clients.)

2. Despite calls for uniformity in licensure laws, the privileged communication provisions in existing laws show considerable variation. The most commonly noted limitations and exceptions to privilege include various combinations of the following:
   a. When clients, or their legal representatives, waive their right to privilege by signing a release of information or by voluntarily testifying.
   b. When counselors suspect child abuse or neglect.
   c. When a client's condition poses a clear and imminent danger to the client or an identifiable third party.
   d. When a client brings a complaint or charge against a counselor to a state regulatory board or court of law.
   e. When the client's physical or mental condition is an issue in legal proceedings.
   f. When the counselor is involved in assessing a client as part of a court-ordered examination.
   g. When there is a need for involuntary hospitalization.
   h. When a client's competency is an issue in a civil or criminal proceeding.
   i. When there are criminal law exceptions (violations or when the client was a crime victim, especially if the victim was a minor). (Note: there are actually only a few states that include this as an exception to privilege and most note that the exception exists if the victim was a minor.)
   j. Other "catch-all" phrases such as "when disclosure is necessary for justice," "by general court order," and "as otherwise required by law."

TABLE 15-1 Privileged Communication Provisions in Statutes and Regulations of Selected Helping Professions

	STATE												
	AL	AK	AZ	AR	CA	CO	CT	DE	FL	GA	HI	ID	IL
Certified School Counselors	no	no	no	no	no	no	yes	no	no	no	no	yes	no
Licensed Professional Counselors	yes	—	—	yes	—	—	—	—	no	nob	—	yes	—
Marriage and Family Therapists	—	—	—	—	yes	—	no	—	no	no	—	—	—
Psychologists	yes	no	yes	yes	yes	yes	yes	yes	no	yes	no	yes	yes
Social Workers	no	—	—	yes	yes	yes	—	yes	no	nob	—	yes	yes

	STATE												
	IN	IA	KS	KY	LA	ME	MD	MA	MI	MN	MS	MO	MT
Certified School Counselors	yes	yes	no	yes	no	yesa	yes	no	yes	no	no	no	yes
Licensed Professional Counselors	—	—	—	—	—	—	no	—	—	—	yes	yes	yes
Marriage and Family Therapists	—	—	—	—	—	—	—	—	yes	—	—	—	—
Psychologists	yes	yes	yes	yes	yes	yes	yes	yes	yes	yes	yes	yes	yes
Social Workers	—	yes	yes	yes	yes	yes	yes	yes	yes	—	—	—	yes

	STATE											
	NE	NV	NH	NJ	NM	NY	NC	ND	OH	OK	OR	PA
Certified School Counselors	no	yes	no	no	no	no	yes	yes	yesb	yes	yes	yes
Licensed Professional Counselors	yes	—	—	—	—	—	yes	—	yesb	yes	—	—
Marriage and Family Therapists	—	no	—	yes	—	—	yes	—	—	—	—	—
Psychologists	no	yes	yes	yes	yes	yes	yes	yes	yes	yes	yes	yes
Social Workers	—	—	yes	—	—	yes	no	no	yesb	yes	yes	—

	STATE											
	RI	SC	SD	TN	TX	UT	VT	VA	WA	WV	WI	WY
Certified School Counselors	no	yesa	yes	no	no	no	no	no	yesa	no	yesa	no
Licensed Professional Counselors	—	nob	—	nob	no	—	—	yes	—	yes	—	—
Marriage and Family Therapists	—	nob	—	nob	—	yes	—	—	—	—	—	—
Psychologists	no	no	yes	yes	yes	yes	no	yes	yes	no	yes	yes
Social Workers	no	no	yes	yes	yes	yes	—	yes	—	yes	—	—

Note. A dash (—) indicates state does not regulate as a separate profession.
aPrivilege limited to student drug and alcohol problems.
bProfessions regulated under same state act.

Fischer and Sorenson (1996) cite Wigmore, the leading authority on the Anglo-American law of evidence, as indicating four requirements.

1. The communications must originate in confidence that they will not be disclosed.
2. The confidentiality must be essential to full and satisfactory maintenance of the relationship between the parties.
3. The relationship must be one which, in the opinion of the community, should be sedulously fostered.
4. The injury to that relation, caused by disclosure, would be greater than the benefit gained to the process of litigation.

These criteria are generally accepted by modern scholars of the law of evidence as the appropriate test for what qualifies as privileged communication.

Judges have been very reluctant to grant or acknowledge such a privilege and more reluctant still to extend it to new relationships. Even with long-recognized exemptions, such as the lawyer-client relationship, courts have demanded that certain conditions be met. (p. 19–20)

Competence and Malpractice

As previously noted, counselors are expected to function within the limits of their professional expertise. This is not only ethically expected but also legally desirable. The dramatic increase in malpractice suits across all the helping professions indicates that our competence may be under legal scrutiny at any time. The governing legal principle in such cases is pointed out by Fischer and Sorenson (1996) as follows.

One who undertakes, gratuitously or for consideration, to render services to another which he should recognize as necessary for the protection of the other person or things, is subject to liability to the other for physical harm resulting from his failure to exercise reasonable care to perform his undertaking, if:

a. His failure to exercise such care increases the risk of harm, or
b. The harm is suffered because of the other's reliance upon the undertaking. (p. 42)

They also note that the most common situations in which legal problems are most likely to occur are these.

- Administering drugs
- Giving birth control advice
- Giving abortion-related advice
- Making statements that might be defamatory
- Assisting in searches of students' lockers
- Violating confidentiality and the privacy of records (p. 51)

Counselors as Expert Witnesses

Counselors are increasingly making court appearances as expert witnesses. Depending on the counselor's work setting, she or he may be called on to testify in cases of child abuse and neglect, sexual abuse, child custody, divorce, and addictions, to name but a few. Being an expert witness and deporting oneself well as a professional cannot be dealt with casually. We, therefore, recommend that practicing counselors review the American Counseling Association

Legal Series monograph *The Counselor as an Expert Witness* (1993) by William Weikel and Paula Hughes, edited by Theodore P. Remley, Jr. In addition, if the counseling organization retains a lawyer for legal advice, it is also advisable to consult with this individual.

Third-Party Payments

A legal issue for many counselors, especially those in private practice or employed by agencies dependent on client payments, is the issue of third-party payments. This is the practice of reimbursement from a third party, usually an insurance company, for services that a counselor (the second party) renders to a client (the first party). "As of 1993, nine states mandated coverage for reimbursement for the services of professional counselors. These were California, Colorado, Connecticut, Florida, Maryland, New Hampshire, Mississippi, Texas, and Virginia" (Strosnider & Grad, 1993, p. 15).

SUMMARY

This chapter has reminded readers of ethical guidelines and expectancies for the profession of counseling. Special attention has been paid to the issues of competence, confidentiality, and personal relationships with clients.

This chapter has also noted the importance of counselors informing themselves of the legal implications and restrictions on their professional activities.

Whether our profession of counseling advances and achieves noble goals will depend very little on textbook writers, past and present, but on *you*, our readers, who will represent our profession in the future. You are our future. We wish you well!

DISCUSSION QUESTIONS

1.   Identify and discuss the lack of or questionable ethics in activities such as sales, advertising, politics, and government.

2.   What are the differences and similarities between ethics and values?

3.   Why are codes of ethics important to the counseling profession?

4.   Are warranties or guarantees for products indications that manufacturers want to treat customers ethically?

5.   Are there any legal concerns you would have as a practicing counselor?

6.   Are you aware of any recent court decisions or pending legislation that could have implications for counselors in schools? In nonschool settings?

7.   How do you intend to keep abreast of legal enactments or court decisions affecting the counseling profession?

CLASS ACTIVITIES

1.   Examine current newspapers and magazines for examples of ethical and legal violations that betray a public trust. Share in class or small groups.

2.   In small groups, share and discuss situations in which you feel you were treated unethically.

3.   Ask a local lawyer to address the class on the topic of professional malpractice.

SELECTED READINGS

Aiello, H., & Humes, C. (1987). Counselor contact of the noncustodial parent: A point of law. *Elementary School Guidance and Counseling, 21*, 177–182.

Caublin, L., & Prout, H. (1983). School counselors and the reporting of child abuse: A survey of state laws and practices. *The School Counselor, 30* (5), 358–367.

Dellinger, A. M. (1983). Legal issues in school health: Part II. *School Law Bulletin, 14* (3), 1, 9–15.

Ethics Committee of APA. (1988). Trends in ethics cases: Common pitfalls and published resources. *American Psychologist, 43* (7), 564–572.

Herlihy, B., Healy, M., Cook, E., & Hudson, P. (1987). Ethical practices of licensed professional counselors: A survey of state licensing boards. *Counselor Education and Supervision, 27* (1), 69–76.

Herlihy, B., & Sheeley, V. (1988). Counselor liability and the duty to warn: Selected cases, standards, trends, and implications for practice. *Counselor Education and Supervision, 27*, 69–76.

Hinkeldey, N., & Spokane, A. (1985). Effects of pressure and legal guideline clarity on counselor decision making in legal and ethical conflict situations. *Journal of Counseling and Development, 64* (4), 240–245.

Huey, W. (1987). Ethical standards for school counselors: Test your knowledge. *The School Counselor, 34* (5), 331–335.

Hummel, D. L. (1985). Law and ethics for practitioners in counseling and guidance. *Educational Perspectives, 23* (3), 3–12.

Ibrahim, F. A. (1996). A multicultural perspective on principle and virtue ethics. *Counseling Psychologist, 24*, 78–85.

Kitchener, K. S. (Ed.). (1984). Ethical decision making in counseling psychology [Special issue]. *Counseling Psychologist, 12* (3), 19–98.

Kitchener, K. S. (1996). There is more to ethics than principles. *Counseling Psychologist, 24*, 92–97.

Krieshok, T. (1987). Psychologists and counselors in the legal system: A dialogue with Theodore Blau. *Journal of Counseling and Development, 66* (2), 69–72.

Mabe, A. R., & Rollin, S. A. (1986). The role of a code of ethical standards in counseling. *Journal of Counseling and Development, 64*, 294–297.

Mappes, D., Robb, G., & Engels, D. (1985). Conflicts between ethics and law in counseling and

psychotherapy. *Journal of Counseling and Development, 64* (4), 246–252.

Monahan, J., & Walker, L. (1988). Social science research in law: A new paradigm. *American Psychologist, 43* (6), 465–472.

Neukrug, E., Lovell, C., & Parker, R. J. (1996). Employing ethical codes and decision-making models: A developmental process. *Counseling and Values, 40*, 98–106.

Remley, T. (1988). More explanation needed in ethical and legal topics. *Mental Health Counseling, 10* (3), 167–170.

Robinson, S. (1988). Counselor competence and malpractice suits: Opposite sides of the same coin. *Counseling and Human Development, 20* (9), 1–7.

Shilloto-Clarke, C. (1996). Ethical issues in counselling psychology. In R. Woolfe & W. Dryden (Eds.), *Handbook of counselling psychology* (pp. 555–580). London: Sage.

VanderCreek, L., & Knapp, S. (1984). Counselors, confidentiality and life-endangering clients. *Counselor Education and Supervision, 24* (1), 51–57.

Welfel, E. R., & Lipsitz, N. E. (1983). Wanted: A comprehensive approach to ethics research and education. *Counselor Education and Supervision, 22* (4), 320–332.

Wilcoxon, S. A. (1987). Client consent in departures from customary and suggested treatment formats. *American Mental Health Counselors Association Journal, 9* (2), 77–83.

RESEARCH OF INTEREST

Borders, L. D., Cashwell, C. S., & Rotter, J. C. (1995). Supervision of counselor licensure applicants: A comparative study. *Counselor Education and Supervision, 35* (1), 54–69.

Abstract

This article provides baseline information about supervision being given to counselor licensure applicants and investigates the impact of regulations on the conduct of this supervision. A comparison study of supervisors was conducted with 107 subjects from South Carolina and 83 from Missouri, the former with recommended supervisor and supervision regulations and the latter without it. Subjects completed questionnaires regarding their supervision practices and rated their supervision knowledge skills. Supervisors in both states were experienced counselors from a variety of fields and indicated altruistic and humanitarian reasons for working with counselor licensure applicants. More of South Carolina supervisors had aligned with counselor education and reported more training experiences. Regulations did not have adverse effects on supervision.

Chu, L., & Duling, J. (1987). Confidentiality and the university counseling center. *NASPA Journal, 24* (3), 50–56.

Abstract

These authors surveyed 160 directors of college and university counseling centers to determine whether there was a consensus regarding confidentiality in terms of personal responsibilities and policies within their center. Results revealed a need for campus counseling centers to look at their policies regarding confidentiality and to keep current with legal implications of the limits of confidential communication.

Geisler, J. S. (1995). The impact of the passage of a counselor licensure law: One state's experience. *Journal of Mental Health Counseling, 17* (2), 188–198.

Abstract

Responses to a questionnaire completed by 764 Licensed Professional Counselors (LPCs) revealed that the majority of LPCs are holding their licenses in reserve waiting to use them at a later date. Fifty-nine percent of LPCs were women, and the mean age of all LPCs was 47 years. Fifty-nine percent of counselors received their undergraduate degrees in the social sciences or education. For those in a fee-for-service setting, the mean fee per session was $69.91 (range $20–$138). Only 9% of LPCs had requested reimbursement. They report having difficulty receiving third-party payments. Those that had been successful had been assertive in marketing their services and had been proactive with HMOs, employee assistance programs, and insurance companies, and had contracts with businesses and managed health care organizations.

Navin, S., Beamish, P., & Johanson, G. (1995). Ethical practices of field-based mental health counselor supervisors. *Journal of Mental Health Counseling, 17* (2), 243–253.

Abstract

This study examined current ethical supervisory practices of 321 field-based mental health supervisors in Ohio as they relate to the Supervisory Role section of the Association for Counselor Education and Supervision ethical standards. Sixty-one percent of respondents held licenses in more than one area. The standards more consistently followed were participating in professional organizations, reviewing legal and ethical responsibilities, establishing procedures for crisis intervention, meeting regularly with and providing ongoing feedback to counseling students, conducting remedial referral, and avoiding sexual contact with students. The standard least consistently followed was training in supervision, suggesting that little formal course work had been completed by clinical supervisors. The standard that produced the most mixed results involved multiple roles.

Stadler, H., & Paul, R. D. (1986). Counselor educator's preparation in ethics. *Journal of Counseling and Development, 64* (5), 328–330.

Abstract

The results of a national survey of department heads in counselor education and counseling psychology are reported. Conclusions are drawn regarding the respondents' training in professional ethics, their perceptions of the adequacy of this training, and their effectiveness in responding to ethical dilemmas.

American School Counselor Association (Adopted July 1990)
Role Statement: The School Counselor

The American School Counselor Association recognizes and supports the implementation of comprehensive developmental counseling programs at all educational levels. The programs are designed to help all students develop their educational, social, career, and personal strengths and to become responsible and productive citizens. School counselors help create and organize these programs, as well as provide appropriate counselor interventions.

School counseling programs are developmental by design, focusing on needs, interests, and issues related to the various stages of student growth. There are objectives, activities, special services and expected outcomes, with an emphasis on helping students to learn more effectively and efficiently. There is a commitment to individual uniqueness and the maximum development of human potential. A counseling program is an integral part of a school's total educational program.

THE SCHOOL COUNSELOR

The school counselor is a certified professional educator who assists students, teachers, parents, and administrators. Three generally recognized helping processes used by the counselor are counseling, consulting, and coordinating: 1) Counseling is a complex helping process in which the counselor establishes a trusting and confidential working relationship. The focus is on problem-solving, decision-making, and discovering personal

meaning related to learning and development; 2) Consultation is a cooperative process in which the counselor-consultant assists others to think through problems and to develop skills that make them more effective in working with students; 3) Coordination is a leadership process in which the counselor helps organize and manage a school's counseling program and related services.

School counselors are employed in elementary, middle/junior high, senior high, and postsecondary schools. Their work is differentiated by attention to age-specific developmental stages of growth and related interests, tasks, and challenges. School counselors are human behavior and relationship specialists who organize their work around fundamental interventions.

Counselor interventions have sometimes been referred to as functions, services, approaches, tasks, activities, or jobs. They have, at times, been viewed as roles themselves, helping to create the image of the counselor. In a comprehensive developmental counseling program, school counselors organize their work schedules around the following basic interventions:

Individual Counseling. Individual counseling is a personal and private interaction between a counselor and a student in which they work together on a problem or topic of interest. A face-to-face, one-to-one meeting with a counselor provides a student maximum privacy in which to freely explore ideas, feelings, and behaviors. School counselors establish trust and build a helping relationship. They respect the privacy of information, always considering actions in terms of the rights, integrity, and welfare of students. Counselors are obligated by law and ethical standards to report and to refer a case when a person's welfare is in jeopardy. It is a counselor's duty to inform an individual of the conditions and limitations under which assistance may be provided.

Small Group Counseling.   Small group counseling involves a counselor working with two or more students together. Group size generally ranges from five to eight members. Group discussions may be relatively unstructured or may be based on structured learning activities. Group members have an opportunity to learn from each other. They can share ideas, give and receive feedback, increase their awareness, gain new knowledge, practice skills, and think about their goals and actions. Group discussions may be problem-centered, where attention is given to particular concerns or problems. Discussions may be growth-centered, where general topics are related to personal and academic development.

Large Group Guidance.   Large group meetings offer the best opportunity to provide guidance to the largest number of students in a school. Counselors first work with students in large groups wherever appropriate because it is the most efficient use of time. Large group work involves cooperative learning methods, in which the larger group is divided into smaller working groups under the supervision of a counselor or teacher. The guidance and counseling curriculum, composed of organized objectives and activities, is delivered by teachers or counselors in classrooms or advisory groups. School counselors and teachers may co-lead some activities. Counselors develop and present special guidance units which give attention to particular developmental issues or areas of concern in their respective schools and they help prepare teachers to deliver part of the guidance and counseling curriculum.

Consultation.   The counselor as a consultant helps people to be more effective in working with others. Consultation helps individuals think through problems and concerns, acquire more knowledge and skill, and become more objective and self-confident. This intervention can take place in individual or group conferences, or through staff-development activities.

Coordination.   Coordination as a counselor intervention is the process of managing various indirect services which benefit students and being a liaison between school and community agencies. It may include organizing special events which involve parents or resource people in the community in guidance projects. It often entails collecting data and disseminating information. Counselors might coordinate a student needs assessment, the interpretation of standardized tests, a child study team, or a guidance related teacher or parent education program.

THE PREPARATION OF SCHOOL COUNSELORS

School counselors are prepared for their work through the study of interpersonal relationships and behavioral sciences in graduate education courses in accredited colleges and universities. Preparation involves special training in counseling theory and skills related to school settings. Particular attention is given to personality and human development theories and research, including career and life-skills development; learning theories, the nature of change and the helping process; theories and approaches to appraisal, multicultural and community awareness; educational environments; curriculum development; professional ethics; and program planning, management, and evaluation.

Counselors are prepared to use the basic interventions in a school setting, with special emphasis on the study of helping relationships, facilitative skills, brief counseling; group dynamics and group learning activities; family systems; peer helper programs, multicultural and cross-cultural helping approaches; and educational and community resources for special school populations.

School counselors are aware of their own professional competencies and responsibilities within the school setting. They know when and how to refer or involve other professionals. They are accountable for their actions and participate in appropriate studies and research related to their work.

RESPONSIBILITY TO THE PROFESSION

To assure high quality practice, counselors are committed to continued professional growth and personal development. They are active members of the American Counseling Association and the American School Counselor Association, as well as state and local professional associations which foster and promote school counseling. They also uphold the ethical and professional standards of these associations.

School counselors meet the state certification standards and abide by the laws in the states where they are working. Counselors work cooperatively with individuals and organizations to promote the overall development of children, youth, and families in their communities.

Appendix B

American Counseling
Association (As Approved
by Governing Council, April 1995;
Effective July 1, 1995)

Code of Ethics
and Standards
of Practice

PREAMBLE

The American Counseling Association is an educational, scientific, and professional organization whose members are dedicated to the enhancement of human development throughout the life span. Association members recognize diversity in our society and embrace a cross-cultural approach in support of the worth, dignity, potential, and uniqueness of each individual.

The specification of a code of ethics enables the association to clarify to current and future members, and to those served by members, the nature of the ethical responsibilities held in common by its members. As the code of ethics of the association, this document establishes principles that define the ethical behavior of association members. All members of the American Counseling Association are required to adhere to the Code of Ethics and the Standards of Practice. The Code of Ethics will serve as the basis for processing ethical complaints initiated against members of the association.

NOTE: For information on ordering the *ACA Code of Ethics and Standards of Practice* write to:
ACA Distribution Center
P.O. Box 531
Annapolis Junction, MD 20701-0531
or call 301-470-4ACA (301-470-4222); toll free 1-800-422-2648; fax (301) 604-0158.

SECTION A: THE COUNSELING RELATIONSHIP

A.1. Client Welfare

a. *Primary Responsibility*

The primary responsibility of counselors is to respect the dignity and to promote the welfare of clients.

b. *Positive Growth and Development*

Counselors encourage client growth and development in ways that foster the clients' interest and welfare; counselors avoid fostering dependent counseling relationships.

c. *Counseling Plans*

Counselors and their clients work jointly in devising integrated, individual counseling plans that offer reasonable promise of success and are consistent with abilities and circumstances of clients. Counselors and clients regularly review counseling plans to ensure their continued viability and effectiveness, respecting clients' freedom of choice. (See A.3.b.)

d. *Family Involvement*

Counselors recognize that families are usually important in clients' lives and strive to enlist family understanding and involvement as a positive resource, when appropriate.

e. *Career and Employment Needs*

Counselors work with their clients in considering employment in jobs and circumstances that are consistent with the clients' overall abilities, vocational limitations, physical restrictions, general temperament, interest and aptitude patterns, social skills, education, general qualifications, and other relevant characteristics and needs. Counselors neither place nor participate in placing clients in positions that will result in damaging the interest and the welfare of clients, employers, or the public.

A.2. Respecting Diversity

a. *Nondiscrimination*

Counselors do not condone or engage in discrimination based on age, color, culture, disability, ethnic group, gender, race, religion, sexual orientation, marital status, or socioeconomic status. (See C.5.a., C.5.b., and D.1.i.)

b. *Respecting Differences*

Counselors will actively attempt to understand the diverse cultural backgrounds of the clients with whom they work. This includes, but is not limited to, learning how the counselor's own cultural/ethnic/racial identity impacts her/his values and beliefs about the counseling process. (See E.8. and F.2.i)

A.3. Client Rights

a. *Disclosure to Clients*

When counseling is initiated, and throughout the counseling process as necessary, counselors inform clients of the purposes, goals, techniques, procedures, limitations, potential risks and benefits of services to be performed, and other pertinent information. Counselors take steps to ensure that clients understand the implications of diagnosis, the intended use of tests and reports, fees, and billing arrangements. Clients have the right to expect confidentiality and to be provided with an explanation of its limitations, including supervision and/or treatment team professionals; to obtain clear information about their case records; to participate in the ongoing counseling plans; and to refuse any recommended services and be advised of the consequences of such refusal. (See E.5.a. and G.2.)

b. *Freedom of Choice*

Counselors offer clients the freedom to choose whether to enter into a counseling relationship and to determine which professional(s) will provide counseling. Restrictions that limit choices of clients are fully explained. (See A.1.c.)

c. *Inability to Give Consent*

When counseling minors or persons unable to give voluntary informed consent, counselors act in these clients' best interests. (See B.3.)

A.4. Clients Served by Others

If a client is receiving services from another mental health professional, counselors, with client consent, inform the professional persons already involved and develop clear agreements to avoid confusion and conflict for the client. (See C.6.c.)

A.5. Personal Needs and Values

a. *Personal Needs*

In the counseling relationship, counselors are aware of the intimacy and responsibilities inherent in the counseling relationship, maintain respect for clients, and avoid actions that seek to meet their personal needs at the expense of clients.

b. *Personal Values*

Counselors are aware of their own values, attitudes, beliefs, and behaviors and how these apply in a diverse society, and avoid imposing their values on clients. (See C.5.a.)

A.6. Dual Relationships

a. *Avoid When Possible*

Counselors are aware of their influential positions with respect to clients, and they avoid exploiting the trust and dependency of clients. Counselors make every effort to avoid dual relationships with clients that could impair professional judgment or increase the risk of harm to clients. (Examples of such relationships include, but are not limited to, familial, social, financial, business, or close personal relationships with clients.) When a dual relationship cannot be avoided, counselors take appropriate professional precautions such as informed consent, consultation, supervision, and documentation to ensure that judgment is not impaired and no exploitation occurs. (See F.1.b.)

b. *Superior/Subordinate Relationships*

Counselors do not accept as clients superiors or subordinates with whom they have administrative, supervisory, or evaluative relationships.

A.7. Sexual Intimacies with Clients

a. *Current Clients*

Counselors do not have any type of sexual intimacies with clients and do not counsel persons with whom they have had a sexual relationship.

b. *Former Clients*

Counselors do not engage in sexual intimacies with former clients within a minimum of two years after terminating the counseling relationship. Counselors who engage in such relationship after two years following termination have the responsibility to thoroughly examine and document that such relations did not have an exploitative nature, based on factors such as duration of counseling, amount of time since counseling, termination circumstances, client's personal history and mental status, adverse impact on the client, and actions by the counselor suggesting a plan to initiate a sexual relationship with the client after termination.

A.8. Multiple Clients

When counselors agree to provide counseling services to two or more persons who have a relationship (such as husband and wife, or parents and children), counselors clarify at the outset which person or persons are clients and the nature of the relationships they will have with each involved person. If it becomes apparent that counselors may be called upon to perform potentially conflicting roles, they clarify, adjust, or withdraw from roles appropriately. (See B.2. and B.4.d.)

A.9. Group Work

a. Screening

Counselors screen prospective group counseling/therapy participants. To the extent possible, counselors select members whose needs and goals are compatible with goals of the group, who will not impede the group process, and whose well-being will not be jeopardized by the group experience.

b. Protecting Clients

In a group setting, counselors take reasonable precautions to protect clients from physical or psychological trauma.

A.10. Fees and Bartering   (See D.3.a. and D.3.b.)

a. Advance Understanding

Counselors clearly explain to clients, prior to entering the counseling relationship, all financial arrangements related to professional services including the use of collection agencies or legal measures for nonpayment. (See A.11.c.)

b. Establishing Fees

In establishing fees for professional counseling services, counselors consider the financial status of clients and locality. In the event that the established fee structure is inappropriate for a client, assistance is provided in attempting to find comparable services of acceptable cost. (See A.10.d., D.3.a., and D.3.b.)

c. Bartering Discouraged

Counselors ordinarily refrain from accepting goods or services from clients in return for counseling services because such arrangements create inherent potential for conflicts, exploitation, and distortion of the professional relationship. Counselors may participate in bartering only if the relationship is not exploitive, if the client requests it, if a clear written contract is established, and if such arrangements are an accepted practice among professionals in the community. (See A.6.a.)

d. Pro Bono Service

Counselors contribute to society by devoting a portion of their professional activity to services for which there is little or no financial return (pro bono).

A.11. Termination and Referral

a. Abandonment Prohibited

Counselors do not abandon or neglect clients in counseling. Counselors assist in making appropriate arrangements for the continuation of treatment, when necessary, during interruptions such as vacations, and following termination.

b. Inability to Assist Clients

If counselors determine an inability to be of professional assistance to clients, they avoid entering or immediately terminate a counseling relationship. Counselors are knowledgeable about referral resources and suggest appropriate alternatives. If clients decline the suggested referral, counselors should discontinue the relationship.

c. Appropriate Termination

Counselors terminate a counseling relationship, securing client agreement when possible, when it is reasonably clear that the client is no longer benefiting, when services are no longer required, when counseling no longer serves the client's needs or interests, when clients do not pay fees charged, or when agency or institution limits do not allow provision of further counseling services. (See A.10.b. and C.2.g.)

A.12. Computer Technology

a. Use of Computers

When computer applications are used in counseling services, counselors ensure that: (1) the client is intellectually, emotionally, and physically capable of using the computer application; (2) the computer application is appropriate for the needs of the client; (3) the client understands the purpose and operation of the computer applications; and (4) a follow-up of client use of a computer application is provided to correct possible misconceptions, discover inappropriate use, and assess subsequent needs.

b. *Explanation of Limitations*

Counselors ensure that clients are provided information as a part of the counseling relationship that adequately explains the limitations of computer technology.

c. *Access to Computer Applications*

Counselors provide for equal access to computer applications in counseling services. (See A.2.a.)

SECTION B: CONFIDENTIALITY

B.1. Right to Privacy

a. *Respect for Privacy*

Counselors respect their clients' right to privacy and avoid illegal and unwarranted disclosures of confidential information. (See A.3.a. and B.6.a.)

b. *Client Waiver*

The right to privacy may be waived by the client or their legally recognized representative.

c. *Exceptions*

The general requirement that counselors keep information confidential does not apply when disclosure is required to prevent clear and imminent danger to the client or others or when legal requirements demand that confidential information be revealed. Counselors consult with other professionals when in doubt as to the validity of an exception.

d. *Contagious, Fatal Diseases*

A counselor who receives information confirming that a client has a disease commonly known to be both communicable and fatal is justified in disclosing information to an identifiable third party, who by his or her relationship with the client is at a high risk of contracting the disease. Prior to making a disclosure the counselor should ascertain that the client has not already informed the third party about his or her disease and that the client is not intending to inform the third party in the immediate future. (See. B.1.c. and B.1.f.)

e. *Court Ordered Disclosure*

When court ordered to release confidential information without a client's permission, counselors request to the court that the disclosure not be required due to potential harm to the client or counseling relationship. (See B.1.c.)

f. *Minimal Disclosure*

When circumstances require the disclosure of confidential information, only essential information is revealed.

To the extent possible, clients are informed before confidential information is disclosed.

g. *Explanation of Limitations*

When counseling is initiated and throughout the counseling process as necessary, counselors inform clients of the limitations of confidentiality and identify foreseeable situations in which confidentiality must be breached. (See G.2.a.)

h. *Subordinates*

Counselors make every effort to ensure that privacy and confidentiality of clients are maintained by subordinates including employees, supervisees, clerical assistants, and volunteers. (See B.1.a.)

i. *Treatment Teams*

If client treatment will involve a continued review by a treatment team, the client will be informed of the team's existence and composition.

B.2. Groups and Families

a. *Group Work*

In group work, counselors clearly define confidentiality and the parameters for the specific group being entered, explain its importance, and discuss the difficulties related to confidentiality involved in group work. The fact that confidentiality cannot be guaranteed is clearly communicated to group members.

b. *Family Counseling*

In family counseling, information about one family member cannot be disclosed to another member without permission. Counselors protect the privacy rights of each family member. (See A.8., B.3., and B.4.d.)

B.3. Minor or Incompetent Clients

When counseling clients who are minors or individuals who are unable to give voluntary, informed consent, parents or guardians may be included in the counseling process as appropriate. Counselors act in the best interests of clients and take measures to safeguard confidentiality. (See A.3.c.)

B.4. Records

a. *Requirement of Records*

Counselors maintain records necessary for rendering professional services to their clients and as required by laws, regulations, or agency or institution procedures.

b. *Confidentiality of Records*

Counselors are responsible for securing the safety and confidentiality of any counseling records they create, maintain, transfer, or destroy whether the records are written, taped, computerized, or stored in any other medium. (See B.1.a.)

c. *Permission to Record or Observe*

Counselors obtain permission from clients prior to electronically recording or observing sessions. (See A.3.a.)

d. *Client Access*

Counselors recognize that counseling records are kept for the benefit of clients, and therefore provide access to records and copies of records when requested by competent clients, unless the records contain information that may be misleading and detrimental to the client. In situations involving multiple clients, access to records is limited to those parts of records that do not include confidential information related to another client. (See A.8., B.1.a., and B.2.b.)

e. *Disclosure or Transfer*

Counselors obtain written permission from clients to disclose or transfer records to legitimate third parties unless exceptions to confidentiality exist as listed in Section B.1. Steps are taken to ensure that receivers of counseling records are sensitive to their confidential nature.

B.5. Research and Training

a. *Data Disguise Required*

Use of data derived from counseling relationships for purposes of training, research, or publication is confined to content that is disguised to ensure the anonymity of the individuals involved. (See B.1.g. and G.3.d.)

b. *Agreement for Identification*

Identification of a client in a presentation or publication is permissible only when the client has reviewed the material and has agreed to its presentation or publication. (See G.3.d.)

B.6. Consultation

a. *Respect for Privacy*

Information obtained in a consulting relationship is discussed for professional purposes only with persons clearly concerned with the case. Written and oral reports present data germane to the purposes of the consultation, and every effort is made to protect client identity and avoid undue invasion of privacy.

b. *Cooperating Agencies*

Before sharing information, counselors make efforts to ensure that there are defined policies in other agencies serving the counselor's clients that effectively protect the confidentiality of information.

SECTION C: PROFESSIONAL RESPONSIBILITY

C.1. Standards Knowledge

Counselors have a responsibility to read, understand, and follow the Code of Ethics and the Standards of Practice.

C.2. Professional Competence

a. *Boundaries of Competence*

Counselors practice only within the boundaries of their competence, based on their education, training, supervised experience, state and national professional credentials, and appropriate professional experience. Counselors will demonstrate a commitment to gain knowledge, personal awareness, sensitivity, and skills pertinent to working with a diverse client population.

b. *New Specialty Areas of Practice*

Counselors practice in specialty areas new to them only after appropriate education, training, and supervised experience. While developing skills in new specialty areas, counselors take steps to ensure the competence of their work and to protect others from possible harm.

c. *Qualified for Employment*

Counselors accept employment only for positions for which they are qualified by education, training, supervised experience, state and national professional credentials, and appropriate professional experience. Counselors hire for professional counseling positions only individuals who are qualified and competent.

d. *Monitor Effectiveness*

Counselors continually monitor their effectiveness as professionals and take steps to improve when necessary. Counselors in private practice take reasonable steps to seek out peer supervision to evaluate their efficacy as counselors.

e. *Ethical Issues Consultation*

Counselors take reasonable steps to consult with other counselors or related professionals when they have questions regarding their ethical obligations or professional practice. (See H.1.)

f. *Continuing Education*

Counselors recognize the need for continuing education to maintain a reasonable level of awareness of current scientific and professional information in their fields of activity. They take steps to maintain competence in the skills they use, are open to new procedures, and keep current with the diverse and/or special populations with whom they work.

g. *Impairment*

Counselors refrain from offering or accepting professional services when their physical, mental, or emotional problems are likely to harm a client or others. They are alert to the signs of impairment, seek assistance for problems, and, if necessary, limit, suspend, or terminate their professional responsibilities. (See A.11.c.)

C.3. Advertising and Soliciting Clients
a. *Accurate Advertising*

There are no restrictions on advertising by counselors except those that can be specifically justified to protect the public from deceptive practices. Counselors advertise or represent their services to the public by identifying their credentials in an accurate manner that is not false, misleading, deceptive, or fraudulent. Counselors may only advertise the highest degree earned which is in counseling or a closely related field from a college or university that was accredited when the degree was awarded by one of the regional accrediting bodies recognized by the Council on Postsecondary Accreditation.

b. *Testimonials*

Counselors who use testimonials do not solicit them from clients or other persons who, because of their particular circumstances, may be vulnerable to undue influence.

c. *Statements by Others*

Counselors make reasonable efforts to ensure that statements made by others about them or the profession of counseling are accurate.

d. *Recruiting Through Employment*

Counselors do not use their places of employment or institutional affiliation to recruit or gain clients, supervisees, or consultees for their private practices. (See C.5.e.)

e. *Products and Training Advertisements*

Counselors who develop products related to their profession or conduct workshops or training events ensure that the advertisements concerning these products or events

are accurate and disclose adequate information for consumers to make informed choices.

f. *Promoting to Those Served*

Counselors do not use counseling, teaching, training, or supervisory relationships to promote their products or training events in a manner that is deceptive or would exert undue influence on individuals who may be vulnerable. Counselors may adopt textbooks they have authored for instruction purposes.

g. *Professional Association Involvement*

Counselors actively participate in local, state, and national associations that foster the development and improvement of counseling.

C.4. Credentials
a. *Credentials Claimed*

Counselors claim or imply only professional credentials possessed and are responsible for correcting any known misrepresentations of their credentials by others. Professional credentials include graduate degrees in counseling or closely related mental health fields, accreditation of graduate programs, national voluntary certifications, government-issued certifications or licenses, ACA professional membership, or any other credential that might indicate to the public specialized knowledge or expertise in counseling.

b. *ACA Professional Membership*

ACA professional members may announce to the public their membership status. Regular members may not announce their ACA membership in a manner that might imply they are credentialed counselors.

c. *Credential Guidelines*

Counselors follow the guidelines for use of credentials that have been established by the entities that issue the credentials.

d. *Misrepresentation of Credentials*

Counselors do not attribute more to their credentials than the credentials represent, and do not imply that other counselors are not qualified because they do not possess certain credentials.

e. *Doctoral Degrees from Other Fields*

Counselors who hold a master's degree in counseling or a closely related mental health field, but hold a doctoral degree from other than counseling or a closely related field do not use the title, "Dr." in their practices and do not announce to the public in relation to their practice or status as a counselor that they hold a doctorate.

C.5. Public Responsibility

a. Nondiscrimination

Counselors do not discriminate against clients, students, or supervisees in a manner that has a negative impact based on their age, color, culture, disability, ethnic group, gender, race, religion, sexual orientation, or socioeconomic status, or for any other reason. (See A.2.a.)

b. Sexual Harassment

Counselors do not engage in sexual harassment. Sexual harassment is defined as sexual solicitation, physical advances, or verbal or nonverbal conduct that is sexual in nature, that occurs in connection with professional activities or roles, and that either: (1) is unwelcome, is offensive, or creates a hostile workplace environment, and counselors know or are told this; or (2) is sufficiently severe or intense to be perceived as harassment to a reasonable person in the context. Sexual harassment can consist of a single intense or severe act or multiple persistent or pervasive acts.

c. Reports to Third Parties

Counselors are accurate, honest, and unbiased in reporting their professional activities and judgments to appropriate third parties including courts, health insurance companies, those who are the recipients of evaluation reports, and others. (See B.1.g.)

d. Media Presentations

When counselors provide advice or comment by means of public lectures, demonstrations, radio or television programs, prerecorded tapes, printed articles, mailed material, or other media, they take reasonable precautions to ensure that (1) the statements are based on appropriate professional counseling literature and practice; (2) the statements are otherwise consistent with the Code of Ethics and the Standards of Practice; and (3) the recipients of the information are not encouraged to infer that a professional counseling relationship has been established. (See C.6.b.)

e. Unjustified Gains

Counselors do not use their professional positions to seek or receive unjustified personal gains, sexual favors, unfair advantage, or unearned goods or services. (See C.3.d.)

C.6. Responsibility to Other Professionals

a. Different Approaches

Counselors are respectful of approaches to professional counseling that differ from their own. Counselors know and take into account the traditions and practices of other professional groups with which they work.

b. Personal Public Statements

When making personal statements in a public context, counselors clarify that they are speaking from their personal perspectives and that they are not speaking on behalf of all counselors or the profession. (See C.5.d.)

c. Clients Served by Others

When counselors learn that their clients are in a professional relationship with another mental health professional, they request release from clients to inform the other professionals and strive to establish positive and collaborative professional relationships. (See A.4.)

SECTION D: RELATIONSHIPS WITH OTHER PROFESSIONALS

D.1. Relationships with Employers and Employees

a. Role Definition

Counselors define and describe for their employers and employees the parameters and levels of their professional roles.

b. Agreements

Counselors establish working agreements with supervisors, colleagues, and subordinates regarding counseling or clinical relationships, confidentiality, adherence to professional standards, distinction between public and private material, maintenance and dissemination of recorded information, workload, and accountability. Working agreements in each instance are specified and made known to those concerned.

c. Negative Conditions

Counselors alert their employers to conditions that may be potentially disruptive or damaging to the counselor's professional responsibilities or that may limit their effectiveness.

d. Evaluation

Counselors submit regularly to professional review and evaluation by their supervisor or the appropriate representative of the employer.

e. *In-Service*

Counselors are responsible for in-service development of self and staff.

f. *Goals*

Counselors inform their staff of goals and programs.

g. *Practices*

Counselors provide personnel and agency practices that respect and enhance the rights and welfare of each employee and recipient of agency services. Counselors strive to maintain the highest levels of professional services.

h. *Personnel Selection and Assignment*

Counselors select competent staff and assign responsibilities compatible with their skills and experiences.

i. *Discrimination*

Counselors, as either employers or employees, do not engage in or condone practices that are inhumane, illegal, or unjustifiable (such as considerations based on age, color, culture, disability, ethnic group, gender, race, religion, sexual orientation, or socioeconomic status) in hiring, promotion, or training. (See A.2.a. and C.5.b.)

j. *Professional Conduct*

Counselors have a responsibility both to clients and to the agency or institution within which services are performed to maintain high standards of professional conduct.

k. *Exploitive Relationships*

Counselors do not engage in exploitive relationships with individuals over whom they have supervisory, evaluative, or instructional control or authority.

l. *Employer Policies*

The acceptance of employment in an agency or institution implies that counselors are in agreement with its general policies and principles. Counselors strive to reach agreement with employers as to acceptable standards of conduct that allow for changes in institutional policy conducive to the growth and development of clients.

D.2. Consultation   (See B.6.)

a. *Consultation as an Option*

Counselors may choose to consult with any other professionally competent persons about their clients. In choosing consultants, counselors avoid placing the consultant in a conflict of interest situation that would preclude the consultant being a proper party to the counselor's efforts to help the client. Should counselors be engaged in a work setting that compromises this consultation standard, they consult with other professionals whenever possible to consider justifiable alternatives.

b. *Consultant Competency*

Counselors are reasonably certain that they have or the organization represented has the necessary competencies and resources for giving the kind of consulting services needed and that appropriate referral resources are available.

c. *Understanding with Clients*

When providing consultation, counselors attempt to develop with their clients a clear understanding of problem definition, goals for change, and predicted consequences of interventions selected.

d. *Consultant Goals*

The consulting relationship is one in which client adaptability and growth toward self-direction are consistently encouraged and cultivated. (See A.1.b.)

D.3. Fees for Referral

a. *Accepting Fees from Agency Clients*

Counselors refuse a private fee or other remuneration for rendering services to persons who are entitled to such services through the counselor's employing agency or institution. The policies of a particular agency may make explicit provisions for agency clients to receive counseling services from members of its staff in private practice. In such instances, the clients must be informed of other options open to them should they seek private counseling services. (See A.10.a., A.11.b., and C.3.d.)

b. *Referral Fees*

Counselors do not accept a referral fee from other professionals.

D.4. Subcontractor Arrangements

When counselors work as subcontractors for counseling services for a third party, they have a duty to inform clients of the limitations of confidentiality that the organization may place on counselors in providing counseling services to clients. The limits of such confidentiality ordinarily are discussed as part of the intake session. (See B.1.e. and B.1.f.)

SECTION E: EVALUATION, ASSESSMENT, AND INTERPRETATION

E.1. General

a. *Appraisal Techniques*

The primary purpose of educational and psychological assessment is to provide measures that are objective and interpretable in either comparative or absolute terms. Counselors recognize the need to interpret the statements in this section as applying to the whole range of appraisal techniques, including test and nontest data.

b. *Client Welfare*

Counselors promote the welfare and best interests of the client in the development, publication, and utilization of educational and psychological assessment techniques. They do not misuse assessment results and interpretations and take reasonable steps to prevent others from misusing the information these techniques provide. They respect the client's right to know the results, the interpretations made, and the bases for their conclusions and recommendations.

E.2. Competence to Use and Interpret Tests

a. *Limits of Competence*

Counselors recognize the limits of their competence and perform only those testing and assessment services for which they have been trained. They are familiar with reliability, validity, related standardization, error of measurement, and proper application of any technique utilized. Counselors using computer-based test interpretations are trained in the construct being measured and the specific instrument being used prior to using this type of computer application. Counselors take reasonable measures to ensure the proper use of psychological assessment techniques by persons under their supervision.

b. *Appropriate Use*

Counselors are responsible for the appropriate application, scoring, interpretation, and use of assessment instruments, whether they score and interpret such tests themselves or use computerized or other services.

c. *Decisions Based on Results*

Counselors responsible for decisions involving individuals or policies that are based on assessment results have a thorough understanding of educational and psychological measurement, including validation criteria, test research, and guidelines for test development and use.

d. *Accurate Information*

Counselors provide accurate information and avoid false claims or misconceptions when making statements about assessment instruments or techniques. Special efforts are made to avoid unwarranted connotations of such terms as IQ and grade equivalent scores. (See C.5.c.)

E.3. Informed Consent

a. *Explanation to Clients*

Prior to assessment, counselors explain the nature and purposes of assessment and the specific use of results in language the client (or other legally authorized person on behalf of the client) can understand, unless an explicit exception to this right has been agreed upon in advance. Regardless of whether scoring and interpretation are completed by counselors, by assistants, or by computer or other outside services, counselors take reasonable steps to ensure that appropriate explanations are given to the client.

b. *Recipients of Results*

The examinee's welfare, explicit understanding, and prior agreement determine the recipients of test results. Counselors include accurate and appropriate interpretations with any release of individual or group test results. (See B.1.a. and C.5.c.)

E.4. Release of Information to Competent Professionals

a. *Misuse of Results*

Counselors do not misuse assessment results, including test results, and interpretations, and take reasonable steps to prevent the misuse of such by others. (See C.5.c.)

b. *Release of Raw Data*

Counselors ordinarily release data (e.g., protocols, counseling or interview notes, or questionnaires) in which the client is identified only with the consent of the client or the client's legal representative. Such data are usually released only to persons recognized by counselors as competent to interpret the data. (See B.1.a.)

E.5. Proper Diagnosis of Mental Disorders

a. *Proper Diagnosis*

Counselors take special care to provide proper diagnosis of mental disorders. Assessment techniques (including personal interview) used to determine client care (e.g., locus of treatment, type of treatment, or recommended follow-up) are carefully selected and appropriately used. (See A.3.a. and C.5.c.)

b. *Cultural Sensitivity*

Counselors recognize that culture affects the manner in which clients' problems are defined. Clients' socioeconomic and cultural experience is considered when diagnosing mental disorders.

E.6. Test Selection

a. *Appropriateness of Instruments*

Counselors carefully consider the validity, reliability, psychometric limitations, and appropriateness of instruments when selecting tests for use in a given situation or with a particular client.

b. *Culturally Diverse Populations*

Counselors are cautious when selecting tests for culturally diverse populations to avoid inappropriateness of testing that may be outside of socialized behavioral or cognitive patterns.

E.7. Conditions of Test Administration

a. *Administration Conditions*

Counselors administer tests under the same conditions that were established in their standardization. When tests are not administered under standard conditions or when unusual behavior or irregularities occur during the testing session, those conditions are noted in interpretation, and the results may be designated as invalid or of questionable validity.

b. *Computer Administration*

Counselors are responsible for ensuring that administration programs function properly to provide clients with accurate results when a computer or other electronic methods are used for test administration. (See A.12.b.)

c. *Unsupervised Test-Taking*

Counselors do not permit unsupervised or inadequately supervised use of tests or assessments unless the tests or assessments are designed, intended, and validated for self-administration and/or scoring.

d. *Disclosure of Favorable Conditions*

Prior to test administration, conditions that produce most favorable test results are made known to the examinee.

E.8. Diversity in Testing

Counselors are cautious in using assessment techniques, making evaluations, and interpreting the performance of populations not represented in the norm group on which an instrument was standardized. They recognize the effects of age, color, culture, disability, ethnic group, gender, race, religion, sexual orientation, and socioeconomic status on test administration and interpretation and place test results in proper perspective with other relevant factors. (See A.2.a.)

E.9. Test Scoring and Interpretation

a. *Reporting Reservations*

In reporting assessment results, counselors indicate any reservations that exist regarding validity or reliability because of the circumstances of the assessment or the inappropriateness of the norms for the person tested.

b. *Research Instruments*

Counselors exercise caution when interpreting the results of research instruments possessing insufficient technical data to support respondent results. The specific purposes for the use of such instruments are stated explicitly to the examinee.

c. *Testing Services*

Counselors who provide test scoring and test interpretation services to support the assessment process confirm the validity of such interpretations. They accurately describe the purpose, norms, validity, reliability, and applications of the procedures and any special qualifications applicable to their use. The public offering of an automated test interpretations service is considered a professional-to-professional consultation. The formal responsibility of the consultant is to the consultee, but the ultimate and overriding responsibility is to the client.

E.10. Test Security

Counselors maintain the integrity and security of tests and other assessment techniques consistent with legal and contractual obligations. Counselors do not appropriate, reproduce, or modify published tests or parts thereof without acknowledgment and permission from the publisher.

E.11. Obsolete Tests and Outdated Results

Counselors do not use data or test results that are obsolete or outdated for the current purpose. Counselors make every effort to prevent the misuse of obsolete measures and test data by others.

E.12. Test Construction

Counselors use established scientific procedures, relevant standards, and current professional knowledge for test design in the development, publication, and utilization of educational and psychological assessment techniques.

SECTION F: TEACHING, TRAINING, AND SUPERVISION

F.1. Counselor Educators and Trainers

a. *Educators as Teachers and Practitioners*

Counselors who are responsible for developing, implementing, and supervising educational programs are skilled as teachers and practitioners. They are knowledgeable regarding the ethical, legal, and regulatory aspects of the profession, are skilled in applying that knowledge, and make students and supervisees aware of their responsibilities. Counselors conduct counselor education and training programs in an ethical manner and serve as role models for professional behavior. Counselor educators should make an effort to infuse material related to human diversity into all courses and/or workshops that are designed to promote the development of professional counselors.

b. *Relationship Boundaries with Students and Supervisees*

Counselors clearly define and maintain ethical, professional, and social relationship boundaries with their students and supervisees. They are aware of the differential in power that exists and the student's or supervisee's possible incomprehension of that power differential. Counselors explain to students and supervisees the potential for the relationship to become exploitive.

c. *Sexual Relationships*

Counselors do not engage in sexual relationships with students or supervisees and do not subject them to sexual harassment. (See A.6. and C.5.b.)

d. *Contributions to Research*

Counselors give credit to students or supervisees for their contributions to research and scholarly projects. Credit is given through coauthorship, acknowledgment, footnote statement, or other appropriate means, in accordance with such contributions. (See G.4.b. and G.4.c.)

e. *Close Relatives*

Counselors do not accept close relatives as students or supervisees.

f. *Supervision Preparation*

Counselors who offer clinical supervision services are adequately prepared in supervision methods and tech-

niques. Counselors who are doctoral students serving as practicum or internship supervisors to master's level students are adequately prepared and supervised by the training program.

g. *Responsibility for Services to Clients*

Counselors who supervise the counseling services of others take reasonable measures to ensure that counseling services provided to clients are professional.

h. *Endorsement*

Counselors do not endorse students or supervisees for certification, licensure, employment, or completion of an academic or training program if they believe students or supervisees are not qualified for the endorsement. Counselors take reasonable steps to assist students or supervisees who are not qualified for endorsement to become qualified.

F.2. Counselor Education and Training Programs

a. *Orientation*

Prior to admission, counselors orient prospective students to the counselor education or training program's expectations, including but not limited to the following: (1) the type and level of skill acquisition required for successful completion of the training, (2) subject matter to be covered, (3) basis for evaluation, (4) training components that encourage self-growth or self-disclosure as part of the training process, (5) the type of supervision settings and requirements of the sites for required clinical field experiences, (6) student and supervisee evaluation and dismissal policies and procedures, and (7) up-to-date employment prospects for graduates.

b. *Integration of Study and Practice*

Counselors establish counselor education and training programs that integrate academic study and supervised practice.

c. *Evaluation*

Counselors clearly state to students and supervisees, in advance of training, the levels of competency expected, appraisal methods, and timing of evaluations for both didactic and experiential components. Counselors provide students and supervisees with periodic performance appraisal and evaluation feedback throughout the training program.

d. *Teaching Ethics*

Counselors make students and supervisees aware of the ethical responsibilities and standards of the profession and the students' and supervisees' ethical responsibilities to the profession. (See C.1. and F.3.e.)

e. *Peer Relationships*

When students or supervisees are assigned to lead counseling groups or provide clinical supervision for their peers, counselors take steps to ensure that students and supervisees placed in these roles do not have personal or adverse relationships with peers and that they understand they have the same ethical obligations as counselor educators, trainers, and supervisors. Counselors make every effort to ensure that the rights of peers are not compromised when students or supervisees are assigned to lead counseling groups or provide clinical supervision.

f. *Varied Theoretical Positions*

Counselors present varied theoretical positions so that students and supervisees may make comparisons and have opportunities to develop their own positions. Counselors provide information concerning the scientific bases of professional practice. (See C.6.a.)

g. *Field Placements*

Counselors develop clear policies within their training program regarding field placement and other clinical experiences. Counselors provide clearly stated roles and responsibilities for the student or supervisee, the site supervisor, and the program supervisor. They confirm that site supervisors are qualified to provide supervision and are informed of their professional and ethical responsibilities in this role.

h. *Dual Relationships as Supervisors*

Counselors avoid dual relationships such as performing the role of site supervisor and training program supervisor in the student's or supervisee's training program. Counselors do not accept any form of professional services, fees, commissions, reimbursement, or remuneration from a site for student or supervisee placement.

i. *Diversity in Programs*

Counselors are responsive to their institution's and program's recruitment and retention needs for training program administrators, faculty, and students with diverse backgrounds and special needs. (See A.2.a.)

F.3. Students and Supervisees

a. *Limitations*

Counselors, through ongoing evaluation and appraisal, are aware of the academic and personal limitations of stu-

dents and supervisees that might impeded performance. Counselors assist students and supervisees in securing remedial assistance when needed, and dismiss from the training program supervisees who are unable to provide competent service due to academic or personal limitations. Counselors seek professional consultation and document their decision to dismiss or refer students or supervisees for assistance. Counselors assure that students and supervisees have recourse to address decisions made, to require them to seek assistance, or to dismiss them.

b. *Self-Growth Experiences*

Counselors use professional judgment when designing training experiences conducted by the counselors themselves that require student and supervisee self-growth or self-disclosure. Safeguards are provided so that students and supervisees are aware of the ramifications their self-disclosure may have, on counselors whose primary role as teacher, trainer, or supervisor requires acting on ethical obligations to the profession. Evaluative components of experiential training experiences explicitly delineate predetermined academic standards that are separate and not dependent on the student's level of self-disclosure. (See A.6.)

c. *Counseling for Students and Supervisees*

If students or supervisees request counseling, supervisors or counselor educators provide them with acceptable referrals. Supervisors or counselor educators do not serve as counselor to students or supervisees over whom they hold administrative, teaching, or evaluative roles unless this is a brief role associated with a training experience. (See A.6.b.)

d. *Clients of Students and Supervisees*

Counselors make every effort to ensure that the clients at field placements are aware of the services rendered and the qualifications of the students and supervisees rendering those services. Clients receive professional disclosure information and are informed of the limits of confidentiality. Client permission is obtained in order for the students and supervisees to use any information concerning the counseling relationship in the training process. (See B.1.e.)

e. *Standards for Students and Supervisees*

Students and supervisees preparing to become counselors adhere to the Code of Ethics and the Standards of Practice. Students and supervisees have the same obligations to clients as those required of counselors. (See H.1.)

SECTION G: RESEARCH AND PUBLICATION

G.1. Research Responsibilities

a. *Use of Human Subjects*

Counselors plan, design, conduct, and report research in a manner consistent with pertinent ethical principles, federal and state laws, host institutional regulations, and scientific standards governing research with human subjects. Counselors design and conduct research that reflects cultural sensitivity appropriateness.

b. *Deviation from Standard Practices*

Counselors seek consultation and observe stringent safeguards to protect the rights of research participants when a research problem suggests a deviation from standard acceptable practices. (See B.6.)

c. *Precautions to Avoid Injury*

Counselors who conduct research with human subjects are responsible for the subjects' welfare throughout the experiment and take reasonable precautions to avoid causing injurious psychological, physical, or social effects to their subjects.

d. *Principal Researcher Responsibility*

The ultimate responsibility for ethical research practice lies with the principal researcher. All others involved in the research activities share ethical obligations and full responsibility for their own actions.

e. *Minimal Interference*

Counselors take reasonable precautions to avoid causing disruptions in subjects' lives due to participation in research.

f. *Diversity*

Counselors are sensitive to diversity and research issues with special populations. They seek consultation when appropriate. (See A.2.a. and B.6.)

G.2. Informed Consent

a. *Topics Disclosed*

In obtaining informed consent for research, counselors use language that is understandable to research participants and that: (1) accurately explains the purpose and procedures to be followed; (2) identifies any procedures that are experimental or relatively untried; (3) describes the attendant discomforts and risks; (4) describes the benefits or changes in individuals or organizations that might be reasonably expected; (5) discloses appropriate alternative procedures that would be advantageous for subjects; (6) offers to answer any inquiries concerning the procedures; (7) describes any limitations on confidentiality; and (8) instructs that subjects are free to withdraw their consent and to discontinue participation in the project at any time. (See B.1.f.)

b. *Deception*

Counselors do not conduct research involving deception unless alternative procedures are not feasible and the prospective value of the research justifies the deception. When the methodological requirements of a study necessitate concealment or deception, the investigator is required to explain clearly the reasons for this action as soon as possible.

c. *Voluntary Participation*

Participation in research is typically voluntary and without any penalty for refusal to participate. Involuntary participation is appropriate only when it can be demonstrated that participation will have no harmful effects on subjects and is essential to the investigation.

d. *Confidentiality of Information*

Information obtained about research participants during the course of an investigation is confidential. When the possibility exists that others may obtain access to such information, ethical research practice requires that the possibility, together with the plans for protecting confidentiality, be explained to participants as a part of the procedure for obtaining informed consent. (See B.1.e.)

e. *Persons Incapable of Giving Informed Consent*

When a person is incapable of giving informed consent, counselors provide an appropriate explanation, obtain agreement for participation and obtain appropriate consent from a legally authorized person.

f. *Commitments to Participants*

Counselors take reasonable measures to honor all commitments to research participants.

g. *Explanations After Data Collection*

After data are collected, counselors provide participants with full clarification of the nature of the study to remove any misconceptions. Where scientific or human values justify delaying or withholding information, counselors take reasonable measures to avoid causing harm.

h. *Agreements to Cooperate*

Counselors who agree to cooperate with another individual in research or publication incur an obligation to cooperate as promised in terms of punctuality of performance and with regard to the completeness and accuracy of the information required.

i. *Informed Consent for Sponsors*

In the pursuit of research, counselors give sponsors, institutions, and publication channels the same respect and opportunity for giving informed consent that they accord to individual research participants. Counselors are aware of their obligation to future research workers and ensure that host institutions are given feedback information and proper acknowledgment.

G.3. Reporting Results

a. *Information Affecting Outcome*

When reporting research results, counselors explicitly mention all variables and conditions known to the investigator that may have affected the outcome of a study or the interpretation of data.

b. *Accurate Results*

Counselors plan, conduct, and report research accurately and in a manner that minimizes the possibility that results will be misleading. They provide thorough discussions of the limitations of their data and alternative hypotheses. Counselors do not engage in fraudulent research, distort data, misrepresent data, or deliberately bias their results.

c. *Obligation to Report Unfavorable Results*

Counselors communicate to other counselors the results of any research judged to be of professional value. Results that reflect unfavorably on institutions, programs, services, prevailing opinions, or vested interests are not withheld.

d. *Identity of Subjects*

Counselors who supply data, aid in the research of another person, report research results, or make original data available take due care to disguise the identity of respective subjects in the absence of specific authorization from the subjects to do otherwise. (See B.1.g. and B.5.a.)

e. *Replication Studies*

Counselors are obligated to make available sufficient original research data to qualified professionals who may wish to replicate the study.

G.4. Publication

a. *Recognition of Others*

When conducting and reporting research, counselors are familiar with and give recognition to previous work on the topic, observe copyright laws, and give full credit to those to whom credit is due. (See F.1.d. and G.4.c.)

b. *Contributors*

Counselors give credit through joint authorship, acknowledgment, footnote statements, or other appropriate means to those who have contributed significantly to research or concept development in accordance with such contributions. The principal contributor is listed first and minor technical or professional contributions are acknowledged in notes or introductory statements.

c. *Student Research*

For an article that is substantially based on a student's dissertation or thesis, the student is listed as the principal author. (See F.1.d. and G.4.a.)

d. *Duplicate Submission*

Counselors submit manuscripts for consideration to only one journal at a time. Manuscripts that are published in whole or in substantial part in another journal or published work are not submitted for publication without acknowledgment and permission from the previous publication.

e. *Professional Review*

Counselors who review material submitted for publication, research, or other scholarly purposes respect the confidentiality and proprietary rights of those who submitted it.

SECTION H: RESOLVING ETHICAL ISSUES

H.1. Knowledge of Standards

Counselors are familiar with the Code of Ethics and the Standards of Practice and other applicable ethics codes from other professional organizations of which they are member, or from certification and licensure bodies. Lack of knowledge or misunderstanding of an ethical responsibility is not a defense against a charge of unethical conduct. (See F.3.e.)

H.2. Suspected Violations

a. *Ethical Behavior Expected*

Counselors expect professional associates to adhere to Code of Ethics. When counselors possess reasonable cause that raises doubts as to whether a counselor is acting in an ethical manner, they take appropriate action. (See H.2.d. and H.2.e.)

b. *Consultation*

When uncertain as to whether a particular situation or course of action may be in violation of Code of Ethics, counselors consult with other counselors who are knowledgeable about ethics, with colleagues, or with appropriate authorities.

c. *Organization Conflicts*

If the demands of an organization with which counselors are affiliated pose a conflict with Code of Ethics, counselors specify the nature of such conflicts and express to their supervisors or other responsible officials their commitment to Code of Ethics. When possible, counselors work toward change within the organization to allow full adherence to Code of Ethics.

d. *Informal Resolution*

When counselors have reasonable cause to believe that another counselor is violating an ethical standard, they attempt to first resolve the issue informally with the other counselor if feasible, providing that such action does not violate confidentiality rights that may be involved.

e. *Reporting Suspected Violations*

When an informal resolution is not appropriate or feasible, counselors, upon reasonable cause, take action such as reporting the suspected ethical violation to state or national ethics committees, unless this action conflicts with confidentiality rights that cannot be resolved.

f. *Unwarranted Complaints*

Counselors do not initiate, participate in, or encourage the filing of ethics complaints that are unwarranted or intend to harm a counselor rather than to protect clients or the public.

H.3. Cooperation with Ethics Committees

Counselors assist in the process of enforcing Code of Ethics. Counselors cooperate with investigations, proceedings, and requirements of the ACA Ethics Committee or ethics committees of other duly constituted associations or boards having jurisdiction over those charged with a violation. Counselors are familiar with the ACA Policies and Procedures and use it as a reference in assisting the enforcement of the Code of Ethics.

STANDARDS OF PRACTICE

All members of the American Counseling Association (ACA) are required to adhere to the Standards of Practice and the Code of Ethics. The Standards of Practice represent minimal behavioral statements of the Code of Ethics. Members should refer to the applicable section of the Code of Ethics for further interpretation and amplification of the applicable Standard of Practice.

SECTION A: THE COUNSELING RELATIONSHIP

Standard of Practice One (SP-1) Nondiscrimination

Counselors respect diversity and must not discriminate against clients because of age, color, culture, disability, ethnic group, gender, race, religion, sexual orientation, marital status, or socioeconomic status. (See A.2.a.)

Standard of Practice Two (SP-2) Disclosure to Clients

Counselors must adequately inform clients, preferably in writing, regarding the counseling process and counseling relationship at or before the time it begins and throughout the relationship. (See A.3.a.)

Standard of Practice Three (SP-3) Dual Relationships

Counselors must make every effort to avoid dual relationships with clients that could impair their professional judgment or increase the risk of harm to clients. When a dual relationship cannot be avoided, counselors must take appropriate steps to ensure that judgment is not impaired and that no exploitation occurs. (See A.6.a. and A.6.b.)

Standard of Practice Four (SP-4) Sexual Intimacies with Clients

Counselors must not engage in any type of sexual intimacies with current clients and must not engage in sexual intimacies with former clients within a minimum of two years after terminating the counseling relationship. Counselors who engage in such relationship after two years following termination have the responsibility to thoroughly examine and document that such relations did not have an exploitative nature.

Standard of Practice Five (SP-5) Protecting Clients During Group Work

Counselors must take steps to protect clients from physical or psychological trauma resulting from interactions during group work. (See A.9.b.)

Standard of Practice Six (SP-6) Advance Understanding of Fees

Counselors must explain to clients, prior to their entering the counseling relationship, financial arrangements related to professional services. (See A.10. a.–d. and A.11.c.)

Standard of Practice Seven (SP-7) Termination

Counselors must assist in making appropriate arrangements for the continuation of treatment of clients, when necessary, following termination of counseling relationships. (See A.11.a.)

Standard of Practice Eight (SP-8) Inability to Assist Clients

Counselors must avoid entering or immediately terminate a counseling relationship if it is determined that they are unable to be of professional assistance to a client. The counselor may assist in making an appropriate referral for the client. (See A.11.b.)

SECTION B: CONFIDENTIALITY

Standard of Practice Nine (SP-9) Confidentiality Requirement

Counselors must keep information related to counseling services confidential unless disclosure is in the best interest of clients, is required for the welfare of others, or is required by law. When disclosure is required, only information that is essential is revealed and the client is informed of such disclosure. (See B.1.a.–f.)

Standard of Practice Ten (SP-10) Confidentiality Requirements for Subordinates

Counselors must take measures to ensure that privacy and confidentiality of clients are maintained by subordinates. (See B.1.h.)

Standard of Practice Eleven (SP-11) Confidentiality in Group Work

Counselors must clearly communicate to group members that confidentiality cannot be guaranteed in group work. (See B.2.a.)

Standard of Practice Twelve (SP-12) Confidentiality in Family Counseling

Counselors must not disclose information about one family member in counseling to another family member without prior consent. (See B.2.b.)

Standard of Practice Thirteen (SP-13) Confidentiality of Records

Counselors must maintain appropriate confidentiality in creating, storing, accessing, transferring, and disposing of counseling records. (See B.4.b.)

Standard of Practice Fourteen (SP-14) Permission to Record or Observe

Counselors must obtain prior consent from clients in order to electronically record or observe sessions. (See B.4.c.)

Standard of Practice Fifteen (SP-15) Disclosure or Transfer of Records

Counselors must obtain client consent to disclose or transfer records to third parties, unless exceptions listed in SP-9 exist. (See B.4.e.)

Standard of Practice Sixteen (SP-16) Data Disguise Required

Counselors must disguise the identity of the client when using data for training, research, or publication. (See B.5.a.)

SECTION C: PROFESSIONAL RESPONSIBILITY

Standard of Practice Seventeen (SP-17) Boundaries of Competence

Counselors must practice only within the boundaries of their competence. (See C.2.a.)

Standard of Practice Eighteen (SP-18) Continuing Education

Counselors must engage in continuing education to maintain their professional competence. (See C.2.f.)

Standard of Practice Nineteen (SP-19) Impairment of Professionals

Counselors must refrain from offering professional services when their personal problems or conflicts may cause harm to a client or others. (See C.2.g.)

Standard of Practice Twenty (SP-20) Accurate Advertising

Counselors must accurately represent their credentials and services when advertising. (See C.3.a.)

Standard of Practice Twenty-one (SP-21) Recruiting Through Employment

Counselors must not use their place of employment or institutional affiliation to recruit clients for their private practices. (See C.3.d.)

Standard of Practice Twenty-two (SP-22) Credentials Claimed

Counselors must claim or imply only professional credentials possessed and must correct any known misrepresentations of their credentials by others. (See C.4.a.)

Standard of Practice Twenty-three (SP-23) Sexual Harassment

Counselors must not engage in sexual harassment. (See C.5.b.)

Standard of Practice Twenty-four (SP-24) Unjustified Gains

Counselors must not use their professional positions to seek or receive unjustified personal gains, sexual favors, unfair advantage, or unearned goods or services. (See C.5.e.)

Standard of Practice Twenty-five (SP-25) Clients Served by Others

With the consent of the client, counselors must inform other mental health professionals serving the same client that a counseling relationship between the counselor and client exists. (See C.6.c.)

Standard of Practice Twenty-six (SP-26) Negative Employment Conditions

Counselors must alert their employers to institutional policy or conditions that may be potentially disruptive or damaging to the counselor's professional responsibilities, or that may limit their effectiveness or deny clients' rights. (See D.1.c.)

Standard of Practice Twenty-seven (SP-27) Personnel Selection and Assignment

Counselors must select competent staff and must assign responsibilities compatible with staff skills and experiences. (See D.1.h.)

Standard of Practice Twenty-eight (SP-28) Exploitive Relationships with Subordinates

Counselors must not engage in exploitive relationships with individuals over whom they have supervisory, evaluative, or instructional control or authority. (See D.1.k.)

SECTION D: RELATIONSHIP WITH OTHER PROFESSIONALS

Standard of Practice Twenty-nine (SP-29) Accepting Fees from Agency Clients

Counselors must not accept fees or other remuneration for consultation with persons entitled to such services through the counselor's employing agency or institution. (See D.3.a.)

Standard of Practice Thirty (SP-30) Referral Fees

Counselors must not accept referral fees. (See D.3.b.)

SECTION E: EVALUATION, ASSESSMENT, AND INTERPRETATION

Standard of Practice Thirty-one (SP-31) Limits of Competence

Counselors must perform only testing and assessment services for which they are competent. Counselors must not allow the use of psychological assessment techniques by unqualified persons under their supervision. (See E.2.a.)

Standard of Practice Thirty-two (SP-32) Appropriate Use of Assessment Instruments

Counselors must use assessment instruments in the manner for which they were intended. (See E.2.b.)

Standard of Practice Thirty-three (SP-33) Assessment Explanations to Clients

Counselors must provide explanations to clients prior to assessment about the nature and purposes of assessment and the specific uses of results. (See E.3.a.)

Standard of Practice Thirty-four (SP-34) Recipients of Test Results

Counselors must ensure that accurate and appropriate interpretations accompany any release of testing and assessment information. (See E.3.b.)

Standard of Practice Thirty-five (SP-35) Obsolete Tests and Outdated Test Results

Counselors must not base their assessment or intervention decisions or recommendations on data or test results that are obsolete or outdated for the current purpose. (See E.11.)

SECTION F: TEACHING, TRAINING, AND SUPERVISION

Standard of Practice Thirty-six (SP-36) Sexual Relationships with Students or Supervisees

Counselors must not engage in sexual relationships with their students and supervisees. (See F.1.c.)

Standard of Practice Thirty-seven (SP-37) Credit for Contributions to Research

Counselors must give credit to students or supervisees for their contributions to research and scholarly projects. (See F.1.d.)

Standard of Practice Thirty-eight (SP-38) Supervision Preparation

Counselors who offer clinical supervision services must be trained and prepared in supervision methods and techniques. (See F.1.f.)

Standard of Practice Thirty-nine (SP-39) Evaluation Information

Counselors must clearly state to students and supervisees in advance of training, the levels of competency expected, appraisal methods, and timing of evaluations. Counselors must provide students and supervisees with periodic performance appraisal and evaluation feedback throughout the training program. (See F.2.c.)

Standard of Practice Forty (SP-40) Peer Relationships in Training

Counselors must make every effort to ensure that the rights of peers are not violated when students and supervisees are assigned to lead counseling groups or provide clinical supervision. (See F.2.e.)

Standard of Practice Forty-one (SP-41) Limitations of Students and Supervisees

Counselors must assist students and supervisees in securing remedial assistance, when needed, and must dismiss from the training program students and supervisees who are unable to provide competent service due to academic or personal limitations. (See F.3.a.)

Standard of Practice Forty-two (SP-42) Self-Growth Experiences

Counselors who conduct experiences for students or supervisees that include self-growth or self disclosure must inform participants of counselors' ethical obligations to the profession and must not grade participants based on their nonacademic performance. (See F.3.b.)

Standard of Practice Forty-three (SP-43) Standards for Students and Supervisees

Students and supervisees preparing to become counselors must adhere to the Code of Ethics and the Standards of Practice of counselors. (See F.3.e.)

SECTION G: RESEARCH AND PUBLICATION

Standard of Practice Forty-four (SP-44) Precautions to Avoid Injury in Research

Counselors must avoid causing physical, social, or psychological harm or injury to subjects in research. (See G.1.c.)

Standard of Practice Forty-five (SP-45) Confidentiality of Research Information

Counselors must keep confidential information obtained about research participants. (See G.2.d.)

Standard of Practice Forty-six (SP-46) Information Affecting Research Outcome

Counselors must report all variables and conditions known to the investigator that may have affected research data or outcomes. (See G.3.a.)

Standard of Practice Forty-seven (SP-47) Accurate Research Results

Counselors must not distort or misrepresent research data, nor fabricate or intentionally bias research results. (See G.3.b.)

Standard of Practice Forty-eight (SP-48) Publication Contributors

Counselors must give appropriate credit to those who have contributed to research. (See G.4.a. and G.4.b.)

SECTION H: RESOLVING ETHICAL ISSUES

Standard of Practice Forty-nine (SP-49) Ethical Behavior Expected

Counselors must take appropriate action when they possess reasonable cause that raises doubts as to whether counselors or other mental health professionals are acting in an ethical manner. (See H.2.a.)

Standard of Practice Fifty (SP-50) Unwarranted Complaints

Counselors must not initiate, participate in, or encourage the filing of ethics complaints that are unwarranted or intended to harm a mental health professional rather than to protect clients or the public. (See H.2.f.)

Standard of Practice Fifty-one (SP-51) Cooperation with Ethics Committees

Counselors must cooperate with investigations, proceedings, and requirements of the ACA Ethics Committee or ethics committees of other duly constituted associations or boards having jurisdiction over those charged with a violation. (See H.3.)

REFERENCES

The following documents are available to counselors as resources to guide them in their practices. These resources are not a part of the Code of Ethics and the Standards of Practice.

American Association for Counseling and Development/Association for Measurement and Evaluation in Counseling and Development. (1989). The responsibilities of users of standardized tests (revised). Washington, DC: Author.

American Counseling Association. (1988). American Counseling Association Ethical Standards. Alexandria, VA: Author.

American Psychological Association. (1985). Standards for educational and psychological testing (revised). Washington, DC: Author.

American Rehabilitation Counseling Association, Commission on Rehabilitation Counselor Certification, and National Rehabilitation Counseling Association. (1995). Code of professional ethics for rehabilitation counselors. Chicago, IL: Author.

American School Counselor Association. (1992). Ethical standards for school counselors. Alexandria, VA: Author.

Joint Committee on Testing Practices. (1988). Code of fair testing practices in education. Washington, DC: Author.

National Board for Certified Counselors. (1989). National Board for Certified Counselors Code of Ethics. Alexandria, VA: Author.

Prediger, D. J. (Ed.). (1993, March). Multicultural assessment standards. Alexandria, VA: Association for Assessment in Counseling.

POLICIES AND PROCEDURES FOR RESPONDING TO MEMBERS' REQUESTS FOR INTERPRETATIONS OF THE ETHICAL STANDARDS

(Revised by Governing Council, April 1994; Effective July 1, 1994)

Section A: Appropriate Requests

1. ACA members may request that the Committee issue formal interpretations of the ACA Code of Ethics for the purpose of guiding the member's own professional behavior.

2. Requests for interpretations will not be considered in the following situations:

a. The individual requesting the interpretation is not an ACA member, or

b. The request is intended to determine whether the behavior of another mental health professional is unethical. In the event an ACA member believes the behavior of another mental

health professional is unethical, the ACA member should resolve the issue directly with the professional, if possible, and should file an ethical complaint if appropriate.

Section B: Procedures

1. Members must send written requests for interpretations to the Committee at ACA Headquarters.

2. Questions should be submitted in the following format: "Does (counselor behavior) violate Sections ____ or any other sections of the ACA Ethical Standards?" Questions should avoid unique details, be general in nature to the extent possible, and be brief.

3. The Committee staff liaison will revise the question, if necessary, and submit it to the Committee Co-Chair for approval.

4. The question will be sent to Committee members who will be asked to respond individually.

5. The Committee Co-Chair will develop a consensus interpretation on behalf of the Committee.

6. The consensus interpretation will be sent to members of the Committee for final approval.

7. The formal interpretation will be sent to the member who submitted the inquiry.

8. The question and the formal interpretation will be published in the ACA newsletter, but the identity of the member requesting the interpretation will not be disclosed.

POLICIES AND PROCEDURES FOR PROCESSING COMPLAINTS OF ETHICAL VIOLATIONS

Section A: General

1. The American Counseling Association, hereafter referred to as the "Association" or "ACA," is dedicated to enhancing human development throughout the life span and promoting the counseling profession.

2. The Association, in furthering its objectives, administers the Code of Ethics that have been developed and approved by the ACA Governing Council.

3. The purpose of this document is to facilitate the work of the ACA Ethics Committee ("Committee") by specifying the procedures for processing cases of alleged violations of the ACA Code of Ethics, codifying options for sanctioning members, and stating appeals procedures. The intent of the Association is to monitor the professional conduct of its members to promote sound ethical practices. ACA does not, however, warrant the performance of any individual.

Section B: Ethics Committee Members

1. The Ethics Committee is a standing committee of the Association. The Committee consists of six (6) appointed members, including two (2) Co-Chairs whose terms overlap. Two members are appointed annually for three (3) year terms by the President-Elect; appointments are subject to confirmation by the ACA Governing Council. Any vacancy occurring on the Committee will be filled by the President in the same manner, and the person appointed shall serve the unexpired term of the member whose place he or she took. Committee members may be reappointed to not more than one (1) additional consecutive term.

2. One (1) of the Committee Co-Chairs is appointed annually by the President-Elect from among the Committee members who have two (2) years of service remaining and serves as Co-Chair for two (2) years, subject to confirmation by the ACA Governing Council.

Section C: Role and Function

1. The Ethics Committee is responsible for:
   a. Educating the membership as to the Association's Code of Ethics;
   b. Periodically reviewing and recommending changes in the Code of Ethics of the Association as well as the Policies and Procedures for Processing Complaints of Ethical Violations;
   c. Receiving and processing complaints of alleged violations of the Code of Ethics of the Association; and,
   d. Receiving and processing questions.

2. The Committee shall meet in person or by telephone conference a minimum of three (3) times per year for processing complaints.

3. In processing complaints about alleged ethical misconduct, the Committee will compile an objective, factual account of the dispute in question and make the best possible recommendation for the resolution of the case. The Committee, in taking any action, shall do so only for cause, shall only take the degree of disciplinary action that is reasonable, shall utilize these procedures with objectivity and fairness, and in general shall act only to further the interests and objectives of the Association and its membership.

4. Of the six (6) voting members of the Committee, a vote of four (4) is necessary to conduct business. In the event a Co-Chair or any other member of the Committee has a personal interest in the case, he or she shall withdraw from reviewing the case.

5. In the event Committee members recuse themselves from a complaint and insufficient voting members are available to conduct business, the President shall appoint former ACA Committee members to decide the complaint.

Section D: Responsibilities of the Committee

1. The Committee members have an obligation to act in an unbiased manner, to work expeditiously, to safeguard the confidentiality of the Committee's activities, and to follow procedures established to protect the rights of all individuals involved.

Section E: Responsibilities of the Co-Chairs Administering the Complaint

1. In the event that one of the Co-Chairs Administering the Complaint; conflict of interest in a particular case, the other Co-Chair shall administer the complaint. The Co-Chair administering the complaint shall not have a vote in the decision.

2. In addition to the above guidelines for members of the Committee, the Co-Chairs, in conjunction with the Headquarters staff liaison, have the responsibilities of:
   a. Receiving, via ACA Headquarters, complaints that have been certified for membership status of the accused;
   b. Determining whether the alleged behavior(s), if true, would violate ACA's Code of Ethics and whether the Committee should review the complaint under these rules;
   c. Notifying the complainant and the accused member of receipt of the case by certified mail return receipt requested;
   d. Notifying the members of the Committee of the case;
   e. Requesting additional information from complainants, accused members, and others;
   f. Presiding over the meetings of the Committee;
   g. Preparing and sending, by certified mail, communications to the complainant and accused member on the recommendations and decisions of the Committee; and

h. Arranging for legal advice with assistance and financial approval of the ACA Executive Director.

Section F: Jurisdiction

1. The Committee will consider whether individuals have violated the ACA Code of Ethics if those individuals:

  a. Are current members of the American Counseling Association; or

  b. Were ACA members when the alleged violations occurred.

2. Ethics committees of divisions, branches, corporate affiliates, or other ACA entities must refer all ethical complaints involving ACA members to the Committee.

Section G: Eligibility to File Complaints

1. The Committee will receive complaints that ACA members have violated one or more sections of the ACA Code of Ethics from the following individuals:

  a. Members of the general public who have reason to believe that ACA members have violated the ACA Code of Ethics.

  b. ACA members, or members of other helping professions, who have reason to believe that other ACA members have violated the ACA Code of Ethics.

  c. The Co-Chair of the Committee on behalf of the ACA membership when the Co-Chair has reason to believe through information received by the Committee that ACA members have violated the ACA Code of Ethics.

2. If possible, individuals should attempt to resolve complaints directly with accused members before filing ethical complaints.

Section H: Time Lines

1. The time lines set forth in these standards are guidelines only and have been established to provide a reasonable time framework for processing complaints.

2. Complainants or accused members may request extensions of deadlines when appropriate. Extensions of deadlines will be granted by the Committee only when justified by unusual circumstance.

Section I: Nature of Communication

1. Only written communications regarding ethical complaints against members will be acceptable. If telephone inquiries from individuals are received regarding the filing of complaints, responding to complaints, or providing information regarding complaints, the individuals calling will be informed of the written communication requirement and asked to comply.

2. All correspondence related to an ethical complaint must be addressed to the Ethics Committee, ACA Headquarters, 5999 Stevenson Avenue, Alexandria, VA 22304, and must be marked "confidential." This process is necessary to protect the confidentiality of the complainant and the accused member.

Section J: Filing Complaints

1. Only written complaints, signed by complainants, will be considered.

2. Individuals eligible to file complaints will send a letter outlining the nature of the complaint to the Committee at the ACA Headquarters.

3. The ACA staff liaison to the Committee will communicate in writing with complainants. Receipt of complaints and confirmation of membership status of accused members as defined in Section F.1., above, will be acknowledged to the complainant. Proposed formal complaints will be sent to complainants after receipt of complaints have been acknowledged.

4. If the complaint does not involve a member as defined in Section F.1., above, the staff liaison shall inform the complainant.

5. The Committee Co-Chair administering a complaint will determine whether the complaint, if true, would violate one or more sections of the ethical standards or if the complaint could be properly decided if accepted. If not, the complaint will not be accepted and the complainant shall be notified.

6. If the Committee Co-Chair administering the complaint determines that there is insufficient information to make a fair determination of whether the behavior alleged in the complaint would be cause for action by the Committee, the ACA staff liaison to the Committee may request further information from the complainant or others.

7. When complaints are accepted, complainants will be informed that copies of the formal complaints plus evidence and documents submitted in support of the complaint will be provided to the accused member and that the complainant must authorize release of such information to the accused member before the complaint process may proceed.

8. The ACA staff liaison, after receiving approval of the Committee Co-Chair administering a complaint, will formulate a formal complaint which will be presented to the complainants for their signature.

  a. The correspondence from complainants will be received and the staff liaison and Committee Co-Chair administering the complaint will identify all ACA Code of Ethics that might have been violated if the accusations are true.

  b. The formal complaint will be sent to complainants with a copy of these Policies and Procedures, a copy of the ACA Code of Ethics, a verification affidavit form, and an authorization and release of information form. Complainants will be asked to sign and return the completed complaint, verification affidavit, and authorization and release information forms. It will be explained to complainants that sections of the codes that might have been violated may be added or deleted by the complainant before signing the formal statement.

  c. If complainants elect to add or delete sections of the ethical standards in the formal complaint, the unsigned formal complaint shall be returned to ACA Headquarters with changes noted and a revised formal complaint will be sent to the complainants for their signature.

9. When the completed formal complaint, verification affidavit form, and authorization and release of information form are presented to complainants for their signature, they will be asked to submit all evidence and documents they wish to be considered by the Committee in reviewing the complaint.

Section K: Notification of Accused Members

1. Once signed formal complaints have been received, accused members will be sent a copy of the formal complaint and copies of all evidence and documents submitted in support of the complaint.

2. Accused members will be asked to respond to the complaint against them. They will be asked to address each section of the ACA Code of Ethics they have been accused of having violated. They will be informed that if they wish to respond they must do so in writing within sixty (60) working days.

3. Accused members will be informed that they must submit all evidence and documents they wish to be considered by the Committee in reviewing the complaint within sixty (60) working days.

4. After accused members have received notification that a complaint has been brought against them, they will be given sixty (60) working days to notify the Committee Co-Chair (via ACA Headquarters) in writing, by certified mail, if they wish to request a formal face-to-face hearing before the Committee. Accused members may waive their right to a formal hearing before the Committee. (See Section P: Hearings).

5. If the Committee Co-Chair determines that there is insufficient information to make a fair determination of whether the behavior alleged in the complaint would be cause for action by the Committee, the ACA staff liaison to the Committee may request further information from the accused member or others. The accused member shall be given thirty (30) working days from receipt of the request to respond.

6. All requests for additional information from others will be accompanied by a verification affidavit form which the information provider will be asked to complete and return.

7. The Committee may, in its discretion, delay or postpone its review of the case with good cause, including if the Committee wishes to obtain additional information. The accused member may request that the Committee delay or postpone its review of the case for good cause if done so in writing.

Section L: Disposition of Complaints

1. After receiving the responses of accused members, Committee members will be provided copies of: (a) the complaint, (b) supporting evidence and documents sent to accused members, (c) the response, and (d) supporting evidence and documents provided by accused members and others.

2. Decisions will be rendered based on the evidence and documents provided by the complainant and accused member or others.

3. The Committee Co-Chair administering a complaint will not participate in deliberations or decisions regarding that particular complaint.

4. At the next meeting of the Committee held no sooner than fifteen (15) working days after members received copies of documents related to a complaint, the Committee will discuss the complaint, response, and supporting documentation, if any, and determine the outcome of the complaint.

5. The Committee will determine whether each Code of Ethics the member has been accused of having violated was violated based on the information provided.

6. After deliberations, the Committee may decide to dismiss the complaint or to dismiss charges within the complaint.

7. In the event it is determined that any of the ACA Code of Ethics have been violated, the Committee will impose for the entire complaint one or a combination of the possible sanctions allowed.

Section M: Withdrawal of Complaints

1. If the complainant and accused member both agree to discontinue the complaint process, the Committee may, at its discretion, complete the adjudication process if available evidence indicates that this is warranted. The Co-Chair of the Committee, on behalf of the ACA membership, shall act as complainant.

Section N: Possible Sanctions

1. Reprinted remedial requirements may be stipulated by the Committee.

2. Probation for a specified period of time subject to Committee review of compliance. Remedial requirements may be imposed to be completed within a specified period of time.

3. Suspension from ACA membership for a specified period of time subject to Committee review of compliance. Remedial requirements may be imposed to be completed within a specified period of time.

4. Permanent expulsion from ACA membership. This sanction requires a unanimous vote of those voting.

5. The penalty for failing to fulfill in a satisfactory manner a remedial requirement imposed by the Committee as a result of a probation sanction will be automatic suspension until the requirement is met, unless the Committee determines that the remedial requirement should be modified based on good cause shown prior to the end of the probationary period.

6. The penalty for failing to fulfill in a satisfactory manner a remedial requirement imposed by the Committee as a result of a suspension sanction will be automatic permanent expulsion unless the Committee determines that the remedial requirement should be modified based on good cause shown prior to the end of the suspension period.

7. Other corrective action.

Section O: Notification of Results

1. Accused members shall be notified of Committee decisions regarding complaints against them.

2. Complainants will be notified of Committee decisions after the deadline for accused members to file appeals or, in the event an appeal is filed, after a filed appeal decision has been rendered.

3. After complainants are notified of the results of their complaints as provided in Section O., Paragraph 2 above, if a violation has been found and accused members have been suspended or expelled, counselor licensure, certification, or registry boards, other mental health licensure, certification, or registry boards, voluntary national certification boards, and appropriate professional associations will also be notified of the results. In addition, ACA divisions, state branches, the ACA Insurance Trust, and other ACA-related entities will also be notified of the results.

4. After complainants have been notified of the results of their complaint as provided in Section O., Paragraph 2, above, if a violation has been found and accused members have been suspended or expelled, a notice of the Committee action that includes the sections of the ACA ethical standards that were found to have been violated and the sanctions imposed will be published in the ACA newsletter.

Section P: Hearings

1. At the discretion of the Committee, a hearing may be conducted when the results of the Committee's preliminary determination indicate that additional information is needed.

2. When accused members, within sixty (60) working days of notification of the complaint, request a formal face-to-face or telephone conference hearing before the Committee a hearing shall be conducted (See Section K.6.)

3. The accused shall bear all their expenses associated with attendance at hearings requested by the accused.

4. The Committee Co-Chair shall schedule a formal hearing on the case at the next scheduled Committee meeting and notify both the complainant and the accused member of their right to attend the hearing in person or by telephone conference call.

5. The hearing will be held before a panel made up of the Committee and if the accused member chooses, a representative of the accused member's primary Division. This representative will be identified by the Division President and will have voting privileges.

Section Q: Hearing Procedures

1. Purpose.

   a. A hearing will be conducted to determine whether a breach of the ethical standards has occurred and, if so, to determine appropriate disciplinary action.

b. The Committee will be guided in its deliberations by principles of basic fairness and professionalism, and will keep its deliberations as confidential as possible, except as provided herein.

2. Notice.

a. The accused members shall be advised in writing by the Co-Chair administering the complaint of the time and place of the hearing and the charges involved at least forty-five (45) working days before the hearing. Notice shall include a formal statement of the complaints lodged against the accused member and supporting evidence.

b. The accused member is under no duty to respond to the notice, but the Committee will not be obligated to delay or postpone its hearing unless the accused so requests in writing, with good cause reviewed at least fifteen (15) working days in advance. In the absence of such 15 day advance notice and postponement by the Committee, if the accused fails to appear at the hearing, the Committee shall decide the complaint on record. Failure of the accused member to appear at the hearing shall not be viewed by the Committee as sufficient grounds alone for taking disciplinary action.

3. Conduct of the Hearing.

a. Accommodations. The location of the hearing shall be determined at the discretion of the Committee. The Committee shall provide a private room to conduct the hearing and no observers or recording devices other than a recording device used by the Committee shall be permitted.

b. Presiding Officer. The Co-Chair in charge of the case shall preside over the hearing and deliberations of the Committee. At the conclusion of the hearing and deliberations of the Committee, the Co-Chair shall promptly notify the accused member and complainant of the Committee's decision in writing as provided in Section O., Paragraphs 1 and 2, above.

c. Record. A record of the hearing shall be made and preserved, together with any documents presented in evidence, at ACA Headquarters for a period of three (3) years. The record shall consist of a summary of testimony received or a verbatim transcript, at the discretion of the Committee.

d. Right to Counsel. The accused member shall be entitled to have legal counsel present to advise and represent them throughout the hearing. Legal counsel for ACA shall also be present at the hearing to advise the Committee and shall have the privilege of the floor.

e. Witnesses. Either party shall have the right to call witnesses to substantiate his or her version of the case.

f. The Committee shall have the right to call witnesses it believes may provide further insight into the matter. ACA shall, in its sole discretion, determine the number and identity of witnesses to be heard.

g. Witnesses shall not be present during the hearing except when they are called upon to testify and shall be excused upon completion of their testimony and any cross-examination.

h. The Co-Chair administering the complaint shall allow questions to be asked of any witness by the opposition or members of the Committee if such questions and testimony are relevant to the issues in the case.

i. The Co-Chair administering the complaint will determine what questions and testimony are relevant to the case. Should the hearing be disturbed by irrelevant testimony, the Co-Chair administering the complaint may call a brief recess until order can be restored.

j. All expenses associated with counsel on behalf of the parties shall be borne by the respective parties. All expenses associated with witnesses on behalf of the accused shall be borne by the accused when the accused requests a hearing. If the Committee requests the hearing, all expenses associated with witnesses shall be borne by ACA.

4. Presentation of Evidence.

a. The staff liaison, or the Co-Chair administering the complaint shall be called upon first to present the charge(s) made against the accused and to briefly describe the evidence supporting the charge. The person presenting the charges shall also be responsible for examining and cross-examining witnesses on behalf of the complainant and for otherwise presenting the matter during the hearing.

b. The complainant or a member of the Committee shall then be called upon to present the case against the accused. Witnesses who can substantiate the case may be called upon to testify and answer questions of the accused and the Committee.

c. If the accused has exercised the right to be present at the hearing, he or she shall be called upon last to present any evidence which refutes the charges against him or her. This includes witnesses as in Subsection (3) above.

d. The accused will not be found guilty simply for refusing to testify. Once the accused member chooses to testify, however, he or she may be cross-examined by the complainant and members of the Committee.

e. The Committee will endeavor to conclude the hearing within a period of approximately three (3) hours. The parties will be requested to be considerate of this time frame in planning their testimony.

f. Testimony that is merely cumulative or repetitious may, at the discretion of the Co-Chair administering the complaint, be excluded.

5. Relevancy of Evidence.

a. The Hearing Committee is not a court of law and is not required to observe formal rules of evidence. Evidence that would be inadmissible in a court of law may be admissible in the hearing before the Committee, if it is relevant to the case. That is, if the evidence offered tends to explain, clarify, or refute any of the important facts of the case, it should generally be considered.

b. The Committee will not consider evidence or testimony for the purpose of supporting any charge that was not set forth in the notice of the hearing or that is not relevant to the issues of the case.

6. Burden of Proof.

a. The burden of proving a violation of the ethical standards is on the complainant and/or the Committee. It is not up to the accused to prove his or her innocence of any wrong-doing.

b. Although the charge(s) need not be proved "beyond a reasonable doubt," the Committee will not find the accused guilty in the absence of substantial, objective, and believable evidence to sustain the charge(s).

7. Deliberation of the Committee.

a. After the hearing is completed, the Committee shall meet in a closed session to review the evidence presented and reach a conclusion. ACA

legal counsel may attend the closed session to advise the Committee if the Committee so desires.

b. The Committee shall be the sole trier of the facts and shall weigh the evidence presented and assess the credibility of the witnesses. The act of a majority of the members of the Committee present shall be the decision of the Committee. A unanimous vote of those voting is required for permanent expulsion from ACA membership.

c. Only members of the Committee who were present throughout the entire hearing shall be eligible to vote.

8. Decision of the Committee.

a. The Committee will first resolve the issue of the guilt or innocence of the accused on each charge. Applying the burden of proof in Subsection (5), above, the Committee will vote by secret ballot, unless the members of the Committee consent to an oral vote.

b. In the event a majority of the members of the Committee do not find the accused guilty, the charges shall be dismissed. If the Committee finds the accused member has violated the Code of Ethics, it must then determine what sanctions, in accordance with Section N: Possible Sanctions, shall be imposed.

c. As provided in Section O., above, the Co-Chair administering the complaint shall notify the accused member and complainant of the Committee's decision in writing.

Section R: Appeals

1. Decisions of the ACA Ethics Committee that members have violated the ACA Code of Ethics may be appealed by the member found to have been in violation based on one or both of the following grounds:

a. The Committee violated its policies and procedures for processing complaints of ethical violations; and/or

b. The decision of the Committee was arbitrary and capricious and was not supported by the materials provided by the complainant and accused member.

2. After members have received notification that they have been found in violation of one or more ACA Code of Ethics, they will be given thirty (30) working days to notify the Committee in writing by certified mail that they are appealing the decision.

3. An appeal may consist only of a letter stating one or both of the grounds of appeal listed in Subsection (1), above, and the reasons for the appeal.

4. Appealing members will be asked to identify the primary ACA division to which he or she belongs. The ACA President will appoint a three (3) person appeals panel consisting of two (2) former ACA Ethics Committee Chairs and the President of the identified division. The ACA attorney shall serve as legal advisor and have the privilege of the floor.

5. The three (3) member appeals panel will be given copies of the materials available to the Committee when it made its decision, a copy of the hearing transcript if a hearing was held, plus a copy of the letter filed by the appealing member.

6. The appeals panel generally will render its decision regarding an appeal which must receive a majority vote within sixty (60) working days of their receipt of the above materials.

7. The decision of the appeals panel may include one of the following:

   a. The decision of the Committee is upheld.

   b. The decision of the Committee is reversed and remanded with guidance to the Committee for a new decision. The reason for this decision will be given to the Committee in detail in writing.

8. When a Committee decision is reversed and remanded, the complainant and accused member will be informed in writing and additional information may be requested first from the complainant and then from the accused member. The Committee will then render another decision without a hearing.

9. Decisions of the appeals panel to uphold the Committee decision are final.

Section S: Substantial New Evidence

1. In the event substantial new evidence is presented in a case in which an appeal was not filed, or in a case which a final decision has been rendered, the case may be reopened by the Committee.

2. The Committee will consider substantial new evidence and if it is found to be substantiated and capable of exonerating a member who was expelled, the Committee will reopen the case and go through the entire complaint process again.

Section T: Records

1. The records of the Committee regarding complaints are confidential except as provided herein.

2. Original copies of complaint records will be maintained in locked files at ACA Headquarters or at an off-site location chosen by ACA.

3. Members of the Committee will keep copies of complaint records confidential and will destroy copies of records after a case has been closed or when they are no longer a member of the Committee.

Section U: Legal Actions Related to Complaints

1. Complaints and accused members are required to notify the Committee if they learn of any type of legal action (civil or criminal) being filed related to the complaint.

2. In the event any type of legal action is filed regarding an accepted complaint, all actions related to the complaint will be stayed until the legal action has been concluded. The Committee will consult with legal counsel concerning whether the processing of the complaint will be stayed if the legal action does not involve the same complainant and the same facts complained of.

3. If actions on a complaint are stayed, the complainant and accused member will be notified.

4. When actions on a complaint are continued after a legal action has been concluded, the complainant and accused member will be notified.

Appendix C

American Psychological Association

Ethical Principles of Psychologists and Code of Conduct

CONTENTS

INTRODUCTION

PREAMBLE

GENERAL PRINCIPLES

Principle A: Competence
Principle B: Integrity
Principle C: Professional and Scientific Responsibility
Principle D: Respect for People's Rights and Dignity
Principle E: Concern for Others' Welfare
Principle F: Social Responsibility

ETHICAL STANDARDS

SOURCE: From American Psychological Association (1992), *Ethical Principles of Psychologists and Code of Conduct.* Copyright © 1992 by the American Psychological Association. Reprinted by permission.

INTRODUCTION

The American Psychological Association's (APA's) Ethical Principles of Psychologists and Code of Conduct (hereinafter referred to as the Ethics Code) consists of an Introduction, a Preamble, six General Principles (A–F), and specific Ethical Standards. The Introduction discusses the intent, organization, procedural considerations, and scope of application of the Ethics Code. The Preamble and General Principles are *aspirational* goals to guide psychologists toward the highest ideals of psychology. Although the Preamble and General Principles are not themselves enforceable rules, they should be considered by psychologists in arriving at an ethical course of action and may be considered by ethics bodies in interpreting the Ethical Standards. The Ethical Standards set forth *enforceable* rules for conduct as psychologists. Most of the Ethical Standards are written broadly, in order to apply to psychologists in varied roles, although the application of an Ethical Standard may vary depending on the context. The Ethical Standards are not exhaustive. The fact that a given conduct is not specifically addressed by the Ethics Code does not mean that it is necessarily either ethical or unethical.

Membership in the APA commits members to adhere to the APA Ethics Code and to the rules and procedures used to implement it. Psychologists and students, whether or not they are APA members, should be aware that the Ethics Code may be applied to them by state psychology boards, courts, or other public bodies.

The Ethics Code applies only to psychologists' work-related activities, that is, activities that are part of the psychologists' scientific and professional functions or

---

This version of the APA Ethics Code was adopted by the American Psychological Association's Council of Representatives during its meeting, August 13 and 16, 1992, and is effective beginning December 1, 1992. Inquiries concerning the substance or interpretation of the APA Ethics Code should be addressed to the Director, Office of Ethics, American Psychological Association, 750 First Street, NE, Washington, DC 20002-4242.

This Code will be used to adjudicate complaints brought concerning alleged conduct occurring on or after the effective date. Complaints regarding conduct occurring prior to the effective date will be adjudicated on the basis of the version of the Code that was in effect at the time the conduct occurred, except that no provisions repealed in June 1989, will be enforced even if an earlier version contains the provision. The Ethics Code will undergo continuing review and study for future revisions; comments on the Code may be sent to the above address.

The APA has previously published its Ethical Standards as follows:

American Psychological Association. (1953). *Ethical standards of psychologists*. Washington, DC: Author.
American Psychological Association. (1958). Standards of ethical behavior for psychologists. *American Psychologist, 13*, 268–271.
American Psychological Association. (1963). Ethical standards of psychologists. *American Psychologist, 18*, 56–60.
American Psychological Association. (1968). Ethical standards of psychologists. *American Psychologist, 23*, 357–361.
American Psychological Association. (1977, March). Ethical standards of psychologists. *APA Monitor*, pp. 22–23.
American Psychological Association. (1979). *Ethical standards of psychologists*. Washington, DC. Author.
American Psychological Association. (1981). Ethical principles of psychologists. *American Psychologist, 36*, 633–638.
American Psychological Association. (1990). Ethical principles of psychologists (amended June 2, 1989). *American Psychologist, 45*, 390–395.

NOTE: Request copies of the APA's Ethical Principles of Psychologists and Code of Conduct from the APA Order Department, 750 First Street, NE, Washington, DC 20002-4242, or phone (202) 336-5510.

---

that are psychological in nature. It includes the clinical or counseling practice of psychology, research, teaching, supervision of trainees, development of assessment instruments, conducting assessments, educational counseling, organizational consulting, social intervention, administration, and other activities as well. These work-related activities can be distinguished from the purely private conduct of a psychologist, which ordinarily is not within the purview of the Ethics Code.

The Ethics Code is intended to provide standards of professional conduct that can be applied by the APA and by other bodies that choose to adopt them. Whether or not a psychologist has violated the Ethics Code does not by itself determine whether he or she is legally liable in a court action, whether a contract is enforceable, or whether other legal consequences occur. These results are based on legal rather than ethical rules. However, compliance with or violation of the Ethics Code may be admissible as evidence in some legal proceedings, depending on the circumstances.

In the process of making decisions regarding their professional behavior, psychologists must consider this Ethics Code, in addition to applicable laws and psychology board regulations. If the Ethics Code establishes a higher standard of conduct than is required by law, psychologists must meet the higher ethical standard. If the Ethics Code standard appears to conflict with the requirements of law, then psychologists make known their commitment to the Ethics Code and take steps to resolve the conflict in a responsible manner. If neither law nor the Ethics Code resolves an issue, psychologists should consider other professional materials[1] and the

---

[1]Professional materials that are most helpful in this regard are guidelines and standards that have been adopted or endorsed by professional psychological organizations. Such guidelines and standards, whether adopted by the American Psychological Association (APA) or its Divisions, are not enforceable as such by this Ethics Code, but are of educative value to psychologists, courts, and professional bodies. Such materials include, but are not limited to, the APA's *General Guidelines for Providers of Psychological Services* (1987), *Specialty Guidelines for the Delivery of Services for Clinical Psychologists, Counseling Psychologists, Industrial/Organizational Psychologists, and School Psychologists* (1981), *Guidelines for Computer Based Tests and Interpretations* (1987), *Standards for Educational and Psychological Testing* (1985), *Ethical Principles in the Conduct of Research with Human Participants* (1982), *Guidelines for Ethical Conduct in the Care and Use of Animals* (1986), *Guidelines for Providers of Psychological Services to Ethnic, Linguistic, and Culturally Diverse Populations* (1990), and *Publication Manual of the American Psychological Association* (3rd ed., 1983). Materials not adopted by APA as a whole include the APA Division 41 (Forensic Psychology)/American Psychology—Law Society's *Specialty Guidelines for Forensic Psychologists* (1991).

dictates of their own conscience, as well as seek consultation with others within the field when this is practical.

The procedures for filing, investigating, and resolving complaints of unethical conduct are described in the current Rules and Procedures of the APA Ethics Committee. The actions that APA may take for violations of the Ethics Code include actions such as reprimand, censure, termination of APA membership, and referral of the matter to other bodies. Complainants who seek remedies such as monetary damages in alleging ethical violations by a psychologist must resort to private negotiation, administrative bodies, or the courts. Actions that violate the Ethics Code may lead to the imposition of sanctions on a psychologist by bodies other than APA, including state psychological associations, other professional groups, psychology boards, other state or federal agencies, and payors for health services. In addition to actions for violation of the Ethics Code, the APA Bylaws provide that APA may take action against a member after his or her conviction of a felony, expulsion or suspension from an affiliated state psychological association, or suspension or loss of licensure.

PREAMBLE

Psychologists work to develop a valid and reliable body of scientific knowledge based on research. They may apply that knowledge to human behavior in a variety of contexts. In doing so, they perform many roles, such as researcher, educator, diagnostician, therapist, supervisor, consultant, administrator, social interventionist, and expert witness. Their goal is to broaden knowledge of behavior and, where appropriate, to apply it pragmatically to improve the condition of both the individual and society. Psychologists respect the central importance of freedom of inquiry and expression in research, teaching, and publication. They also strive to help the public in developing informed judgments and choices concerning human behavior. This Ethics Code provides a common set of values upon which psychologists build their professional and scientific work.

The Code is intended to provide both the general principles and the decision rules to cover most situations encountered by psychologists. It has as its primary goal the welfare and protection of the individuals and groups with whom psychologists work. It is the individual responsibility of each psychologist to aspire to the highest possible standards of conduct. Psychologists respect and protect human and civil rights, and do not knowingly participate in or condone unfair discriminatory practices.

The development of a dynamic set of ethical standards for a psychologist's work-related conduct requires a personal commitment to a lifelong effort to act ethically; to encourage ethical behavior by students, supervisees, employees, and colleagues, as appropriate; and to consult with others, as needed, concerning ethical problems. Each psychologist supplements, but does not violate, the Ethics Code's values and rules on the basis of guidance drawn from personal values, culture, and experience.

GENERAL PRINCIPLES

Principle A: Competence

Psychologists strive to maintain high standards of competence in their work. They recognize the boundaries of their particular competencies and the limitations of their expertise. They provide only those services and use only those techniques for which they are qualified by education, training, or experience. Psychologists are cognizant of the fact that the competencies required in serving, teaching, and/or studying groups of people vary with the distinctive characteristics of those groups. In those areas in which recognized professional standards do not yet exist, psychologists exercise careful judgment and take appropriate precautions to protect the welfare of those with whom they work. They maintain knowledge of relevant scientific and professional information related to the services they render, and they recognize the need for ongoing education. Psychologists make appropriate use of scientific, professional, technical, and administrative resources.

Principle B: Integrity

Psychologists seek to promote integrity in the science, teaching, and practice of psychology. In these activities psychologists are honest, fair, and respectful of others. In describing or reporting their qualifications, services, products, fees, research, or teaching, they do not make statements that are false, misleading, or deceptive. Psychologists strive to be aware of their own belief systems, values, needs, and limitations and the effect of these on their work. To the extent feasible, they attempt to clarify for relevant parties the roles they are performing and to function appropriately in accordance with those roles. Psychologists avoid improper and potentially harmful dual relationships.

Principle C: Professional and Scientific Responsibility

Psychologists uphold professional standards of conduct, clarify their professional roles and obligations, accept appropriate responsibility for their behavior, and adapt their methods to the needs of different populations.

Psychologists consult with, refer to, or cooperate with the other professionals and institutions to the extent needed to serve the best interests of their patients, clients, or other recipients of their services. Psychologists' moral standards and conduct are personal matters to the same degree as is true for any other person, except as psychologists' conduct may compromise their professional responsibilities or reduce the public's trust in psychology and psychologists. Psychologists are concerned about the ethical compliance of their colleagues' scientific and professional conduct. When appropriate, they consult with colleagues in order to prevent or avoid unethical conduct.

Principle D: Respect for People's Rights and Dignity

Psychologists accord appropriate respect to the fundamental rights, dignity, and worth of all people. They respect the rights of individuals to privacy, confidentiality, self-determination, and autonomy, mindful that legal and other obligations may lead to inconsistency and conflict with the exercise of these rights. Psychologists are aware of cultural, individual, and role differences, including those due to age, gender, race ethnicity, national origin, religion, sexual orientation, disability, language, and socioeconomic status. Psychologists try to eliminate the effect on their work of biases based on those factors, and they do not knowingly participate in or condone unfair discriminatory practices.

Principle E: Concern for Others' Welfare

Psychologists seek to contribute to the welfare of those with whom they interact professionally. In their professional actions, psychologists weigh the welfare and rights of their patients or clients, students, supervisees, human research participants, and other affected persons, and the welfare of animal subjects of research. When conflicts occur among psychologists' obligations or concerns, they attempt to resolve these conflicts and to perform their roles in a responsible fashion that avoids or minimizes harm. Psychologists are sensitive to real and ascribed differences in power between themselves and others, and they do not exploit or mislead other people during or after professional relationships.

Principle F: Social Responsibility

Psychologists are aware of their professional and scientific responsibilities to the community and the society in which they work and live. They apply and make public their knowledge of psychology in order to contribute to human welfare. Psychologists are concerned about and work to mitigate the causes of human suffering. When undertaking research, they strive to advance human welfare and the science of psychology. Psychologists try to avoid misuse of their work. Psychologists comply with the law and encourage the development of law and social policy that serve the interests of their patients and clients and the public. They are encouraged to contribute a portion of their professional time for little or no personal advantage.

ETHICAL STANDARDS

1. *General Standards*

These General Standards are potentially applicable to the professional and scientific activities of all psychologists.

1.01 Applicability of the Ethics Code

The activity of a psychologist subject to the Ethics Code may be reviewed under these Ethical Standards only if the activity is part of his or her work-related functions or the activity is psychological in nature. Personal activities having no connection to or effect on psychological roles are not subject to the Ethics Code.

1.02 Relationship of Ethics and Law

If psychologists' ethical responsibilities conflict with law, psychologists make known their commitment to the Ethics Code and take steps to resolve the conflict in a responsible manner.

1.03 Professional and Scientific Relationship

Psychologists provide diagnostic, therapeutic, teaching, research, supervisory, consultative, or other psychological services only in the context of a defined professional or scientific relationship or role. (See also Standards 2.01, Evaluation, Diagnosis, and Interventions in Professional Context, and 7.02, Forensic Assessments.)

1.04 Boundaries of Competence

(a) Psychologists provide services, teach, and conduct research only within the boundaries of their competence, based on their education, training, supervised experience, or appropriate professional experience.

(b) Psychologists provide services, teach, or conduct research in new areas or involving new techniques only after first undertaking appropriate study, training, supervision, and/or consultation from persons who are competent in those areas or techniques.

(c) In those emerging areas in which generally recognized standards for preparatory training do not yet exist, psychologists nevertheless take reasonable steps to ensure the competence of their work and to protect patients, clients, students, research participants, and others from harm.

1.05 Maintaining Expertise

Psychologists who engage in assessment, therapy, teaching, research, organizational consulting, or other professional activities maintain a reasonable level of awareness of current scientific and professional information in their fields of activity, and undertake ongoing efforts to maintain competence in the skills they use.

1.06 Basis for Scientific and Professional Judgments

Psychologists rely on scientifically and professionally derived knowledge when making scientific or professional judgments or when engaging in scholarly or professional endeavors.

1.07 Describing the Nature and Results of Psychological Services

(a) When psychologists provide assessment, evaluation, treatment, counseling, supervision, teaching, consultation, research, or other psychological services to an individual, a group, or an organization, they provide, using language that is reasonably understandable to the recipient of those services, appropriate information beforehand about the nature of such services and appropriate information later about results and conclusions. (See also Standard 2.09, Explaining Assessment Results.)

(b) If psychologists will be precluded by law or by organizational roles from providing such information to particular individuals or groups, they so inform those individuals or groups at the outset of the service.

1.08 Human Differences

Where differences of age, gender, race, ethnicity, national origin, religion, sexual orientation, disability, language, or socioeconomic status significantly affect psychologists' work concerning particular individuals or groups, psychologists obtain the training, experience, consultation, or supervision necessary to ensure the competence of their services, or they make appropriate referrals.

1.09 Respecting Others

In their work-related activities, psychologists respect the rights of others to hold values, attitudes, and opinions that differ from their own.

1.10 Nondiscrimination

In their work-related activities, psychologists do not engage in unfair discrimination based on age, gender, race, ethnicity, national origin, religion, sexual orientation, disability, socioeconomic status, or any basis proscribed by law.

1.11 Sexual Harassment

(a) Psychologists do not engage in sexual harassment. Sexual harassment is sexual solicitation, physical advances, or verbal or nonverbal conduct that is sexual in nature, that occurs in connection with the psychologist's activities or roles as a psychologist, and that either: (1) is unwelcome, is offensive, or creates a hostile workplace environment, and the psychologist knows or is told this; or (2) is sufficiently severe or intense as to be abusive to a reasonable person in the context. Sexual harassment can consist of a single intense or severe act or of multiple persistent or pervasive acts.

(b) Psychologists accord sexual-harassment complainants and respondents dignity and respect. Psychologists do not participate in denying a person admittance or advancement, employment, tenure, or promotion, based solely upon their having made, or their being the subject of, sexual harassment charges. This does not preclude taking action based upon the outcome of such proceedings or consideration of other appropriate information.

1.12 Other Harassment

Psychologists do not knowingly engage in behavior that is harassing or demeaning to persons with whom they interact in their work based on factors such as those persons' age, gender, race, ethnicity, national origin, religion, sexual orientation, disability, language, or socioeconomic status.

1.13 Personal Problems and Conflicts

(a) Psychologists recognize that their personal problems and conflicts may interfere with their effectiveness. Accordingly, they refrain from undertaking an activity when they know or should know that their personal problems are likely to lead to harm to a patient, client, colleague, student, research participant, or other person to whom they may owe a professional or scientific obligation.

(b) In addition, psychologists have an obligation to be alert to signs of, and to obtain assistance for, their personal problems at an early stage, in order to prevent significantly impaired performance.

(c) When psychologists become aware of personal problems that may interfere with their performing work-related duties adequately, they take appropriate measures, such as obtaining professional consultation or assistance, and determine whether they should limit, suspend, or terminate their work-related duties.

1.14 Avoiding Harm

Psychologists take reasonable steps to avoid harming their patients or clients, research participants, students, and others with whom they work, and to minimize harm where it is foreseeable and unavoidable.

1.15 Misuse of Psychologists' Influence

Because psychologists' scientific and professional judgments and actions may affect the lives of others, they are alert to and guard against personal, financial, social, organizational, or political factors that might lead to misuse of their influence.

1.16 Misuse of Psychologists' Work

(a) Psychologists do not participate in activities in which it appears likely that their skills or data will be misused by others, unless corrective mechanisms are available. (See also Standard 7.04, Truthfulness and Candor.)

(b) If psychologists learn of misuse or misrepresentation of their work, they take reasonable steps to correct or minimize the misuse or misrepresentation.

1.17 Multiple Relationships

(a) In many communities and situations, it may not be feasible or reasonable for psychologists to avoid social or other nonprofessional contacts with persons such as patients, clients, students, supervisees, or research participants. Psychologists must always be sensitive to the potential harmful effects of other contacts on their work and on those persons with whom they deal. A psychologist refrains from entering into or promising another personal, scientific, professional, financial, or other relationship with such persons if it appears likely that such a relationship reasonably might impair the psychologist's objectivity or otherwise interfere with the psychologist's effectively performing his or her functions as a psychologist, or might harm or exploit the other party.

(b) Likewise, whenever feasible, a psychologist refrains from taking on professional or scientific obligations when preexisting relationships would create a risk of such harm.

(c) If a psychologist finds that, due to unforeseen factors, a potentially harmful multiple relationship has arisen, the psychologist attempts to resolve it with due regard for the best interests of the affected person and maximal compliance with the Ethics Code.

1.18 Barter (with Patients or Clients)

Psychologists ordinarily refrain from accepting goods, services, or other nonmonetary remuneration from patients or clients in return for psychological services because such arrangements create inherent potential for conflicts, exploitation, and distortion of the professional relationship. A psychologist may participate in bartering *only* if (1) it is not clinically contraindicated, *and* (2) the relationship is not exploitative. (See also Standards 1.17, Multiple Relationships, and 1.25, Fees and Financial Arrangements.)

1.19 Exploitative Relationships

(a) Psychologists do not exploit persons over whom they have supervisory, evaluative, or other authority such as students, supervisors, employees, research participants, and clients or patients. (See also Standards 4.05–4.07 regarding sexual involvement with clients or patients.)

(b) Psychologists do not engage in sexual relationships with students or supervisees in training over whom the psychologist has evaluative or direct authority, because such relationships are so likely to impair judgment or be exploitative.

1.20 Consultations and Referrals

(a) Psychologists arrange for appropriate consultations and referrals based principally on the best interests of their patients or clients, with appropriate consent, and subject to other relevant considerations, including applicable law and contractual obligations. (See also Standards 5.01, Discussing the Limits of Confidentiality, and 5.06, Consultations.)

(b) When indicated and professionally appropriate, psychologists cooperate with other professionals in order to serve their patients or clients effectively and appropriately.

(c) Psychologists' referral practices are consistent with law.

1.21 Third-Party Requests for Services

(a) When a psychologist agrees to provide services to a person or entity at the request of a third party, the psychologist clarifies to the extent feasible, at the outset of the service, the nature of the relationship with each party. This clarification includes the role of the psychologist (such as therapist, organizational consultant, diagnostician, or expert witness), the probable uses of the services provided or the information obtained, and the fact that there may be limits to confidentiality.

(b) If there is a foreseeable risk of the psychologist's being called upon to perform conflicting roles because of the involvement of a third party, the psychologist clarifies the nature and direction of his or her responsibilities, keeps all parties appropriately informed as matters develop, and resolves the situation in accordance with this Ethics Code.

1.22 Delegation to and Supervision of Subordinates

(a) Psychologists delegate to their employees, supervisees, and research assistants only those responsibilities that such persons can reasonably be expected to perform competently, on the basis of their education, training, or experience, either independently or with the level of supervision being provided.

(b) Psychologists provide proper training and supervision to their employees or supervisees and take reasonable steps to see that such persons perform services responsibly, competently, and ethically.

(c) If institutional policies, procedures, or practices prevent fulfillment of this obligation, psychologists attempt to modify their role or to correct the situation to the extent feasible.

1.23 Documentation of Professional and Scientific Work

(a) Psychologists appropriately document their professional and scientific work in order to facilitate provision of services later by them or by other professionals, to ensure accountability, and to meet other requirements of institutions or the law.

(b) When psychologists have reason to believe that records of their professional services will be used in legal proceedings involving recipients of or participants in their work, they have a responsibility to create and maintain documentation in the kind of detail and quality that would be consistent with reasonable scrutiny in an adjudicative forum. (See also Standard 7.01, Professionalism, under Forensic Activities.)

1.24 Records and Data

Psychologists create, maintain, disseminate, store, retain, and dispose of records and data relating to their research, practice, and other work in accordance with law and in a manner that permits compliance with the requirements of this Ethics Code. (See also Standard 5.04, Maintenance of Records.)

1.25 Fees and Financial Arrangements

(a) As early as is feasible in a professional or scientific relationship, the psychologist and the patient, client, or other appropriate recipient of psychological services reach an agreement specifying the compensation and the billing arrangements.

(b) Psychologists do not exploit recipients of services or payors with respect to fees.

(c) Psychologists' fee practices are consistent with law.

(d) Psychologists do not misrepresent their fees.

(e) If limitations to services can be anticipated because of limitations in financing, this is discussed with the patient, client, or other appropriate recipient of services as early as is feasible. (See also Standard 4.08, Interruption of Services.)

(f) If the patient, client, or other recipient of services does not pay for services as agreed, and if the psychologist wishes to use collection agencies or legal measures to collect the fees, the psychologist first informs the person that such measures will be taken and provides that person an opportunity to make prompt payment. (See also Standard 5.11, Withholding Records for Nonpayment.)

1.26 Accuracy in Reports to Payors and Funding Sources

In their reports to payors for services or sources of research funding, psychologists accurately state the nature of the research or service provided, the fees or charges, and where applicable, the identity of the provider, the findings, and the diagnosis. (See also Standard 5.05, Disclosures.)

1.27 Referrals and Fees

When a psychologist pays, receives payment from, or divides fees with another professional other than in an employer-employee relationship, the payment to each is based on the services (clinical, consultative, administrative, or other) provided and is not based on the referral itself.

2. *Evaluation, Assessment, or Intervention*

2.01 Evaluation, Diagnosis, and Interventions in Professional Context

(a) Psychologists perform evaluations, diagnostic services, or interventions only within the context of a defined professional relationship. (See also Standard 1.03, Professional and Scientific Relationship.)

(b) Psychologists' assessments, recommendations, reports, and psychological diagnostic or evaluative statements are based on information and techniques (including personal interviews of the individual when appropriate) sufficient to provide appropriate substantiation for their findings. (See also Standard 7.02, Forensic Assessments.)

2.02 Competence and Appropriate Use of Assessments and Interventions

(a) Psychologists who develop, administer, score, interpret, or use psychological assessment techniques, interviews, tests, or instruments do so in a manner and for purposes that are appropriate in light of the research on or evidence of the usefulness and proper application of the techniques.

(b) Psychologists refrain from misuse of assessment techniques, interventions, results, and interpretations and take reasonable steps to prevent others from misusing the information these techniques provide. This includes refraining from releasing raw test results or raw data to persons, other than to patients or clients as appropriate, who are not qualified to use such information. (See also Standards 1.02, Relationship of Ethics and Law, and 1.04, Boundaries of Competence.)

2.03 Test Construction

Psychologists who develop and conduct research with tests and other assessment techniques use scientific procedures and current professional knowledge for test design, standardization, validation, reduction or elimination of bias, and recommendations for use.

2.04 Use of Assessment in General and with Special Populations

(a) Psychologists who perform interventions or administer, score, interpret, or use assessment techniques are familiar with the reliability, validation, and related standardization or outcome studies of, and proper applications and uses of, the techniques they use.

(b) Psychologists recognize limits to the certainty with which diagnoses, judgments, or predictions can be made about individuals.

(c) Psychologists attempt to identify situations in which particular interventions or assessment techniques or norms may not be applicable or may require adjustment in administration or interpretation because of factors such as individuals' gender, age, race, ethnicity, national origin, religion, sexual orientation, disability, language, or socioeconomic status.

2.05 Interpreting Assessment Results

When interpreting assessment results, including automated interpretations, psychologists take into account the various test factors and characteristics of the person being assessed that might affect psychologists' judgments or reduce the accuracy of their interpretations. They indicate any significant reservations they have about the accuracy or limitations of their interpretations.

2.06 Unqualified Persons

Psychologists do not promote the use of psychological assessment techniques by unqualified persons. (See also Standard 1.22, Delegation to and Supervision of Subordinates.)

2.07 Obsolete Tests and Outdated Test Results

(a) Psychologists do not base their assessment or intervention decisions or recommendations on data or test results that are outdated for the current purpose.

(b) Similarly, psychologists do not base such decisions or recommendations on tests and measures that are obsolete and not useful for the current purpose.

2.08 Test Scoring and Interpretation Services

(a) Psychologists who offer assessment or scoring procedures to other professionals accurately describe the purpose, norms, validity, reliability, and applications of the procedures and any special qualifications applicable to their use.

(b) Psychologists select scoring and interpretation services (including automated services) on the basis of evidence of the validity of the program and procedures as well as on other appropriate considerations.

(c) Psychologists retain appropriate responsibility for the appropriate application, interpretation, and use of assessment instruments, whether they score and interpret such tests themselves or use automated or other services.

2.09 Explaining Assessment Results

Unless the nature of the relationship is clearly explained to the person being assessed in advance and precludes provision of an explanation of results (such as in some organizational consulting, preemployment or security screenings, and forensic evaluations), psychologists ensure that an explanation of the results is provided using language that is reasonably understandable to the person assessed or to another legally authorized person on behalf of the client. Regardless of whether the scoring and interpretation are done by the psychologist, by assistants, or by automated or other outside services, psychologists take reasonable steps to ensure that appropriate explanations of results are given.

2.10 Maintaining Test Security

Psychologists make reasonable efforts to maintain the integrity and security of tests and other assessment techniques consistent with law, contractual obligations, and in a manner that permits compliance with the requirements of this Ethics Code. (See also Standard 1.02, Relationship of Ethics and Law.)

3. *Advertising and Other Public Statements*

3.01 Definition of Public Statements

Psychologists comply with this Ethics Code in public statements relating to their professional services, products, or publications or to the field of psychology. Public statements include but are not limited to paid or unpaid advertising, brochures, printed matter, directory listings, personal resumes or curricula vitae, interviews or comments for use in media, statements in legal proceedings, lectures and public oral presentations, and published materials.

3.02 Statements by Others

(a) Psychologists who engage others to create or place public statements that promote their professional practice, products, or activities retain professional responsibility for such statements.

(b) In addition, psychologists make reasonable efforts to prevent others whom they do not control (such as employers, publishers, sponsors, organizational clients, and representatives of the print or broadcast media) from making deceptive statements concerning psychologists' practice or professional or scientific activities.

(c) If psychologists learn of deceptive statements about their work made by others, psychologists make reasonable efforts to correct such statements.

(d) Psychologists do not compensate employees of press, radio, television, or other communication media in return for publicity in a news item.

(e) A paid advertisement relating to the psychologist's activities must be identified as such, unless it is already apparent from the context.

3.03 Avoidance of False or Deceptive Statements

(a) Psychologists do not make public statements that are false, deceptive, misleading, or fraudulent, either because of what they state, convey, or suggest or because of what they omit, concerning their research, practice, or other work activities or those of persons or organizations with which they are affiliated. As examples (and not in limitation) of this standard, psychologists do not make false or deceptive statements concerning (1) their training, experience, or competence; (2) their academic degrees; (3) their credentials; (4) their institutional or association affiliations; (5) their services; (6) the scientific or clinical basis for, or results or degree of success of their services; (7) their fees; or (8) their publications or research findings. (See also Standards 6.15, Deception in Research, and 6.18, Providing Participants with Information about the Study.)

(b) Psychologists claim as credentials for their psychological work, only degrees that (1) were earned from a regionally accredited educational institution or (2) were the basis for psychology licensure by the state in which they practice.

3.04 Media Presentations

When psychologists provide advice or comment by means of public lectures, demonstrations, radio or television programs, prerecorded tapes, printed articles, mailed material, or other media, they take reasonable precautions to ensure that (1) the statements are based on appropriate psychological literature and practice, (2) the statements are otherwise consistent with this Ethics Code, and (3) the recipients of the information are not encouraged to infer that a relationship has been established with them personally.

3.05 Testimonials

Psychologists do not solicit testimonials from current psychotherapy clients or patients or other persons who because of their particular circumstances are vulnerable to undue influence.

3.06 In-Person Solicitation

Psychologists do not engage, directly or through agents, in uninvited in-person solicitation of business from actual or potential psychotherapy patients or clients or other persons who because of their particular circumstances are vulnerable to undue influence. However, this does not preclude attempting to implement appropriate collateral contacts with significant others for the purpose of benefiting an already engaged therapy patient.

4. *Therapy*

4.01 Structuring the Relationship

(a) Psychologists discuss with clients or patients as early as is feasible in the therapeutic relationship appropriate issues, such as the nature and anticipated course of therapy, fees, and confidentiality. (See also Standards 1.25, Fees and Financial Arrangements, and 5.01, Discussing the Limits of Confidentiality.)

(b) When the psychologist's work with clients or patients will be supervised, the above discussion includes that fact, and the name of the supervisor, when the supervisor has legal responsibility for the case.

(c) When the therapist is a student intern, the client or patient is informed of that fact.

(d) Psychologists make reasonable efforts to answer patients' questions and to avoid apparent misunderstandings about therapy. Whenever possible, psychologists provide oral and/or written information, using language that is reasonably understandable to the patient or client.

4.02 Informed Consent to Therapy

(a) Psychologists obtain appropriate informed consent to therapy or related procedures, using language that is reasonably understandable to participants. The content of informed consent will vary depending on many circumstances; however, informed consent generally implies that the person (1) has the capacity to consent, (2) has been informed of significant information concerning the procedure, (3) has freely and without undue influence expressed consent, and (4) consent has been appropriately documented.

(b) When persons are legally incapable of giving informed consent, psychologists obtain informed permission from a legally authorized person, if such substitute consent is permitted by law.

(c) In addition, psychologists (1) inform those persons who are legally incapable of giving informed consent about the proposed interventions in a manner commensurate with the persons' psychological capacities, (2) seek their assent to those interventions, and (3) consider such persons' preferences and best interests.

4.03 Couple and Family Relationships

(a) When a psychologist agrees to provide services to several persons who have a relationship (such as husband and wife or parents and children), the psychologist attempts to clarify at the outset (1) which of the individuals are patients or clients and (2) the relationship the psychologist will have with each person. This clarification includes the role of the psychologist and the probable uses of the services provided or the information obtained. (See also Standard 5.01, Discussing the Limits of Confidentiality.)

(b) As soon as it becomes apparent that the psychologist may be called on to perform potentially conflicting roles (such as marital counselor to husband and wife, and then witness for one party in a divorce proceeding), the psychologist attempts to clarify and adjust, or withdraw from roles, appropriately. (See also Standard 7.03, Clarification of Role, under Forensic Activities.)

4.04 Providing Mental Health Services to Those Served by Others

In deciding whether to offer or provide services to those already receiving mental health services elsewhere, psychologists carefully consider the treatment issues and the potential patient's or client's welfare. The psychologist discusses these issues with the patient or client, or another legally authorized person on behalf of the client, in order to minimize the risk of confusion and conflict, consults with the service providers when appropriate, and proceeds with caution and sensitivity to the therapeutic issues.

4.05 Sexual Intimacies with Current Patients or Clients

Psychologists do not engage in sexual intimacies with current patients or clients.

4.06 Therapy with Former Sexual Partners

Psychologists do not accept as therapy patients or clients persons with whom they have engaged in sexual intimacies.

4.07 Sexual Intimacies with Former Therapy Patients

(a) Psychologists do not engage in sexual intimacies with a former therapy patient or client for at least two years after cessation or termination of professional services.

(b) Because sexual intimacies with a former therapy patient or client are so frequently harmful to the patient or client, and because such intimacies undermine public confidence in the psychology profession and thereby deter the public's use of needed services, psychologists do not engage in sexual intimacies with former therapy patients and clients even after a two-year interval except in the most unusual circumstances. The psychologist who engages in such activity after the two years following cessation or termination of treatment bears the burden of demonstrating that there has been no exploitation, in light of all relevant factors, including (1) the amount of time that has passed since therapy terminated, (2) the nature and duration of the therapy, (3) the circumstances of termination, (4) the patient's or client's personal history, (5) the patient's or client's current mental status, (6) the likelihood of adverse impact on the patient or client or others, and (7) any statements or actions made by the therapist during the course of therapy suggesting or inviting the possibility of a posttermination sexual or romantic relationship with the patient or client. (See also Standard 1.17, Multiple Relationships.)

4.08 Interruption of Services

(a) Psychologists make reasonable efforts to plan for facilitating care in the event that psychological services are interrupted by factors such as the psychologist's illness, death, unavailability, or relocation or by the client's relocation or financial limitations. (See also Standard 5.09, Preserving Records and Data.)

(b) When entering into employment or contractual relationships, psychologists provide for orderly and appropriate resolution of responsibility for patient or client care in the event that the employment or contractual relationship ends, with paramount consideration given to the welfare of the patient or client.

4.09 Terminating the Professional Relationship

(a) Psychologists do not abandon patients or clients. (See also Standard 1.25e, under Fees and Financial Arrangements.)

(b) Psychologists terminate a professional relationship when it becomes reasonably clear that the patient or client no longer needs the service, is not benefiting, or is being harmed by continued service.

(c) Prior to termination for whatever reason, except where precluded by the patient's or client's conduct, the psychologist discusses the patient's or client's views and needs, provides appropriate pretermination counseling, suggests alternative service providers as appropriate, and takes other reasonable steps to facilitate transfer of responsibility to another provider if the patient or client needs one immediately.

5. *Privacy and Confidentiality*

These Standards are potentially applicable to the professional and scientific activities of all psychologists.

5.01 Discussing the Limits of Confidentiality

(a) Psychologists discuss with persons and organizations with whom they establish a scientific or professional relationship (including, to the extent feasible, minors and their legal representatives) (1) the relevant limitations on confidentiality, including limitations where applicable in group, marital, and family therapy or in organizational consulting, and (2) the foreseeable uses of the information generated through their services.

(b) Unless it is not feasible or is contraindicated, the discussion of confidentiality occurs at the outset of the relationship and thereafter as new circumstances may warrant.

(c) Permission for electronic recording of interviews is secured from clients and patients.

5.02 Maintaining Confidentiality

Psychologists have a primary obligation and take reasonable precautions to respect the confidentiality rights of those with whom they work or consult, recognizing that confidentiality may be established by law, institutional rules, or professional or scientific relationships. (See also Standard 6.26, Professional Reviewers.)

5.03 Minimizing Intrusions on Privacy

(a) In order to minimize intrusions on privacy, psychologists include in written and oral reports, consultations, and the like, only information germane to the purpose for which the communication is made.

(b) Psychologists discuss confidential information obtained in clinical or consulting relationships, or evaluative data concerning patients, individual or organizational clients, students, research participants, supervisees, and employees, only for appropriate scientific or professional purposes and only with persons clearly concerned with such matters.

5.04 Maintenance of Records

Psychologists maintain appropriate confidentiality in creating, storing, accessing, transferring, and disposing of records under their control, whether these are written, automated, or in any other medium. Psychologists maintain and dispose of records in accordance with law and in a manner that permits compliance with the requirements of this Ethics Code.

5.05 Disclosures

(a) Psychologists disclose confidential information without the consent of the individual only as mandated by law, or where permitted by law for a valid purpose, such as (1) to provide needed professional services to the patient or the individual or organizational client, (2) to obtain appropriate professional consultations, (3) to protect the patient or client or others from harm, or (4) to obtain payment for services, in which instance disclosure is limited to the minimum that is necessary to achieve the purpose.

(b) Psychologists also may disclose confidential information with the appropriate consent of the patient or the individual or organizational client (or of another legally authorized person on behalf of the patient or client), unless prohibited by law.

5.06 Consultations

When consulting with colleagues, (1) psychologists do not share confidential information that reasonably could lead to the identification of a patient, client, research participant, or other person or organization with whom they have a confidential relationship unless they have obtained the prior consent of the person or organization or the disclosure cannot be avoided, and (2) they share information only to the extent necessary to achieve the purposes of the consultation. (See also Standard 5.02, Maintaining Confidentiality.)

5.07 Confidential Information in Databases

(a) If confidential information concerning recipients of psychological services is to be entered into databases or systems of records available to persons whose access has not been consented to by the recipient, then psychologists use coding or other techniques to avoid the inclusion of personal identifiers.

(b) If a research protocol approved by an institutional review board or similar body requires the inclusion of personal identifiers, such identifiers are deleted before the information is made accessible to persons other than those of whom the subject was advised.

(c) If such deletion is not feasible, then before psychologists transfer such data to others or review such data collected by others, they take reasonable steps to determine that appropriate consent of personally identifiable individuals has been obtained.

5.08 Use of Confidential Information for Didactic or Other Purposes

(a) Psychologists do not disclose in their writings, lectures, or other public media, confidential, personally identifiable information concerning their patients, individual or organizational clients, students, research participants, or other recipients of their services that they obtained during the course of their work, unless the person or organization has consented in writing or unless there is other ethical or legal authorization for doing so.

(b) Ordinarily, in such scientific and professional presentations, psychologists disguise confidential information concerning such persons or organizations so that they are not individually identifiable to others and so that discussions do not cause harm to subjects who might identify themselves.

5.09 Preserving Records and Data

A psychologist makes plans in advance so that confidentiality of records and data is protected in the event of the psychologist's death, incapacity, or withdrawal from the position or practice.

5.10 Ownership of Records and Data

Recognizing that ownership of records and data is governed by legal principles, psychologists take reasonable

and lawful steps so that records and data remain available to the extent needed to serve the best interests of patients, individual or organizational clients, research participants, or appropriate others.

5.11 Withholding Records for Nonpayment

Psychologists may not withhold records under their control that are requested and imminently needed for a patient's or client's treatment solely because payment has not been received, except as otherwise provided by law.

6. *Teaching, Training Supervision, Research, and Publishing*

6.01 Design of Education and Training Programs

Psychologists who are responsible for education and training programs seek to ensure that the programs are competently designed, provide the proper experiences, and meet the requirements for licensure, certification, or other goals for which claims are made by the program.

6.02 Descriptions of Education and Training Programs

(a) Psychologists responsible for education and training programs seek to ensure that there is a current and accurate description of the program content, training goals and objectives, and requirements that must be met for satisfactory completion of the program. This information must be made readily available to all interested parties.

(b) Psychologists seek to ensure that statements concerning their course outlines are accurate and not misleading, particularly regarding the subject matter to be covered, bases for evaluating progress, and the nature of course experiences. (See also Standard 3.03, Avoidance of False or Deceptive Statements.)

(c) To the degree to which they exercise control, psychologists responsible for announcements, catalogs, brochures, or advertisements describing workshops, seminars, or other non-degree-granting educational programs ensure that they accurately describe the audience for which the program is intended, the educational objectives, the presenters, and the fees involved.

6.03 Accuracy and Objectivity in Teaching

(a) When engaged in teaching or training, psychologists present psychological information accurately and with a reasonable degree of objectivity.

(b) When engaged in teaching or training, psychologists recognize the power they hold over students or supervisees and therefore make reasonable efforts to avoid engaging in conduct that is personally demeaning to students or supervisees. (See also Standards 1.09, Respecting Others, and 1.12, Other Harassment.)

6.04 Limitation on Teaching

Psychologists do not teach the use of techniques or procedures that require specialized training, licensure, or expertise, including but not limited to hypnosis, biofeedback, and projective techniques, to individuals who lack the prerequisite training, legal scope of practice, or expertise.

6.05 Assessing Student and Supervisee Performance

(a) In academic and supervisory relationships, psychologists establish an appropriate process for providing feedback to students and supervisees.

(b) Psychologists evaluate students and supervisees on the basis of their actual performance on relevant and established program requirements.

6.06 Planning Research

(a) Psychologists design, conduct, and report research in accordance with recognized standards of scientific competence and ethical research.

(b) Psychologists plan their research so as to minimize the possibility that results will be misleading.

(c) In planning research, psychologists consider its ethical acceptability under the Ethics Code. If an ethical issue is unclear, psychologists seek to resolve the issue through consultation with institutional review boards, animal care and use committees, peer consultations, or other proper mechanisms.

(d) Psychologists take reasonable steps to implement appropriate protections for the rights and welfare of human participants, other persons affected by the research, and the welfare of animal subjects.

6.07 Responsibility

(a) Psychologists conduct research competently and with due concern for the dignity and welfare of the participants.

(b) Psychologists are responsible for the ethical conduct of research conducted by them or by others under their supervision or control.

(c) Researchers and assistants are permitted to perform only those tasks for which they are appropriately trained and prepared.

(d) As part of the process of development and implementation of research projects, psychologists consult those with expertise concerning any special population under investigation or most likely to be affected.

6.08 Compliance with Law and Standards

Psychologists plan and conduct research in a manner consistent with federal and state law and regulations, as well as professional standards governing the conduct of research, and particularly those standards governing research with human participants and animal subjects.

6.09 Institutional Approval

Psychologists obtain from host institutions or organizations appropriate approval prior to conducting research, and they provide accurate information about their research proposals. They conduct the research in accordance with the approved research protocol.

6.10 Research Responsibilities

Prior to conducting research (except research involving only anonymous surveys, naturalistic observations, or similar research), psychologists enter into an agreement with participants that clarifies the nature of the research and the responsibilities of each party.

6.11 Informed Consent to Research

(a) Psychologists use language that is reasonably understandable to research participants in obtaining their appropriate informed consent (except as provided in Standard 6.12, Dispensing with Informed Consent). Such informed consent is appropriately documented.

(b) Using language that is reasonably understandable to participants, psychologists inform participants of the nature of the research; they inform participants that they are free to participate or to decline to participate or to withdraw from the research; they explain the foreseeable consequences of declining or withdrawing; they inform participants of significant factors that may be expected to influence their willingness to participate (such as risks, discomfort, adverse effects, or limitations on confidentiality, except as provided in Standard 6.15, Deception in Research); and they explain other aspects about which the prospective participants inquire.

(c) When psychologists conduct research with individuals such as students or subordinates, psychologists take special care to protect the prospective participants from adverse consequences of declining or withdrawing from participation.

(d) When research participation is a course requirement or opportunity for extra credit, the prospective participant is given the choice of equitable alternative activities.

(e) For persons who are legally incapable of giving informed consent, psychologists nevertheless (1) provide an appropriate explanation, (2) obtain the participant's assent, and (3) obtain appropriate permission from a legally authorized person, if such substitute consent is permitted by law.

6.12 Dispensing with Informed Consent

Before determining that planned research (such as research involving only anonymous questionnaires, naturalistic observations, or certain kinds of archival research) does not require the informed consent of research participants, psychologists consider applicable regulations and institutional review board requirements, and they consult with colleagues as appropriate.

6.13 Informed Consent in Research Filming or Recording

Psychologists obtain informed consent from research participants prior to filming or recording them in any form, unless the research involves simply naturalistic observations in public places and it is not anticipated that the recording will be used in a manner that could cause personal identification or harm.

6.14 Offering Inducements for Research Participants

(a) In offering professional services as an inducement to obtain research participants, psychologists make clear the nature of the services, as well as the risks, obligations, and limitations. (See also Standard 1.18, Barter [with Patients or Clients].)

(b) Psychologists do not offer excessive or inappropriate financial or other inducements to obtain research participants, particularly when it might tend to coerce participation.

6.15 Deception in Research

(a) Psychologists do not conduct a study involving deception unless they have determined that the use of deceptive techniques is justified by the study's prospective scientific, educational, or applied value and that equally effective alternative procedures that do not use deception are not feasible.

(b) Psychologists never deceive research participants about significant aspects that would affect their willingness to participate, such as physical risks, discomfort, or unpleasant emotional experiences.

(c) Any other deception that is an integral feature of the design and conduct of an experiment must be explained to participants as early as is feasible, preferably at the conclusion of their participation, but no later than at the conclusion of the research. (See also Standard 6.18, Providing Participants with Information about the Study.)

6.16 Sharing and Utilizing Data

Psychologists inform research participants of their anticipated sharing or further use of personally identifiable research data and of the possibility of unanticipated future uses.

6.17 Minimizing Invasiveness

In conducting research, psychologists interfere with the participants or milieu from which data are collected only in a manner that is warranted by an appropriate research design and that is consistent with psychologists' roles as scientific investigators.

6.18 Providing Participants with Information about the Study

(a) Psychologists provide a prompt opportunity for participants to obtain appropriate information about the nature, results, and conclusions of the research, and psychologists attempt to correct any misconceptions that participants may have.

(b) If scientific or humane values justify delaying or withholding this information, psychologists take reasonable measures to reduce the risk of harm.

6.19 Honoring Commitments

Psychologists take reasonable measures to honor all commitments they have made to research participants.

6.20 Care and Use of Animals in Research

(a) Psychologists who conduct research involving animals treat them humanely.

(b) Psychologists acquire, care for, use, and dispose of animals in compliance with current federal, state, and local laws and regulations, and with professional standards.

(c) Psychologists trained in research methods and experienced in the care of laboratory animals supervise all procedures involving animals and are responsible for ensuring appropriate consideration of their comfort, health, and humane treatment.

(d) Psychologists ensure that all individuals using animals under their supervision have received instruction in research methods and in the care, maintenance, and handling of the species being used, to the extent appropriate to their role.

(e) Responsibilities and activities of individuals assisting in a research project are consistent with their respective competencies.

(f) Psychologists make reasonable efforts to minimize the discomfort, infection, illness, and pain of animal subjects.

(g) A procedure subjecting animals to pain, stress, or privation is used only when an alternative procedure is unavailable and the goal is justified by its prospective scientific, education, or applied value.

(h) Surgical procedures are performed under appropriate anesthesia; techniques to avoid infection and minimize pain are followed during and after surgery.

(i) When it is appropriate that the animal's life be terminated, it is done rapidly, with an effort to minimize pain, and in accordance with accepted procedures.

6.21 Reporting of Results

(a) Psychologists do not fabricate data or falsify results in their publications.

(b) If psychologists discover significant errors in their published data, they take reasonable steps to correct such errors in a correction, retraction, erratum, or other appropriate publication means.

6.22 Plagiarism

Psychologists do not present substantial portions or elements of another's work or data as their own, even if the other work or data source is cited occasionally.

6.23 Publication Credit

(a) Psychologists take responsibility and credit, including authorship credit, only for work they have actually performed or to which they have contributed.

(b) Principal authorship and other publication credits accurately reflect the relative scientific or professional contributions of the individuals involved, regardless of their relative status. Mere possession of an institutional position, such as Department Chair, does not justify authorship credit. Minor contributions to the research or to the writing for publications are appropriately acknowledged, such as in footnotes or in an introductory statement.

(c) A student is usually listed as principal author on any multiple-authored article that is substantially based on the student's dissertation or thesis.

6.24 Duplicate Publication of Data

Psychologists do not publish, as original data, data that have been previously published. This does not preclude republishing data when they are accompanied by proper acknowledgment.

6.25 Sharing Data

After research results are published, psychologists do not withhold the data on which their conclusions are based from other competent professionals who seek to verify the substantive claims through reanalysis and who intend to use such data only for that purpose, provided that the confidentiality of the participants can be protected and unless legal rights concerning proprietary data preclude their release.

6.26 Professional Reviewers

Psychologists who review material submitted for publication, grant, or other research proposal review respect the confidentiality of and the proprietary rights in such information of those who submitted it.

7. *Forensic Activities*

7.01 Professionalism

Psychologists who perform forensic functions, such as assessments, interviews, consultations, reports, or expert testimony, must comply with all other provisions of this Ethics Code to the extent that they apply to such activities. In addition, psychologists base their forensic work on appropriate knowledge of and competence in the areas underlying such work, including specialized knowledge concerning special populations. (See also Standards 1.06, Basis for Scientific and Professional Judgments; 1.08, Human Differences; 1.15, Misuse of Psychologists' Influence; and 1.23, Documentation of Professional and Scientific Work.)

7.02 Forensic Assessments

(a) Psychologists' forensic assessments, recommendations, and reports are based on information and techniques (including personal interviews of the individual, when appropriate) sufficient to provide appropriate substantiation for their findings. (See also Standards 1.03, Professional and Scientific Relationship; 1.23, Documentation of Professional and Scientific Work; 2.01, Evaluation, Diagnosis, and Interventions in Professional Context; and 2.05, Interpreting Assessment Results.)

(b) Except as noted in (c), below, psychologists provide written or oral forensic reports or testimony of the psychological characteristics of an individual only after they have conducted an examination of the individual adequate to support their statements or conclusions.

(c) When, despite reasonable efforts, such an examination is not feasible, psychologists clarify the impact of their limited information on the reliability and validity of their reports and testimony, and they appropriately limit the nature and extent of their conclusions or recommendations.

7.03 Clarification of Role

In most circumstances, psychologists avoid performing multiple and potentially conflicting roles in forensic matters. When psychologists may be called on to serve in more than one role in a legal proceeding—for example, as consultant or expert for one party or for the court and as a fact witness—they clarify role expectations and the extent of confidentiality in advance to the extent feasible, and thereafter as changes occur, in order to avoid compromising their professional judgment and objectivity and in order to avoid misleading others regarding their role.

7.04 Truthfulness and Candor

(a) In forensic testimony and reports, psychologists testify truthfully, honestly, and candidly and, consistent with applicable legal procedures, describe fairly the bases for their testimony and conclusions.

(b) Whenever necessary to avoid misleading, psychologists acknowledge the limits of their data or conclusions.

7.05 Prior Relationships

A prior professional relationship with a party does not preclude psychologists from testifying as fact witnesses or from testifying to their services to the extent permitted by applicable law. Psychologists appropriately take into account ways in which the prior relationship might affect their professional objectivity or opinions and disclose the potential conflict to the relevant parties.

7.06 Compliance with Law and Rules

In performing forensic roles, psychologists are reasonably familiar with the rules governing their roles. Psychologists are aware of the occasionally competing demands placed upon them by these principles and the requirements of the court system, and attempt to resolve these conflicts by making known their commitment to this Ethics Code and taking steps to resolve the conflict in a responsible manner. (See also Standard 1.02, Relationship of Ethics and Law.)

8. *Resolving Ethical Issues*

8.01 Familiarity with Ethics Code

Psychologists have an obligation to be familiar with this Ethics Code, other applicable ethics codes, and their application to psychologists' work. Lack of awareness or misunderstanding of an ethical standard is not itself a defense to a charge of unethical conduct.

8.02 Confronting Ethical Issues

When a psychologist is uncertain whether a particular situation or course of action would violate this Ethics Code, the psychologist ordinarily consults with other psychologists knowledgeable about ethical issues, with state or national psychology ethics committees, or with other appropriate authorities in order to choose a proper response.

8.03 Conflicts Between Ethics and Organizational Demands

If the demands of an organization with which psychologists are affiliated conflict with this Ethics Code, psychologists clarify the nature of the conflict, make known their commitment to the Ethics Code, and to the extent feasible, seek to resolve the conflict in a way that permits the fullest adherence to the Ethics Code.

8.04 Informal Resolution of Ethical Violations

When psychologists believe that there may have been an ethical violation by another psychologist, they attempt to resolve the issue by bringing it to the attention of that individual if an informal resolution appears appropriate and the intervention does not violate any confidentiality rights that may be involved.

8.05 Reporting Ethical Violations

If an apparent ethical violation is not appropriate for informal resolution under Standard 8.04 or is not resolved properly in that fashion, psychologists take further action appropriate to the situation, unless such action conflicts with confidentiality rights in ways that cannot be resolved. Such action might include referral to state or national committees on professional ethics or to state licensing boards.

8.06 Cooperating with Ethics Committees

Psychologists cooperate in ethics investigations, proceedings, and resulting requirements of the APA or any affiliated state psychological association to which they belong. In doing so, they make reasonable efforts to resolve any issues as to confidentiality. Failure to cooperate is itself an ethics violation.

8.07 Improper Complaints

Psychologists do not file or encourage the filing of ethics complaints that are frivolous and are intended to harm the respondent rather than to protect the public.

Appendix D

Public Law 93-380

Protection of the Rights and Privacy of Parents and Students—Family Educational Rights and Privacy Act of 1974

Sec. 513.(a) Part C of the General Education Provisions Act is further amended by adding at the end thereof the following new section:

PROTECTION OF THE RIGHTS AND PRIVACY OF PARENTS AND STUDENTS

Sec. 438.(a)(1) No funds shall be made available under any applicable program to any State or local educational agency, any institution of higher education, any community college, any school, any agency offering a preschool program, or any other educational institution which has a policy of denying, or which effectively prevents, the parents of students attending any school of such agency, or attending such institution of higher education, community college, school, preschool, or other educational institution, the right to inspect and review any and all official records, files, and data directly related to their children, including all material that is incorporated into each student's cumulative record folder, and intended for school use or to be available to parties outside the school or school system, and specifically including, but not necessarily limited to, identifying data, academic work completed, level

of achievement (grades, standardized achievement test scores), attendance data, scores on standardized intelligence, aptitude, and psychological tests, interest inventory results, health data, family background information, teacher or counselor ratings of serious or recurrent behavior patterns. Where such records or data include information on more than one student, the parents of any student shall be entitled to receive, or be informed of, that part of such record or data as pertains to their child. Each recipient shall establish appropriate procedures for the granting of a request by parents for access to their child's school records within a reasonable period of time, but in no case more than forty-five days after the request has been made.

(2) Parents shall have an opportunity for a hearing to challenge the content of their child's school records, to insure that the records are not inaccurate, misleading, or otherwise in violation of the privacy or other rights of students, and to provide an opportunity for the correction or deletion of any such inaccurate, misleading, or otherwise inappropriate data contained therein.

(b)(1) No funds shall be made available under any applicable program to any State or local educational agency, any institution of higher education, any community college, any school, any agency offering a preschool program, or any other educational institution which has a policy of permitting the release of personally identifiable records or files (or personal information contained therein) of students without the written consent of their parents to any individual, agency, or organization, other than to the following—

(A) other school officials, including teachers within the educational institution or local educational agency who have legitimate educational interests;

(B) officials of other schools or school systems in which the student intends to enroll, upon condition that the student's parents be notified of the transfer, receive a copy of the record if desired, and have an opportunity for a hearing to challenge the content of the record;

(C) authorized representatives of (i) the Comptroller General of the United States, (ii) the Secretary, (iii) an administrative head of an educational agency (as defined in section 409 of this Act), or (iv) State educational authorities, under the conditions set forth in paragraph (3) of this subsection; and

(D) in connection with a student's application for, or receipt of, financial aid.

(2) No funds shall be made available under any applicable program to any State or local educational agency, any institution of higher education, any community college, any school, agency offering a preschool program, or any other educational institution which has a policy of practice of furnishing, in any form, any personally identifiable information contained in personal school records, to any persons other than those listed in subsection (b)(1) unless—

(A) there is written consent from the student's parents specifying records to be released, the reasons for such release, and to whom, and with a copy of the records to be released to the student's parents and the student if desired by the parents, or

(B) such information is furnished in compliance with judicial order, or pursuant to any lawfully issued subpoena, upon condition that parents and the student are notified of all such orders or subpoenas in advance of the compliance therewith by the educational institution or agency.

(3) Nothing contained in this section shall preclude authorized representatives of (A) the Comptroller General of the United States, (B) the Secretary, (C) an administrative head of an educational agency or (D) State educational authorities from having access to student or other records which may be necessary in connection with the audit and evaluation of Federally-supported education programs, or in connection with the enforcement of the Federal legal requirements which relate to such programs: *Provided* that, except when collection of personally identifiable data is specifically authorized by Federal law, any data collected by such officials with respect to individual students shall not include information (including social security numbers) which would permit the personal identification of such students or their parents after the data so obtained has been collected.

(4)(A) With respect to subsections (c)(1) and (c)(2) and (c)(3), all persons, agencies, or organizations desiring access to the records of a student shall be required to sign a written form which shall be kept permanently with the file of the student, but only for inspection by the parents or student, indicating specifically the legitimate educational or other interest that each person, agency, or organization has in seeking this information. Such form shall be available to parents and to the school official responsible for record maintenance as a means of auditing the operation of the system.

(B) With respect to this subsection, personal information shall only be transferred to a third party on the condition that such party will not permit any other party to have access to such information without the written consent of the parents of the student.

(c) The Secretary shall adopt appropriate regulations to protect the rights of privacy of students and their families in connection with any surveys or data-gathering activities conducted, assisted, or authorized by the Secretary or an administrative head of an education agency. Regulations established under this subsection shall include provisions controlling the use, dissemination, and protection of such data. No survey or data-gathering activities shall be conducted by the Secretary, or an administrative head of an education agency under an applicable program, unless such activities are authorized by law.

(d) For the purpose of this section, whenever a student has attained eighteen years of age, or is attending an institution of postsecondary education the permission or consent required of and the rights accorded to the parents of the student shall thereafter be required of and accorded to the student.

(e) No funds shall be made available under any applicable program unless the recipient of such funds informs the parents of students, or the students, if they are eighteen years of age or older, or are attending an institution of postsecondary education, of the rights accorded them by this section.

(f) The Secretary, or an administrative head of an education agency, shall take appropriate actions to enforce provisions of this section and to deal with violations of this section, according to the provisions of this Act, except that action to terminate assistance may be taken only if the Secretary finds that there has been a failure to comply with the provisions of this section, and he has determined that compliance cannot be secured by voluntary means.

(g) The secretary shall establish or designate an office and review board within the Department of Health, Education, and Welfare for the purpose of investigating, processing, reviewing, and adjusting violations of the provisions of this section and complaints which may be filed concerning alleged violations of this section, according to the procedures contained in sections 434 and 437 of this Act.

(b)(1)(i) The provisions of this section shall become effective ninety days after the date of enactment of section 438 of the General Education Provisions Act.

(2)(i) This section may be cited as the "Family Educational Rights and Privacy Act of 1974."

PROTECTION OF PUPIL RIGHTS

Sec. 514.(a) Part C of the General Education Provisions Act is further amended by adding after section 438 the following new section:

Protection of Pupil Rights

Sec. 439.(a) All instructional material, including teacher's manuals, films, tapes, or other supplementary instructional material which will be used in connection with any research or experimentation program or project shall be available for inspection by the parents or guardians of the children engaged in such program or project. For the purpose of this section "research or experimentation program or project" means any program or project in any applicable program designed to explore or develop new or unproven teaching methods or techniques.

(b) The amendment made by subsection (a) shall be effective upon enactment of this Act.

Appendix

American School Counselor Association
The School Counselor and Comprehensive School Counseling Programs

THE POSITION STATEMENT OF THE AMERICAN SCHOOL COUNSELOR ASSOCIATION (ASCA)

ASCA endorses comprehensive school counseling programs that promote and enhance student learning. The focus of the program is on the three broad and interrelated areas of student development: academic, career, and personal/social development. Each encompasses a variety of desired student learning competencies, which form the foundation of the developmental school counseling program. The school counselor uses a variety of activities and resources to promote the desired student development. School counselor responsibilities include organization, implementation, and coordination of the program.

THE RATIONALE

A comprehensive school counseling program is developmental in nature. It is systematic, sequential, clearly defined, and accountable. The foundation of the program is developmental psychology, educational philosophy, and counseling methodology. Proactive and preventative in focus, the school counseling program is integral to the educational program. It assists students in acquiring and using life-long skills through the development of acade-

SOURCE: From American School Counselor Association (1997), *The School Counselor and Comprehensive School Counseling Programs*. Position Statement. American School Counselor Association. Reprinted by permission.

mic, career, self-awareness, and interpersonal communication skills. The goal of the comprehensive school counseling program is to provide all students with life success skills.

The school counseling program has characteristics similar to other educational programs, including a scope and sequence; student competencies or outcomes; activities and processes to assist students in achieving the outcomes; professionally credentialed personnel; materials and resources; and national standards for evaluation.

We recognize that our educational system is being challenged by the increasing needs of today's students and the rising expectations of society. Many of our children enter school with emotional, physical, and interpersonal barriers to learning. Although comprehensive school counseling programs include necessary crisis-oriented responsive services, the emphasis is on the developmental skill building for all students beginning when students enter school and continuing as they progress through the grades.

Effective school counseling programs are a collaborative effort between the counselor and other educators to create an environment which promotes school success. Staff and counselors value and respond to the diversity and individual differences in our society and communities. Comprehensive school counseling programs help ensure equal opportunities for all students to participate fully in the educational process.

This school counseling model is compatible with the *National Education Goals* and the *National Standards for School Counseling Programs*.

THE COUNSELOR'S ROLE

Within a comprehensive school counseling program, counselors will focus their skills, time, and energy on direct service to students, staff, and families. ASCA recommends a realistic counselor-student ratio to be 1:250. School counselors will spend 70% of their time in direct service to students. Indirect services will include counseling program planning, maintenance and evaluation, participation in school site planning and implementation, partnerships and alliances with postsecondary institutions, businesses, and community agencies, and other tasks which enhance the mission of the program.

The comprehensive school counseling program balances many components. It requires counselors to deliver individual and small group counseling and large group guidance; to teach skill development in academic, career, and personal/social areas; to provide consultation and case management; and to coordinate, manage, and evaluate the school counseling program.

As student advocates, school counselors participate as members of the educational team. They consult and collaborate with teachers, administrators, and families to assist students to be successful academically, vocationally, and personally. School counselors are indispensable partners with the instructional staff in the development of contributing members of society. They assure, on behalf of students and their families, that all school programs facilitate the educational process and offer the opportunity for school success.

SUMMARY

A written comprehensive, developmentally based preK–12 school counseling program should be implemented in every school district. It should include a systematic and planned program delivery that productively involves all students and promotes and enhances the learning process.

The comprehensive school counseling program facilitates student development in three areas:

- academic development which includes the acquisition of skills, attitudes, and knowledge which contributes to effective learning in school and throughout the life span;
- career development which includes the foundation for the acquisition of skills, attitudes, and knowledge which will enable students to make a successful transition from school to careers;
- personal/social development which includes the acquisition of skills, attitudes, and knowledge to help students understand and respect self and others, acquire effective interpersonal skills, understand and practice safety and survival skills, and develop into contributing members of society.

The comprehensive school counseling program should be supported by appropriate resources and implemented and coordinated by a credentialed professional school counselor.

RUST Statement Revised (AACD/AMECD Policy Statement)

Responsibilities of Users of Standardized Tests

I. INTRODUCTION

Background

At the 1976 AACD (then APGA) Convention, the Board of Directors requested the development of a statement on the responsible use of standardized tests to promote proper test use, reflecting the advantages of assessment along with concerns about negative effects, and to help its members employ safeguards against misuse of tests. A committee representing all AACD Divisions and Regions spent two years studying the issues and developed a statement, published in the October 1978 issue of *Guidepost*, entitled "Responsibilities of Users of Standardized Tests." The Association for Measurement and Evaluation in Counseling and Development was charged with maintaining ongoing review of the so-called RUST Statement. The present statement has grown out of that review.

Target Audience

The statement is intended to address the needs of the members of AACD and its Divisions, Branches, and Regions, including counselors and other human service workers. Although it may interest test developers, teachers, administrators, parents, the press, or the general public, it is not specifically designed for these audiences.

Organization and Focus

The statement is organized into eight sections: Introduction, Test Decisions, Qualification of Test Users, Test Se-

lection, Test Administration, Test Scoring, Test Interpretation, and Communicating Test Results. Basic to the statement is the assumption that test data are merely numbers and that guidelines can help to promote their constructive use. The statement specifies general principles and activities which constitute responsible practice. These are grouped around similar issues and are indexed for ease of reference.

II. TEST DECISIONS

Decisions should be based on data. In general, test data improve the quality of decisions. However, deciding whether or not to test creates the possibility of three kinds of errors. First, a decision not to test can result in misjudgments that stem from inadequate or subjective data. Second, tests may produce data which could improve accuracy in decisions affecting the client, but which are not used in counseling. Third, tests may be misused. The responsible practitioner will determine, in advance, the purpose for administering a given test, considering protections and benefits for the client, practitioner, and agency.

A. Define purposes for testing by developing specific objectives and limits for the use of test data in relation to the particular assessment purpose:

1. Placement: If the purpose is selection or placement, the test user should understand the programs or institutions into which the client may be placed and be able to judge the consequences of inclusion or exclusion decisions for the client.

2. Prediction: If the purpose is prediction, the test user should understand the need for predictive data as well as possible negative consequences (e.g., stereotyping).

3. Description: If the purpose is diagnosis or description, the test user should understand the general domain being measured and be able to identify those aspects which are adequately measured and those which are not.

4. Growth: If the purpose is to examine growth or change, the test user should understand the practical and theoretical difficulties associated with such measurement.

5. Program Evaluation: If the purpose of assessment is the evaluation of an agency's programs, the test user should be aware of the various information needs for the evaluation and of the limitations of each instrument used to assess those needs, as well as how the evaluation will be used.

B. Determine Information Needs and Assessment Needs:

1. Determine whether testing is intended to assess individuals, groups, or both.

2. Identify the particular individual and/or group to be tested with regard to the agency's purposes and capabilities.

3. Determine the limitations to testing created by an individual's age; racial, sexual, ethnic, and cultural background; or other characteristics.

4. Avoid unnecessary testing by identifying decisions which can be made with existing information.

5. Assess the consequences for clients of deciding either to test or not to test.

6. Limit data gathering to the variables that are needed for the particular purpose.

7. Cross-validate test data using other available information whenever possible.

III. QUALIFICATIONS OF TEST USERS

While all professional counselors and personnel workers should have formal training in psychological and educational measurement and testing, this training does not necessarily make one an expert, and even an expert does not have all the knowledge and skills appropriate to some particular situations or instruments. Questions of user qualifications should always be addressed when testing is being considered.

Lack of proper qualifications can lead to errors and subsequent harm to clients. Each professional is responsible for making judgements on this in each situation and cannot leave that responsibility either to clients or to

others in authority. It is incumbent upon the individual test user to obtain appropriate training or arrange for proper supervision and assistance when engaged in testing. Qualifications for test users depend on four factors:

A. Purposes of Testing: Technically proper testing for ill-understood purposes may constitute misuse. Because the purposes of testing dictate how the results are used, qualifications of test users are needed beyond general testing competencies to interpret and apply data.

B. Characteristics of Tests: Understanding the nature and limitations of each instrument used is needed by test users.

C. Settings and Conditions of Test Use: Assessment of the quality and relevance of test user knowledge and skill to the situation is needed before deciding to test or to participate in a testing program.

D. Roles of Test Selectors, Administrators, Scorers, and Interpreters: Test users must be engaged in only those testing activities for which their training and experience qualify them.

IV. TEST SELECTION

The selection of tests should be guided by information obtained from a careful analysis of the characteristics of the population to be tested; the knowledge, skills, abilities, or attitudes to be assessed; the purposes for testing; and the eventual use and interpretation of the test scores. Use of tests should also be guided by criteria for technical quality recommended by measurement professionals (i.e., the APA/AERA/NCME "Standards for Educational and Psychological Tests" and the APA/AERA/NCME/AACD/ ASHA "Code of Fair Testing Practices in Education").

A. Relate Validity to Usage:

1. Determine the validity of a test (whether the test measures what is meant to be measured) through evidence of the constructs used in developing the test, the correlation of the test performance with other appraisals of the characteristics being measured, and/or the predictions of specified behaviors from the test performance.

2. Determine whether a test is congruent with the users' definition of the characteristics of human performance to be appraised.

3. Use tests for selection purposes only when they show predictive validity for the specific tasks or competencies needed in an educational or employment experience and when they maintain legal and ethical prescriptions for non-discriminatory

practices in program selection, employment, or placement.

B. Use Appropriate Tests:

1. Document tests as appropriate for the characteristics of the population to be tested.

2. Only use tests within the level of skills of the practitioner.

3. Use tests consistent with local needs:

   a. Give attention to how the test is designed to handle variation of motivation, working speed, language facility, and experiential background among persons taking it; bias in response to its content; and effects of guessing in response to its questions.

   b. Determine whether a common test or different tests are required for accurate measurement of groups with special characteristics.

      i. Recognize that the use of different tests for cultural, ethnic, and racial groups may constitute ineffective means for making corrections for differences.

      ii. Determine whether persons or groups that use different languages should be tested in either or both languages and in some instances, tested first for bilingualism or language dominance.

C. Consider Technical Characteristics:

1. Select only tests that have documented evidence of reliability or consistency.

2. Select only tests that have adequate documented evidence of the effectiveness of the measure for the purpose to be served and justification of the inferences based on the results.

3. Scrutinize standardization and norming procedures for relevance to the local population and use of the data.

4. Use separate norms for men and women or other subgroups when empirical evidence indicates they are appropriate.

5. Determine the degree of technical quality demanded of a test on the basis of the nature of the decisions to be made.

6. Include ease and accuracy of the procedures for scoring, summarizing, and communicating test performance among the criteria for selecting a test.

7. Consider practical constraints of cost, conditions, and time for testing as secondary test selection criteria.

D. Employ User Participation in Test Selection: Actively involve everyone who will be using the assessments (administering, scoring, summarizing, interpreting, making decisions) as appropriate in the selection of tests so that they are congruent with local purposes, conditions, and uses.

V. TEST ADMINISTRATION

Test administration includes procedures to ensure that the test is used in the manner specified by the test developers and that the individuals being tested are working within conditions which maximize opportunity for optimum, comparable performance.

A. Provide Proper Orientation:

1. Inform testing candidates, parents, and institutions or agencies in the community as appropriate about the testing procedures. The orientation should make the test meaningful for the individual or group being tested, and should include the purposes of the test, the kinds of tasks it involves, how it is administered and how the scores will be reported and used.

2. Provide persons being tested sufficient practice experiences prior to the test.

3. Prior to testing, check all test takers' ability to record their responses adequately (e.g., in the use of machine-scorable answer sheets).

4. Provide periodic training by qualified personnel for test administrators within agencies or institutions using tests.

5. Review test materials and administration sites and procedures prior to the time for testing to ensure standardized conditions and appropriate response to any irregularities which may occur.

B. Use Qualified Test Administrators:

1. Acquire any training required to administer the test.

2. Ensure that individuals taking self-administered or self-scored instruments have the necessary understanding and competencies.

C. Provide Appropriate Testing Conditions:

1. Ensure that the testing environment (seating, work surfaces, lighting, heating, freedom from distractions, etc.) and psychological climate are conducive to the best possible performance of the test takers.

2. Carefully observe, record, and attach to the test record any deviation from prescribed test administration procedures.

3. Use a systematic and objective procedure for observing and recording environmental, health, or emotional factors, or other elements which may invalidate test performance. This record should be attached to the test scores of the persons tested.

4. Use sufficiently trained personnel to provide uniform conditions and to observe the conduct of the examinees when large groups of individuals are tested.

D. Give Proper Directions:

1. Present each test in the manner prescribed in the test manual to ensure that it is fair to each test taker.

2. Administer standardized tests with the verbatim instructions, exact sequence and timing, and identical materials that were used in the test standardization.

E. Demonstrate Professional Collaboration:
In settings where skill and knowledge are pooled and responsibility shared, consider the qualifications of the testing team as a whole as more important than those of individuals. However, coordination and consistency of responsibilities with expertise must be maintained.

VI. TEST SCORING

Accurate measurement of human performance necessitates adequate procedures for scoring the responses of examinees. These procedures must be audited as necessary to ensure consistency and accuracy of application.

A. Consider Accuracy and Interpretability: Select a test scoring process that maximizes accuracy and interpretability.

B. Rescore Samples: Routinely rescore samples of examinee responses to monitor the accuracy of the scoring process.

C. Screen Test Results: Screen reports of test results using personnel competent to recognize unreasonable or impossible scores.

D. Verify Scores and Norms: Verify the accuracy of computation of raw scores and conversion to normative scales prior to release of such information to examinees or users of test results.

E. Communicative Deviations: Report as part of the official record any deviation from normal conditions and examinee behaviors.

F. Label Results: Clearly label the date of test administration along with the scores.

VII. TEST INTERPRETATION

Test interpretation encompasses all the ways that meaning is assigned to the scores. Proper interpretation requires knowledge about the test which can be obtained by studying its manual and other materials along with current research literature with respect to its use; no one should undertake the interpretation of scores on any test without such study.

A. Consider Reliability: Reliability is important because it is a prerequisite to validity and because the degree to which a score may vary due to measurement error is an important factor in its interpretation.

1. Estimate test stability using a reliability (or other appropriate) coefficient.

2. Use the standard error of measurement to estimate the amount of variation due to random error in individual scores and to evaluate the precision of cut-scores in selection decisions.

3. Consider, in relationship to the uses being made of the scores, variance components attributed to error in the reliability index.

4. Evaluate reliability estimates with regard to factors that may have artificially raised or lowered them (e.g., test speededness, biases in population sampling).

5. Distinguish indices of objectivity (i.e., scorer reliability) from rest reliability.

B. Consider Validity: Proper test interpretation requires knowledge of the validity evidence available for the intended use of the test. Its validity for other uses is not relevant. Indeed, use of a measure for a purpose for which it was not designed may constitute misuse. The nature of the validity evidence required for a test depends upon its use.

1. Use for Placement: Predictive validity is the usual basis for valid placement.

a. Obtain adequate information about the programs or institutions in which the client may be placed to judge the consequences of such placement.

b. Use all available evidence to infer the validity of an individual's score. A single test score should not be the sole basis for a placement or selection recommendation. Other items of information about an individual (e.g., teacher report, counselor opinion) frequently improve the likelihood that proper judgments and decisions will be made.

c. Consider validity for each alternative (i.e., each placement option) when interpreting test scores and other evidence.

d. Examine the possibility that a client's group membership (socioeconomic status, gender, subculture, etc.) may affect test performance and, consequently, validity.

e. Estimate the probability of favorable outcomes for each possible placement before making recommendations.

f. Consider the possibility that outcomes favorable from an institutional point of view may differ from those that are favorable from the individual's point of view.

2. Use for Prediction: The relationship of the test scores to an independently developed criterion measure is the basis for predictive validity.

a. Consider the reliability and validity of the criterion measure(s) used.

b. Consider the validity of a measure in the context of other predictors available (i.e., does the test make a valid contribution to prediction beyond that provided by other measures).

c. Use cross-validation to judge the validity of prediction processes.

d. Consider the effects of labeling, stereotyping, and prejudging people (e.g., self-fulfilling prophecies that may result from labeling are usually undesirable).

e. If a statistically valid predictor lacks both construct and content validity, analyze the mechanism by which it operates to determine whether or not its predictive validity is spurious.

3. Use for Description: Comprehensiveness of information is fundamental to effective description, since no set of test scores completely describes an individual.

a. Clearly identify the domain assessed by any measure and the adequacy of the content sampling procedures used in developing items.

b. Clarify the dimensions being measured when multiple scores from a battery or inventory are used for description.

i. Examine the content and/or construct validity of each score separately.

ii. Consider the relative importance of each of the separate elements for interpretation.

iii. Give appropriate weights to reflect the variabilities (e.g., standard deviations) and relationships (e.g., correlations) of scores which are to be combined.

c. Distinguish characteristics that can be validated only empirically and those for which content specifications exist.

4. Use for Assessment of Growth: Assessment of growth or change requires valid tests as well as a valid procedure for combining them.

a. Specifically evaluate the reliability of differences between scores as measures of change.

b. Establish the validities of the measures used to establish change in relation to one another as well as individually.

c. Consider comparability of intervals in scales used to assess change.

i. Evaluate derived or extrapolated scores (e.g., grade equivalents) for possible different meanings at different score levels.

ii. Consider problems in interpretation and comparability of tests (e.g., floor or ceiling effects, content changes from level to level, poor articulation in multilevel tests, lack of comparability of alternate forms, inadequacy of score-equating across forms, and differences in administration and timing of tests from that of their norming).

d. Assess potential for undesirable correlations of difference scores with the measures entering into their calculations (e.g., regression toward the mean).

e. Recognize the potential lack of comparability between norms for differences derived from norms and norms for differences derived from differences (i.e., mathematically derived norms for differences are not necessarily equivalent to norms based on distributions of actual differences).

5. Use for Program Evaluation: Assessments of group differences (between groups or within groups over time) are based on research designs which to varying degrees admit competing interpretations of the results.

a. Use procedures in the evaluation which ensure that no factors other than those being studied have major influence on the results (i.e., internal validity).

b. Use statistical procedures which are appropriate and have all assumptions met by the data being analyzed.

c. Evaluate the generalizability (external validity) of the results for different individuals, settings, tests, and variables.

C. Scores, Norms, and Related Technical Features: The result of scoring a test or subtest is usually a number called a raw score which by itself is not interpretable. Additional steps are needed to translate the number directly into either a verbal description (e.g., pass or fail) or into a derived score (e.g., a standard score). Less than full understanding of these procedures is likely to produce errors in interpretation and ultimately in counseling or other uses.

1. Examine appropriate test materials (e.g., manuals, handbooks, users' guides, and technical reports) to identify the descriptions or derived scores produced and their unique characteristics.

   a. Know the operational procedures for translating raw scores into descriptions or derived scores.

   b. Know specific psychological or educational concepts or theories before interpreting the scores of tests based on them.

   c. Consider differential validity along with equating error when different tests, different test forms, or scores on the same test administered at different times are compared.

2. Clarify arbitrary standards used in interpretation (e.g., mastery or nonmastery for criterion-referenced tests).

   a. Recognize that when a score is interpreted based on a proportion score (e.g., percent correct), its elements are being given arbitrary weights.

   b. Recognize that the difficulty of a fixed standard (e.g., 80 percent right) varies widely and thus does not have the same meaning for different content areas and for different assessment methods.

   c. Report the number (or percentage) of items right in addition to the interpretation when it

will help others understand the quality of the examinees' performance.

3. Employ derived scores based on norms which fit the needs of the current use of the test.

   a. Evaluate whether available norm groups are appropriate as part of the process of interpreting the scores of clients.

      i. Use norms for the group to which the client belongs.

      ii. Recognize that derived scores based on different norm groups may not be comparable.

      iii. Use local norms and derived scores based on them whenever possible.

   b. Choose a score based on its intended use.

      i. Consider relative standing scores (e.g., percentile ranks) for comparison of individuals to the norm or reference group.

      ii. Consider standard or scaled scores whenever means and variances or other arithmetic operations are appropriate.

      iii. When using a statistical technique, use the test's derived score which best meets the assumptions of the analysis.

D. Administration and Scoring Variation: Stated criteria for score interpretation assume standard procedures for administering and scoring the test. Departures from standard conditions and procedures modify and often invalidate these criteria.

1. Evaluate unusual circumstances peculiar to the administration and scoring of the test.

   a. Examine reports from administrators, proctors, and scorers concerning irregularities or unusual conditions (e.g., excessive anxiety) for possible effects on test performance.

   b. Consider potential effects of examiner-examinee differences in ethnic and cultural background, attitudes, and values based on available relevant research.

   c. Consider any reports of examinee behavior indicating the responses were made on some basis other than that intended.

   d. Consider differences among clients in their reaction to instructions about guessing and scoring.

2. Evaluate scoring irregularities (e.g., machine scoring errors) and bias and judgment effects when subjective elements enter into scoring.

VIII. COMMUNICATING TEST RESULTS

The responsible counselor or other practitioner reports test data with a concern for the individual's need for information and the purposes of the information. There must also be protection of the right of the person tested to be informed about how the results will be used and what safeguards exist to prevent misuse (right to information) and about who will have access to the results (right to privacy).

A. Decisions about Individuals: Where test data are used to enhance decisions about an individual, the practitioner's responsibilities include:

1. Limitations on Communication:

   a. Inform the examinee of possible actions that may be taken by any person or agency who will be using the results.

   b. Limit access to users specifically authorized by the law or by the client.

   c. Obtain the consent of the examinee before using test results for any purpose other than those advanced prior to testing.

2. Practitioner Communication Skills:

   a. Develop the ability to interpret test results accurately before attempting to communicate them.

   b. Develop appropriate communication skills, particularly with respect to concepts that are commonly misunderstood by the intended audience, before attempting to explain test results to clients, the public, or other recipients of the information.

3. Communication of Limitations of the Assessment:

   a. Inform persons receiving test information that scores are not perfectly accurate and indicate the degree of inaccuracy in some way, such as by reporting score intervals.

   b. Inform persons receiving test information of any circumstances that could have affected the validity or reliability of the results.

   c. Inform persons receiving test information of any factors necessary to understand potential sources of bias for a given test result.

   d. Communicate clearly that test data represent just one source of information and should rarely, if ever, be used alone for decision making.

4. Communication of Client Rights:

   a. Provide test takers or their parents or guardians with information about any rights they may have to obtain test copies and/or their completed answer sheets, to retake tests, to have tests rescored, or to cancel test scores.

   b. Inform test takers or their parents or guardians, about how long the test scores will remain on file along with the person to whom, and circumstances under which, they may be released.

   c. Describe the procedures test takers or their parents or guardians may use to register complaints or have problems resolved.

B. Decisions about Groups: Where standardized test data are being used to describe groups for the purpose of evaluation, the practitioner's responsibilities include:

1. Background Information:

   a. Identify the purposes for which the reported data are appropriate.

   b. Include additional information (e.g., population characteristics) if it can improve accuracy of understanding.

2. Averages and Norms:

   a. Clarify the amount of meaning that can be attached to differences between groups (e.g., statistical significance should not be taken as a judgment of importance).

   b. Qualify norms based on their appropriateness for the group being tested.

3. Use obsolescence schedules so that stored data are systematically relocated to historic files or destroyed.

4. Process data used for research or program evaluation to assure individual anonymity (e.g., released only in aggregated form).

5. Political Usage:

   a. Emphasize that test data should be used only for the test's stated purposes.

   b. Public release of test information provides data for many purposes. Take steps to minimize those which may be adverse to the interests of those tested.

6. Agency Policies:

   a. Advocate agency test-reporting policies designed to benefit the groups being measured.

   b. Advocate the establishment of procedures for periodic review of test use.

IX. EXTENSIONS OF THESE PRINCIPLES

This statement is intended to address current and emerging problems and concerns that are generic to all AACD divisions, branches, and regions by formulating principles that are specific enough to serve as a template for more closely focused statements addressed to specific situations. Individual divisions, branches, and regions are encouraged to elaborate upon this statement to reflect principles, procedures, and examples appropriate to their members.

This revision of the 1978 RUST Statement was prepared by a standing committee of AMECD chaired by William D. Schafer. Participating in the revision were Esther E. Diamond, Charles G. Eberly, Patricia B. Elmore, Jo-Ida C. Hansen, William A. Mehrens, Jane E. Myers, Larry Rawlins, and Alan G. Robertson.

Additional copies of the RUST Statement may be obtained from the American Association for Counseling and Development, 5999 Stevenson Avenue, Alexandria, VA 22304. Single copies are free.

Appendix **G**

American Mental Health Counselors Association (Last Amended April 23, 1987) AMHCA Code of Ethics

PREAMBLE

Mental health counselors believe in the dignity and worth of the individual. They are committed to increasing knowledge of human behavior and understanding of themselves and others. While pursuing these endeavors, they make every reasonable effort to protect the welfare of those who seek their services or of any subject that may be the object of study. They use their skills only for purposes consistent with these values and do not knowingly permit their misuse by others. While demanding for themselves freedom of inquiry and community, mental health counselors accept the responsibility this freedom confers: competence, objectivity in the application of skills, and concern for the best interests of clients, colleagues, and society in general. In the pursuit of these ideals, mental health counselors subscribe to the following principles:

Principle 1. Responsibility

In their commitment to the understanding of human behavior, mental health counselors value objectivity and integrity, and in providing services they maintain the highest standards. They accept responsibility for the consequences of their work and make every effort to insure that their services are used appropriately.

518

a. Mental health counselors accept ultimate responsibility for selecting appropriate areas for investigation and the methods relevant to minimize the possibility that their findings will be misleading. They provide thorough discussion of the limitations of their data and alternative hypotheses, especially where their work touches on social policy or might be misconstrued to the detriment of specific age, sex, ethnic, socioeconomic, or other social categories. In publishing reports of their work, they never discard observations that may modify the interpretation of results. Mental health counselors take credit only for the work they have actually done. In pursuing research, mental health counselors ascertain that their efforts will not lead to changes in individuals or organizations unless such changes are part of the agreement at the time of obtaining informal consent. Mental health counselors clarify in advance the expectations for sharing and utilizing research data. They avoid dual relationships which may limit objectivity, whether theoretical, political, or monetary, so that interference with data, subjects, and milieu is kept to a minimum.

b. As employees of an institution or agency, mental health counselors have the responsibility of remaining alert to institutional pressures which may distort reports of counseling findings or use them in ways counter to the promotion of human welfare.

c. When serving as members of governmental or other organizational bodies, mental health counselors remain accountable as individuals to the Code of Ethics of the American Mental Health Counselors Association (AMHCA).

d. As teachers, mental health counselors recognize their primary obligation to help others acquire knowledge and skill. They maintain high standards of scholarship and objectivity by presenting counseling information fully and accurately, and by giving appropriate recognition to alternative viewpoints.

e. As practitioners, mental health counselors know that they bear a heavy social responsibility because their recommendations and professional actions may alter the lives of others. They, therefore, remain fully cognizant of their impact and alert to personal, social, organizational, financial, or political situations or pressures which might lead to misuse of their influence.

f. Mental health counselors provide reasonable and timely feedback to employees, trainees, supervisors, students, clients, and others whose work they may evaluate.

Principle 2. Competence

The maintenance of high standards of professional competence is a responsibility shared by all mental health counselors in the interest of the public and the profession as a whole. Mental health counselors recognize the boundaries of their competence and the limitations of their techniques and only provide services, use techniques, or offer opinions as professionals that meet recognized standards. Throughout their careers, mental health counselors maintain knowledge of professional information related to the services they render.

a. Mental health counselors accurately represent their competence, education, training, and experience.

b. As teachers, mental health counselors perform their duties based on careful preparation so that their instruction is accurate, up-to-date, and scholarly.

c. Mental health counselors recognize the need for continuing training to prepare themselves to serve persons of all ages and cultural backgrounds. They are open to new procedures and sensitive to differences between groups of people and changes in expectations and values over time.

d. Mental health counselors with the responsibility for decisions involving individuals or policies based on test results should know and understand literature relevant to the tests used and testing problems with which they deal.

e. Mental health counselors and practitioners recognize that their effectiveness depends in part upon their ability to maintain sound interpersonal relations, that temporary or more enduring aberrations on their part may interfere with their abilities or distort their appraisals of others. Therefore, they refrain from undertaking any activity in which their personal problems are likely to lead to inadequate professional services or harm to a client, or, if they are already engaged in such activity when they become aware of their personal problems, they would seek competent professional assistance to determine whether they should suspend or terminate services to one or all of their clients.

f. The mental health counselor has a responsibility both to the individual who is served and to the institution with which the service is performed to maintain high standards of professional conduct. The mental health counselor strives to maintain the highest levels of professional services offered to the individuals to be served. The mental health counselor also strives to assist the agency, organization, or institution in providing the highest caliber of professional services. The acceptance of employment in an institution implies that the mental health counselor is in substantial agreement with the general policies and principles of the institution. If, despite concerted efforts, the member cannot reach agreement with the employer as to acceptable standards of conduct that allow for changes in institutional policy conducive to the positive growth and development of counselees, then terminating the affiliation should be seriously considered.

g. Ethical behavior among professional associates, mental health counselors and non–mental health counselors is expected at all times. When information is possessed which raises serious doubt as to the ethical behavior of professional colleagues, whether Association members or not, the mental health counselor is obligated to take action to attempt to rectify such a condition. Such action shall utilize the institution's channels first and then utilize procedures established by the state, division, or Association.

h. The mental health counselor is aware of the intimacy of the counseling relationship and maintains a healthy respect for the personhood of the client and avoids engaging in activities that seek to meet the mental health counselor's personal needs at the expense of the client. Through awareness of the negative impact of both racial and sexual stereotyping and discrimination, the member strives to ensure the individual rights and personal dignity of the client in the counseling relationship.

Principle 3. Moral and Legal Standards

Mental health counselors' moral, ethical, and legal standards of behavior are a personal matter to the same degree as they are for any other citizen, except as these may compromise the fulfillment of their professional responsibilities, or reduce the trust in counseling or counselors held by the general public. Regarding their own behavior, mental health counselors should be aware of the prevailing community standards and of the possible impact upon the quality of professional services provided by their conformance to or deviation from these standards. Mental health counselors should also be aware of the possible impact of their public behavior upon the ability of colleagues to perform their professional duties.

a. To protect public confidence in the profession of counseling, mental health counselors will avoid public behavior that is clearly in violation of accepted moral and legal standards.

b. To protect students, mental health counselors/teachers will be aware of the diverse backgrounds of students and, when dealing with topics that may give offense, will see that the material is treated objectively, that it is clearly relevant to the course, and that it is treated in a manner for which the student is prepared.

c. Providers of counseling services conform to the statutes relating to such services as established by their state and its regulating professional board(s).

d. As employees, mental health counselors refuse to participate in employer's practices which are inconsistent with the moral and legal standards established by federal or state legislation regarding the treatment of employees or of the public. In particular and for example, mental health counselors will not condone practices which result in illegal or otherwise unjustifiable discrimination on the basis of race, sex, religion, or national origin in hiring, promotion, or training.

e. In providing counseling services to clients mental health counselors avoid any action that will violate or diminish the legal and civil rights of clients or of others who may be affected by the action.

f. Sexual conduct, not limited to sexual intercourse, between mental health counselors and clients is specifically in violation of this code of ethics. This does not, however, prohibit the use of explicit instructional aids including films and video tapes. Such use is within accepted practices of trained and competent sex therapists.

Principle 4. Public Statements

Mental health counselors in their professional roles may be expected or required to make public statements providing counseling information, professional opinions, or supply information about the availability of counseling products and services. In making such statements, mental health counselors take full account of the limits and uncertainties of present counseling knowledge and techniques. They represent, as objectively as possible, their professional qualifications, affiliations, and functions, as well as those of the institutions or organizations with which the statements may be associated. All public statements, announcements of services, and promotional activities should serve the purpose of providing sufficient information to aid the consumer public in making informed judgments and choices on matters that concern it.

a. When announcing professional counseling services, mental health counselors limit the information to: name, highest relevant degree conferred, certification or licensure, address, telephone number, office hours, cost of services, and a brief explanation of the other types of services offered but not evaluative as to their quality or uniqueness. They will not contain testimonials by implication. They will not claim uniqueness of skill or methods beyond those acceptable and public scientific evidence.

b. In announcing the availability of counseling services or products, mental health counselors will not display their affiliations with organizations or agencies in a manner that implies the sponsorship or certification of the organization or agency. They will not name their employer or professional associations unless the services are in fact to be provided by or under the responsible, direct supervision and continuing control of such organizations or agencies.

c. Mental health counselors associated with the development of promotion of counseling devices, books, or other products offered for commercial sale will make every effort to ensure that announcements and advertisements are presented in a professional and factually informative manner without unsupported claims of superiority and must be supported by scientifically acceptable evidence or by willingness to aid and encourage independent professional scrutiny or scientific tests.

d. Mental health counselors engaged in radio, television, or other public media activities will not participate in commercial announcements recommending to the general public the purchase or use of any proprietary or single-source product or service.

e. Mental health counselors who describe counseling or the services of professional counselors to the general public accept the obligation to present the material fairly and accurately, avoiding misrepresentation through sensationalism, exaggeration, or superficiality. Mental health counselors will be guided by the primary obligation to aid the public in forming their own informed judgments, opinions, and choices.

f. As teachers, mental health counselors ensure their statements in catalogs and course outlines are accurate, particularly in terms of subject matter to be covered, bases for grading, and nature of classroom experiences.

g. Mental health counselors accept the obligation to correct others who may represent their professional qualifications or associations with products or services in a manner incompatible with these guidelines.

h. Mental health counselors providing consultation, workshops, training, and other technical services may refer to previous satisfied clients in their advertising, provided there is no implication that such advertising refers to counseling services.

Principle 5. Confidentiality

Mental health counselors have a primary obligation to safeguard information about individuals obtained in the course of teaching, practice, or research. Personal information is communicated to others only with the person's written consent or in those circumstances where there is clear and imminent danger to the client, to others, or to society. Disclosures of counseling information are restricted to what is necessary, relevant, and verifiable.

a. All materials in the official record shall be shared with the client, who shall have the right to decide what information may be shared with anyone beyond the immediate provider of service and to be informed of the implications of the materials to be shared.

b. The anonymity of clients served in public and other agencies is preserved, if at all possible, by withholding names and personal identifying data. If external conditions require reporting such information, the client shall be so informed.

c. Information received in confidence by one agency or person shall not be forwarded to another person or agency without the client's written permission.

d. Service providers have a responsibility to ensure the accuracy and to indicate the validity of data shared with their parties.

e. Case reports presented in classes, professional meetings, or in publications shall be so disguised that no identification is possible unless the client or responsible authority has read the report and agreed in writing to its presentation or publication.

f. Counseling reports and records are maintained under conditions of security and provisions are made for their destruction when they have outlived their usefulness. Mental health counselors ensure that privacy and confidentiality are maintained by all persons in the employ or volunteers and community aides.

g. Mental health counselors who ask that an individual reveal personal information in the course of interviewing, testing, or evaluation, or who allow such information to be divulged, do so only after making certain that the person or authorized representative is fully aware of the purposes of the interview, testing, or evaluation and of the ways in which the information will be used.

h. Sessions with clients are taped or otherwise recorded only with their written permission or the written permission of a responsible guardian. Even with guardian written consent one should not record a session against the expressed wishes of a client.

i. Where a child or adolescent is the primary client, the interests of the minor shall be paramount.

j. In work with families, the rights of each family member should be safeguarded. The provider of service also has the responsibility to discuss the contents of the record with the parent and/or child, as appropriate, and to keep separate those parts which should remain the property of each family member.

Principle 6. Welfare of the Consumer

Mental health counselors respect the integrity and protect the welfare of the people and groups with whom they work. When there is a conflict of interest between the client and the mental health counselors' employing institution, the mental health counselors clarify the nature and direction of their loyalties and responsibilities and keep all parties informed of their commitments. Mental health counselors fully inform consumers as to the purpose and nature of any evaluative, treatment, educational, or training procedure, and they freely acknowledge that clients, students, or subjects have freedom of choice with regard to participation.

a. Mental health counselors are continually cognizant both of their own needs and of their inherently powerful position "vis-a-vis" clients, in order to avoid exploiting the client's trust and dependency. Mental health counselors make every effort to avoid dual relationships with clients and/or relationships which might impair their professional judgment or increase the risk of client exploitation. Examples of such dual relationships include treating an employee or supervisor, treating a close friend or family relative, and sexual relationships with clients.

b. Where mental health counselors work with members of an organization goes beyond reasonable conditions of employment, mental health counselors recognize possible conflicts of interest that may arise. When such conflicts occur, mental health counselors clarify the nature of the conflict and inform all parties of the nature and directions of the loyalties and responsibilities involved.

c. When acting as supervisors, trainers, or employers, mental health counselors accord recipients informed choice, confidentiality, and protection from physical and mental harm.

d. Financial arrangements in professional practice are in accord with professional standards that safeguard the best interests of the client and that are clearly understood by the client in advance of billing. This may best be done by the use of a contract. Mental health counselors are responsible for assisting clients in finding needed services in those instances where payment of the usual fee would be a hardship. No commission or rebate or other form of remuneration may be given or received for referral of clients for professional services, whether by an individual or by an agency.

e. Mental health counselors are responsible for making their services readily accessible to clients in a manner that facilitates the client's ability to make an informed choice when selecting a service provider. This responsibility includes a clear description of what the client may expect in the way of tests, reports, billing, therapeutic regime, and schedules and the use of the mental health counselor's Statement of Professional Disclosure.

f. Mental health counselors who find that their services are not beneficial to the client have the responsibility to make this known to the responsible persons.

g. Mental health counselors are accountable to the parties who refer and support counseling services and to the general public and are cognizant of the indirect or long-range effects of their intervention.

h. The mental health counselor attempts to terminate a private service or consulting relationship when it is reasonably clear to the mental health counselor that the consumer is not benefiting from it. If a consumer is receiving services from another mental health professional, mental health counselors do not offer their services directly to the consumer without informing the professional persons already involved in order to avoid confusion and conflict for the consumer.

i. The mental health counselor has the responsibility to screen prospective group participants, especially when the emphasis is on self-understanding and growth through self-disclosure. The member should maintain an awareness of the group participants' compatibility throughout the life of the group.

j. The mental health counselor may choose to consult with any other professionally competent person about a client. In choosing a consultant, the mental health counselor should avoid placing the consultant in a conflict of interest situation that would preclude the consultant's being a proper party to the mental health counselors' efforts to help the clients.

k. If the mental health counselor is unable to be of professional assistance to the client, the mental health counselor should avoid initiating the counseling relationship or the mental health counselor terminates the relationship. In either event, the member is obligated to suggest appropriate alternatives. (It is incumbent upon the mental health counselors to be knowledgeable about referral resources so that a satisfactory referral can be initiated.) In the event the client declines the suggested referral, the mental health counselor is not obligated to continue the relationship.

l. When the mental health counselor has other relationships, particularly of an administrative, supervisory, and/or evaluative nature, with an individual seeking counseling services, the mental health counselor should not serve as the counselor but should refer the individual to another professional. Only in instances where such an alternative is unavailable and where the individual's situation definitely warrants counseling intervention should the mental health counselor enter into and/or maintain a counseling relationship. Dual relationships with clients which might impair the member's objectivity and professional judgment (such as with close friends or relatives, sexual intimacies with any client, etc.) must be avoided and/or the counseling relationship terminated through referral to another competent professional.

m. All experimental methods of treatment must be clearly indicated to prospective recipients, and safety precautions are to be adhered to by the mental health counselor instituting treatment.

n. When the member is engaged in short-term group treatment/training programs, e.g., marathons and other encounter-type or growth groups, the member ensures that there is professional assistance available during and following the group experience.

Principle 7. Professional Relationship

Mental health counselors act with due regard to the needs and feelings of their colleagues in counseling and other professions. Mental health counselors respect the prerogatives and obligations of the institutions or organizations with which they are associated.

a. Mental health counselors understand the areas of competence of related professions and make full use of other professional, technical, and administrative resources which best serve the interests of consumers. The absence of formal relationships with other professional workers does not relieve mental health counselors from the responsibility of securing for their clients the best possible professional service; indeed, this circumstance presents a challenge to the professional competence of mental health counselors, requiring special sensitivity to problems outside their areas of training, and foresight, diligence, and tact in obtaining the professional assistance needed by clients.

b. Mental health counselors know and take into account the traditions and practices of other professional groups with which they work and cooperate fully with members of such groups when research, services, and other functions are shared or in working for the benefit of public welfare.

c. Mental health counselors strive to provide positive conditions for those they employ and they spell out clearly the conditions of such employment. They encourage their employees to engage in activities that facilitate their further professional development.

d. Mental health counselors respect the viability, reputation, and the proprietary right of organizations which they serve. Mental health counselors show due regard for the interest of their present or prospective employers. In those instances where they are critical of policies, they attempt to effect change by constructive action within the organization.

e. In the pursuit of research, mental health counselors give sponsoring agencies, host institutions, and publication channels the same respect and opportunity for giving informed consent that they accord to individual research participants. They are aware of their obligation to future research workers and ensure that host institutions are given feedback information and proper acknowledgment.

f. Credit is assigned to those who have contributed to a publication, in proportion to their contribution.

g. When a mental health counselor violates ethical standards, mental health counselors who know first-hand of such activities should, if possible, attempt to rectify the situation. Failing an informal solution, mental health counselors should bring such unethical activities to the attention of the appropriate state and/or national committee on ethics and professional conduct. Only after all professional alternatives have been utilized will a mental health counselor begin legal action for resolution.

Principle 8. Utilization of Assessment Techniques

In the development, publication, and utilization of counseling assessment techniques, mental health counselors follow relevant standards. Individuals examined, or their legal guardians, have the right to know the results, the interpretations made, and where appropriate, the partic-

ulars on which final judgment was based. Test users should take precautions to protect test security but not at the expense of an individual's right to understand the basis for decisions that adversely affect that individual or that individual's dependents.

a. The client has the right to have and the provider has the responsibility to give explanations of test results in language the client can understand.

b. When a test is published or otherwise made available for operational use, it should be accompanied by a manual (or other published or readily available information) that makes every reasonable effort to describe fully the development of the test, the rationale, and specifications followed in writing items analysis or other research. The test, the manual, the record forms, and other accompanying material should help users make correct interpretations of the test results and should warn against common misuses. The test manual should state explicitly the purposes and applications for which the test is recommended and identify any special qualifications required to administer the test and to interpret it properly. Evidence of validity and reliability, along with other relevant research data, should be presented in support of any claims made.

c. Norms presented in test manuals should refer to defined and clearly described populations. These populations should be the groups with whom users of the test will ordinarily wish to compare the persons tested. Test users should consider the possibility of bias in tests or in test items. When indicated, there should be an investigation of possible differences in validity for ethnic, sex, or other subsamples that can be identified when the test is given.

d. Mental health counselors who have the responsibility for decisions about individuals or policies that are based on test results should have a thorough understanding of counseling or educational measurement and of validation and other test research.

e. Mental health counselors should develop procedures for systematically eliminating from data files test score information that has, because of the lapse of time, become obsolete.

f. Any individual or organization offering test scoring and interpretation services must be able to demonstrate that their programs are based on appropriate research to establish the validity of the programs and procedures used in arriving at interpretations. The public offering of an automated test interpretation service will be considered as a professional-to-professional consultation. In this the formal responsibility of the consultant is to the consultee but his/her ultimate and overriding responsibility is to the client.

g. Counseling services for the purpose of diagnosis, treatment, or personalized advice are provided only in the context of a professional relationship, and are not given by means of public lectures or demonstrations, news-papers or magazine articles, radio or television programs, mail, or similar media. The preparation of personnel re-ports and recommendations based on test data secured solely by mail is unethical unless such appraisals are an in-tegral part of a continuing client relationship with a com-pany, as a result of which the consulting clinical mental health counselor has intimate knowledge of the client's personal situation and can be assured thereby that his written appraisals will be adequate to the purpose and will be properly interpreted by the client. These reports must not be embellished with such detailed analyses of the sub-ject's personality traits as would be appropriate only for intensive interviews with the subjects.

Principle 9. Pursuit of
Research Activities

The decision to undertake research should rest upon a considered judgment by the individual mental health counselor about how best to contribute to counseling and to human welfare. Mental health counselors carry out their investigations with respect for the people who par-ticipate and with concern for their dignity and welfare.

a. In planning a study the investigator has the per-sonal responsibility to make a careful evaluation of its ethical acceptability, taking into account the following principles for research with human beings. To the extent that this appraisal, weighing scientific and humane val-ues, suggests a deviation from any principle, the investi-gator incurs an increasingly serious obligation to seek ethical advice and to observe more stringent safeguards to protect the rights of the human research participants.

b. Mental health counselors know and take into ac-count the traditions and practices of other professional groups with members of such groups when research, ser-vices, and other functions are shared or in working for the benefit of public welfare.

c. Ethical practice requires the investigator to inform the participant of all features of the research that reason-ably might be expected to influence willingness to par-ticipate, and to explain all other aspects of the research about which the participant inquires. Failure to make full disclosure gives added emphasis to the investigator's abiding responsibility to protect the welfare and dignity of the research participant.

d. Openness and honesty are essential characteristics of the relationship between investigator and research par-ticipant. When the methodological requirements of a study necessitate concealment or deception, the investiga-tor is required to ensure as soon as possible the participant's understanding of the reasons for this action and to restore the quality of the relationship with the investigator.

e. In the pursuit of research, mental health coun-selors give sponsoring agencies, host institutions, and publication channels the same respect and opportunity for giving informed consent that they accord to individ-ual research participants. They are aware of their obliga-tion to future research workers and ensure that host institutions are given feedback information and proper acknowledgment.

f. Credit is assigned to those who have contributed to a publication, in proportion to their contribution.

g. The ethical investigator protects participants from physical and mental discomfort, harm, and danger. If the risk of such consequences exists, the investigator is re-quired to inform the participant of that fact, secure con-sent before proceeding, and take all possible measures to minimize distress. A research procedure may not be used if it is likely to cause serious and lasting harm to participants.

h. After the data are collected, ethical practice re-quires the investigator to provide the participant with a full clarification of the nature of the study and to remove any misconceptions that may have arisen. Where scien-tific or humane values justify delaying or withholding in-formation the investigator acquires a special responsibility to assure that there are no damaging consequences for the participants.

i. Where research procedure may result in undesir-able consequences for the participant, the investigator has the responsibility to detect and remove or correct these consequences, including, where relevant, long-term aftereffects.

j. Information obtained about the research partici-pants during the course of an investigation is confiden-tial. When the possibility exists that others may obtain access to such information, ethical research practice re-quires that the possibility, together with the plans for pro-tecting confidentiality, be explained to the participants as a part of the procedure for obtaining informed consent.

Principle 10. Private Practice

a. A mental health counselor should assist where per-mitted by legislation or judicial decision the profession in fulfilling its duty to make counseling services available in private settings.

b. In advertising services as a private practitioner the mental health counselor should advertise the services in such a manner so as to accurately inform the public as to services, expertise, profession, and techniques of counseling in a professional manner. A mental health counselor who assumes an executive leadership role in the organization shall not permit his/her name to be used in professional notices during periods when not actively engaged in the private practice of counseling.

The mental health counselor may list the following: Highest relevant degree, type and level of certification or license, type and/or description of services and other relevant information. Such information should not contain false, inaccurate, misleading, partial, out-of-context, or deceptive material or statements.

c. The mental health counselor may join in partnership/corporation with other mental health counselors and/or other professionals provided that each mental health counselor of the partnership or corporation makes clear the separate specialties by name in compliance with the regulations of the locality.

d. A mental health counselor has an obligation to withdraw from a counseling relationship if it is believed that employment will result in violation of the code of ethics, if their mental capacity or physical condition renders it difficult to carry out an effective professional relationship, or if the mental health counselor is discharged by the client because the counseling relationship is no longer productive for the client.

e. A mental health counselor should adhere to and support the regulations for private practice of the locality where the services are offered.

f. Mental health counselors are discouraged from deliberate attempts to utilize one's institutional affiliation to recruit clients for one's private practice. Mental health counselors are to refrain from offering their services in the private sector, when they are employed by an institution in which this is prohibited by stated policies reflecting conditions for employment.

g. In establishing fees for professional counseling services, mental health counselors should consider the financial status of clients and locality. In the event that the established fee structure is inappropriate for a client, assistance should be provided in finding services of acceptable cost.

Principle 11. Consulting

a. The mental health counselor acting as consultant must have a high degree of self-awareness of his/her own values, knowledge, skills, and needs in entering a helping relationship which involves human and/or organizational change and that the focus of the relationship be on the issues to be resolved and not on the person(s) presenting the problem.

b. There should be understanding and agreement between the mental health counselor and client for the problem definition, change goals, and predicted consequences of interventions selected.

c. The mental health counselor must be reasonably certain that she/he or the organization represented have the necessary competencies and resources for giving the kind of help which is needed now or may develop later and that appropriate referral resources are available to the consultant, if needed later.

d. The mental health counselor relationship must be one in which client adaptability and growth toward self-direction are encouraged and cultivated. The mental health counselor must maintain this role consistently and not become a decision maker or substitute for the client.

e. When announcing consultant availability for services, the mental health counselor conscientiously adheres to professional standards.

f. The mental health counselor is expected to refuse a private fee or other remuneration for consultation with persons who are entitled to these services through the members' employing institution or agency. The policies of a particular agency may make explicit provisions for private practice with agency counselees by members of its staff. In such instances, the counselees must be apprised of other options open to them should they seek private counseling services.

Principle 12. Client's Rights

The following apply to all consumers of mental health services, including both in and out-patients in all state, county, local, and private care mental health facilities, as well as patients/clients of mental health practitioners in private practice.

The client has the right:

a. to be treated with consideration and respect;

b. to expect quality service provided by concerned, competent staff;

c. to a clear statement of the purposes, goals, techniques, rules of procedure, and limitations as well as potential dangers of the services to be performed and all other information related to or likely to affect the ongoing counseling relationship;

d. to obtain information about their case record and to have this information explained clearly and directly;

e. to full, knowledgeable, and responsible participation in the on-going treatment plan, to the maximum feasible extent;

f. to expect complete confidentiality and that no information will be released without written consent;

g. to see and discuss their charges and payment records; and

h. to refuse any recommended services and be advised of the consequences of this action.

American Association for
Marriage and Family Therapy
(Effective August 1, 1991)
AAMFT Code
of Ethics

The Board of Directors of the American Association for Marriage and Family Therapy (AAMFT) hereby promulgates, pursuant to Article 2, Section 2.013 of the Association's Bylaws, the Revised AAMFT Code of Ethics, effective August 1, 1991.

The AAMFT Code of Ethics is binding on Members of AAMFT in all membership categories, AAMFT Approved Supervisors, and applicants for membership and the Approved Supervisor designation (hereafter, AAMFT Member).

If an AAMFT Member resigns in anticipation of, or during the course of an ethics investigation, the Ethics Committee will complete its investigation. Any publication of action taken by the Association will include the fact that the Member attempted to resign during the investigation.

Marriage and family therapists are strongly encouraged to report alleged unethical behavior of colleagues to appropriate professional associations and state regulatory bodies.

SOURCE: This Code is published by:
American Association for Marriage and Family Therapy
1100 17th Street, NW, 10th Floor
Washington, DC 20036-4601
(202) 452-0109

Violations of this Code should be brought in writing to the attention of the AAMFT Ethics Committee, 1100 17th Street, NW, The Tenth Floor, Washington, DC 20036-4601 (telephone 202/452-0109).

1. RESPONSIBILITY TO CLIENTS

Marriage and family therapists advance the welfare of families and individuals. They respect the rights of those persons seeking their assistance, and make reasonable efforts to ensure that their services are used appropriately.

1.1 Marriage and family therapists do not discriminate against or refuse professional service to anyone on the basis of race, gender, religion, national origin, or sexual orientation.

1.2 Marriage and family therapists are aware of their influential position with respect to clients, and they avoid exploiting the trust and dependency of such persons. Therapists, therefore, make every effort to avoid dual relationships with clients that could impair professional judgment or increase the risk of exploitation. When a dual relationship cannot be avoided, therapists take appropriate professional precautions to ensure judgment is not impaired and no exploitation occurs. Examples of such dual relationships include, but are not limited to, business or close personal relationships with clients. Sexual intimacy with clients is prohibited. Sexual intimacy with former clients for two years following the termination of therapy is prohibited.

1.3 Marriage and family therapists do not use their professional relationships with clients to further their own interests.

1.4 Marriage and family therapists respect the right of clients to make decisions and help them to understand the consequences of these decisions. Therapists clearly advise a client that a decision on marital status is the responsibility of the client.

1.5 Marriage and family therapists continue therapeutic relationships only so long as it is reasonably clear that clients are benefiting from the relationship.

527

1.6 Marriage and family therapists assist persons in obtaining other therapeutic services if the therapist is unable or unwilling, for appropriate reasons, to provide professional help.

1.7 Marriage and family therapists do not abandon or neglect clients in treatment without making reasonable arrangements for the continuation of such treatment.

1.8 Marriage and family therapists obtain written informed consent from clients before videotaping, audio recording, or permitting third party observation.

2. CONFIDENTIALITY

Marriage and family therapists have unique confidentiality concerns because the client in a therapeutic relationship may be more than one person. Therapists respect and guard confidences of each individual client.

2.1 Marriage and family therapists may not disclose client confidences except: (a) as mandated by law; (b) to prevent a clear and immediate danger to a person or persons; (c) where the therapist is a defendant in a civil, criminal, or disciplinary action arising from the therapy (in which case client confidences may be disclosed only in the course of that action); or (d) if there is a waiver previously obtained in writing, and then such information may be revealed only in accordance with the terms of the waiver. In circumstances where more than one person in a family receives therapy, each such family member who is legally competent to execute a waiver must agree to the waiver required by subparagraph (d). Without such a waiver from each family member legally competent to execute a waiver, a therapist cannot disclose information received from any family member.

2.2 Marriage and family therapists use client and/or clinical materials in teaching, writing, and public presentations only if a written waiver has been obtained in accordance with Subprinciple 2.1(d), or when appropriate steps have been taken to protect client identity and confidentiality.

2.3 Marriage and family therapists store or dispose of client records in ways that maintain confidentiality.

3. PROFESSIONAL COMPETENCE AND INTEGRITY

Marriage and family therapists maintain high standards of professional competence and integrity.

3.1 Marriage and family therapists are in violation of this Code and subject to termination of membership or other appropriate action if they: (a) are convicted of any felony; (b) are convicted of a misdemeanor related to their qualifications or functions; (c) engage in conduct which could lead to conviction of a felony, or a misdemeanor related to their qualifications or functions; (d) are expelled from or disciplined by other professional organizations; (e) have their licenses or certificates suspended or revoked or are otherwise disciplined by regulatory bodies; (f) are no longer competent to practice marriage and family therapy because they are impaired due to physical or mental causes or the abuse of alcohol or other substances; or (g) fail to cooperate with the Association at any point from the inception of an ethical complaint through the completion of all proceedings regarding that complaint.

3.2 Marriage and family therapists seek appropriate professional assistance for their personal problems or conflicts that may impair work performance or clinical judgment.

3.3 Marriage and family therapists, as teachers, supervisors, and researchers, are dedicated to high standards of scholarship and present accurate information.

3.4 Marriage and family therapists remain abreast of new developments in family therapy knowledge and practice through educational activities.

3.5 Marriage and family therapists do not engage in sexual or other harassment or exploitation of clients, students, trainees, supervisees, employees, colleagues, research subjects, or actual or potential witnesses or complainants in investigations and ethical proceedings.

3.6 Marriage and family therapists, because of their ability to influence and alter the lives of others, exercise special care when making public their professional recommendations and opinions through testimony or other public statements.

4. RESPONSIBILITY TO STUDENTS, EMPLOYEES, AND SUPERVISEES

Marriage and family therapists do not exploit the trust and dependency of students, employees, and supervisees.

4.1 Marriage and family therapists are aware of their influential position with respect to students, employees, and supervisees, and they avoid exploiting the trust and dependency of such persons. Therapists, therefore, make every effort to avoid dual relationships that could impair professional judgment or increase the risk of exploitation. When a dual relationship cannot be avoided, therapists take appropriate professional precautions to ensure judgment is not impaired and no exploitation occurs. Examples of such dual relationships include, but are not limited to, business or close personal relationships with students, employees, or supervisees. Provision of therapy to students, employees, or supervisees is prohibited. Sexual intimacy with students or supervisees is prohibited.

4.2 Marriage and family therapists do not permit students, employees, or supervisees to perform or to hold themselves out as competent to perform professional services beyond their training, level of experience, and competence.

4.3 Marriage and family therapists do not disclose supervisee confidences except: (a) as mandated by law; (b) to prevent a clear and immediate danger to a person or persons; (c) where the therapist is a defendant in a civil, criminal, or disciplinary action arising from the supervision (in which case supervisee confidences may be disclosed only in the course of that action); (d) in educational or training settings where there are multiple supervisors, and then only to other professional colleagues who share responsibility for the training of the supervisee; or (e) if there is a waiver previously obtained in writing, and then such information may be revealed only in accordance with the terms of the waiver.

5. RESPONSIBILITY TO RESEARCH PARTICIPANTS

Investigators respect the dignity and protect the welfare of participants in research and are aware of federal and state laws and regulations and professional standards governing the conduct of research.

5.1 Investigations are responsible for making careful examinations of ethical acceptability in planning studies. To the extent that services to research participants may be compromised by participation in research, investigators seek the ethical advice of qualified professionals not directly involved in the investigation and observe safeguards to protect the rights of research participants.

5.2 Investigators requesting participants' involvement in research inform them of all aspects of the research that might reasonably be expected to influence willingness to participate. Investigators are especially sensitive to the possibility of diminished consent when participants are also receiving clinical services, have impairments which limit understanding and/or communication, or when participants are children.

5.3 Investigators respect participants' freedom to decline participation in or to withdraw from a research study at any time. This obligation requires special thought and consideration when investigators or other members of the research team are in positions of authority or influence over participants. Marriage and family therapists, there-

fore, make every effort to avoid dual relationships with research participants that could impair professional judgment or increase the risk of exploitation.

5.4 Information obtained about a research participant during the course of an investigation is confidential unless there is a waiver previously obtained in writing. When the possibility exists that others, including family members, may obtain access to such information, this possibility, together with the plan for protecting confidentiality, is explained as part of the procedure for obtaining informed consent.

6. RESPONSIBILITY TO THE PROFESSION

Marriage and family therapists respect the rights and responsibilities of professional colleagues and participate in activities which advance the goals of the profession.

6.1 Marriage and family therapists remain accountable to the standards of the profession when acting as members or employees of organizations.

6.2 Marriage and family therapists assign publication credit to those who have contributed to a publication in proportion to their contributions and in accordance with customary professional publication practices.

6.3 Marriage and family therapists who are the authors of books or other materials that are published or distributed cite persons to whom credit for original ideas is due.

6.4 Marriage and family therapists who are the authors of books or other materials published or distributed by an organization take reasonable precautions to ensure that the organization promotes and advertises the materials accurately and factually.

6.5 Marriage and family therapists participate in activities that contribute to a better community and society, including devoting a portion of their professional activity to services for which there is little or no financial return.

6.6 Marriage and family therapists are concerned with developing laws and regulations pertaining to marriage and family therapy that serve the public interest, and with altering such laws and regulations that are not in the public interest.

6.7 Marriage and family therapists encourage public participation in the design and delivery of professional services and in the regulation of practitioners.

7. FINANCIAL ARRANGEMENTS

Marriage and family therapists make financial arrangements with clients, third party payors, and supervisees that are reasonably understandable and conform to accepted professional practices.

7.1 Marriage and family therapists do not offer or accept payment for referrals.

7.2 Marriage and family therapists do not charge excessive fees for services.

7.3 Marriage and family therapists disclose their fees to clients and supervisees at the beginning of services.

7.4 Marriage and family therapists represent facts truthfully to clients, third party payors, and supervisees regarding services rendered.

8. ADVERTISING

Marriage and family therapists engage in appropriate informational activities, including those that enable laypersons to choose professional services on an informed basis.

General Advertising

8.1 Marriage and family therapists accurately represent their competence, education, training, and experience relevant to their practice of marriage and family therapy.

8.2 Marriage and family therapists assure that advertisements and publications in any media (such as directories, announcements, business cards, newspapers, radio, television, and facsimiles) convey information that is necessary for the public to make an appropriate selection of professional services. Information could include: (a) office information, such as name, address, telephone number, credit card acceptability, fees, languages spoken, and office hours; (b) appropriate degrees, state licensure and/or certification, and AAMFT Clinical Member status; and (c) description of practice. (For requirements for advertising under the AAMFT name, logo, and/or the abbreviated initials AAMFT, see Subprinciple 8.15, below.)

8.3 Marriage and family therapists do not use a name which could mislead the public concerning the identity, responsibility, sources, and status of those practicing under that name and do not hold themselves out as being partners or associates of a firm if they are not.

8.4 Marriage and family therapists do not use any professional identification (such as a business card, office sign, letterhead, or telephone or association directory listing) if it includes a statement of claim that is false, fraudulent, misleading, or deceptive. A statement is false, fraudulent, misleading, or deceptive if it (a) contains a material misrepresentation of fact; (b) fails to state any material fact necessary to make the statement, in light of

all circumstances, not misleading; or (c) is intended to or is likely to create an unjustified expectation.

8.5 Marriage and family therapists correct, wherever possible, false, misleading, or inaccurate information and representations made by others concerning the therapist's qualifications, services, or products.

8.6 Marriage and family therapists make certain that the qualifications of persons in their employ are represented in a manner that is not false, misleading, or deceptive.

8.7 Marriage and family therapists may represent themselves as specializing within a limited area of marriage and family therapy, but only if they have the education and supervised experience in settings which meet recognized professional standards to practice in that specialty area.

Advertising Using AAMFT Designations

8.8 The AAMFT designations of Clinical Member, Approved Supervisor, and Fellow may be used in public information or advertising materials only by persons holding such designations. Persons holding such designations may, for example, advertise in the following manner:

- *Jane Doe, Ph.D., a Clinical Member of the American Association for Marriage and Family Therapy.* Alternately, the advertisement could read: *Jane Doe, Ph.D., AAMFT Clinical Member.*
- *John Doe, Ph.D., an Approved Supervisor of the American Association for Marriage and Family Therapy.* Alternately, the advertisement could read: *John Doe, Ph.D., AAMFT Approved Supervisor.*
- *Jane Doe, Ph.D., a Fellow of the American Association for Marriage and Family Therapy.* Alternately, the advertisement could read: *Jane Doe, Ph.D., AAMFT Fellow.* More than one designation may be used if held by the AAMFT Member.

8.9 Marriage and family therapists who hold the AAMFT Approved Supervisor or the Fellow designation may not represent the designation as an advanced clinical status.

8.10 Student, Associate, and Affiliate Members may not use their AAMFT membership status in public information or advertising materials. Such listings on professional resumes are not considered advertisements.

8.11 Persons applying for AAMFT membership may not list their application status on any resume or advertisement.

8.12 In conjunction with their AAMFT membership, marriage and family therapists claim as evidence of educational qualifications only those degrees (a) from regionally accredited institutions or (b) from institutions recognized by states which license or certify marriage and family therapists, but only if such state regulation is recognized by AAMFT.

8.13 Marriage and family therapists may not use the initials AAMFT following their name in the manner of an academic degree.

8.14 Marriage and family therapists may not use the AAMFT name, logo, and/or the abbreviated initials AAMFT or make any other such representation that would imply that they speak for or represent the Association. The Association is the sole owner of its name, logo, and the abbreviated initials AAMFT. Its committees and divisions, operation as such, may use the name, logo, and/or the abbreviated initials, AAMFT, in accordance with AAMFT policies.

8.15 Authorized advertisements of Clinical Members under the AAMFT name, logo, and/or the abbreviated initials AAMFT may include the following: the Clinical Member's name, degree, license or certificate held when required by state law, name of business, address, and telephone number. If a business is listed, it must follow, not precede, the Clinical Member's name. Such listings may not include AAMFT offices held by the Clinical Member, nor any specializations, since such a listing under the AAMFT name, logo, and/or the abbreviated initials, AAMFT, would imply that this specialization has been credentialed by AAMFT.

8.16 Marriage and family therapists use their membership in AAMFT only in connection with their clinical and professional activities.

8.17 Only AAMFT divisions and programs accredited by the AAMFT Commission on Accreditation for Marriage and Family Therapy Education, not businesses nor organizations, may use any AAMFT-related designation or affiliation in public information or advertising materials, and then only in accordance with AAMFT policies.

8.18 Programs accredited by the AAMFT Commission on Accreditation for Marriage and Family Therapy Education may not use the AAMFT name, logo, and/or the abbreviated initials, AAMFT. Instead, they may have printed on their stationery and other appropriate materials a statement such as:

> The (name of program) of the (name of institution) is accredited by the AAMFT Commission on Accreditation for Marriage and Family Therapy Education.

8.19 Programs not accredited by the AAMFT Commission on Accreditation for Marriage and Family Therapy Education may not use the AAMFT name, logo, and/or the abbreviated initials, AAMFT. They may not state in printed program materials, program advertisements, and student advisement that their courses and training opportunities are accepted by AAMFT to meet AAMFT membership requirements.

Appendix I

American Psychological Association Committee on Professional Standards, Board of Professional Affairs
General Guidelines for Providers of Psychological Services

PREAMBLE

A set of practices and implicitly recognized principles of conduct evolves over the history of every profession. Such principles guide the relationships of the members of the profession to their users, to each other, and to the community of which both professionals and users are members. Making such guiding principles and practices explicit is a sign of the profession's maturity and serves the best interests of the profession, its users, and the community at large.

These General Guidelines were revised by the Committee on Professional Standards (COPS) in consultation with the Board of Professional Affairs (BPA) and providers of psychological services from throughout the American Psychological Association (APA). The assistance of APA staff is gratefully acknowledged. The names of members and staff who supported this effort are included in Footnote 4. This document was approved by the APA Council of Representatives in February 1987.

Comments or questions on these General Guidelines should be addressed to the Committee on Professional Standards, American Psychological Association, 1200 Seventeenth Street, NW, Washington, DC 20036.

SOURCE: Copyright © 1987 by the American Psychological Association, Inc. Reprinted by permission of the publisher.

Copies may be ordered from: Order Department, American Psychological Association, P.O. Box 92984, Washington, DC 20090.

Because psychology is a continually evolving science and profession, guidelines for practice are living documents that require periodic review and revision. The *General Guidelines for Providers of Psychological Services*[1,2] represents an important milestone in the evolutionary development of professional psychology.

These General Guidelines are a set of aspirational statements for psychologists that encourage continual improvement in the quality of practice and service. Some of these General Guidelines have been derived from specific APA Ethical Principles (APA, 1981a).[3] Providers of psychological services have the same responsibility to uphold these specific General Guidelines as they would the corresponding Ethical Principles. The language of the other General Guidelines must at all times be interpreted in light of their aspirational intent.

These General Guidelines are general in nature and, as such, are intended for use by all providers of psychological services; they are supplemented by the *Specialty Guidelines for the Delivery of Services by Clinical (Counseling, Industrial/Organizational, and School) Psychologists* (APA, 1981b).

INTRODUCTION

This version of the *General Guidelines* is the second revision of the principles originally adopted by the American Psychological Association on September 4, 1974, and first revised in 1977.[4] The *General Guidelines* are intended to improve the quality, effectiveness, and accessibility of psychological services.

Since 1970, the American Psychological Association has worked to develop and codify a uniform set of guidelines for psychological practice that would serve the respective needs of users, providers, third-party purchasers, and other sanctioners of psychological services. In addition, the APA has established a Committee on Professional Standards, which is charged with keeping the General Guidelines responsive to the needs of these groups and with upgrading and extending them as the profession and science of psychology continue to develop knowledge, improved methods, and additional modes of psychological service. These General Guidelines have been established by organized psychology as a means of self-regulation in the public interest.

When providing any of the covered psychological service functions at any time and in any setting, whether public or private, profit or nonprofit, any persons representing themselves as psychologists are expected, where feasible, to observe these General Guidelines of practice to promote the best interests and welfare of the users of such services. Functions and activities related to the teaching of psychology, the writing or editing of scholarly or scientific manuscripts, and the conduct of scientific research do not fall within the purview of the present *General Guidelines*.[5]

Underlying Principles

Six basic principles have guided the development of these General Guidelines:

1. These General Guidelines apply to psychological service functions offered by psychologists, regardless of their specialty, of the setting, or of the form of remuneration given to them. Professional psychology has a uniform set of guidelines just as it has a common code of ethics (APA, 1981a). These General Guidelines apply equally to individual practitioners and to those who work in a group practice, an institutional agency, or another organizational setting.

2. Guidelines describe levels of quality for covered psychological services that providers strive to attain, regardless of the nature of the users, purchasers, or sanctioners of such covered services.

3. Those people who provide psychological services meet acceptable levels of education, training, and experience that are consistent and appropriate to the functions they perform. The final responsibility and accountability for defining qualifications and supervision

requirements for service rest with a professional psychologist[6] (see Definitions).

4. Guidelines do not constrain psychologists from employing new methods (see Guideline 1.8) or from making flexible use of support personnel in staffing the delivery of services. The General Guidelines illuminate potential weaknesses in the delivery of psychological services and point to their correction. Some settings may require additional guidelines for specific areas of service delivery than those herein proposed. There is no intent to diminish the scope or quality of psychological services that exceed these General Guidelines. Systematically applied, these General Guidelines serve to establish desirable levels of psychological service. They serve to establish a more effective and consistent basis for evaluating the performance of individual service providers, and they serve to guide the organizing of psychological service units in human service settings.

5. It is recognized that there are significant differences among the established fields of professional psychology in regard to education and training, technical methodology, user populations served, and methods and settings of service delivery. The *Specialty Guidelines for the Delivery of Services* (APA, 1981b) provides acknowledgment of these differences while conforming to the guiding principles delineated by the General Guidelines.

6. These General Guidelines have been developed with the understanding that psychological services must be planned and implemented so that they are sensitive to factors related to life in a pluralistic society such as age, gender, affectional orientation, culture, and ethnicity.

Implications of Guidelines

The General Guidelines presented here have broad implications both for members of the public who use psychological services and for providers of such services.

1. The Guidelines furnish a basis for a mutual understanding between providers and users. Further, they facilitate improved quality of services and more effective evaluation of these services and their outcomes.

2. The Guidelines are an important step toward greater uniformity in legislative and regulatory actions involving providers of psychological services, and provide a model for the development of accreditation procedures for service facilities.

3. The Guidelines give specific content to the profession's concept of ethical practice as reflected in the APA *Ethical Principles of Psychologists* (1981a).

4. The Guidelines have significant impact on training models for both professional and support personnel in psychology.

5. Guidelines for the provision of psychological services influence what is considered desirable organizational structure, budgeting, and staffing patterns in these facilities.

Definitions

Providers of Psychological Services
This term subsumes two categories of providers of psychological services. The two categories are as follows:

A. Professional psychologists. Psychologists have a doctoral degree in psychology from an organized, sequential program in a regionally accredited university or professional school.[6,7,8] Specific definitions of professional psychologists by each of the recognized specialties are provided in the *Specialty Guidelines for the Delivery of Services* (APA, 1981b).

B. Other persons who provide psychological services. Qualifications and supervision for these persons are commensurate with their responsibilities and are further delineated in these policies[9] and in the *Specialty Guidelines for the Delivery of Services*.

Psychological Services
This term refers to one or more of the following:[10]

A. Evaluation, diagnosis,[11] and assessment of the functioning of individuals, groups, and organizations.

B. Interventions, preventive and ameliorative, that facilitate the functioning of individuals, groups, and organizations.[12]

C. Consultation relating to A and B.

D. Program development services in the areas of A, B, and C.[13]

E. Administration and supervision of psychological services.[14]

F. Evaluation of all psychological services.

Psychological Service Unit
This is the functional unit through which psychological services are provided:

A. A psychological service unit is a unit that provides predominantly psychological services and is composed of one or more professional psychologists and support staff.

B. A psychological service unit may operate as a functional or geographic component of a larger governmental, educational, correctional, health, training, industrial, or commercial organizational unit, or as an independent professional service unit.[15]

C. A psychological service unit may take the form of one or more psychologists providing professional services in a multidisciplinary setting.

D. A psychological service unit also may be an individual or group of individuals in a private practice or a psychological consulting firm.

Users
Users include the following:

A. Direct users or recipients of psychological services.

B. Public and private institutions, facilities, or organizations receiving psychological services.

Sanctioners
Sanctioners include the following:

A. Direct users or recipients of psychological services.

B. Public and private institutions, facilities, or organizations receiving psychological services.

C. Any other individual, group, organization, institution, or governing body having legitimate interaction with a psychologist functioning in a professional capacity.

GENERAL GUIDELINE 1: PROVIDERS

1.1 Each psychological service unit offering psychological services has available at least one professional psychologist and as many more professional psychologists as are necessary to assure the quality of services offered.[16]

Illustrative Statement.[17] The intent of this General Guideline is that one or more providers of psychological services in any psychological service unit meet the levels of training and experience of professional psychologists as specified in the preceding definitions.[18] When a professional psychologist is not available on a full-time basis, the facility retains the services of one or more professional psychologists on a regular part-time basis to supervise the psychological services provided. The psychologist who is so retained has authority and participates sufficiently to enable him or her to assess the needs for services, to review the content of services provided, and to assume professional responsibility and accountability for them.

1.2 Providers of psychological services who do not meet the requirements for professional psychologists are supervised, directed, and evaluated by a professional psychologist to the extent required by the tasks assigned (see Definitions and the *Specialty Guidelines for the Delivery of Services*, APA, 1981b). Tasks assigned to these providers are in keeping with their demonstrated areas of competence. The level and extent of supervision may vary from task to task, as long as the professional psychologist retains a close relationship that is sufficient to meet this General Guideline. In situations in which those providers work in a fair, autonomous fashion, they maintain an appropriate level of consultation and supervisory support from a professional psychologist.

Illustrative Statement: For example, in health care settings, support personnel may be assigned varying levels of responsibility for providing designated functions within their demonstrated areas of competence. Support personnel are considered to be responsible for their functions and behavior when assisting in the provision of psychological services and are accountable to a professional psychologist. Ultimate professional responsibility and accountability for the services provided require that the supervisor review reports and test protocols and review and discuss intervention plans, strategies, and outcomes. In these settings, the nature and extent of supervision is determined by the professional psychologist to assure the adequacy of psychological services provided.

To facilitate the effectiveness of the psychological service unit, the nature of the supervisory relationship is clearly and explicitly communicated to support personnel, preferably in writing. Such communications describe and delineate the duties of the employees, such as the range and type of services to be provided. The limits of independent action and decision making are defined. Descriptions of responsibilities specify the means by which employees will contact the professional psychologist in the event of emergency or crisis situations.

1.3 Wherever a psychological service unit exists, a professional psychologist is responsible for planning, directing, and reviewing the provision of psychological services.

Illustrative Statement: The psychologist who directs or coordinates the unit maintains an ongoing or periodic review of the adequacy of services and plans in accordance with the results of such evaluation. This psychologist coordinates the activities of the psychological service unit with other professional, administrative, and technical groups, both within and outside the facility. This psy-

chologist, who may be the director, chief, or coordinator of the psychological service unit, has related responsibilities including, but not limited to, recruiting qualified staff, directing training and research activities of the service, maintaining a high level of professional and ethical practice, and assuring that staff members function only within the areas of their competence.

To facilitate the effectiveness of services by increasing the level of staff sensitivity and professional skills, the psychologist who is designated as director participates in the selection of professional and support personnel whose qualifications include sensitivity and consideration for the language, cultural and experiential background, affectional orientation, ethnic identification, age, and gender of the users, and whose professional skills are directly relevant to the needs and characteristics of these users. Additionally, the director ensures that professional and support personnel do not provide services in any manner that is discriminatory or exploitative to users.

In other institutional and organizational settings, psychologists may be administratively responsible to individuals from disciplines other than psychology. In these instances, the psychologist should seek to sensitize the administrator to the need to allow participation of the psychologist in planning, directing, and reviewing the provision of psychological services.

1.4 When functioning within an organizational setting, professional psychologists seek, whenever appropriate and feasible, to bring their education, training, experience, and skills to bear upon the goals of the organization by participating in the planning and development of overall operations.

Illustrative Statement: One way psychologists maintain high professional standards is by being active representatives on boards and committees concerned with service delivery and overall operation of their facility. These activities may include but are not limited to active participation as voting and as office-holding members, on the governance staff as well as on executive, planning, and evaluation boards and committees.

1.5 All providers of psychological services attempt to maintain and apply current knowledge of scientific and professional developments that are directly related to the services they render. This includes knowledge relating to special populations (such as ethnic or other minorities) that may compose a part of their practice.

Illustrative Statement: Methods through which knowledge of scientific and professional developments may be gained include, but are not limited to, continuing education, attendance at workshops, participation in staff development programs, formal and informal on-the-job training, and reading scientific and professional publications. All providers have access to reference material related to the provisions of psychological services. All providers are prepared to show evidence periodically that they are staying abreast of and utilizing current knowledge and practices.

1.6 Professional psychologists limit their practice, including supervision, to their demonstrated areas of professional competence. Special proficiency supervision of psychologists may be provided by professionals from other disciplines whose competence in the given area has been demonstrated by previous education, training, and experience.

Illustrative Statement: Psychological services are offered in accordance with the providers' areas of competence as defined by verifiable education, training, and experience. Before offering professional services beyond the range of their experience and usual practice (e.g., providing services to culturally/linguistically diverse populations), psychologists strive to obtain pertinent knowledge through such means as education, training, reading, and appropriate professional consultation.

1.7 Psychologists who change or add a specialty meet the same requirement with respect to subject matter and professional skills that apply to doctoral education, training, and experience in the new specialty.[19]

Illustrative Statement: Retraining psychologists to qualify them for a change in specialty must be under the auspices of a program in a regionally accredited university or professional school that offers the doctoral degree in that specialty. Such education and training are individualized, due credit being given for relevant coursework or requirements that have previously been satisfied. Merely taking an internship or acquiring experience in a practicum setting or in an employment setting is not considered adequate preparation for becoming a clinical, counseling, industrial/organizational, or school psychologist. Fulfillment of such an individualized training program is attested to by official certification by the supervising department or professional school indicating the successful completion of education preparation in the particular specialty. Specific requirements for retraining in each of the recognized specialties are detailed in the

Specialty Guidelines for the Delivery of Services (APA, 1981b).

1.8 Psychologists are encouraged to develop and/or apply and evaluate innovative theories and procedures, to provide appropriate theoretical or empirical support for their innovations, and to disseminate their results to others.

Illustrative Statement: A profession rooted in a science continually explores, studies, conducts, and evaluates applications of theories and procedures with a view toward developing, verifying, and documenting new and improved ways of serving users.

GENERAL GUIDELINE 2: PROGRAMS

2.1 Composition and organization of a psychological service unit

2.1.1 The composition and programs of a psychological service unit strive to be responsive to the needs of the people and settings served.

Illustrative Statement: A psychological service unit is structured to facilitate effective and economical delivery of services. For example, a psychological service unit serving a predominantly low-income or ethnic minority group has a staffing pattern and service program adapted to the linguistic, experiential, attitudinal, and financial characteristics of the user population.

2.1.2 A psychological service unit strives to include sufficient numbers of professional psychologists and support personnel to achieve its goals, objectives, and purposes.

Illustrative Statement: The workload, diversity of the psychological services required, and the specific goals and objectives of the setting determine the numbers and qualifications of professional psychologists and support personnel in the psychological service unit. Where shortages in personnel exist, so that psychological services cannot be rendered in a professional manner, the director of the psychological service unit initiates action to modify appropriately the specific goals, objectives, and timetables of the service. If necessary, the director appropriately modifies the scope or workload of the unit to maintain the quality of the services and, at the same time, makes continued efforts to devise alternative systems for delivery of services.

2.2 Policies

2.2.1 A written description of roles, objectives, and scope of services is developed by multi-provider psychological service units as well as by psychological service units that are a component of an organization, unless the unit has a specific alternative approach. The written description or alternative approach is reviewed annually and is available to the staff of the unit and to users and sanctioners upon request.

Illustrative Statement: The psychological service unit reviews its objectives and scope of services annually and makes revisions as necessary to ensure that the psychological services offered are consistent with staff competencies and current psychological knowledge and practice. This statement is discussed with staff, reviewed by the appropriate administrator, and distributed to users and sanctioners upon request and whenever appropriate. Psychologists strive to be aware of management theories and practices that will aid in the delivery of psychological services.

2.2.2 Providers of psychological services avoid any action that will violate or diminish the legal and civil rights of users or of others who may be affected by their actions.[20]

Illustrative Statement: Providers of psychological services are continually sensitive to the issue of confidentiality of information; they strive to be sensitive to the potential impact of their decisions and recommendations, and to other matters pertaining to individual, legal, and civil rights. Providers of psychological services strive to be aware of issues such as self-incrimination in judicial proceedings, involuntary commitment to hospitals, protection of minors, protection of legal incompetents, discriminatory practices in employment selection procedures, recommendations for special education provisions, information relative to adverse personnel actions in the armed services, and adjudication of domestic relations disputes in divorce and custodial proceedings. Providers of psychological services are encouraged to make themselves available to local committees, review boards, and similar advisory groups established to safeguard the human, civil, and legal rights of service users.

2.2.3 Providers of psychological services are familiar with and abide by the American Psychological Association's *Ethical Principles of Psychologists* (1981a), *Specialty Guidelines for the Delivery of Services* (1981b), *Standards for Educational and Psychological Testing* (1985), *Ethical Principles in the Conduct of Research with Human Participants* (1982), *Guidelines for Computer-Based Tests and Interpretations* (1986), "Guidelines for Psychologists Conducting Growth Groups" (1973), and other APA policy statements relevant to guidelines for professional services issued by the Association.[21]

Illustrative Statement: Psychological service units have available a copy of each of these documents, and providers maintain current knowledge of relevant APA guidelines and principles.

2.2.4 Providers of psychological services seek to conform to relevant statutes established by federal, state, and local governments. At times psychologists may seek to challenge legal constraints that they reasonably and honestly believe unduly infringe on the rights of their users or on the right of psychologists to practice their profession; however, any such challenges should conform to appropriate legal procedures.

Illustrative Statement: All providers of psychological services seek to be familiar with and practice in conformity with relevant statutes that relate directly to the practice of psychology. They also endeavor to be informed about governmental agency regulations that have the force of law and that relate to the delivery of psychological services (e.g., evaluation for disability retirement or for special education placements). In addition, all providers seek to be aware that federal agencies such as the Veterans Administration, the Department of Education, and the Department of Health and Human Services have policy statements regarding psychological services. Providers of psychological services attempt to be familiar with other statutes and regulations, including those addressed to the civil and legal rights of users (e.g., those promulgated by the federal Equal Employment Opportunity Commission) that are pertinent to their scope of practice.

2.2.5 In recognizing the matrix of personal and societal problems, providers make available, when appropriate, information regarding additional human services, such as specialized psychological services, legal aid societies, social services, employment agencies, health resources, and educational and recreational facilities.

Illustrative Statement: Psychologists and support personnel are sensitive to the broader context of human needs. They refer to such resources and are encouraged, when appropriate, to intervene actively on behalf of the users. Providers make appropriate use of other professional, research, technical, and administrative resources whenever these serve the best interests of the users, and they establish and maintain cooperative or collaborative arrangements with such other resources as are required to meet the needs of users.

2.2.6 In the best interest of the users, providers of psychological services endeavor to consult and collaborate with professional colleagues in the planning and delivery of services when such consultation is deemed appropriate.

Illustrative Statement: Psychologists recognize the areas of special competence of other psychologists and of other professionals for consultation and referral purposes.

2.3   Procedures

2.3.1 Each psychological service unit is guided by a set of procedural guidelines for the delivery of psychological services.

Illustrative Statement: Depending on the nature of the setting, and whenever feasible, providers are prepared to provide a statement of procedural guidelines in oral and/or written form that can be understood by users as well as sanctioners. This statement may describe the current methods, forms, procedures, and techniques being used to achieve the objectives and goals for psychological services.

This statement is communicated to staff and, when appropriate, to users and sanctioners. The psychological service unit provides for the annual review of its procedures for the delivery of psychological services.

2.3.2 Psychologists develop plans for psychological services appropriate to the problems presented by the users.

Illustrative Statement: Ideally, a plan for intervention or consultation is in written form and serves as a basis for accountability. Regardless of the type of setting or users involved, a plan that describes the psychological services indicated and the manner in which they will be provided is developed and agreed upon by the providers and users.[22] A psychologist who provides services as one member of a collaborative effort participates in the development and implementation of the overall service plan and provides for its periodic review.

2.3.3 There is a mutually acceptable understanding between a provider and a user or that user's responsible agent regarding the delivery of service.

Illustrative Statement: A psychologist discusses the plan for the provision of psychological services with the user, noting procedures that will be used and respective responsibilities of provider and user. This interaction is repeated whenever major changes occur in the plan for service. This understanding may be oral or written, but in any event, the psychologist documents the nature of the understanding.[23]

2.3.4 Professional psychologists clarify early on to users and sanctioners the exact fee structure or financial arrangements and payment schedule when providing services for a fee. (See Ethical Principle 6d.)

Illustrative Statement: Psychologists inform users of their payment policies and of their willingness to assist users in obtaining reimbursement. Those who accept reimbursement from a third party are acquainted with the appropriate statutes and regulations, instruct their users on proper procedures for submitting claims, and inform them of limits on confidentiality of claims information, in accordance with pertinent statutes.

2.3.5 Accurate, current, and pertinent records of essential psychological services are maintained.

Illustrative Statement: At a minimum, records kept of psychological services should include identifying data, dates of services, and types of services, and where appropriate, may include a record of significant actions taken.[24] Providers make all reasonable efforts to record essential information concerning psychological services within a reasonable time of their conception.

2.3.6 Each psychological service unit follows an established policy for the retention and disposition of records.[25]

Illustrative Statement: Such a policy conforms to government statutes and regulations, or to organizational or institutional regulations, policies, or practices where such are applicable.

2.3.7 Psychologists establish and maintain a system that protects the confidentiality of their users' records.[26]

Illustrative Statement: Psychologists establish and maintain the confidentiality of information about the users of services, whether obtained by themselves or by those they supervise. If directed otherwise by statute, by regulations with the force of law, or by court order, psychologists seek a resolution that is both ethically and legally feasible and appropriate; for example, psychologists might request in camera (judge's chambers) hearings when they are required by the court to produce records. All people who are supervised by psychologists, including nonprofessional personnel and students, and who have access to records of psychological services are also expected to maintain this confidentiality of information. Psychologists do not release confidential information, except with the written consent of the user involved, or of his or her legal representative, guardian, or other holder of the privilege on behalf of the user, and only after being assured by whatever means may be required that the user has been assisted in understanding the implications of the release. Even after the consent has been obtained for release, psychologists clearly identify such information as confidential for the recipient of the information.

Users are informed in advance of any limits in the setting for maintaining the confidentiality of psychological information. For instance, psychologists in hospital settings inform their patients that psychological information in a patient's clinical record may be available to other hospital personnel without the patient's written consent. Similar limitations on confidentiality of psychological information may be present in certain school, industrial, business, government, or military settings or in instances where the user has waived confidentiality for purposes of third-party payment. When the user's intention to waive confidentiality is judged by a professional psychologist to be contrary to the user's best interest or to be in conflict with that person's legal or civil rights, it is the responsibility of the psychologist to discuss the implications of releasing the psychological information and to assist the user in limiting disclosure by specifying the nature of the information, the recipients, and the time period during which the release is in effect, recognizing, however, that the ultimate decision concerning release of information is that of the user. Providers of psychological services are sensitive to both the benefits and the possible misuse of information regarding individuals that is stored in computerized data banks. Providers take necessary measures to ensure that such information is used in a socially responsible manner.

Users have the right to information in their agency records and to be informed as to any regulations that govern the release of such information. However, the records are the property of the psychologist or of the facility in which the psychologist works and are, therefore, under the control of the psychologist or of the facility. Users have the right to examine such psychological records. Preferably such examination should be in the presence of a psychologist who judges how best to explain the material in a meaningful and useful manner.

In school settings, parents have the legal right to examine such psychological records, preferably in the presence of a psychologist. In the event that a family moves to another school system, the parents have the legal right to examine a copy of such records from the former school in the new school setting. In either circumstance, the rationale for allowing parents to examine such records is to assure that parents are not in a disadvantaged position if they choose to challenge a

school's decision regarding the child. Disclosure of such psychological information in the records from a former school is conducted under secure conditions; such records have been transmitted to the new school to a psychologist under whose supervision the records may be examined. Psychologists and the institutions in which they work have written policy regarding the storage and access of pupils' records. Parents are informed of the results of a psychological assessment of their child in a form most meaningful and useful to the parents.

Raw psychological data (e.g., test protocols, therapy or interview notes, or questionnaire returns) in which a user is identified are ordinarily released only with the written consent of the user or of the user's legal representative, and are released only to a person recognized by the psychologist as competent to interpret the data. Any use of made of psychological reports, records, or data for research or training purposes is consistent with this General Guideline. Additionally, providers of psychological services comply with statutory confidentiality requirements and with those embodied in the *Ethical Principles of Psychologists* (APA, 1981a).

2.3.8 Providers of psychological services do not use privileged information received in the course of their work for competitive advantage or personal gain. (See Ethical Principle 5.)

Illustrative Statement: Providers of psychological services often obtain privileged information through their work with users, or while reviewing the proposals of competing practitioners or agencies. Such information may include but not be limited to users' or user associates' business interests, or the interests of competing colleagues or practitioners. When providers acquire such information and it is protected by applicable law or through agreement, it is held confidential and shall not be used for competitive advantage. Further, information that is potentially harmful to users or their associates, or to professional colleagues, should not be used for personal advantage.

2.4 Environment

2.4.1 Providers of psychological services promote the development of a physical, organizational, and social environment in the service setting that facilitates optimal human functioning.

Illustrative Statement: As providers of services, professional psychologists are concerned with the environment of their service unit, especially as it affects the quality of service, but also as it impinges on human functioning in the larger unit of an organization when the service unit is included in such a larger context. Attention is given to the comfort and, where relevant, to the privacy of providers and users. Federal, state, and local requirements for safety, health, and sanitation are observed. Physical arrangements and organizational policies and procedures are conducive to the human dignity, self-respect, and optimal functioning of users and to the effective delivery of service. The atmosphere in which psychological services are rendered is appropriate to the service and to the users, whether in an office, clinic, school, college, university, industrial setting, or other organizational or institutional setting.

GENERAL GUIDELINE 3: ACCOUNTABILITY

3.1 The promotion of human welfare is the primary principle guiding the professional activities of all members of the psychological service unit.

Illustrative Statement: Providers of psychological services are expected to interact with users in a manner that is considerate, effective, economical, and humane; to be mindful of their accountability to the sanctioners of psychological services and to the general public; and to see that appropriate steps are taken to protect the confidentiality of the service relationship.

The psychological service unit does not withhold services to a potential user on the basis of that user's national or ethnic origin, religion, gender, affectional orientation, or age; nor does it provide services in a discriminatory or exploitative fashion. However, this does not preclude psychologists from serving agencies whose publicly declared policy restricts users to membership of a particular religious, ethnic, or other specified group, as long as that policy does not constitute unlawful discrimination.[27] Professional psychologists who find that psychological services are being provided in a manner that is discriminatory or exploitative of users or that is contrary to these General Guidelines or to government statutes or regulations take appropriate corrective actions, which may include the refusal to provide services. When conflicts of interest arise, psychologists are guided in the resolution of differences by the principles set forth in the *Ethical Principles of Psychologists* (APA, 1981a).

Recognition is given to the following considerations in regard to the withholding of services: (1) the professional right of psychologists to limit their practice to a specific category of users with whom they have achieved demonstrated competence (e.g., individuals, families, groups, ethnic minorities, or organizations); (2) the right and responsibility of psychologists to withhold an assessment procedure when not validly applicable; (3) the right and responsibility of psychologists to withhold services in specific instances in which their own limitations or user characteristics might impair the quality of the services; (4) the obligation of psychologists to seek to ameliorate through peer review, consultation, therapeutic procedures, or other procedures those factors that inhibit the provision of services to particular individuals, families, groups, ethnic minorities, or organizations; and (5) the obligation of psychologists who withhold services to assist the users in obtaining services from another source.

3.2 Psychologists pursue their activities as members of the independent, autonomous profession of psychology.

Illustrative Statement: Psychologists, as members of an independent profession, are responsible both to the public and to their peers through established review mechanisms. Psychologists are aware of the implications of their activities for the profession as a whole. They seek to eliminate discriminatory practices instituted for self-serving purposes that are not in the interest of the users (e.g., arbitrary requirements for referral and supervision or sign-off by another profession). They are cognizant of their responsibilities for the development of the profession. They participate where possible in the training and career development of students and other providers, participate as appropriate in the training of support personnel or other professionals, and integrate their contributions within the structure established for delivering psychological services. They facilitate the development of and participate in professional standards review mechanisms and seek to work with other professionals in a cooperative manner for the good of the users and for the benefit of the general public.

Psychologists recognize that it is their responsibility to keep supervisors, administrators, and other agency personnel informed of APA guidelines, principles, standards, policies, and other criteria related to their professional functioning. This information is imparted at times that are appropriate in the individual setting. This may include statements of policy procedures, disclaimers, and so forth. Psychologists are responsible for defining and developing their profession, consistent with the general canons of science and with the public welfare.[28]

3.3 There are periodic, systematic, and effective evaluations of psychological services.

Illustrative Statement: When the psychological service unit is a component of a larger organization, regular assessment of progress in achieving goals is provided in the service delivery plan. Such evaluation could include consideration of the effectiveness of psychological services relative to costs in terms of time, money, and the availability of professional and support personnel. Evaluation of the psychological service delivery system could be conducted both internally and, when possible, under independent auspices. Descriptions of therapeutic procedures and other services as well as outcome measures should be as detailed as possible. This evaluation might include an assessment of effectiveness (to determine what the service accomplished), costs, continuity (to ensure that the services are appropriately linked to other human services), availability (to determine appropriate levels and distribution of services and personnel), accessibility (to ensure that the services are barrier-free to users), and adequacy (to determine whether the services meet the identified needs of users). In such evaluations, care is taken to maintain confidentiality of records and privacy of users. It is highly desirable that there be a periodic reexamination of review mechanisms to ensure that these attempts at public safeguards are effective and cost-efficient and do not place unnecessary encumbrances on providers or unnecessary additional expenses on users or sanctioners for services rendered.

3.4   Professional psychologists are accountable for all aspects of the services they provide and are appropriately responsive to those people who are concerned with these services.

Illustrative Statement: Depending upon the settings, accurate and full information is made available to prospective individual or organizational users regarding the qualifications of providers, the nature and extent of services offered, and, where appropriate, financial costs and potential risks. In recognizing their responsibilities to users, sanctioners, third-party purchasers, and other providers, wherever appropriate and consistent with the users' legal rights and privileged communications, professional psychologists make available information about initiation, continuation, modification, termination, and evaluation of psychological services and provide counsel to users regarding their decisions about such issues.

3.5   In the public interest, professional psychologists may wish to provide some services to individuals or organizations for little or no financial return.

Illustrative Statement: Professional psychologists are encouraged to contribute a portion of their services and work for which they receive little or no financial return, according to the *Ethical Principles of Psychologists* (APA, 1981a), and to encourage those they supervise to perform services on a similar basis.

FOOTNOTES

[1]The footnotes to these General Guidelines represent an attempt to provide a coherent context of other policy statements of the APA regarding professional practice. The General Guidelines extend these previous policy statements where necessary to reflect current concerns of the public and of the profession.

[2]Note that the title and emphasis of these General Guidelines have been changed from the 1977 version of the *Standards for Providers of Psychological Services.* This has been done to reflect the development and adoption of the *Specialty Guidelines for the Delivery of Services* by the APA in 1980. The profession continues to grow in a variety of areas in which specific guidelines are not yet necessary. These General Guidelines are intended to support practitioners in these areas.

As stated later in the Preamble, the General Guidelines are aspirational in nature. The change in title is meant to signify that the professional practice of psychology is constantly changing. No collection of principles can adequately direct these changes, and there is no intent to limit future development even though this collection represents the consensus of the profession at this time.

[3]The Ethical Principles from which the General Guidelines have been derived are noted in parentheses at the end of the corresponding General Guidelines.

[4]Early in 1970, acting at the direction of the APA's Council of Representatives, the Board of Professional Affairs (BPA) appointed a task force composed of practicing psychologists with specialized knowledge in at least one of every major class of human service facility and with experience relevant to the setting of standards. The task force's charge was to develop a set of standards for psychological practice. Soon thereafter, partial support for this activity was obtained through a grant from the National Institute of Mental Health (NIMH Grant MH 21696).

The task force promptly established liaison with national groups already active in setting and accrediting standards. It was therefore able to influence two groups of the Joint Commission on Accreditation of Hospitals (JCAH), the Accreditation Council for Facilities for the Mentally Retarded (JCAH, 1971) and the Accreditation Council for Psychiatric Facilities (JCAH, 1972), in their adoption of certain basic principles and in their wording of their standards for psychological services. It also contributed substantially to the "constitutionally required minimum standards for adequate treatment of the mentally ill" ordered by the U.S. District Court in Alabama in the case of *Wyatt v. Stickney* (1972). In concert with other APA committees, the task force also represented the APA in national-level deliberations with government groups and insurance carriers that defined the qualifications necessary for psychologists involved in providing health services.

These interim outcomes involved influence by the APA on actions by groups of nonpsychologists that directly affected the manner in which psychological services were employed, particularly in health and rehabilitation settings. However, these measures did not relieve the Association from exercising its responsibility to speak out directly and authoritatively on what standards for psychological practice should be throughout a broad range of human service settings.

In September 1974, after more than four years of study and broad consultations, the task force completed the APA's first edition of the *Standards for Providers of Psychological Services* (1974). The task of collecting, analyzing, and synthesizing reactions to the original Standards fell to two successive committees. They were charged similarly to review and revise the Standards and to suggest means to implement them, including their acceptance by relevant government and private accreditation groups. The dedicated work of the psychologists who served on both of those committees is gratefully acknowledged. Also recognized with thanks are the several hundred comments received from scores of interested persons representing professional, academic, and scientific psychology; from consumer groups; from administrators of facilities; and from others.

Members of the Task Force on Standards for Service Facilities, which submitted the original Standards in September 1974, were Milton L. Blum, Jacqueline C. Bouhoutsos, Jerry H. Clark, Harold A. Edgerton, Marian D. Hall, Durand F. Jacobs (1972–1974 Chair), Floyd H. Martinez, John E. Muthard, Asher R. Pacht, William D. Pierce, Sue A. Warren, and Alfred M. Wellner (1970–1971 Chair). Staff liaisons from the APA Office of Professional Affairs were John J. McMillan (1970–1971), Gottlieb Simon (1971–1973), and Arthur Centor (1973–1974).

In January 1975, the APA Council of Representatives created the original Committee on Standards for Providers of Psychological Services. The Committee was charged with updating and revising the Standards adopted in September 1974. Members of the Committee were Jacqueline C. Bouhoutsos, Leon Hall, Marian D. Hall, Mary Henle, Durand F. Jacobs (Chair), Abel Ossorio, and Wayne Sorenson. The task force liaison was Jerry H. Clark, and the APA Central Office liaison was Arthur Centor.

In January 1976, the Council modified its charge to the Committee to review the Standards and to recommend revisions needed to reflect the varying needs of only those psychologists engaged in the activities of clinical psychology, counseling psychology, industrial/organizational psychology, and school psychology. The Committee was reconstituted with one member representing each of the four applied activities, plus one member representing institutional practice and one representing the public interest. Members were Jules Barron (later replaced by Morris Goodman), clinical; Barbara A. Kirk (later replaced by Milton Schwebel), counseling; Virginia Schein (later replaced by Frank Friedlander), industrial/organizational; Durand F. Jacobs (Chair), institutional practice; M. Brewster Smith (later re-

placed by Pearl Mayo Dansby), public interest; Marian D. Hall (later replaced by Jack I. Bardon and Nadine M. Lambert), school. Arthur Centor and Richard Kilburg were the APA Central Office liaisons. The revised *Standards for Providers of Psychological Services* was approved by the APA Council of Representatives in January 1977 (APA, 1977).

In January 1980, the APA Council of Representatives instructed the Board of Professional Affairs to amend the 1977 Standards in keeping with the principles enunciated by the Council in connection with its action approving the four sets of *Specialty Guidelines for the Delivery of Services* (APA, 1981b). The BPA referred the task of revising the 1977 Standards to the newly created Committee on Professional Standards, composed of Juanita Braddock, public member; Judy E. Hall, experimental/mental retardation; Nadine M. Lambert, school; David Mills (Chair, January–April 1981), clinical/counseling; Milton Schwebel counseling; Gilfred Tanabe (1980 Chair), clinical; and Murphy Thomas (Chair, May–December 1981), clinical. Subsequent members of the Committee on Professional Standards included William Chestnut, counseling; Lorraine D. Eyde, industrial/organizational; Morris Goodman (1982–1983 Chair), clinical; John H. Jackson, school; Caroline Miller, public member, William Schofield (1984 Chair), clinical; and Barbara Wand, social. These past members of the Committee on Professional Standards were responsible for completing the 1984 revision of the Standards. Central Office staff assistance was provided by Richard Kilburg and Joy Burke (1980), Sharon Shueman and Pam Juhl (1980–1982), Jutta N. Hagner (1982–1984), and Patricia J. Aletky (1982–1985).

The 1985 draft revision was prepared by Committee on Professional Standards members Susan Robbins Berger, school; LaMaurice Gardner, clinical; Jo-Ida Hansen, counseling; Marlene Muse, public member; Lyle Schoenfeldt, industrial/organizational; William Schofield (1985 Chair), clinical; and Barbara Wand (1985 Vice-Chair), social. Central Office staff assistance was provided by Patricia J. Aletky, Patricia Brown, and Rizalina Mendiola. Between March 1985 and June 1985, a BPA work group on the Standards (composed of John H. Jackson, Chair; Morris Goodman; and William Schofield) reviewed and modified the 1985 draft revision. Central Office staff assistance was provided by Patricia J. Aletky, Patricia Brown, and Rizalina Mendiola.

In November 1985, BPA approved a revised effort that involved Committee on Professional Standards members and work groups representing each of the recognized specialties. The Committee on Professional Standards members participating were Lyle Schoenfeldt (1986 Chair), industrial/organizational; Susan Robbins Berger (1986 Vice-Chair), school; LaMaurice Gardner, clinical; Jo-Ida Hansen, counseling; Richard Kilburg, clinical; and Alan Malyon, clinical. Work group participants, by specialty area and Division, were as follows: Clinical: Robert Weitz (Division 12); Patricia Hannigan and Gerald Koocher (Division 29); Donna Copeland, Marlene Eisen, and Billie S. Strauss (Division 30); Arthur Bodin (Divisions 31, 38, 39, 42, 43); Ronald Kurz (Division 38); and Florence Kaslow (Divisions 41 and 43); Counseling: Ricki Bander, John Corrigan, Thomas Dowd, David Fago, and Milton Schwebel (Division 17); Industrial/Organizational: Hannah R. Hirsh and Manuel London (Division 14); School: Judith Alpert, John H. Jackson, and Ralph D. Wenger (Division 16); and Milton Shore (Division 37). Central Office assistance was provided by Pam Juhl, Sheila Lane Forsyth, Russell Newman, and Mary Lisa Debraggio.

[5]These General Guidelines are designed to be consistent with existing APA policies. One APA policy governing this issue is the 1987 Model Act for State Licensure of Psychologists, prepared by a subcommittee of APA's Committee on Professional Practice and adopted by the APA Council of Representatives in February 1987.

[6]People who met the following criteria on or before the date of adoption of the original Standards on September 4, 1974, shall also be considered professional psychologists: (a) a master's degree in a program primarily psychological in content from a regionally accredited university or professional school; (b) appropriate education, training, and experience in the area of service offered; (c) a license or certificate in the state in which they practice, conferred by a state board of psychological examiners; or, in the absence of statutory regulation, the endorsement of the state psychological association through voluntary certification; or, for practice in primary and secondary schools, a state department of education certificate as a school psychologist provided that the certificate required at least two graduate years. Wherever the term *psychologist* is used in these General Guidelines, it refers to *professional psychologist*.

Within the specialty of school psychology, those persons who met the following criteria on or before, but not beyond, January 31, 1985, are also recognized as professional school psychologists: (a) a master's or higher degree, requiring at least two years of full-time graduate study in school psychology, from a regionally accredited university or professional school; (b) at least three additional years of training and experience in school psychological services, including a minimum of 1,200 hours in school settings; and (c) a license or certificate conferred by a state board of psychological examiners or a state educational agency for practice in elementary or secondary schools.

[7]Some federal and state legislation uses the term *clinical psychologist* to identify a set of service providers that is not limited to clinical psychologists as defined by the APA in the *Specialty Guidelines for the Delivery of Services by Clinical Psychologists* (APA, 1981b). APA defines the term *clinical psychologist* in health service delivery legislation in a generic sense to include all qualified professional psychologists who provide relevant services. Intraprofessionally, as represented by its *Specialty Guidelines*, APA currently supports specific and meaningful differentiation in the education, training, and practices of the specialties of clinical psychology, counseling psychology, industrial/organizational psychology, and school psychology.

[8]This definition is similar to the recommended statutory language in the "Requirements for Licensure" section of the 1987 APA Model Act for State Licensure of Psychologists (APA, 1987b), a policy statement setting forth model state legislation affecting the practice of psychology and recognizing the doctor-

ate as the minimum educational requirement for entry into professional practice as a psychologist:

> Applicants for licensure shall possess a doctoral degree in psychology from an institution of higher education. The degree shall be obtained from a recognized program of graduate study in psychology as defined by the rules and regulations of the Board.

> By 1995 applicants for licensure shall have completed a doctoral program in psychology that is accredited by the American Psychological Association (APA). In areas where no accreditation exists, applicants for licensure shall have completed a doctoral program in psychology that meets recognized acceptable professional standards as determined by the Board. When a new specialty of professional psychology is recognized as being within the accreditation scope of the APA, doctoral programs within that specialty will be afforded a transition period of eight years from their first class of students to the time of their accreditation. During that transition period, graduates of such programs may sit for licensure examination whether or not the program has been accredited. The same principle applies as well to new doctoral programs of specialties previously recognized within the scope of APA accreditation.

> Applicants trained in institutions outside the United States shall meet requirements established by the Board. (APA, 1987b, p. 698)

In addition to the above educational requirements, the following experience requirements also appear in the 1987 APA Model Act for State Licensure of Psychologists:

> For admission to the licensure examination, applicants shall demonstrate that they have completed two years of supervised professional experience, one year of which shall be postdoctoral. The criteria for appropriate supervision shall be in accordance with regulations to be promulgated by the Board. Postdoctoral experience shall be compatible with the knowledge and skills acquired during formal doctoral or postdoctoral education in accordance with professional requirements and relevant to the intended area of practice. Applicants shall be required to show evidence of good character, that is, that they have not been convicted of a criminal offense that bears directly on the fitness of the individual to be licensed. (APA, 1987b, p. 698)

[9]With regard to the roles, responsibilities, and supervision process for other persons who provide psychological services, a professional psychologist should consider the following issues and suggestions:

a. A professional psychologist is identified as the ethically responsible agent in all advertising, public announcements, and billings for supervised psychological services.

b. A supervising psychologist reviews and is responsible for all reports prepared by the assistant.

c. Professional psychologists set a reasonable limit on the number of assistants who are employed and supervised by a single supervisor.

d. Professional psychologists must be sufficiently available to ensure adequate evaluation or assessment, intervention planning, direction, and consultation.

e. Assistants provide services or carry out activities at the direction of the psychologist employer/supervisor who is responsible for those services or activities.

f. Assistants work in reasonably close physical proximity to the supervising psychologist so as to have available regular and continuing supervision.

[10]As was noted in the opening section of the General Guidelines, functions and activities of psychologists relating to the teaching of psychology, the writing or editing of scholarly or scientific manuscripts, the conduct of scientific research, and the activities of members of other professions do not fall within the purview of the General Guidelines.

[11]For the purposes of these General Guidelines and consistent with the 1987 APA Model Act for State Licensure of Psychologists, the term *diagnosis* may include the diagnosis of mental, emotional, nervous, or behavioral disorders or conditions of individuals and groups by professionals trained to do so, such as clinical, counseling, school, rehabilitation, and health psychologists (see Footnote 13).

[12]Consistent with the 1987 APA Model Act for State Licensure of Psychologists, such interventions include, but are not limited to, psychotherapy and counseling (see Footnote 13), and other interventions may include vocational development, cognitive rehabilitation, process consultation, psychological skills training, techniques of health psychology, selection and placement of personnel, and organizational development.

Specific definitions of interventions by each of the recognized specialties are provided in the *Specialty Guidelines for the Delivery of Services* (APA, 1981b).

[13]These definitions should be compared to the 1987 APA Model Act for State Licensure of Psychologists (APA, 1987b, p. 697), which includes definitions of *psychologist* and *practice of psychology* as follows:

Psychologist: A person represents himself or herself to be a psychologist if that person uses any title or description of services incorporating the words *psychology, psychological,* or *psychologist,* or if he or she possess expert qualification in any area of psychology or if that person offers to the public or renders to individuals or to groups of individuals services defined as the practice of psychology in this Act.

Practice of Psychology is defined as the observation, description, evaluation, interpretation, and modification of human behavior by the application of psychological principles, methods, and procedures, for the purpose of preventing or eliminating symptomatic, maladaptive, or undesired behavior and of enhancing interpersonal relationships, work and life adjustment, personal effectiveness, behavioral health, and mental health. The practice of psychology includes, but is not limited to, psychological testing and the evaluation or assessment of personal characteristics such as intelligence, personality, abilities, interests, aptitudes and neuropsychological functioning; counseling, psychoanalysis, psychotherapy, hypnosis, biofeedback, and behavior analysis and therapy; diagnosis and treatment of mental and emotional disorder or disability, alcoholism and substance abuse, disorders of habit or conduct, as well as of the psychological aspects of physical illness, accident, injury or disability; and psychoeducational evaluation, therapy, remediation and consultation. Psychological services may be rendered to individuals, families, groups, and the public. The practice of psychology shall be construed within the meaning of this definition without regard to whether payment is received for services rendered. (See Section J for exemptions.)

[14]As indicated in the *Ethical Principles of Psychologists* (APA, 1981a), especially Principle 1 (Responsibility) and Principle 3 (Moral and Legal Guidelines), when functioning as an administrator or manager in an organization or unit that is not a psychological services unit, psychologists apply their knowledge, skills, and abilities in furtherance of the objectives of that organization while remaining aware of the requirements of their profession's ethics and guidelines.

[15]The relation of a psychological service unit to a larger facility or institution is also addressed indirectly in the APA *Guidelines for Conditions of Employment of Psychologists* (APA, 1987a), which emphasizes the roles, responsibilities, and prerogatives of the psychologist when he or she is employed by or provides services for another agency, institution, or business.

[16]At the time of the adoption of these General Guidelines, there were four state statutes that did not require a doctoral degree for unsupervised provision of psychological services. Therefore, the goal of having the highest level of training for psychological practitioners is not, at the current time, fully achievable. (See Footnote 18 and Guideline 2.2.4.)

In addition to the small minority of states that recognize nondoctoral psychologists as independent providers of psychological services, almost all states recognize nondoctoral school psychologists who meet the requisite education, training, and experience prescribed by state departments of education as independent practitioners within local, regional, and state school systems.

[17]These illustrative statements have been selected to clarify how these General Guidelines might be implemented or apply in particular situations, and/or the importance of particular implications of the General Guidelines. The APA recognizes that there

may be a variety of implications of and methods for implementing a specific General Guideline depending on the situation in a given setting.

[18]This General Guideline reflects changes in the 1987 revision of the Model Act for State Licensure of Psychologists adopted by the APA Council of Representatives in February 1987 (APA, 1987b). Guideline 1.1 expresses the goal of the APA that psychological service units in all organizations have at least one professional psychologist available to assure the quality of services offered.

[19]This General Guideline follows closely the statement regarding "Policy on Training for Psychologists Wishing to Change Their Specialty" adopted by the APA Council of Representatives in January 1976 and revised by the Council in January 1982. Included therein is the implementing provision that "this policy statement shall be incorporated in the guidelines of the Committee on Accreditation so that appropriate sanctions can be brought to bear on university and internship training programs which violate [it]" (Conger, 1976, p. 424).

[20]See also *Ethical Principles in the Conduct of Research with Human Participants* (APA, 1982) and *Principles Concerning the Counseling and Therapy of Women* (APA, 1978).

[21]These documents are available from the American Psychological Association, 1200 Seventeenth Street, NW, Washington, DC 20036.

[22]Another example of a specific application of this principle is found in Guideline 2 in "Guidelines for Psychologists Conducting Growth Groups" (APA, 1973):

2. The following information should be made available in writing to all prospective participants:

   a. An explicit statement of the purpose of the group;

   b. Types of techniques that may be employed;

   c. The education, training, and experience of the leader or leaders;

   d. The fee and any additional expense that may be incurred;

   e. A statement as to whether or not a follow-up service is included in the fee;

   f. Goals of the group experience and techniques to be used;

   g. Amounts and kinds of responsibility to be assumed by the leader and by the participants. For example, (i) the degree to which a participant is free not to follow suggestions and prescriptions of the group leader and other group members (ii) any restrictions on a participant's freedom to leave the group at any time; and

   h. issues of confidentiality. (p. 933)

[23]When the user of the service is a child, it is desirable that both parent (or legal guardian) and child, to the extent possible, be involved in this understanding.

[24]Health care providers hold widely varying views about the wisdom of written records relating to the content of the psychotherapeutic relationship.

[25]In the absence of such, the policy is as follows:

1. Retain the full record intact for a specified period of time, if not in perpetuity. Some records need to be retained during the lifetime of an individual, either by the provider or by some other agency through arrangement by the provider. These records are necessary in special circumstances, such as in the case of handicapped individuals who need to comply with requests from the Social Security Administration for information on documented disabilities during their childhood years.

2. If a full record is not retained following completion of service delivery, a summary of the record is maintained for a specified period of time.

3. A record or the summary of a record may be disposed of only after a specified period of time following completion of planned services or the date of last contact, whichever comes later. (See the relevant sections of the *Specialty Guidelines for the Delivery of Services*, APA, 1981b, for specific retention and disposition guidelines. These are Guidelines 2.3.4 for clinical, counseling, and school psychologists.) In the event of the death of or the incapacity of a psychologist in independent practice, special procedures are necessary to assure the continuity of active service to the user and the safeguarding of records in accordance with this Guideline. For this reason, with the approval of the affected user, it is appropriate for another psychologist, acting under the auspices of the Professional Standards Review Committee (PSRC) or the Ethics Committee of the state, where such a committee is available, to review the record with that user and recommend a course of action for continuing professional service, if needed. Depending on local circumstances, appropriate arrangements for record retention and disposal are also recommended by the reviewing psychologist. This General Guideline has been developed to address a variety of circumstances that may arise, often years after a set of psychological services has been completed. Increasingly, records are being utilized in forensic matters, for peer review, for investigation of ethical complaints, and in response to requests from users, other professionals, or other legitimate parties requiring accurate information about the exact dates, nature, course, and outcome of a set of psychological services.

[26]Support for the principle of privileged communication is found in the Model Act for State Licensure of Psychologists (APA, 1987b):

In judicial proceedings, whether civil, criminal, or juvenile; in legislative and administrative proceedings; and in proceedings preliminary and ancillary thereto, a patient or client, or his or her guardian or personal representative, may refuse to disclose or prevent the disclosure of confidential information, including information contained in administrative records, communicated to a psychologist licensed or otherwise authorized to practice psychology under the laws of this jurisdiction, or to persons reasonably believed by the patient or client to be so licensed, and their agents, for the purpose of diagnosis, evaluation, or treatment of any mental or emotional condition or disorder. In the absence of evidence to the contrary, the psychologist is presumed authorized to claim the privilege on the patient's or client's behalf.

This privilege may not be claimed by the patient or client, or on his or her behalf by authorized persons, in the following circumstances:

1. where abuse or harmful neglect of children, the elderly, or disabled or incompetent individuals is known or reasonably suspected;

2. where the validity of a will of a former patient or client is contested;

3. where such information is necessary for the psychologist to defend against a malpractice action brought by the patient or client;

4. where an immediate threat of physical violence against a readily identifiable victim is disclosed to the psychologist;

5. in the context of civil commitment proceedings, where an immediate threat of self-inflicted damage is disclosed to the psychologist;

6. where the patient or client, by alleging mental or emotional damages in litigation, puts his or her mental state at issue;

7. where the patient or client is examined pursuant to court order; or

8. in the context of investigations and hearings brought by the patient or client and conducted by the Board, where violations of this Act are at issue. (pp. 702–703)

Specific provisions for the maintenance of confidentiality are spelled out in each of the Specialty Guidelines for the Delivery of Services (APA, 1981b).

[27]Examples of such agencies are clinics for battered women, clinics for Spanish-speaking users, and clinics for members of a specific religious faith or church.

[28]The APA is prepared to provide appropriate assistance to responsible members who are subjected to unreasonable limitations upon their opportunities to function as practitioners, administrators, or consultants. The APA is prepared to cooperate with any responsible professional psychological organization in opposing any unreasonable limitations on the professional functions of the members of that organization. This insistence upon professional autonomy has been upheld over the years by the affirmative actions of the courts and of other public and private bodies in support of the right of psychologists to pursue those functions that they are trained and qualified to perform. Psychologists recognize that other professions and other groups will, from time to time, seek to define the roles and responsibilities of psychologists. The APA opposes such attempts.

REFERENCES

American Psychological Association. (1973). Guidelines for psychologists conducting growth groups. American Psychologist, 28, 933.

American Psychological Association. (1974). Standards for providers of psychological services. Washington, DC: Author.

American Psychological Association. (1977). Standards for providers of psychological services. American Psychologist, 32, 495–505.

American Psychological Association. (1978). Principles concerning the counseling and therapy of women. Counseling Psychologist, 7 (4), 74–76.

American Psychological Association. (1981a). Ethical principles of psychologists. American Psychologist, 36, 633–638.

American Psychological Association. (1981b). Specialty guidelines for the delivery of services by clinical (counseling, industrial/organizational, and school) psychologists. American Psychologist, 36, 639–681.

American Psychological Association. (1982). Ethical principles in the conduct of research with human participants. Washington, DC: Author.

American Psychological Association. (1986). Guidelines for computer-based tests and interpretations. Washington, DC: Author.

American Psychological Association. (1987a). Guidelines for conditions of employment of psychologists. American Psychologist, 42, 724–729.

American Psychological Association. (1987b). Model act for state licensure of psychologists. American Psychologist, 42, 696–703.

Conger, J. J. (1976). Proceedings of the American Psychological Association, Incorporated, for the year 1975: Minutes of the annual meeting of the Council of Representatives. American Psychologist, 31, 406–434.

Joint Commission on Accreditation of Hospitals, Accreditation Council for Psychiatric Facilities. (1972). Accreditation manual for psychiatric facilities: 1972. Chicago, IL: Author.

Joint Commission on Accreditation of Hospitals, Accreditation Council for Facilities for the Mentally Retarded.

(1971). *Standards for residential facilities for the mentally retarded.* Chicago IL: Author.

Standards for educational and psychological testing. (1985). Washington, DC: American Psychological Association.

Wyatt v. Stickney, 325 F. Supp. (M.D. Ala. 1971), 334 F. Supp. 1341 (M.D. Ala.), 344 F. Supp. 373 (M.D. Ala. 1972), *aff'd sub nom. Wyatt v. Aderholt,* 503 F.2d 1305 (5th Cir. 1974).

Ethical Principles of Psychologists: Amendments June 2, 1989

The Board of Directors of the American Psychological Association, on June 2, 1989, rescinded and will no longer enforce the following sections of APA's Ethical Principles:

Rescinded June 1989: Principle 4.b.iii
Principle 4.b.v.
Principle 4.b.vi
Principle 4.b.vii
Principle 4.b.viii

The following portions of Principle 6.d. and Principle 7.b. have also been **rescinded:**

Principle 6.d.: "They neither give nor receive any renumeration for referring clients for professional services."

Principle 7.b.: "If a person is receiving similar services from another professional, psychologists do not offer their own services directly to such a person."

American Counseling Association
Multicultural/Diversity Agenda

CORE VALUES

- The phenomenon of multiculturalism and diversity are the essence of all that we do as a profession and as professionals. They are core competencies of the American Counseling Association and stepping stones on the path to social justice.
- Valuing diversity and multiculturalism is an obligation of a competent professional counselor, an association leader, all counselor educators, students and counselor education programs, and institutions that deliver consulting services in the public and private sector.
- Addressing the dynamics of oppression and privilege are key to institutional and individual change.
- Advocating for diversity and multiculturalism to the society at large is an obligation of professional counselors, counselor educators and the American Counseling Association.
- Achieving multicultural/diversity outcomes has no end point but is an ongoing process both for the association and for the members.
- People need to feel safe and be welcome wherever they are in their own developmental process throughout the association and its stakeholders.
- The profession exists to serve multicultural/diverse populations.

- The terms multiculturalism and diversity are evolving in their meanings and applications but encompass inclusivity and the celebration of human differences.

PRINCIPLES AND GOALS

Principle I

ACA will foster an appreciation of diversity and multiculturalism and has an obligation to work toward creating conditions in which leaders and members are encouraged to engage in issues of multiculturalism and diversity.

Goal 1: To ensure that ACA's Code of Ethics, Standards of Practice, credentialing, and accreditation standards reflect diversity and multiculturalism as core competencies.

Goal 2: To engage in political processes, public policy, and advocacy to uphold the core values of diversity and multiculturalism.

Goal 3: For ACA leaders, members, and staff to actively model and advocate for the core values of multiculturalism and diversity.

Goal 4: To ensure the leadership and membership throughout ACA reflects a multicultural and diverse society.

Goal 5: To identify and promulgate the attributes of counselor education programs and continuing education initiatives that successfully promote the development of diversity and multiculturalism core values.

Goal 6: To encourage ACA members to provide pro bono counseling services to people in need.

Principle II

ACA values and respects the development, recruitment, retention, and involvement of a multiculturally diverse membership.

Goal 1:   To develop ACA as a multiculturally competent association.

Goal 2:   To increase the number of leaders from underrepresented groups.

Goal 3:   To expand and retain the membership of ACA to reflect a multicultural and diverse society.

Goal 4:   To ensure an organizational environment that is safe, inviting, and nurturing to individuals from varied backgrounds/cultures.

Goal 5:   To ensure that opportunities for acquiring diversity/multicultural competencies are available to all ACA members.

Principle III

ACA values and encourages professional counselors who integrate multicultural diversity knowledge and skills into their practices. Therefore, it is the responsibility of ACA members to be professional and competent in multicultural/diversity issues.

Goal 1:   To provide multicultural diversity education and training to ACA members.

Goal 2:   To identify and recognize counselors, who have demonstrated exemplary competencies in the area of multiculturalism and/or diversity.

Goal 3:   To provide a wide range of professional resources on multicultural diversity issues for counselors.

Goal 4:   To provide electronic access to multicultural/diversity resources.

Goal 5.   To build bridges internationally.

Principle IV

ACA values and respects a joyful expansion of leadership that is diverse across the membership and the practice of counseling.

Goal 1:   To develop a cadre of emerging leaders.

Goal 2:   To promote diversity in all fields of counseling practice.

Goal 3:   To expand leadership opportunities within ACA.

Goal 4:   To reflect diversity, interest, *and* expertise in national, divisional, and branch committee membership.

Appendix K

American School Counselor Association
The National Standards for School Counseling Programs

EXECUTIVE SUMMARY

After extensive research and review, the American School Counselor Association announces the establishment of The National Standards for School Counseling Programs.

NATIONAL STANDARDS

- help school systems identify what students will know and be able to do as a result of participating in a school counseling program;
- establish similar goals, expectations, support systems, and experiences for all students;
- serve as an organizational tool to identify and prioritize the elements of an effective school counseling program; and
- provide an opportunity to discuss the role of counseling programs in school to enhance student learning.

WHY SCHOOL COUNSELING PROGRAMS?

The purpose of a counseling program in a school setting is to promote and enhance the learning process. The goal of the program is to enable all students to achieve success in school and to develop into contributing members of our society. A school counseling program based on national standards provides all the necessary elements for students to achieve success in school. This programmatic approach helps school counselors to continuously assess

their students' needs, identify the barriers and obstacles that may be hindering student success, and advocate programmatic efforts to eliminate these barriers.

School success requires that students make successful transitions and acquire the attitudes, skills, and knowledge that are essential to the competitive workplace of the 21st century.

WHAT ARE THE NATIONAL STANDARDS?

The National Standards for School Counseling Programs facilitate student development in three broad areas:

- Academic Development
- Career Development
- Personal/Social Development

Within each area are three standards, which provide guidance and a framework for states, school systems, and individual schools to develop effective school counseling programs. The nine standards are followed by a list of student competencies or desired student learning outcomes, which define the specific knowledge, attitudes, and skills students should obtain or demonstrate as a result of participating in a school counseling program. These competencies form a foundation on which to construct measurable indicators of student performance.

Academic Development

Standard A. Students will acquire the attitudes, knowledge, and skills that contribute to effective learning in school and across the life span.

Standard B. Students will complete school with the academic preparation essential to choose from a wide

SOURCE: American School Counselor Association (1997), *The National Standards for School Counseling Programs*. Executive Summary. American School Counselor Association. Reprinted by permission.

550

range of substantial postsecondary options, including college.

Standard C.   Students will understand the relationship of academics to the world of work, and to life at home and in the community.

Career Development

Standard A.   Students will acquire the skills to investigate the world of work in relation to knowledge of self and to make informed career decisions.

Standard B.   Students will employ strategies to achieve future career success and satisfaction.

Standard C.   Students will understand the relationship between personal qualities, education and training, and the world of work.

Personal/Social Development

Standard A.   Students will acquire the attitudes, knowledge, and interpersonal skills to help them understand and respect self and others.

Standard B.   Students will make decisions, set goals, and take necessary action to achieve goals.

Standard C.   Students will understand safety and survival skills.

The National Standards for School Counseling Programs help school counselors, school and district administrators, faculty and staff, counselor educators, state associations, businesses, communities, and policy makers to provide effective school counseling programs for all students.

The National Standards for School Counseling Programs are supported by implementation and evaluation tools to assist in their redesign of current school counseling programs to meet the needs of students in the 21st century.

The American School Counselor Association is dedicated to assisting school counselors to help students reach their full potential.

American School Counselor Association
801 N. Fairfax St., Suite 310
Alexandria, VA 22314
703-683-2722
800-306-4722

National Board for Certified Counselors (Approved July 1, 1982; Amended February 21, 1987, January 6, 1989, and October 31, 1997)

NBCC Code of Ethics

PREAMBLE

The National Board for Certified Counselors (NBCC) is a professional certification board which certifies counselors as having met standards for the general and specialty practice of professional counseling established by the Board. The counselors certified by NBCC may identify with different professional associations and are often licensed by jurisdictions which promulgate codes of ethics. The NBCC Code of Ethics provides a minimal ethical standard for the professional behavior of all NBCC certificants. This code provides an expectation of and assurance for the ethical practice for all who use the professional services of an NBCC certificant. In addition, it serves the purpose of having an enforceable standard for all NBCC certificants and assures those served of some resource in case of a perceived ethical violation.

The NBCC Ethical Code applies to all those certified by NBCC regardless of any other professional affiliation. Persons who receive professional services from certified counselors may elect to use other ethical codes which apply to their counselor. Although NBCC cooperates with professional associations and credentialing organizations, it can bring actions to discipline or sanction NBCC certificants only if the provisions of the NBCC Code are found to have been violated.

The National Board for Certified Counselors, Inc. (NBCC), promotes counseling through certification. In pursuit of this mission, the NBCC:

SOURCE: From National Board for Certified Counselors (1998), *Code of Ethics*. Copyright © 1998 National Board for Certified Counselors, Inc. Reprinted by permission. No further reproduction authorized without written permission of the NBCC.

- Promotes quality assurance in counseling practice
- Promotes the value of counseling
- Promotes public awareness of quality counseling practice
- Promotes professionalism in counseling
- Promotes leadership in credentialing

Section A: General

1. Certified counselors engage in continuous efforts to improve professional practices, services, and research. Certified counselors are guided in their work by evidence of the best professional practices.

2. Certified counselors have a responsibility to the clients they serve and to the institutions within which the services are performed. Certified counselors also strive to assist the respective agency, organization, or institution in providing competent and ethical professional services. The acceptance of employment in an institution implies that the certified counselor is in agreement with the general policies and principles of the institution. Therefore, the professional activities of the certified counselor are in accord with the objectives of the institution. If the certified counselor and the employer do not agree and cannot reach agreement on policies that are consistent with appropriate counselor ethical practice that is conducive to client growth and development, the employment should be terminated. If the situation warrants further action, the certified counselor should work through professional organizations to have the unethical practice changed.

3. Ethical behavior among professional associates (i.e., both certified and noncertified counselors) must be expected at all times. When a certified counselor has

552

doubts as to the ethical behavior of professional colleagues, the certified counselor must take action to attempt to rectify this condition. Such action uses the respective institution's channels first and then uses procedures established by the NBCC or the perceived violator's profession.

4. Certified counselors must refuse remuneration for consultation or counseling with persons who are entitled to these services through the certified counselor's employing institution or agency. Certified counselors must not divert to their private practices, without the mutual consent of the institution and the client, legitimate clients in their primary agencies or the institutions with which they are affiliated.

5. In establishing fees for professional counseling services, certified counselors must consider the financial status of clients. In the event that the established fee status is inappropriate for a client, assistance must be provided in finding comparable services at acceptable cost.

6. Certified counselors offer only professional services for which they are trained or have supervised experience. No diagnosis, assessment, or treatment should be performed without prior training or supervision. Certified counselors are responsible for correcting any misrepresentations of their qualifications by others.

7. Certified counselors recognize their limitations and provide services or use techniques for which they are qualified by training and/or supervision. Certified counselors recognize the need for and seek continuing education to assure competent services.

8. Certified counselors are aware of the intimacy in the counseling relationship and maintain respect for the client. Counselors must not engage in activities that seek to meet their personal or professional needs at the expense of the client.

9. Certified counselors must ensure that they do not engage in personal, social, organizational, financial, or political activities which might lead to a misuse of their influence.

10. Sexual intimacy with clients is unethical. Certified counselors will not be sexually, physically, or romantically intimate with clients, and they will not engage in sexual, physical, or romantic intimacy with clients within a minimum of two years after terminating the counseling relationship.

11. Certified counselors do not condone or engage in sexual harassment, which is defined as unwelcome comments, gestures, or physical contact of a sexual nature.

12. Through an awareness of the impact of stereotyping and unwarranted discrimination (e.g., biases based on age, disability, ethnicity, gender, race, religion, or sexual orientation), certified counselors guard the individual rights and personal dignity of the client in the counseling relationship.

13. Certified counselors are accountable at all times for their behavior. They must be aware that all actions and behaviors of the counselor reflect on professional integrity and, when inappropriate, can damage the public trust in the counseling profession. To protect public confidence in the counseling profession, certified counselors avoid behavior that is clearly in violation of accepted moral and legal standards.

14. Products or services provided by certified counselors by means of classroom instruction, public lectures, demonstrations, written articles, radio or television programs or other types of media must meet the criteria cited in this code.

15. Certified counselors have an obligation to withdraw from the practice of counseling if they violate the Code of Ethics, or if the mental or physical condition of the certified counselor renders it unlikely that a professional relationship will be maintained.

Section B: Counseling Relationship

1. The primary obligation of certified counselors is to respect the integrity and promote the welfare of clients, whether they are assisted individually, in family units, or in group counseling. In a group setting, the certified counselor is also responsible for taking reasonable precautions to protect individuals from physical and/or psychological trauma resulting from interaction within the group.

2. Certified counselors know and take into account the traditions and practices of other professional disciplines with whom they work and cooperate fully with such. If a person is receiving similar services from another professional, certified counselors do not offer their own services directly to such a person. If a certified counselor is contacted by a person who is already receiving similar services from another professional, the certified counselor carefully considers that professional relationship as well as the client's welfare and proceeds with caution and sensitivity to the therapeutic issues. When certified counselors learn that their clients are in a professional relationship with another counselor or mental health professional, they request release from the clients to inform the other counselor or mental health professional of their relationship with the client and strive to establish positive and collaborative professional relationships that are

in the best interest of the client. Certified counselors discuss these issues with clients and the counselor or professional so as to minimize the risk of confusion and conflict and encourage clients to inform other professionals of the new professional relationship.

3. Certified counselors may choose to consult with any other professionally competent person about a client and must notify clients of this right. Certified counselors avoid placing a consultant in a conflict-of-interest situation that would preclude the consultant serving as a proper party to the efforts of the certified counselor to help the client.

4. When a client's condition indicates that there is a clear and imminent danger to the client or others, the certified counselor must take reasonable action to inform potential victims and/or inform responsible authorities. Consultation with other professionals must be used when possible. The assumption of responsibility for the client's behavior must be taken only after careful deliberation, and the client must be involved in the resumption of responsibility as quickly as possible.

5. Records of the counseling relationship, including interview notes, test data, correspondence, audio or visual tape recordings, electronic data storage, and other documents are to be considered professional information for use in counseling. Records should contain accurate factual data. The physical records are property of the certified counselors or their employers. The information contained in the records belongs to the client and therefore may not be released to others without the consent of the client or when the counselor has exhausted challenges to a court order. The certified counselors are responsible to ensure that their employees handle confidential information appropriately. Confidentiality must be maintained during the storage and disposition of records. Records should be maintained for a period of at least five (5) years after the last counselor/client contact, including cases in which the client is deceased. All records must be released to the client upon request.

6. Certified counselors must ensure that data maintained in electronic storage are secure. By using the best computer security methods available, the data must be limited to information that is appropriate and necessary for the services being provided and accessible only to appropriate staff members involved in the provision of services. Certified counselors must also ensure that the electronically stored data are destroyed when the information is no longer of value in providing services or required as part of clients' records.

7. Any data derived from a client relationship and used in training or research shall be so disguised that the informed client's identity is fully protected. Any data which cannot be so disguised may be used only as expressly authorized by the client's informed and uncoerced consent.

8. When counseling is initiated, and throughout the counseling process as necessary, counselors inform clients of the purposes, goals, techniques, procedures, limitations, potential risks and benefits of services to be performed, and clearly indicate limitations that may affect the relationship as well as any other pertinent information. Counselors take reasonable steps to ensure that clients understand the implications of any diagnosis, the intended use of tests and reports, methods of treatment and safety precautions that must be taken in their use, fees, and billing arrangements.

9. Certified counselors who have an administrative, supervisory, and/or evaluative relationship with individuals seeking counseling services must not serve as the counselor and should refer the individuals to other professionals. Exceptions are made only in instances where an individual's situation warrants counseling intervention and another alternative is unavailable. Dual relationships that might impair the certified counselor's objectivity and professional judgment must be avoided and/or the counseling relationship terminated through referral to a competent professional.

10. When certified counselors determine an inability to be of professional assistance to a potential or existing client, they must, respectively, not initiate the counseling relationship or immediately terminate the relationship. In either event, the certified counselor must suggest appropriate alternatives. Certified counselors must be knowledgeable about referral resources so that a satisfactory referral can be initiated. In the event that the client declines a suggested referral, the certified counselor is not obligated to continue the relationship.

11. When certified counselors are engaged in intensive, short-term counseling, they must ensure that professional assistance is available at normal costs to clients during and following the short-term counseling.

12. Counselors using electronic means in which counselor and client are not in immediate proximity must present clients with local sources of care before establishing a continued short- or long-term relationship. Counselors who communicate with clients via Internet are governed by NBCC standards for Web-Counseling.

13. Counselors must document permission to practice counseling by electronic means in all governmental jurisdictions where such counseling takes place.

14. When electronic data and systems are used as a component of counseling services, certified counselors must ensure that the computer application, and any information it contains, is appropriate for the respective needs of clients and is nondiscriminatory. Certified counselors must ensure that they themselves have acquired a facilitation level of knowledge with any system they use including hands-on application, and understanding of the uses of all aspects of the computer-based system. In selecting and/or maintaining computer-based systems that contain career information, counselors must ensure that the system provides current, accurate, and locally relevant information. Certified counselors must also ensure that clients are intellectually, emotionally, and physically compatible with computer applications and understand their purpose and operation. Client use of a computer application must be evaluated to correct possible problems and assess subsequent needs.

15. Certified counselors who develop self-help/stand-alone computer software for use by the general public, must first ensure that it is designed to function in a stand-alone manner that is appropriate and safe for all clients for which it is intended. A manual is required. The manual must provide the user with intended outcomes, suggestions for using the software, descriptions of inappropriately used applications, and descriptions of when and how other forms of counseling services might be beneficial. Finally, the manual must include the qualifications of the developer, the development process, validation date, and operating procedures.

16. The counseling relationship and information resulting from it remains confidential, consistent with the legal and ethical obligations of certified counselors. In group counseling, counselors clearly define confidentiality and the parameters for the specific group being entered, explain the importance of confidentiality, and discuss the difficulties related to confidentially involved in group work. The fact that confidentiality cannot be guaranteed is clearly communicated to group members. However, counselors should give assurance about their professional responsibility to keep all group communications confidential.

17. Certified counselors must screen prospective group counseling participants to ensure compatibility with group objectives. This is especially important when the emphasis is on self-understanding and growth through self-disclosure. Certified counselors must maintain an awareness of the welfare of each participant throughout the group process.

Section C: Measurement and Evaluation

1. Because many types of assessment techniques exist, certified counselors must recognize the limits of their competence and perform only those assessment functions for which they have received appropriate training or supervision.

2. Certified counselors who utilize assessment instruments to assist them with diagnoses must have appropriate training skills in educational and psychological measurement, validation criteria, test research, and guidelines for test development and use.

3. Certified counselors must provide instrument specific orientation or information to an examinee prior to and following the administration of assessment instruments or techniques so that the results may be placed in proper perspective with other relevant factors. The purpose of testing and the explicit use of the results must be made known to an examinee prior to testing.

4. In selecting assessment instruments or techniques for use in a given situation or with a particular client, certified counselors must carefully evaluate the specific theoretical bases and characteristics, validity, reliability and appropriateness of the instrument.

5. When making statements to the public about assessment instruments or techniques, certified counselors must provide accurate information and avoid false claims or misconceptions concerning the meaning of the instrument's reliability and validity terms.

6. Counselors must follow all directions and researched procedures for selection, administration, and interpretation of all evaluation instruments and use them only within proper contexts.

7. Certified counselors must be cautious when interpreting the results of instruments that possess insufficient technical data, and must explicitly state to examinees the specific limitations and purposes for the use of such instruments.

8. Certified counselors must proceed with caution when attempting to evaluate and interpret performances of any person who cannot be appropriately compared to the norms for the instrument.

9. Because prior coaching or dissemination of test materials can invalidate test results, certified counselors are professionally obligated to maintain test security.

10. Certified counselors must consider psychometric limitations when selecting and using an instrument, and must be cognizant of the limitations when interpreting the results. When tests are used to classify clients, certified counselors must ensure that periodic review and/or retesting are made to prevent client stereotyping.

11. An examinee's welfare, explicit prior understanding, and consent are the factors used when determining who receives the test results. Certified counselors must see that appropriate interpretation accompanies any release of individual or group test date (e.g., limitations of instrument and norms).

12. Certified counselors must ensure that computer-generated test administration and scoring programs function properly thereby providing clients with accurate test results.

13. Certified counselors who develop computer-based test interpretations to support the assessment process must ensure that the validity of the interpretations is established prior to the commercial distribution of the computer application.

14. Certified counselors recognize that test results may become obsolete, and avoid the misuse of obsolete data.

15. Certified counselors must not appropriate, reproduce, or modify published tests or parts thereof without acknowledgment and permission from the publisher, except as permitted by the fair educational use provisions of the U.S. copyright law.

Section D: Research and Publication

1. Certified counselors will adhere to applicable legal and professional guidelines on research with human subjects.

2. In planning research activities involving human subjects, certified counselors must be aware of and responsive to all pertinent ethical principles and ensure that the research problem, design, and execution are in full compliance with any pertinent institutional or governmental regulations.

3. The ultimate responsibility for ethical research lies with the principal researcher, although others involved in the research activities are ethically obligated and responsible for their own actions.

4. Certified counselors who conduct research with human subjects are responsible for the welfare of the subjects throughout the experiment and must take all reasonable precautions to avoid causing injurious psychological, physical, or social effects on their subjects.

5. Certified counselors who conduct research must abide by the basic elements of informed consent:

    a. fair explanation of the procedures to be followed, including an identification of those which are experimental

    b. description of the attendant discomforts and risks

    c. description of the benefits to be expected

    d. disclosure of appropriate alternative procedures that would be advantageous for subjects with an offer to answer any inquiries concerning the procedures

    e. an instruction that subjects are free to withdraw their consent and to discontinue participation in the project or activity at any time

6. When reporting research results, explicit mention must be made of all the variables and conditions known to the investigator that may have affected the outcome of the study or the interpretation of the data.

7. Certified counselors who conduct and report research investigations must do so in a manner that minimizes the possibility that the results will be misleading.

8. Certified counselors are obligated to make available sufficient original research data to qualified others who may wish to replicate the study.

9. Certified counselors who supply data, aid in the research of another person, report research results, or make original data available, must take due care to disguise the identity of respective subjects in the absence of specific authorization from the subjects to do otherwise.

10. When conducting and reporting research, certified counselors must be familiar with and give recognition to previous work on the topic, must observe all copyright laws, and must follow the principles of giving full credit to those to whom credit is due.

11. Certified counselors must give due credit through joint authorship, acknowledgment, footnote statements, or other appropriate means to those who have contributed to the research and/or publication, in accordance with such contributions.

12. Certified counselors should communicate to other counselors the results of any research judged to be of professional value. Results that reflect unfavorably on institutions, programs, services, or vested interests must not be withheld.

13. Certified counselors who agree to cooperate with another individual in research and/or publication incur an obligation to cooperate as promised in terms of punc-

tuality of performance and with full regard to the completeness and accuracy of the information required.

14. Certified counselors must not submit the same manuscript, or one essentially similar in content, for simultaneous publication consideration by two or more journals. In addition, manuscripts that have been published in whole or substantial part should not be submitted for additional publication without acknowledgment and permission from any previous publisher.

Section E: Consulting

Consultation refers to a voluntary relationship between a profession helper and a help-needing individual, group, or social unit in which the consultant is providing help to the client(s) in defining and solving a work-related problem or potential work-related problem with a client or client system.

1. Certified counselors, acting as consultants, must have a high degree of self-awareness of their own values, knowledge, skills, limitations, and needs in entering a helping relationship that involves human and/or organizational change. The focus of the consulting relationship must be on the issues to be resolved and not on the person(s) presenting the problem.

2. In the consulting relationship, the certified counselor and client must understand and agree upon the problem definition, subsequent goals, and predicted consequences of interventions selected.

3. Certified counselors acting as consultants must be reasonably certain that they, or the organization represented, have the necessary competencies and resources for giving the kind of help that is needed or that may develop later, and that appropriate referral resources are available.

4. Certified counselors in a consulting relationship must encourage and cultivate client adaptability and growth toward self-direction. Certified counselors must maintain this role consistently and not become a decision maker for clients or create a future dependency on the consultant.

Section F: Private Practice

1. In advertising services as a private practitioner, certified counselors must advertise in a manner that accurately informs the public of the professional services, expertise, and techniques of counseling available.

2. Certified counselors who assume an executive leadership role in a private practice organization do not permit their names to be used in professional notices during periods of time when they are not actively engaged in the private practice of counseling unless their executive roles are clearly stated.

3. Certified counselors must make available their highest degree (described by discipline), type and level of certification and/or license, address, telephone number, office hours, type and/or description of services, and other relevant information. Listed information must not contain false, inaccurate, misleading, partial, out-of-context, or otherwise deceptive material or statements.

4. Certified counselors who are involved in a partnership/corporation with other certified counselors and/or other professionals, must clearly specify all relevant specialties of each member of the partnership or corporation.

Appendix: Certification Examination

Applicants for the NBCC Certification Examination must have fulfilled all current eligibility requirements, and are responsible for the accuracy and validity of all information and/or materials provided by themselves or by others for fulfillment of eligibility criteria.

Approved on July 1, 1982

Amended on February 21, 1987, January 6, 1989, and October 31, 1997

Acknowledgment

Reference documents, statements, and sources for the development of the NBCC Code of Ethics were as follows:

The Ethical Standards of the American Counseling Association (ACA), Responsible Uses for Standardized Testing (AMECD), codes of ethics for the American Psychological Association, and the National Career Development Association, Handbook of Standards for Computer-Based Career Information Systems (ACSCI); and Guidelines for the Use of Computer-Based Career Information and Guidance Systems (ACSCI).

National Board for Certified Counselors
NBCC Standards for the Ethical Practice of WebCounseling

The relative newness of the use of the Internet for service and product delivery leaves authors of standards at a loss when beginning to create ethical practices on the Internet. This document, like all codes of conduct, will change as information and circumstances not yet foreseen evolve. However, each version of this code of ethics is the current best standard of conduct passed by the NBCC Board of Directors. As with any code, and especially with a code such as this, created for an evolving field of work, NBCC and CCE welcome comments and ideas for further discussion and inclusion.

Further, the development of these WebCounseling standards has been guided by the following principles:

These standards are intended to address practices which are unique to WebCounseling and WebCounselors,

These standards are not to duplicate non–Internet-based standards adopted in other codes of ethics,

Recognizing that significant new technology emerges continuously, these standards should be reviewed frequently,

WebCounseling ethics cases should be reviewed in light of delivery systems existing at the moment rather than at the time the standards were adopted.

WebCounselors who are not National Certified Counselors may indicate at their WebSite their adherence to these standards, but may not publish these stan-

dards in their entirety without written permission of the National Board for Certified Counselors.

The *Practice of WebCounseling* shall be defined as "the practice of professional counseling and information delivery that occurs when client(s) and counselor are in separate or remote locations and utilize electronic means to communicate over the Internet."

In addition to following the NBCC Code of Ethics pertaining to the practices of professional counseling, WebCounselors shall:

1. Review pertinent legal and ethical codes for possible violations emanating from the practice of Web-Counseling and supervision.

> *Liability insurance policies should also be reviewed to determine if the practice of WebCounseling is a covered activity. Local, state, provincial, and national statutes as well as the codes of professional membership organizations, professional certifying bodies, and state or provincial licensing boards need to be reviewed. Also, as no definitive answers are known to questions pertaining to whether WebCounseling takes place in the WebCounselor's location or the WebClient's location, WebCounselors should consider carefully local customs regarding age of consent and child abuse reporting.*

2. Inform WebClients of encryption methods being used to help ensure the security of client/counselor/supervisor communications.

> *Encryption methods should be used whenever possible. If encryption is not made available to clients, clients must be informed of the potential hazards of unsecured communication on the Internet. Hazards may include authorized or unauthorized monitoring of transmissions and/or records of WebCounseling sessions.*

3. Inform clients if, how and how long session data are being preserved.

Session data may include WebCounselor/WebClient e-mail, test results, audio/video session recordings, session notes, and counselor/supervisor communications. The likelihood of electronic sessions being preserved is greater because of the ease and decreased costs involved in recording. Thus, its potential use in supervision, research, and legal proceedings increases.

4. In situations where it is difficult to verify the identity of WebCounselor or WebClient, take steps to address impostor concerns, such as by using code words, numbers, or graphics.

5. When parent/guardian consent is required to provide WebCounseling to minors, verify the identity of the consenting person.

6. Follow appropriate procedures regarding the release of information for sharing WebClient information with other electronic sources.

Because of the relative ease with which e-mail messages can be forwarded to formal and casual referral sources, WebCounselors must work to ensure the confidentiality of the WebCounseling relationship.

7. Carefully consider the extent of self-disclosure presented to the WebClient and provide rational for WebCounselor's level of disclosure.

WebCounselors may wish to ensure that, minimally, the WebClient has the same data available about his/her service provider as would be available if the counseling were to take place face to face (i.e., possibly ethnicity, gender, etc.). Compelling reasons for limiting disclosure should be presented. WebCounselors will remember to protect themselves from unscrupulous users of the Internet by limiting potentially harmful disclosure about self and family.

8. Provide links to WebSites of all appropriate certification bodies and licensure boards to facilitate consumer protection.

9. Contact NBCC/CEE or the WebClient's state or provincial licensing board to obtain the name of at least one Counselor-On-Call within the WebClient's geographical region.

WebCounselors who have contacted an individual to determine his or her willingness to serve as a Counselor-On-Call (either in person, over the phone, or via e-mail) should also ensure that the WebClient is provided with local crisis intervention hotline numbers, 911 and similar numbers in the event that the Counselor-On-Call is unavailable.

10. Discuss with their WebClients procedures for contacting the WebCounselor when he or she is off-line.

This means explaining exactly how often e-mail messages are to be checked by the WebCounselor.

11. Mention at their WebSites those presenting problems they believe to be inappropriate for WebCounseling.

While no conclusive research has been conducted to date, those topics might include: sexual abuse as a primary issue, violent relationships, eating disorders, and psychiatric disorders that involve distortions of reality.

12. Explain to clients the possibility of technology failure.

The WebCounselor

- *gives instructions to WebClients about calling if problems arise,*
- *discusses the appropriateness of the client calling collect when the call might be originating from around the world,*
- *mentions differences in time zones,*
- *talks about dealing with response delays in sending and receiving e-mail messages*

13. Explain to clients how to cope with potential misunderstandings arising from the lack of visual cues from WebCounselor or WebClient.

For example, suggesting the other person simply say, "Because I couldn't see your face or hear your tone of voice in your e-mail message, I'm not sure how to interpret that last message."

Appendix

American School Counselor Association (Adopted 1981; Revised 1985, 1993)

The School Counselor and Child Abuse/ Neglect Prevention

THE POSITION OF THE AMERICAN SCHOOL COUNSELOR ASSOCIATION (ASCA)

It is the responsibility of the school counselor to report suspected cases of child abuse/neglect to the proper authorities. Recognizing that the abuse of children is not limited to the home and that corporal punishment by school authorities might well be considered child abuse, the ASCA supports any legislation which specifically bans the use of corporal punishment as a disciplinary tool within the schools.

THE RATIONALE

The incidence of reported child abuse and child neglect has increased significantly, both nationally and statewide, during the past several years. Generally, state laws require people in the helping professions, who have reasonable cause to believe that a child is suffering serious physical or emotional injury, to report this situation to the appropriate authorities. School counselors are mandated reporters and need policies, referral procedures, and information. It is a legal, moral, and ethical responsibility to report child abuse.

There are social beliefs and values that parents have the right to discipline their children as they choose.

SOURCE: From American School Counselor Association (1993), *The School Counselor and Child Abuse/Neglect Prevention.* Position Statement. American School Counselor Association. Reprinted by permission.

Research shows, however, that a large percentage of abusive parents were abused children, perpetuating the cycle of abuse. The consequences of such beliefs and the cycle of abuse are physical and/or emotional harm, and lowered self-esteem.

Definitions

Abuse: The infliction by other than accidental means of physical harm upon the body of a child, continual psychological damage or denial of emotional needs; e.g., extensive bruises/patterns; burns/patterns; lacerations, welts or abrasions; injuries inconsistent with information offered; sexual abuse involving molestation or exploitation, including but not limited to rape, carnal knowledge, sodomy, or unnatural sexual practices; emotional disturbance caused by continuous friction in the home, marital discord, or mentally ill parents; cruel treatment.

Neglect: The failure to provide necessary food, care, clothing, shelter, supervision, or medical attention for a child; e.g., malnourished, ill-clad, dirty, without proper shelter or sleeping arrangements, lacking appropriate health care; unattended, lacking adequate supervision; ill and lacking essential medical attention; irregular/illegal absences from school; exploited, overworked; lacking essential psychological/emotional nurturance; abandonment.

Corporal Punishment: Any act of physical force upon a pupil for the purpose of punishing that pupil. This definition specifically excludes any reasonable force exercised by a school employee which is used in self-defense, in defense of other persons or property or to restrain or remove a pupil who is disrupting school functions and who refuses to comply with a request to stop.

THE COUNSELOR'S ROLE

ASCA recognizes that it is the absolute responsibility of school counselors to report suspected cases of child abuse/neglect to the proper authorities. Responsible action by the counselor can be achieved through the recognition and understanding of the problem, knowing the reporting procedures, and participating in available child abuse information programs. Counselors with such understanding aid in early detection of the problem. We also recognize that the abuse of children is not limited to the home and that corporal punishment by school authorities might well be considered child abuse.

Counselors must commit themselves to providing strategies to help break the cycle of child abuse. It is the responsibility of school counselors to help children and adults cope with abusive behavior, facilitate behavioral changes, and develop positive interpersonal relationships as well as to prepare for parenting styles. Counselors must coordinate team efforts on behalf of the child; provide support to teachers and other school personnel; work to reestablish trust and to provide or refer to ongoing counseling services; provide developmental workshops and/or support groups enhancing parenting skills; and provide programs and inservices designed to help prevent child abuse.

SUMMARY

School counselors are key people in the child abuse prevention network. The school counselor must be able to guide and help, and to provide all appropriate services during a crisis situation. Up-to-date information can sometimes mean a turning point in the life and behavior of an abusive family.

References

Abbe, A. E. (1961). Consultation to a school guidance program. *Elementary School Journal, 61*, 331–337.

Abramowitz, S. I., & Murray, J. (1983). Race Effects in Psychotherapy. In J. Murray & P. R. Abramson. (Eds.) *Bias in psychotherapy*. New York: Praeger.

Aiken, L. R. (1988). *Psychological testing and assessment* (5th ed.). Boston: Allyn & Bacon.

Ailes, R. (1988). *You are the message*. Homewood, IL: Dow, Jones-Brown.

Allen, G. J., Chinsky, J. M., Larsen, S. W., Lochman, J. E., & Selinger, H. V. (1976). *Community psychology and the schools*. Hillsdale, NJ: Erlbaum.

Allsopp, A., & Prosen, S. (1988). Teacher reactions to a child sexual abuse training program. *Elementary School Guidance and Counseling, 22*, 299–305.

American Counseling Association. (1995). *Code of ethics and standards of practice*. Alexandria, VA: Author.

American Psychiatric Association. (1994). *Diagnostic and statistical manual of mental disorders* (4th ed.). Washington, DC: Author.

American Psychological Association. (1992). *Ethical principles of psychologists and code of conduct*. Washington, DC: Author.

American School Counselor Association. (1964). *Statement of policy for secondary school counselors*. Washington, DC: Author.

American School Counselor Association. (1988). The school counselor and child abuse/neglect prevention. *Elementary School Guidance and Counseling, 22*, 261–263.

Americans with Disabilities Act handbook. (1991). Washington, DC: U.S. Government Printing Office.

Anastasi, A. (1988). *Psychological testing* (6th ed.). New York: Macmillan.

Anastasi, A. (1992). Tests and assessment: What counselors should know about the use and interpretations of psychological tests. *Journal of Counseling and Development, 70* (5), 610–615.

Anastasi, A., & Urbina, S. (1997). *Psychological testing.* (7th ed.). Upper Saddle River, NJ: Prentice-Hall.

Anderson, D. J., & Cranston-Gingras, A. (1991). Sensitizing counselors and educators to multicultural issues: An interactive approach. *Journal of Counseling and Development, 70*, 91–98.

Arredondo, P. M. (1986). Immigration as a historical moment leading to an identity crisis. *Journal of Counseling and Human Service Professionals, 1* (1), 79–87.

Arredondo, P. M. (1991). Counseling Latinas. In C. C. Lee, & B. L. Richardson (Eds.), *Multicultural issues in counseling: New approaches to diversity* (pp. 143–156). Alexandria, VA: American Association for Counseling and Development.

Arthur, G. L., Jr., & Swanson, C. D. (1993). Confidentiality and privileged communication. In T. P. Remley, Jr. (Ed.), *ACA Legal Series*, 6. Alexandria, VA: American Counseling Association.

Association for Specialists in Group Work. (1990). *Ethical guidelines for group counselors and professional standards for the training of group workers* (rev. ed.). Alexandria, VA: Author.

Atkinson, D. R. (1983). Ethnic Similarity in Counseling Psychology: A Review of Research. *The Counseling Psychologist, 11* (3), 79–92.

Aubrey, R. F. (1977). Historical development of guidance and counseling and implications for the future. *Personnel and Guidance Journal, 55*, 288–295.

Baker, S. B. (1977). An argument for constructive accountability. *Personnel and Guidance Journal, 56* (1), 53–55.

Baker, S. B. (1996). *School counseling for the twenty-first century*. Columbus, OH: Merrill.

Baker, S. B., Swisher, P., Nadenichek, P., & Popowitz, C. (1984). Primary effects of primary prevention strategies. *Personnel and Guidance Journal, 62*, 459–464.

Bandura, A. (1982). The psychology of chance encounters and life paths. *The American Psychologist, 37* (7), 747–755.

Barclay, J. R. (1984a). Primary prevention in schools [Special issue]. *Personnel and Guidance Journal, 62* (8).

Barclay, J. R. (1984b). Primary prevention on campuses and in communities [Special issue]. *Personnel and Guidance Journal, 62* (9).

Basile, S. K. (1996). A guide to solution-focused brief therapy. *Counseling and Human Development, 29* (4).

Beers, C. (1908). *A mind that found itself*. New York: Longmans Green; republished by Doubleday, 1953.

Belkin, G. S. (1975). *Practical counseling in the schools*. Dubuque, IA: Brown.

Belkin, G. S. (1988). *Introduction to counseling* (3rd ed.). Madison, WI: Brown & Benchmark.

Bell, T. (1983). *A nation at risk: The imperative for educational reform*. Washington, DC: The National Commission on Excellence in Education.

Berk, J., & Berk, S. (1991). *Managing effectively: A handbook for first-time managers*. New York: Sterling.

Biggs, D., & Blocher, D. (1987). *Foundations of ethical counseling*. New York: Springer.

Bissel, L., & Royce, J. E. (1992). Ethics for addiction professionals. *Professional Counselor, 6* (4).

Blanchard, K. H. (1982). *The one minute manager*. New York: Morrow.

Blau, P. M., Gustad, J. W., Jessor, R., Parnes, H. S., & Wilcock, R. G. (1956). Occupational choice: A conception framework. *Industrial and Labor Relations Review, 9*, 531–543.

Blocher, D. H. (1987). *The professional counselor*. New York: Macmillan.

Blocher, D. H., & Biggs, D. A. (1983). *Counseling psychology in community settings*. New York: Springer.

Bloom, B. L. (1984). *Community mental health: A general introduction* (2nd ed.). Belmont, CA: Brooks/Cole.

Bloom, B. S. (1976). *Human characteristics and school learning*. New York: McGraw-Hill.

Bloom, J., Gerstein, L., Tarvydas, V., Conaster, J., Davis, E., Kater, D., Sherrard, P., & Esposito, R. (1990). Model legislation for licensed professional counselors. *Journal of Counseling and Development, 68*, 511–523.

Blum, L. (1986). Building constructive counselor-teacher relationships. *Elementary School Guidance and Counseling, 20*, 236–239.

Borow, H. (1964). *Man in a world at work*. Ellicott City, MD: National Career Development Association.

Bowman, S. L. (1993). Career intervention strategies for ethnic minorities. *Career Development Quarterly, 42*, 14–25.

Brammer, L. M. (1988). *The helping relationship: Process and skills* (4th ed.). Englewood Cliffs, NJ: Prentice-Hall.

Brammer, L. M., Shostrom, E. L., & Abrego, P. J. (1989). *Therapeutic psychology: Fundamentals of counseling and psychotherapy* (5th ed.). Englewood Cliffs, NJ: Prentice-Hall.

Brandt, J. E., & Hood, A. B. (1968). Effect of personality adjustment on the predictive validity of the Strong Vocational Interest Blank. *Journal of Counseling Psychology, 15,* 547–551.

Braucht, S., & Weime, B. (1990). Establishing a rural school counseling agenda: A multiagency needs-assessment model. *The School Counselor, 37,* 179–183.

Brewer, J. M. (1932). *Education as guidance.* New York: Macmillan.

Brown, D., & Kurpius, D. J. (Eds.). (1985). Consultation. *The Counseling Psychologist, 13* (3).

Brown, D., Kurpius, D. J., & Morris, J. R. (1988). *Handbook of consultation with individuals and small groups.* Alexandria, VA: Association for Counselor Education and Supervision.

Brown, D., & Srebalus, D. J. (1988). *An introduction to the counseling profession.* Englewood Cliffs: Prentice-Hall.

Brown, J. H., & Christensen, D. N. (1986). *Family therapy: Theory and practice.* Monterey, CA: Brooks/Cole.

Bruce, P. (1984). Continuum of counseling goals: A framework for differentiating counseling strategies. *Personnel and Guidance Journal, 62,* 259–263.

Burnette, C., Williams, R. L., & Law, J. G. (1987). Therapeutic and lifestyle reduction of aggressiveness in Vietnam veterans, *Group, 11* (1), 3–14.

Burnham, S., & Satcher, J. (1990). *Guide to community colleges serving students with learning disabilities (Mississippi, Alabama, Georgia, Tennessee, and Florida).* (ERIC Document Reproduction Service No. ED 320098).

Burns, J. M. (1978). *Leadership.* New York: Harper & Row.

Campbell, N. J., & Dobson, J. E. (1987). An inventory of student computer anxiety. *Elementary School Guidance and Counseling, 22,* 149–156.

Caplan, G. (1963). Types of mental health consultation. *American Journal of Orthopsychiatry, 33,* 470–481.

Caplan, G. (1970). *The theory and practice of mental health consultation.* New York: Basic Books.

Capuzzi, D., & Gross, D. R. (1997). *Introduction to the counseling profession* (2nd ed.). Boston: Allyn & Bacon.

Carlson, J. (1993). Marriage and family counseling. In G. R. Walz & J. C. Bleuer (Eds.), *Counselor efficacy: Assessing and using counseling outcome research.* Ann Arbor, MI: ERIC Counseling and Personnel Services Clearinghouse.

Casey, J., & Ramsammy, R. (1992, February). *Mac-Mentoring: Using technology and counseling with at-risk youth.* Paper presented at the Annual Conference of the California Association for Counseling and Development, San Francisco.

Centers for Disease Control and Prevention. (1995). *Morbidity and mortality weekly report: A compilation of 1995 MMWR articles on HIV infection and AIDS.* November 24, 1995, Vol. 44 (46), pp. 849–853.

Centers for Disease Control and Prevention. (1997). *HIV/AIDS surveillance report.* U.S. HIV and AIDS cases reported through June 1997. Midyear Edition, Vol. 9 (1), pp. 16 and 25.

Centers for Disease Control and Prevention. (1997). *Morbidity and mortality weekly report.* February 28, 1997, Vol. 46 (8).

Chase, C. I. (1984). *Elementary statistical procedures* (3rd ed.). New York: McGraw-Hill.

Christensen, S. P. (1989). Cross-cultural awareness development: A conceptual model. *Counselor Education and Supervision, 28,* 270–287.

Cohen, R. I., Montague, P., Nathanson, L. S., & Swerdlik, M. E. (1988). *Psychological testing: An introduction to tests and measurement.* Mountain View, CA: Mayfield.

College Entrance Examination Board (1986, October). *Keeping the options open: Recommendations.* New York: Final report of the Commission on Precollege Guidance and Counseling.

Conyne, R. K. (1987). *Primary preventative counseling*. Muncie, IN: Accelerated Development.

Cooney, J. (1991). *Coping with sexual abuse*. New York: Rosen Publishing Group.

Corey, G. (1995). *Theory and practice of group counseling* (4th ed.). Pacific Grove, CA:Brooks/Cole.

Corey, G. (1995). *Theory and practice of group counseling* (4th ed.). Belmont, CA: Wadsworth, Inc.

Corey, M. S., & Corey, G. (1997). *Groups: Process and practice* (5th ed.). Pacific Grove, CA: Brooks/Cole.

Cormier, L. S., & Hackney, H. (1993). *The professional counselor: A process guide to helping*. Boston: Allyn & Bacon.

Crocker, E. C. (1964). Depth consultation with parents. *Young Children, 20*, 91–99.

Crosbie-Burnett, M. C., & Pulvino, C. J. (1990). Protech: A multimodal group intervention for children with reluctance to use computers. *Elementary School Guidance and Counseling, 24*, 272–280.

Crouch, R. C. (1979). Social work defined. *Social Work, 24*, 46–48.

Crow, L. D., & Crow, A. (1960). *An introduction to guidance* (2nd ed.). New York: American.

Cubberly, E. P. (1934). *Public education in the United States*. Boston: Houghton Mifflin.

Daly, M. (1979). How good is your child's school counselor? *Better Homes and Gardens, 57*, 15–22.

Delco, W. (1988). *Access plus quality: The formula for student success*. Paper presented at the Third Annual Harry S. Truman Lecture, Washington, DC.

Dolliver, R. H. (1982). Review of card sorts. In J. T. Kapes & M. M. Mastie (Eds.), *A counselor's guide to vocational guidance instruments* (pp. 147–160). Falls Church, VA: National Vocational Guidance Association.

Donovan, C. E. (1959). A new era of guidance. *School and Society, 87*, 241.

Drasgow, J., & Carkhuff, R. R. (1964). Juder neuropsychiatric keys before and after psychotherapy. *Journal of Counseling Psychology, 11*, 67–69.

Driver, H. I. (1958). *Counseling and learning through small group discussions*. Madison, WI: Monona.

Drummond, R. J. (1996). *Appraisal procedures for counselors and helping professionals* (3rd. ed.). Englewood Cliffs, NJ: Prentice-Hall.

Dziekan, K. I., & Okocha, A. A. G. (1993, June). Accessibility of rehabilitation services: Comparison by racial-ethnic status. *Rehabilitation Counseling Bulletin, 36*, 183–189.

Eckerson, L., & Smith, H. (1962). *Elementary school guidance: The consultant*. (Reprint of three articles in *School Life*). Washington, DC: U.S. Department of Health, Education and Welfare, Office of Education.

Egan, G. (1977). *You and me: The skills of communicating and relating to others*. Monterey, CA: Brooks/Cole.

Ewing, D. B. (1975). Direct from Minnesota—E. G. Williamson. *Personnel and Guidance Journal, 54*, 77–87.

Exum, H. A., & Moore, Q. L. (1993). Transcultural counseling from African-American perspectives. In J. McFadden (Ed.). *Transcultural counseling: Bilateral and international perspectives*. (pp. 193–212). Alexandria, VA: American Counseling Association

Fagan, T. K., & Wise, P. S. (1994). *School psychology: Past, present and future*. New York: Longman.

Fassinger, R. E. (1991). The hidden minority: Issues and challenges in working with lesbian women and gay men. *Counseling Psychologist, 19*, 157–176.

Faust, V. B. (1967). The counselor as a consultant to teachers. *Elementary School Guidance and Counseling, 1*, 112–117.

Faust, V. B. (1968). *The history of elementary school counseling: Overview and critique*. Boston: Houghton Mifflin.

Feingold, G. A. (1947). A new approach to guidance. *School Review, 4*, 542–550.

Felner, R. D., Jason, L. A., Moritsugu, J. N., & Farber, S. S. (Eds.). (1983). *Preventive psychology: Theory, research, and practice*. New York: Pergamon.

Fischer, L., & Sorenson, G. P. (1996). *School law for counselors, psychologists and social workers*. New York: Longman.

Fiske, E. B. (1988). America's test mania. *New York Times*, Education Life, Section 12, 16–20.

Flygare, T. (1975). *The legal rights of students*. Bloomington, IN: Phi Delta Kappa Educational Foundation.

Fong, M. L., & Amatea, E. S. (1992). Stress and single professional women: An exploration of causal factors. *Journal of Mental Health Counseling, 14*, 20–29.

Fretz, B. R. (1988). Third National Conference for Counseling Psychology: Planning the future. *Counseling Psychologist, 16* (3).

Frieden, B. (1993). *The fountain of age*. New York: Simon & Schuster.

Froehlich, C. P. (1958). *Guidance services in schools* (2nd ed.). New York: McGraw-Hill.

Fuqua, D. R., & Kurpius, D. J. (1993). Conceptual models in organization consultation. *Journal of Counseling and Development, 71* (6), 607–618.

Gandara, P. (1989, January). Those children are ours: Moving towards community. *National Education Journal*, 38–43.

Garmezy, N. (1978, spring–summer). DSM III: Never mind the psychologists—Is it good for the children? *Clinical Psychologist, 31* (3–4), 1, 4–6.

Gazda, G. M. (1984). *Group counseling: A developmental approach* (3rd ed.). Boston: Allyn & Bacon.

Gazda, G. M. (1989). *Group counseling: A developmental approach* (3rd ed.). Boston: Allyn & Bacon.

Gazda, G. M., Asbury, F. R., Balzer, F. J., Childers, W. C., & Walters, R. P. (1977). *Human relations development: A manual for educators*. Boston: Allyn & Bacon.

Gelso, C. J., & Fretz, B. R. (1992). *Counseling psychology*. New York: Harcourt Brace Jovanovich.

George, R. L., & Cristiani, T. S. (1995). *Counseling: Theory and practice* (4th ed.). Englewood Cliffs, NJ: Prentice-Hall.

George, R. L., & Dustin, D. (1988). *Group counseling: Theory and practice*. Englewood Cliffs, NJ: Prentice-Hall.

Gerler, E. R., Jr. (1995). Advancing elementary and middle school counseling through computer technology. *Elementary School Guidance and Counseling, 30* (1), 8–15.

Getson, R., & Schweid, R. (1976). School counselors and the Buckley Amendment—Ethical Standards squeeze. *The School Counselor, 24*, 56–58.

Gibbs, J. T., Huang, L., & Associates. (1989). *Children of color: Psychological intervention with minority youth*. San Francisco: Jossey-Bass.

Gibson, R. L. (1973). The counselor as curriculum consultant. *American Vocational Journal, 48*, 50–51, 54.

Gibson, R. L. (1977). Counseling and annual guidance committee report. Unpublished manuscript. North Central Association of Colleges and Schools.

Gibson, R. L. (1989). Prevention and the elementary school counselor. *Elementary School Guidance and Counseling, 24* (1), 30–36.

Gibson, R. L. (1990). Teachers' opinions of high school counseling and guidance programs: Then and now. *The School Counselor, 37*, 248–255.

Gibson, R. L., & Higgins, R. E. (1966). *Techniques of guidance: An approach to pupil analysis*. Chicago: Science Research Associates.

Gibson, R. L., & Mitchell, M. H. (1976). *Identification of effective concepts in placement and follow-up: A technical report*. Indianapolis: State of Indiana and Indiana University.

Gibson, R. L., Mitchell, M. H., & Basile, S. K. (1993). *Counseling in the elementary school: A comprehensive approach*. Boston: Allyn & Bacon.

Gibson, R. L., Mitchell, M. H., & Higgins, R. E. (1983). *Development and management of counseling programs and guidance services*. New York: Macmillan.

Gifford, B. R. (1991, August). The learning society: Serious play. *Chronicle of Higher Education*, p. 7.

Gilbride, D. D. (1993). Parental attitudes toward their child with a disability: Implications for rehabilitation counselors. *Rehabilitation Counseling Bulletin, 36,* 139–150.

Gill, S. J., & Barry, R. A. (1982). Group-focused counseling: Classifying the essential skills. *Personnel and Guidance Journal, 60,* 302–305.

Gilliland, B. E., James, R. K., Bowman, J. T. (1989). *Theories and strategies in counseling and psychotherapy* (2nd ed.). Englewood Cliffs, NJ: Prentice-Hall.

Ginzberg, E. (1972). Restatement of the theory of occupational choice. *Vocational Guidance Quarterly, 20* (3), 169–176.

Ginzberg, E., Ginsburg, S. W., Axelrad, S., & Herma, J. L. (1951). *Occupational choice: An approach to a general theory.* New York: Columbia University Press.

Glasser, W. (1965). *Reality therapy.* New York: Harper & Row.

Glasser, W. (1981). *Stations of the mind.* New York: Harper & Row.

Glasser, W. (1984). Reality therapy. In R. J. Corsini (Ed.), *Current psychotherapies* (3rd ed., pp. 320–353). Itasca, IL: Peacock.

Glasser, W. (1989). Control theory in the practice of reality therapy. In N. Glasser (Ed.), *Control theory in the practice of reality therapy: Case studies.* New York: Harper & Row.

Goldenberg, I., & Goldenberg, H. (1991). *Family therapy: An overview.* Pacific Grove, CA: Brooks/Cole.

Goodwin, D. K. (1978, October). True leadership. *Psychology Today,* 46–48, 50, 53–54, 57–58, 110.

Goshen, C. E. (1967). *Documentary history of psychiatry: A sourcebook on history principles* (pp. 501–504). New York: Philosophical Library.

Gracenin, D. On their own terms. *The Executive Educator* (October 1993).

Gross, B., & Gross, R. (1974). *Will it grow in a classroom?* New York: Dell.

Gross, M. L. (1963). *The brain watchers.* New York: Signet Books.

Gysbers, N. C., & Henderson, P. (1994). *Developing and managing your school guidance program* (2nd ed.). Alexandria, VA: American Counseling Association.

Gysbers, N. C., Hughey, K. F., Starr, M., & Lapan, R. T. (1992). Improving school guidance programs: A framework for program, personnel, and results evaluation. *Journal of Counseling and Development, 70* (5), 565–570.

Hackney, H. L., & Cormier, L. S. (1996). *The professional counselor: A process guide to helping* (3rd ed.). Boston: Allyn & Bacon.

Hadley, R. G., & Mitchell, L. K. (1995). *Counseling research and program evaluation.* Pacific Grove, CA: Brooks/Cole.

Hagedorn, H. J., Beck, K. J., Neubert, S. F., & Werlin, S. H. (1976). *Working manual of simple program evaluation techniques for community mental health centers.* Rockville, MD: Arthur D. Little (for National Institute of Mental Health).

Hansen, J. C., Stevic, R. R., & Warner, R. W., Jr. (1986). *Counseling: Theory and process* (4th ed.). Boston: Allyn & Bacon.

Hansen, J. C., Warner, R. W., & Smith, E. M. (1980). *Group counseling: Theory and process* (2nd ed.). Englewood Cliffs, NJ: Prentice-Hall.

Hardesty, P. H., & Dillard, J. M. (1994). The role of elementary school counselors compared with their middle and secondary school counterparts. *Elementary School Guidance and Counseling, 29* (2), 83–91.

Harrison, D. K. Race as a counselor-client variable in counseling and psychotherapy: A review of the research. *The Counseling Psychologist, 5* (1), 124–133.

Hatch, R. N., & Costar, J. W. (1961). *Guidance services in the elementary school.* Dubuque, IA: Brown.

Havighurst, R. J. (1953). *Human development and education.* New York: Longmans, Green.

Havighurst, R. J. (1964). Youth in exploration and man emergent. In H. Borow (Ed.), *Man in a world at work* (pp. 215–236). Alexandria, VA: National Career Development Association.

Hawes, G. R. (1973). Criterion referenced testing—No more losers, no more norms, no more parents raising storms. *Nation's Schools, 91* (2), 35–41.

Hawks, B. K., & Muha, D. (1991). Facilitating the career development of minorities: Doing it differently this time. *Career Developoment Quarterly, 39,* 251–260.

Henderson, A. (1988, October). Best friends. *Phi Delta Kappan,* 149–153.

Heppner, P. P., Kivlighan, D. M., Jr., & Wampold, B. E. (1992). *Research design in counseling.* Pacific Grove, CA: Brooks/Cole.

Herlihy, B., & Glosoff, H. (1994). Licensure, registration, or certification for counselors. Personal communication to authors.

Herlihy, B., Healy, M., Cook, E. P., & Hudson, P. (1987). Ethical practices of licensed professional counselors: A survey of state licensing boards. *Counselor Education and Supervision, 27* (1), 69–76.

Herlihy, B., & Sheeley, V. L. (1987). Privileged communication in selected helping professions: A comparison among statues. *Journal of Counseling and Development, 65* (19), 479–483.

Herndon, T. (1976). Standardized tests: Are they worth the cost? *Educational Digest, 42,* 13–16.

Herr, E. L. (1979). *Guidance and counseling in the schools: The past, present, and future.* Falls Church, VA: American Personnel and Guidance Association.

Herr, E. L., & Cramer, S. H. (1996). *Career guidance and counseling through the life span: Systematic approaches* (5th ed.). New York: HarperCollins.

Higbee, J. L., Dwinell, P. L., McAdams, C. R., GoldbergBelle, E., & Tardola, M. E. (1991). Serving underprepared students in institutions of higher education. *Journal of Humanistic Education and Development, 30,* 73–80.

Hinshaw, R. P. (1942). The concept of adjustment and problems of norms. *Psychological Review, 49,* 284–292.

Hirshberg, D. (1991). *The role of the community college in economic and workforce development.* Los Angeles, CA: ERIC Clearinghouse for Junior Colleges. (ERIC Document Reproduction Service No. ED 339443).

Holland, J. L. (1966). *The psychology of vocational choice.* Lexington, MA: Blaisdell/Ginn.

Holland, J. L. (1973). *Making vocational choices: A theory of careers.* Englewood Cliffs, NJ: Prentice-Hall.

Holland, J. L. (1985a). *Making vocational choices: A theory of careers* (2nd ed.). Englewood Cliffs, NJ: Prentice-Hall.

Holland, J. L. (1985b). *The self-directed search: Professional manual—1985 edition.* Odessa, FL: Psychological Assessment Resources.

Hollis, J. W. (1997). *Counselor preparation: 1996–1998. Programs, faculty trends* (9th ed.). Washington, DC: Accelerated Development & National Board for Certified Counselors.

Hollis, J. W., & Wantz, R. A. (1994). *Counselor preparation 1993–95: Vol. II. Status, trends, and implications* (8th ed.). Muncie, IN: Accelerated Development.

Hood, A. B., & Johnson, R. W. (1991). *Assessment in counseling: A guide to the use of psychological assessment procedures.* Alexandria, VA: American Association for Counseling and Development.

Hopkins, B. R., & Anderson, B. S. (1990). *The counselor and the law* (3rd. ed.). Alexandria, VA: American Association for Counseling and Development.

Hopkins, K. D., & Stanley, J. C. (1981). *Eduational and psychological measurement and evaluation* (6th ed.). Englewood Cliffs, NJ: Prentice-Hall.

Hotchkiss, L., & Borow, H. (1990). Sociological perspectives on work and career development. In D. Brown, L. Brooks, & Associates (Eds.), *Career choice and development* (2nd ed.). San Francisco: Jossey-Bass.

Hoyt, K. (1993). Guidance is not a dirty word. *The School Counselor, 40* (4), 267–274.

Humes, C. W. (1987). *Contemporary counseling: Services, applications, issues.* Muncie, IN: Accelerated Development.

Humes, C. W., II. (1978). School counselors and PL 94-142. *The School Counselor, 25,* 193–195.

Humes, C. W., & Hohenshil, T. H. (1987). Elementary counselors, school psychologists, school social workers: Who does what? *Elementary School Guidance and Counseling, 22,* 37–45.

Hummel, D. L., & Humes, C. W. (1984). *Pupil services: Development, coordination, administration.* New York: Macmillan

Hutson, P. W. (1958). *The guidance function in education.* New York: Appleton-Century-Crofts.

Iacocca, L., & Novack, W. (1984). *Iacocca: An autobiography.* New York: Bantam Books.

Imanuri, K. (1995). *A passion for success.* New York: McGraw-Hill.

Inamori, K. (1995). *A passion for success.* New York: McGraw Hill.

Isaacson, L. E. (1985). *Basics of career counseling.* Boston: Allyn & Bacon.

Isaacson, L. E., & Brown, D. (1993). *Career information, career counseling, and career development.* Boston: Allyn & Bacon.

Ishisaka, H. A., Nguyen, Q. T., & Okimoto, J. T. (1985). The role in the mental health treatment of Indochinese refugees. In T. C. Owan (Ed.), *Southeast Asian mental health treatment, prevention services, training, and research.* Washington, DC: National Institute of Mental Health.

Ivey, A. E., Ivey, M. B., & Simek-Downing, L. (1987). *Counseling and psychotherapy: Integrating skills, theory, and practice* (2nd ed.). Englewood Cliffs, NJ: Prentice-Hall.

Ivey, A. E., Ivey, M. B., & Simek-Morgan, L. (1993). *Counseling and psychotherapy: A multicultural perspective* (3rd ed.). Boston: Allyn & Bacon.

Ivey, A. E., Ivey, M. B., & Simek-Morgan, L. (1997). *Counseling and psychotherapy: A multicultural perspective* (4th ed.). Boston: Allyn & Bacon.

Jacques, M. E. (1969). *Rehabilitation counseling: Scope and services.* Boston: Houghton Mifflin.

James, W. (1890). *The principles of psychology: Vol. I.* New York: Holt.

Jeger, A. M., & Slotnick, R. S. (1982). *Community mental health and behavioral ecology: A handbook of theory, research and practice.* New York: Plenum.

Jemerin, M. D., & Philips, I. (1988). Changes in inpatient child psychiatry: Consequences and recommendations. *Journal of the American Academy of Child and Adolescent Psychiatry, 27,* 397–493.

Jenkins, D. E. (1985). Ethical and legal dilemmas of working with students with special needs. *Elementary School Guidance and Counseling, 19,* 202–209.

Jenkins, W., Patterson, J. B., & Szymanski, E. M. (1992). Philosophical, historic, and legislative aspects of the rehabilitation counseling profession. In R. M. Parker & E. M. Szymanski (Eds.), *Rehabilitation counseling: Basics and beyond* (2nd ed., 1–41). Austin, TX: PRO-ED.

Johansen, J. H., Collins, H. W., & Johnson, J. A. (1975). *American Education* (2nd ed.). Dubuque, IA: Brown.

Johansson, C. B., & Campbell, D. P. (1971). Stability of the Strong Vocational Interest Blank for Men. *Journal of Applied Psychology, 55,* 34–36.

Johnson, M. L. (1993). *An American imperative: higher expectations for higher education: an open letter to those concerned about the American future.* Report of the Wingspread Group on Higher Education. Racine, WI: Johnson Foundation.

Jones, A. J. (1963). *Principles of guidance* (5th ed.). New York: McGraw-Hill.

Kameen, M. C., Robinson, E. H., & Rotter, J. C. (1985). Coordination activities: A study of perception of elementary and middle school counselors. *Elementary School Guidance and Counseling, 20,* 97–104.

Kazdin, A. E. (1981). Behavioral observation. In A. S. Bellack & M. Hersen (Eds.), *Behavioral assessment: A practical handbook* (2nd ed., pp. 101–124). Boston: Allyn & Bacon.

Kennedy, E. M. (1990, November). Community-based care for the mentally ill: Simple justice. *American Psychologist, 45* (11), 1238–1240.

Keyes, R. (1976). *Is there life after high school?* Boston: Little, Brown.

Kielder, T. (1993). *Old friends.* Boston: Houghton Mifflin.

Kinney, J., & Leaton, G. (1978). *Loosening the grip: A handbook of alcohol information.* St. Louis: Mosby.

Klopf, G. (1960). The expanding role of the high-school counselor. *School and Society, 88,* 417–419.

Kotter, J. (1988). *The leadership factor.* New York: Free Press.

Kottler, J. A., & Brown, R. W. (1985). *Introduction to therapeutic counseling.* Monterey, CA: Brooks/Cole.

Krumboltz, J. D. (Ed.). (1966). *Revolution in counseling: Implications of behavioral science.* Boston: Houghton Mifflin.

Krumboltz, J. D., Mitchell, A., & Gelatt, H. G. (1975). Applications of social learning theory of career selection. *Focus on Guidance, 8,* 1–16.

Kurpius, D. J. (1978). Consultation theory and process: An integrated model. *Personnel and Guidance Journal, 56,* 335–338.

Kurpius, D. J., & Brown, D. (1988). *Handbook of consultation: An intervention for advocacy and outreach.* Alexandria, VA: Association for Counselor Education and Supervision.

Kurpius, D. J., & Fuqua, D. R. (Eds.). (1993a). Consultation: A paradigm for helping: Consultation I: Conceptual, structural and operational dimensions [Special issue]. *Journal of Counseling and Development, 71* (6).

Kurpius, D. J., & Fuqua, D. R. (Eds.). (1993b). Fundamental issues in defining consultation. *Journal of Counseling and Development, 71,* 598–600.

Kurpius, D. J., & Robinson, S. E. (Eds.). (1978). Consultation I: Definition-models-programs [Special issue]. *Personnel and Guidance Journal, 56* (6).

LaFromboise, T. D., & Rowe, W. (1983). Skills training for bicultural competence: Rationale and application. *Journal of Counseling Psychology, 30,* 589–595.

Lambert, R. G., & Lambert, M. J. (1984). The effects of role preparation for psychotherapy on immigrant clients seeking mental health services in Hawaii. *Journal of Community Psychology, 12,* 263–275.

Lazarus, A. A. (1989). *The practice of multimodal therapy.* Baltimore: Johns Hopkins University Press.

Lazarus, A. A., & Beutler, L. E. (1993). On technical eclecticism. *Journal of Counseling and Development, 71,* 381–385.

Leahy, M. J., & Szymanski, E. M. (1995, November/December). Rehabilitation counseling: Evolution and current status. *Journal of Counseling and Development, 74* (2), 163–166.

Leahy, M. J., Szymanski, E. M., & Linkowski, D. C. (1993). Knowledge importance in rehabilitation counseling. *Rehabilitation Counseling Bulletin, 37,* 130–145.

Lee, C. C. (1991). Multicultural counseling: New perspectives for the 1990s and beyond. *Counseling and Human Development, 23* (5), 1–8.

Leitenberg, H., Agras, W. S., Thompson, L. D., & Wright D. E. (1968). Feedback in behavior modification: An experimental analysis in two phobic cases. *Journal of Applied Behavior Analysis, 1,* 131–137.

Lessinger, L., Cunningham, E., & Sabine, D. D. (1973). *Accountability: Systems planning in education.* Homewood, IL: ETC.

Lewin, K. (1936). *Principles of topological psychology.* New York: McGraw-Hill.

Lewis, J. A., Lewis, M. D., & Souflee, F., Jr. (1993). *Management of human service programs.* Pacific Grove, CA: Brooks/Cole.

Lewis, M. D., Hayes, R. L., & Lewis, J. A. (1986). *An introduction to the counseling profession.* Itasca, IL: Peacock.

Lewis, M. D., & Lewis, J. A. (1991). *Management of human service programs* (2nd ed.) Pacific Grove, CA: Brooks/Cole.

Lieberman, M., Yalom, I., & Miles, M. (1973). *Encounter groups: First facts.* New York: Basic Books.

Lorenzo, M. K., & Adler, D. A. (1984). Mental health services for Chinese in a community health center. *Social Casework, 65,* 600–610.

Lucking, R., & Mitchum, N. (1990). Desktop publishing for counselors. *The School Counselor, 37,* 270–272.

Mallart, M. (1955). *The history of the guidance movement: Western civilization—1955.* Cleveland: Collins & World.

Mannino, F. V., & MacLennan, B. W. (1978). *Monitoring and evaluating mental health consultation and education services.* DHEW Pub. No. (ADM) 77-550. Washington, DC: U.S. Government Printing Office.

Marshall, J. (1983). Reducing the effects of work-oriented values on the lives of male American workers. *Vocational Guidance Quarterly, 32,* 109–115.

Maslow, A. H. (1970). *Motivation and personality* (2nd ed.). New York: Harper & Row.

Matarazzo, J. D. (1986). Computerized clinical and psychological test interpretations: Unvalidated plus all mean and no sigma. *American Psychologist, 41,* 14–24.

McCandless, B. R., & Coop, R. H. (1979). *Adolescents: Behavior and development* (2nd ed.). New York: Holt, Rinehart & Winston.

McCully, C. H. (1962). The school counselor: Strategy for professionalization. *Personnel and Guidance Journal, 61,* 597–601.

McCully, C. H. (1965). The counselor: Instrument of change. *Teachers College Record, 66,* 405–412.

McCully, C. H. (1969). *Challenges for change in counselor education.* (Compiled by L. L. Miller.) Minneapolis, MN: Burgess.

McFadden, J. (Ed.) (1993). *Transcultural counseling: Bilateral and international perspectives.* Alexandria, VA: American Counseling Association.

McKown, H. C. (1934). *Home room guidance.* New York: McGraw-Hill.

Meares, P. A. (1977). Analysis of tasks in school social work. *Social Work, 22,* 196–201 .

Meichenbaum, D. (1991). Evolution of cognitive behavior therapy. In J. Zeig (Ed.), *The evolution of psychology, II.* New York: Brunner/Mazel.

Meichenbaum, D. (1993). Stress inoculation training: A twenty-year update. In R. Wolfolk, & P. Lehrer (Eds.), *Principles and practices of stress management.* New York: Guilford.

Mitchell, L. K., & Krumboltz, J. D. (1990). Social learning approach to career decision making: Krumboltz's theory. In D. Brown & L. Brooks (Eds.), *Career choice and development: Applying contemporary theories to practice* (2nd ed.) (pp. 145–196). San Francisco: Jossey-Bass.

Mitchell, L. K., & Krumboltz, J. D. (1996). Krumboltz's learning theory of career choice and counseling. In D. Brown, L. Brooks & Associates (Eds.), *Career choice and development* (3rd ed.) (pp. 233–276). San Francisco: Jossey-Bass.

Moles, O. C. (1991). Guidance programs in American high schools: A descriptive portrait. *The School Counselor, 38* (3), 163–173.

Moreno, J. L. (Ed.). (1960). *The sociometry reader.* New York: Free Press.

Moses, A., & Hawkins, R. (1982). *Counseling lesbian women and gay men: A life issues approach.* St. Louis: Mosby.

Mueller, C. G. (1979). Some origins of psychology as science. In M. R. Rosenzweig & L. W. Porter (Eds.), *Annual Review of Pychology* (Vol. 30, pp. 9–29). Palo Alto, CA: Annual Reviews.

Munson, H. L. (1971). *Foundation of developmental guidance.* Boston: Allyn & Bacon.

Murray, H., Barrett, W. G., & Honburger, E. (1938). *Explorations in personality: A clinical and experimental study of fifty men of college age.* New York: Oxford University Press.

Myers, J. E. (1990, July). Aging: An overview for mental health counselors. *Journal of Mental Health Counseling, 12* (3), 245–259.

Myers, J. E. (1992). Competencies, credentialing, and standards for gerontological counselors:

Implications for counselor education. *Counselor Education and Supervision, 32,* 34–41.

Myers, J. E., Emmerling, D., & Leafgren, F. (1992). Wellness throughout the lifespan [Special issue]. *Journal of Counseling and Development, 71* (2).

Naisbitt, J., & Aburdene, P. (1990). *Megatrends 2000.* New York: Morrow.

National Commission on Excellence in Education (1983). *A nation at risk: The imperative for educational reform.* Washington, DC: U.S. Government Printing Office.

National Commission on Testing and Public Policy (1990). *From gatekeeper to gateway: Transforming testing in America.* Washington, DC: Author.

National Commission on the Reform of Secondary Education (1973). *The Reform of Secondary Education.* New York: McGraw-Hill.

National Employment Counseling Association. (1975). Role of the employment counselor. *Journal of Employment Counseling, 12,* 148–153.

National Vocational Guidance Association. (1973). *Career development: NVGA–AVA position paper.* Washington, DC: American Personnel and Guidance Association.

Nelson, R. C. (1992). Spa in counseling. *Journal of Counseling and Development, 71* (2), 214–220.

New York State Teachers Association. (1935). *Guidance in the secondary school.* New York State Teachers Association Educational Monograph #3. New York: Author.

Nidorf, J. F. (1985). Mental health and refugee youths: A model for diagnostic training. In T. C. Owan (Ed.), *Southeast Asian mental health treatment, prevention services, training, and research.* Washington, DC: National Institute of Mental Health.

Nolte, M. C. (1975). Use and misuse of tests in education: Legal implications. *Evaluation Horizons, 54,* 10–16.

Obermann, C. E. (1965). *A history of vocational rehabilitation in America.* Minneapolis: Denison.

Ohlsen, M. M. (1955). *Guidance: An introduction.* New York: Harcourt Brace Jovanovich.

Omizo, M. M., Omizo, S. A., & D'Andrea, M. J. (1992). Promoting wellness among elementary school children. *Journal of Counseling and Development, 71* (2), 194–198.

Ornstein, A. C. (1976). IQ tests and the culture issue. *Phi Delta Kappan, 57,* 403–404.

Paradise, L. V., & Long, T. J. (1981). *Counseling in the community college.* New York: Praeger.

Parsons, F. (1909). *Choosing a vocation.* Boston: Houghton Mifflin.

Partin, R. L. (1993). School counselors' time: Where does it go? *The School Counselor, 40* (4), 274–281.

Passons, W. R. (1975). *Gestalt approaches in counseling.* New York: Holt, Rinehart & Winston.

Patton, M. J. (1984). Managing social interaction in counseling: A contribution from the philosophy of science. *Journal of Counseling Psychology, 17,* 442–456.

Pedersen, P. (1988). *A handbook for developing multicultural awareness.* Alexandria, VA: American Association for Counseling and Development.

Pedersen, P. B. (Ed.). (1991). Multiculturism as a fourth force in counseling [Special issue]. *Journal of Counseling and Development, 70* (1).

Peeks, B. (1993). Revolutions in counseling and education: A systems perspective in the schools. *Elementary School Guidance and Counseling, 27,* 245–251.

Peregoy, J. J. (1993). Transcultural counseling with American Indians and Alaskan Natives: Contemporary issues for consideration. In J. McFadden (Ed.), *Transcultural counseling: Bilateral and international perspectives* (pp. 163–191). Alexandria, VA: American Counseling Association.

Perls, F. (1948). Theory and technique of personality integration. *American Journal of Psychotherapy, 2,* 565–586.

Peter, L. I., & Hull, R. (1959). *The Peter principle.* New York: Harper & Row.

Peters, T. J., & Waterman, R. H., Jr. (1982). *In search of excellence.* New York: Harper & Row.

Phelps, R. J., Peer, G. G., & Canada, R. M. (1973). Training employment personnel in basic counseling skills. *Journal of Employment Counseling, 10,* 173–179.

Phillips, E. L. (1968). Achievement place: Token reinforcement procedures in a home-style rehabilitation setting for "pre-delinquent" boys. *Journal of Applied Behavior Analysis, 1,* 213–223.

Ponzo, Z. (1992). Promoting successful aging: Problems, opportunities, and counseling guidelines. *Journal of Counseling and Development, 71* (2), 210–213.

Proctor, W. M., Benefield, W., & Wrenn, C. G. (1931). *Workbook in vocations.* Boston: Houghton Mifflin.

Pyszowski, I. S. (1986). Moral values and the schools: Is there a way out of the maze? *Chronicle Guidance, 107* (1), 87–92.

Quimbita, G. (1991). *Preparing women and minorities for careers in math and science: The role of community colleges.* Los Angeles: ERIC Clearinghouse for Junior Colleges. (ERIC Document Reproduction Service No. ED 333943.)

Rapoport, R., & Rapoport, R. N. (1976). *Dual-career families re-examined: New interpretations of work and family.* London: Martin Robertson.

Raths, L. E., Harmin, M., & Simon, S. B. (1978). *Values and teaching: Working with values in the classroom.* Columbus, OH: Merrill.

Remley, T. P., Jr. (1991, August). On being different. *Guidepost,* p. 2.

Remley, T. P., Jr. (1993). Consultation contracts. *Journal of Counseling and Development, 72,* 157–159.

Rencken, R. H. (1989). *Intervention strategies for sexual abuse.* Alexandria, VA: American Association for Counseling and Development.

Reschly, D. J., & Wilson, M. S. (1993). *Demographics, job satisfaction, system reform, and current/ideal roles: 1986–1995 comparisons.* Unpublished manuscript.

Ridley, C. R. (1995). *Overcoming unintentional racism in counseling and therapy: A practitioner's guide to intentional intervention.* Thousand Oaks: Sage.

Robinson, S. E. (1983). Nader versus ETS: Who should we believe? *Personnel and Guidance Journal, 61,* 260–262.

Robinson, S. E., & Roth, S. L. (1992). Women and health [Special issue]. *Journal of Mental Health Counseling, 14* (1).

Rockwell, P. J., & Rothney, J. W. M. (1961). Some social ideas of pioneers in the guidance movement. *Personnel and Guidance Journal, 40,* 349–354.

Roe, A. (1956). *The psychology of occupation.* New York: Wiley.

Roe, A., & Klas, D. (1972). Classifications of occupations. In J. W. Whiteley & A. Resnikoff (Eds.), *Perspectives on Vocational Development* (pp. 199–221). Washington, DC: American Personnel and Guidance Association.

Rogers, C. R. (1942). *Counseling and psychotherapy.* Cambridge, MA: Riverside.

Rogers, C. R. (1951). *Client-centered therapy.* Boston: Houghton Mifflin.

Rogers, C. R. (1959a). A theory of therapy, personality and interpersonal relationships as developed in the client-centered framework. In S. Koch (Ed.), *Psychology: A study of science: Vol. 3* (pp. 184–256). New York: McGraw-Hill.

Rogers, C. R. (1959b). Significant learning: In theory and in education. *Educational Leadership, 16,* 232–242.

Rogers, C. R. (1967a). The conditions of change from a client-centered viewpoint. In B. G. Berenson & R. R. Carkhuff (Eds.), *Sources of gain in counseling and psychotherapy.* New York: Holt, Rinehart & Winston.

Rogers, C. R. (1967b). The process of the basic encounter group. In J. F. T. Bugental (Ed.), *Challenges of humanistic psychology* (pp. 261–276). New York: McGraw-Hill.

Rowntree, D. (1987). *Assessing students: How shall we know them?* London: Nichols.

Rude, S. S., Weissberg, M., & Gazda, G. M. (1988). Looking to the future: Themes from the third national conference for counseling psychology. *The Counseling Psychologist, 16*, 423–430.

Rutter, M. (1980). School influences on children's behavior and development: The 1979 Kenneth Blackfan Lecture, Children's Hospital Medical Center, Boston. *Pediatrics, 65* (2), 208–220.

Sampson, J. P., Jr., Kolodinsky, R. W., & Green, B. P. (1997). Counseling on the information highway: Future possibilities and potential problems. *Journal of Counseling and Development, 75* (3), 203–212.

Sampson, J. P., Jr., & Pyle, K. R. (1983). Ethical issues involved with the use of computer-assisted counseling, testing and guidance systems. *Personnel and Guidance Journal, 61*, 283–287.

Sattler, J. M. (1992). *Assessment of children* (3rd ed.). San Diego, CA: Sattler.

Schein, E. H. (1978). The role of the consultant: Content expert or process facilitator? *Personnel and Guidance Journal, 56*, 339–345.

Schein, E. H. (1991). Process consultation. *Consulting Psychology Bulletin, 43*, 16–18.

Schmidt, J. J. (1993). *Counseling in schools: Essential services and comprehensive programs*. Boston: Allyn & Bacon.

Schmolling, P., Jr., Youkeles, M., & Burger, W. R. (1989). *Human services in contemporary America* (2nd ed.). Pacific Grove, CA: Brooks/Cole.

Sekaran, U. (1986). *Dual-career families*. San Francisco: Jossey-Bass.

Seligman, L. (1983). An introduction to the new DSM-II. *Personnel and Guidance Journal, 61* (10), 601–605.

Shanker, A. (1988, April 24). Where we stand. Time for truth in testing: Exams fail the test. *New York Times*, p. E7.

Shertzer, B., & Stone, S. C. (1981). *Fundamentals of guidance* (4th ed.). Boston: Houghton Mifflin.

Shifron, R., Dye, A., & Shifron, G. (1983). Implications for counseling the unemployed in a recessionary economy. *Personnel and Guidance Journal, 61*, 527–529.

Simon, S. B., & deSherbinin, P. (1975). Values clarification: It can start gently and grow deep. *Phi Delta Kappan, 56*, 679–683.

Smead, R. (1995). *Skills and techniques for group work with children and adolescents*. Champaign, IL: Research Press.

Smith, D. K. (1984). Practicing school psychologists: Their characteristics, activities, and populations served. *Professional Psychology: Research and Practice, 15*, 798–810.

Solomon, C., & Jackson-Jobe, P. (Eds.). (1992). *Helping homeless people: Unique challenges and solutions*. Alexandria, VA: American Association for Counseling and Development.

Spivack, G., & Shure, M. B. (1974). *Social adjustment of young children*. San Francisco: Jossey-Bass.

Sprinthall, N. A. (1990). Counseling psychology from Greyston to Atlanta: On the road to Armageddon? *The Counseling Psychology, 18*, 454–462.

St. John, W. D., & Walden, J. (1976). Keeping student confidence. *Phi Delta Kappan, 57*, 682–684.

Stevens, R., & Phil, R. O. (1982). The identification of the student-at-risk for failure. *Journal of Clinical Psychology, 38* (2), 298–301.

Stockton, R. (1980). The education of group leaders: A review of the literature with suggestions for the future. *Journal for Specialists in Group Work, 5*, 55–62.

Stockton, R., Barr, J. E., & Klein, R. (1981). Identifying the group dropout: A review of the literature. *Journal for Specialists in Group Work, 6*, 75–82.

Stockton, R., & Morran, D. K. (1982). Review and perspective of critical dimensions in therapeutic small group research. In G. M. Gazda (Ed.), *Basic approaches to group psychotherapy and group counseling* (3rd ed.). Springfield, IL: Charles C. Thomas.

Stockton, R., & Toth, P. (1993). Small group counseling in school settings. In J. Wittmer (Ed.),

Managing your school counseling program: K–12 developmental strategies. Minneapolis: Educational Media Corporation.

Stolz-Loike, M. (1992). *Dual-career couples: New perspectives in counseling.* Alexandria, VA: American Association for Counseling and Development.

Strosnider, J. S., & Grad, J. D. (1993). Third-party payments. *ACA Legal Series,* 9. Alexandria, VA: American Counseling Association.

Sturtevant, S. M. (1937). Some questions regarding the developing guidance movement. *School Review,* 58, 14–23.

Sue, D. W. (1978). Editorial. *Personnel and Guidance Journal,* 56 (8), 451.

Sue, D. W. (1981). *Counseling the culturally different: Theory and practice.* New York: Wiley.

Sue, D. W., & Sue, D. M. (1989). Multicultural counseling. *Counseling and Human Development,* 22 (3), 1–12.

Sue, D. W., & Sue, D. M. (1990). *Counseling the culturally different: Theory and practice* (2nd ed.). New York: Wiley.

Super, D. E. (1975). *The psychology of careers.* New York: Harper & Row.

Super, D. E. (1990). A life-span, life-space approach to career development. In D. Brown, L. Brooks, & Associates (Eds.), *Career choice and development* (2nd ed.). San Francisco: Jossey-Bass.

Super, D. E., Starishevsky, R., Matlin, N., & Jordaan, J. P. (1963). *Career development: Self-concept theory.* New York: College Entrance Examination Board.

Tableman, B., Marceniak, D., Johnson, D., & Rodgers, R. (1982). Stress management training for women on public assistance. *American Journal of Community Psychology,* 10, 357–367.

Taylor, S. E., Falke, R. L., Shapton, S. J., & Lichtman, R. R. (1986). Social support, support groups, and the cancer patient. *Journal of Consulting and Clinical Psychology,* 54, 608–615.

Teague, J. B. (1992). Issues related to the treatment of adolescent lesbians and homosexuals. *Journal of Mental Health Counseling,* 14, 422–439.

Texas Rehabilitation Commission. (1984). *Eligibility requirements of rehabilitation.* Austin: Author.

Tharp, R. G., & Wetzel, R. (1969). *Behavior modification in the natural environment.* New York: Academic Press.

Thomas, D. R. (1973). *The schools next time.* New York: McGraw-Hill.

Thomson-Rountree, P., & Woodruff, A. E. (1982). An examination of Project Aware: The effects on children's attitudes toward themselves, others and school. *Journal of School Psychology,* 20, 20–31.

Tinsley, H. E. A., Hinson, J. A., Tinsley, D. J., & Holt, M. S. (1993). Attributes of leisure and work experiences. *Journal of Counseling Psychology,* 40, 447–455.

Tinsley, H. E. A., & Tinsley, D. J. (1986). A theory of the attributes, benefits and causes of leisure experience. *Leisure Sciences,* 8, 1–45.

Tinsley, H. E. A., & Tinsley, D. J. (1988). An expanded context for the study of career decision-making, development, and maturity. In W. B. Walsh & S. H. Osipow (Eds.), *Career decision making* (pp. 213–264). Hillsdale, NJ: Erlbaum.

Toomer, J. E. (1982). Counseling psychologists in business and industry. *The Counseling Psychologist,* 10 (3), 9–18.

Traxler, A. E. (1950). Emerging trends in guidance. *School Review,* 58, 14–23.

Turnbull, A. P., & Turnbull, H. R. (1990). *Families, professionals and exceptionality: A special partnership.* Columbus, OH: Merrill.

Tung, T. M. (1985). Psychiatric care for southeast Asians: How different is different? In T. C. Owan (Ed.), *Southeast Asian mental health, treatment, prevention services, training, and research.* Washington, DC: National Institute of Mental Health.

Tyler, L. E. (1980). The next twenty years. *The Counseling Psychologist,* 8 (4), 19–21.

U.S. Bureau of Census. (1980). *Census of population supplementary report.* (PC 80–513). Washington, DC: U.S. Government Printing Office.

U.S. Bureau of Census. (1993). *1992 economic census: Geographic reference manual.* (EC93-R-1). Washington, DC: U.S. Government Printing Office.

U.S. Bureau of Census. (1995). *Current Population Reports.* (Series P-20). Washington, DC: U.S. Government Printing Office.

Veninga, R. L., & Spradley, J. P. (1981). *The work stress connection: How to cope with job burnout.* Boston: Little, Brown.

Wallace, W. A. (1986). *Theories of counseling and psychotherapy: A basic issues approach.* Boston: Allyn & Bacon.

Watson, J. B. (1913). Psychology as the behaviorist views it. *Psychological Review, 20,* 159–170.

Weikel, W. J., & Hughes, P. R. (1993). The counselor as expert witness. *ACA Legal Series, 5.* Alexandria, VA: American Counseling Association.

Weissberg, R. P., & Gesten, E. L. (1982). Considerations for developing effective school-based social problem solving (SPS) training programs. *School Psychology Review, 11* (1), 56–63.

Werner, J. L. (1978). Community mental health consultation with agencies. *Personnel and Guidance Journal 56,* 364–368.

Werner, J. L., & Tyler, M. M. (1993). Community-based interventions: A return to community mental health centers' origins. *Journal of Counseling and Development, 71* (6), 689–692.

White, B. L. (1985). The first three years of life. Englewood Cliffs, NJ: Prentice-Hall.

Whitely, J. M. (1980). Counseling psychology in the year 2000 A.D. *The Counseling Psychologist, 8* (4), 2–8

Wigmore, 89 Evidence § 2192 at 70, 73 (McNaughton revision, 3rd ed. 1961).

Wilcoxon, S. A., & Puleo, S. G. (1992). Professional development needs of mental health counselors: Results of a national survey. *Journal of Mental Health Counseling, 14,* 187–195.

Williamson, E. G. (1939). *How to counsel students: A manual of techniques for clinical counselors.* New York: McGraw-Hill.

Windle, C., & Neigher, W. (1978). Ethical problems in program evaluation: Advice for trapped evaluators. *Evaluation and Program Planning, 1* (2), 97–107.

Woody, R. H., Hansen, J. C., & Rossberg, R. H. (1989). *Counseling psychology: Strategies and services.* Pacific Grove, CA: Brooks/Cole.

Worthen, B. R., White, K. R., & Borg, W. R. (1993). *Measurement and evaluation in the schools.* New York: Longman.

Wrenn, C. G. (1962). *The counselor in a changing world.* Washington, DC: American Personnel and Guidance Association.

Wrenn, C. G. (1973). *The world of the contemporary counselor.* Boston: Houghton Mifflin.

Yalom, I. D. (1995). *The theory and practice of group psychotherapy* (4th ed.). New York: Basic Books.

Zeran, F. R., & Riccio, A. C. (1962). *Organization and administration of guidance services.* Skokie, IL: Rand McNally.

Zirbes, L. (1949). Why guidance? *Childhood Education, 25,* 197–201.

Zunker, V. G. (1994). *Career counseling: Applied concepts of life planning* (4th ed.). Pacific Grove, CA: Brooks/Cole.

Zunker, V. G. (1998). *Career counseling: Applied concepts of life planning* (5th ed.). Pacific Grove, CA: Brooks/Cole.

Zytowski, D. G. (1972). Four hundred years before Parsons. *Personnel and Guidance Journal, 50,* 443–450.

Author Index

Abbe, A. E., 359
Abrego, P. J., 138, 140
Aburdene, P., 87
Adler, D. A., 185
Agras, W. S., 279
Aiken, L. R., 250
Ailes, R., 415
Allen, G. J., 36
Allsopp, A., 170
Amatea, E. S., 385
American Association for Counseling and Development, 480
American Association for Marriage and Family Therapy, 527
American Association of Retired Persons, 112
American Counseling Association, 450–451, 460, 462, 480, 510, 518
American Psychiatric Association, 267
American Psychological Association, 445, 480, 488, 490, 532, 537, 539, 542
American Rehabilitation Counseling Association, 480
American School Counselor Association, 13, 171, 480, 508
Americans with Disabilities Act Handbook, 332
Anastasi, A., 229, 243, 250
Anderson, B. S., 448–449
Anderson, D. J., 180
Arredondo, P. M., 184, 187
Arthur, G. L., Jr., 446
Asbury, F. R., 152, 157
Association for Measurement and Evaluation in Counseling and Development, 480
Association for Specialists in Group Work, 199
Axelrad, S., 316

Baker, S. B., 170, 381, 422
Balzer, F. J., 152, 157
Bandura, A., 324
Barr, J. E., 210
Barrett, W. G., 252
Barry, R. A., 212–213
Basile, S. K., 57, 136, 145, 158, 170, 181, 368, 407
Beck, K. J., 422, 430
Beers, C., 15, 21
Belkin, G. S., 4
Bell, T., 14
Bellack, A. S., 278
Benefield, W., 10
Berk, J., 406
Berk, S., 406
Berne, E., 135
Beutler, L. E., 141
Biggs, D. A., 31, 263, 445
Bissell, L., 446
Blanchard, K. H., 395

Blau, P. M., 317
Blocher, D. H., 31, 263, 266, 363, 370, 445
Bloom, B. L., 16, 19, 38, 71, 369–370, 448
Bloom, J., 453
Blum, L., 71
Borg, W. R., 253, 425, 429
Borow, H., 17
Bowman, J. T., 132
Bowman, S. L., 330
Brammer, L. M., 138, 140, 147
Brandt, J. E., 248
Braucht, S., 410
Brewer, J., 10
Brown, D., 331, 360
Brown, J. H., 18
Brown, R. W., 267
Bruce, P., 145–146
Bruges, 4
Burger, W. R., 378
Burnette, C., 381
Burnham, S., 68
Burns, J. M., 206

Campbell, D. P., 248
Campbell, N. J., 77
Caplan, G., 369
Capuzzi, D., 110, 280
Carkhuff, R. R., 248
Carlson, J., 111
Casey, J., 77
Centers for Disease Control and Prevention, 162, 165, 169
Cetron, M. J., 89
Chase, C. I., 236
Childers, W. C., 152, 157
Chinsky, J. M., 36
Christensen, D. N., 18
Christensen, S. P., 180
Cohen, R. I., 252
College Entrance Examination Board, 15, 87–88
Collins, H. W., 5
Commission on Rehabilitation Counselor Certification, 480
Conyne, R. K., 90
Cook, E. P., 447
Cooney, J., 171
Coop, R. H., 220
Corey, G., 202, 204, 207
Corey, M. S., 207
Cormier, L. S., 132–133, 146, 294
Costar, J. W., 30
Council for Accreditation of Counseling and Related Educational Programs, 99
Cramer, S. H., 324–325, 332, 345

Subject Index